Raymond Yop

# DATABASE SECURITY

**ACM PRESS BOOKS**

This book is published as part of ACM Press Books – a collaboration between the Association for Computing Machinery and Addison-Wesley Publishing Company. ACM is the oldest and largest educational and scientific society in the information technology field. Through its high-quality publications and services, ACM is a major force in advancing the skills and knowledge of IT professionals throughout the world. For further information about ACM contact:

**ACM Member Services**
1515 Broadway, 17th Floor
New York, NY 10036-5701
Phone: 1-212-626-0500
Fax: 1-212-944-1318
E-mail: ACMHELP@ACM.org

**ACM European Service Center**
Avenue Marcel Thiry 204
1200 Brussels, Belgium
Phone: 32-2-774-9602
Fax: 32-2-774-9690
E-mail: ACM_Europe@ACM.org

**OTHER TITLES IN THE SERIES**

Object-Oriented Reuse, Concurrency and Distribution *Colin Atkinson*
Algebraic Specification *J.A. Bergstra, J. Heering and P. Klint (Eds)*
Multimedia Programming: Objects and Environments *Simon Gibbs and Dionysios Tsichritzis*
The Set Model for Database and Information Systems *Mikhail Gilula*
Object-Oriented Software Engineering: A Use Case Driven Approach *Ivar Jacobson, Magnus Christerson, Patrik Jonnson and Gunnar Övergaard*
The Object Advantage: Business Process Reengineering with Object Technology *Ivar Jacobson, Maria Ericson and Agneta Jacobson*
Object-Oriented Concepts, Databases and Applications *Won Kim and Frederick H. Lochovsky (Eds)*
Object-Oriented Programming in the BETA Programming Language *O. Lehrmann Madsen, B. Moller-Pederson and K. Nygaard*
Distributed Systems (2nd edn) *Sape Mullender (Ed.)*
Design Patterns for Object-Oriented Software Development *Wolfgang Pree*
The Oberon System: User Guide and Programmer's Manual *Martin Reiser*
Programming in Oberon: Steps Beyond Pascal and Modula *Martin Reiser and Niklaus Wirth*
Software Quality: A Framework for Success in Software Development and Support *Joc Sanders and Eugene Curran*
Advanced Animation and Rendering Techniques *Alan Watt and Mark Watt*
Project Oberon: The Design of an Operating System and Compiler *Niklaus Wirth and Jürg Gutknecht*

# DATABASE SECURITY

**Silvana Castano**
*Dipartimento di Scienze dell'Informazione*
*Università di Milano*

**Maria Grazia Fugini**
*Dipartimento di Informatica e Sistemistica*
*Università di Pavia*

**Giancarlo Martella**
*Dipartimento di Scienze dell'Informazione*
*Università di Milano*

**Pierangela Samarati**
*Dipartimento di Scienze dell'Informazione*
*Università di Milano*

**ADDISON-WESLEY PUBLISHING COMPANY**

Wokingham, England • Reading, Massachusetts • Menlo Park, California • New York
Don Mills, Ontario • Amsterdam • Bonn • Sydney • Singapore
Tokyo • Madrid • San Juan • Milan • Paris • Mexico City • Seoul • Taipei

Translated from the Italian edition *Sicurezza delle Basi di Dati: Techniche, Strumenti e Metodologie*



Cover designed by Designers & Partners of Oxford and
printed by The Riverside Printing Co. (Reading) Ltd.
Typeset by Meridian Phototypesetting Limited, Pangbourne.
Printed in Great Britain by T. J. Press, Padstow, Cornwall.

First printed 1994

**British Library Cataloguing in Publication Data is available.**

**Library of Congress Cataloging in Publication Data**

Sicurezza del basi di dati. English
Database security/Silvano Castano...[et al.].
p. cm.
Translation of: Sicurezza del basi di dati.
Includes bibliographical references and index.
ISBN 0-201-59375-0
1. Database security. I. Castano, Silvano. II. Title.
QA76.9.D314S55 1994
005.8--dc20 94-26279

# Dedication

Silvana Castano: to my husband Mario

Maria Grazia Fugini: to my family

Giancarlo Martella: to my wife Maurizia

Pierangela Samarati: to my parents Dino and Francesca

# Foreword

Computer security is defined as protection of information processed by a computer against unauthorized observation, unauthorized or improper modification, and denial of service (ensuring no authorized use of the information is denied). Assuring computer security is not a trivial task; suitable methods and tools are required for developing secure systems. The task of providing effective protection in database management systems is particularly difficult, since they process large amounts of information in complex ways and require a fine granularity of control over data.

Fortunately, there has been a great deal of research activity in the database security area in the last ten years. Several design approaches have emerged from this research, and some of them are finding their way into commercial products. It will be interesting to see which of these approaches will eventually survive in the marketplace.

This book gives an authoritative and complete perspective on the field of database security. It contains background material for the beginner (such as formal security models and features necessary to build secure operating systems), material related to its theoretical foundation (such as various secure data models and inferences in statistical databases), and descriptions of research prototypes and commercial products. It also covers data protection in advanced database environments, and novel data modelling paradigms and related topics such as intrusion detection.

This book can serve as a textbook in an undergraduate or graduate course as well as a source of reference for research. Until now, the only way to get a comprehensive view of the field was through articles scattered in many different journals and conference proceedings. At last, there is a single publication that covers database security issues thoroughly.

Sushil Jajodia
Fairfax, Virginia
September 1994

# Foreword

# Preface

Database (DB) security comprises a set of measures, policies and mechanisms to provide secrecy, integrity and availability of data and to combat possible attacks on the system (*threats*) from insiders and outsiders, both malicious and accidental. DB security encompasses *physical, logical* and *organizational* issues. Physical DB security focuses on tools, devices, and hardware/software techniques able to prevent or detect unauthorized physical accesses to data storage facilities, and to provide DB backup/recovery. Logical DB security consists of control measures, models and techniques to prevent, detect or deter unauthorized logical (that is, via software) accesses to data. Organizational DB security concentrates on management constraints, operational procedures, and supplementary controls established to provide DB protection. This book is concerned mainly with *logical* DB security.

The *design of logical security* is relevant when planning the security of a DB system, because of its influence on the correctness and performance of the target information system. The design first analyses the threats (that is, possible attacks) and the vulnerabilities (that is, weaknesses that may be exploited to cause loss or harm). Second, the risks to which the DB is exposed are assessed: that is, a measure is taken of the possibility of security breaches and of the severity of the consequent damage. In this way, the design identifies the security policies and requirements of the organization, and states the access needs of the users. The resulting design aims to ensure the correct use of information through a set of security measures that, while providing the users with the complete set of resources they are cleared for, limit the accesses to the authorized subjects, monitor the user activities, and try to limit the loss and damage deriving from potential attacks.

For a long time, security of a DB was considered an *additional* problem to be addressed when the need arose, and after threats to the secrecy and integrity of data had occurred. Therefore, while DB design, organization and management is now considered a sound discipline, security of DBs is seen as an 'optional' feature to be added when the system reveals risks; this approach necessarily penalizes the system performance. With hindsight, after threats and attacks on DB systems in recent years, it has been recognized that security is a feature that should be taken into account in the early phases of DB design, so that data protection can be incorporated efficiently into the system.

Early systems where DB security has been a concern are critical environments, where data management must occur in a proven secure manner, such as military or governmental systems. In this application area, models and techniques have been studied thoroughly, and have produced a set of reference concepts and techniques. Security developed for military systems is classed as 'mandatory' because access privileges of users on system data cannot be modified during the system lifetime and are subject to user clearances and data-classification controls.

Owing to the spread of DBs in a variety of environments where a strict mandatory control policy cannot be applied, commercial DB security has been the object of research in many studies conducted in the military environment. In commercial DBs, access privileges are based on the concept of 'data owner' who can, in a discretionary way, delegate some access privileges to other users. Therefore, although based on some basic concepts developed for military DBs, security of commercial DBs is basically of discretionary type for which a set of models and techniques have been developed.

Other goals in DB security relate to how well the system achieves the security goals (assurance), the relationship between the security mechanisms provided by the operating system and those provided by the DB system, the architecture of a secure DBMS and the problem of inference – particularly in statistical DBs. Some security models and techniques have been developed specifically for DBs, others have been derived as an extension of early results achieved in the field of operating system security. Recently, some *standards* for security of DBs have started to emerge, as well as structures for authorization mechanisms for discretionary security in commercial database management systems (DBMSs). Meanwhile, research is active in the field of next-generation DBs; indeed with advances in DB models and technologies, new security requirements arise.

## Purpose of this book

The basic goals of this book are the following:

(1) To provide a modelling, technological and methodological framework for security system development in DBs, which is an increasing necessity in many organizations.

(2) To detail the security properties that need to be considered during the definition and design phases of a DB. In particular, security policies for dealing with authorization, grant and revocation of access rights, information flow, aggregation and inference links, integrity and secrecy constraints are examined.

(3) To outline the *modelling phase* of DB security, which provides the ability to include security features in DB design methodologies and in software-development methods. The definition of a secure DB from a semantic viewpoint affects the implementation structure of the DB; suitable security models and design techniques are surveyed.

(4) To illustrate the security *mechanisms* on which a DB can rely, such as operating system mechanisms of access control, verification techniques applicable to operating system kernels, authentication, audit and intrusion/detection techniques. Issues in the verification and enforcement of security checks are presented; DB/operating system interfacing techniques are also illustrated.
(5) To describe the security issues typical of a special kind of DB, *statistical DBs*: that is, systems storing data to be used for statistical purposes; these are exposed to particular risks, such as statistical inference, owing to the nature of their data and the operations that can be executable on it.
(6) To provide a survey of current trends in DB security, in particular in the field of security modelling in object-oriented DBs, where relevant research efforts are giving some stable results.
(7) To provide teaching support to DB and information system practitioners and students, in terms of comparisons of different techniques and of references to significant literature.

## Outline of the book

In essence this book covers three topics. One (in Chapters 2, 4 and 7) is devoted to security development: security models, design techniques and system architectures, standards, security software and emerging models and systems. The second topic (Chapters 3 and 6) relates to the security mechanisms underlying DB security: that is, the measures for user authentication and for access control to the system resources. Authentication techniques, file and main memory protection, intrusion/detection techniques, auditing and a survey of security issues in some commercial operating systems are discussed here. The third topic (Chapter 5) concerns the issue of inference in statistical DBs.

In detail, Chapter 1 illustrates the security problems of DBs; after reviewing briefly some concepts of DBs and of DBMS, threats and controls are classified; the basic concepts of policies and mechanisms are introduced. As a reference DB model, the relational model is described and then used to give examples.

In Chapter 2 the basic security models for access control are described and classified. Some derive from operating system security models, some were especially conceived for DBMSs; mandatory- and discretionary-oriented models are distinguished. Then, the basic model for control of information flow among the system resources is presented. Each model is described according to its features, the supported system policies, the protection levels, the items considered, the access modalities, the enabled operations and the axioms and constraints defined. A comparison of models is provided.

Chapter 3 deals with the security functions offered by operating systems, with reference to the mechanisms for user and resource identification and authentication, protection of memory and of resources, flow control, and isolation and confinement. The security features of the most common operating systems are described and compared. The US Department of Defense (DoD) criteria are illustrated.

Chapter 4 tackles the design of security software and security mechanisms. After analysing the main desirable criteria and requirements, the development process for secure systems is illustrated. Secure DBMSs and DBs are also examined. Development processes are presented in terms of methods, available techniques and solutions and international standards. Finally, the security functions offered by some basic security software and by some commercial DBMSs are presented, together with emerging standards in the field.

Chapter 5 deals with protection of statistical DBs. Problems in this area affect governmental bodies, as natural users of this type of DB, as well as public and private organizations which often need statistical data. *Inference* attacks could easily take place and lead to disclosure of private records. After reviewing briefly the necessary concepts of statistics, methodologies of attack are analysed, and protection techniques are presented, classified and discussed.

In Chapter 6, the use of expert system techniques for system auditing is also illustrated with some prototypes.

So long as traditional DBs prove inadequate for more advanced and complex application environments, new models and technologies for data management will emerge; new data models require new protection techniques, some of which are presented in Chapter 7. Among the new trends, object-orientation is considered, owing to the availability of meaningful research results in security management for object DBMSs.

## Audience

The basic activities to be performed for securing a DB are to *understand the attacks* that may come from the environment, to *state the security policies* of the organization, and to *model the security requirements* using a suitable model, or combination of models. In addition, secure data *design and implementation* have to be tackled, with proper *verification* that the system can meet the security requirements and with mechanisms chosen to comply with the degree of security and performance expected from the system. These activities involve expert users, knowledgeable in both DB design and security, such as DB administrators, consultants, analysts, designers, programmers, and operators involved in security design and maintenance. We believe the book can be a valid support in approaching in a systematic way most of the problems that can be encountered.

A management audience is also addressed, in that it can benefit from an introductory survey of the risks to which their DBs might be exposed and of the existing standards and available packages. For this audience, however, the introductory paragraphs of each chapter are suggested. Users who need a foundation from which to evaluate the risks and protection measures of the DB that they operate can gain sufficient knowledge to understand the meaning of security measures present in their DBs, and to suggest possible modifications.

The community of researchers can find a helpful framework for studying the existing models and mechanisms, and the current research trends, in a comparative and structured way.

Finally, students of DBs, information systems, and operating systems courses can find a support in terms of concepts and references to meaningful literature.

The book is self-contained: DB and operating systems concepts and statistical fundamentals have been inserted respectively in Chapters 1, 3 and 5. However, a familiarity with DB and operating system concepts is recommended. For other aspects of security, such as physical and organizational security or communication security (mainly based on cryptography), the reader is referred to the several good texts existing on these topics; DB recovery techniques following system failures are contained in almost all DB books.

*Silvana Castano, Maria Grazia Fugini, Giancarlo Martella, Pierangela Samarati,*
*April 1994*

## Acknowledgments

The authors would like to thank all the people who contributed directly and indirectly to the completion of this book. In particular, the subject of DB security has been studied initially by the authors within National Research Projects developed in Italy from 1980, sponsored by the Italian Government, and later in the framework of the 'Progetto Finalizzato Informatica e Calcolo Parallelo' sponsored by the National Research Council, from 1989. We thank our colleagues in the projects for a useful exchange of ideas.

Preliminary versions of this book have been tested through workshops and courses. We acknowledge in particular the ideas exchanged within IFIP TC11 Working Group on Database Security (WG11:3), in the Italian Group 'Security' of AICA (Italian Computer Association), and at the Polytechnic of Vienna, Austria, within the COMETT Initiative of the EC. The methodology for secure DB design has been tested by Arthur Andersen Consultants, Italy, in projects on security of banking institutions.

The authors are grateful to Elisa Bertino, Sushil Jajodia and Ravi Sandhu for their suggestions about the book organization and contents.

Obviously, all errors and omissions are the full responsibility of the authors, whose names appear in alphabetical order.

3.3 Memory protection . . . 151
- 3.3.1 Fence address . . . 152
- 3.3.2 Relocation . . . 153
- 3.3.3 Register-based protection . . . 155
- 3.3.4 Paging . . . 159
- 3.3.5 Segmentation . . . 161

3.4 Access control to resources . . . 164
- 3.4.1 Access control mechanisms . . . 164

3.5 Flow-control mechanisms . . . 173
- 3.5.1 Control mechanisms at run time . . . 174
- 3.5.2 Control mechanisms at compile time . . . 175

3.6 Isolation . . . 177

3.7 Security functions in some operating systems . . . 179
- 3.7.1 IBM MVS . . . 179
- 3.7.2 UNIX . . . 180
- 3.7.3 VAX/VMS . . . 184
- 3.7.4 IBM VM/SP . . . 185
- 3.7.5 OS/400 . . . 187

3.8 Security packages . . . 189
- 3.8.1 RACF . . . 189
- 3.8.2 CA-ACF2 . . . 193
- 3.8.3 CA-TOP SECRET . . . 196

3.9 Security standards . . . 199
- 3.9.1 The DoD criteria . . . 203
- 3.9.2 Classification of some systems according to the DoD criteria . . . 213

3.10 Design of secure operating systems . . . 218
- 3.10.1 Kernel-based approach . . . 219
- 3.10.2 UCLA Secure UNIX . . . 223
- 3.10.3 Kernelized Secure Operating System (KSOS) . . . 225
- 3.10.4 Secure Xenix . . . 226
- 3.10.5 VAX Security Kernel . . . 227

**4 Database security design . . . 237**

4.1 Introduction . . . 237

4.2 Secure DBMS design . . . 238
- 4.2.1 Security mechanisms in DBMSs . . . 239
- 4.2.2 The System R authorization model . . . 245
- 4.2.3 Secure DBMS architectures . . . 253
- 4.2.4 Research prototypes . . . 262
- 4.2.5 Commercial products . . . 265

4.3 Design of secure databases . . . 273
- 4.3.1 Preliminary analysis . . . 276
- 4.3.2 Requirement analysis and security policy selection . . . 277
- 4.3.3 Conceptual design . . . 281
- 4.3.4 Logical design . . . 282

4.3.5 Physical design . . . 283
4.3.6 Implementation of security mechanisms . . . 283
4.3.7 Verification and testing . . . 288

**5 Statistical database security . . . 291**
5.1 Introduction . . . 291
5.2 Basic concepts and assumptions . . . 293
5.3 Inference protection techniques . . . 296
5.3.1 Conceptual techniques . . . 298
5.3.2 Restriction-based techniques . . . 304
5.3.3 Perturbation-based techniques . . . 319
5.4 A general framework for comparing inference protection techniques . . . 335

**6 Intrusion detection . . . 343**
6.1 Introduction . . . 343
6.2 Automated tools for intrusion detection . . . 344
6.3 Expert-systems-based approach: the IDES system . . . 348
6.3.1 Foundations . . . 348
6.3.2 IDES model . . . 356
6.3.3 System architecture . . . 361
6.4 The Haystack system . . . 365
6.4.1 Intrusion types . . . 366
6.4.2 Analysis of the audit trail . . . 367
6.4.3 Design principles and system architecture . . . 367
6.5 The Multics Intrusion Detection and Alerting System (MIDAS) . . . 369
6.5.1 Rules . . . 369
6.5.2 MIDAS operation . . . 370
6.6 Audit in Trusted Database Management Systems (TDBMS) . . . 372
6.6.1 Study results . . . 373
6.7 The Wisdom and Sense (W&S) anomaly detection system . . . 374
6.7.1 Approach: the rule base . . . 375
6.7.2 Data model . . . 375
6.7.3 Evaluation of rules for anomaly detection . . . 376
6.7.4 Implementation . . . 376
6.8 The Time-based Inductive Machine (TIM) approach . . . 377
6.8.1 Input data and rules . . . 378
6.8.2 Anomaly detection . . . 378
6.8.3 System considerations . . . 379
6.9 Trends in intrusion detection . . . 380
6.9.1 Machine Learning (ML) . . . 380
6.9.2 Software engineering techniques . . . 381
6.9.3 Neural naturals . . . 382

**7 Security models for next-generation databases . . . . . . . . . . . . . 385**
7.1 Introduction . . . . . . . . . . . . . . . . . . . . . . . . . . . . 385
7.1.1 Elements of active databases . . . . . . . . . . . . . . 386
7.1.2 Elements of object-oriented databases . . . . . . . . . . 387
7.2 Security in active databases . . . . . . . . . . . . . . . . . . . 390
7.3 Security in object-oriented databases. . . . . . . . . . . . . . . 394
7.4 The ORION authorization model . . . . . . . . . . . . . . . . . 396
7.4.1 Subjects . . . . . . . . . . . . . . . . . . . . . . . . . 396
7.4.2 Objects . . . . . . . . . . . . . . . . . . . . . . . . . 397
7.4.3 Access modes . . . . . . . . . . . . . . . . . . . . . . 399
7.4.4 Authorizations. . . . . . . . . . . . . . . . . . . . . . 401
7.4.5 Rules for the derivation of implicit authorizations and access control. . . . . . . . . . . . . . . . . . . . . 404
7.4.6 Inheritance hierarchies, composite objects and versions . . . . . . . . . . . . . . . . . . . . . . . . . 406
7.5 The Bertino–Weigand model. . . . . . . . . . . . . . . . . . . 408
7.6 Authorization models based on methods . . . . . . . . . . . . . 410
7.6.1 The Iris authorization model . . . . . . . . . . . . . . . 410
7.6.2 The data-hiding model . . . . . . . . . . . . . . . . . . 412
7.7 The message filter . . . . . . . . . . . . . . . . . . . . . . . . 413
7.7.1 Entities of the model . . . . . . . . . . . . . . . . . . . 414
7.7.2 Information flow . . . . . . . . . . . . . . . . . . . . . 414
7.7.3 Message-filtering algorithm . . . . . . . . . . . . . . . 415
7.7.4 Classification requirement representation . . . . . . . . . 417
7.8 SORION model . . . . . . . . . . . . . . . . . . . . . . . . . 418
7.8.1 Entities of the model . . . . . . . . . . . . . . . . . . . 420
7.8.2 Security policy axioms. . . . . . . . . . . . . . . . . . 420
7.8.3 Classification axioms. . . . . . . . . . . . . . . . . . . 421
7.8.4 Classification requirement representation . . . . . . . . . 423
7.9 The Millen–Lunt model. . . . . . . . . . . . . . . . . . . . . . 426
7.9.1 Entities of the model . . . . . . . . . . . . . . . . . . . 426
7.9.2 Axioms . . . . . . . . . . . . . . . . . . . . . . . . . 427
7.9.3 Classification requirement representation . . . . . . . . . 429
7.10 Modelling multilevel entities through single-level objects . . . . . . . . . . . . . . . . . . . . . . . . . . . . . 430
7.11 Observations on OODBMS security . . . . . . . . . . . . . . . 432

Index . . . . . . . . . . . . . . . . . . . . . . . . . . . . . . . 439

# 1 Information security

## 1.1 Introduction

The increasing development of information technology in the past few years has led to the widespread use of computer systems in various public and private organizations, such as banks, universities, manufacturing or service companies, hospitals, libraries, central or distributed administration and so on. The increased reliability now offered in hardware and software technologies, coupled with the continuous reduction of costs, the increasing professional expertise of information specialists and the availability of support tools, have all contributed to encourage the widespread use of computing services.

This has meant that more data than ever before is now stored and managed by computer systems, or rather by the tools and techniques capable of supporting and meeting these application requirements. Such requirements have been largely satisfied by database technology employing *Database Management Systems (DBMSs)*.

A database (Ullman, 1988; Date, 1990) is a collection of permanent data, managed by the DBMS software. Database design methodologies have been developed to support the different information requirements and operation environments of applications. Conceptual and logical data models have been studied, with the associated languages and tools for data definition, manipulation and querying. The target has been the production of DBMSs able to access efficiently application-defined subsets of data in a database.

A further basic feature of a DBMS is its ability to manage transactions simultaneously on behalf of concurrent applications; thus, each application has the view of a virtually dedicated database. This feature turns out to be relevant when considering, for example, a banking database and its several on-line users, or an airline or railway database and its related booking activities.

Distributed processing has also contributed to advances in the development and automation of information systems. Today, the processing units of an organization and its remote branches can communicate rapidly with each other via computer networks, personal computers and workstations, thus allowing a rapid transfer of a large amount of data.

Although the increasingly widespread use of both centralized and distributed databases has proved necessary to support business functions, it has also posed serious problems of data security (Denning and Denning, 1979; Parker, 1984). In fact, damage in a database environment does not only affect a single user or application but rather the whole information system: hence, consequences are *a priori* unpredictable (Dobkin *et al.*, 1979). Advances in information processing techniques (tools and languages) aimed at a simplification of human/machine interfaces have served to make databases available to different types of user; consequently, more serious security problems arise (Denning, 1990). Therefore, in computer-based information systems, technologies, tools and procedures concerning security are essential both to assure system continuity and reliability and to protect data and programs from intrusions, modifications, theft and unauthorized disclosure (Saltzer and Schroeder, 1975; Summers, 1984).

The complexity of the design and implementation of a secure information system depends on the number of factors to be taken into account, such as the heterogeneity of system users, the granularity and territorial extension of information systems (both at national and international levels), the uncontrollable and unpredictable consequences of loss of information, and the difficulties in modelling, specifying and verifying data security (Fernandez, *et al.*, 1981; Denning, 1982; Perry, 1982; Pfleeger, 1989; Hruska and Jackson, 1990; McLean, 1990).

### 1.1.1 Database security

*Information security* in a database includes three main aspects: *secrecy, integrity, and availability* (Russell and Gangemi, 1991). Note that in this book, the terms authorization, protection and security will be used interchangeably. More precisely, authorization is used in database systems, protection is typical of operating systems, and security is the most general term. We use the same term employed by the literature regarding each model or system considered.

Ensuring **secrecy** means preventing/detecting/deterring the improper disclosure of information. In general, secrecy properly refers to protection of data involved in highly protected environments, such as military environments or departments of commercial environments. *Privacy* refers to information about individuals, and is sometimes defined as 'the right of an individual, group or institution to determine when, how and for what purpose information concerning himself/itself can be collected, stored and released to other people or entities'. Therefore, privacy refers to environments where data about people or legal individuals is maintained; privacy is ensured by laws and rules in many countries. *Secrecy* is a most relevant aspect of security-critical environments. For example, the target coordinates of a missile should not be improperly disclosed. In commercial environments, secrecy of information is strictly coupled with the application environment and with the internal policies or market strategies and regulations of the organization (Sterne *et al.*, 1991). Consequently, in such environments, secrecy will be ensured only for a portion of data that is defined as *critical* for the organization. As another example, a general policy of commercial environments is that employees should not come to know the salaries of their managers.

Ensuring **integrity** of information means preventing/detecting/deterring the improper modification of information (Sandhu and Jajodia, 1990). For example, in a military environment, the target coordinates of a missile should not be improperly modified. Also, in commercial environments, data integrity is a relevant aspect: the good working of an organization depends on correct operations on correct and coherent data. For example, an employee should not be able to modify his or her own salary, or improperly alter data regarding an electronic payment.

Ensuring **system availability** (that is, avoiding *denial of service*) means preventing/detecting/deterring improper denial of access to services provided by the system (Courtney, 1990). For example, in a commercial environment, payment orders regarding taxes should be made on time as fixed by law. Analogously, in a military environment, when the proper command is issued, the missile should fire.

In many environments, such as public institutions, secrecy and integrity are often needed in combination. For example, in hospitals, airline companies or credit institutions, both secrecy and integrity are required since, besides privacy constraints, correctness of data is vital. Wrong data would entail heavy damage ranging from financial loss to loss of human lives.

## 1.2 A survey of database concepts

A database is a collection of mutually correlated data permanently stored on persistent storage supports. It is used within an organization by different applications, each one having its own aims and purposes. In a database, data (*entities*) and entity associations that characterize an organization are described.

Data management functions, usually supplied by an operating system, are extended through a set of programs globally called the **Database Management System (DBMS)**. Great quantities of data can be accessed rapidly and efficiently by a DBMS which supplies a set of targeted functions, such as schema management, concurrent transaction management, data access control, logging, recovery of the database after system failures. This is useful for both the database and the application management. Management of a *logical model* describing data and associations among data is a further basic feature of a DBMS, which makes high-level languages available for this purpose.

In database design, a *conceptual phase* and a *logical phase* are distinguished, where *conceptual and logical models* are respectively used for describing the structure of the database. Of these **data models**, the logical model is DBMS dependent (for example, relational or hierarchical), while the conceptual model is used for *conceptual design* independent of the particular DBMS to be used. The *Entity–Relationship* model is one of the most popular conceptual models, based on the concepts of *entity*, as a class of real-world objects to be described in the database, and of *relationship*, modelling associations between two or more entities.

During logical design, the conceptual schema is translated into a *logical schema* describing data according to the logical model supported by the selected DBMS. Hierarchical, network and relational models are the logical models managed by traditional DBMS technology.

The **languages** available in a DBMS comprise a *Data Definition Language (DDL)*, a *Data Manipulation Language (DML)*, and a *Query Language (QL)*. The DDL supports the definition of the logical database schema. Operations on data are specified using the DML or the QL. Database operations are concerned with data retrieval, insertion, deletion and update. The DML, which generally requires full knowledge of the logical model and schema (procedural properties), is used by specialized users, such as application developers. Query languages, on the contrary, are declarative languages oriented to support non-practitioner end-users. DML languages can be 'hosted' within an ordinary programming language, called the host language. Thus, applications using programming languages can include DML instructions for data-oriented operations.

### 1.2.1 Components of a DBMS

The typical architecture of a DBMS is shown in Figure 1.1.

The modules of Figure 1.1 correspond to the following functionalities (Ullman, 1988):

- DDL compilation
- DML language processing
- Database querying
- Database management
- File management.

A set of data supports the functionality of these modules:

- Database description tables
- Authorization tables
- Concurrent access tables.

Sets of data in a database are requested by end users or application programs through DML instructions or via QL instructions. These instructions are then interpreted by the DBMS through the DML and QL processor. The purpose is query optimization according to the database schema, described in a set of database description tables. These are defined through DDL instructions compiled by the DDL compiler. Optimized queries are processed by the database manager and translated into operations on the physical files of data.

The database manager also checks the users' or programs' authorizations to data access by consulting the authorization tables. Authorized operations are

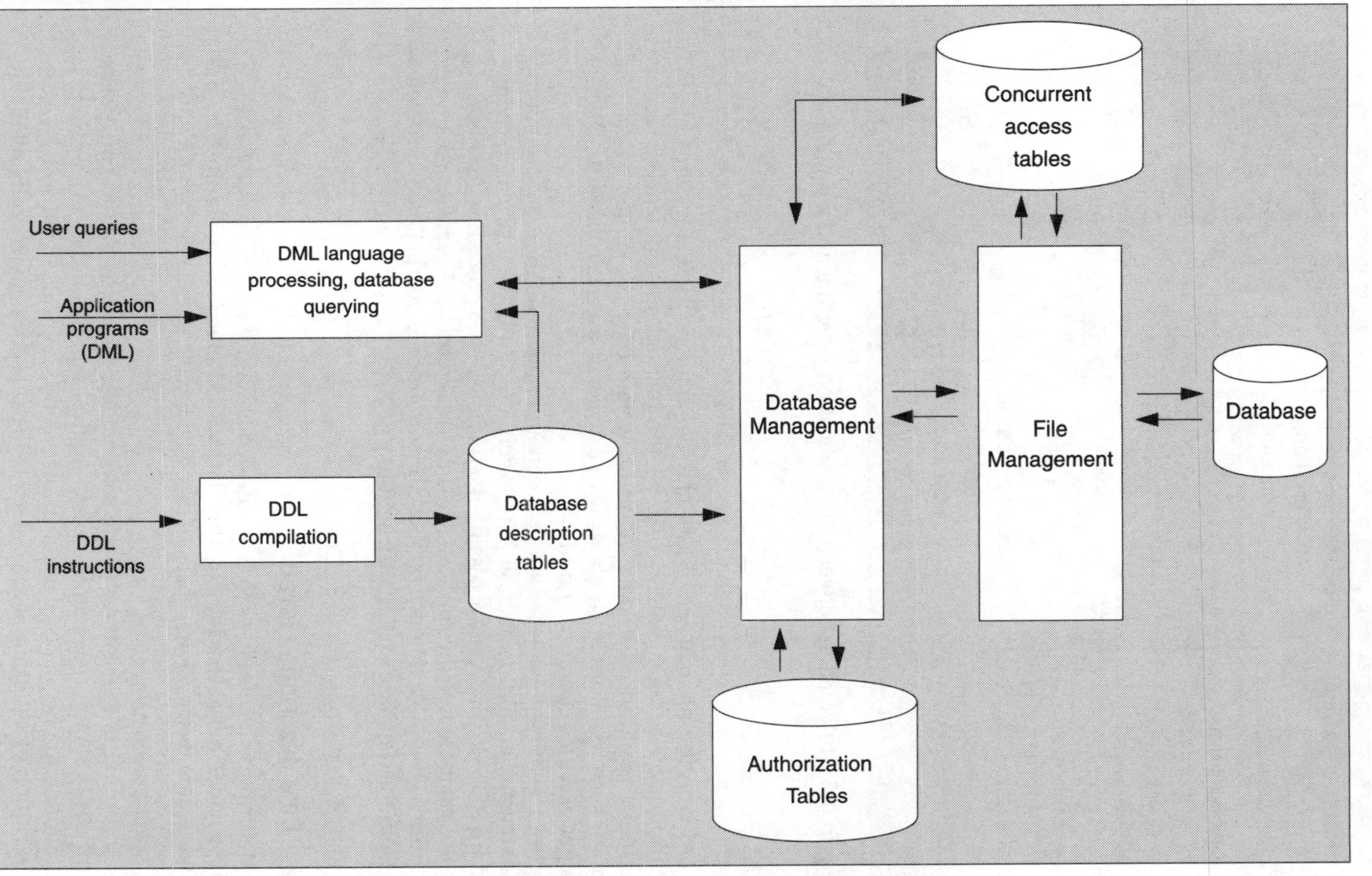


*Figure 1.1* DBMS architecture.

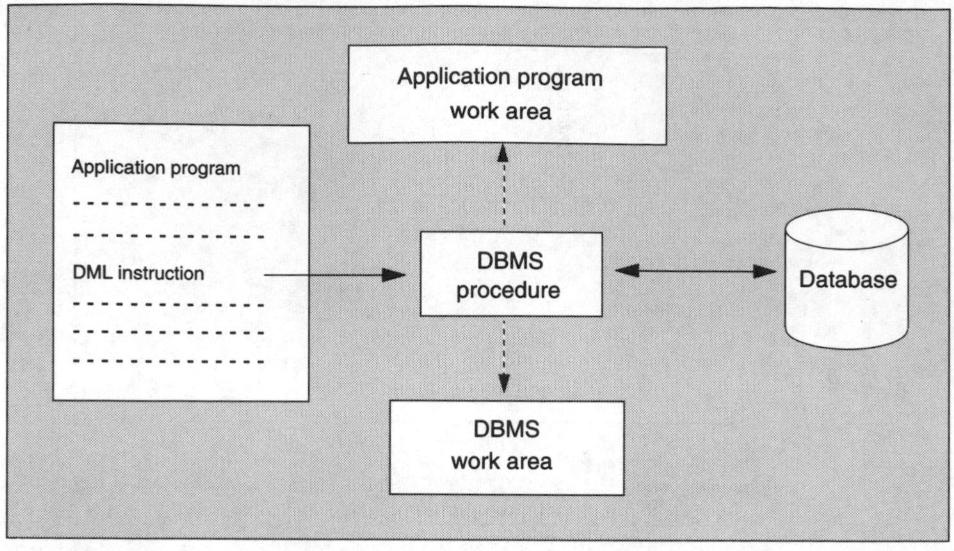


*Figure 1.2* Interaction between an application program and a database.

forwarded to the file manager. The database manager is also responsible for concurrent access management: that is, for managing simultaneous access requests by applications to data. A set of system data is maintained for this purpose, such as information about active locks at a certain instant. The file manager executes operations on files.

Figure 1.2 shows the interaction between an application program containing DML statements, and a database. The execution of a DML instruction corresponds to a DBMS procedure accessing the database. The procedure fetches data from the database into the application work area (retrieval instructions), moves data from a work area into the database (insert, update instructions), or deletes data from the database (delete instructions).

### 1.2.2 Data description levels

Data description levels of a DBMS are shown in Figure 1.3 (Ullman, 1988). Each level provides an abstraction of the database. Referring to Figure 1.3, the following data description levels can be considered in a DBMS:

- *Logical views*
  According to the features of the selected logical model and the purposes of applications, views on the whole logical schema of data are provided, tailored to the various application needs. Logical views are the description of a portion of the database logical schema. Generally available

are a DDL to define logical views, and a DML to operate on the logical views. The DDL for logical views is often similar to the DDL for logical schemes. DDL instructions are compiled by the DDL compilation module, to obtain the database description tables.

- *Logical data schema*
  At this level, all the data of the database is described using the logical model of the selected DBMS (hierarchical, network, relational). All data and its relationships are described through the DDL of the selected DBMS, and the various operations on the logical schema are specified through the DML of that DBMS.

- *Physical data schema*
  At this level, the storage structure of data within the files in secondary memory is described. Data is physically stored as records (of fixed or variable length) and record pointers.

The different levels allowed by a DBMS in the description of data support the notion of **logical and physical independence of data**.

Logical independence means that a logical schema can be modified without modifying the application programs operating on that schema. In this case modifications of the logical schema correspond to redefining the correspondence between the logical schema and the logical views of the applications on that schema.

Physical independence means that the physical data schema can be modified without modifying the applications accessing that data. Sometimes it also means that the physical structures for data storage can be modified without affecting the description of the logical data schema. This is due to the presence of an intermediate level between the logical schema level and the physical level (in the ANSI/SPARC proposals, this is called 'internal level') that directly interfaces these modifications to the logical schema.

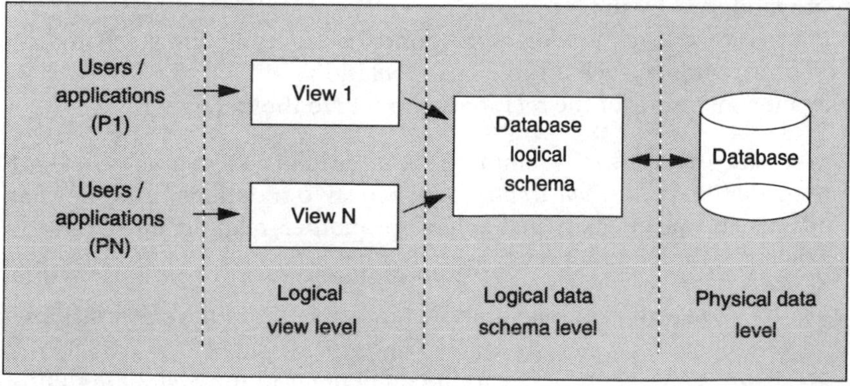


*Figure 1.3* Data description levels.

### 1.2.3 Elements of the relational data model

DBMSs based on the relational model are, nowadays, the most up-to-date commercially used technology for DBMSs. The reason for this is that they rely on a formal model, which provides high independence of the physical structures of data (Atzeni and De Antonellis, 1993). Additionally, the model is flexible in that it allows a variety of operations and queries that are not bound to the underlying physical features, unlike the hierarchical and network models.

The basis of the relational model is the mathematical concept of ***relation***, which, according to the set theory, is a subset of the Cartesian product $D_1 \times D_2 \times ... \times D_n$, (where $D_1, D_2, ..., D_n$ is a set of domains). A relation is, therefore, a set of $n$-tuples $(d_1, d_2,..., d_n)$ such that:

$$d_1 \in D_1, d_2 \in D_2, ..., d_n \in D_n$$

The number $n$ of domains, on which the relation is defined, is named the *degree* of the relation. The number of $n$-tuples of the relation is the *cardinality* of the relation. Each value $d_i$ in the $n$-tuple is named the *component*.

A relational database is a collection of tables, where a table corresponds to a relation. The table rows correspond to the $n$-tuples of the relation. The table columns correspond to the components of the $n$-tuples. The table columns are often assigned unique names, the *attributes*. Tables rows are all different and univocally identified by the values of one or more attributes called the *key* of the relation.

A *functional dependency* exists between two single-valued attributes $A_1$ and $A_2$ of a relation $r$ if and only if to every value of $A_1$ in $r$ there corresponds only one value of $A_2$ in $r$ (symbolically denoted by $A_1 \rightarrow A_2$).

The *relational schema* is composed of the relation name and the set of the relation attribute names. The *schema* of a relational database is the set of the relational schemas of all the relations defined for the representation of the entities and the relationships between entities of the database. An example of a relational database schema is reported in Figure 1.4, where the `Student` and `Course` entities and the 'many-to-many' relationship named `Enrolment` among them are modelled by three relations.

At the **instance** level, a table corresponds to each relational schema, and a record corresponds to each $n$-tuple of the relation.

Relevant constraints of the relational model are the following:

- *entity integrity constraint*, stating that no primary key value can be null;
- *referential integrity constraint*, between two relations, stating that an $n$-tuple in one relation that refers to another relation must refer to an existing $n$-tuple in that relation.

Figure 1.5 shows an example of an instance related to the schema shown in Figure 1.4.

As an example, we show a declaration statement in the SQL **data definition language** (Structured Query Language), defined for **relational** DBMSs. The declaration of the `Student` relation of Figure 1.4 has the following form in SQL:

```
Student ( StudNum, Name, Birthdate )
Course ( CourseCode, Teacher )
Enrolment ( StudNum, CourseCode, Grade )
```

*Figure 1.4* Sample relational schema.

```
CREATE TABLE Student
(StudNum NUMBER (6.0) NOT NULL,
Name CHAR (20),
Birthdate DATE);
CREATE INDEX FOR Student ON Name
```

| StudNum | Name | Birthdate |
|---|---|---|
| 306318 | Smith | 05-24-65 |
| 316804 | Johnson | 12-28-64 |
| 305700 | Bradford | 11-3-65 |
| 319887 | Partridge | 11-9-65 |

| CourseCode | Teacher |
|---|---|
| CS 130 | Brown |
| CS 104 | Schoen |
| CS 125 | Debson |

| StudNum | CourseCode | Grade |
|---|---|---|
| 306318 | CS 130 | A |
| 305700 | CS 130 | B |
| 319887 | CS 125 | A |
| 319887 | CS 104 | C |
| 319887 | CS 125 | D |

*Figure 1.5* An example of the schema of Figure 1.4.

This declaration means that a **Student** relation exists, with **StudNum, Name,** and **Birthdate** attributes for which the domain values are specified. In addition, a value must be always defined for **StudNum** in the database records, because this attribute is the relation key (primary key). The definition of an index on **Name** is useful for searching the student records more efficiently at the physical level.

As an example, the SQL instructions respectively corresponding to search, insert, delete and data update operations in the database are listed in the following **query and update** example:

```
SELECT Name FROM Student
WHERE StudNum > '316056' AND < '324567'
```

to find all the student names whose **StudNum** is in the given range of values.

```
INSERT INTO Student
VALUES (307240, 'Ferg', '09-25-65')
```

to insert into the **Student** table the new record corresponding to the student **Ferg** with the specified values.

```
DELETE FROM Student
WHERE StudNum = '306318'
```

to delete from the **Student** table a record with the specified key.

```
UPDATE Student
SET Birthdate = '11-28-63'
WHERE StudNum = '319887'
```

to update the **Birthdate** attribute of the record whose **StudNum** value is **319887** to the new value specified in the **SET** clause.

Since a formal basis is available (the concept of 'relation'), *query languages* can be defined for the relational model to express formally operations on the relations. The best known query language of this type is the **relational algebra** which is a procedural language with a set of operators whose operands are relations. All the relational algebra operators are applied on relations and give relations as a result. The main operators on sets of the relational algebra are:

- *Union*: applied to $r$ and $s$, returns a new relation $t$ defined as the set of the $n$-tuples belonging to $r$ or to $s$;
- *Difference* $r - s$: applied to $r$ and $s$ returns a new relation $t$ defined as the set of the $n$-tuples belonging to $r$ and not to $s$;
- *Intersection*: applied to $r$ and $s$ returns a new relation $t$ defined as the set of the $n$-tuples belonging to $r$ and to $s$;
- *Cartesian product*: applied to $r$ and $s$, returns a new relation $t$ defined as the set of the $n$-tuples that are a combination of the $n$-tuples of $r$ and $s$.

The basic relational algebra operators specifically defined for relations are:

- *Selection* $\sigma$: applied to a relation $r$, returns a new relation $s$ formed of the $n$-tuples of $r$ verifying a predicate (expressed through a formula involving constants, and comparison operators). It implements the horizontal decomposition of $r$;
- *Projection* $\pi$: applied to a relation $r$, returns a relation $s$ containing the $n$-tuples of $r$ defined on a subset of the attributes of $r$. It implements the vertical decomposition of $r$;
- *Natural join*, $r \bowtie s$: let $r(YX)$ and $s(XZ)$ be two relations, such that $YX \cap XZ = X$; the natural join of $r$ and $s$ is a relation $t$ defined on Y X Z consisting of the set of the $n$-tuples resulting from the concatenation of $n$-tuples in $r$ with $n$-tuples in $s$ that have identical values for the attributes X.

## 1.3 Security problems in databases

In database environments, the different applications and users of an organization refer to a unique integrated set of data through the DBMS. On the one hand, this solves problems like duplication, data inconsistency, or dependence between the programs and the data structures; on the other hand, security threats become a more serious and important issue in database environments.

Achieving security in a database environment means identifying the threats and choosing the proper *policies* ('what' the security system is expected to do) (Olson and Marshall, 1990) and *mechanisms* ('how' the security system should achieve the security goals) (Bell, 1990). It also involves the provision of *security system assurance* ('how well' the security system meets the protection requirements and executes the expected functions) (Andrews and MacEwen, 1990).

### 1.3.1 Threats to database security

A *threat* can be defined as a hostile agent that, either casually or by using a specialized technique, can disclose or modify the information managed by a system.

Violations to database security consist of improper readings, modifications or deletions of data. Events that bring violations to databases are called threats (Hinke, 1988). Consequences of violations can be grouped into three categories.

- *Improper release of information* caused by reading of data from intentional or accidental access by improper users. Included in this category are violations to secrecy deriving from authorized observation of data that could be used to infer unauthorized information.
- *Improper modification of data.* This involves all violations to data integrity through improper data handling or modifications. Improper modifications do not necessarily involve unauthorized reading, as data can be tampered with without being read.
- *Denial of service.* This involves those actions that could prevent users from accessing data or using resources.

Security threats can also be classified according to the way they can occur: that is, as *non-fraudulent* (accidental) and *fraudulent* (intentional) threats.

Non-fraudulent threats are casual accidents independent of a determined will to cause damage. These involve:

- *Natural or accidental disasters*, such as earthquakes, water damage or fire. These accidents can damage the system hardware and the stored data; they always cause an integrity violation or denial of service.
- *Errors or bugs in hardware or software*. This may lead to incorrect application of the security policies and, therefore, to unauthorized access, reading or modification of data, or to denial of access to authorized users.
- *Human errors* causing unintentional violations such as incorrect input or incorrect use of applications: the consequences are analogous to those caused by errors or bugs.

Fraudulent or intentional factors denote an explicit and determined fraudulent will to cause damage. Violations involve two classes of user:

(1) *Authorized users* who can abuse their privileges and authority.
(2) *Hostile agents*, namely, improper users (outsiders and insiders) executing actions of vandalism to the software and/or system hardware, or improperly reading or writing data. In both cases 'legal' tasks or 'legal' use of applications can mask the real fraudulent purpose. Typically, viruses, Trojan Horses and trapdoors are attacks of hostile agents. A virus is a code able to copy itself and to damage permanently and often irreparably the environment where it gets reproduced. A Trojan Horse is a program which, under an apparent utility, collects information for its own, possibly fraudulent, use. It can be software installed unwittingly by authorized users which, in addition to the desired functionalities, exploits the user's legitimate privileges to cause a security breach. A trapdoor is a code segment hidden within a program; a special input will start this segment and allow its owner to skip the protection mechanisms and to access the system resources beyond his or her privileges.

## 1.3.2 Database protection requirements

Protecting a database from possible threats means protecting resources, particularly stored data, from accidental or intentional unauthorized reading and/or updates (Fernandez *et al.*, 1981). Database protection requirements can be summarized as follows.

#### *Protection from improper access*

This is a primary problem to which this book devotes major attention. It consists of granting access to a database only to authorized users. Access requests have to be checked by the DBMS against the user's or application's authorizations. Access controls are more complex for databases than for files managed by an operating system. Controls need to apply to objects of a finer granularity such as records, attributes and values. Additionally, data within a database is semantically related, thus allowing a user to come to know the value of a data item without accessing it directly, but by inferring it from known values.

***Protection from inference***

Inference denotes the possibility of obtaining confidential information from non-confidential data. In particular, inference problems affect statistical databases where users must be prevented from tracing back to information on individual entities starting from statistical aggregated information. For example, suppose a user first queries the database for the average salary of women employees, and later for the number of women employees. If this last value is 1, the user is enabled to draw (infer) the woman's salary using only statistical queries (average and counting).

***Integrity of the database***

This requirement concerns database protection from unauthorized access that could modify the contents of data, as well as from errors, viruses, sabotage or *failures* in the system that could damage stored data. This kind of protection is partly carried out by the DBMS through proper system controls, and various backup and recovery procedures, and partly through *ad hoc* security procedures.

Backup and recovery procedures are widely investigated in DBMS literature (Korth and Silberschatz, 1988). Hereafter, we summarize briefly the relevant concepts. In case of failure, the state of the database may no longer be consistent. To preserve consistency, we require that each transaction be atomic. Atomicity means that a transaction can only:

(1) Terminate correctly, modifying the accessed data;
(2) Terminate unsuccessfully without modifying the accessed data.

After a transaction has terminated correctly, the data modifications are made permanent (durability).

The *recovery system* uses a log journal, namely, a file containing a sequence of records stored into stable storage. For each transaction, the log journal records the operations that have been performed on data (read, write, insert, delete) as well as transaction control operations ('begin transaction', 'commit' – correct termination, 'abort' – unsuccessful termination, 'end transaction'), also the old value and the new value of the records involved.

Basically, the recovery system reads the log file to determine the transactions to be undone (i.e., all noncommitted transactions), and the transactions to be redone (i.e., transactions having a 'commit' in the log). To undo a transaction means to copy the old value of each operation in the involved record. To redo a transaction means to copy the new value of each operation in the record.

**Ad-hoc security procedures** aim to protect data from unauthorized modifications, alterations, insertions and erasures. Modelling, design and enforcement of these procedures is one of the goals of the logical security of a database, as illustrated extensively in this book.

### *Operational integrity of data*

This requirement aims to ensure the logical consistency of data in a database during concurrent transactions. The **concurrency manager** is the DBMS subsystem that fulfils this requirement.

The concurrency manager ensures the *serializability* and *isolation* properties of transactions. Serializability means that the outcome of a concurrent run of a set of transactions is the same as the one produced by a strict sequence of these transactions. *Isolation* means mutual independence among transactions, thus avoiding 'domino effects', where an 'abort transaction' causes other transactions to abort in a cascade.

The problem of ensuring that concurrent access to the same data item by different transactions does not lead to data inconsistency is commonly solved through **locking** techniques.

*Lock and unlock* techniques consist, respectively, in blocking data items for the time needed to execute an operation, and in releasing the items once the operation has been completed. In this way, a transaction can lock a data item, making it inaccessible to other transactions. The item is accessible again at release time.

However, it is not possible to ensure serializability sufficiently by locking techniques alone: the *two-phases locking* protocol overcomes this problem. According to this protocol, lock and unlock operations must be executed to prevent a transaction from blocking other resources (that is, demanding further blocks) after releasing some item. This assures transaction serializability through a growing phase for lock acquisition and a decreasing phase for lock releasing. According to a second principle of this protocol, a transaction is prevented from releasing resources (that is, a lock) before commit, abort or writing operations have been executed for this transaction. Owing to this principle, commit or abort operations are executed by a transaction only when all the required resources are actually available.

### *Semantic integrity of data*

The problem is to ensure the logical consistency of modified data by controlling data values in the allowed range. Restrictions on data values (for example, attribute values in a relational database) are expressed as *integrity constraints*.

Constraints can be defined for the whole database (conditions defining the correct state of a database), or for transitions (conditions to be verified in order to execute a modification to the database).

### *Accountability and auditing*

This requirement consists of the possibility of recording all accesses to data, for both 'read' and 'write' operations (Bonium, 1988). Auditing and accountability are useful deterrent tools for data physical integrity, as well as for subsequent analysis of access sequences to a database. The granularity level of the registered operations could be a problem for a database; it might be useful to record operations involving the single value inside a record, but this is impractical from the viewpoint of time and cost.

#### *User authentication*

This requirement concerns the necessity of identifying uniquely the database users. User identification is the basis of every authorization mechanism. Users are allowed access to data when identified as 'authorized' users by the system.

#### *Management and protection of sensitive data*

Databases may contain *sensitive data* that should not to be made public; some databases contain only sensitive data (for example, military databases), while others are completely public (for example, library databases). Databases containing mixed data, that is, both sensitive and ordinary data, exhibit more complex protection problems. A data item is sensitive in various circumstances: by itself; when combined with other data; for being contained in records that are declared as sensitive or for being declared sensitive by the *Database Administrator (DBA)*.

Access control for databases containing mixed data consists primarily in protecting the confidentiality of sensitive data, allowing access only to authorized users (generally a small portion of the user population); these users are granted a set of operations on sensitive data and are prevented from propagating their privileges.

In addition, access control allows users who are authorized for sensitive data to work on non-sensitive data as well, together with other users, with no interferences.

Finally, situations may arise where authorized users can access a given set of sensitive data separately, although they cannot access all data concurrently.

#### *Multilevel protection*

'Multilevel protection' means a set of protection requirements. Information may need to be classified at various levels of protection: for example, in military databases, where a finer classification is needed than simply 'sensitive' and 'ordinary' data. In these environments, sensitive levels can be different even among items of the same record, or values of the same attribute. In this sense, multilevel protection is intended both as the assignment of classification levels to different information items and as the assignment of different accesses to single items according to their classification.

A further requirement in multilevel protection concerns the possibility of assigning a level to aggregated information to express that sensitivity is higher or lower for aggregated items than for the single items participating in the aggregation. Secrecy and integrity of multilevel information is met by assigning a clearance to users and by allowing a user to access data classified at the user clearance level.

#### *Confinement*

Confinement is intended as the necessity to avoid undesired *information transfer* between system programs: for example, transfer of 'critical' data to unauthorized programs. Information transfer occurs along **authorized**

**channels**, **memory channels**, and **covert channels**. Authorized channels supply output information via authorized actions: for example, editing or compiling a file. Memory channels are memory areas where data stored by a program can be read by other programs. A covert channel is a communication channel based on the use of system resources not normally intended for communication between the subjects (processes) of the system. For example, a program that varies its pagination rate when processing some critical data could transfer information to another program which can trace back the critical data by examining those variations. As another example, a covert channel between a 'high' subject and a 'low' subject can occur via Trojan Horses included respectively in 'high' and 'low' software, which leak information, unbeknown to the 'high' subject. The concern of covert channels is mainly with subjects (not users) which might contain infected code (Levin *et al.*, 1990).

## 1.4 Security controls

Database protection can be obtained through security measures for:

- Flow control
- Inference control
- Access control.

To these controls, *cryptographic techniques* can be added, which consist of coding stored data under a secret enciphering key. Through these techniques secrecy of information is assured by making data visible to anyone but only understandable to authorized users (Denning, 1982).

### 1.4.1 Flow control

Flow controls regulate the distribution (flow) of information among accessible objects (Denning, 1976, 1977, 1982). A flow between object X and object Y occurs when a statement reads values from X and writes values into Y. Flow controls check that information 'contained' in some objects (for example, reports) does not flow explicitly (through a copy) or implicitly (via groups of instructions involving intermediate objects) into less protected objects. Should this occur, a user could indirectly get in Y what he cannot get directly from X, thus leading to secrecy violation.

Copying data from X to Y is the typical example of information flow (from X to Y). Moreover, partial information flow occurs when part of the information in X is copied or when data moved to Y is not exactly data contained in X but can provide information about it. An example is a test operation on X: by observing the result of this test, information can be inferred on the value of X.

Flow-control policies require admissible flows to be listed or regulated. A flow violation occurs via a request for data transfer between two objects for which, on the basis of admitted flows, that transfer is unauthorized. Control mechanisms should deny the execution of these requests.

Often, flow-control problems are faced by classifying the system elements: that is, objects and subjects. 'Read' and 'write' operations among these are authorized on the basis of relationships among the classes. Higher-class objects are more protected during 'read' access than lower-class objects: here flow controls prevent violations consisting of information transfer to lower levels, that is, to more accessible levels. Instead, transfer to higher levels, namely to more protected levels, is allowed. The risk is to over-classify information with more protection than is appropriate for its actual sensitivity. This problem in flow-control policies has been solved by defining operations that allow transfer of objects to lower levels, while keeping unaltered the sensitivity of data in these objects.

### 1.4.2 Inference control

Inference controls aim at protecting data from indirect detection (Denning and Schlorer, 1983). This occurs when a set X of data items to be read by a user can be used to obtain the set Y of data as $Y = f(X)$, that is, by applying a function $f$ to X.

An **inference channel** is a channel where users can find an item X and then use X to derive Y as $Y= f(X)$.

The main inference channels in a system are:

(1) *Indirect access*. This occurs when an unauthorized user succeeds in knowing the set of data Y (for which he is not authorized) through a query on the set of data X visible to him, and undergoing conditions on Y. For example, the following query:

```
SELECT X FROM r WHERE Y = value
```

reveals that $n$-tuples may exist in the relation $r$ verifying the condition Y=value.

Another example is the insertion of a record with an $n$-tuple having the same key of an already existing $n$-tuple not visible to the user performing the insertion. Upon system denial, the user infers the existence of an $n$-tuple that he cannot access, holding that specific key value. Indirect access is a flow violation, and problems concerning flow violations can sometimes be included in inference controls.

(2) *Correlated data*. Correlated data is the typical inference channel where visible X data is semantically connected to invisible Y data. Consequently, information about Y can be obtained by reading X. For example, in $z = t \times k$, $t$ and $k$ being visible, and $z$ invisible, the value of $z$ can be inferred from the existing 'times' arithmetical relation. Decreasing the uncertainty degree about a data value as a result of authorized requests can also be considered as inference.

(3) *Missing data.* A channel of missing data is an inference channel through which users can come to know the existence of a set of data X. Typically, a user can get an object name, although he or she may be prevented from access to the information contained therein. Another example is answering a user query about a relation by displaying, together with authorized information, null values which mask the sensitive inaccessible information. These null values make it possible to infer the existence of the masked item value (sometimes the value itself), or at least decrease the uncertainty about it.

**Statistical inference** is a further aspect involving deduction of data. The basic aspects of statistical inference are presented in Denning (1982) and Denning and Schlorer (1983): the issue is typical of databases releasing statistics about groups of individuals. In these databases, access to individual data is not allowed; instead, data is accessible only via *statistical functions.* However, traces of the original items contained in data obtained via statistics could be obtained by skilful users. Statistical attacks can be faced by two types of control:

(1) *Data perturbation.* This control is performed directly on the protected data. For example, it is achieved by grouping sensitive information and by replacing the original items by microstatistics so that the resulting global value is unchanged, but no single items are left in the database. As another method, information on single records can be biased through a proper perturbation function; this preserves data privacy without affecting the global statistics appreciably.

(2) *Query controls.* These are the most widely used. Most of them are based on the 'size' (number of records) of the query set (namely the set of records verifying the query). A well-known technique is the 'query-set size control' consisting in returning data only about sets sized between $k$ and $n - k$, $n$ being the total size of the database, and $k > 1$ a selected parameter. Query controls are also implemented by determining the sensitivity degree of information. To this purpose, the user's previous knowledge about data must be taken into account when processing a new query, in order to compute the total amount of information that the user would finally get and what damage to data secrecy could result from this. Despite satisfactory results, this kind of control proves to be expensive and difficult to manage. Quantifying the users' knowledge of information is difficult, since it depends on sources external to the system, or released formerly and no longer belonging to the system.

### 1.4.3 Access control

Access controls in information systems are responsible for ensuring that all direct accesses to the system objects occur exclusively according to the modes and rules fixed by protection policies. An *access control system* (Figure 1.6) includes subjects (users, processes) who access objects (data, programs) through operations ('read', 'write', 'run'). Functionally, it consists of two components:

(1) A *set of access policies and rules:* information stored in the system, stating the access modes to be followed by subjects upon access to objects.
(2) A *set of control procedures (security mechanisms)* that check the queries (access requests) against the stated rules (query validation process); queries may then be allowed, denied or modified, filtering out unauthorized data.

***Security policies***

The security policies of a system are high-level guidelines concerning design and management of authorization systems (Fernandez *et al.*, 1981). Generally, they express the basic choices taken by an organization for its own data security. The definition of security policies leads to the explicit formulation of security *strategies*, thus giving security its rightful relevance instead of the fragmentary and approximate consideration it is often given. In fact, a clear and complete description of security strategies of an organization allows critical points and possible conflicts to be discussed and solved, and the objectives to be analysed and correlated.

Security policies define the *principles* on which access is granted or denied. Sometimes besides 'if', they state 'how' an access should be granted, or that the queries can return partial results, filtering out unauthorized data.

Authorization rules (access rules) are the expression of security policies; they determine the system behaviour at run time. The security policies should also state how the set of authorization rules (insertion, modification) is administered. Examples of security policies follow.

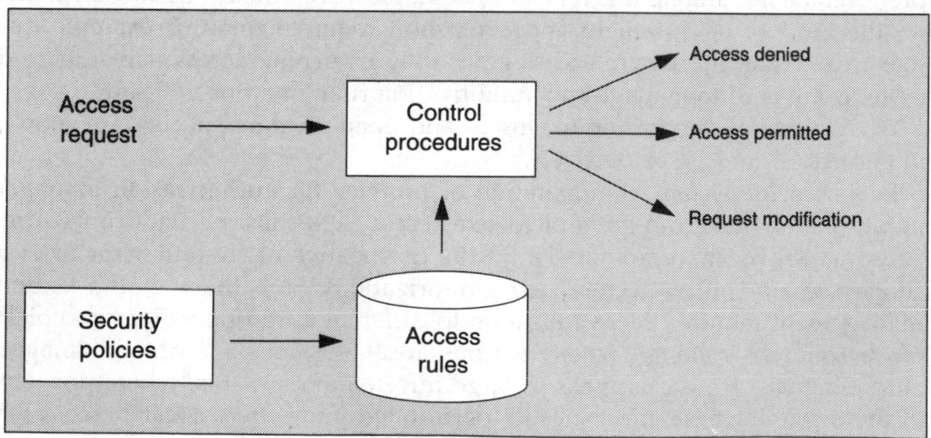


***Figure 1.6*** Access control system.

The question, 'How much information is accessible to each subject?' involves the problem of **access limitation**. Two basic policies exist:

(1) *Minimum privilege policy,* also called 'need-to-know' policy. According to this policy, system subjects should use the minimum quantity of information needed for their activity. This assumes a definable minimum that is sometimes hard to evaluate. A drawback of this policy is that overlimiting may lead to strong and useless restrictions for innocuous subjects.
(2) *Maximum privilege policy,* based on the principle of the 'maximum availability' of data in a database, so that sharing is maximized. This policy is adequate for environments such as universities or research centres, where strict protection is not particularly needed, because of both the reliability of users and the data-exchange requirements.

In a **closed system** only explicitly authorized accesses are allowed. In an **open system** accesses that are not explicitly forbidden are allowed. A closed system policy states that, for each subject, authorization rules exist specifying the access privileges of that subject on the system objects. These will be the only rights this subject is granted by the control mechanism. An open system policy states that, for each subject, authorization rules exist specifying the privileges that subject does not hold on the system objects. These will be the only rights this subject will be denied by the control mechanism.

Open and closed systems are mutually exclusive. When deciding upon security strategies, the choice depends on the features and requirements of the database environment, users, applications, organizational aspects, and so on. A closed system enforces the minimum privilege policy, whereas an open system enforces maximized sharing. Protection is higher in closed systems: errors such as a missing rule can deny authorized access but cause no damage, whereas in open systems this same event can grant unauthorized access.

Closed systems allow an easier evaluation of the authorization state of a system, that is, the privileges held by all users, and, for this reason, are often the preferred choice among this type of system. However, the choice also depends on the kind of environment and protection requirements; for example, for maximized sharing, where access grant may overcome access denial, closed systems are hard to manage and authorization rules onerous to insert.

Access controls, according to closed- and open-systems policies, are shown in Figures 1.7 and 1.8 respectively.

In a security system, the definition of **policies for authorization management**, that is, 'who' can grant or revoke access rights, is a relevant procedure. Grant and revocation are not always the prerogative of an authorizer or of a single security officer (centralized authorization). Sometimes, authorization management requires decentralization to different authorizers. This is typical of distributed systems, where various local systems are often managed autonomously. It also happens in large information systems, where portions of the same database are 'logically' partitioned into different databases, each managed by a local DBA.

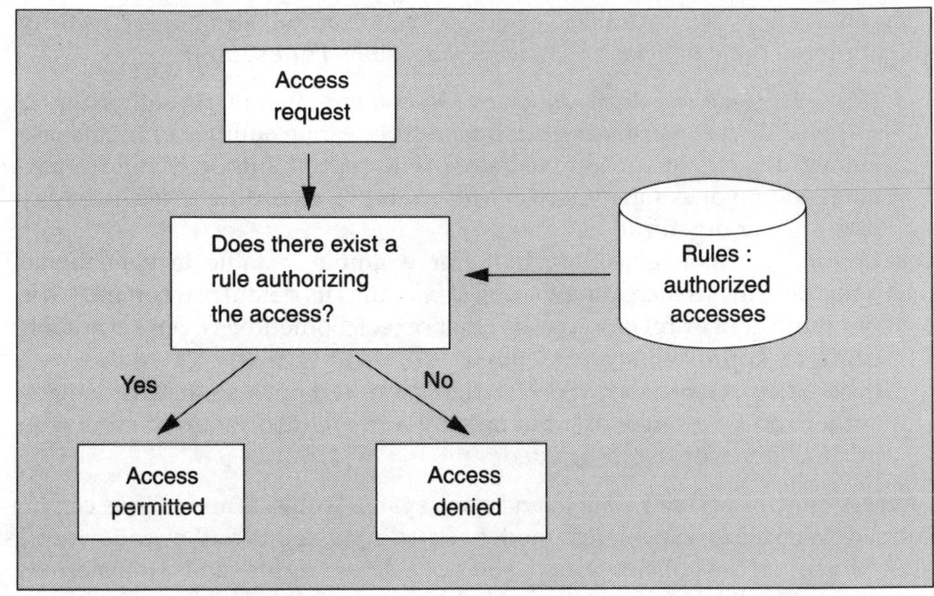


*Figure 1.7* Access control: closed system.

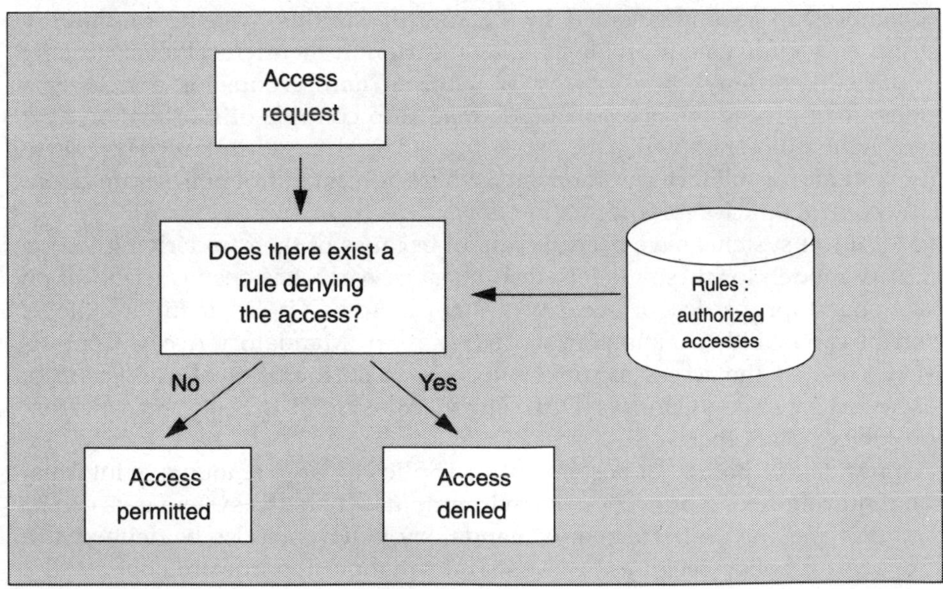


*Figure 1.8* Access control: open system.

The choice between centralized or decentralized administration is a security policy. Intermediate policies are, however, possible. For example:

- *Hierarchical decentralized authorization*, where a central authorizer is responsible for distributing administrative responsibilities of a database among dependent subadministrators. The central authorizer thus nominates and revokes subauthorizers, for example, according to the hierarchy of his or her organization.
- *Ownership*. Upon object creation (for example, a table in a relational database), the user creating the object becomes its default owner; he or she can thus grant or revoke access to that object. Sometimes a central administrator's approval may be required.
- *Cooperative authorization*. Special rights on certain resources cannot be authorized by a single user but only by a predefined group of users who must all agree on access granted.

**Access-control policies** state if, and how, system subjects and objects can be grouped, in order to share access modes according to given authorizations and rules. Moreover, the policies state if, and how, access rights can be transferred.

Grouping or classifying users who hold some privileges, or resources that share common protection requirements, greatly simplifies the specification of the security policies and the implementation of the security mechanisms. Therefore, various grouping criteria have been proposed.

Problems related to group management comprise, at the design level, the consequences of a user being a member of different groups and, at the implementation level, how to manage changing group membership.

Membership is implemented by default in various systems to simplify design and enforcement problems. Classification in hierarchical levels (totally or partially ordered) for groups of subjects and groups of objects is a widespread procedure; access controls map into controls of information flow among the different levels. This procedure is largely used in **multilevel security systems** for military environments, where access control policies are essentially control policies for information flow.

Multilevel systems have been successful because of their underlying formal security model; for these models, theoretical research has been carried out on the general properties of security systems. Access policies for multilevel systems can be either mandatory or discretionary. Mandatory Access Controls (MAC) restrict the access of subjects to objects on the basis of *security labels*. Discretionary Access Controls (DAC) allow access rights to be propagated from one subject to another.

A **mandatory policy** for access control applies to large amounts of information requiring strong protection in environments where the system data can be classified and the users cleared. A mandatory policy can also be defined as a flow-control policy because it prevents information flow towards objects of a lower classification. Access to data is determined by a mandatory policy through definition of subject and object security classes. The two main features of an object security class are: the *classification level*, which reflects the information it contains, and the category (application area) to which object information refers. Classification levels are, for example:

```
0 = Unclassified
1 = Confidential
2 = Secret
3 = Top secret
```

Categories tend to reflect the system areas or departments of the organization. In military environments, for example, the following could be areas:

```
Nuclear - Nato - Intelligence
```

while in industrial environments areas could be:

```
Production - Personnel - Engineering - Administration
```

For $m$ system areas, possible categories derivable from their associations would be $2^m$.

A relation of partial order is defined on the Security Classes *SC* defined as:

$SC = (A,C)$

*A* being the classification level, and C a category. This relation states that, given two security classes, $SC = (A, C)$ and $SC' = (A', C')$:

$SC \leq SC'$

if, and only if, the following conditions are verified:

$A \leq A'$ and $C' \supset C$

Thus, for example, the relation:

(2, *Nuclear*) ≤ (3, (*Nuclear, Nato*))

is verified, while:

(2, (*Nuclear, Nato*)) ≤ (3, *Nato*)

is not verified.

Each subject and each object is assigned a security class comprising a sensitivity level and a set of categories. These two components correspond, both for subjects and objects, to their role in the system.

A subject classification reflects the degree of trust that can be assigned to that subject, and the application area where it operates. An object classification reflects the sensitivity of the information contained in the object, i.e., the potential damage that could result from unauthorized disclosure of information.

A set of axioms determines the relations to be verified between the subject class and the object class in order to allow subjects to access objects according to security criteria. These relations depend on the access mode.

With regard to access right transfer, assigned rights cannot be changed and modifications are permitted only to the authorizer. This means that full control on the authorization system is kept by the authorizer. Access control through mandatory policies is depicted in Figure 1.9.

**Discretionary policies** require that, for each *subject, authorization rules* be defined specifying the *privileges* owned on the system *objects*. Access requests are checked by the discretionary control mechanism and access is granted only to subjects for which an authorization rule exists and is verified (Figure 1.10).

Discretionary policies are based on the identification of the user requesting the access. 'Discretionary' means that the possibility exists for users to grant and revoke access rights on some objects. This implies the decentralization of the administrative control through ownership. However, a discretionary policy is also well suited for centralized administration. In this case, authorizations will be managed by the system administrator: decentralized administration implies discretionary control policies, while the contrary does not normally hold. Discretionary policies need more complex authorization mechanisms, also aimed at avoiding loss of control on right *propagation* from the authorizer or other responsible persons.

*Revocation of propagated rights* is a further problem. For each revoked right, the user(s) who subsequently granted or received it must be identified by the system. Various revocation policies exist for this purpose. DAC has some

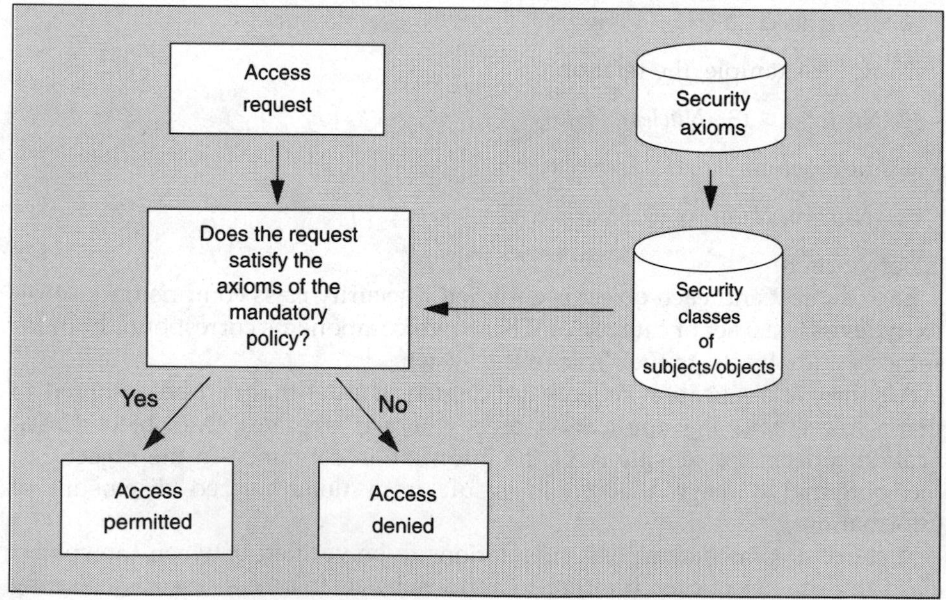


*Figure 1.9* Mandatory access control.

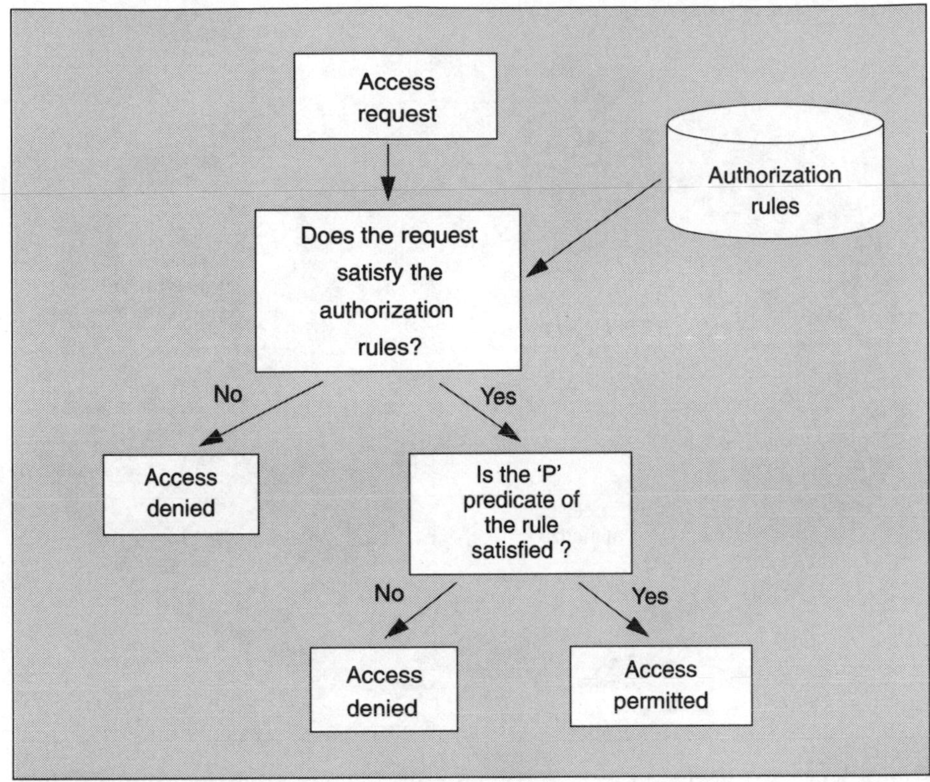


*Figure 1.10* Discretionary access control.

inherent weaknesses: it allows information from an object that can be read to flow to any other object that can be written by the subject; even if the user is trusted not to do that deliberately, it is still possible for Trojan Horses to copy information from one object to another.

Mandatory policies and discretionary policies are not mutually exclusive. They can be combined: the mandatory policy applies to the authorization control, while the discretionary policy applies to access control. If an access query meets the discretionary controls, for example, if authorizations exist for this query, it will also meet the mandatory policy axioms for the controlled authorizations (Figure 1.11).

#### *Authorization rules*

As described before, translating requirements and security policies into a set of authorization rules is the authorizer's task. Normally, security requirements are both determined by the organization and identified by the users, on the basis of their own experience.

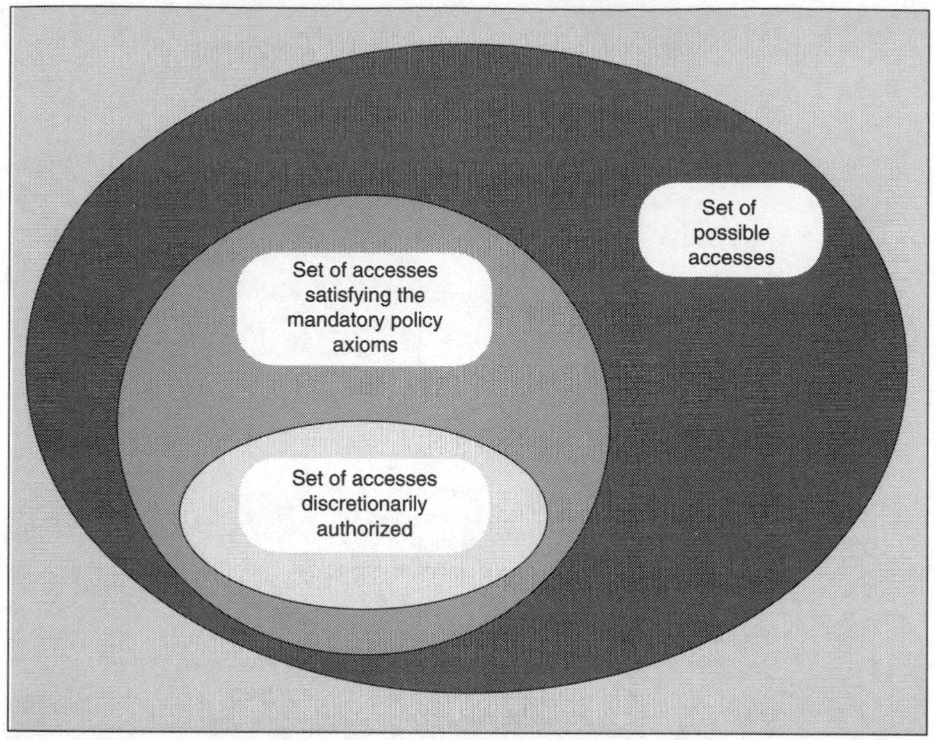


*Figure 1.11* Authorized rights in contemporaneous application of mandatory and discretionary policies.

Authorization rules are expressed in compliance with the hardware/software environments of the protection system, and the adopted security policies. The design process of a security system must supply a model supporting the authorizer when mapping requirements into the rules, according to the security policies that have been considered (Figure 1.12). Since single entities of the system are taken into consideration at the requirement specification level (for example, user `'Smith'`, file `'filename.ext'`, program library of application `'A1'`), the amount of associated requirements and access rules tends to be large. Different security models exist (see Chapter 2) supporting the representation of access rules as a structured and formalized design activity (Landwehr, 1981; Millen and Cerniglia, 1984). As an example, in the access matrix model, the set of security rules of a system is represented as a matrix *A* called *Authorization, or Access Matrix*, whose rows represent system subjects and columns represent system objects. An entry $A[i,j]$ represents the type of access allowed for subject $s_i$ to object $o_j$.

An example of authorization matrix is depicted in Table 1.1, where R = Read, W = Write, EXEC = Execute, CR = Create, and DEL = Delete. This is a simple case of **access control** based on the object name, called *name-dependent* access.

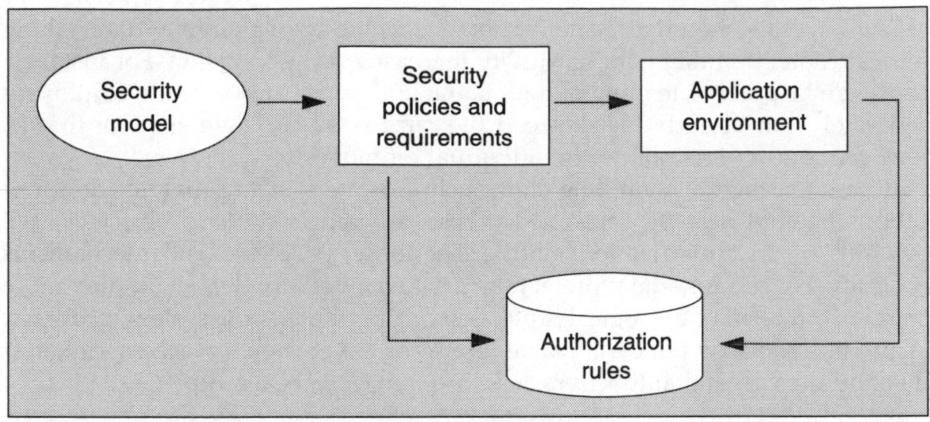


*Figure 1.12* Design of authorization rules.

*A*[*i,j*] may contain more complex security rules specifying access constraints between subjects and objects (for example, depending on the contents of *j*).

The following rule: 'User 1 can read record Y only if the third field of Y is < 100' is an example of *content-dependent control*. In this case, the matrix entries need to be 'extended' through a predicate expressing a constraint on the privilege. A security rule can be represented as a quadruple (Fernandez *et al.*, 1981; Bussolati and Martella, 1982):

$\langle s,o,t,p \rangle$

where $s$ = subject, $o$ = object, $t$ = type of access right and $p$ = (optional) predicate.

A predicate may also refer to some system variables, such as the date, time and query source, thus establishing the basis for *context-dependent control*. An example of context-dependent control is: 'classified information cannot be accessed via a remote login', or 'salary information can be updated only at the end of the year'. Content-dependent controls are beyond the scope of operating systems and are provided by the DBMS. Context-dependent controls can be partially provided by the operating system and partially by the DBMS. More sophisticated controls (such as controls based on the past history of accesses) require database support.

**Table 1.1** Authorization matrix.

| | | **Objects** | |
|---|---|---|---|
| **Subjects** | **File F1** | **File F2** | **File F3** |
| **User 1** | R, W | EXEC | EXEC |
| **User 2** | – | – | CR, DEL |
| **Program P1** | R, W | R | – |

Security rules should also specify non-accessible aggregations of data, taking into consideration that data sensitivity increases via aggregation. For instance, users can be granted reading of both name and salary values of the employees separately, but be forbidden to read the `'name-salary'` aggregation: that is, they cannot correlate salaries to individual employees.

Access to programs handling data, such as some system programs or applications, should also be controlled. These are represented as objects in the columns of an authorization matrix. Therefore, problems and mechanisms typically concerning data protection are extended to deal with the more complex problem of the logical protection of the whole of the system resources. With discretionary policies, where grant or revocation of access rights is demanded to several authorizers, a security rule can be a 6-tuple:

$$\langle a, s, o, t, p, f \rangle$$

where $a$ is an authorizer subject who granted $s$ the right $\langle o, t, p \rangle$, while $f$ is a copy flag describing the possibility for $s$ to further transfer $\langle o, t, p \rangle$ to other subjects. The security policies **(access rules management)** concerning access right transfer determine the presence of this flag and its use. For example, in some systems the flag is reset upon $n$ subsequent grants, thus allowing an $n$-deep privilege transfer.

Sometimes, a set of Auxiliary Procedures (AP) is associated to a security rule, to define which actions can be possibly undertaken by the security system, should an access query partially meet a rule. For each $AP_i$ belonging to a set $AP$, a condition $C_i$ is specified which can be a function of other components of the rule, or of system variables. A more complete form of an authorization rule is then the following:

$$\langle a,s,t,o,p,f, \{C_i, AP_i\} \rangle$$

### *Security mechanisms*

An access control system relies on security mechanisms that are functions implementing the security rules and policies (Denning, 1982). Security mechanisms concern the *prevention* of improper access (access control mechanisms), and the *detection* of improper access (auditing and intrusion detection mechanisms). Good prevention and detection require good authentication mechanisms. Access control mechanisms are more fundamental because prevention is preferred. However, sometimes, detection is the only option: for example, accountability in proper use of privileges or against modification of messages in a network.

Security mechanisms can be implemented via hardware, software or through administrative procedures (Landwehr 1983, Myers 1990). During the development of a security system, policies and mechanisms should be separated, making it possible to:

- Discuss access rules independently of the implementation mechanisms. This allows designers to focus on the correctness of the security requirements being captured and on the consistency of the security policies;

- Compare different access control policies or different implementation mechanisms for the same policy;
- Design mechanisms with the ability to implement different policies. This is necessary when policies need dynamic changes to accord with modifications to the application environment, and consequently with protection requirements. Should security policies be strictly related to implementation mechanisms, changes to policies must be adequate for the implementation of the control system.

The achievement of mechanisms complying with the designed policies is a crucial issue. In fact, the incorrect implementation of a security policy leads to incorrect access rules or to insufficient support of protection policies. Two basic types of system fault can derive from incorrect implementation:

(1) *Denial of allowed access.*
(2) *Grant of forbidden access.*

#### External mechanisms

These consist of administrative and physical control measures able to prevent undesired access to the physical resources (rooms, terminals, devices), so that only authorized accesses are allowed. Devices providing protection against accidental threats like short circuits, fire, earthquakes or environment conditions can also be included among external protection mechanisms. However, full protection cannot be assured, particularly in those environments where accidental attacks or violations can hardly be foreseen. The target is then to minimize possible damages. This means:

- Minimize possible violations;
- Minimize possible consequent damages;
- Provide recovery procedures.

#### Internal mechanisms

These are protection measures to be applied once a user bypasses, or receives authorized access by, the external controls. Authentication of user identity and verification of the legitimacy of the required actions according to the user authorizations are the basic actions. Internal protection consists of three principal mechanisms:

(1) *Authentication.* This mechanism prevents unauthorized users from using a system by checking their identity through:
    - Something a user is acquainted with (passwords, codes, etc.);
    - Something the user owns (magnetic cards, badges, etc.);
    - Physical characteristics of the user (fingerprints, signature, voice, etc.).

(2) *Access controls.* Upon successful authentication, queries entered by users can be answered only according to existing authorizations for these users.

(3) *Auditing mechanisms*. These monitor the utilization of the system resources from its users. Auditing mechanisms consist of two phases:
   - A *logging phase*, where all the access queries and related answers (both authorized and denied) are recorded;
   - A *reporting phase*, where reports from the previous phase are checked to detect possible violations or attacks.

   Auditing mechanisms are relevant for data protection because they support:
   - The evaluation of the *system reactions* in the face of some types of threat; this also helps to detect system leaks or inadequacies;
   - The *detection of violation attempts* executed through sequences of queries.

   Moreover, attempts or threats are discouraged because of the users' consciousness of auditing procedures monitoring every operation.

An overall view of the architecture of a DBMS including security features appears in Figure 1.13, where modules and users are shown (the figure is an elaboration of that contained in Fernandez *et al.* (1981) of a reference secure DBMS architecture). It is assumed that protected data is accessible only via DBMS functions. After user login and authentication, each subsequent access query to the database (generally made through an application program) is mediated by the Authorization System (AS) procedures, which consult the files of the authorization rules to check query compliance with these rules. Access is allowed upon query-rules match. Otherwise, an error message can be sent to the user, and/or violations can be registered in a log file together with references (for example, date, time, user) by the AS. This log file is periodically examined by the auditor, to detect possible suspect behaviours or to verify recurring types of violations.

A specialist, the security administrator, is responsible for defining the authorization rules derived from the security requirements of the organization. The authorizer may be the same auditor and/or the DBA.

Authorized access queries are translated into program calls from the library of applications, processed by the transaction manager and then transformed into data access requests (processed by the data manager). Further controls can be made by the operating system (such as the control of file access) and the hardware, to ensure that data is exclusively transferred into the work area of a requesting user. Crypto-techniques and backup copies are the usual means for the protection of physical data and the program storage system.

The secure DBMS module manages all the queries. It includes the *authorization rules* (for discretionary controls) and the *security axioms* (for mandatory controls); one, or both, is used by the AS, depending on the system protection policies. In the same module, the DB schemas are included since these are also protected objects.

The following roles are involved in the management of a security system:

- The *application manager*, responsible for the development and maintenance of library programs;

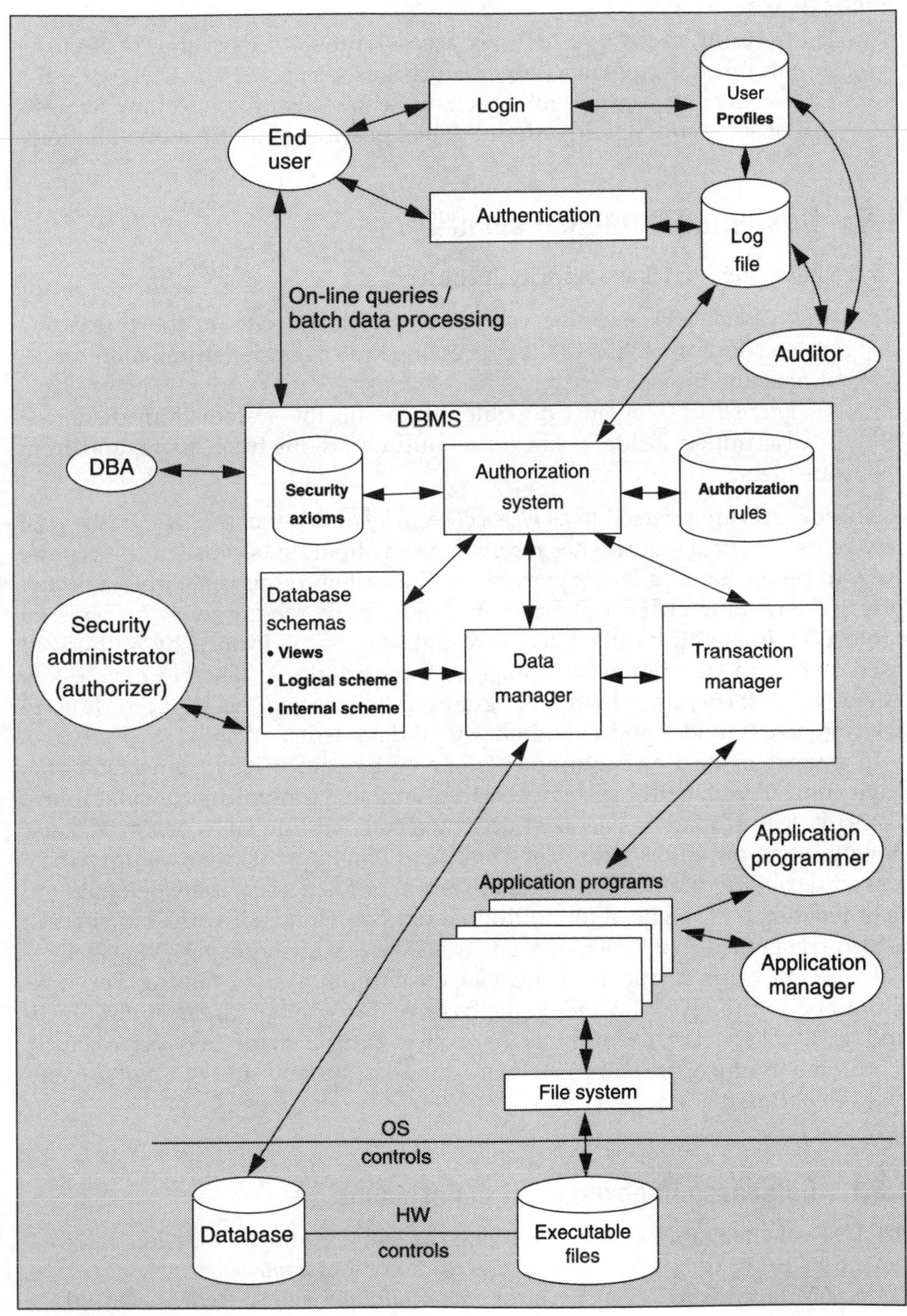


*Figure 1.13* Architecture of a DBMS including security features.

- The *DBA*, who manages the conceptual and internal schemas of the database;
- The *security officer*, who defines access authorizations and/or security axioms through rules in a proper language (sometimes, the DDL or DML);
- The *auditor*, responsible for checking sequences of connection requests and of access queries, in order to detect possible authorization violations.

## 1.5 Designing database security

As we have seen, database security includes:

(1) An *external level*, meaning control of physical access to the processing system, and protection of the processing system from natural, man-made, or machine disasters;

(2) An *internal level*, against possible attacks on the system from dishonest or disgruntled insiders, and errors and omissions by insiders, and from outsiders.

These levels are referred to as *physical security* and *logical security*. In the past few years, physical security has received great attention because of the general view of protection as a *'locking process'* of the system resources within a secure physical environment. Security cannot be assured by relying solely on physical protection. In fact, fraudulent access to data can be performed by authorized users, who can take unfair advantage of their privileges. Therefore, access to 'sensitive' information should be granted to selected users, according to selected access modes and to limited sets of data items.

In general, **protection requirements** of a system are strictly connected to the environment where the system is used, and to economical considerations. Security features are recognized to constitute additional costs and cause downgrading of performance. They also lead to a higher system complexity; a loss in flexibility; the need for human resources for design, management, and maintenance; and the need for additional hardware and software. However, it is also recognized that a lack of security measures, by exposing the system to risks, might bring about much heavier costs upon system failure. The risks should be accurately estimated on the basis of the typology of the environment and of its users. For example, a distinction can be made between security requirements of private/commercial information systems and those of government departments.

### 1.5.1 Databases in government departments

Analysis of database security problems in some countries has led to some databases being classified according to their contents: *vital information*, that is, necessary to national security, and *non-vital information*, which should be granted under proper controls or authorizations. Databases containing these types of information are called **classified databases**. Data therein is classified at different security levels (secret, confidential, etc.) according to its level of sensitivity. Access is granted to users and transactions properly *cleared* for a given correct security level. Databases belonging to the Department of Defense, State Department, Department of Treasury, and Department of Industry and Justice are usually included in this category (Landwehr, 1988).

In these environments, penetration attempts are hardly detectable. Individuals wishing to infiltrate the database would be highly motivated and would use sophisticated traceless tools. Information integrity and denial of service (which means preventing authorized users from employing the system resources) are relevant problems in this type of database.

Currently, software environments and DBMSs offering *provable* protection to classified databases seem to be hardly realizable. Great research efforts are being devoted to achieve *trusted* database management software. Hale and Coates (1985) describe the basic requirements of such software, while Schell and Denning (1986) illustrate the integrity aspects of trusted databases.

A viable approach for classified databases is to make access authorizations dependent on the personal identity and certifiable reliability of users.

The described type of protection has long since been recognized to be inappropriate for public, unclassified databases (Lipner, 1982). Their contents refer, for example, to energy plants, to census, social, fiscal or criminal information, to commercial data, such as economic indicators, budget, forecast and development plans of great interest to companies applying for public contracts and competitions.

Cost quantification from unauthorized access to these databases is hardly estimable: for example, how can the damage caused to the individual derived from disclosure and diffusion of personal (medical, fiscal) data be evaluated?

### 1.5.2 Commercial databases

At first sight, damage estimation is easier for *information systems* of commercial organizations. As a matter of fact, sensitivity degrees of data are directly stated by the organization (for example, industry, financial or insurance body), by distinguishing between data that is vital for the organization, and ordinary data requiring low protection. So far, security design has rarely been given primary consideration in commercial databases and the related security problems have received limited attention in the literature.

Within these environments, security problems arise from authorized users; in fact, a preliminary check on the users' reliability seems almost impossible to achieve methodically. Consequently the procedures for authorization grant are often inadequate, and control techniques and tools for checking that users access only data and programs that they are authorized for are rather poor.

Moreover, the complexity of security problems depends on the *semantic nature* of a database. The entity to be protected is not a physical resource or device, such as a file or a terminal, but rather a set of items representing information with a global meaning. Therefore, protection requirements are not only *selective*, that is, dependent on the user identity or on the access mode, but also sensitive to the contents of data, or dependent on elements such as system parameters, access history and data aggregation. This makes the design, interpretation and enforcement of an authorization model for databases a complex task.

Finally, consider that access grant and revocation should be able to follow the dynamics of an organization: to this purpose, the consistency of the set of authorizations in the system not only needs continuous checks against the protection requirements, but also needs possible modifications.

The degree of security provided by current commercial DBMS technology is rather low. Practically, databases appear to be extremely vulnerable even to simple attacks, let alone sophisticated attacks like Trojan Horses, inference threats, worms, trackers or trapdoors. Note that all these terms are typical of the literature on computer security – see, for example, Denning (1990, 1982).

Protection techniques for both unclassified public databases and commercial databases are substantially similar, being based on hardware/software tools and on organizational measures. Attempts are being made to adapt trusted DBMS techniques to commercial environments (see, for example, Turn (1982) for a discussion). However, they often appear inflexible and inadequate; moreover, they turn out to be totally inadequate in the face of threats like Trojan Horses and trapdoors embedded in application software (Hinke, 1988).

Specialized DBMS architectures, called *multilevel secure DBMS architectures*, have been proposed to meet multilevel protection requirements. Some multilevel architectures are the Integrity Lock architecture, the Kernelized architecture, the Replicated architecture (as proposed in the Woods Hole Study performed in Summer 1982), and the Trusted Subject architecture. The Replicated architecture exists as a research prototype developed at NRL (Naval Research Laboratory) and no commercial systems are currently available. The Integrity Lock architecture has been studied at the Mitre Corporation and is available as a commercial product (Trudata). The Kernelized architecture has been studied at SRI (Stanford Research Institute) and is embedded in one secure version of Oracle. Most of the commercially secure DBMS products (for example, Sybase, Rubix, Informix, Oracle, Dec) implement the trusted subject architecture as developed in a research prototype (ASD-TRW). Some techniques used in these prototypes are: the partitioning of multilevel databases into various one-level databases (thus producing redundancy and inconsistency); the application of crypto-techniques on sensitive data; the *integrity lock* techniques specifying sensitivity level and checking unauthorized modifications (through *checksum* techniques); and mechanisms based on 'sensitivity keys', which are a combination of an identifier with a sensitivity level of the data item. Further techniques introduce a front end between the user and the DBMS, so that multilevel protection is managed without altering the DBMS protection features. Alternatively, a user/DBMS filter is employed, or views are defined, containing only the information a user is authorized for.

## 1.6 Concluding remarks

Access control in a system is guided by *access policies* stating who can access which objects of that system. Access policies should be independent of the mechanisms that will implement the physical control of access: this allows control mechanisms to be available for different polices. Access policies specify *access requirements*: that is, detailed access modes can be expressed for access by a subject (or group of subjects) to an object (or group of objects).

Requirements are then translated into access rules on the basis of the adopted policies. This is a crucial phase in secure system development. Correctness and completeness of the rules and of the corresponding implementation mechanisms are involved. A mapping process should be performed using modelling techniques for security requirements and policies: a model allows the designers to clearly represent and verify the security properties of the system.

The variety of possible threats to database secrecy and integrity makes database protection a complex problem. Therefore, protection needs a set of measures involving humans, software and hardware. Weakness in any one of these might compromise the whole system security. Moreover, data protection, as a part of a more complex security system, raises issues of system reliability.

In summary, in secure system development one needs to consider some crucial aspects, such as:

- The features of the actual storage and processing environment. A careful analysis is essential to state the degree of protection offered and required by the system: these are the security requirements;
- The protection mechanisms external to the processing environment. These are the administrative and physical control measures that contribute to the effectiveness of operational security measures;
- The internal DB protection mechanisms. These act once the controls (login and authentication) have been passed successfully by the user;
- The physical organization of stored information;
- The security features provided by the operating system and by the hardware;
- The reliability of hardware and software;
- The administrative, human and organizational aspects.

## References

Andrews D.J. and MacEwen G. (1990). *A Review of Tools and Methods for System Assurance.* Andyne Computing Ltd

Atzeni P. and De Antonellis V. (1993). *Relational Database Theory.* Benjamin Cummings

Bell D.E. (1990). Lattices, policies, and implementations. In *Proc. 13th National Computer Security Conf.* October 1990

Bonium D.A. (1988). Logging and accountability in database management systems. In *Database Security: Status and Prospects* (Landwehr C.E., ed.), Elsevier North-Holland, IFIP

Bussolati U. and Martella G. (1982). Data security management in distributed databases. *Information Systems,* **7**(3)

Courtney R.H. (1990). Factors affecting the availability of security measures in data processing system components. In *Proc. 13th National Computer Security Conf.* October 1990

Date C.J. (1990). *An Introduction to Database Systems* 5th edn. Addison-Wesley

Denning D.E. (1976). A lattice model of secure information flow. *Comm. ACM,* **19**(5)

Denning D.E. (1977). Certification of programs for secure information flow. *Comm. ACM,* **20**(7)

Denning D.E. (1982). *Cryptography and Data Security.* Addison-Wesley

Denning D.E. and Denning P.J. (1979). Data security. *ACM Computing Surveys,* **11**(3)

Denning D.E. and Schlorer J. (1983). Inference controls for statistical databases. *IEEE Computer,* **16**(2)

Denning F.J. ed. (1990). *Computers under Attack: Intruders, Worms, and Viruses.* Addison-Wesley

Dobkin D.A., Jones A.J. and Lipton R. (1979). Protection against user influence. *ACM Trans. Database Systems,* **4**(1)

Fernandez E.B., Summers R.C. and Wood C. (1981). *Database Security and Integrity.* Addison-Wesley

Hale M.W. and Coates C.L. (1985). *Trusted Database Management Systems.* Draft of Department of Defense

Hinke T.H. (1988). DBMS technology vs. threats. In *Database Security: Status and Prospects* (C.E. Landwehr, ed.) Amsterdam: Elsevier Science (North-Holland)

Hruska J. and Jackson K.H. (1990). *Computer Security Solutions.* Oxford: Blackwell Scientific Publications

Korth H.F. and Silberschatz A. (1988). *Database System Concepts,* Computer Science Series. Maidenhead: McGraw-Hill

Landwehr C.E. (1981). Formal models for computer security. *ACM Computing Surveys,* **13**(3)

Landwehr C.E. (1983). The best available technologies for computer security. *IEEE Computer,* **16**(7)

Landwehr C.E. (1988) Database security: where are we? In *Database Security: Status and Prospects* (Landwehr C.E., ed.). Amsterdam: Elsevier Science (North-Holland)

Levin T.E., Tao A. and Padilla S.J. (1990). Covert storage channel analysis: a worked example. In *Proc. 13th National Computer Security Conf.* October 1990

Lipner S.B. (1982). Non-discretionary controls for commercial applications. In *Proc. IEEE Symposium on Security and Privacy,* Oakland, April 1982

McLean J. (1990). The specification and modelling of computer security. *IEEE Computer,* **23**(1)

Millen J.K. and Cerniglia C.M. (1984). Computer security models. *MITRE Technical Report*, MITRE Corporation

Myers E.D. (1990). A categorization of processor protection mechanims. In *Proc. 13th National Computer Security Conf.* October 1990

Olson I. and Marshall A. (1990). Computer access control policy choices. *Computers & Security*, Elsevier Science (North-Holland), **9**(8)

Parker D.B. (1984). The many faces of data vulnerability. *IEEE Spectrum*, **21**(5)

Perry W.E. (1982). Developing a computer security and control strategy. *Computers & Security*, Elsevier Science (North-Holland), **1**(1)

Pfleeger C.P. (1989). *Security in Computing*. Prentice-Hall

Russell D. and Gangemi G.T. (1991). *Computer Security Basics*. O'Reill & Associates

Saltzer J.D. and Schroeder M.D. (1975). The protection of information in computer systems. *Proc. IEEE*, **63**(9)

Sandhu R.S. and Jajodia S. (1990). Integrity mechanisms in database management systems. In *Proc. 13th National Computer Security Conf.* October 1990

Schell R.R. and Denning D.E. (1986). Integrity in trusted database systems. In *Proc. 9th National Computer Security Conf.* Gaithersburg, 1986

Sterne D.F. *et al.* (1991). An analysis of application specific security policies. *Proc. 14th National Computer Security Conf.* October 1991

Summers R.C. (1984). An overview of computer security. *IBM Systems Journal*, **23**(24)

Turn R (1982). Private sector needs for trusted/secure computer systems. *Proc. AFIPS Conf.* **51**

Ullman J.D. (1988). *Principles of Database and Knowledge-Base Systems*. Computer Science Press

# 2 Security models

## 2.1 Introduction

The objective of security modelling is to produce a high-level, software-independent, conceptual model, starting from requirements specifications that describe the protection needs of the system (Jones, 1978; Landwer 1981; Millen and Cerniglia, 1984; Fugini and Martella, 1988; McLean, 1990). A security model provides a semantically rich representation in that it allows functional and structural properties of the security system to be described. A security model allows the developers to give a high-level definition of the protection requirements and system policies as well as producing a concise and precise description of the desired system behaviour. Moreover, it enables one to demonstrate that the security system satisfies some properties by proving that the abstract model satisfies those properties, that the system model, or a formal specification, corresponds to the abstract model, and that the implementation enforces the system model.

Many security models have been proposed in the literature. Security models can be broadly classified in two categories: discretionary and non-discretionary (or mandatory) models.

*Discretionary security models* govern the access of users to the information on the basis of the users's identity and of rules that specify, for each user and object in the system, the types of access the user is allowed for the object. The request of a user to access an object is checked against the specified authorizations; if there exists an authorization stating that the user can access the object in the specific mode, the access is granted, otherwise it is denied. Discretionary protection models generally allow users to grant other users authorizations to access the objects. The most common form of administration is the *ownership* policy, where the creator of an object is allowed to grant and revoke other users' accesses (and the privilege of administering them) to the object created. Discretionary access control therefore represents a flexible way to enforce different protection requirements.

*Mandatory security models* govern the access to the information by the individuals on the basis of the classifications of *subjects* and *objects* in the system. Objects are the passive entities storing information, such as data files, records, fields in records, etc. Subjects are active entities that access the objects. Generally, a subject is considered to be an active process operating on behalf of a user.

Access classes are associated with every subject and object in the system, and the access of a subject to an object is granted if some relationship, depending on the access mode, is satisfied between the classifications of the subject and the object.

In this chapter we review some discretionary and mandatory security models proposed for the protection of information in operating systems and in database systems (see Table 2.1).

As for discretionary security, the access matrix model (Lampson, 1971; Graham and Denning, 1973; Harrison *et al.*, 1976) represents the milestone. This model is the first proposal aimed at formalizing security with the purpose of addressing theoretical issues, such as the safety problem, and practical problems, such as privileges storage aspects. The access matrix model views the security system in terms of states. A state is characterized by a set of subjects, objects, and authorizations. Analysis procedures check that modifications to the system state (transitions) respect the defined security properties. Most discretionary models can be considered an extension of the access matrix model. The Take–Grant model (Jones *et al.*, 1976), which uses a graph structure to represent the system state, focuses on the problem of propagation of privileges. Some variations have been proposed to this model aimed at refining the mechanism of privilege propagation control. Among these, the Action-Entity model (Bussolati *et al.*, 1983; Fugini and Martella, 1984) considers a richer set of administrative privileges and supports predicates in authorizations.

Some other models have been specifically targeted to the protection of information in database systems. Among these, the model of Wood *et al.* (1979) refers to the ANSI/SPARC architecture and considers the problem of authorizations in multilevel-schema relational databases. The model is based on rules for the derivation and the consistency controls of authorizations at the different schema levels.

As for mandatory security the milestone is represented by the model of Bell and LaPadula (1973, 1974a, 1974b, 1975). This model, which is based on the object–subject classification paradigm, has stated the two key principles for preserving information secrecy. These principles safeguard secrecy by preventing high-secrecy (sensitive) information from flowing into low-secrecy objects. The Bell–LaPadula model describes the system in terms of states. Properties (axioms) are then defined which govern the changes (transitions) to the system state. A similar security model has been proposed by Biba (1977) for the purpose of safeguarding information integrity. Biba's model is based on principles which preserve information integrity by preventing low-integrity information from flowing to high-integrity objects. The Bell–LaPadula and Biba principles have been merged to preserve secrecy as well as integrity of the information in the Dion model (Dion, 1981). A generalization of the mandatory access control policies is represented by the information flow system of Denning (1976). The information flow system is based on a lattice of security classes. Each object in the system is assigned a security class. Information in an object is allowed to flow (either directly or indirectly) only to objects with a higher access class. Determining and restricting flows among objects requires examination of the code operating on the objects.

**Table 2.1** Security models.

| Models | OS security | DB security | Discretionary policy | Mandatory policy: Secrecy | Mandatory policy: Integrity | Indirect access or information-flow control | Access control |
|---|---|---|---|---|---|---|---|
| Access Matrix | x | x | x | | | | x |
| Take–Grant | x | x | x | | | | x |
| Action–Entity | x | x | x | | | | x |
| Wood *et al.* | | x | x | | | | x |
| Bell–La Padula | x | | x | x | | x | x |
| Biba | x | | x | x | x | x | x |
| Dion | x | | | x | x | x | x |
| Sea View | | x | x | x | x | x | x |
| Jajodia–Sandhu | | x | | x | | x | x |
| Smith–Winslett | | x | | x | | x | x |
| Lattice | x | | | | | x | |

The application of the Bell–LaPadula model to the protection of relational databases introduces new protection requirements. In particular, the problem arises of dealing with the multiple occurrence of an entity at different classification levels (*polyinstantiation*). These requirements, originally studied in the MULTICS project (Hinke and Schaefer, 1975), have been addressed by various models. These models extend the concept of relation to the consideration of security classifications. The main difference among the various models is how they deal with the problem of polyinstantiation. Among the various approaches are the Sea View model (Denning, 1987; Denning *et al.*, 1986, 1987, 1988), which was developed as a research prototype at SRI, Palo Alto; the Jajodia and Sandhu model (Jajodia and Sandhu, 1991a, 1991b; Sandhu and Jajodia, 1991, 1992b), which proposes a formalization of the relational model with the consideration of security classification; and the Smith and Winslett model (Smith, 1992; Smith and Winslett, 1992; Winslett *et al.*, 1994), which proposes a model based on the theory of belief.

Besides the discretionary and mandatory categorizations, the models can be classified according to the following aspects:

- The *target system:* for example, models for OS protection, models for DB security or for both; depending on the target system, different resources are protected and different access modes considered.
- The *type of policy*: mandatory or discretionary.
- The *addressed security aspects:* secrecy or integrity.
- The *type of control:* some models are oriented to direct access control, others allow control of indirect access or flow of information.

Accordingly, the choice of a security model in the development of a security system depends on the target environment, on the security aspects involved, on the security policies and on the intended controls.

Sometimes, one model is insufficient to represent complex and/or diversified protection needs, whereas a combination of models can be used more satisfactorily. *Ad hoc* models can be defined as specializations or extensions of existing models, when no models, or combinations thereof, are capable of describing exhaustively the protection requirements for a specific problem.

In this chapter we present some of the security models mentioned above. In the description of security models, the following aspects are examined for each model (see Figure 2.1):

- *Subjects.* These are the active entities of the system, which request access to objects. These requests must be controlled to ensure they match the security requirements. Subjects represent possible threats to information security.
- *Objects.* These are the passive entities of the system, which contain information to be protected from unauthorized accesses or modifications.
- *Access modes.* These represent the types of access subjects can exercise on objects. The execution of an access mode causes an information flow from the object to the subject and vice versa.

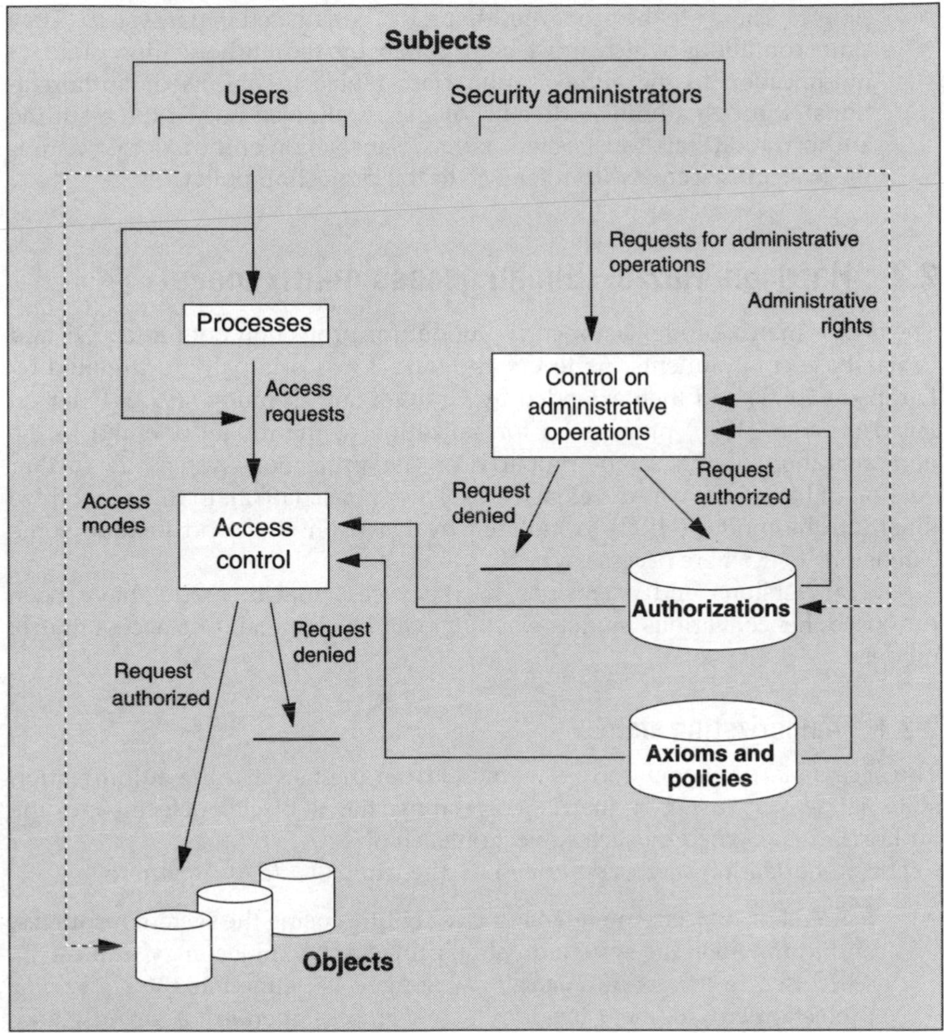


*Figure 2.1* Elements of the security model in a security system.

- *Policies.* These are the 'laws' according to which accesses are controlled.
- *Authorizations.* These state the accesses that subjects are allowed to execute on the objects of the system. The authorization state consists of the set of accesses users are authorized to execute.
- *Administrative rights.* These privileges (implemented by primitives such as 'grant', 'revoke', 'own') allow the modification of the authorizations: that is, of the access modes subjects are allowed to execute on objects. In discretionary systems, the possession of administrative privileges by subjects enables them to grant and revoke privileges (authorizations) to other subjects.

- *Axioms*. These are the properties that must be satisfied in the system. They state conditions which must be satisfied by the authorization state. A modification to the authorization state (subjects, objects or authorizations), through administrative privileges, is allowed only if the resulting authorization state satisfies the axioms. Satisfaction of the axioms ensures the system is secure with reference to the protection policy.

## 2.2 Harrison–Ruzzo–Ullman access matrix model

The access matrix model is a security model for protection both in an OS and in database environments. As to OS, the model was originally formulated by Lampson (1971) and then extended by Graham and Denning (1972). Later on Harrison *et al.* (1976) proposed a formalization of the model oriented to the demonstration of the safety property of the protection system. A further version of the model was developed by Conway *et al.* (1972). In this section we illustrate the model (HRU) formulated by Harrison *et al.* and include some extensions to it where necessary.

Several versions and extensions of the access matrix model have been proposed; hence, various models exist that can be classifiable as access matrix models.

### 2.2.1 Authorization state

The access matrix model derives its name from the fact that the authorization state is defined using a matrix correlating the subjects, objects and the authorizations owned by each subject on each object.

The authorization state is described by the triple $Q = (S,O,A)$, where:

- $S$ is a set of subjects, intended as active entities using the system resources, and from which the system must be protected. A subject may be a *user*, a *set of users*, a *process* or a *domain*. A domain is defined as the context or protection environment inside which a process operates. A process may be associated to different domains during its execution, therefore it may hold different privileges.
- $O$ is the set of objects, intended as entities that must be protected. This set consists both of passive entities (the system resources) and of active entities (subjects). Also subjects are viewed as objects to be protected. Therefore $O \subset S$. Each object is univocally identified by a name.

  In operating system environments, objects are typically: files, memory segments, and processes (program activations). In the database interpretation, the objects may be: databases, relations, attributes, records, and fields in a record.
- $A$ is the access matrix. The matrix rows correspond to the subjects and the columns to the objects. Since objects include subjects, the matrix is rectangular. Entry $A[s,o]$ contains the access modes for which subject $s$ is authorized on object $o$. The matrix structure is reported in Table 2.2.

**Table 2.2** Access matrix.

| Subjects | Objects | | | |
|---|---|---|---|---|
| | $O_1$ | ... | $O_j$ | ... | $O_m$ |
| $S_1$ | $A[s_1, o_1]$ | | $A[s_1, o_j]$ | | $A[s_1, o_m]$ |
| . | | | | | |
| . | | | | | |
| $S_i$ | $A[s_i, o_1]$ | | $A[s_i, o_j]$ | | $A[s_i, o_m]$ |
| . | | | | | |
| . | | | | | |
| $S_n$ | $A[s_n, o_1]$ | | $A[s_n, o_j]$ | | $A[s_n, o_m]$ |

In the application to database systems, the model can be extended by considering, in the specification of the authorizations, conditions which must be satisfied in order for the objects to use the authorizations (Denning, 1982). In this case, each entry *A[s,o]* of the matrix is a decision rule which specifies, besides the access modes *s* is authorized for on *o*, also the conditions to be satisfied in order for *s* to exercise the access modes. Possible conditions that can be expressed are:

- *Data-dependent* conditions, specifying constraints on the value of the accessed data. For example, a subject may be authorized to read from the EMPLOYEE table only those employees whose salary is ≤1000.
- *Time-dependent* conditions, specifying constraints on the time an access can take place. For example, a subject may be authorized to read from the EMPLOYEE table only between 8:00am and 5:00pm.
- *Context-dependent* conditions, specifying constraints on combinations of data which can be accessed. For example, a subject may be authorized to read the names of the employees and the salaries of the employees, but he cannot read the two fields together and get the association pairs 'name–salary'.
- *History-dependent* conditions, specifying constraints dependent on previously performed accesses. For example, a subject may be authorized to read the salaries of the employees if he has not previously read the names of the employees.

### 2.2.2 Access modes

The set of access modes depends on the type of the considered objects and of the system functionalities. Generally, they are: *read, write, append, execute,* and the *'own'* privilege (indicating ownership). If the matrix entry *A[s,o]* contains the 'own' access mode, *s* is considered the owner of *o* and, as such, is allowed to administer authorizations on *o*.

**Table 2.3** Primitive operations of the access matrix model.

| **Operation** | **Conditions** | **Resulting state Q′ = (S′, O′, A′)** |
|---|---|---|
| enter r into $A[s_i, o_j]$ | $s_i \in S$<br>$o_j \in O$ | $S' = S$<br>$O' = O$<br>$A'[s_i, o_j] = A[s_i, o_j] \cup \{r\}$<br>$A'[s_m, o_k] = A[s_m, o_k]\ \ k \neq j, m \neq i,$ |
| delete r from $A[s_i, o_j]$ | $s_i \in S$<br>$o_j \in O$ | $S' = S$<br>$O' = O$<br>$A'[s_i, o_j] = A[s_i, o_j] - \{r\}$<br>$A'[s_m, o_k] = A[s_m, o_k]\ \ k \neq j, m \neq i,$ |
| create subject $s_i$ | $s_i \notin S$ | $S' = S \cup \{s_i\}$<br>$O' = O \cup \{s_i\}$<br>$A'[s, o] = A[s, o]\ \ s \in S, o \in O$<br>$A'[s_i, o] = \emptyset\ \ o \in O'$<br>$A'[s, o_j] = \emptyset\ \ s \in S'$ |
| create object $o_j$ | $o_i \notin O$ | $S' = S$<br>$O' = O \cup \{o_j\}$<br>$A'[s, o] = A[s, o]\ \ s \in S, o \in O$<br>$A'[s_i, o_j] = \emptyset\ \ s \in S'$ |
| destroy subject $s_i$ | $s_i \in S$ | $S' = S - \{s_i\}$<br>$O' = O - \{s_i\}$<br>$A'[s, o] = A[s, o]\ \ s \in S', o \in O'$ |
| destroy object $o_j$ | $o_i \in O$<br>$o_i \notin S$ | $S' = S$<br>$O' = O - \{o_j\}$<br>$A'[s, o] = A[s, o]\ \ s \in S', o \in O'$ |

In some versions of the model, for the protection of systems where processes are allowed to create subprocesses, the access mode Control is also considered. The access mode can be specified for a process on another process. If a process $p_1$ holds the Control authorization on a process $p_2$, then $p_2$ is subordinate to (son of) $p_1$, and $p_1$ can control the authorizations of $p_2$: that is, $p_1$ can grant and revoke any of $p_2$'s authorizations (including those granted to $p_2$ by other subjects).

## 2.2.3 Operations

The state $Q$ of the system can be modified by a set of commands. Commands are composed of a sequence of primitive operations that modify the access matrix. Six primitive operations (*op*) have been identified by Harrison *et al.* (1976):

- *Enter r into A[s,o]* grants subject *s* the authorization for the access mode *r* on object *o*. The matrix is modified by adding the *r* access mode to entry *A[s,o]*.
- *Delete r from A[s,o]* revokes from subject *s* the authorization for the access mode *r* on *o* (it is the inverse of the previous operation). The *r* access mode is removed from the entry *A[s,o]*.

- *Create subject s* adds a new subject *s* to the system. This command adds a new row and a new column to the access matrix.
- *Destroy subject s* removes subject *s* from the system. This entails deleting from the matrix the row and column corresponding to *s*.
- *Create object o* defines a new protected object *o*. This entails adding a new column to the access matrix.
- *Destroy object o* destroys object *o*. The operation has the effect of removing the corresponding column from the matrix.

The application of an operation *op* to a state $Q = (S,O,A)$ causes a transition from $Q$ to $Q' = (S',O',A')$ where $Q'$ differs from $Q$ for the value of at least one of the three components.

A state transition is indicated by $Q \vdash_{op} Q'$ to be read as: $Q'$ is derivable from $Q$ by applying the operation *op*. The effects of *op* on the system state $Q(S,A,O)$ are shown in Table 2.3, where the 'conditions' column indicates the conditions to be satisfied for the operation to be allowed. If these conditions are not satisfied, then the operation has no effect and $Q = Q'$.

## 2.2.4 Commands

A system state is modified through commands. Harrison *et al.* consider commands consisting of two parts: a conditional part and an operational part. The conditional part specifies the constraints to be satisfied for the operations indicated in the second part to be enforced. The conditions typically test the values of some entries of the access matrix.

A command has the following form:

```
command c(x1,..., xk)
        if r1 in A[xs1, xo1] and
           r2 in A[xs2, xo2] and
           .
           .
           rm in A[xsm, xom]
        then op1
           op2
           .
           .
           opn
end
```

where $r_1,...,r_m$ are access modes, and $s_1,...,s_m$ and $o_1,...,o_m$ are integers between 1 and $k$. If $m$=0, the command has no conditional part.

The execution of a command $c(x_1,...,x_k)$ on the state $Q = (S,O,A)$ causes the transition to state $Q'$, such that a set of states exist $Q_0, Q_1, ..., Q_n$ for which:

$$Q = Q_0 \vdash op_1^* \, Q_1 \vdash op_2^* \, ... \vdash op_n^* \, Q_n = Q'$$

where $op_j^*$ indicates the primitive *op*eration *op*, and the formal parameters ($x_1$, ..., $x_k$) in the definition are replaced by the actual parameters supplied at the command call. If the conditional part of the command is not satisfied, then the command has no effect and

$$Q = Q'.$$

By using the six predefined operations, different commands can be specified which provide the functionalities that best suit the protection requirements of the system.

For example, the following three commands allow a process respectively to create a new file, thus acquiring the ownership privilege on it, and to grant and revoke other users the privileges on this file. The model allows only objects to be specified as parameters in a command. The access mode cannot be provided as a parameter. A command must therefore be specified for each possible access mode to be considered. The following examples refer to the read privilege.

```
command CREATE(process,file)
        create object file
        enter O into (process,file)
end.
command CONFERread(owner,friend,file)
        if O in (owner,file)
then enter R into A[friend,file]
end.
command REVOKEread(owner,friend,file)
        if O in A[owner,file]
then delete R from A[exfriend,file]
end.
```

The *create* command allows a process to create a file and acquire, in the file, the read, write and 'own' privileges.

```
command NEWCREATE(process,file)
        create object file
        enter O into A[process,file]
        enter R into A[process,file]
        enter W into A[process,file]
end.
```

### 2.2.5 Administration of authorizations

The inclusion of the 'own' privilege allows the ownership policy to be enforced by the model, allowing subjects to administer authorizations on the objects they have created. The owner of an object may grant/revoke other subjects any privilege on the object (except for the 'own' privilege, which cannot be transferred). The owner of an object can grant to other subjects the authorization for an access mode on the object even if he or she does not personally hold the authorization for that access mode. Note that this violates the principle of *attenuation of privileges,* which states that subjects should not be able to increase their privileges or grant to other subjects privileges they themselves do not own. In the access matrix model, this principle can be violated by the owner of an object with respect to authorizations on the object. However, the principle applies to non-owners.

In some systems, the privilege enabling propagation of access rights can also be held by subjects other than the owner. These subjects must be explicitly authorized for the 'grant' of an access mode. The access matrix model represents this by allowing a flag to be associated with a specific privilege held by a subject on an object stating that the subject is allowed to grant other users the privilege on the object. In particular, two types of flag are defined (Denning, 1982), corresponding to different grant modalities: the *copy flag*, denoted by '*', and the *transfer flag* denoted by '+'.

Let $m$ be a generic access mode:

- Authorization $m^*$ in $A[s,o]$ of the matrix indicates that $s$ is authorized to grant privilege $m$ on the object $o$ to other subjects. However, $s$ can grant only the privilege; he cannot grant the flag on the privilege. If a subject $s_1$ has a privilege with the copy flag on object $o$ and it grants the privilege on $o$ to subject $s_2$, then the privilege is added to entry $A[s_2,o]$. The transfer of privilege does not have any effect on the authorizations of $s_1$.

  For example, the transfer of the read privilege on an object can be obtained through a command as follows:

```
command TRANSFER_read(subject1,subject2,file)
        if R* in A[subject1,file]
then enter R into A[subject2,file]
end.
```

- authorization $m^+$ in entry $A[s,o]$ of the matrix indicates that $s$ can transfer other subjects' privilege $m$ on object $\sigma$, but so doing it loses the privilege and the possibility to grant it. The privilege and the ability of administering it are transferred to the grantee. As an example, the transfer of the read privilege owned by the grantor with only the 'transfer' flag can be expressed by the following command:

```
command TRANSFER-ONLY_read(subject1,subject2,file)
        if R+ in A[subject1,file]
        then delete R+ from A[subject1,file]
             enter R+ into A[subject2,file]
end.
```

If the owner of an object grants a subject a privilege with the copy flag, then the subject can grant the privilege to any other subject in the system. Hence, the set of subjects allowed to exercise the privilege can potentially increase regardless of the owner's will. By contrast, suppose the owner of an object grants another subject a privilege on the subject with the transfer flag; then, if this subject grants the privilege to another subject, the granting subject will lose it. Hence, although the subject allowed for the privilege may change, the number of subjects allowed for the privilege cannot.

Transfer of privileges may also take place upon creation of subordinated processes. In particular, if a process $p_1$ creates a subordinated process $p_2$ holding a memory segment $m$, then $p_1$ can grant to $p_2$ all access modes on $m$.

Authorization for privileges on an object, granted by the owner or by any subject holding a copy or a transfer flag, can be revoked only by the owner of the object. If the object is a process, these authorizations can be revoked by the process controlling it.

### 2.2.6 Model implementation

The states of the access matrix represent the authorizations holding in the system: that is, the access modes each subject can exercise on each object. Then, every request from a subject to access an object in a given mode is mediated by the access control mechanisms which will allow the access if, and only if, the subject owns the access mode on the object: that is, the corresponding entry in the matrix contains the access mode. If conditional authorization can be specified, then the request will be granted only if the condition in the authorization (that is, the conditions associated with the right in the subject/object entry) is satisfied.

It must be noted that storing a matrix as a bidimensional array proves ineffective, since the matrix, even if sparse, takes a large memory area. A possible storage method consists in a global table of triples $\langle s_i, o_j, A[s_i,o_j]\rangle$ with several elements equal to non-null entries of $A$ (see Figure 2.2a). However, this approach has some disadvantages:

- It may be not convenient to keep a whole authorization table in main memory because there may be many inactive subjects/objects. Thus, more memory than necessary is occupied.
- The considered level of granularity for objects and subjects can cause the table to be very heavy in terms of memory. A simple example is a public file (that is, accessible to all subjects): with this approach, the table contains one triple storing the authorizations on the object for each system subject.
- The examination of the table does not provide an immediate visibility either of the set of the objects accessible by a given subject or of the set of subjects which can access a given object.

The most common alternatives for the implementation of the access matrix are storing by rows and storing by columns.

- *Storing by rows.* A list is associated to each subject. Each element of the list indicates a system object and the privileges held by the subject. To each subject $S_i$ in the access matrix, a list of pairs $\langle O_j, A[S_i,O_j]\rangle$ is associated for each object $O_j$ such that $A[S_i,O_j]$ is not null. Therefore, the elements of the

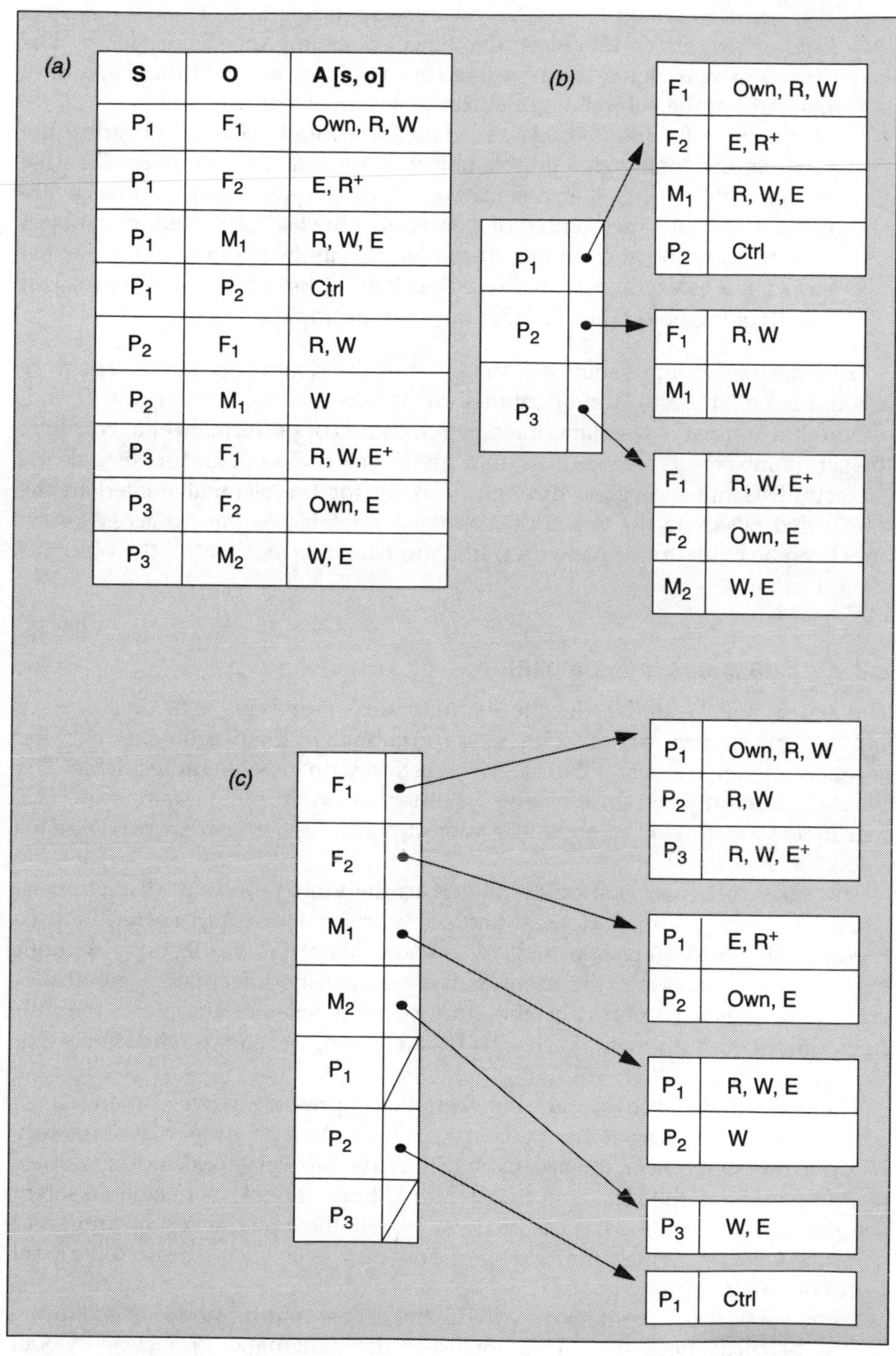


***Figure 2.2*** Alternative storing methods for an access matrix: (a) table with fields $<S_i, O_j, A[s_i, o_j]>$; (b) capability list; (c) access control list.

lists are non-null entries of the row corresponding to $S_i$. Thus, if a subject holds no rights on an object, this object does not appear in the list. The objects/access rights list associated to a subject is called the Capability List (CL) of the subject. Figure 2.2b shows an example of CLs.

- *Storing by columns.* A list is associated with each object, indicating the subjects and their rights on this object. Therefore, to each object $O_j$, a list of pairs $\langle S_i, A[S_i,O_j]\rangle$ is associated. Only non-null matrix entries are considered; thus the number of elements of the list associated to an object $O_j$ is equal to the number of non-null entries in the column for $O_j$. The list associated to each object is the authorization list or Access-Control List (ACL) of the object. Figure 2.2c shows an example of ACLs.

Both approaches have some advantages and disadvantages: in the capability list approach, subjects' authorizations on objects can be immediately found, although it is a heavy task (and inefficient in terms of performance) to compute the set of subjects granted access on a given object. To obtain this list, all the subjects' lists must be gone through, looking for the element related to the demanded object. In the access list approach, all subjects granted access on an object can be easily found; however, it is inefficient to look for all the objects a subject can access.

### 2.2.7 Extensions to the model

The access matrix model, despite its generality, represents a flexible way to express and control access rules to information. A main problem with the access matrix model is that the 'safety' question is, in general, undecidable. The 'safety' question consists of asking whether, given an initial state, there is a reachable state in which a particular subject possesses a particular privilege for a specific object.

The safety problem is strongly related to the vulnerability of discretionary access controls to Trojan Horses. Indeed, a Trojan Horse can surreptitiously modify the protection state (e.g. by adding a new authorization) without explicit instruction from the users. However, any modification to the authorization state is constrained by the authorization scheme. Therefore, the vulnerability of the authorization state to Trojan Horses depends on the effects that these can have on it.

There is an intrinsic conflict between the expressive power of an access control model and tractability of safety analysis. As a consequence of its very broad expressive power, the access matrix model has very weak safety properties. In particular, the Harrison, Ruzzo and Ullman model has decidable safety for the mono-operational case: that is, where the body of each command consists only of a single primitive operation. However, such a restricted model is not of any practical use.

Some work has been done to extend the access matrix model to make the safety problem decidable. This includes the Schematic Protection Model proposed by Sandhu (Sandhu, 1988, 1992a; Sandhu and Share, 1986) and its extension to the Extended Schematic Protection Model by Ammann and Sandhu (1991, 1992). Another model that extends the access matrix model to provide interesting cases where the safety question is decidable is the Typed Access Matrix model (Sandhu, 1992b). The Typed Access Matrix model extends the HRU model with the consideration of types for subjects and objects. Each object (subject) in the system is assigned, at creation time, a type which remains constant for the whole life of the object (subject). Types and access modes are not predefined in the model but are part of the system definition: they are defined when a system is initialized and thereafter remain constant. The restriction of the Typed Access Matrix model to monotonic operations (that is, revocation of authorization is not considered) has been shown to have decidable safety cases identified on the basis of the types of subjects and objects involved in the operations.

## 2.3 Take–Grant model

The Take–Grant model, proposed by Jones *et al.* (1976), can be considered as an extension of the access matrix model. The model uses a graph structure to represent the authorizations in the system. However, the graph can be easily represented by its adjacency matrix whose entries represent the values of the arcs labels. This model can be used to protect both OS and database environments.

### 2.3.1 Authorization state

The system state is described by the triple (*S*,*O*,*G*), where:

- *S* is a set of *subjects* (or *active objects*). The considered subjects are: users, *processes*, and *programs acting on behalf of users*.
- *O* is a set of (passive) objects. Objects may be either operating system resources resources (*files*, *memory segments*, and so on), and database objects (*databases*, *relations*, *records*, and *fields*).
- G is the *graph* describing the system authorization state. The *nodes* of the graph represent the subjects and objects of the system. In the following, subjects are represented by a filled-in circle, and objects by a white circle; a barred circle indicates a generic node (either a subject or an object). The graph is directed and access authorizations are represented by *labelled arcs*. An arc from a subject (or object) towards another subject (or object), labelled with one or more access rights, indicates that the source node is authorized to perform the rights expressed by the label on the destination node.

In the first version of the model (Jones *et al.*, 1976) access authorizations could be specified only for subjects. A subsequent version (Jones, 1978) allows access authorizations to be specified for objects as well.

Formally, G is defined as $G = (S,O,E)$, where $V = S \cup O$ is the set of vertexes, with $S \cap O = \emptyset$, and $E$ is the set of arcs. In the following, $x \xrightarrow{r} y$ denotes the arc labelled with $r$ and oriented from node $x$ to node $y$ ($x$ is also named source node, and $y$ destination node).

### 2.3.2 Access modes

The model considers the following four privileges:

- *Read*. An arc labelled with 'read' from node *A* to node *B* indicates that the subject (or object) represented by node *A* can read the information contained in the object represented by node *B*.
- *Write*. An arc labelled with 'write' from node *A* to node *B* indicates that the subject (or object) represented by node *A* can write into the object represented by node *B*.
- *Take*. An arc labelled with 'take' from node *A* to node *B* indicates that *A* is enabled to 'take' any right held by *B* on other subjects or objects in the system.
- *Grant*. An arc labelled with 'grant' from node *A* to node *B* indicates that *A* can 'grant' to *B* any of the rights held by *A* on other subjects or objects in the system.

The first two rights are called *inert*, in that they do not modify the system authorization/protection state. The last two, by allowing right transfer and therefore graph modification, are called *transport rights*.

'Take' and 'grant' rights can be held exclusively by subjects, even in the extended version of the model where rights can also be specified also for objects: this means that source nodes of arcs labelled as 'take'/'grant' must be subjects.

### 2.3.3 Operations and transfer of privileges

The authorization graph can be modified through some operations. These operations are modelled as graph rewriting rules. The application of an operation *op* to a graph $G = (S,O,E)$ results in a transition to graph $G' = (S',O',E')$, which differs from the previous one by at least one component. This transformation is denoted by:

$G \vdash_{op} G'$.

The model considers four operations:

- *take (d,s,x,y)*. The subject *s* takes the right *d* on the object (subject) *y* from the object (subject) *x*. For the operation to be successful, the following conditions must be satisfied: *(i)* *s* must hold the take privilege upon *x*, and *(ii)* *x* must hold *d* on *y*. The effect of the operation is the addition of an arc labelled *d* from *s* to *y* (Figure 2.3).
- *grant (d,s,x,y)*. The subject *s* grants the right *d* on the object (subject) *y* to the object (subject) *x*. For the operation to be successful, the following conditions must be satisfied: *(i)* *s* must hold the grant privilege on *x*, and *(ii)* *x* must hold *d* on *y*. The effect of the grant operation is the addition of an arc labelled *d* from *s* to *y* (Figure 2.4).
- *create* $\{subject_p \mid object_p\}(s,x)$. Subject *s* creates subject (object) *x* and is granted the set of rights *p* on *x*. The result of this operation is the addition to the graph of a new node representing the subject (object) *x* and of an arc labelled with *p* directed from *s* to *x* (Figure 2.5).

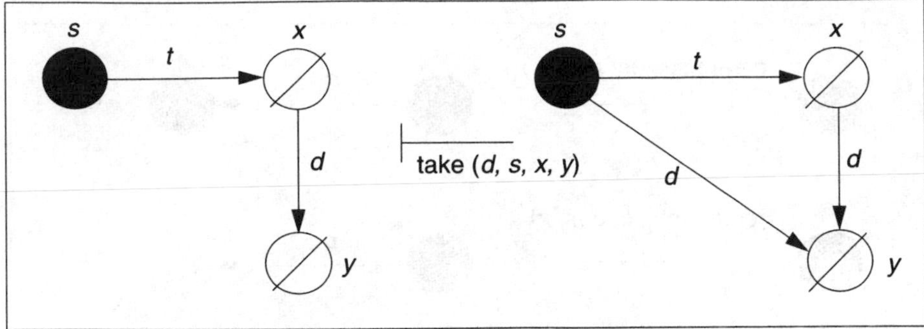


*Figure* 2.3 Effect of a take $(d, s, x, y)$.

- *remove*$_p$ $(s,x)$. Subject $s$ is revoked the $p$ rights it has been granted on object (subject) $x$. The result of this operation entails the deletion of the elements contained in the set $p$ from the label of the arc between $s$ and $x$ (Figure 2.6). When, consequent to this operation, the label is null, $s$ does not have any privilege on $x$, and the arc is removed.

Note that both the 'read'/'write' inert rights, and the 'take'/'grant' transport rights, can be taken, granted, or added by creation, and can be revoked. The effects of these operations on the authorization graph are shown in Table 2.4.

Note that, when the table indicates the addition of a labelled arc, if the arc exists already, its label must be updated by adding the elements contained in the new label. Analogously, the arc removal indicates the unwanted rights removal from the label. Only if the new label is null is the arc actually removed.

Let us see some examples of graph transformations entailed by the operations. Consider the authorization graph $G$ of Figure 2.7(a).

- *create object* $_{\{r,w\}}(s_1,o_2)$ leads to the authorization graph $G_1$ depicted in Figure 2.7(b).
- *grant* $(r, s_1, o_1, o_2)$ on $G_1$ leads to the authorization graph $G_2$ depicted in Figure 2.7(c).
- *take* $(r, s_2, o_1, o_2)$ on $G_2$ leads to the authorization graph $G_3$ (Figure 2.7(d)).
- *remove*$_w(s_1, o_2)$ on $G_3$ leads to the authorization graph $G_4$ (Figure 2.7(e)).

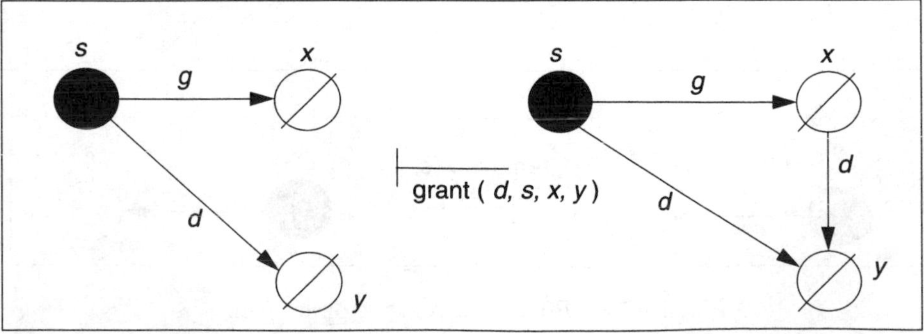


*Figure* 2.4 Effect of a grant $(d, s, x, y)$ operation.

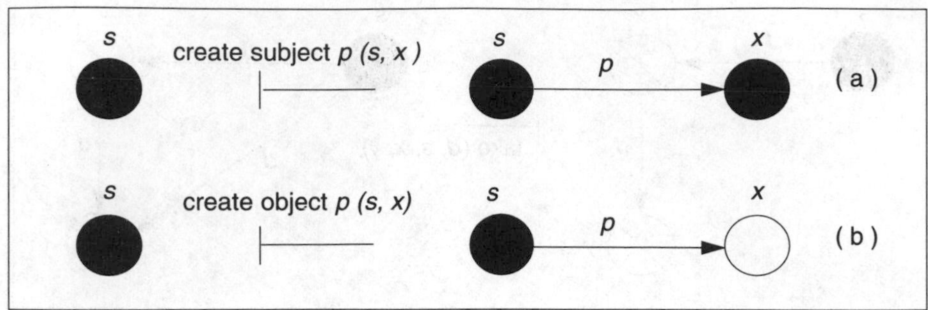


*Figure 2.5* Effect of a create operation of a subject (a) and of an object (b).

Note that subject *s*, who granted the read right on $o_2$ to $o_1$, loses control on the subsequent transfers of this right.

**Table 2.4** Operations of the Take–Grant model.

| **Operation** | **Conditions** | **Resulting state G′ = (S′, O′, E′)** |
|---|---|---|
| take (d, s, x, y) | s∈S<br>s - t - x∈E<br>s - d - y∈E<br>s ≠ y | S′ = S<br>O′ = O<br>E′ = E ∪ {s - d - y} |
| grant (d, s, x, y) | s∈S<br>s - g - x∈E<br>s - d - y∈E<br>x ≠ y | S′ = S<br>O′ = O<br>E′ = E ∪ {x - d - y} |
| create subject$_p$ (s, x) | s∈S<br>x∉S | S′ = S ∪ {x}<br>O′ = O<br>E′ = E ∪ {s - p - x} |
| create object$_p$ (s, x) | s∈S<br>x∉O | S′ = S<br>O′ = O ∪ {x}<br>E′ = E ∪ {s - p - x} |
| remove$_p$ (s, x) | s∈S<br>x∈S ∪ O<br>s - e - x∈E<br>p ⊆ e | S′ = S<br>O′ = O<br>E′ = E − {s - p - x} |

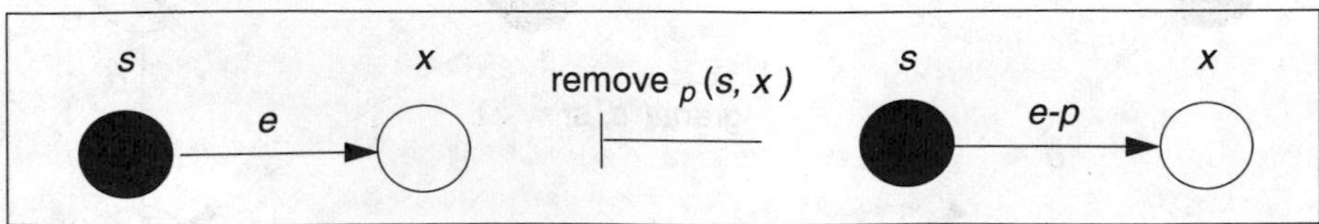


*Figure 2.6* Effect of a remove operation.

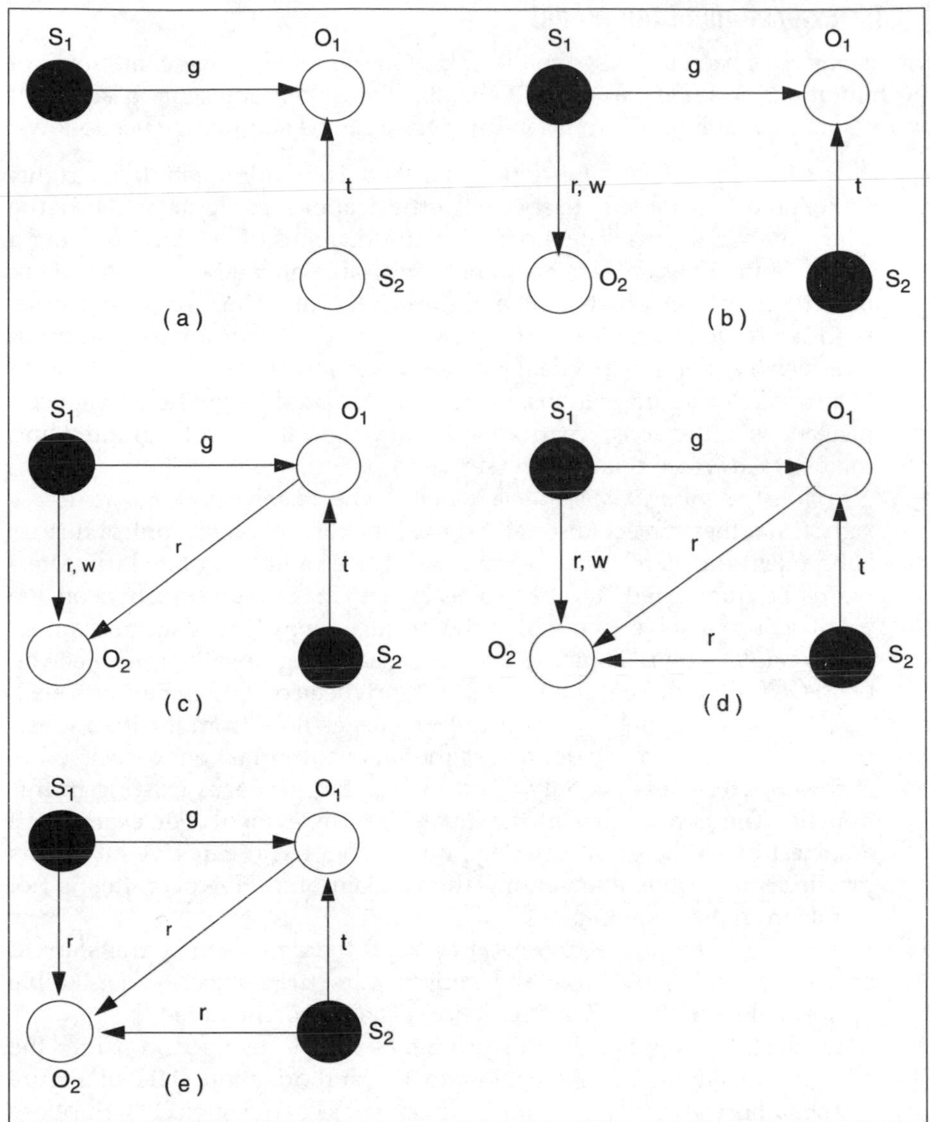


*Figure* 2.7 Execution of a sequence of operations on an authorization graph: (a) authorization graph $G$; (b) authorization graph $G_1$; (c) authorization graph $G_2$; (d) authorization graph $G_3$; (e) authorization graph $G_4$.

Regarding implementation, as the Take–Grant model is classifiable as an access matrix model, the same considerations presented for the access matrix model hold. In particular, the graph can be directly represented as a capability system, where an arc represents a specific capability. As a matter of fact, arcs in the graph relate only to non-null entries of the access matrix; these arcs connect each subject to all the objects (subjects) on which the subject holds a right, represented through the label.

### 2.3.4 Extensions to the model

Extensions have been proposed to the Take–Grant model to overcome some of the limitations it suffers from. In fact, the Take–Grant presents a series of disadvantages that limit its applicability. These can be summarized as follows:

- *Non-selectivity of administrative rights.* The administrative rights (take/grant) do not refer to specific authorizations, but to the whole of the user's authorizations. Therefore, all authorizations of a subject owning a 'grant' authorization can be transferred, and all authorizations of an object (subject) on which a 'take' right is held can be taken. For example, with reference to graph (b) of Figure 2.7, $S_1$ can grant any of its authorizations (i.e., for any privilege, on any object) to $O_1$ and $S_2$ can take from $O_1$ any of $O_1$'s authorizations. Generally, it should be possible to specify instead, as in the access matrix model, the right that can be granted and the object to which this right refers.
- *No control on propagation of authorizations.* When a subject grants an access right to another subject (also inert rights), he can no longer control further subsequent transfers of this right. Indeed, the right he granted can afterwards be transferred to other subjects with 'take' authorization on the grantee or to a subject on which the grantee owns 'grant' authorization. For example, with reference to Figure 2.7, after $S_1$ grants the *r* privilege on $O_2$ to $O_1$, no subsequent transfer of the *r* privilege on $O_2$ can be controlled.
- *Non locality.* A model is local if the privileges flow from, or to, a given domain (a domain being defined as the set of authorizations associated to each subject) is possible only if authorized by privileges existing in this domain. The non-locality of the Take–Grant is evident. For example, if a subject owns the grant privilege on an object *x*, it can give any of its privileges to *x*, thus augmenting the domain of *x*. However, this is not visible from the domain of *x*.
- *Reversibility of the privileges transport flow.* If the rights can be transferred, directly or indirectly, from the subject *x* to the subject *y*, a possible opposite flow of the rights (from *y* to *x*) cannot be prevented.

  To illustrate how the flow of privileges can be reversed, consider the example in Figure 2.8. According to the authorization state of Figure 2.8(a) authorizations can be moved from subject $s_1$ to subject $s_2$. Suppose now that subject $s_1$ creates an object *o* and grants to itself the grant and take privileges on this object by requiring operation

  create object$_{\{g,t\}}$($s_1$,*o*).

  The resulting authorization graph is shown in Figure 2.8(b).

  Suppose now that subject $s_1$ requires operation

  grant($g$,$s_1$,$s_2$,$o$)

  thus giving $s_2$ the 'grant' privilege on *o*. The resulting authorization graph is shown in Figure 2.8(c). As illustrated in this graph, privileges can now flow from $s_2$ to $s_1$ (by passing through *o*). That is, $s_2$ grants

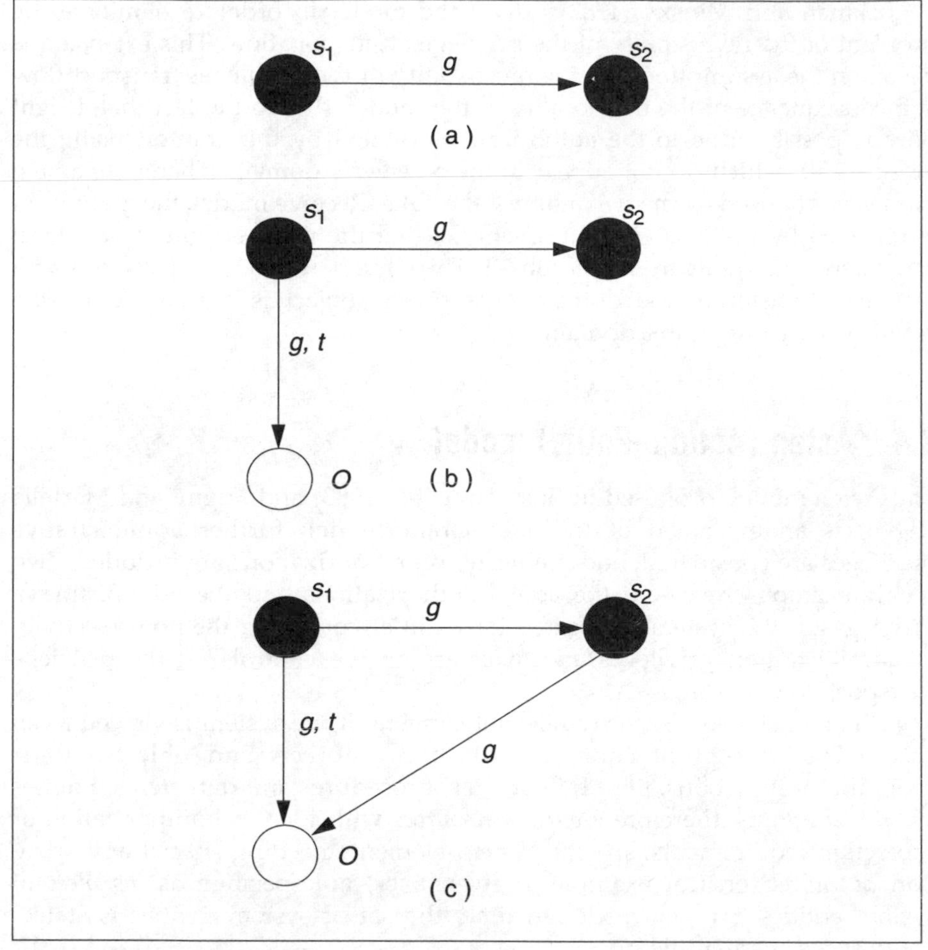


*Figure 2.8* Example of reversibility in Take–Grant: (a) moving authorizations from $s_1$ to $s_2$; (b) $s_1$ obtains grant right of object $o$; (c) $s_1$ gives $s_2$ grant right of object $o$.

them to $o$ (with a grant operation) and $s_1$ takes them from $o$ (with a take operation).

To overcome some of these drawbacks, Jones (the original author of the model) extends the model to the specification, in the declaration of the 'take' and 'grant' privileges of both access modes and objects (subjects) to which these privileges are referred (Jones, 1978). Jones also introduces a new object, the 'procedure', and a new right, the 'fork' right, used for procedure calls. The extended model, besides eliminating the problem of the non-selectivity of the Take–Grant, can be used, according to Jones, as a tool to verify the correctness of the security mechanisms.

Lockman and Minsky (1982) extend the model in order to eliminate the problem of the reversibility of the privileges transport flow. This extension is based on the assumption that the reversibility of the privileges transport flow is a consequence of the non-locality of the model, due to the fact that a right flow is possible due to the authorizations owned by the grantor (using the grant right), which do not appear in the receiver's domain. Therefore, a new model is proposed by the two authors, the Take–Receive model: the grant right is replaced by the receive right. Users holding the receive right on a subject can receive the rights from this subject. Thus, the new model is local, in that a privilege transfer in the domain of a given subject is authorized by the privileges existing in this domain.

## 2.4 Acten (Action–Entity) model

The Acten model, proposed in Bussolati *et al.* (1983) and Fugini and Martella (1984), is an extension of the Take–Grant model: further administrative privileges are considered, and predicates on authorizations are included. Two separate graphs represent the access authorizations and the administrative privileges in the system. The extensions aim at correcting the non-selectivity of administration privileges and at enlarging the controls on the privilege transport flow.

In the model, every security-relevant element of the system is viewed as an entity. The concept of entity regards both **subjects** and **objects**: users, programs, transactions, files, I/O devices, procedures and data items. Entities are *resource types*, therefore *groups of resources* with identical authorization or protection requirements; specific system elements needing special authorization or protection (for example, a given user) are specified as *instances* of system entities. At system design time, the set of system entities is stated; entity types are identified.

### 2.4.1 Access modes

The model distinguishes between *static* access modes and *dynamic* access modes; both are called *actions*. The execution of static actions does not modify the *authorization state* of the system; the execution of dynamic actions modifies the authorization state because they add or delete privileges. The *static access modes* are:

- *Use*: this is the typical access mode between users, user groups, operators and programmers on one side, and I/O resources and application programs on the other. The 'use' privilege on an application program allows the program to be executed by the requester.
- *Read*: to access the contents of an entity.
- *Update:* to modify or manipulate an entity.
- *Create:* to add entities in the system.
- *Delete:* to remove entities from the system.

The dynamic access modes are:

- *Grant/Revoke.* The grant (revoke) privilege held by an entity $E_i$ *towards* an entity $E_j$, *related to* a static access mode $m$, and *referred to* an entity $E_k$ allows $E_i$ to grant $E_j$ – and later revoke – $m$ on $E_k$. An entity can administer a privilege only if it holds that privilege. $E_k$ is called the *parameter* of the authorization.
- *Delegate/Abrogate.* The delegate (abrogate) privilege held by $E_i$ *towards* $E_j$, *related to* a static access mode $m$, and *referred to* an entity $E_k$ allows $E_i$ to grant – and later revoke – the dynamic authorization 'grant' related to $m$ on $E_k$. The authorizations to the delegate and abrogate privileges are limited to a few system entities. If the delegator $E_i$ does not hold the authorization for $m$ for which it receives the grant, the authorization for $m$ is automatically granted. $E_k$ is called the *parameter* of the authorization.

If an entity $E_i$ holds the highest level access mode (create/delete), and the delegate/abrogate authorization upon an entity $E_j$, then $E_i$ is the *owner* of $E_j$. The owner of an entity is unique. The authorizations for the delegate/abrogate access modes are given exclusively to the owner.

The access modes are hierarchically ordered by assigning a *level* to each mode. The levels assigned to the static and dynamic access modes are reported in Tables 2.5 and 2.6 respectively.

If an entity $E_i$ is authorized to access $E_j$ in mode at level $L'$, it is also enabled by default to access $E_j$ according to all the access modes classified at levels $L'' \leq L'$. This implies, in particular, that if an entity is authorized for the grant (delegate) privilege on a given authorization, it is also enabled for the revoke (abrogate) privilege related to the same authorization.

This ordering of access modes simplifies the grant and revocation of access rights. When an access mode is granted on an entity, all the modes at a lower classification are granted by default. Analogously, when an access mode is revoked, all the modes at a higher classification are revoked. It is also possible to specify the maximum level of the access mode executable by an entity, thus assigning clearances to entities, and similarly to the models for mandatory policies.

**Table 2.5** Static access modes and their classification in the Acten model.

| **Access mode** | **Level** |
|---|---|
| Create/Delete | 4 |
| Update | 3 |
| Read | 2 |
| Use | 1 |

**Table 2.6** Administrative privileges and their classification in the Acten model.

| **Administration right** | **Level** |
|---|---|
| Delegate/abrogate | 2 |
| Grant/revoke | 1 |

### 2.4.2 Authorizations

An authorization is a binary relation between entities. It is characterized by the involved *entities* and *access mode*, by a *direction*, and by one or more attributes called *predicates*. The direction specifies which entity can execute the denoted access and which entity undergoes this access. The predicates are conditions to be satisfied for access to be allowed. Formally, a static authorization is indicated as:

$$A_{ij} = a \sim \{p_{ij}\}$$

where $a$ denotes the access mode that entity $E_i$ holds on $E_j$ if the conditions expressed in $\{p_{ij}\}$ are matched. In the predicates, the model considers only system conditions, for example, time or origin location of a request, or generally those conditions that can be evaluated externally to the requested data. Data-dependent conditions are considered at the level of entity definition. In particular, for each condition that can be imposed on the contents of a given entity, two entities are considered, one containing the data verifying the condition, and one containing the data not verifying the condition. The authorization to access an entity for which a value-dependent condition is expressed is specified by defining a proper entity and by referring access to this entity.

For example, if a user is authorized to read the EMPLOYEE table only for those tuples where the 'salary' field is lower than a given value (value-dependent constraint), a new entity is defined for EMPLOYEE, with the tuples where the 'salary' is lower than *value*. The user is then authorized to access only the new entity. Therefore, to each database object, several model entities can correspond.

The authorizations to execute the dynamic access modes are characterized by an expression of the form:

$$A_{i_{j/k}} = a \sim \{p_{ij}\}$$

where $a$ denotes the access mode that can be administered, $E_k$ the parameter entity to which access is referred, $E_i$ the entity administering the access, and $E_j$ the entity to which the authorization for the access mode (or for its administration) can be granted or revoked. Also in this case, the predicate expresses the conditions to be satisfied in order for the request for the authorization to be granted.

For each entity $E_i$, two sets are defined, the *authorization state* $S_a$ and the *protection state* $S_p$ of an entity. Their definition is as follows:

$$S_a(E_i) = \{A_{i,j}^{h_j}\ E_i\}\ j = 1,\ldots, N, j \neq i, h_j \geq 1$$
$$S_p(E_i) = \{A_{j,i}^{m_j}\ E_i\}\ j = 1,\ldots, N, j \neq i, m_j \geq 1$$

where:

- $N$ is the total number of entities in the system.
- $S_a(E_i)$ is the *authorization state* of entity $E_i$. It denotes all the authorizations that the considered entity holds on all the other system entities. It is composed of all the authorizations $\{A_{i,j}^{h_j}, E_i\}$ where $A_{i,j}^{h_j}$ is the $h$-th action that $E_i$ can execute on $E_j$.
- $S_p(E_i)$ is the *protection state* of $E_i$. It denotes all the authorizations held by the system entities onto $E_i$. It is composed of all the authorizations $\{A_{j,i}^{m_j}, E_i\}$ where $A_{j,i}^{m_j}$ is the $m$-th action that $E_i$ can undergo from $E_j$.

- The number of different values of $j$ in $S_a(E_i)$ is the number $n_i$ of all the entities onto which $E_i$ can execute actions. These values are grouped in a set denoted as $J$. The number of different values of $j$ in $S_p(E_i)$ is the number $p_i$ of all the entities that can execute actions on $E_i$. These values are grouped in a set denoted as $Y$.
- $h_j$ and $m_j$ are the number of actions between $E_i$ and $E_j$ in $S_a(E_i)$ and $S_p(E_i)$ respectively:

  $| S_a(E_i) | = \Sigma_j h_j \; \forall j \in J$
  $| S_p(E_i) | = \Sigma_j m_j \; \forall j \in Y$

where the sums are computed on the different values of $j$ in $S_a(E_i)$ and $S_p(E_i)$ respectively.

### 2.4.3 Entity classification

On the basis of the sets $S_a(E_i)$ and $S_p(E_i)$, the model classifies every entity $E_i$ in the system as:

- *Active entity:* if $S_a(E_i) \neq 0$. An active entity is an entity that can execute actions on other system entities.
- *Passive entity*: if $S_p(E_i) \neq 0$. A passive entity is an entity that can only undergo actions from other system entities.
- *Active and passive entity:* if $S_a(E_i) \neq 0$ and $S_p(E_i) \neq 0$. This means that $E_i$ can both execute and undergo actions.

Examples of active entities are the DBA, the 'root' in a UNIX system: they can read, create, update data, or grant and revoke access rights to users. Examples of passive entities are data files and items: they can be read, updated, created, and so on but cannot perform any action in the system (they do not hold or access administration rights). Typical examples of active and passive entities are programs and processes, or database transactions: they can access data (active behaviour) and can also be used, created and controlled by a user or by another program (passive behaviour).

### 2.4.4 Model structures

The model elements are represented in two graphs:

- *Static Graph* SG, containing the authorizations for static actions;
- *Dynamic Graph* DG, containing the authorizations for dynamic actions.

The static graph SG comprises nodes, corresponding to the system entities, and arcs, corresponding to the authorizations between entities to execute static actions. Arcs are labelled: an arc labelled with $a$ from $E_i$ to $E_j$ denotes that $E_i$ holds the authorization for the access mode (static action) $a$ upon $E_j$. If the authorization is constrained by some predicates, the arc is crossed (the associated predicate is then reported separately). Figure 2.9 shows a sample SG.

The dynamic graph DG is analogously defined as a set of nodes corresponding to the system entities, and arcs corresponding to the authorizations between entities to execute dynamic actions. Arcs are labelled: a label has the form *"DA SA {M}"*, where *DA* denotes the authorization for the administration (dynamic action)

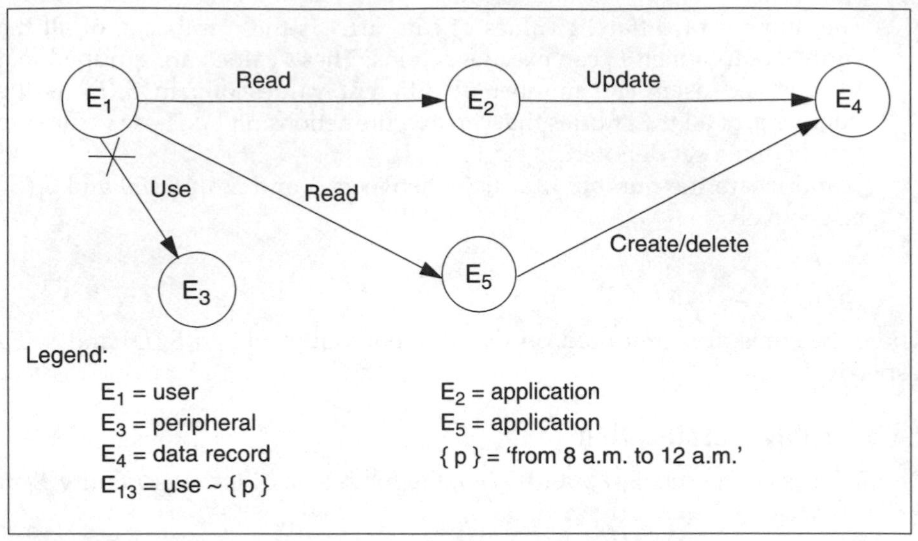


*Figure 2.9* An example of a static graph.

of the access *SA* (static action) upon the destination entity. The set {*M*} is specified only for the delegate and abrogate modes and denotes the entities upon which the transferred administration privilege 'grant' can be performed. The administered entity is represented by a labelled bar on the arc. If the authorization is constrained by some predicates, the arc is barred. For example, in the DG of Figure 2.10, the

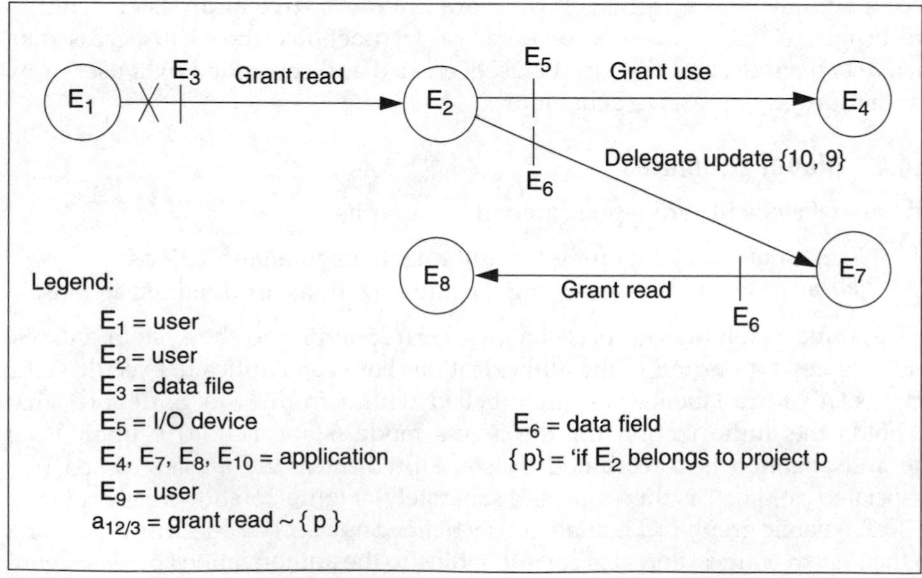


*Figure 2.10* An example of a dynamic graph.

arc between $E_2$ and $E_7$ denotes that $E_2$ can transfer to $E_7$ the grant privilege for the update access mode upon $E_6$; it also shows that $E_7$ can further transfer this privilege to entities $E_9$ and $E_{10}$ ($E_9$ and $E_{10}$ are the elements of set $\{M\}$).

The model introduces the following tables:

- *Table of security classes*. This provides, for each entity $E_i$, the following information:
  - the static action $A_i^+$ at the highest level that $E_i$ can execute on the system entities. This action is called the *active potentiality* of $E_i$.
  - the dynamic action $A_i^-$ at the lowest level that can be executed by the system entities on $E_i$. This action is called the *passive potentiality* of $E_i$.

  No active potentiality is defined for passive entities; conversely, no passive potentiality is defined for active entities. The potentialities are stated by the security administrators and the authorizations must comply with these definitions. The table of security classes allows the administrators to assign an authority level and a protection level to each system entity according to its physical nature and its functional position in the system, or according to the role played by an entity within a project or in the organization. Table 2.7 gives a sample table of security classes.
- *Table of entity states.* This shows the entities that own some other entities in the system and the list of the owned entities. The table may be examined to verify the legitimacy of requests of grant/revocation of dynamic actions. In fact, these requests can be authorized only to the owner of the entity to which the involved access mode is referred. A sample state table is shown in Table 2.8 where entity $E_2$, owned by $E_7$, is indirectly owned by $E_1$, $E_1$ being the owner of $E_7$.
- *Tables of action hierarchy.* These are the two tables listing the static action levels and the dynamic action levels. They are depicted in Tables 2.5 and 2.6.

**Table 2.7** Security class table.

| | Potentiality | Action |
|---|---|---|
| $E_1$ | $A_1^+$ | Update |
| | $A_1^-$ | – |
| $E_2$ | $A_2^+$ | Update |
| | $A_2^-$ | Create/Delete |
| $E_3$ | $A_3^+$ | Create/Delete |
| | $A_3^-$ | Use |
| $E_4$ | $A_4^+$ | – |
| | $A_4^-$ | Create/Delete |
| $E_5$ | $A_5^+$ | Create/Delete |
| | $A_5^-$ | Create/Delete |

Legend:
$E_1$ = user   $E_3$ = peripheral
$E_2$, $E_5$ = application   $E_4$ = data record

**Table 2.8** Entity state table.

| Owner entity | Owned entities |
|---|---|
| $E_1$ | $E_8$, $E_5$, $E_7$ |
| $E_4$ | $E_6$ |
| $E_7$ | $E_3$, $E_2$ |

Legend: $E_1$ = project manager, $E_2$ = application, $E_3$ = terminal, $E_4$ = COBOL programmer, $E_5$ = data file, $E_6$ = COBOL library, $E_7$ = programmers, $E_8$ = data file

## 2.4.5 Consistency and transformation rules

The model specifies the rules to be respected during the system life cycle:

- *Internal consistency rules.* The structure of both graphs SG and DG should be consistent with the structure, nature and security relationships of the represented protected system.
- *Mutual consistency rules.* The SG and the DG should be consistent in representing the privileges, for example: a privilege cannot be propagated if the grantor does not hold that privilege. These rules reflect the protection strategies and policies for the system.
- *Transformation rules.* These control the indirect authorizations and the access right propagation.

In the following, the consistency rules are illustrated.

### *Internal consistency rules for SG*

A system entity can execute or undergo only those access modes which are compatible with its type and role in the system. For example, the 'delete' mode cannot be executed upon peripheral devices, and the 'use' mode is ambiguous for files. Each mode has to be excluded or *interpreted* for a given resource: for the file, 'use' can be interpreted as 'execute' with no 'read' or 'write' of the file contents.

The internal consistency rules express the operational semantics of the authorizations specified in the system. In particular, they ensure that the modifications to the SG due to new authorizations are consistent with the table of security classes. The rules are expressed in a 'filter' function that evaluates each requested modification to the SG against the table of security classes and the table of entity states.

### *Internal consistency rules for DG*

The internal consistency rules for the DG ensure the consistency of dynamic authorizations with the requirements for administration privileges fixed by the system policies. The basic rules are:

- *Rule I.1.* Let $E_j$ be the owner entity of $E_k$. No other entities $E_i$, $\forall i, k \neq j, k \neq i$, can hold the authorization $A_{ij/k}$ of type **'GRANT SA'**, where SA is any static action. In fact, since $E_j$ is the owner of $E_k$, it is enabled to execute the SA at the highest level (create/delete) and no other entities are enabled to administer the authorizations on $E_k$.
- *Rule I.2.* An entity $E_i$ can be authorized for the delegate/abrogate actions on $E_k$ only if $E_i$ is the owner of $E_k$ (also indirect). This rule expresses the policy that only the entity owner is enabled to administer the authorizations on that entity.
- *Rule I.3.* Let $E_j$ be an entity authorized to grant to an entity $E_m$ a static action of level $L'$ with parameter $E_k$. $E_i$, owner of $E_k$, can execute on $E_j$ the dynamic action $A_{ij/k}$ of type **'DELEGATE SA'** only if $L(\text{SA}) > L'$.
- *Rule I.4.* An entity $E_j$, recipient of a static action SA of level $L$ through a delegate action, can grant this SA only to entities $E_m$ whose active potentiality $A^+$ has level $L' \geq L$. This conditions are checked when the delegate/abrogate authorization is specified, to verify that $E_m$ (with the associated set $\{M\}$) is consistent with the requirement expressed by this rule.

#### *Transformation rules for SG*

The purpose of these rules is to show all the privileges held indirectly by an entity on the other system entities. In fact, it may happen that an entity $E_i$ can execute an action on an entity $E_j$ although no direct arcs exist on the SG from $E_i$ to $E_j$. The direct arcs would express an explicitly authorized action. Instead, a path (set of arcs and nodes) may exist in SG providing $E_i$ with an implicit privilege which must be checked. Transformation rules are defined for groups of three entities $E_i$, $E_j$, $E_z$, and two authorizations $A_{ij}$ and $A_{jz}$. Each rule determines the static action $A_{iz}$ that can be executed via an authorization chain $A_{ij}-A_{jz}$. A transformation rule is defined as a function $F$ which, given four arguments $(A_{ij}, A_{jz}, E_i, E_z)$ returns $A_{iz}$ obtained as a combination of the argument actions. $F$ is a function of $A_{ij}$ and of $A_{jz}$ in that $A_{iz}$ depends on the type and hierarchical level of the access modes in the authorizations of the three entities. $F$ is also a function of $E_i$ and $E_z$ in that $A_{iz}$ must be consistent with the nature and role of the involved entities $E_i$ and $E_z$. In particular, the level of $A_{iz}$ cannot be higher than the level of the active potentiality of $E_i$ nor lower than the level of the passive potentiality of $E_j$; both levels are stated in the table of security classes.

The algorithm for $F$ is as follows.

(1) Compare $L(A_{ij})$ and $L(A_{jz})$.

(2) If $L(A_{ij}) > L(A_{jz})$ then $L(A_{iz}) = L(A_{jz})$.

(3) If $L(A_{ij}) \leq L(A_{jz})$ then check the active potentiality of $E_i$ in the table of security classes:

$$L(A_{iz}) = \begin{cases} L(A_i^+) \text{ if } L(A_{jz}) > L(A_i^+) \\ L(A_{jz}) \text{ if } L(A_{jz}) < L(A_i^+) \end{cases}$$

where $L(A)$ denotes the level of authorization $A$.

This function does not consider the passive potentiality of $E_z$ in that the check on the level of $A_{jz}$ in steps 2 and 3 ensures that this potentiality is never violated.

If $A_{ij}$ and $A_{jz}$ are constrained by some predicates, say $p_{ij}$ and $p_{jz}$, then the predicate $p_{iz}$ on the derived authorization $A_{iz}$ is obtained as the intersection of the two predicates: $p_{iz} = p_{ij} \wedge p_{jz}$.

When the path between $E_i$ and $E_z$ includes various entities, the algorithm for $F$ is applied to groups of two entities at a time, each time considering the computed derived action.

Figure 2.11 shows two sample computations of an indirect authorization: the authorization state is the same in both cases of the figure (indirect rights are shown by dotted-line arcs).

#### *Transformation rules for DG*

These rules control the *flow of privileges* in the system: that is, the flow of static and dynamic actions due to the execution of dynamic actions. For example, if a user $E_1$ can grant to another user $E_2$ the privilege to update a data file $E_3$, and $E_2$ can grant the read privilege on the same file $E_3$ to an application program $E_4$, then $E_1$ can indirectly grant a privilege to $E_4$ through the chain comprising entities $E_1$, $E_2$, and $E_4$, and the authorizations among these entities. The authorizations that could derive as a consequence of the execution of one or more dynamic actions are called *indirect authorizations*. These have to be checked at design time to verify their consistency with the security requirements.

Transformation rules are defined for groups of three entities $E_i$, $E_j$, $E_z$, and of two dynamic actions $A_{ij/k}$ and $A_{jz/k}$ defined on the same parameter entity $E_k$. Rules determine the indirect authorization $A_{iz/k}$. Indirect authorizations are not always defined: it is when the authorization $A_{jz/k}$ 'depends' on $A_{ij/k}$ that the possibility to execute $A_{jz/k}$ is *subordinated* to the possibility to execute $A_{ij/k}$. A dynamic authorization $A_{jz/k}$ of kind `'GRANT SA'` is subordinated to another authorization $A_{ij/k}$ if the following conditions are satisfied:

(1) $E_j$ and $E_k$ are not linked by any authorization $A_{jk}$ in the static graph.
(2) If an authorization $A_{ij}$ exists in the static graph, then $L(A_{jk}) < L(\text{SA})$.
(3) The static action SA, granted or delegated through $A_{ij/k}$, is at level $L' \geq L(\text{SA})$.

Figure 2.12 shows a DG where no indirect dynamic authorization can be derived. In Figure 2.13 some dynamic authorizations are shown: one subordinated action is represented on the DG with a boldface arc. Subordinated actions are the authorizations for the 'grant' mode which do not satisfy the requirement that an entity must be authorized for an access mode in order to administer that mode. For example, in Figure 2.13 the authorization $A_{34/2}$ is inconsistent since $E_3$, authorized to grant the read mode on $E_2$, is not authorized to the read access. $A_{34/2}$ will be consistent only after the grant by $E_1$ to $E_3$ of the authorization for update on $E_2$.

The transformation rule for the DG is as follows.

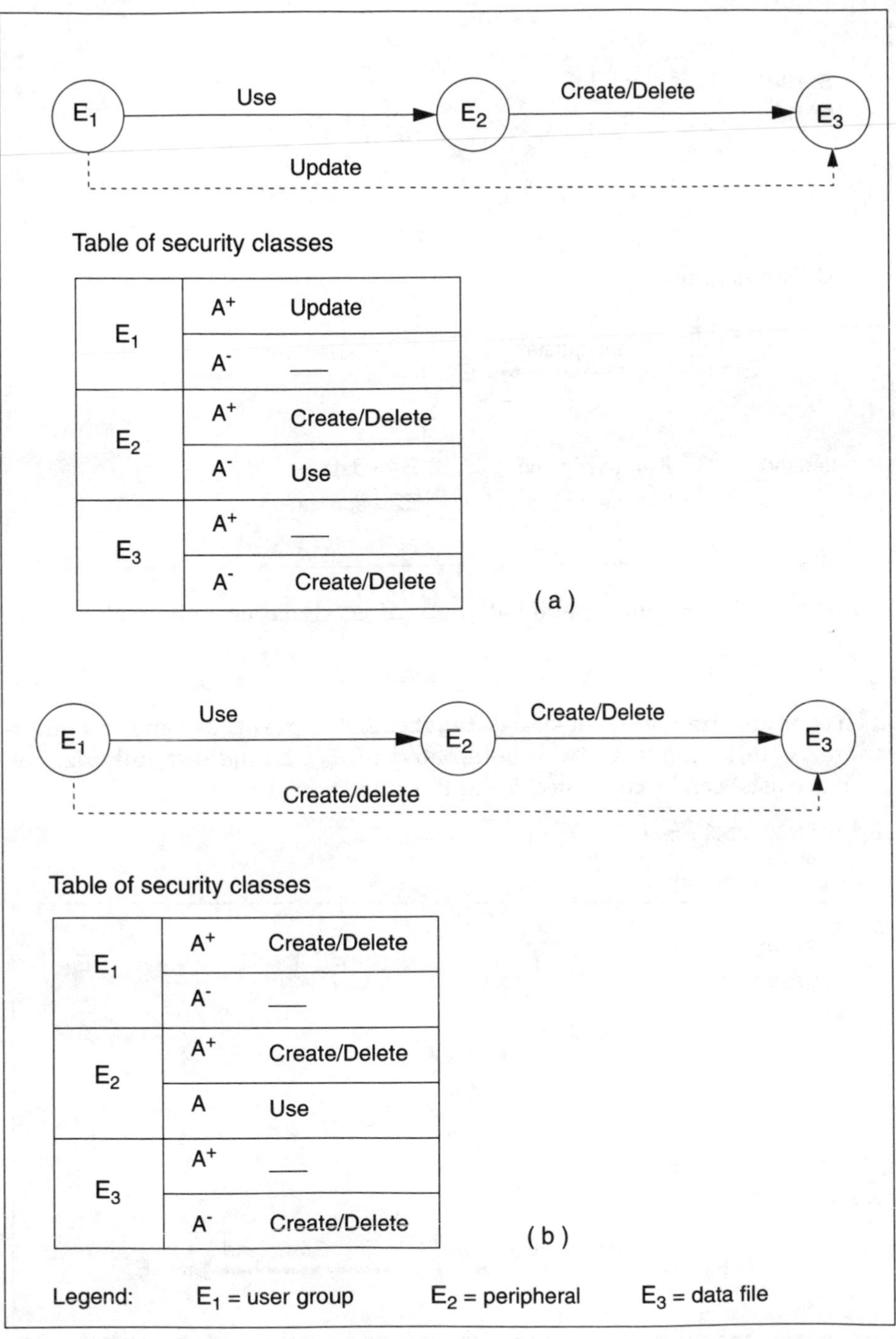


*Figure 2.11* Applications of algorithm for indirect action computation: (a) Update; (b) Create/Delete.

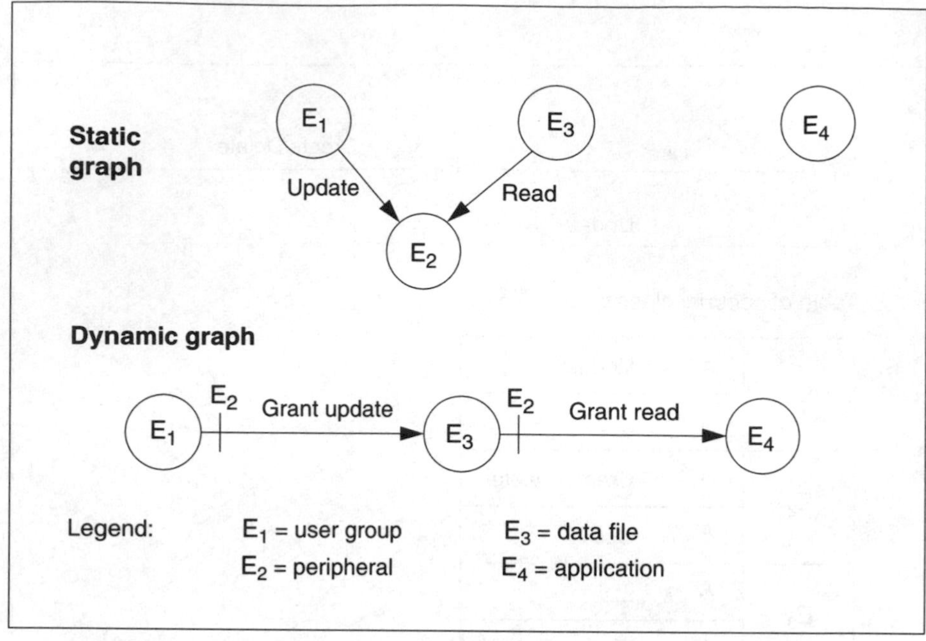


*Figure 2.12* Dynamic graph with no indirect dynamic authorizations.

*Rule T.1*

Given an authorization $A_{ij/k}$ of kind `delegate SA"` or `grant SA"` and an authorization $A_{jz/k}$ of kind `grant SA'` subordinated to $A_{ij/k}$, an indirect authorization $A_{iz/k}$ (if it exists) can be computed using the rule:

$$SA = F(SA'', SA', E_i, E_z)$$

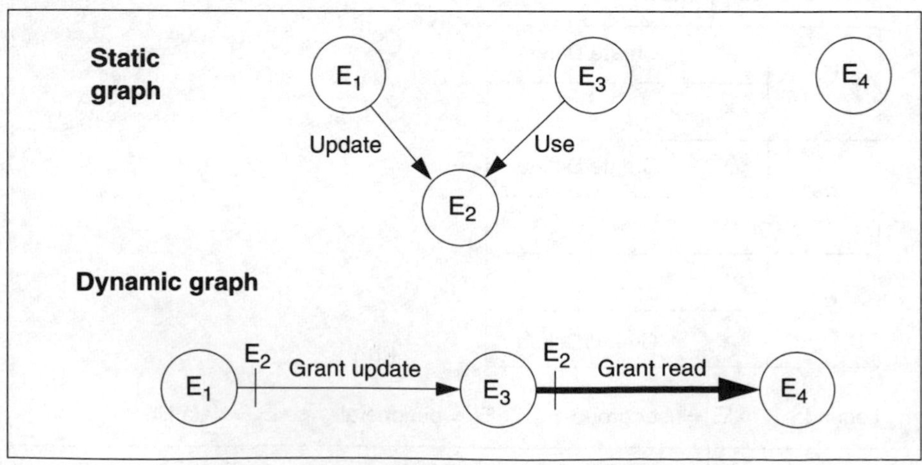


*Figure 2.13* Example of a subordinated action.

where $F$ is a function of its four arguments, analogous to the transformation rule for the SG. $S_a$ is determined by an algorithm similar to the algorithm for the SG. In particular, given condition 2 on subordinated actions, which must be satisfied in order to apply the rule, SA is always computed through step 2 of algorithm $F$. Therefore, SA = SA'.

Analogous to that seen for SG, if the original authorizations are constrained by predicates, the indirect authorization gets the predicate computed via the intersection operation.

The rule can be applied to more than three entities and two actions only if the considered entities and actions belong to a *grant/revoke chain*. This chain on $E_k$ is defined as a path of DG including an authorization $A_{ij/k}$ of kind **delegate SA** or **grant SA**, and of one or more subordinated authorizations $A_{lm/k}$ of kind SA. A chain has the following properties:

- Only the first arc in the chain can be labelled as **delegate SA**. In fact, the other arcs are subordinated authorizations, and authorization of type **'delegate/abrogate'** cannot be subordinated (they are source authorizations).
- The hierarchical level of static authorizations along the chain cannot increase. This property is a consequence of point 3 in the definition of subordinated actions.

The transformation rule can thus be applied incrementally to a grant/revoke chain by substituting, at each step, the authorization derived at the preceding step. A sample application of the transformation rule of DG to a grant/revoke chain is shown in Figure 2.14.

#### Mutual consistency rules for SG and DG

These rules ensure that dynamic privileges are consistent with the state of authorizations for access modes, and vice versa.

*Rule M.1*

$E_i$ can grant $E_j$ the privilege to execute a static action SA of level $L$ upon $E_k$ only if, in the SG, $E_i$ can execute SA' of level $L' \geq L$ on $E_k$. This rule translates the requirement that an entity must hold the access privilege in order to be enabled to administer this privilege.

*Rule M.2*

If $E_j$ can execute a static action $A_{jk}$ of level $L$, then in the DG $E_i$ can grant to $E_j$ the privilege to execute only static authorizations of level $L' > L$ on $E_k$. This rule is analogous to rule I.3.

*Rule M.3*

For each authorization $A_{ij/k}$ of type **delegate SA**, the corresponding authorization $A_{ij}$ must exist in the SG, of type create/delete. This rule translates the requirement that the delegate and abrogate rights for access modes on an entity can be executed only by the owner of this entity. The owner must hold the create and delete rights on the entity.

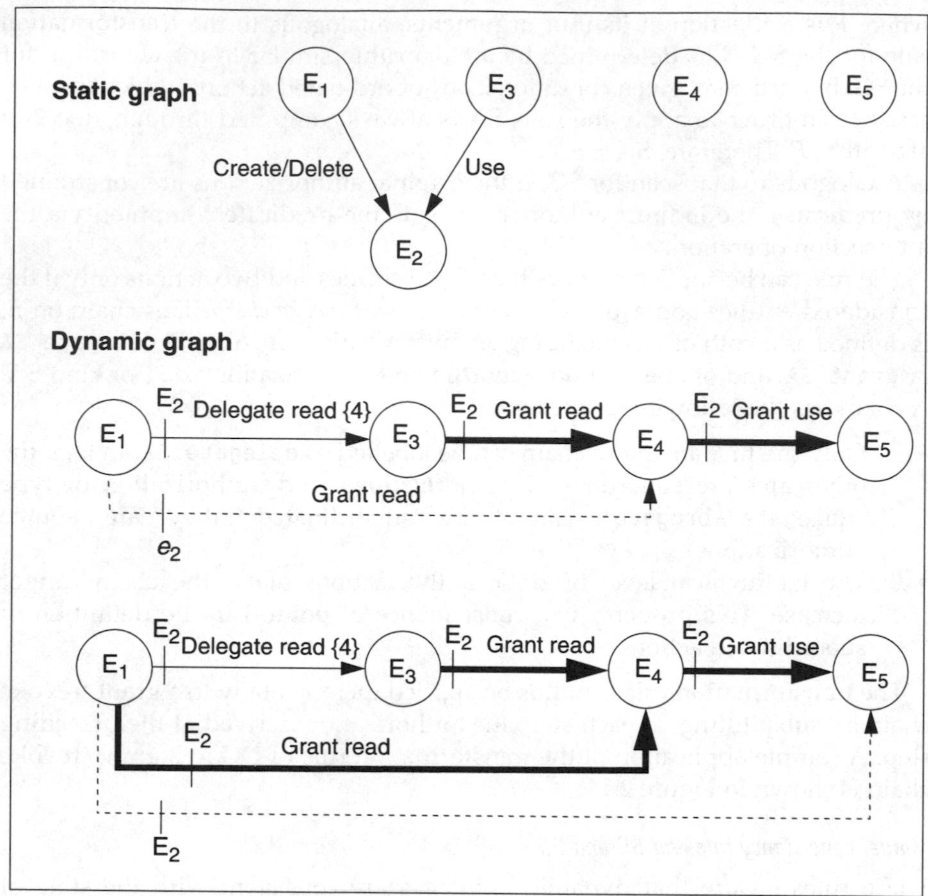


*Figure 2.14* Chain of subordinated actions.

An interpretation of Acten in the UNIX discretionary mechanisms is provided in Fugini *et al.* (1991). A hierarchy of authorizers is defined, a specification language based on the UNIX shell is defined as an authorization language, and a prototype implementation is described.

## 2.5 Wood *et al.* model

In this section we present a model, proposed by Wood *et al.* (1979), which is oriented to authorization management and access control in multilevel-schema databases. Note that this must be distinguished from 'multilevel security' models or architectures, which refer to data/users classification in mandatory systems. The model considers the three-level architecture of the ANSI/SPARC proposal for databases (1977), which is briefly reviewed here. The model treats the problems of authorizations at different levels and inter-level consistency as well as the issue of access decisions.

## 2.5.1 ANSI/SPARC architecture

The ANSI/SPARC architecture is based on a three-level view of the database. The three levels are as follows.

(1) *External level.* This is the nearest to the user; it is the user's view on the database. External schemas, which are oriented to specific applications, are sets of views over the underlying conceptual object types.
(2) *Conceptual level.* This is the representation of the data stored in the database. A conceptual object type may support multiple external object types.
(3) *Internal level.* This is the closest to the physical storing: that is, the low-level representation of the data stored in the database. Note that, although close to the physical storage method, the internal level does not coincide with the physical level. In fact, the internal level does not consider physical blocks, neither is it bound to hardware elements.

According to this architecture, a database is characterized by an internal schema, a conceptual schema, and a number of external schemas (see Figure 2.15). Each of the schemas may be based on a different data model and specify a number of object types. Requests by users to access objects of the external schema are translated into corresponding operations on objects at the lower levels.

The model of Wood *et al.* considers the problem of authorizations in multilevel-schema databases with particular attention to the problem of *consistency* among authorization rules at different levels and to the *validation* of access requests against these rules. The model considers a relational database model for the external level, and an entity-relationship model for the conceptual level.

## 2.5.2 Subjects and objects

The model subjects are the users accessing the system. In particular, two types of users are distinguished: the *authorizers*, who administer the authorizations (i.e. grants and revokes), and the *users*, who access data according to the authorizations specified by the authorizers.

Different protection objects are considered in the two levels and each level considers different type categories. Some categories refer to types, others to the instances or occurrences of these types.

(1) *Conceptual-level objects.* Each object $o$ in the system belongs to the type category. A function $n$ is defined, associated with each object $o$: its type category $n(o)$. This function is applied both to conceptual-level objects and to external-level objects.

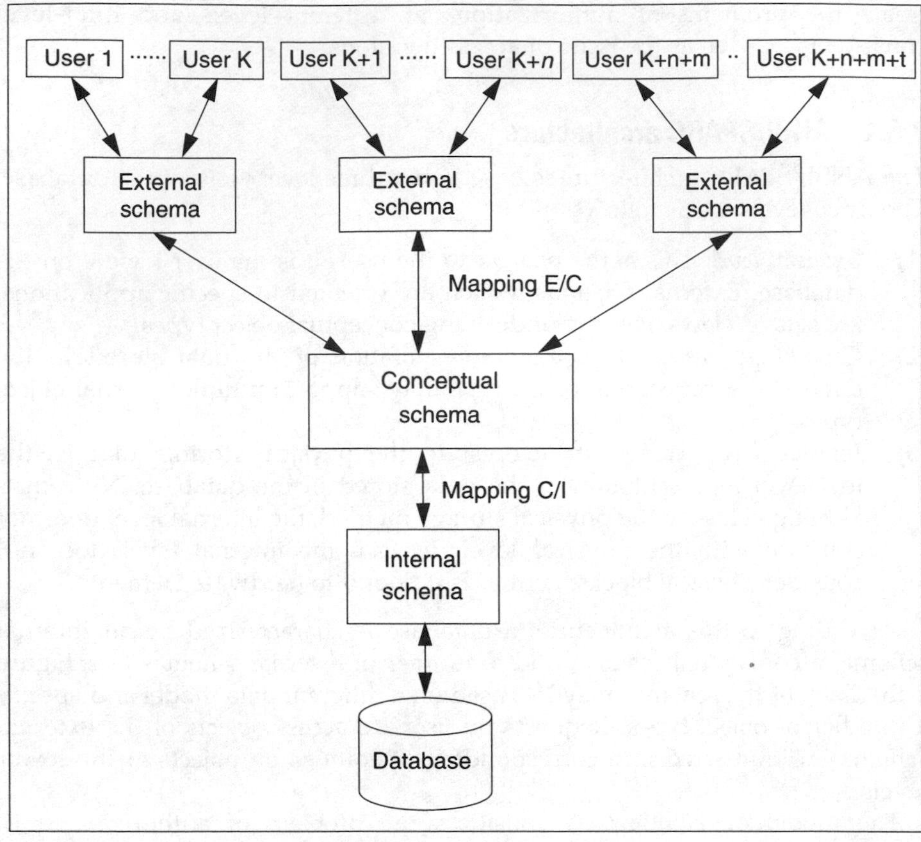


*Figure 2.15* Three-level database architecture in the ANSI/SPARC proposal.

(2) *External-level objects.* The type categories at the conceptual level are: entity set, relationship type, and attribute. Attributes may be associated with one entity set. An attribute maps an entity set to a value set. A relationship type is a bidirectional association between two entity sets. The relationship type may have two names, corresponding to its two directions. The type categories are: table, view, and field (column). Tables can be described in terms of conceptual-level objects. In the following, the notation 'x.y' indicates field y of table x.

### 2.5.3 Access modes

At each level (conceptual and external), a set *TP* of operations (that is, access modes) is defined for each type category. The access modes considered at each level are as follows.

(1) *Conceptual-level access modes.* The access modes $TP_C$ applicable to type category C at the conceptul level are:

- $TP_{entity}$ = {insert, delete};
- $TP_{attribute}$ = {update, read, use};
- $TP_{relation}$ = {insert, delete, use}.

In the following, *C* denotes the set of all conceptual level object types, and $T_C$ denotes the access modes applicable to the conceptual level objects. Therefore:

- C = {entity, attribute, relation}
- $T_C = TP_{entity} \cup TP_{attribute} \cup TP_{relation}$ = {insert, delete, update, use}

(2) *External-level access modes.* The access modes $TP_C$ applicable to type category C at the external level are:

- $TP_{table}$ = {insert, delete};
- $TP_{field}$ = {update, read, use}.

In the following, *E* denotes the set of all external-level object types, and $T_E$ denotes the set of all access modes applicable to external-level objects. Therefore:

- *E* = {table, field};
- $T_E = TP_{table} \cup TP_{field}$ = {insert, delete, update, use}.

In the model, the update right does not imply the read right.

### 2.5.4 Mapping function

The model assumes that any operation on an external object *e* can be mapped to a set of operations on one or more conceptual objects *c*.

A mapping function $\phi^v$ is defined for each table *v* in the system. $\phi^v$ maps operations on external-level objects to a set of operations on conceptual-level objects. More precisely, $\phi^v$ maps external-level pairs ⟨access type, object⟩ to a set of conceptual-level pairs ⟨access type, object⟩.

Function $\phi^v$ can be formally defined as follows:

$$\phi^v: T_E \times E \rightarrow T_C \times C$$

At the element level, this transformation is:

$$\phi^v: \langle t_r, e_i \rangle \rightarrow \langle t_s^k, c_j^k \rangle \ \forall k,\ t_s^k = \in T_{cj}^k$$

Generally, database management systems allow the specification of predicates in the access request. A predicate in an access request on entity *e* determines the subset of the set of occurrences of *e* to be accessed. Like access types, predicates referred to external objects must be mapped to predicates on conceptual objects.

The mapping function, extended to consider data predicates, becomes as follows:

$$\phi^v : \langle t_r, e_i : p_l \rangle \rightarrow \{\langle t_s^k, c_j^k : p_m^k \rangle\}.$$

### 2.5.5 Authorization state

Authorizations are described by *access rules*. Access rules are 4-tuples of the form $\langle s,o,t,p \rangle$. Access rule $\langle s,o,t,p \rangle$ states that subject $s$ can exercise the access mode $t$ on object $o$ under conditions expressed by predicate $p$. Access rules are defined by an authorizer, who is in charge of applying the security policies of the organization.

Basic access rules should be specified at the conceptual level, since that level provides a global view of the data of an organization. Moreover, the definer of an external object has the option of specifying the allowed access types for that object. To do this, a table definition includes access constraints, specifying which access types are legal for each external object $e$: that is, for each table and its fields. These constraints are stored in an *Access Constraint table (AC)* with two columns, one for the external objects, and one for the access types $t$.

The tuple $\langle e_i, t_j \rangle$ in AC states that access type $t_j$ is allowed on the external object $e_i$. An example of an AC table is illustrated in Table 2.9.

The table lists the access constraints for the EMPLOYEE table. According to the specified constraints, rows of EMPLOYEE may be deleted or inserted and all its fields can be read, but only the MANAGER and SALARY fields can be updated.

Obviously, the access type specified in the access constraint table for an external object must belong to the set of the possible access types defined for the category of that object. This is formally expressed as follows:

$$AC.t\ (e_i, *) \in TP_{n(e_i)}\ \forall e_i \in AC.t$$

where '*' is the wildcard symbol.

Access rules specified on conceptual objects are transformed into access rules on external objects. The authorizer can specify a user's access to external objects in either of two ways:

(1) By accepting the access rules that are derived from conceptual level rules;
(2) By defining some new, more restrictive rules.

Ideally, the system displays the derived rules so that the authorizer can then determine if more restrictive rules are needed. If new rules are defined, the system checks if they are consistent with the conceptual-level rules. A rule specified at the external level is consistent if it is at least as restrictive as the existing rules for the underlying objects.

Figure 2.16 shows the relationship of access rules at different levels.

### 2.5.6 Access rules at the conceptual level

Access rules of the form $\langle s,o,t,p \rangle$ are specified for all conceptual-level objects (that is, all entity sets, attributes and relationship types). These rules, called conceptual-level access rules, are stored in the *Conceptual Rule (CR)* table. CR has four columns, one for each rule element (subject, conceptual object, access types and predicate). An example of a CR table is illustrated in Table 2.10.

For a conceptual-level access rule, the specified access type must belong to the set of legal access types defined for the corresponding conceptual category.

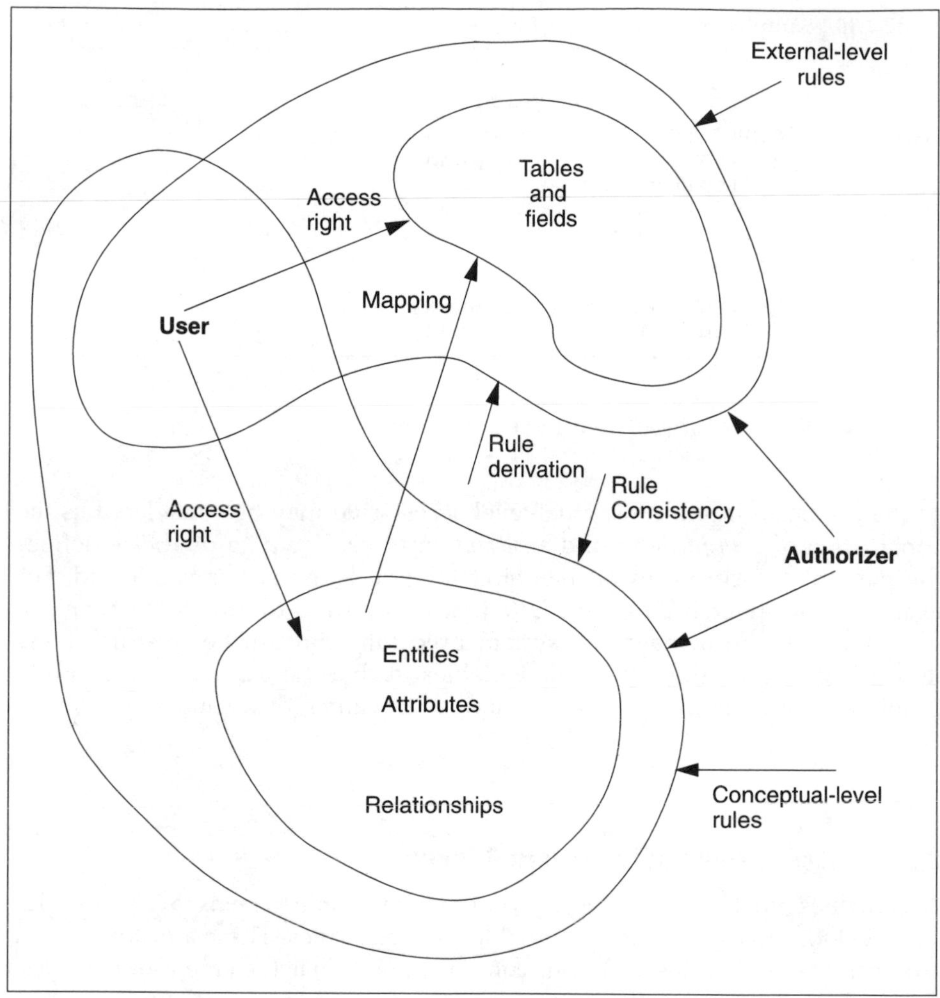


*Figure 2.16* Relationship between rules at various levels.

**Table 2.9** A sample AC table.

| C | T |
|---|---|
| EMPLOYEE | delete |
| EMPLOYEE | insert |
| EMPLOYEE.name | read |
| EMPLOYEE.ssn | read |
| EMPLOYEE.manager | read |
| EMPLOYEE.salary | read |
| EMPLOYEE.manager | update |
| EMPLOYEE.salary | update |

**Table 2.10** Sample conceptual rule table.

| S | C | T | P |
|---|---|---|---|
| Jones | EMPLOYEE.name | read | — |
| Jones | EMPLOYEE.ssn | read | — |
| Jones | EMPLOYEE.manager | read | — |
| Jones | EMPLOYEE.salary | read | — |
| Jones | EMPLOYEE.salary | update | where EMPLOYEE.manager = Jones |
| Smith | EMPLOYEE.name | read | — |
| Smith | EMPLOYEE.ssn | read | — |

The constraint is formally expressed as follows:

$$CR.t\ (*, c_j, *, *) \in TP_{n(c_j)}\ \forall c_j \in CR.c$$

The predicate in the conceptual-level access rule may be considered as the conjunction of *data predicate* and a *system predicate*. The data predicate defines the particular occurrences of the object for which the access is allowed. For example, with reference to Table 2.10, Jones is allowed to update the salary of the employees he manages. A system predicate may further restrict access depending on the values of certain variables, such as time of day or location of terminal. These conditions can be viewed as values of attributes of system entity sets.

## 2.5.7 Access rules at the external level

Access rules must exist for a table in order for that table to be used. Access rules specified for tables are called external level access rules. These are stored in an *External Rules (ER)* table with four columns, one for each element of the rules. External-level rules are either explicitly defined or else derived from the underlying conceptual-level access rules. For each external rule, the specified access type must belong to the set of legal access types defined for the corresponding external category.

This constraint is formally expressed as follows.

$$ER.t\ (*, e_i, *, *) \in TP_{n(e_i)}\ \forall e_i \in ER.e$$

As for conceptual-access rules, the predicate in a rule is the conjunction of a system predicate and a data predicate.

When an external-level rule is defined, it must be checked for consistency with both the access constraints (stated in the AC table) and the underlying conceptual access rules. Access rule predicates can be ignored in the procedure because they will be intersected at access rule evaluation time.

Let $\langle s_i, e_i, t_i, p_i \rangle$ be an external access rule, where $e_i$ is either a table $r$ or one of its fields. The following two conditions must be satisfied for consistency:

(1) **Consistency of the access rule with the access constraints specified for table *t*.**
*The access type specified in the external rule for an external object must be one of the allowable accesses to that object specified in table AC.*
This condition is formally expressed as follows:
$ER.t\ (s_i,e_i,t_i,*) \in AC.t\ (e_i,*)$

(2) **Consistency of the access rule with underlying conceptual-level rules.**
*The* ⟨*access type, object*⟩ *pairs produced by the mapping function* $\Phi^v$ *must be contained in the conceptual level rules for* $s_i$.
This constraint is formally expressed as follows:
$t_s^k \in CR.t\ (s_i,c_j^k,*,*)\ \forall < t_s^k,c_j^k > \in \Phi^v\ (<t_i,e_i>)$.

If both conditions 1 and 2 are satisfied, the rule is consistent with all underlying rules. In the case where the external rule is derived from the conceptual-level rules, only condition 1 need be tested.

### 2.5.8 Access control

An access request is a 4-tuple of the form ⟨*s′,o′,t′,p′*⟩, where s′ is the subject submitting the request, *o′* is the database object that *s′* intends to access in a way defined by access type *t′*, and *p′* selects the specific occurrences of *o′* requested by *s′*.

The model considers a closed policy. Absence of a rule granting a subject access to a conceptual object implies that this subject has no access to any of the occurrences of that object through any external view. Therefore, upon an access request ⟨*s′,o′,t′,p′*⟩, the system controls the existence of an external access rule ⟨*s,o,t,p*⟩ where *s* = *s′*, *o* = *o′*, and *t* = *t′*. If such a rule exists, the access is granted for the occurrences of *o′* satisfying both the predicate *p′* given by the user and the predicate *p* stated in the access rule. To restrict the user access only to the occurrences of the object which satisfy both the predicates, the rule predicate is appended via the `AND` operator to the query *(query modification)*.

Consider an access request ⟨*s′, e′, t′, p′*⟩ submitted by subject *s′* for access *t′* to external object *e′* with restriction *p′*. The access control process is composed of the following steps:

(1) The request is checked against the external-level rules. If no rule exists, then some predefined enforcement procedure is invoked and the algorithm terminates (there is no need to examine the conceptual-level rules, since these have been transformed into external-level rules).
(2) The intersection of predicate *p′* given by the user and predicate *p* of the access rule is computed and the result is substituted to *p′* in the query (query modification).
(3) The query on the external object *e′* is transformed, using the mapping function $\Phi^v$, into the set of ⟨`operation,object-subset`⟩ pairs, where an

object-subset is a set of occurrences of a conceptual-level object corresponding to external object $e'_i$.

(4) Each ⟨`operation,object-subset`⟩ pair is then modified by restricting the object-subset to the occurrences satisfying the predicates expressed in the corresponding conceptual-level rules.

Figure 2.17 illustrates the access control steps.

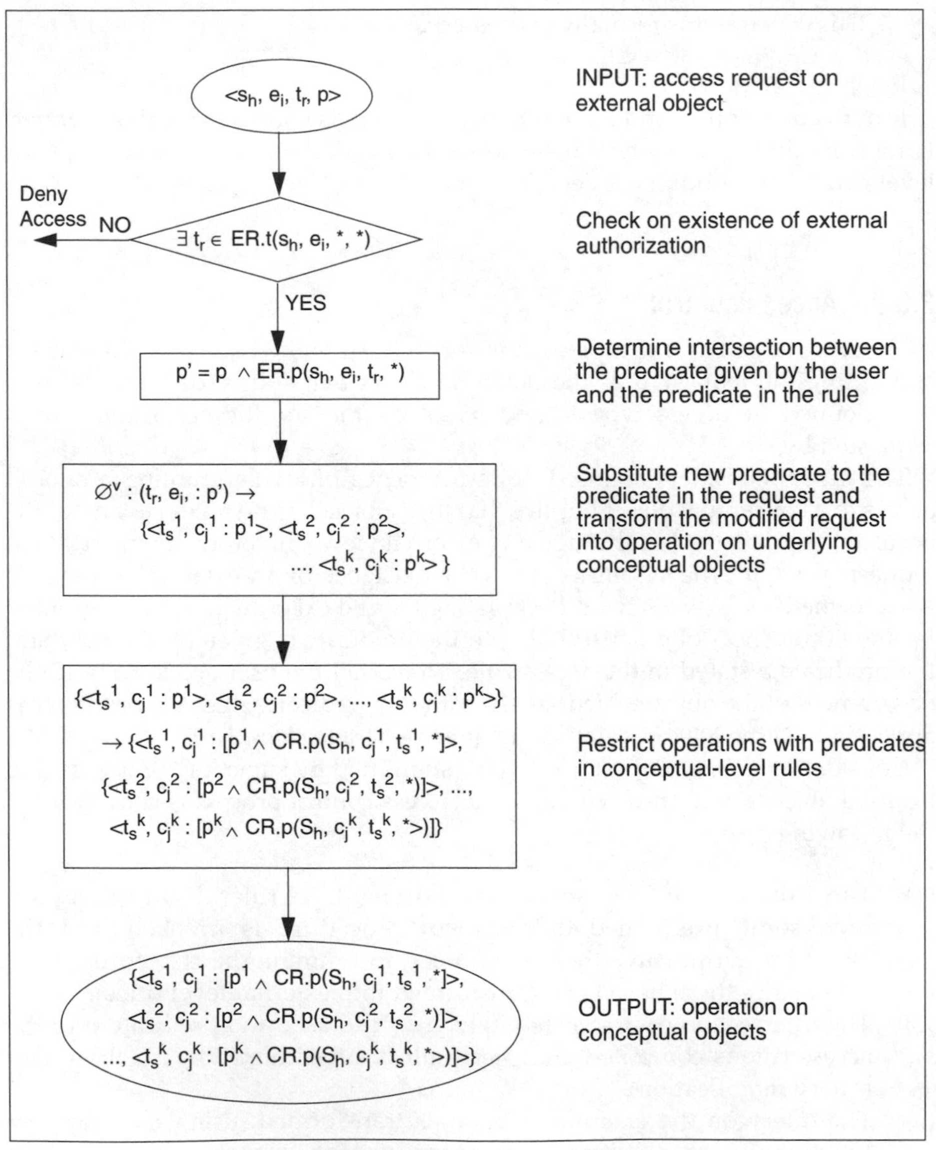


*Figure 2.17* Access control steps.

## 2.6 Discussion on discretionary models

The models proposed so far govern the access to the information on the basis of discretionary protection policies. These policies (which govern the access of users to the information on the basis of the user's identity and of rules specifying, for each user and each object in the system, the types of accesses the user is allowed on the object) have the advantage of being flexible and therefore suitable for various types of system and application. For these reasons, they have been widely used in a variety of implementations, especially in the commercial and industrial environments. However, discretionary access control policies have a drawback in that they do not provide a real assurance on the satisfaction of the protection requirements. Although each access is controlled and allowed only if authorized, it is easily possible to bypass the access restrictions stated through the authorizations. For example, a user who is permitted to read data can pass it to other users who are not authorized to read it without the cognizance of the data's owner. Therefore, it is possible for a user who is not authorized to read and acquire data despite the discretionary control. The main problem is that discretionary policies do not impose any restriction on the usage of information once it is obtained by a user: that is, dissemination of information is not controlled. This makes discretionary control vulnerable to malicious attacks such as Trojan Horses embedded in programs. A Trojan Horse is a computer program with an actual or apparently useful function, which contains additional *hidden functions* that surreptitiously exploit the legitimate authorizations of the invoking process.

To understand how a Trojan Horse can leak information to unauthorized users despite the discretionary access control, consider the following example. Suppose user $x$ creates file $f_1$ and writes some information in it. Suppose now user $y$ creates file $f_2$. User $y$ is the owner of the file and therefore allowed to execute any operation on the file. In particular, $y$ can grant other users authorizations on the file. Suppose then that $y$ grants $x$ the write privilege on file $f_2$. Consider now a program $P$ (a Trojan Horse), which performs some utility function. Moreover, suppose that program $P$ contains a hidden piece of code composed of a read operation on file $f_1$ and a write operation on file $f_2$ (Figure 2.18a). Suppose now that $x$ invokes program $P$. The process that executes program $P$ runs with the privileges of the calling user $x$: that is, all access requests are checked against the authorizations of user $x$. Consider in particular the execution of the hidden code. First the read operation on file $f_1$ is requested. Since $x$ is the owner of the file the operation is granted. Then, the write operation on file $f_2$ is requested. Since $x$ owns the write privilege on $f_2$, the write operation is also granted. As a consequence, during execution of program $P$ some information has been read from file $f_1$, on which user $y$ does not have read authorization, and written into file $f_2$, on which user $y$ has read authorization (Figure 2.18b). Then, an illegal transmission of information to unauthorized user $y$ has been performed despite the discretionary access control.

This simple example illustrates how easily the restrictions stated by the discretionary authorizations can be bypassed and therefore produce a lack of

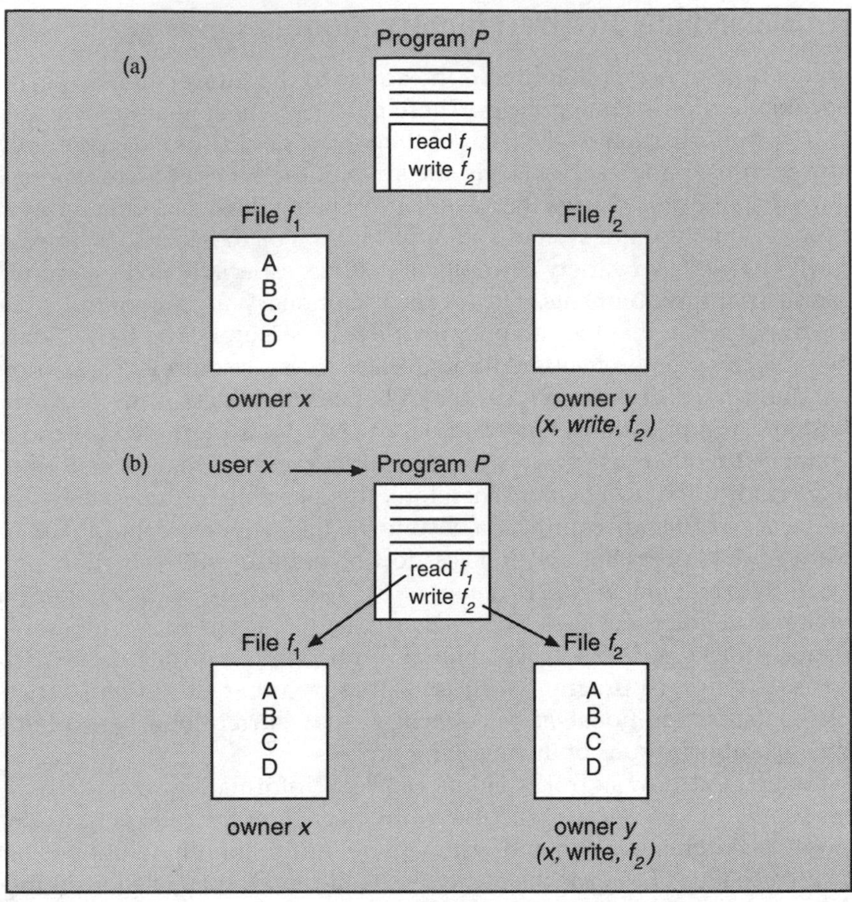


*Figure 2.18* Example of a Trojan Horse: (a) program $P$ contains hidden code to access files $f_1$ and $f_2$; $y$ can grant 'write' on $f_2$; (b) after user $x$ runs the program, user $y$ has access to information transferred from file $f_1$ (to which user $y$ does not have read access) to $f_2$ (which he can read).

assurance on the satisfaction of authorizations imposed by the discretionary policy.

This type of Trojan Horse can be foiled by using mandatory policies that govern the access to information on the basis of classifications assigned to subjects and objects in the system. In the remainder of this chapter we illustrate some models that enforce mandatory policies. We will then show how mandatory policies can be used to protect against Trojan Horses.

## 2.7 Bell–LaPadula model

The Bell–La Padula model (Bell and La Padula, 1973, 1974a, 1974b, 1976) is an extension of the access matrix model oriented to the definition of security requirements in complex systems, where system elements can be classified. The model, essentially oriented to protection in OS environments, faces the problem of *information secrecy*. Secrecy is expressed as a set of rules (axioms) that must be satisfied during the working of the system. The Bell–LaPadula model represents the reference model for data protection under mandatory policies.

The model is based on the classification of the system elements. Classifications are expressed by security levels. Each security level is defined by two components: a *classification* and a *set of categories*. The classification is an element of a set composed of four elements: Top Secret (TS); Secret (S); Confidential (C); Unclassified (U). This set is fully ordered: TS > S > C > U.

The set of categories is a subset of a non-hierarchical set of elements. The elements of this set depend on the considered environment and refer to the application area to which information pertains or where data is to be used. Examples of categories are Nato, Nuclear, and Crypto. The set of the security levels forms a *lattice*, which is partially ordered according to the dominance (≥) relationship.

A security level $L_1 = (C_1,S_1)$ is higher or equal to (*dominates*) level $L_2 = (C_2,S_2)$ if and only if the following relationships are valid:

$$C_1 \geq C_2$$
$$S_1 \supseteq S_2$$

If both relationships are strictly verified, then $L_1$ is higher (>) than $L_2$.

The definitions for < and ≤ are analogous.

If, given two levels $L_1$ and $L_2$, neither the relationship $L_1 \geq L_2$ nor the relationship $L_2 \geq L_1$ holds, the two levels are said to be *incomparable*.

The model is based on a **subject–object** paradigm. Subjects are active elements of the system that can execute actions. Objects are passive elements of the system that contain information.

Subjects are processes acting on behalf of users. Each user is assigned a security level named *clearance*. The clearance assigned to a user reflects the user's trustworthiness not to disclose sensitive information to individuals who do not hold the appropriate clearance. A user can log into the system at any level dominated by clearance. Processes activated by a user will be assigned the security level of that user.

The model, which is targeted to the protection of information in OSs, considers files, memory areas and programs, as objects to be protected. Each object is assigned a *security level*. The security level of an object reflects the sensitivity of the information stored therein, and therefore the potential damage which could result from unauthorized disclosure of information to individuals not cleared for that information.

The model considers the following **access modes** executable by subjects on objects:

- *Read-only*: to read the information contained in an object. This mode is generally referred to as 'read'.
- *Append:* to append information to an object without seeing its contents: that is, writing without reading.
- *Execute:* to execute an object (program).
- *Read–write:* to write into an object. This mode allows the subject also to see the contents of the object. It is generally referred to as 'write'.

The model supports decentralized administration of privileges on objects through ownership. In particular, the creator of an object is considered the object owner and, as such, is allowed to grant and revoke authorizations to access the object to other users. Every privilege can be granted, except for the ownership privilege, which is not transferable.

### 2.7.1 System state

The state of the system is described by the 4-tuple *(b,M,f,H)*, where:

- *b* is the *current access set*. This set is composed of triples of the form ⟨subject, object, access-mode⟩. A triple ⟨*s,o,m*⟩ in *b* indicates that subject *s* has current access to object *o* in *m* mode.
- *M* is the access matrix. This is the same matrix of the access matrix model (of which Bell–LaPadula is an extension). The matrix describes the access modes each subject can execute on each object. In particular, the entry *M(s,o)* indicates the access mode subject *s* is authorized for on object *o*.
- *f* is a *level function* that associates with each subject and object in the system, its security level. Formally:
  $$f: O \cup S \rightarrow L$$
  where *O* is the set of objects, *S* is the set of objects, and *L* the set of security levels.
  
  To each object only one security level is associated (assigned upon object creation). The security level of *o* is indicated by $f_o$.
  
  To each user two security levels are associated: its *clearance*, indicated by $f_s$, and its *current level*, indicated by $f_c$. The clearance of a user is the security level assigned to the user when it is created. The current level of a user is the security level at which the user is actually operating. The current security level may change during the subject's lifetime. However, it must always be dominated by the user clearance: that is, for each subject $s \in S$, the following relationship must always be verified:
  $$f_c(s) \leq f_s(s)$$
  In particular this means that a user can log into the system at any security level dominated by his or her clearance. The security level at which the user logs into the system is the current security level and determines the accesses that the user can execute.
- *H* is the *current objects hierarchy*. The hierarchy is a directed rooted tree whose nodes correspond to objects in the system. Objects which are 'inactive' and not accessible are not included in the hierarchy. The model requires the hierarchy to satisfy the compatibility property which states that the security level of an object must dominate the security level of its parent.

### 2.7.2 Operations

The system state can be changed by executing operations. The execution of an operation on a state *(b,M,f,H)* causes the transition to state *(b′,M′,f′,H′)* where at least one of the components differs from the corresponding component in the initial state.

In the following, *access* indicates any of the access modes applicable to an object (that is, read, append, execute, and write). The operations causing state transitions are as follows:

- *Get access.* To initiate access to an object in the requested mode. The execution of this operation modifies the current access set $b$, by adding the triple of the elements involved in the access.
- *Release access.* To terminate the access previously started by 'get'. This is the inverse of the 'get' operation. The execution of this operation modifies the state of the current accesses $b$ by removing the corresponding triple.
- *Give access.* To grant an access mode on an object to a subject. It allows access rights to be transferred among subjects. The execution of this operation modifies the access matrix by inserting, in the entry corresponding to the given subject and object, the access mode being granted. The operation is performed only if the insertion of the authorization respects the axioms of the mandatory policy. A subject can receive the discretionary authorization for an access mode on an object only if the authorization respects the mandatory policy.
- *Rescind access.* To revoke an access previously granted with the 'give' operation. This is the inverse of the 'give' operation. In order for the operation to be executed, the subject requiring it must have write access to the parent of the requested object in the objects hierarchy $H$. The execution of the operation modifies the access matrix $M$ by deleting the entry corresponding to the authorization being revoked. Moreover, the execution of the operation modifies the current access set $b$ since rescinding permissions has the side-effect of forcing access release.
- *Create object.* This is used for inactive objects: that is, to add them to the object hierarchy. An object may be in two stages:
  - the object exists but is *inactive*; as such some accesses cannot occur on it;
  - the object exists and is *active*, thus accessible, and is in the object hierarchy.

  An object can migrate among stages during its lifetime. The 'create' operation activates an inactive object to make it accessible. This operation modifies the objects hierarchy $H$ by adding the node corresponding to the activated object.
- *Delete object.* To deactivate an active object. This is the inverse of the 'create' operation. The execution of this operation modifies the objects hierarchy $H$, by removing the node corresponding to the object and all its descendant nodes. Additionally, it modifies the current access set $b$, since deleting an object has the side-effect of releasing all accesses to it.
- *Change subject security level.* To change the current security level $f$ of a subject. The execution of this operation by a subject modifies the function $f$ by associating to the subject the new current level. The current security level of the subject must be dominated by the subject's clearance.

- *Change object security level.* To change the security level of an object. This operation can be executed only on inactive objects and has the effect of changing the function *f* by associating the new security level to the object. The security level of an object can only be upgraded: that is, the new security level must dominate the previous security level of the object. Moreover, the new security level of the object must be dominated by the clearance of the subject requesting the change: that is, $f_s \geq f_o$.

### 2.7.3 Axioms

The model defines a set of properties which must be satisfied in order for the system to be secure. A system state is secure if, and only if, it satisfies the properties. Each required operation is controlled by a reference monitor and its execution is allowed if, and only if, the system state which would result is secure: that is, it satisfies all properties of the model. The model develops the notion of *trusted subject*. This is a subject that can be relied on not to compromise security. Some constraints are enforced only on requests made by *untrusted subjects*.

**(1) Simple security (ss) property**
*A subject may have read or write access to an object only if the clearance of the subject dominates the security level of the object.*

A system state v = (b, M, f, H) satisfies the ss-property if, and only if, for each element M[s,o] containing the 'read' or 'write' access mode: $f_s(s) \geq f_o(o)$

The aim of this property is to prevent subjects from reading information that has a higher classification than the subject's clearance; it prevents subjects from directly accessing information for which they are not cleared to the necessary level.

**(2) Star (*) property**
*An untrusted subject may have append access to an object if the security level of the object dominates the security level of the subject. An untrusted subject may have write access to an object only if the security level of the object is equal to the current security level of the subject. An untrusted subject may have read access to an object only if the security level of the object is dominated by the current security level of the subject.*

A system state $v = (b,M,f,H)$ satisfies the *-property if, and only if, for each subject $s \in S'$, where $S' \subseteq S$ is the set of untrusted subjects and for all objects $o \in O$:

- *append* $\in M[s,o] \Rightarrow f_c(s) \leq f_o(o)$
- *write* $\in M[s,o] \Rightarrow f_c(s) = f_o(o)$
- *read* $\in M[s,o] \Rightarrow f_c(s) \geq f_o(o)$

Note that, with respect to untrusted subjects, the *-property includes the ss-property: that is, the satisfaction of the *- property implies also the satisfaction of the ss-property. Indeed, let *s* be an untrusted subject and *o* be an object. Consider an authorization for an access mode $m \in M[s',o]$ which satisfies the *-property. Let us show that this also satisfies the ss-property. If *m*=append or execute, the ss-property is trivially satisfied in that it does not impose any restriction on them. Consider $m$=write; since the *-property is satisfied, $f_c(s') = f_o(o)$. Then, since $f_s(s') \geq f_c(s')$ we have $f_s(s') \geq f_o(o')$. Hence, the ss-property is satisfied.

Consider $m$=read. Since the *-property is satisfied, $f_c(s') \geq f_o(o)$. Then, again, since the current level of a subject must always be dominated by the clearance of the subject, $f_s(s') \geq f_c(s')$. Then, $f_s(s') \geq f_o(o)$ and the ss-property is satisfied. Note, however, that both properties are required. The ss-property is required to hold for any subjects, while the *-property is required to hold for untrusted subjects (which is a subset of the subjects in the system).

The two properties mentioned have been summarized in two basic principles:

(1) No read-up secrecy. A subject can only read objects whose security level is dominated by the level of the subject.

(2) No write-down secrecy. A subject can only write objects whose security level dominates the security level of the subject.

These principles have been adopted by all models applying a mandatory policy for information protection. The satisfaction of the principles controls the flow of information in the system by ensuring that information will not become accessible by subjects who do not hold the necessary clearance.

(3) **Tranquillity principle**
*No subject can modify the classification of an active object.*
This axiom, defined in the original version of the model, has been subsequently removed; current versions allow the modification of the classification of active objects. The rules controlling the classification change depend on the specific applications and vary from system to system.

(4) **Discretionary security property (ds-property)**
*Every current access must be present in the access matrix: that is, a subject can exercise only accesses for which it has the necessary authorization. A system state satisfies the discretionary property if and only if for all subjects s, objects o, and access mode m:*

$$<s,o,m> \in b \Rightarrow m \in M[s,o].$$

The discretionary security property states that only accesses for which there exists the corresponding discretionary authorization can be allowed.

The properties above represent the key principles of the Bell–LaPadula model. A system state is considered to be secure only if it satisfies these properties. State transition is allowed only if the resulting state is secure.

In an extended version of the model by Feiertag *et al.* (1977), other properties have been added which impose constraints on the accessibility of inactive objects and the state of newly activated objects. These properties are as follows:

(5) **Non-accessibility of inactive objects.**
*A subject cannot read the contents of an inactive object.*
This property states that objects which do not appear in the objects hierarchy $H$ are not accessible through privileges that imply the read access (read and update). This principle can be formally expressed as follows.

A system state $v = (b,M,f,H)$ satisfies the non-accessibility axiom of inactive objects if, and only if, for any subject *s* and any inactive object *o*: $(s,o,r) \in b \Rightarrow r \neq$ *"read"* $\wedge\, r \neq$ *"write"*.

(6) **Rewriting of inactive objects.**
*A newly activated object is assigned an initial state independent of the previous activations of the object.*

## 2.8 Biba model

The Bell–LaPadula model aims at achieving secrecy by preventing unauthorized release of information. However, it does not protect the system from unauthorized modifications of information. The model proposed by Biba (1977) applies principles similar to those of the Bell–LaPadula model for the protection of information integrity. Like the Bell–LaPadula model, the Biba model is based on the notions of subjects and objects and on their classifications. The concepts of subject and object are the same as in the Bell-LaPadula model. Each subject and each object in the system is assigned a classification named *integrity level*.

Each integrity level consists of two elements: a *classification* and a *set of categories*. A classification is an element of a hierarchical set of elements. It consists of these elements: *Crucial (C), Very Important (VI) and Important (I)*, for which C > VI > I. The set of categories is a subset of a non-hierarchical set. This is analogous to the set of categories in the Bell–LaPadula model.

The integrity levels form a lattice with respect to the partial ordering dominance relationship (≥). Integrity level $L_1 = (C_1, S_1)$ dominates (≥) integrity level $L_2 = (C_2, S_2)$ if, and only if, the following relationships are both satisfied:

$$C_1 \geq C_2 \textit{ and } S_1 \supseteq S_2.$$

If the strict inequality holds in both relations (> and ⊃), then $L_1 > L_2$. The < and ≤ definitions are analogous. If, given the integrity levels $L_1$ and $L_2$ neither $L_1 \geq L_2$ nor $L_2 \geq L_1$ holds, $L_1$ and $L_2$ are said to be *incomparable*.

The model considers as **subjects** all the active system elements that can access information: typically, processes acting on behalf of users. Each user in the system is assigned an integrity level. A process acting on behalf of a user is assigned the integrity level of the user. The integrity level assigned to a user reflects the user's trustworthiness for inserting, modifying or deleting information.

**Objects** considered in the model are all the passive system elements for which access can be requested: files, programs, and so on. Each object in the system is assigned an integrity level. The integrity level assigned to an object reflects both the degree of trust that can be placed in the information stored in the object and the potential damage that could result from unauthorized modification of the information (Denning, 1986).

The model considers the following **access modes**:

- *Modify*: to write information in an object. It is analogous to the 'write' mode of the other models;

- *Invoke*: this differs from the previous modes, which were applicable to objects, in that it applies to subjects. The presence of an 'invoke' right between two subjects allows these subjects to communicate;
- *Observe*: to read information in an object. It is analogous to the 'read' mode of the other models;
- *Execute*: to execute an object (program).

The model does not address the problem of administration of authorizations. In particular, unlike the Bell–LaPadula model, ownership is not considered in Biba.

## 2.8.1 Axioms

The model does not provide any administrative operations for grant and revocation of the authorization state. Hence, changes to the authorization state are possible only through direct modification of the ACLs associated with the objects; the policy axioms govern the change.

The Biba model does not specify a unique security policy. A family of policies is proposed, each adopting different conditions to ensure information integrity. The policies of the Biba model can be grouped in two major groups: non-discretionary and discretionary policies (Millen and Cerniglia, 1984).

#### *Non-discretionary policies*

Non-discretionary policies determine the accesses executable by the subjects on the objects on the basis of the security levels assigned to them. The model considers the following non-discretionary policies.

(1) *Low-watermark policy for subjects.* This policy is based on the following axioms:

- A subject can hold the 'modify' access to an object only if the integrity level of the subject dominates (≥) the integrity level of the object.
- A subject can hold the 'invoke' access to another subject only if the integrity level of the first subject dominates the integrity level of the second subject.
- A subject can hold the 'observe' access to whatever object. After an observe operation by a subject on an object, the integrity level of the subject is set equal to the least upper bound between the subject's and object's integrity levels before the access.

This policy is said to be *dynamic*, since it possibly decreases the integrity level of a subject upon each observe operation on objects with lower, or incomparable, integrity levels.

The main drawback of this policy consists in the fact that access to the system may depend on the order of submission of access requests. In particular, the set of objects modifiable by a given subject changes upon each observe access executed by the subject on an object at a lower or incomparable integrity level. As a result, 'modify' or 'invoke' requests of a subject may be denied because they appear after observe requests which decrease the subject's integrity level. It is therefore possible for a subject to sabotage its own processing because objects which are necessary for its own functions may become inaccessible.

(2) *Low-watermark policy for objects.* This policy is based on the following axioms:

- A subject can hold the 'modify' access to objects at whatever integrity level. After each 'modify' access by a subject on an object, the integrity level of the object is set equal to the greatest lower bound between the integrity level of the subject and integrity level of the object held before the access.

The policy is said to be *dynamic* since it allows the integrity level of modified objects to change. Instead of preventing a subject from modifying higher or incomparable integrity objects, this policy lowers the integrity of the modified objects to that of the subject who has modified it. The main drawback of this policy is that it allows improper modifications. Improper modifications are made apparent when the integrity level of improperly modified objects is downgraded. Hence, this policy cannot be considered as satisfactory since information is fully exposed to threats. Allowing improper modifications may result in replacing high-integrity information with low-integrity information and the impossibility of recovering the high-level data which has been altered.

(3) *Low-watermark integrity audit policy.* This policy is based on the following axiom:

- A subject can 'modify' objects at whatever integrity level. If a subject modifies an object at higher or incomparable integrity level, the security violations are recorded in an audit trail.

The policy is a variant of the low-watermark policy for objects in which integrity levels are fixed. Like the previous policy, this policy does not prevent improper modifications of information but only makes them apparent. The real integrity level, or 'current corruption level', of each object can be computed by examining the audit trail. The drawback of this policy, like the previous one, is that it permits improper modifications to take place.

(4) *Ring policy.* In this policy, integrity levels of both subject and objects are fixed during their lifetime. It is based on the following axioms:

- A subject can hold the 'modify' access to an object only if the integrity level of the subject dominates the integrity level of the object.
- A subject can hold the 'invoke' access to another subject only if the integrity level of the first subject is dominated by the integrity level of the second subject.
- A subject can hold the 'observe' access to objects at whatever integrity level.

This policy prevents subjects from modifying information in objects at higher or incomparable integrity levels. However, since 'observe' accesses are not constrained, improper 'modify' operations can occur indirectly. Indeed, a high-level subject can'observe' an object at a lower integrity level and then modify that object at its own security level. Hence, information can flow from low to higher or incomparable integrity levels. To avoid this, a subject needs to be cautious when using data from a lower-integrity object.

(5) *Strict integrity policy.* This policy is based on the following axioms:
   - Integrity *-property: a subject can hold the 'modify' access to an object only if the integrity level of the subject dominates the integrity level of the object.
   - Invocation property: a subject can hold the 'invoke' access to another subject only if the integrity level of the first subject dominates the integrity level of the second subject.
   - Simple integrity condition: a subject can hold the 'observe' access to an object only if the integrity level of the subject is dominated by the integrity level of the object.

   This policy is the dual of the Bell–LaPadula security policy for the integrity problem. The first two properties are respectively analogous to the security property and the *-property of Bell–LaPadula, but with the inverse of the relationship holding among the levels. The fact that the 'append' access mode is not considered, and that the object integrity level is unique, simplifies the *-property, which is partially cancelled and partially absorbed by the simple property. The strict integrity policy prevents information from being transferred from low-integrity objects to objects at higher or incomparable integrity levels, assuming that information flow results only from observe and modify accesses.

   The axioms of the strict integrity policy have been summarized in two basic principles: *No Read-Down Integrity* and *No Write-Up Integrity*. The principles are the dual of the No Read-Up and No Write-Down principles of the Bell–LaPadula model.

### Discretionary policies

The model considers the following different discretionary access control policies.

(1) *Access control lists.* Each object is assigned an access control list indicating the subjects that can access the object and the access modes each subject can exercise. The access control list of an object can be modified by subjects holding the 'modify' access to the object in which the ACL list is contained.

(2) *Objects hierarchy.* Objects are organized in a hierarchy using a rooted tree structure. The ancestors of an object are the objects on a path between it and the root. To access an object a subject must have 'observe' access to all its ancestors.

(3) *Ring.* Each subject is assigned a privilege attribute (ring). Rings are numbered. Lower-number rings represent higher privileges.
The policy requires the following axioms to hold:
- A subject can hold the 'modify' access to objects only in an allowed range of rings.
- A subject can hold the 'invoke' access to subjects of greater privilege only in an allowed range of rings. A subject can hold the 'invoke' access to any subject with lower or equal privilege.
- A subject can hold the 'observe' access to objects only in an allowed range of rings.

## 2.9 Dion model

The model of Dion (1981) proposes a mandatory policy which protects the secrecy as well as the integrity of data. The model basically combines the principles for controlling secrecy of the Bell–LaPadula model with the principles of the strict integrity policy of the Biba model.

This model does not provide any discretionary policy. Hence, all accesses satisfying the mandatory policy are considered authorized. It differs from the other models in that Dion does not allow information transfer from objects to subjects (for example, through write operations). Data flow is allowed only between objects, never between objects and subjects. To this aim, the model introduces the concept of *connection,* which is the link a subject must establish between two objects to allow information to flow between them.

The model is based on a classification of subjects and objects which includes both security and integrity levels. The security levels, and their semantics, are the same as in the Bell–LaPadula model. The integrity levels and their semantics are the same as in the Biba model. We refer the reader to these models for the explanation of classification levels.

### 2.9.1 Subjects and their classification

The model considers as subjects those programs executing in the system and acting on behalf of users. Each system subject is assigned *three security levels* and *three integrity levels.*

- *Absolute Security Level (ASL)* is the security level given to the subject upon its creation. It is fixed for the whole life cycle of the subject. Typically, this level will be the security level of the user on behalf of whom the subject is acting.
- *Read Security Level (RSL)* is the highest security level from which the subject is allowed to read.
- *Write Security Level (WSL)* is the lowest security level to which the subject is allowed to write.

- *Absolute Integrity Level (AIL)* is the integrity level given to the subject upon its creation. It is fixed for the whole life cycle of the subject. Typically, this level will be the integrity level of the user on behalf of whom the subject is acting.
- *Read Integrity Level (RIL)* is the lowest integrity level from which the subject is allowed to read.
- *Write Integrity Level (WIL)* is the highest integrity level to which the subject is allowed to write.

For each system subject *s*, the following relationship must be satisfied:

$WSL(s) \leq ASL(s) \leq RSL(s);$
$RIL(s) \leq AIL(s) \leq WIL(s).$

A subject for which at least one inequality is strictly satisfied is said to be *trusted*. A subject can be trusted from the viewpoint of secrecy, integrity, or both, depending on the number of strictly satisfied inequalities. Subjects for which the above four relations are satisfied by equality are said to be *untrusted*.

### 2.9.2 Objects and their classification

The model considers as objects any data storage entity in the system. Each object is assigned three security levels and three integrity levels as follows.

- *Absolute Security Level (ASL)* is the security level of the data contained in the object. It is fixed for the whole life cycle of the object.
- *Migration Security Level (MSL)* is the highest security level to which the data in the object may flow.
- *Corruption Security Level (CSL)* is the lowest security level from which data may flow into the object.
- *Absolute Integrity Level (AIL)* is the integrity level of the data contained in the object. It is fixed for the whole life cycle of the object.
- *Migration Integrity Level (MIL)* is the lowest integrity level to which data in the object may flow.
- *Corruption Integrity Level (CIL)* is the highest integrity level from which data may flow into the object.

For each system object *o*, the following relationship must be satisfied:

$CSL(o) \leq ASL(o) \leq MSL(o);$
$MIL(o) \leq AIL(o) \leq CIL(o).$

### 2.9.3 Axioms

When a subject wishes to transfer data between two objects, it must establish an explicit connection between them. Once an *explicit connection* is established between two objects, a subject can then cause data to flow by making the appropriate system call. All explicit connections are unidirectional.

The request by subject $s$ to establish a connection between object $o_1$ and object $o_2$ is granted only if the levels of the subjects and the objects satisfy the restrictions stated in the model axioms. Once the connection has been established, no further constraints are enforced. The axioms, which are summarized in Figure 2.19, are as follows.

(1) **Migration property**
*The migration levels of the object where information is written ($o_2$) must be at least as restrictive as those of the object from which information is read ($o_1$).* Formally, the relationships to be satisfied among the migration levels of $o_1$ and $o_2$ are as follows.
$MSL(o_1) \geq MSL(o_2)$
$MIL(o_1) \leq MIL(o_2)$.

The migration property ensures that the migration, security, and integrity levels of $o_1$ will not be circumvented. If the migration property were not satisfied, data in $o_1$ would be allowed to migrate improperly to security levels not allowed through the mediation of object $o_2$. Indeed, transfer of data to an object with a lower migration security level or a higher migration integrity level would allow the data to migrate to objects to which $o_1$ cannot directly transfer data.

(2) **Corruption property**
*The corruption levels of the object from which information is read ($o_1$) must be at least as restrictive as those of the object where information is written ($o_2$).*

Formally, the relationships to be satisfied among the corruption levels of $o_1$ and $o_2$ are as follows.
$CSL(o_1) \geq CSL(o_2)$
$CIL(o_1) \leq CIL(o_2)$.

This property ensures that the corruption security and integrity level of $o_2$ will not be circumvented. If the property were not satisfied, data which should not be allowed to flow into $o_2$ would be able to flow through the mediation of $o_1$.

(3) **Security property**
*The subject establishing the connection must have read access to the object from which information is read ($o_1$), and write access to the object in which information is written ($o_2$). The 'read security' level of the subject must dominate the 'absolute security' level of the object from which the information is read.*

*The 'write security' level of the subject requesting a connection must be dominated by the 'absolute security' level of the object to which information is transferred.*

Formally, the relationships to be satisfied are as follows:
$RSL(s) \geq ASL(o_1)$
$WSL(s) \leq ASL(o_2)$.

This property corresponds to the No Read-Up and No Write-Down secrecy of the Bell–LaPadula model.

(4) **Integrity property**
*The subject s establishing the connection must have read access to the object from which information is read ($o_1$), and write access to the object in which informa-*

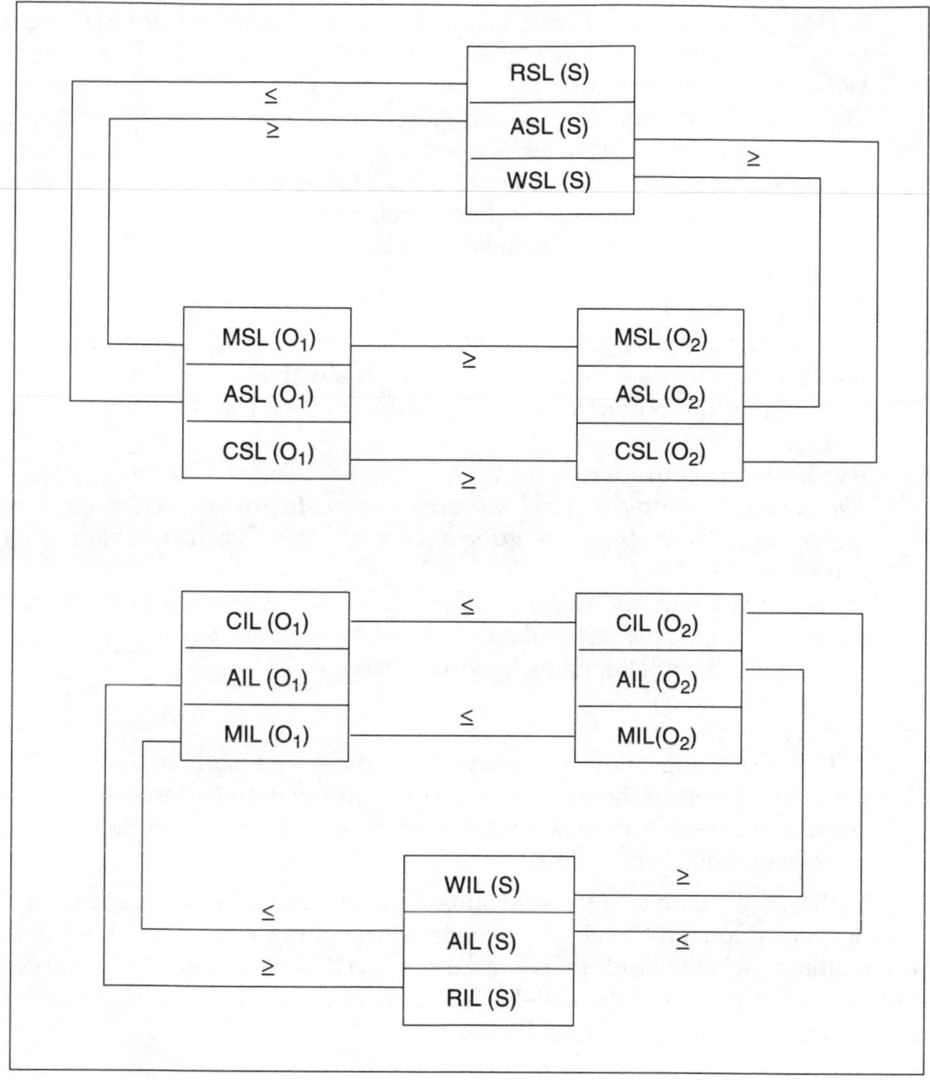


*Figure 2.19* Dion axioms (RSC = read security level; WSL = write security level; CSL = corruption security level; AIL = absolute integrity level; ASL = absolute security level; MSL = migration security level; RIL = read integrity level; WIL = write integrity level).

*tion is written ($o_2$). Then, the 'read integrity' level of the subject must be dominated by the 'absolute integrity' level of the object from which information flows. The 'write integrity' level of the subject must dominate the 'absolute integrity' level of the object to which information is transferred.*

Formally, the relationships to be satisfied are as follows:

$RIL(s) \leq AIL(o_1)$

$WIL(s) \geq AIL(o_2)$.

This property corresponds to the No Read-Down and No Write-Up integrity of the strict integrity policy of the Biba model.

(5) **Write/corruption property**
*The 'absolute security' level of the subject must dominate the 'corruption security' level of the object to which information is transferred ($o_2$). The 'absolute integrity' level of the subject must be dominated by the 'corruption integrity' level of the object to which information is transferred ($o_2$).*

Formally, the relationships to be satisfied are:

$ASL(s) \geq CSL(o_2)$

$AIL(s) \leq CIL(o_2)$.

This property guarantees the satisfaction of the corruption levels of the object to which information is transferred ($o_2$) with respect to the subject $s$ making the connection. It derives directly from the way levels have been defined.

(6) **Read/migration property**
*The 'absolute security' level of the subject requesting a connection must be dominated by the 'migration security' level of the object from which information is transferred ($o_1$).*

*The 'absolute integrity' level of the subject requesting a connection must dominate the 'migration integrity' level of the object from which information is transferred ($o_1$).*

Formally, the relationships to be satisfied are:

$ASL(s) \leq MSL(o_1)$

$AIL(s) \geq MIL(o_1)$.

The read/migration property guarantees the satisfaction of the migration levels of the object from which information is transferred with respect to the subject $s$ making the connection. It derives directly from the way levels have been defined.

Note that in the case of untrusted subjects, that is, subjects whose read and write levels are equal to the absolute levels, the resulting axioms are simplified. As a matter of fact, the last four axioms are reduced to the No Read-Up and No Write-Down principles of the Bell–LaPadula model, and to the No Read-Down and No Write-Up integrity of the Biba model.

## 2.10 The Sea View model

The Sea View (SEcure dAta VIEW) model (Denning, 1987; Denning *et al.*, 1986, 1987, 1988) is a security model for the protection of relational database systems developed by Denning *et al.* at the Stanford Research Institute (SRI). The model governs access to the data stored in the database on the basis of mandatory as well as discretionary policies.

The Sea View model is formulated in two layers: the MAC (Mandatory Access Control) model, and the TCB (Trusted Computing Base) model. The MAC model corresponds to a reference monitor that enforces the mandatory security policy of the Bell–LaPadula model. The TCB model defines the concept of multilevel relations, supports discretionary controls for multilevel relations and views, and formalizes the supporting policies. The TCB model is layered on top of the MAC model: all the information of the TCB is stored in objects mediated by the MAC reference monitor.

### 2.10.1 The MAC model

The MAC model provides a formal statement of the Sea View mandatory policy which states that no user is to be given access to classified or other sensitive information unless that user has been determined to possess the requisite secrecy and integrity authorizations (clearances) for the information, based on the information classification.

The Sea View mandatory policy, which summarizes the axioms of the Bell–La Padula and Biba models illustrated previously, is formalized in terms of subjects, objects and access classes.

#### *Access classes*

An access class has a secrecy component, called *secrecy class*, and an integrity component, called *integrity class*. The secrecy class corresponds to the security level of the Bell–La Padula model. The integrity class corresponds to the integrity level of the Biba model. We refer the reader to these models for the meaning of the secrecy and integrity classes and the definition of the ordering relations among them.

Access classes of the Sea View model form a lattice according to a partial ordering relationship called *dominates* (≥). An access class $C_1$ *dominates* (≥) an access class $C_2$ if, and only if, the secrecy component of $C_1$ dominates the secrecy component of $C_2$ and the integrity component of $C_1$ is dominated by the integrity component of $C_2$. Formally, given two classes $C_1 = \langle X_1,Y_1 \rangle$, and $C_2 = \langle X_2,Y_2 \rangle$, $C_1 \geq C_2$ if, and only if, $X_1 \geq X_2$ and $Y_1 \leq Y_2$. If any of the two inequalities is strictly verified (that is, > or <), $C_1$ is said to strictly dominate (>) $C_2$. If, given two classes $C_1$ and $C_2$, neither $C_1 \geq C_2$ nor $C_1 \leq C_2$ holds, the two classes are said to be incomparable. For example, access class ⟨(TS,Nato), (I,Nato)⟩ dominates access class ⟨(S,Nato), (VI,Nato)⟩; classes ⟨(TS,Nato), (VI,Nato)⟩ and ⟨(S,Nato), (I,Nato)⟩ are incomparable.

#### *Objects*

Objects of the MAC model are the information containers *(files)* to which access must be controlled. Each object is associated to a unique identifier and a unique access class. The identifier and access class of an object are fixed for the whole life of the object. Note that the objects protected by the MAC model are not abstract structures of the database; they are single-level files of the underlying operating system into which database information is mapped. This allows the model to specify and control the mandatory policy constraints with reference to single-level objects.

#### *Subjects*

Subjects of the MAC model are *processes* acting on behalf of users. Each user in the system is assigned a range of secrecy and integrity classes in which he or she is permitted to operate. Subjects operating on behalf of a user are assigned the classification of that user. Each user is assigned minimal secrecy and integrity classes, denoted *minsecrecy* and *minintegrity* respectively, in addition to the standard maximal secrecy and integrity classes, denoted *maxsecrecy* and *maxintegrity* secrecy. The pair ⟨*minsecrecy, maxintegrity*⟩ is called the *writeclass* of the subject. The pair ⟨*maxsecrecy, minintegrity*⟩ is called the *readclass* of the subject. For each subject, the readclass must dominate the writeclass.

If the readclass of a subject *s* strictly dominates the writeclass of the subject the subject is said to be *trusted*. If the strict inequality is verified for the secrecy classes, then the subject is trusted with respect to secrecy. If the strict inequality is verified for the integrity classes, then the subject is trusted with respect to integrity. Subjects that are trusted with respect to secrecy are allowed to write data at a secrecy class that may be lower than that of some of the data read. In this case it must be shown that the subjects will not convey the information downward. Subjects that are trusted with respect to integrity are allowed to read data at an integrity class that may be lower than some of the data written. In this case it must be shown that they will not use lower-integrity information to contaminate the information they write. Subjects who are not trusted are said to be *untrusted*. Untrusted subjects have equal readclass and writeclass.

Note that not all subjects are considered to be trusted subjects. Only those subjects requiring trusted status it for their operation (for example, sanitization) can be granted the privilege of being a trusted subject.

### Access modes

The mandatory policy controls only a restricted set of access modes corresponding to the elementary accesses executable on the objects of the operating systems underlying the database. The mandatory access modes are as follows:

- *Read:* to read information stored in an object;
- *Write:* to write information into an object;
- *Execute:* to execute an object.

### Axioms

Execution of the access modes on the objects of the MAC model is governed by a set of axioms. These axioms, which summarize the principle of the Bell–LaPadula model and of the Biba model, are as follows.

(1) **Read property**

*A subject s can read an object o only if its readclass dominates the access class of the object. Formally, s can read o only if readclass(s) ≥ access class(o).*

This property corresponds to requiring the maxsecrecy component of the subject to dominate the secrecy class of the object and the minintegrity component of the subject to be dominated by the integrity class of the object. The read property is the formulation of the No Read-Up secrecy principle of the Bell–LaPadula model, and the No Read-Down integrity principle of the strict integrity policy of the Biba model.

(2) **Write property**
*A subject s can write an object o only if its writeclass is dominated by the access class of the object. Formally, s can write o only if writeclass(s) ≤ access class(o).*

This property corresponds to requiring the minsecrecy component of the subject to be dominated by the secrecy class of the object and the maxintegrity component of the subject to dominate the integrity class of the object. The write property is the formulation of the No Write Down secrecy principle of the Bell–LaPadula model, and the No Write Up integrity principle of the strict integrity policy of the Biba model.

(3) **Execute property**
*A subject s can execute an object o only if its maxintegrity is less than or equal to the integrity class of the object, and its maxsecrecy is greater than or equal to the secrecy class of the object.*

This property is required because the strict integrity policy principles of the Biba model may be too restrictive for database systems. Indeed, high-integrity database subjects that manage the database can be trusted to read low-integrity data without contaminating data of a higher integrity class provided they do not execute program objects of lesser integrity (which could damage the database). However, this is not allowed by the axioms of the Biba model. The Sea View model overcomes this limitation by distinguishing execute access from read access, allowing trusted subjects to read data of lesser integrity level than their *maxintegrity*, and restricting execute access for all subjects to programs of greater or equal integrity. The distinction between read and execute access is not relevant for secrecy classes because the secrecy class of a program object does not reflect its trustworthiness not to contaminate information.

Figure 2.20 illustrates the combination of read and write properties for trusted subjects.

## 2.10.2 The TCB model

The TCB model defines *multilevel relations* and formalizes the *discretionary security* policy. Moreover, the TCB includes *supporting policies* for data consistency, accountability, labelling, aggregation, sanitization, and reclassification. In this section we illustrate how multilevel relations are modelled and the discretionary access control policies which govern the access to data stored in multilevel relations in the TCB model.

#### Multilevel relations

To deal with multilevel data, the model extends the concept of relation to include classification labels. Classifications can be assigned to single elements of a relation: that is, to each specific attribute's value.

A *multilevel relation* is defined as any relation where there exist classification attributes $C_i$ for each data attribute $A_i$ and a classification attribute for each

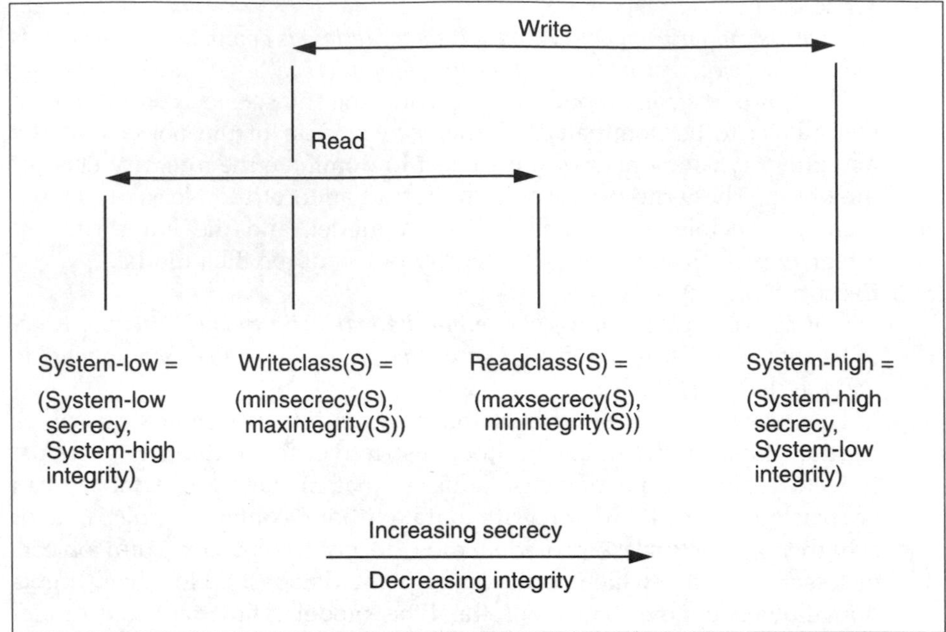


***Figure 2.20*** The combined properties for trusted subjects (Denning *et al.*, 1986).

tuple. Formally, a multilevel relation is represented by a schema $R(A_1,C_1,\ldots, A_n, C_n,T_C)$. An attribute $A_i$ and corresponding $C_i$ of a multilevel relation is single level if, and only if, $C_i$ is defined on a domain represented by a single class in the access class lattice; otherwise it is multilevel. A multilevel relation is single level if all attributes are single-level and of the same class.

Each tuple in a multilevel relation has the form $\langle a_1 \mid c_1,\ldots, a_n \mid c_k, t\rangle$, where $a_i \mid c_i$ indicate respectively the value and the classification of attribute $i$. Element $t$ indicates the access class associated with the tuple: that is, the access class of the information in (or encoded in) the tuple. For simplicity, in multilevel relations only the security levels are considered (i.e., V, C, S or TS).

Figure 2.21 shows an example of a multilevel relation. A multilevel relation has potentially different instances at different access classes. The instance of a relation at a given access class $c$ contains all elements whose classification is dominated by $c$. The instance of a relation at class $c$ represents the information in the relation accessible by users at class $c$ (values not accessible by users at class $c$ are replaced by null values). Therefore, subjects with different readclasses may retrieve data from the multilevel relation, but will see different version of that data. Figure 2.22 illustrates the instances of the multilevel relation of Figure 2.21.

The different instances of a relation must be such that every tuple that appears in the instance of a relation at a given class must also appear in instances of higher classes, although null elements of the low instance may be

| Name | $C_{Name}$ | Department | $C_{Department}$ | Salary | $C_{Salary}$ | TC |
|---|---|---|---|---|---|---|
| Bob | S | Dept1 | S | 10K | S | S |
| Ann | S | Dept2 | S | 20K | TS | TS |
| Sam | TS | Dept2 | TS | 30K | TS | TS |

*Figure 2.21* An example of a multilevel relation.

replaced with non-null elements in the higher-instances *(Inter-Instance Property)*.

The schema of a multilevel relation is also assigned an access class. This access class applies to the relation name as well as to all attributes, names and type definitions for the schema. The classification of objects in the Sea View model must satisfy the following properties.

(1) **Database class integrity**
*The access class of a relation schema must dominate the access class of the name of the database to which it belongs.*

If this constraint were not satisfied, then relations with a class lower than the class of the database name would not be available to users at an access class lower than the class of the database. Moreover, single-level subjects would not be able to write the low relation into the high database.

| Name | $C_{Name}$ | Department | $C_{Department}$ | Salary | $C_{Salary}$ | TC |
|---|---|---|---|---|---|---|
| Bob | S | Dept1 | S | 10K | S | S |
| Ann | S | Dept2 | S | – | S | S |
| Sam | TS | Dept2 | TS | 30K | TS | S |

*S*-Instance

| Name | $C_{Name}$ | Department | $C_{Department}$ | Salary | $C_{Salary}$ | TC |
|---|---|---|---|---|---|---|
| Bob | S | Dept1 | S | 10K | S | S |
| Ann | S | Dept2 | S | 20K | TS | TS |
| Sam | TS | Dept2 | TS | 30K | TS | TS |

*TS*-Instance

*Figure 2.22* Instances of the multilevel relation of Figure 2.21.

This principle follows the compatibility constraint for the object hierarchy of the Bell–La Padula model, which requires that the access class of an object (the extension) dominate the access class of its parent (the intension).

(2) **Visible data property**

*The access class of the relation schema must be dominated by the access class of the lowest data that can be stored in the relation. The greatest lower bound of the range of access classes specified for an attribute must dominate the access class of the relation schema.*

This constraint follows from the principle that the class of the extension must dominate the class of the intension. If the classification schema were not dominated by the classification of the data contained in the relation, then the data in the relation with a classification lower than that of the relation schema would not be available to users at the lower access class, because those users would have no way to reference the relation (its existence would be hidden from them). Moreover, a single-level subject would not be able to write the lower access class data into the relation, because it would need to read the (high) relation schema in order to write the (low) data.

(3) **View class integrity**

*The access class of a view definition must dominate the access class of any relation or view named in the view definition.*

This constraint is a consequence of the mandatory policy. If this constraint did not hold, then the mandatory policy would prohibit a view definition from referencing its underlying relations and views.

The SeaView model defines a set of properties that must be satisfied on the classifications of multilevel relations.

(1) **Multilevel entity integrity**

*Let AK be the set of data attributes forming the primary key of a relation R. All classification attributes $C_i$ corresponding to data attributes $A_i \in AK$ have the same value within any given tuple of R, and this class is dominated by the value of each classification attribute $C_j$ whose data attribute $A_j \notin AK$. No tuple in an instance of R can have null values for any of the primary key attributes.*

The multilevel entity integrity property states that the values for the attributes forming the primary key must have the same access class within any tuple, and that the access class of the primary key value must be dominated by the access class of every other element in the tuple. The constraint that the classification of the primary key be dominated by the classification of the other elements follows from the entity integrity requirement of the relational model (see Chapter 1): that is, the primary key of a tuple should be completely defined (no nulls) and unchangeable. If the constraint were not satisfied then some instances of the relation would have undefined key attributes. The reason for requiring the attributes forming the primary key to be uniformly classified is that otherwise a trusted subject would be needed to add a tuple to a relation (the key must be completely defined at the time a tuple is added to a relation). If a relation has no primary key defined for it, all elements in a tuple must have the same classification, which is the class of the tuple.

(2) **Multilevel referential integrity**
*No tuple in a relation can have a non-null secondary key unless a tuple exists in the referenced relation with the corresponding primary key. Within a tuple, the access class of each element comprising a secondary key must be the same (that is, the secondary key attributes must be uniformly classified) and must dominate the access class of the primary key element(s) in the tuple referenced.*

The multilevel referential integrity property states that if a foreign key is visible at a given access class, then a tuple containing the referenced primary key must also be visible at that access class, and that the class of the foreign key element must dominate the class of the referenced primary key: that is, all references must be downward in access class.

In the standard relational model, each tuple is uniformly identified by the value of its key attributes. When security classes are considered, there may be the need for the simultaneous presence of multiple tuples with the same value for the key attributes but with different classification.

*Polyinstantiation* refers to the simultaneous existence of multiple data objects with the same name, where the multiple instantiations are distinguished by their access classes. Polyinstantiation can affect relations (or complete databases), tuples and data elements:

- *Polyinstantiated relations* are relations identified by relation name but whose schemas have different access classes.
- *Polyinstantiated tuples* (also called *entity polyinstantiation*) are tuples with the same primary key but with different access classes associated to the primary keys.
- *Polyinstantiated elements* (also called *attribute polyinstantiation*) are elements of an attribute which have different access classes but are associated with the same primary key and key class.

Figure 2.23 illustrates an example of a polyinstantiated tuple. Figure 2.24 illustrates an example of a polyinstantiated element. With reference to Figure 2.24, if two tuples referred to as 'Ann' exist both with an attribute key classified as secret, a secret subject will see only one tuple, as illustrated in Figure 2.25.

Polyinstantiation arises because subjects with different classes are allowed to operate on the same relations. If a subject attempts to insert new data into a relation and data already exists (invisibly) with the same name at the higher class then the insertion cannot be refused because the low user would infer the existence of the higher data. The new data must be inserted. In order not to compromise integrity, the old higher data must also be maintained. The contemporaneous presence of the data gives rise to polyinstantiation. The same can happen when a subject attempts to insert data which already exists at lower level. Replacing the old data would introduce a downward channel, so the high and the low data must coexist, therefore introducing polyinstantiation.

| Name | $C_{Name}$ | Department | $C_{Department}$ | Salary | $C_{Salary}$ | TC |
|---|---|---|---|---|---|---|
| Bob | S | Dept1 | S | 10K | S | S |
| Ann | S | Dept2 | S | 20K | TS | TS |
| Sam | TS | Dept2 | TS | 30K | TS | TS |
| Sam | S | Dept1 | S | 10K | S | S |

*Figure 2.23* An example of a polyinstantiated tuple.

In the Sea View model, poylinstantiation is regulated by the following property.

- **Polyinstantiation integrity**
  *Given a relation R with apparent key AK and key class CK, the following functional dependency holds for each attribute $A_i$ that is not in AK:*
  $AK, CK, C_i \rightarrow A_i$.
  *In addition, R satisfies the following multivalued dependency for each attribute $A_i$ that is not in AK:*
  $AK, CK \rightarrow \rightarrow A_i, C_i$
  The polyinstantiation integrity property states that there is a functional dependency from the primary key (including the key class) and the *i*-th element class to the *i*-th element values. There is a multivalued dependency from the primary key to the *i*-th element class and value. Satisfaction of this property ensures that there will never be two tuples with the same primary key unless they represent polyinstantiated tuples or elements.

### Access to multilevel relations

In this section we illustrate how write operations (insert and update) are dealt with in the Sea View model and show how polyinstantiation may arise upon execution of these operations.

| Name | $C_{Name}$ | Department | $C_{Department}$ | Salary | $C_{Salary}$ | TC |
|---|---|---|---|---|---|---|
| Bob | S | Dept1 | S | 10K | S | S |
| Ann | S | Dept2 | S | 30K | TS | TS |
| Ann | S | Dept2 | S | 20K | S | S |
| Sam | TS | Dept2 | TS | 30K | TS | TS |

*Figure 2.24* An example of a polyinstantiated element.

| Name | $C_{Name}$ | Department | $C_{Department}$ | Salary | $C_{Salary}$ | TC |
|---|---|---|---|---|---|---|
| Bob | S | Dept1 | S | 10K | S | S |
| Ann | S | Dept2 | S | 20K | S | S |

*Figure 2.25* View of an S-subject on the multilevel relation of Figure 2.24.

For read operations, subjects have read access to instances of multilevel relations at their level, thus accessing data at their level or below.

For write operations, the problem arises of assigning a single attribute different values at different access classes.

Consider a write operation (insert or update) by a subject on an attribute for which there already exists a value with a different classification from that of the subject. The model distinguishes the cases where the subject clearance is dominated by, dominates or is incomparable with the access class of the pre-existing data as follows.

(1) **The subject clearance is dominated by (or incomparable with) the access class of the data.**
This case arises when a subject needs to insert new data into a relation, and data with the same name already exists (invisibly) at a higher class. Obviously, the subject cannot be informed of the presence of the higher data, and therefore the insertion must be accepted. However, to preserve integrity the high (or incomparable) data should not be deleted. Therefore, polyinstantiation arises.

More precisely:

- A polyinstantiated tuple arises whenever a subject inserts a tuple that has the same primary key values as an existing but invisible tuple.
- A polyinstantiated element arises whenever a subject updates what appears to be a null element in a tuple, but which actually hides data with a higher (or incomparable) access class.

For example, consider the multilevel relation of Figure 2.21 and suppose that an S-subject requires the following operation.

```
INSERT INTO Employee
VALUES Sam, Dept1, 10K
```

The resulting relation, which contains a polyinstantiated tuple, is illustrated in Figure 2.23.

As another example, consider again the multilevel relation of Figure 2.21 and suppose an S-subject requires the following operation.

```
UPDATE Employee
SET Salary = "20K"
WHERE Name = "Ann"
```

The resulting relation, which contains a polyinstantiated element, is illustrated in Figure 2.24.

(2) **The subject clearance dominates the access class of the data.**
If a subject attempts to insert a tuple that has the same primary key as that of an existing tuple with a lower access class, either the operation can be denied and the subject notified of the conflict, or the operation can be executed. In the latter case, since the subject cannot delete or overwrite data at lower level, polyinstantiation will arise. More precisely:

- A polyinstantiated tuple arises whenever a subject inserts a tuple that has the same primary key values as an existing tuple at a lower level;
- A polyinstantiated element arises whenever a subject updates an attribute which has a value classified at a lower level.

For example, consider the relation illustrated in Figure 2.24 and suppose a *TS*-subject requires the following operation.

```
UPDATE Employee
SET Department = "Dept1"
WHERE Name = "Ann"
```

The resulting relation is as illustrated in Figure 2.26, where two tuples have been added.

As illustrated by this example, a single insert (update) operation may introduce, to respect the properties of the model, multiple tuples.

As another example, consider again the relation illustrated in Figure 2.24 and suppose that a *TS*-subject requires the following operation.

```
UPDATE Employee
SET Department = "Dept2", Salary = "20K"
WHERE Name = "Bob"
```

The resulting relation is as illustrated in Figure 2.27, where three tuples have been added. Note that in this case, in order to respect the polyinstantiation properties, tuples have been added which will actually not appear in any of the instances of the relation at different levels (second and third tuple in Figure 2.27).

| Name | $C_{Name}$ | Department | $C_{Department}$ | Salary | $C_{Salary}$ | TC |
|---|---|---|---|---|---|---|
| Bob | S | Dept1 | S | 10K | S | S |
| Ann | S | Dept2 | S | 30K | TS | TS |
| Ann | S | Dept2 | S | 20K | S | S |
| Ann | S | Dept1 | TS | 30K | TS | TS |
| Ann | S | Dept1 | TS | 20K | S | S |
| Sam | S | Dept1 | S | 10K | S | S |

*Figure 2.26* Example of a multilevel relation showing polyinstantiation.

| Name | $C_{Name}$ | Department | $C_{Department}$ | Salary | $C_{Salary}$ | TC |
|---|---|---|---|---|---|---|
| Bob | S | Dept1 | S | 10K | S | S |
| Bob | S | Dept2 | TS | 10K | S | TS |
| Bob | S | Dept1 | S | 20K | TS | TS |
| Bob | S | Dept2 | TS | 20K | TS | TS |
| Ann | S | Dept2 | S | 30K | TS | TS |
| Ann | S | Dept2 | S | 20K | S | S |
| Sam | S | Dept1 | S | 10K | S | S |

*Figure 2.27* Another example of a polyinstantiated multilevel relation.

In the Sea View model a write operation can produce a number of tuples exponential in the number of non-key attributes in a relation. More precisely, the number of manufactured tuples materialized grows at the rate of $|\text{access-classes}|^k$, where $k$ is the number of non-key attributes in the relation. Jajodia and Sandhu (1990) argue that these tuples are spurious. The introduction of these spurious tuples is due to the polyinstantiation integrity property which requires the key and its classification to determine each attribute and its classification via multivalued dependency. To overcome this drawback of the model, the polyinstantiation property has been revised by Lunt and Hsieh (1990), who developed a semantics for write operations on multilevel relations. The new definition of polyinstantiation integrity is composed of two properties: a *state* property, containing the same functional dependency component, and a *transition* property, concerning a new dynamic multivalued dependency component. Whenever an update operation involves some, but not all, of the non-key attributes of a multilevel relation, certain dynamic multivalued dependencies are enforced in the relation. The way in which an update occurs determines whether or not the multivalued dependency should be enforced. In particular, if two or more attributes are updated in a single update statement the multivalued dependency is not enforced. By contrast, if two or more attributes are updated in two or more independent operations, the multivalued dependency is enforced.

#### Discretionary security policy

The discretionary policy allows users to specify which users and groups are authorized for specific modes of access to particular database objects, as well as which users and groups are specifically denied authorization for particular database objects. Negative authorizations cannot be specified for a specific access mode. Instead, a special mode, called null, is used to signify negation. If a subject has the authorization for the null access mode on an object, then the subject cannot exercise any access mode on the object.

The discretionary policy considers *users* and *groups* of users of the system to be subjects. Groups need not be disjoint: that is, a user may belong to more than one group. However, members of groups can only be users: that is, groups cannot be defined on other groups.

Objects protected by the discretionary policy, on which authorizations are specified and against which access control is executed, are: *databases, database relations* (real relations, views, and snapshots) and *MAC objects* (that is, low-level objects of the MAC model where information is contained).

Different access modes are specified according to the different types of considered object. These are as follows:

(1) **Database access modes**

- *Null:* to deny any access on an object;
- *List:* to obtain the names and schemas of the multilevel relations belonging to a database;
- *Create-mrelation:* to create a multilevel relation in a database;
- *Delete-db:* to drop a database;
- *Grant:* to grant other users the authorizations for any access mode (other than grant and give grant) on a database;
- *Give-grant:* to grant other users the authorizations for any access mode (including grant and give grant) on a database.

(2) **Discretionary access modes** (applicable to individual relations and views)

- *Null*: to deny any access to a relation;
- *Select:* to retrieve tuples from a relation;
- *Insert:* to insert tuples in a relation;
- *Update(i):* to modify the *i*th data attribute of a relation;
- *Delete-tuple:* to delete tuples from a relation;
- *Create-view:* to create a view on top of a relation;
- *Delete-mrelation:* to drop a relation;
- *Reference:* to refer to a relation; this is necessary in order to access views defined on top of the relation;
- *Grant:* to grant other users the authorizations for any access mode (other than grant and give grant) on a relation;
- *Give-grant:* to grant other users the authorizations for any access mode (including grant and give grant) on a relation.

(3) **MAC objects access modes**

- *Read:* to read an object;
- *Write:* to write an object;
- *Null:* to deny any access on an object;
- *Grant:* to grant other users the authorizations for any access mode (other than grant and give grant) on an object;
- *Give-grant:* to grant other users the authorizations for any access mode (including grant and give grant) on an object.

The term 'mrelation' in the access modes denotes that the relation to which the mode is referred is a multilevel relation.

### Access control

Access control determines whether a user request must be granted or denied by checking it against the specified authorizations. Since authorizations may be specified for users as well as for groups (and groups may be not disjoint), conflicts may arise among positive and negative authorizations. Conflicts are solved according to the *most specific rule*, meaning that authorizations of a user take precedence over the authorizations of the groups to which the user belongs. Moreover, negative authorizations specified for a subject take precedence over positive authorizations specified for the same subjects.

More precisely, the discretionary access control follows the following priority rules:

- If a user is explicitly denied access to an object, this denial takes precedence over any authorization this user might own either personally or as a member of a group.
- If a user does not personally own any negative authorization on an object but does personally own the positive authorization for some access modes on the object, then he or she is granted only these accesses, and no other accesses owned by the groups to which he or she belongs.
- If nothing has been specified for a user on an object, and if the user is a member of a group that is not denied access to this object, then he or she holds the access rights specified for the group.

According to the rules above a user will be able to use the authorizations specified for a group to which he or she belongs only if nothing has been explicitly specified for the user and no negation has been specified for the group. For example, if an individual user has 'insert' and 'delete' authorization for a database object, and is not denied authorization for the object, then he or she can exercise the 'insert' and 'delete' accesses on the object, but not any additional authorizations that he might hold as a member of a group.

Note that a user who belongs to a group that is denied the access to an object will still be able to exercise his or her personal authorizations as well as authorizations specified for all other groups for which no negation on the object is specified. For example, suppose that a user belongs to group $G_1$ which is authorized for the select access mode on an object and to group $G_2$ which has the null authorization on the same object. Then, the user can exercise the select privilege on the object by employing a subject whose associated group is $G_1$.

### Administration of authorizations

Users can grant and revoke authorizations to access objects and authorizations to administer access to other users and groups. The propagation of authorizations is controlled through the 'grant' and 'give-grant' access modes. These access modes can be referred only to objects and not to single access modes on the objects (that is, the ability to administer accesses to an object is referred to all accesses executable on the object). If a user has the 'grant' access mode for a database object *o*, then the user can grant and revoke any access mode, other than 'grant' and 'give-grant', for the object to and from users and groups. The user can also deny (by granting the null access mode) other users and groups any access on the object. If a user has the 'give-grant' access mode on an object then the user can grant and revoke any access mode (including 'grant' and 'give-grant') on the object to other users and groups. The user can also deny the access on the object by granting the null access mode.

A user authorized for the 'grant' or the 'give-grant' access mode on an object can revoke any authorization on the object, including the authorizations which he or she did not originally grant. The revocation of an authorization from a user does not affect authorizations to any copies of the data that the user may have made, or to any authorization that the user may have granted (that is, revocation is not recursively propagated).

When a user creates a database object other than a view, the user may be given the authorization for all access modes (except null) to the object. For example, if a user creates a relation, the user may receive all discretionary access modes on the relation but the null access mode. The specific set of access modes to be granted to the user is not specified in the model; it is assumed to be a design choice.

When a user creates a view, only the access modes he or she holds on each table directly referenced by the view may be acquired (that is, those relations and views named in the view formula). Thus, the set of authorizations for a newly created view is a subset of the intersection of the authorizations the user holds on all the relations directly referenced by the view. Moreover, the user may be authorized for update access mode on an attribute of the view only if he or she holds the update attribute on each underlying attribute from which the attribute of the view is derived. Note that some views and view attributes may not be updatable. The model allows the user to gain the authorization for the update access mode on these views and attributes as well. However, the user is not guaranteed the update capability on them. For example, suppose that *s* creates a view $V$ on relations $R_1$ and $R_2$. Moreover, suppose that *s* is authorized for the 'select' and 'insert' modes on relation $R_1$. Moreover, *s* is authorized for the 'select' mode (but not the 'insert' mode) on relation $R_2$. Also, suppose that *s* is authorized for the update access mode on attribute $R_1.A$, $R_1.B$ and on attribute $R_2.A$, and that attribute $V.A$ is derived from $R_1.A$ and $R_2.A$ and attribute $V.B$ is derived from $R_1.B$ and $R_2.B$. Then the user may receive on the view only the 'select' access mode ( but not the 'insert' access mode) and may be authorized to update attribute $V.A$ but not attribute $V.B$.

The authorizations of the user creating a view on the view are established at the time that view is created. If a user is granted additional authorizations for the underlying relations, he or she does not gain the corresponding authorizations for the views defined on those relations.

If a user holds the 'grant' or the 'give-grant' modes on the view, then he or she can grant and revoke authorizations on the view to other users and groups. It is not necessary for these users to be authorized for the same access modes on the underlying tables in order to exercise an access mode on the view. However, in order to exercise any access mode on a view, a user must be authorized for the 'reference' access mode on all multilevel relations directly and indirectly referenced by the view.

The authorization to access a database is necessary (but not sufficient) to read the definitions of the relations, views and constraints in the database, as well as to operate on the database. Then, a user or group can be denied access to all the relations in a database simply by being denied the right to access it. To create a relation, view or constraint, a user needs authorizations to create relations ('create-mrelation' mode) in the appropriate database. The authorization to grant and revoke access rights on a database or to delete a database does not imply the corresponding authorizations to the relations, views and constraints contained in the database. Neither are they necessary in order to grant and revoke access rights for, or to delete, relations, views and constraints.

### 2.10.3 Representation of multilevel relations

The Sea View policy requires that the security mechanisms of a system that enforce discretionary security and all supporting policies be constrained by a security kernel, which enforces mandatory security. Then subjects running within the TCB or outside the TCB cannot violate mandatory security. In order to satisfy this requirement all information used by the TCB must be stored in objects of the MAC model and access to it controlled against the mandatory policy. In particular, every multilevel relation must be stored in objects of the MAC model. Since objects of the MAC model are single level, each multilevel relation is decomposed and the data in it stored in different objects, according to their access class. The SeaView model provides a method for decomposing multilevel relations into standard (single-level) base relation of the relational model. In the decomposition all attributes that are uniformly classified are handled as a unit. A multilevel relation is seen as a view over its underlying base relations. Each multilevel relation is then mapped onto one or more single-level storage objects (for example, files or segments) which are protected by a reference monitor that enforces mandatory policy (MAC). Therefore, a subject will be unable to access any data in an underlying relation (in order to derive a multilevel relation) unless the readclass of the subject dominates the class of the object that contains the stored data. A recovery method (Denning, 1985) reconstructs the multilevel relation from the single-level objects in which its data is stored.

## 2.11 The Jajodia and Sandhu model

A model for the application of mandatory policies in relational database systems has been proposed by Jajodia and Sandhu (1991a). The model extends the standard relational model to the consideration of security classifications and provides a formalization of such an extended model. The model is based on the security classifications introduced in the Bell–LaPadula model. Therefore, we refer the reader to this model for the definition of security classes and the relationship between them.

In this section we illustrate how the model formalizes multilevel relations and the operations executable on them.

### 2.11.1 Multilevel relations

To deal with multilevel data, the model extends the standard relational model to include classification labels. A relation, extended with the security classifications, is referred to as a *multilevel relation*. A multilevel relation consists of the following two parts:

(1) A state-independent multilevel *relation scheme* $R(A_1, C_1, \ldots, A_n, C_n, TC)$, where each $A_i$ is a *data attribute* defined over domain $D_i$, each $C_i$ is a *classification attribute* for $A_i$, and *TC* is the *tuple-class* attribute. The domain of $C_i$ is specified by a range $[L_i, H_i]$, which defines a sub-lattice of access classes ranging from $L_i$ up to $H_i$. The domain of *TC* is also a range with the lowest and highest elements equal to the least upper bound of the lowest and highest elements respectively of the classification domains of the attributes. Formally, the domain of *TC* is $[\text{lub}\{L_i : i = 1,\ldots,n\}, \text{lub}\{H_i : i = 1,\ldots, n\}]$.

(2) A collection of state-dependent *relation instances* $R_c(A_1, C_1, \ldots, A_n, C_n, TC)$, one for each access class *c* in the given lattice. Each instance is a set of distinct tuples of the form $(a_1, c_1, \ldots, a_n, c_n, tc)$ where each element $a_i$ is either a value of domain $D_i$ or null, each $c_i$ is a value of the specified range and smaller than *c*, that is, $c_i \in, [L_i, H_i]\ c_i \leq c$, and *tc* is the least upper bound of the classes of the attribute in the tuple: that is, $tc = \text{lub}\{c_i : i = 1, \ldots, n\}$.

The instance of a relation at a given class represents the version of the relation at that class. Basically, each element $t[A_i]$ in a tuple *t* is visible in instances at access class $t[C_i]$ or higher; $t[A_i]$ is replaced by a null value in an instance at a lower access class. Figures 2.28 and 2.29 illustrate an example of multilevel relation and the instances at the different access classes respectively.

#### *Properties of the model*

Read and write operations on the relations are controlled and restricted to the satisfaction of the No Read-Up and No Write-Down principles.

To ensure satisfaction of the mandatory principles, other constraints are put on the classifications of the elements in multilevel relations and to regulate polyinstantiation.

#### (1) Entity integrity

*Let AK be the apparent key of a relation R. A multilevel relation R satisfies entity integrity if, and only if, for all instances $R_c$ of R and $t \in R_c$*

| Name | $C_{Name}$ | Department | $C_{Department}$ | Salary | $C_{Salary}$ | TC |
|---|---|---|---|---|---|---|
| Bob | S | Dept1 | S | 10K | S | S |
| Ann | S | Dept2 | S | 20K | TS | TS |
| Sam | TS | Dept2 | TS | 30K | TS | S |

*Figure 2.28* Example of a multilevel relation EMPLOYEE.

(1) $A_i \in AK \Rightarrow t[A_i] \neq null$,
(2) $A_i, A_j \in AK \Rightarrow t[C_i] = t[C_j]$, *i.e. AK is uniformly classified, and*
(3) $A_i \notin AK\ t[C_i] \geq t[C_{AK}]$ *(where $C_{AK}$ is defined as the classification of the apparent key).*

The property is the extension of the entity integrity property of the standard relational model to deal with security classifications. The first requirement derives directly from the standard relational model and ensures that no tuple in $R_c$ has a null value for any attribute in the apparent key. The second requirement asserts that all key attributes must have the same classification. This will ensure that all key attributes are either entirely visible or entirely null at a specific access class *c*. Finally, the third requirement states that in any tuple the class of the non-key attributes must be dominated by the class of the key attributes. These requirements ensure that non-null attributes will never be associated with a null primary key.

In multilevel relations, null values have may have a double meaning. Null values at a given instance can correspond to real null values or to attributes at

| Name | $C_{Name}$ | Department | $C_{Department}$ | Salary | $C_{Salary}$ | TC |
|---|---|---|---|---|---|---|
| Bob | S | Dept1 | S | 10K | S | S |
| Ann | S | Dept2 | S | - | S | S |

*S*-Instance

| Name | $C_{Name}$ | Department | $C_{Department}$ | Salary | $C_{Salary}$ | TC |
|---|---|---|---|---|---|---|
| Bob | S | Dept1 | S | 10K | S | S |
| Ann | S | Dept2 | S | 20K | TS | TS |
| Sam | TS | Dept2 | TS | 30K | TS | TS |

*TS*-Instance

*Figure 2.29* Instances at the S-level and TS-level of the EMPLOYEE relation shown in Figure 2.28.

a classification higher than the classification of the instance. To formalize the relationship between a tuple and the same tuple with some attribute values hidden (that is, turned to null), the model introduces the *subsumption* relationship between tuples. A tuple $t$ *subsumes* tuple $s$ if for every attribute $A_i$, either

(1) $t[A_i, C_i] = s[A_i, C_i]$ or
(2) $t[A_i] \neq$ null and $s[A_i]$ = null.

For example, with reference to the instances of Figure 2.29, the tuple referred to 'Ann' in the TS-instance subsumes the tuple referred to 'Ann' in the S-instance.

The following property regulates null values and their classification.

**(2) Null integrity**

*A multilevel relation R satisfies null integrity if and only if for each instance $R_c$ of R both the following conditions are satisfied:*

(1) *For all $t \in R_c$, $t[A_i] = null \Rightarrow t[C_i] = t[C_{AK}]$: that is, null values are classified at the level of the key*
(2) *$R_c$ is subsumption free in the sense that it does not contain two distinct tuples such that one subsumes the other.*

The property requires that the null values in a tuple be classified at the same level of the key attributes of the tuple, and that a null value be subsumed by a non-null value independently of the classification of this non-null value.

Instances of a multilevel relation at the different access classes are related. Each instance at an access class $c$ is intended to represent the version of the reality which is appropriate for access class $c$. The following property controls the consistency among the different instances of a relation.

**(3) Inter-instance integrity**

*A multilevel relation R satisfies inter-instance integrity if and only if for all $c' \leq c$, $R_{c'} = \sigma(R_c, c')$, where the filter function $\sigma$ produces the c'-instance $R_c'$ from $R_c$ as follows:*

(1) *For every tuple $t \in R_c$ such that $t[C_{AK}] \leq c'$, there is a tuple $t' \in R_{c'}$, with $t'[AK, C_{AK}] = t[AK, C_{AK}]$ and for $A_i \notin AK$*

$$t'[A_i, C_i] = \begin{cases} t[A_i, C_i] & \text{if } t[C_i] \leq c' \\ \langle null, t[CAK] \rangle & \text{otherwise} \end{cases}$$

(2) *There are no tuples in $R_{c'}$ other than those derived by the above rule.*
(3) *The end result is made subsumption free by exhaustive elimination of subsumed tuples.*

The filter function maps a multilevel relation into different instances, one for each access class. This function restricts each user to the data he or she is cleared for. The inter-instance integrity property states that a tuple present in an instance of a relation must be present also in all other instances of the relation. In instances with access class lower than the class of the tuple some attribute values may be substituted by null values (to hide them from users who do not have the necessary clearance) and given an access class equal to the key class. Moreover, two tuples must not exist in a relation instance such that one subsumes the other.

In the standard relational model, the definition of key is based on functional dependencies: the value of key attributes functionally determines the values of all the other attributes. Therefore, two tuples must not exist in a relation with the same values for the primary key attributes. As already discussed, requiring this constraint to hold in multilevel relations may cause indirect release of sensitive information to users lacking the necessary clearance. The model distinguishes between the *apparent primary key* and actual *primary key* of a relation. The apparent primary key is the key defined in the relation scheme. The actual primary key is defined according to the following property.

**(4) Polyinstantiation integrity property**

*A multilevel relation R satisfies polyinstantiation integrity if, and only if, for every* $R_c$*, for all* $A_i$*:* $AK, C_{AK}, C_i \rightarrow A_i$.

This property asserts that the apparent key specified by a user, together with the classification of this key and the classification of an attribute, functionally determines the value of this attribute. This property implicitly defines the primary key of a multilevel relation as the union of the key attributes, their classifications and the classifications of all the non-key attributes. Formally, the key is formed of $AK \cup C_{AK} \cup C_R$ (where $C_R$ is the set of classification attributes for non-key data attributes). Then, the above property can be expressed as $AK \cup C_{AK} \cup C_R \rightarrow A_R$ (where $A_R$ denotes the set of all non-key attributes). Note that for single-level relations the class of the key attributes ($C_{AK}$) and the class of the non-key attributes ($C_R$) are the same in all tuples. In this case the above definition reduces to $AK \rightarrow A_R$ which is the definition of the primary key in the standard relational model.

This property corresponds to the analogous polyinstantiation property of the Sea View model. However, in the model of Jajodia and Sandhu the requirements of the multivalued dependency $AK, C_{AK} \rightarrow\rightarrow A_i, C_i$ has been taken away because of the drawbacks illustrated in 2.10.

***Access to multilevel relations***

In this section we discuss how the model of Jajodia and Sandhu deals with write operations (that is, insert,update, and delete). Read operations (select) are not considered in that they produce no effect on the state of a database. Read access is controlled according to the No Read-Up principle of the Bell and La Padula model. A user is granted read access to the instance of a multilevel relation at his or her level. Then, from the properties above, he or she will see only data at his or her own level or below.

The effects of operations that modify the state of a database are not only those requested by users; further modifications need to be made for the resulting state to satisfy the properties required by the model.

Consider a user with access class *c*. This user can directly see, and operate on, the instance $R_c$ of a multilevel relation *R*. From this user viewpoint, the remaining instances of $R$ fall into three classes: those strictly dominated by $c$, those that strictly dominate $c$, and those incomparable with $c$. Formally, these classes can be expressed as follows:

$$R_{c'<c} \equiv R'_c \text{ such that } c'<c$$
$$R_{c'>c} \equiv R'_c \text{ such that } c'>c$$
$$R_{c'\sim c} \equiv R'_c \text{ such that } c' \text{ is incomparable with } c.$$

To obey the No Write-Down principle, a $c$-user cannot affect in any way instances of a relation with classification lower than, or incomparable with, his user clearance. Therefore, a $c$ classified user must be prevented from directly or indirectly (that is, as a side-effect) inserting, updating or deleting tuples in each relation instance $R_{c'<c}$ and $R_{c'\sim c}$. Moreover, the actions of a $c$ user must be confined to the tuples in $R_c$ with tuple class equal to $c$. Then, to satisfy the inter-instance property, the effects of these actions must be propagated to the instances at higher classes.

### *Insert operation*

The insert operation, from a $c$-user, has the following form:

```
INSERT INTO Rc[(Ai[, Aj]...)]
VALUES (ai[, aj]...)
```

where the elements in rectangular brackets indicate optional items and '...' signifies repetition. If the list of the attributes is omitted, it is assumed that all the data attributes in $R_c$ are specified. Only data attributes $A_i$ can be explicitly given values. The classification attributes $C_i$ are all implicitly given the value $c$.

Let $t$ be a tuple such that $t[A_i] = a_i$, if $A_i$ is included in the list of attributes of the insert statement, $t[A_i]$ = "null", if $A_i$ is not in the list, and $t[C_l] = c$ for $1 \leq l \leq n$. The insert operation is granted if, and only if, the following conditions are satisfied:

(1) $t[AK]$ does not contain any nulls
(2) For all $u \in R_c : u[AK] \neq t[AK]$.

If these conditions are satisfied, the tuple $t$ is inserted into $R_c$ and consequently into all the instances $R_{c'>c}$. This is the only visible effect of the insertion in the instances $R_{c'>c}$.

As an example, consider the multilevel relation shown in Figure 2.28. Suppose that a $TS$-subject requests the following insert operation:

```
INSERT INTO Employee
VALUES "John, Dept2, 20"
```

The result of the operation on the different instances of the relation is illustrated in Figure 2.30. Consider the relation whose instances are illustrated here and suppose a $TS$-subject requires the operation:

```
INSERT INTO Employee
VALUES "Bob, Dept2, 20K"
```

| Name | $C_{Name}$ | Department | $C_{Department}$ | Salary | $C_{Salary}$ | TC |
|---|---|---|---|---|---|---|
| Bob | S | Dept1 | S | 10K | S | S |
| Ann | S | Dept2 | S | - | S | S |
| John | S | Dept2 | S | 20K | S | S |

*S*-Instance

| Name | $C_{Name}$ | Department | $C_{Department}$ | Salary | $C_{Salary}$ | TC |
|---|---|---|---|---|---|---|
| Bob | S | Dept1 | S | 10K | S | S |
| Ann | S | Dept2 | S | 20K | TS | TS |
| Sam | TS | Dept2 | TS | 30K | TS | TS |
| John | S | Dept2 | S | 20K | S | TS |

*S*-Instance

*Figure 2.30* Result of the operation INSERT VALUES "John,Dept2,20K" on S and TS instances of EMPLOYEE from TS subject.

This operation requires the insertion of a new tuple with a primary key equal to the primary key of an existing tuple. In this case the insertion may be denied, indicating to the user the presence of a tuple with the same primary key, or accepted, in which case the relation contains two tuples with the same apparent primary key, but different access classes (polyinstantiated tuples). The relation which would result from the execution of the operation is shown in Figure 2.31. Note that in this case polyinstantiation was not strictly necessary; the user could have been informed about the conflict. For this reason, in the model, this type of polyinstantiation is referred to as *optional*.

As another example, consider the relation in Figure 2.31 and suppose that an *S*-subject requires the following insertion:

```
INSERT INTO Employee
VALUES "Sam, Dept2, 20K"
```

In this case, a tuple with the same primary key as the one of the tuple to be inserted already exists in the relation. The existing tuple is, however, not visible to the user requesting the insertion. Hence, in this case the user cannot be informed of the already existing tuple and, therefore, the new tuple must be inserted, introducing polyinstantiation (Figure 2.32). This type of polyinstantiation is referred to as *necessary polyinstantiation*, in that it cannot be avoided.

| Name | $C_{Name}$ | Department | $C_{Department}$ | Salary | $C_{Salary}$ | TC |
|---|---|---|---|---|---|---|
| Bob | S | Dept1 | S | 10K | S | S |
| Ann | S | Dept2 | S | - | S | S |
| John | S | Dept2 | S | 20K | S | S |

*S*-Instance

| Name | $C_{Name}$ | Department | $C_{Department}$ | Salary | $C_{Salary}$ | TC |
|---|---|---|---|---|---|---|
| Bob | S | Dept1 | S | 10K | S | S |
| Bob | TS | Dept2 | TS | 20K | TS | TS |
| Ann | S | Dept2 | S | 20K | TS | TS |
| Sam | TS | Dept2 | TS | 30K | TS | TS |
| John | S | Dept2 | S | 20K | S | S |

*TS*-Instance

*Figure 2.31* Result of the operation INSERT VALUES "Bob,Dept2,20K" on S and TS instances of EMPLOYEE from TS subject.

#### *Update operation*

An update operation from a *c* user has the following form:

```
UPDATE R_c
SET A_i = s_i[, A_j = s_j]...
[WHERE p]
```

where each $s_i$ is a scalar expression, and $p$ is a predicate expression which identifies those tuples in $R_c$ that are to be modified. Predicate $p$ may include, besides the usual conditions on data attributes, conditions on classification attributes. The assignment in the **SET** clause, however, can involve only data attributes. The classification of the attributes that are to be inserted is considered to be the class *c* of the user requiring the update.

The effect of the update operation in the standard relational model is to modify $t[A_i]$ to $s_i$ in those tuples $t$ in $R_c$ which satisfy the condition in predicate $p$. Additionally, in multilevel relations, other effects have to be produced on the relation being modified to prevent illegal information flow. If the operation completes, its effect will be visible at instance $R_c$ as well as at all instances $R_{c'>c}$, as indicated in the following.

| Name | $C_{Name}$ | Department | $C_{Department}$ | Salary | $C_{Salary}$ | TC |
|---|---|---|---|---|---|---|
| Bob | S | Dept1 | S | 10K | S | S |
| Ann | S | Dept2 | S | - | S | S |
| Sam | S | Dept2 | S | 20K | S | S |
| John | S | Dept2 | S | 20K | S | S |

*S*-Instance

| Name | $C_{Name}$ | Department | $C_{Department}$ | Salary | $C_{Salary}$ | TC |
|---|---|---|---|---|---|---|
| Bob | S | Dept1 | S | 10K | S | S |
| Bob | TS | Dept2 | TS | 30K | TS | TS |
| Ann | S | Dept2 | S | 20K | TS | TS |
| Sam | TS | Dept2 | TS | 30K | TS | TS |
| Sam | S | Dept2 | S | 20K | S | S |
| John | S | Dept2 | S | 20K | S | S |

*TS*-Instance

***Figure* 2.32** Result of the operation INSERT VALUES "Sam,Dept2,20K" on S and TS instances of EMPLOYEE from S subject.

*Effect of the update on instance $R_c$*

Let $S$ be the set of the tuples in $R_c$ which satisfy predicate $p$. Formally $S = \{t \in R_c \mid t$ satisfies predicate $p\}$. The effect of the update on each tuple $t \in S$ is twofold.

(1) As requested by the user, tuple $t$ must be replaced by tuple $t'$ which is identical to $t$ except for those data attributes which are assigned new values in the **SET** clause. Formally,

$$t'[A_i, C_i] = \begin{cases} t[A_i, C_i] & \text{if } A_i \notin \text{SET clause} \\ \langle s_i, c \rangle & \text{if } A_i \in \text{SET clause} \end{cases}$$

(2) To avoid covert channels, an additional tuple may be inserted to hide the modifications from users classified at a lower level than the class $c$ of the user requesting the update. The insertion of this tuple is needed every time there is an attribute $A_i$ in the **SET** clause such that $t[A_i] < c$. The reason for this is to preserve the original value of $t[A_i]$ *in* $t''$. The new tuple $t''$ to be inserted is formally defined as:

$$t''[A_i, C_i] = \begin{cases} t[A_i, C_i] & \text{if } t[C_i] < c \\ \langle \text{null}, t[AK] \rangle & \text{if } t[C_i] = c \end{cases}$$

Therefore, each tuple $t \in S$ is replaced by a tuple $t'$ and occasionally by a further tuple $t''$. If the resulting relation satisfies polyinstantiation integrity, the update operation is successfully completed. Otherwise, the update is rejected and the relation left unchanged. The effect of the update operation is the combination of all the effects on each tuple $t$ in the **SET** clause.

*Effect of the update on instances $R_{c'}$*

Updates on instance $R_c$ are propagated to higher instances $R_{c'>c}$ according to the *minimum propagation policy*: only those tuples which are needed to preserve the inter-instance property are inserted in $R_{c'>c}$. The tuples to be inserted are the modified tuple $t'$ and possibly the additional tuple $t''$ (this latter only if not subsumed).

To illustrate the effect of the update in instances above the user clearance consider again a tuple $t \in S$ separately. Let $A_i$ be an attribute in the **SET** clause such that $t[C_i]=c$ and $t[A_i] = x$, where $x$ is a non-null value. Suppose that a $c$-user requires to change the value of attribute $t[A_i]$ from $x$ to $s_i$. Owing to polyinstantiation, there may be several tuples $u$ in $R_{c'>c}$ with the same apparent primary key as $t$ and the same value and classification for attribute $A_i$. That is, several tuples may exist for which: $u[A_{AK}, C_{AK}] = t[A_{AK}, C_{AK}]$ and $u[A_i, C_i] = t[A_i, C_i]$.

To meet the polyinstantiation integrity in these tuples the value of $A_i$ must be changed from $x$ to $s_i$. This requirement is formally expressed as follows:

(1) For every $A_i \in$ **SET** clause with $t[A_i] \neq$ null let
$U = \{u \in R_{c'>c} \mid u[A_{AK}, C_{AK}] = t[A_{AK}, C_{AK}],\ u[A_i, C_i] = t[A_i, C_i]\}$.
Replace each tuple $u \in U$ by a tuple $u'$ equal to $u$, except for the attribute to be modified, for which $u'[A_i, C_i] = (s_i, c)$. This rule is applied to each attribute $A_i$ in the **SET** clause.

(2) Insert in $R_{c'>c}$ tuples t' and t'' (the latter only if it exists and is not subsumed).

As an example, consider the multilevel relation of Figure 2.29 and suppose a *TS* user requires the following operation:

```
UPDATE Employee
SET Salary = "30K"
WHERE Name = "Ann"
```

The resulting relation is as illustrated in Figure 2.33: only the modification requested by the user has been executed. No further modifications are needed because the resulting relation satisfies the properties of the model.

Consider now the relation of Figure 2.33 and suppose a *TS*-user requires the following operation

```
UPDATE Employee
SET Department = "Dept1"
WHERE Name = "Ann"
```

| Name | $C_{Name}$ | Department | $C_{Department}$ | Salary | $C_{Salary}$ | TC |
|---|---|---|---|---|---|---|
| Bob | S | Dept1 | S | 10K | S | S |
| Ann | S | Dept2 | S | - | S | S |

*S*-Instance

| Name | $C_{Name}$ | Department | $C_{Department}$ | Salary | $C_{Salary}$ | TC |
|---|---|---|---|---|---|---|
| Bob | S | Dept1 | S | 10K | S | S |
| Ann | S | Dept2 | S | 30K | TS | TS |
| Sam | TS | Dept2 | TS | 30K | TS | TS |

*TS*-Instance

*Figure 2.33* Result of the operation UPDATE Salary = "30K" WHERE Name = "Ann" on S and TS instances of EMPLOYEE from TS subject.

The resulting relation is as illustrated in Figure 2.34. The first tuple regarding "Ann" in the *TS*-instance reflects the update required by the user. The second tuple is the tuple $t''$ introduced to add the effect of the update to *S*-users and maintain inter-instance integrity.

| Name | $C_{Name}$ | Department | $C_{Department}$ | Salary | $C_{Salary}$ | TC |
|---|---|---|---|---|---|---|
| Bob | S | Dept1 | S | 10K | S | S |
| Ann | S | Dept2 | S | - | S | S |

*S*-Instance

| Name | $C_{Name}$ | Department | $C_{Department}$ | Salary | $C_{Salary}$ | TC |
|---|---|---|---|---|---|---|
| Bob | S | Dept1 | S | 10K | S | S |
| Ann | S | Dept1 | TS | 30K | TS | TS |
| Ann | S | Dept2 | S | - | S | S |
| Ann | TS | Dept2 | TS | 30K | TS | TS |

*TS*-Instance

*Figure 2.34* Result of the operation UPDATE Department = "Dept1" WHERE Name = "Ann" on S and TS instances of EMPLOYEE from TS subject.

As another example, consider the relation of Figure 2.29 and suppose a *TS*-subject requires the following operation

```
UPDATE Employee
SET Department = "Dept2", Salary = "20K"
WHERE Name = "Bob"
```

The resulting relation is as illustrated in Figure 2.35. The first tuple regarding "Bob" in the *TS*-instance has been introduced to reflect the update of the user. The second tuple is the tuple $t''$ introduced to maintain inter-instance integrity property. Note that the same update in the Sea View model led to the insertion of three tuples, two of which were considered spurious (Figure 2.27).

### Delete operation

The delete operation has the following form:

```
DELETE FROM R_c [WHERE p]
```

where $p$ is a predicate expression which identifies those tuples in $R_c$ that are to be deleted. As in the case of the update operation, predicate $p$ may also include, besides the usual conditions on data attributes, conditions on classification attributes.

The effect of the delete operation according to the semantics of the delete in the standard relational model is to delete those tuples in $R_c$ which satisfy predicate $p$. However, as in the case of the update, the consideration of classification may require further actions to be executed. In particular, it may be necessary to delete polyinstantiated tuples in $R_{c'>c}$ corresponding to the tuples being deleted (to preserve inter-instance integrity).

Let $t$ be a tuple which satisfies the predicate in the delete statements:

| Name | $C_{Name}$ | Department | $C_{Department}$ | Salary | $C_{Salary}$ | TC |
|---|---|---|---|---|---|---|
| Bob | S | Dept1 | S | 10K | S | S |
| Ann | S | Dept2 | S | - | S | S |

*S*-Instance

| Name | $C_{Name}$ | Department | $C_{Department}$ | Salary | $C_{Salary}$ | TC |
|---|---|---|---|---|---|---|
| Bob | S | Dept1 | S | 10K | S | S |
| Bob | S | Dept2 | TS | 20K | TS | S |
| Ann | S | Dept2 | S | 20K | TS | TS |
| Sam | TS | Dept2 | TS | 30K | TS | TS |

*TS*-Instance

*Figure 2.35* Result of the operation UPDATE Department = "Dept2", Salary = "20K" WHERE Name = "Bob" on S and TS instances of EMPLOYEE from TS subject.

- If $t[AK] = c$, any polyinstantiated tuple in $R_{c'>c}$ will also be deleted.
- If $t[AK] < c$, the tuple will continue to exist in all instances $R_{c' \geq t[AK]}$.

### 2.11.2 Extensions to the model

Some extensions have been proposed to the model in order to solve the problem of polyinstantiation.

Some work has been done in order to eliminate polyinstantiation. Sandhu and Jajodia (1992a) introduce three basic techniques for eliminating *entity* and *attribute* polyinstantiation. Remember that entity polyinstantiation refers to tuples with the same values for the attributes in the apparent primary key but a different key class, whereas attribute polyinstantiation refers to tuples with the same apparent primary key and key class but with different values for one or more remaining attributes. The solutions for eliminating polyinstantiation are as follows:

#### *Entity polyinstantiation*

(1) *Make all keys visible.* In this approach the apparent primary key of the relation must always have an access class equal to the lowest class at which the relation is visible.

(2) *Partition the domain of the primary key.* In this approach the domain of the primary key must be partitioned among the various access classes possible for the primary key. This eliminates the possibility that two users at different access class may try to insert tuples with same apparent primary key.

(3) *Limit insertion to be done by trusted subjects.* In this approach all insertions must be done by a system-high user (or a user to whom all tuples are visible), with a write down occurring as part of the insert operation.

(4) *Use 'restricted' values.* This approach is based on the introduction of a special value, called 'restricted'. When an attribute has a value at a given class, the value of the attribute will be 'restricted' at any access class dominated by or incomparable with the class of the actual value. Value 'restricted' cannot be updated.

Other approaches to limiting polyinstantiation have been proposed. Sandhu and Jajodia (1992b) define a particular semantics of polyinstantiation, called polyinstantiation for covert stories (PCS). PCS allows two alternatives for each attribute (or group of attributes) of a multilevel tuple. These are: no polyinstantiation, or polyinstantiation at the explicit request of a user to whom the polyinstantiation is visible. This approach limits the extent of polyinstantiation by requiring that each real-world entity be modelled in a multilevel relation by, at most, one tuple per security class.

## 2.12 Smith and Winslett model

Another model which considers the application of mandatory policies in relational database systems has been proposed by Smith and Winslett (1992a, 1992b; Winslett *et al.*, 1994). The model is based on the concept of *belief*.

### 2.12.1 Basic properties

A multilevel database is seen as a set of ordinary relational databases, one database for each level in the security lattice. All the databases share the same schema, and each database is assigned a security class or level. The database at a given level contains the total *beliefs* of the subjects of that level about the state of the world reflected in the schema. A subject *believes* the contents of the database at its own level. A subject sees what it and the subjects at lower levels believe. A subject may see many tuples that it does not itself believe. This concept is illustrated in Figure 2.36.

A null value in a tuple means that the subjects at that level believe that a value exists for that attribute, but do not know what that value is.

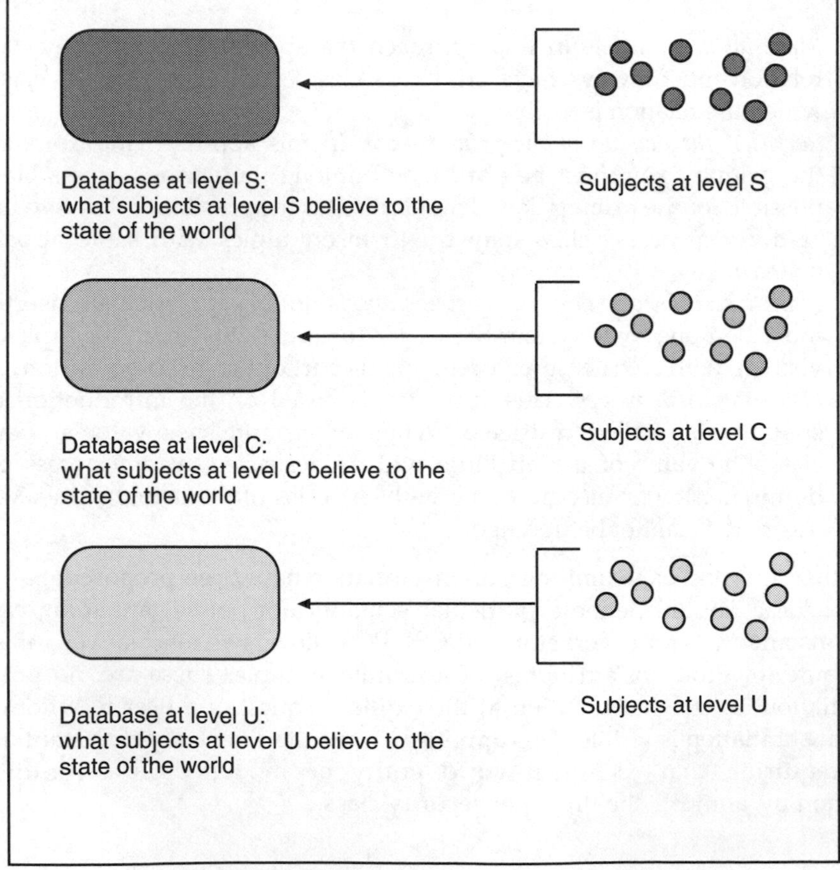


*Figure 2.36* Relationships between subjects and databases of different levels (Winslett *et al.*, 1994).

The following axioms regulate the access of the subjects to the database:

(1) **Update access**
*A database update request (insert, delete, update) from a subject can only alter data in the interpretation at the subject's own level. Data at a particular level can only be altered by subjects at that level.*

The update access rule corresponds to the No Write-Down principle. However, it is stronger than the Bell–La Padula constraints in that writing up is not allowed. The update access rule states that a subject can change its own beliefs, but no one else's.

(2) **Read access**
*A query from a subject at level l can access data from exactly those databases whose label is dominated by l.*

The Read Access rule corresponds to the Bell-LaPadula No Read-Up principle: a subject can retrieve exactly what it can see that someone believes.

### *Multilevel relations*

Unlike the Sea View and the Jajodia and Sandhu models, the Smith and Winslett model does not support classification at the level of each single attribute. By contrast, access classes can be assigned only to key attributes and to tuples as a whole. As argued by the authors of tuple classification, this method is as powerful as attribute classification. Tuples with attributes at different classifications, which cannot be modelled as tuples where only the tuple access class is considered, correspond to tuples which do not have clear semantics (Smith and Winslett, 1992; Smith, 1992). Moreover, the Smith and Winslett model eliminates the problem of proliferation of tuples due to updating in previous models.

A multilevel relation is characterized by a scheme $R(K,KC,A_1,\ldots,A_n,TC)$ where $K$ is the set of key attributes, each $A_i$ is an attribute in the relation, and $KC$ and $TC$ are the security levels of the key attribute and of the tuple respectively. Pair $K$, $KC$ is referred to as the identifier of the entity (eid). The following property defines multilevel relations.

#### *Key and tuple classification property*

*The schema for every relation R must include a 'key classification' attribute KC, representing the security level of the information in K, and a 'tuple classification' attribute TC, representing the security level of the remainder of the tuple: $R(K,KC,A_1,\ldots,A_m,TC)$. The domain of TC and KC is the set of security levels, with the restriction that in a particular tuple, the attribute value for TC must dominate that for KC. Furthermore, K | KC | TC must functionally determine all the attributes of R, and together for the key of relation R.*

Figure 2.37 illustrates an example of a multilevel relation.

Each multilevel relation is then mapped into single-level relations at the different access classes. The relation schemas of these single-level relations are all equal and are the same as the schema of the multilevel relation, except that attribute $TC$ is dropped. The instance of $R$ in the interpretation at level $l$ is

| Name | KC | Department | Salary | TC |
|---|---|---|---|---|
| Bob | U | Dept1 | 10K | U |
| Ann | U | Dept1 | 10K | U |
| Ann | U | Dept2 | 20K | C |
| Sam | S | Dept2 | 20K | S |

*Figure 2.37* Example of a multilevel relation EMPLOYEE.

obtained by selecting all those tuples of *R* which have value *l* for tuple *TC* and then projecting out *TC*.

As an example, consider the multilevel relation EMPLOYEE illustrated in Figure 2.37. Its interpretation at the different levels is illustrated in Figure 2.38.

In the belief-based model, tuples with the same values but different classification for key attributes represent different real-world entities. Tuples with the same values and classification for key attributes but a different classification for the non-key attributes represent different beliefs about the same real-world entity. A tuple at level *l* that contains all null values except for the entity's eid means that the subjects at level *l* believe that the entity exists, but have no beliefs about what its values are. If no tuple for a particular eid appears at level *l*, then the subjects at that level do not believe that the entity exists. At the time

| Name | KC | Department | Salary |
|---|---|---|---|
| Bob | S | Dept1 | 10K |
| Ann | U | Dept1 | 10K |

*U*-Instance

| Name | KC | Department | Salary |
|---|---|---|---|
| Ann | U | Dept2 | 20K |

*C*-Instance

| Name | KC | Department | Salary |
|---|---|---|---|
| Sam | S | Dept2 | 20K |

*S*-Instance

*Figure 2.38* Interpretation at different levels of the EMPLOYEE relation shown in Figure 2.37.

a multilevel entity first appears in the database, it must have a *base tuple*, namely a tuple whose key class and tuple class are equal. A base tuple is the lowest level of database tuple where the existence of an entity is asserted.

### 2.12.2 Access to multilevel relations

In this section we illustrate how write operations are dealt with in the model.

#### *Select operation*

The select statement has the following form:

```
SELECT A_i [A_j] *
FROM R_k [R_l] *
WHERE P
[BELIEVED BY L]
```

where the symbol '*' denotes repetition, and the square brackets denote optional items. Attribute *TC* may not appear in the select clause; it is an implicit part of the answer to every query.

The clause **BELIEVED BY** indicates the level of the data against which the query must be evaluated. Nested select statements cannot have a **BELIEVED BY** clause. The reason for this is to prevent joins between tuples with different security levels. *L* is a list of one or more security levels. Variables 'self' and 'anyone' can be used instead of explicitly listing the security levels. Variable 'self' is used to indicate the level of the user requiring the select. Variable 'anyone' is used to indicate all security levels dominated by the level of the user requiring the select.

The result of the select operation is defined in terms of the database interpretation as follows. The entire query (except the **BELIEVED BY** clause) is evaluated separately against the database at each level *L*. Each answer is then added to the tuple class *TC* of the level of the database producing it. Finally, the tuples so found are unioned.

Note that the operation can be directly executed on a multilevel relation by using the standard select operation and modifying the query by adding to the **WHERE** clause the condition requiring equalities of the tuple class with any of the levels *L* in the **BELIEVED BY** clause.

As an example, consider the multilevel relation illustrated in Figure 2.37 and consider the following query:

```
SELECT All
FROM Employee
WHERE Name = "Ann"
BELIEVED BY Anyone
```

The query would return tuple ⟨**Ann(U),Dept1,10K(U)**⟩ for U-users. The query would return both tuples ⟨**Ann(U),Dept1,10K(U)**⟩ and ⟨**Ann(U),Dept2,20K(C)**⟩ for users classified C or higher.

**Insert operation**

The insert statement has the following form:

```
INSERT INTO R[(Aᵢ[,Aⱼ]*)]
VALUES V
```

where $V$ is a set of tuple values of the form $(a_i[,a_j]*)$.

The insert operation asserts the existence of a new entity at the level of the user requiring the insert. For each tuple value in $V$, a new tuple is inserted such that attribute $A_i$ is given the constant value $a_i$. The key and tuple classes are placed equal to the class of the user requiring the insert.

To respect the key and tuple classification property, if a base tuple already exists with eid matching that of the inserted tuple, the insertion is rejected. Since the value of the existing tuple is visible to the user requiring the insertion, this rejection does not open any covert channel.

As an example, consider the multilevel relation illustrated in Figure 2.37 and suppose an $S$-user requires the following insertion

```
INSERT INTO Employee
VALUES "Ann, Dept2, 30K".
```

Since entity "Ann(U)" does not exist already, the corresponding tuple is inserted. The resulting relation is illustrated in Figure 2.39. Note that 'Ann(U)' and 'Ann(S)' are considered as two different entities.

The model requires users not to reuse old entity keys for new entities. Satisfaction of this requirement guarantees that after deletion of an entity at a lower level, higher-level users can continue to believe in that same entity, with no confusion between the old entity and new entities introduced later on at lower levels.

**Update operation**

The update statement has the following form:

```
UPDATE R
SET Aᵢ=aᵢ[Aⱼ=aⱼ]*
WHERE P
[BELIEVED BY L]
```

| Name | KC | Department | Salary | TC |
|---|---|---|---|---|
| Bob | U | Dept1 | 10K | U |
| Ann | U | Dept1 | 10K | U |
| Ann | U | Dept2 | 20K | C |
| Ann | S | Dept2 | 20K | S |
| Sam | S | Dept2 | 20K | S |

*Figure 2.39* EMPLOYEE: an example of a multilevel relation.

The update operation modifies the beliefs regarding pre-existing multilevel entities at the level of the user requiring the update.

As in the select statement, the **WHERE** and **BELIEVED BY** clauses select tuples of $R$ to which the operation is referred. However, owing to the update access property, only the tuples with the same level as the user requiring the update can be modified. Therefore, the set of tuples updated may be a subset of the tuples which satisfy the conditions in the statement.

If no tuple exists in the relation that matches the condition in the statement, a new tuple is inserted in the database at the level of the query issuer stating the belief expressed in the **SET** clause. Consider an entity $E$ which satisfies the **WHERE** and **BELIEVED BY** clauses of an update statement. For each relational variable $a_i$ mentioned in the **SET** clause, the following process is followed to determine how to update $a_i$ in entity $E$.

(1) If the level of the user requiring the update is contained in $L$, a value is sought in a qualified tuple at the level of the user who required the update.

(2) If no value is available at the level of the user, and a list of levels is given in the **BELIEVED BY** clause, the list is searched sequentially. For each unbound relational variable in $a_i$, the value is used from the first level encountered containing a tuple which supplies a value.

(3) If the security variable 'Anyone' is used, a predetermined traversal of the security sub-lattice dominated by the user is made. The order can be determined by the DBMS, or specified by the user.

(4) If none of the above produces a value suitable for the expression $a_i$, entity $E$ is not updated.

This approach restricts the scope of an update, narrowing it to a single entity by specifying a **WHERE** clause which is satisfied only by one eid. This avoids the problem of tuple proliferation present in the Sea View and Jajodia and Sandhu models.

As an example of how an update statement can generate new tuples, consider the multilevel relation illustrated in Figure 2.37 and suppose an $S$-user issues the command

```
UPDATE Employee
SET Salary = "30K"
WHERE Salary = "20K"
BELIEVED BY Anyone.
```

The meaning of this statement is that all employees whom everyone believes to earn "20K", are now believed to earn "30K" by the $S$ user. Employee "Ann" satisfies the condition in the statement. However, the $S$-user does not have any belief about it. Therefore, a new tuple is inserted for "Ann" at level $S$. As for employee Sam, the value of the attribute is updated. No tuples need to be inserted in this case. The resulting relation is illustrated in Figure 2.40.

As another example, consider the multilevel relation illustrated in Figure 2.37 and consider an $S$-user requiring the following operation:

| Name | KC | Department | Salary | TC |
|---|---|---|---|---|
| Bob | U | Dept1 | 10K | U |
| Ann | U | Dept1 | 10K | U |
| Ann | U | Dept2 | 20K | C |
| Ann | U | Dept2 | 30K | S |
| Sam | S | Dept2 | 30K | S |

*Figure 2.40* EMPLOYEE: an example of a multilevel relation.

```
UPDATE Employee
SET Salary = "20K"
WHERE Name = "Ann"
```

Again, the *S* user has no belief about Ann (U), therefore a new tuple for Ann (U) must be inserted at level *S*. The resulting relation is illustrated in Figure 2.41.

***Delete operation***

The delete statement has the following form:

```
DELETE
FROM R
WHERE P
[BELIEVED BY L]
```

As in the case of the select and update statements, the **WHERE** and **BELIEVED BY** clauses qualify the set of entities which are intended to be deleted. The delete operation, at the level of the user requiring the delete, removes the beliefs about the set of multilevel entities satisfying the conditions in the statement. The result of the operation is that all entities satisfying the conditions are removed from the database as interpreted at the level of the issuer. If a deleted tuple was a base tuple, the entity will still be present at higher levels: that is, higher-level users will still believe the entity exists.

| Name | KC | Department | Salary | TC |
|---|---|---|---|---|
| Bob | U | Dept1 | 10K | U |
| Ann | U | Dept1 | 10K | U |
| Ann | U | Dept2 | 20K | C |
| Ann | U | Dept2 | 30K | S |
| Sam | S | Dept2 | 20K | S |

*Figure 2.41* EMPLOYEE: an example of a multilevel relation.

| Name | KC | Department | Salary | TC |
|---|---|---|---|---|
| Bob | U | Dept1 | 10K | U |
| Ann | U | Dept2 | 20K | C |
| Sam | S | Dept2 | 20K | S |

*Figure 2.42* EMPLOYEE: an example of a multilevel relation.

For instance, consider the multilevel relation illustrated in Figure 2.37 and consider a *U*-user requires the following operation:

```
DELETE
FROM Employee
WHERE Name = "Ann"
BELIEVED BY Anyone
```

The meaning of the operation is that the *U*-user no longer believes that Employee "Ann" exists. The result of the operation is illustrated in Figure 2.42.

## 2.13 The lattice model for flow control

The models considered so far, particularly those adopting discretionary policies, are mainly oriented to control of direct access to information rather than to control of information flow in the system. Lack of control on information flow would make it possible for a subject *s*, who is prevented from reading information from an object, to get this information by collaborating with users who are authorized to access the object, for example to obtain copies of the object.

A requirement of secure flow is that users are not only unable to directly read data they are not authorized for, but also unable to indirectly access such data via other system users or objects.

The lattice model for flow control, proposed by Denning (1975, 1976, 1982) takes into account information flows implied by given sets of access rights. The model is centred around a mathematical structure (a lattice) to formulate the requirements needed for secure information flows. The model is formulated on the basis of 'flow relations' stating allowed information flows in the system. The model was developed to permit the expression of security requirements of existing systems, to support the design of flow control mechanisms and to construct computer-supported programs for certification of secure flow.

The flow relations are expressed by organizing information into classes, and by indicating secure flows among these classes.

### 2.13.1 Formal definition

A model for information flow *FM* is formally defined by the 5-tuple:

$$FM = \langle N, P, SC, \oplus, \rightarrow \rangle$$

where:

- $N = \{a, b, \ldots\}$ is a set of *objects* containing information. Objects in $N$ are both logical structures (files, file records, or program variables) and physical structures (memory locations, address/instruction registers), depending on the control level. System users can also be regarded as objects.
- $P = \{p, q, \ldots\}$ is a set of *processes*. Processes are the active entities accessing the objects, thus responsible for all information flows.
- $SC = \{A, B, \ldots\}$ is a set of *security classes* corresponding to disjoint information classes. These comprise the concepts of **classifications**, **security categories** and **need-to-know**. Each object $a$ in the system is assigned an access class, denoted by $\underline{a}$, specifying the security class of information in $a$.

  An object may be linked to a class via a *static or a dynamic binding*. In the first case, the security class assigned to an object will be fixed all along the object life cycle. In the second case, the security class may change according to the object contents.

  Users may also be assigned a security class, the 'clearance'. This is a fixed class (static link) that cannot be modified. Each process $p$ may be assigned a security class, denoted by $\underline{p}$, derived either from the clearance of the user holding the process, or from the history of the security classes of the objects accessed by $p$.
- $\oplus$ is a binary operator for *class combination*. It enjoys the associative and commutative properties. Given any two operand classes, $\underline{a}$ and $\underline{b}$, the $\oplus$ operator indicates the class that must be assigned to the result of any binary function $f$ applied to values from the $\underline{a}$ and $\underline{b}$ classes. The repeated application of the operator leads to the immediate definition of its extension to $n$ elements. Therefore, $\underline{a}_1 \oplus a_2 \ldots \oplus \underline{a}_n$ indicates the class to be assigned to the result of an $n$-ary function $f$ applied to objects $a_1, a_2 \ldots, a_n$. It is assumed that the $\oplus$ operator is independent of the function used to combine values.

  The set of security classes is closed under the $\oplus$ operator, meaning that, given two classes $a$ and $b$, it is:

  $\underline{a}$ and $\underline{b} \in SC \Rightarrow \underline{a} \oplus \underline{b} \in SC$.
- $\rightarrow$ is a *flow relation* defined on pairs of security classes. Given two classes $\underline{a}$ and $\underline{b}$, the relation $\underline{a} \rightarrow \underline{b}$ is valid if, and only if, information in $\underline{a}$ is allowed to flow into $\underline{b}$. An information flow from $\underline{a}$ to $\underline{b}$ occurs when information associated with $\underline{a}$ affects the value of information associated with $\underline{b}$. This flow results from (sequences of) operations that cause information transfer from one object to another.

  Examples of such operations are: copies, assignments, I/O operations, parameter passing, message sending. The flow definition given in the lattice model includes only flows from legitimate and storage channels; covert channels are excluded.

### 2.13.2 Secure model definition

A flow model *FM* is secure if, and only if, no sequence of operations exists that can originate a flow that violates the '$\rightarrow$' relation. Therefore, if a value $f(a_1, a_2,\ldots,a_n)$ flows into an object $b$ which is statically linked to the security class $\underline{b}$, then the relation $\underline{a_1} \oplus \underline{a_2} \ldots \oplus \underline{a_n} \rightarrow \underline{b}$ must be verified.

If the value $f(a_1, a_2,\ldots, a_n)$ flows into a dynamically classified object $b$, then the class of $b$ must be updated, if necessary, so that the relation $\underline{a_1} \oplus \underline{a_2}\ldots \oplus \underline{a_n} \rightarrow \underline{b}$ is verified.

Assuming '$\rightarrow$' is transitive, the security of single operations implies the security of arbitrary sequences of operations.

### 2.13.3 Lattice derivation

The model requires permitted flows to be consistent, meaning that all flows implied by a permitted flow be allowed by the flow relation. For example, if both $\underline{a} \rightarrow \underline{b}$ and $\underline{b} \rightarrow \underline{c}$ are secure, then $\underline{a} \rightarrow \underline{c}$ is also secure.

This assumption is imperative, otherwise single secure operations could compromise the system security if combined together. Under the above hypothesis, the triple $\langle SC, \rightarrow, \oplus\rangle$ forms a **universally bounded lattice**.

A universally bounded lattice is a structure consisting of a finite set of elements, partially ordered, with least upper bound and greatest lower bound operators on the set.

$\langle SC, \rightarrow\rangle$ is a lattice because it satisfies the properties illustrated in the following.

(1) $\langle SC, \rightarrow\rangle$ is a *partially ordered set*. This occurs because the relation defined on $SC$ enjoys the properties of:

- *reflexivity*: $\forall \underline{a} \in SC$ it is $\underline{a} \rightarrow \underline{a}$. Reflexivity is implied by the hypothesis of consistency. Since the security of instruction $a{:=}a$ is trivial, inconsistency would occur if, for a class $\underline{a}$ in $SC$, $\underline{a} \rightarrow \underline{a}$ were not valid.
- *transitivity*: $\forall \underline{a}, \underline{b}, \underline{c} \in SC$: $\underline{a} \rightarrow \underline{b} \wedge \underline{b} \rightarrow \underline{c} \Rightarrow \underline{a} \rightarrow \underline{c}$. This also derives from the hypothesis of consistency. In fact, $\underline{a} \rightarrow \underline{b}$ implies that a value $x$ can move from $\underline{a}$ to $\underline{b}$, and consequently $x$ can indirectly flow from class $\underline{a}$ to class $\underline{c}$ passing through $\underline{b}$. Inconsistency would occur should $\underline{a} \rightarrow \underline{c}$ not be valid. The assumption of the transitivity implies that a sequence of operations is secure if each single operation is secure.
- *antisymmetricity:* $\forall \underline{a}, \underline{b} \in SC : \underline{a} \wedge \underline{b} \rightarrow \underline{a} \Rightarrow \underline{a} = \underline{b}$. Antisymmetricity derives from the hypothesis that classes are not redundant. In fact, the simultaneous validity of the relations $\underline{a} \rightarrow \underline{b}$ and $\underline{b} \rightarrow \underline{a}$ between the classes $\underline{a}$ and $\underline{b}$ implies that information in one class can flow into another; therefore one of them is not necessary.

(2) *SC* is finite. This requirement does not limit the model generality and applicability, since the limitation in the number of security classes is a property of all systems based on classifications.

(3) *SC* has a lower bound $L : L \,|\!\rightarrow A$ for all $A \in SC$. This assumption can be made without losing generality. In fact, any constant can be posed as *L* (Low). Even if constants must be shared among several classes, objects with class *L* need not necessarily exist.

(4) $\oplus$ is a least upper bound operator on *SC*. This is implied by the fact that, for each $\underline{a}, \underline{b}, \underline{c} \in SC$, the following two relations are satisfied:

- $\underline{a} \rightarrow \underline{a} \oplus \underline{b}$ and $\underline{b} \rightarrow \underline{a} \oplus \underline{b}$. These restrictions are posed for consistency. Should they not be satisfied, operands could not flow into a result generated from themselves, which is absurd. Besides, inconsistency would occur. For instance, $c := a + b$ might be allowed, while $c := a$ might not. This generates an inconsistency, since the last operation can be performed by executing the former with $b$=0.

Actually, if this restriction is not met, the inconsistency does not always hold, because information obtained from combining several values may be less sensitive than the values themselves. For example, a statistic is, generally, less sensitive than the single data items out of which it was calculated (see Chapter 5).

- $\underline{a} \rightarrow \underline{c}$ and $\underline{b} \rightarrow \underline{c} \Rightarrow \underline{a} \oplus \underline{b} \rightarrow \underline{c}$. If both the relations on the left-hand side of the implication hold, then information derived from the combination of $\underline{a}$ and $\underline{b}$ can be transferred into $\underline{c}$. Therefore the relation on the right-hand side of the implication is semantically implied and must be made explicit in the flow relation (all allowed flows must be made explicit).

  The example given in by Denning (1976) refers to the program fragment:

  $c_1 := a;$
  $c_2 := b;$
  $c := c_1 * c_2;$

  whose execution assigns to the variable $c$ the values in $a$ and $b$. Therefore, the flow $\underline{a} \oplus \underline{b} \rightarrow \underline{c}$ is semantically implied. Consistency requires that the flow relation reflects this. Therefore, $\forall \underline{a}, \underline{b} \in SC$, $\underline{a} \oplus \underline{b}$ is the least upper bound, called the *join* of $\underline{a}$ and $\underline{b}$. This assumption does not consider the problem of aggregation, namely the fact that sensitiveness in aggregated information may be higher than the sensitiveness of single information items. Moreover, this assumption does not consider the sensitiveness of the function that combines $\underline{a}$ and $\underline{b}$.

Given a security class *SC*, its least upper bound, *H* (High), is obtained as $H = \oplus SC$; the greatest lower bound, denoted by *L* (low), is obtained as $L = \oplus SC$. Therefore, the $\oplus$ operator is also a least upper bound operator, and a greatest lower bound operator on the security classes.

The values of the $\oplus$ operator applied to a set $X \in SC$ are the lower bound $L$, if $X$ is empty, and the least upper bound of the classes in $X$ otherwise.

Given a set $X = \{\underline{a}_1, \underline{a}_2, \ldots, \underline{a}_n\}$, then $\oplus X = \underline{a}_1 \oplus \underline{a}_2 \oplus \ldots \underline{a}_n$ .

Meeting the properties listed in 1 to 4 above implies the existence of a *greatest lower bound* operator on the security classes, denoted by $\otimes$. Given two security classes $\underline{a}$ and $\underline{b}$, it is $\underline{a} \otimes \underline{b} = \oplus L(\underline{a},\underline{b}) = \{\underline{c} \mid \underline{c} \rightarrow \underline{a} \wedge \underline{c} \rightarrow \underline{b}\}$.

Given a set $X \in SC$, let $\otimes X$ be $H$ (the highest class) if $X$ is empty, otherwise the greatest lower bound of the classes in X. Then, for $n > 1$ and $X = \{\underline{b}_1, \ldots, \underline{b}_n\}$, $\otimes X = b_1 \otimes \ldots \otimes b_n$; moreover, $\underline{a} \rightarrow \underline{b}_i$ $(1 \leq i \leq n)$ if, and only if, $\underline{a} \rightarrow \otimes X$, or $\underline{a} \rightarrow \underline{b}_1 \otimes \ldots \underline{b}_n$.

The value of the expression $\oplus X$ is $H$ (least upper bound) if $X$ is empty, otherwise it is the greatest lower bound of the classes belonging to X.

Figures 2.43 and 2.44 show two sample lattices in terms of description and representation.

It is interesting to show how the classifications of multilevel models can be represented by a lattice. For example, given a set of security levels, defined on the set of security classes C of the Bell–LaPadula model, and on a set of categories S, the lattice is described by:

(C1, S1) $\leq$ (C2,S2) $\Leftrightarrow$ C1 $\leq$ C2, S1 $\subset$ S2
(C1, S1) $\oplus$ (C2, S2) = (*max* (C1,C2), S1 $\cup$ S2)
(C1, S1) $\otimes$ (C2, S2) = (*min* (C1,C2), S1 $\cap$ S2)
$L$ = (Unclassified, {})
$H$ = (Top Secret, S).

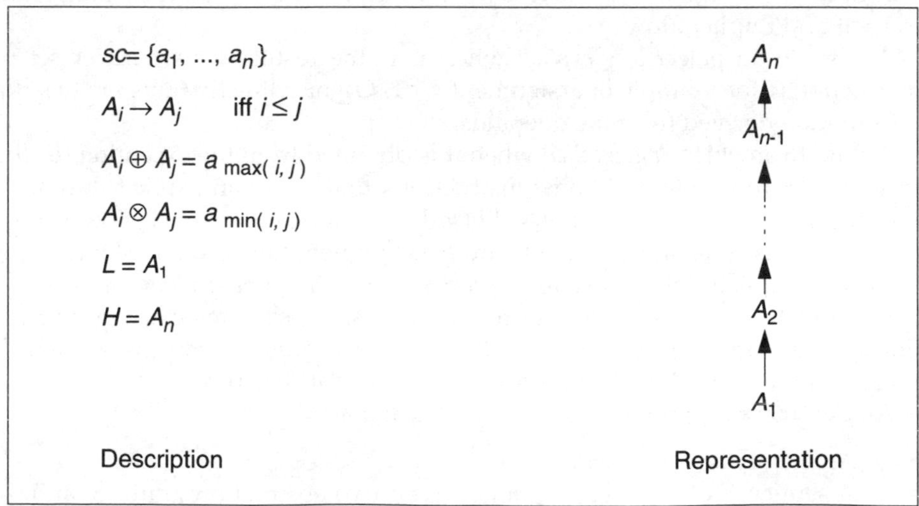


*Figure 2.43* Ordered linear lattice.

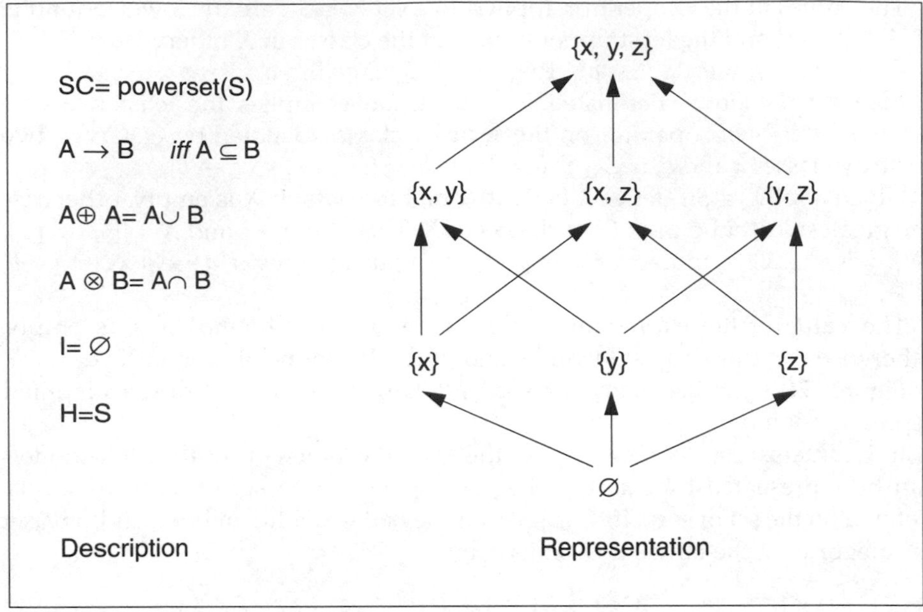


*Figure 2.44* Lattice of the subsets of $S = \{x, y, z\}$

## 2.13.4 Implicit and explicit flow

By applying the lattice model for flow control, the analysis of all information flows existing in a program can be complex, since not all the flows in a program are explicitly specified. For this reason, the model introduces the definitions of explicit and implicit flow.

A flow to an object $b$ is *explicit* when it is the result of a whatever set of instructions ( for example of assignment, or I/O) that directly transfers to $b$ the information derived from the operands.

A flow to an object $b$ is *implicit* when it is obtained from the execution (or the missed execution) of conditional instructions that cause an explicit flow to $b$. For instance, the instruction *if* $a = 0$ *then* $b := c$ causes an explicit flow from $c$ to $b$ when $a$ is null, and hence when the assignment is executed. Moreover, it causes an implicit flow from $a$ to $b$ independent of $a$=0 being true.

In order to specify the security requirements of programs causing implicit flows, an abstract representation of the programs must be considered, which preserves the flows (but not necessarily the original structures).

An **abstract program** $S$ is recursively defined as:

- An elementary instruction;
- A sequence of abstract programs: given two abstract programs $S_1$ and $S_2$, '$S = S_1 ; S_2$' is an abstract program;
- A conditional structure where the value of an $n$-valued variable $c$ affects the selection among alternative abstract programs.

Given $n$ abstract programs $S_1, S_2, \ldots, S_n$ and an $n$-valued variable $c$ such that $S = c: S_1, S_2, \ldots, S_n$ is an abstract program, where "$c : S_1, S_2, \ldots, S_n$" indicates the conditional instruction determining the program that must be executed on the basis of the value of the variable $c$.

For example, "$c{:}S_1$" may represent the instruction "`if c then S1`" or the instruction "`while c do S1`"; "`c:S1, S2`" may represent the instruction "`if c then S1 else S2`" or the instruction "`do case c of S1; S2`".

For each type of abstract program, the conditions that must be satisfied to have a **secure abstract program** are as follows.

- An elementary instruction $S$ is secure if any explicit flow caused by $S$ is secure. In particular, if $S$ writes in an object $b$ a value derived from objects $a_1, a_2, \ldots, a_n$, then the relation $\underline{a_1} \oplus \ldots \underline{a_n} \rightarrow \underline{b}$ holds after executing $S$. If the object $b$ is dynamically bounded to its security class, it may be necessary to modify its class after executing $S$.
- A sequence "$S = S_1{:}S_2$" is secure if $S_1$ and $S_2$ are each secure. This assumption is implied by the transitivity of the flow relation.
- A conditional structure "$S = c{:}S_1, S_2, \ldots, S_n$ " is secure if each $S_k$ is secure and all implicit flows from $c$ are secure. In particular, $b_1, b_2, \ldots b_n$ are the objects where $S$ specifies explicit flow (for each $b_i$, there is an operation in at least one $S_k$ causing an explicit flow into $b_i$). The implicit flow is secure if $\underline{c} \rightarrow \underline{b_i}$ for $i = 1, \ldots, n$, (namely, if $\underline{c} \rightarrow \underline{b_1} \otimes \underline{b_2} \otimes \ldots \underline{b_n}$, after executing $S$. If $b_i$ is dynamically linked to its security class, then it may be necessary to modify its class so that $b_i := \underline{b_i} \oplus \underline{c}$.

## 2.14 Discussion on mandatory models

The advantages of mandatory policies derive basically from their suitability to certain kinds of environment where the users and objects can be classified. Moreover, they provide a high level of certification for security, being based on unforgeable labels. Mandatory control models and flow control models allow one to track the flow of information, therefore providing some kind of protection in the face of the Trojan Horse problem (see 2.6, the discussion on discretionary models). With reference to the example of Figure 2.18, if a mandatory policy or an information flow policy is applied, files $f_1$ and $f_2$, which have different protection requirements, will have a different classification level. Thus, if the classification of program $P$ (that is, of the user running the program) is such that the program can read file $f_1$, $P$ will not be able to write $f_2$. The write operation will be therefore blocked by the reference monitor enforcing the mandatory policy (see Chapter 3 for an explanation of the reference monitor).

However, the mandatory access control policies have the drawback of being too rigid and therefore unapplicable to some environments. In particular, it is not always possible to assign clearances to users of a commercial information system or to assign sensitivity levels to data. However, the current trend is to build security models that integrate mandatory and discretionary control policies. One example of this is the Sea View model. Other examples are some emerging DBMS models and technologies that will be illustrated in Chapters 4 and 7.

Some work has been performed on extending discretionary access control models with a form of access constraints which resemble the mandatory policy approach. Most of this work has been specifically aimed at eliminating, or at least limiting, the vulnerability of the discretionary control to Trojan Horses (Walter *et al.*, 1974; Boebert and Ferguson, 1985; Karger, 1987). Walter *et al.* (1974) propose the application of a strict need-to-know policy for limiting information flow during process execution in the operating system environment. A process is allowed to copy information from one object to another only if the set of users allowed to read the second object is a subset of the set of users allowed to read the first object.

Another approach, proposed by Karger (1987), controls the effects of Trojan Horses in discretionary systems by limiting the files accessible by the application programs on the basis of some knowledge on the program themselves. The control requires the specification, for each application program to be controlled, of name patterns describing the objects to be accessed by an application. All accesses required by an application are mediated by a message checker. The message checker compares the name of the object to be accessed against the pattern specified for the application. If the object's name satisfies the pattern, the access is granted, otherwise the user running the program is queried about the access requested. For example, a Fortran compiler can have as input only files whose name ends with '.for' and can only create and write into files whose name ends with '.obj' or '.lis'. Therefore, if the compiler tries to access files not satisfying these name constraints, an exception is raised.

Bertino *et al.* (1993) propose the use of a strict need-to-know policy for overcoming the vulnerability of discretionary control policies in object-oriented systems. The fact that the status of objects can only be accessed by sending messages to the objects makes information flow in such systems have a concrete and natural embodiment in the form of messages and their replies. As a result, information flow can be controlled by mediating the transmission of messages exchanged between objects. The satisfaction of the strict need-to-know policy ensures that no information is leaked to objects accessible by users who do not have the necessary clearance. The model allows for different options in the application of the policy, therefore making the policy more flexible and adaptable to the specific situations.

Other research efforts have been aimed at extending the discretionary access control with forms of access constraints which cannot be enforced within discretionary authorization models (Stoughton, 1981; Graubart, 1989; McCollum *et al.*, 1990). McCollum *et al.*, (1990) propose a new form of access control which allows the enforcement of control on the flow of information in the system. The control allows the owner of a file to retain control on the dissemination of the information contained in the file. The approach consists of associating a data object with an access control list ,which is propagated, through subject and object labels, to all objects into which the content of the data object may flow. A similar approach has been proposed by Stoughton (1981). In this proposal, each object is associated with two protection attributes: the current access and the potential access. The current access attribute describes what can be done by whom on the object. The potential access attribute describes what can be done by whom to the information in the object, information that, in the future, may be contained in any object. Hence, potential access provides a means of propagating possible access restrictions to the information once it has been released.

## References


Ammann P.E. and Sandhu R.S. (1991). Safety analysis for the Extended Schematic Protection Model. In *Proc. IEEE Symp Security and Privacy*, Oakland, CA, May 1991

Ammann P.E. and Sandhu R.S. (1992). The Extended Schematic Protection Model. *The Journal of Computer Security,* **1**(3, 4)

ANSI/X3/SPARC (1977). DBMS framework report of the study group on database management systems (Tsichritzis D. and Klug A., eds.) *AFIPS Press*

Bell D.E. and La Padula L.J. (1973). Secure computer systems: mathematical foundations. *ESD-TR-73-278*, vol. 1-2, ESD/AFSC, Hanscom AFB, Bedford, MA, November 1973 (MTR-2547, vol. 1-2, MITRE Corp., Bedford, MA)

Bell D. E. and La Padula L. J. (1974a). Secure computer systems: a refinement of the mathematical model. *Technical Report ESD-TR-73-278*, vol. 3, ESD/AFSC, Hanscom AFB, Bedford, MA, April 1974 (MTR-2547, vol. 3, MITRE Corp., Bedford, MA)

Bell D.E. and La Padula L.J. (1974b). Secure computer systems: mathematical foundations and model. *Technical Report M74-244,* The MITRE Corp., Bedford, MA

Bell D.E. and La Padula L.J. (1975). Secure computer systems: unified exposition and Multics interpretation. The MITRE Corp., Bedford, MA

Bertino E., Samarati P. and Jajodia S. (1993.) High assurance discretionary access control in object bases. In *Proc. First ACM Conf. on Computer and Communications Security,* Fairfax, VA, November 1993

Biba K. J. (1977). Integrity considerations for secure computer systems. *ESD-TR-76-372*, ESD/AFSC, Hanscom AFB, Bedford, MA, April 1977 (The MITRE Corp., MTR-3153)

Boebert W.E. and Ferguson C.T. (1985). A partial solution to the discretionary Trojan Horse problem. In *Proc. of the 8th Nat. Computer Security Conf,* Gaithersburg, MD, October 1985

Bussolati U. and Martella G. (1981). Access control and management in multi-level database models. *Trends in Information Processing Systems*. Springer Verlag

Bussolati U., Fugini M.G. and G. Martella. (1983). A conceptual framework for security system design. In *Proc. 9th IFIP World Conf.,* Paris, September 1983

Conway R.W., Maxwell W.L. and Morgan H.L. (1972). On the implementation of security measures in information systems. *Comm. ACM*, **15** (4)

Denning D.E. (1975). Secure information flow in computer systems. *PhD Thesis*, University of Purdue

Denning D.E. (1976). A lattice model of secure information flow. *Comm. ACM*, **19** (5)

Denning D.E. (1982). *Cryptography and Data Security*. Addison-Wesley

Denning D.E. (1985). Commutative filters for reducing inference threats in multilevel database systems. In *Proc. IEEE Symp. on Security and Privacy*, Oakland, CA April, 1985

Denning D.E. (1987). Secure distributed data views: the Sea View formal security model. *Technical Report A003* SRI International

Denning D.E. (1988). Lessons learned from modelling a secure multilevel relational database system. In *Database Security: Status and Prospects* (Landwehr C. E., ed.) Elsevier (North-Holland)

Denning D.E. *et al.* (1986). Secure distributed data view: security policy and interpretation for class A1 multilevel secure relational database system. *Technical Report A002* SRI International

Denning D.E. *et al.* (1987). Views for multilevel database security. *IEEE Trans. Software Eng.* **13** (2)

Denning D.E. *et al.* (1988). The Sea View security model. In *Proc. IEEE Symp. on Security and Privacy*, Oakland, CA, April 1988

Dion L.C. (1981). A complete protection model. In *Proc. IEEE Symp. on Security and Privacy*, Oakland, CA, April 1981

Feiertag R.J., Levitt K.N. and Robinson L. (1987). Proving multilevel security of a system design. In *Proc. 6th ACM Symp. on Operating System Principles*

Fugini M.G. and Martella G. (1984). ACTEN: a conceptual model for security system design. *Computers & Security*, Elsevier (North-Holland), **3**(3)

Fugini M.G. and Martella G. (1988). A Petri net model of access control mechanisms. *Information Systems*, Pergamon Press, **13**(1)

Fugini M.G., Bellinzona R. and Martella G. (1991). An extension to Unix protection mechanims for flexible resource sharing. *Information Systems*, Pergamon Press, **16** (5)

Graham G.S. and Denning P.J. (1972). Protection – principles and practice. In *Proc. Spring Joint. Comp. Conf*, **40** *AFIPS Press*

Graubart R. (1989). On the need for a third form of access control. In *Proc. 12th Nat. Computer Security Conf.* Gaithersburg, MD, October 1989

Harrison M. A., Ruzzo W. L. and Ullman J. D. (1976). Protection in operating systems. *Comm. ACM*, **19**(8)

Hinke T.H. and Schaefer M. (1975). Secure data management system. *Technical Report RADC-TR-75-266*, System Development Corporation

Jajodia S. and Sandhu R. (1990). Polyinstantiation integrity in multilevel relations. In *Proc. IEEE Symp. on Security and Privacy*, Oakland, CA, May 1990

Jajodia S. and Sandhu R. (1991a). Toward a multilevel relational data model. In *Proc. ACM-SIGMOD Conf.*, Denver, CO, May 1991

Jajodia S. and Sandhu R. (1991b). Enforcing primary key requirements in multilevel relations. In *Proc. 4th RADC Workshop on Multilevel Database Security*, Little Compton, Rhode Island, April 1991

Jones A.K. (1978). Protection mechanism models: their usefulness. In *Foundations of Secure Computation* (Lipton R.J., Jones A.K., Dobkin D.P. and DeMillo R.A., eds.)

Jones A.K., Lipton R.J. and Snyder L. (1976). A linear time algorithm for deciding security. In *Proc. 17th Annual Symp. on Foundations of Computer Science*

Karger P.A., (1987). Limiting the damage potential of discretionary Trojan Horses. In *Proc. IEEE Symp. on Security and Privacy*, Oakland, CA, May 1987

Lampson B.W. (1974). Protection. In *Proc. 5th Symp. on Information Sciences and Systems*, Princeton University, March 1971, reprinted in *Operating System Review*, **8**(1) January 1974

Landwer C.E. (1981). Formal models for computer security. *ACM Computing Surveys*, **13** (3)

Lockman A. and Minsky N. (1982). Unidirectional transport of rights and Take-Grant control. *IEEE Trans. on Software Engineering*, **8** (6)

Lunt T.F. and Hsieh D. (1991). Update semantics for a multilevel relational database. In *Database Security IV: Status and Prospects* (Jajodia S. and Landwehr C.E., eds.), North-Holland

McCollum C.J., Messing J.R. and Notargiacomo L. (1990). Beyond the pale of MAC and DAC – defining new forms of access control. In *Proc. IEEE Symp. on Security and Privacy*, Oakland CA, May 1990

McLean J. (1990). The specification and modelling of computer security. *IEEE Computer*, **23**(7)

Millen J.K. and Cerniglia C.M. (1984). Computer security models. *Technical Report n. MTR9531*, The MITRE Corporation, Bedford MA, September

Sandhu R.S. (1988). The schematic protection model: its definition and analysis for acyclic attenuating scheme. *Journal of ACM*, **35** (2)

Sandhu R.S. (1992a). Expressive power of the schematic protection model. *Journal of Computer Security*, **1**

Sandhu R.S. (1992b). The typed access matrix model. In *Proc. IEEE Symposium on Security and Privacy*, Oakland CA, April 1992

Sandhu R. and Jajodia S. (1991). Honest databases that can keep secrets. In *Proc. 14th NIST-NCSC National Computer Security Conference*, Washington DC, October 1991

Sandhu R. and Jajodia S. (1992a). Eliminating polyinstantiation securely. *Computers & Security*, Elsevier (North-Holland), **11**

Sandhu R. and Jajodia S. (1992b). Polyinstantiation for cover stories. In *Proc. European Symposium on Research in Computer Security*, Toulouse, France, Springer-Verlag LNCS **648**

Sandhu R.S. and Share M.E. (1986). Some owner-based scheme with dynamic groups in schematic protection model. In *Proc. IEEE Symp. on Security and Privacy*, Oakland, CA, April 1986

Smith K. (1992) Managing rules in active databases, *PhD thesis* Department of Computer Science, University of Illinois at Urbana-Champaign

Smith K. and Winslett M. (1992). Entity modelling in the MLS relational model. In *Proc. VLDB Conf.*, Vancouver, British Columbia, Canada, 1992

Stoughton A. (1981). Access flow: a protection model which integrates access control and information flow. In *Proc. IEEE Symp. on Security and Privacy*, Oakland CA, May 1981.

Walter K.G., Ogden W.F., Rounds W.C., Bradshaw F.T., Ames S.R. and Sumaway D.G. (1974). Primitive models for computer security. *Technical. Report ESD-TR-4-117*, Case Western Reserve University, Cleveland OH, January 1974

Winslett M., Smith K. and Qian X. (1994). Formal query languages for secure relational databases. To appear in *ACM-Trans. on Database Systems*, 1994

Wood C., Summers R. C. and Fernandez E. B. (1979). Authorization in multilevel database models. *Information Systems*, Pergamon Press, **4**(2)

# 3 Basic security mechanisms and software

## 3.1 Introduction

A security model defines the set of 'abstract' authorized states of a security system; if the system can exist exclusively in these states, it can be defined as secure, according to the principles of that model. Compliance between physical states of a system and authorized states of a model is ensured by the *security mechanisms*: that is, by the hardware and software tools implementing the authorization rules stated by the model. The security mechanisms provided to a processing system and to its applications are based firstly on the security functions available in its Operating System (OS). Security in OSs emerged as a research area in the early 1970s (Needham, 1973), and since then has produced sound results (see, for example, Lampson, 1974; Harrison *et al.*, 1976; Lampson *et al.*, 1977; Hsiao and Kerr, 1978). A set of basic security mechanisms is available both for classified/trusted systems and for commercial OSs (see Landwehr, 1983, for an overview); they constitute the grounds for database security. However, considering database applications, the OS-provided protection functions prove mostly insufficient to support database security policies, owing to the different kind of resources to be protected in a database (Spooner and Gudes, 1984). The inadequacy of security functionalities at the usual OS level and the need to meet the emerging security standard proposals have led to the extension of the OS security mechanism, either by the design of secure OSs and/or by using additional special-purpose security software.

This chapter first describes the resource protection mechanisms provided at the OS level. Next, the security functions of common OSs are described. Then, the functionalities of special-purpose security software are illustrated, and finally, enhancements to the basic OS security mechanisms and the design of secure OSs are described, according to the various security standards, which are also presented.

### 3.1.1 Operating systems concepts

Operating systems are usually viewed as hierarchies of abstractions of functions, starting from the lowest level (the hardware level) of the physical connections and electronic components: this level provides primitive functions (Silberschatz *et al.*, 1991).

Above the hardware level, other abstraction levels of the system functions are defined, up to the application level which supplies a view of the system related to its use. Each level manages and controls its own resources through its own primitives; the implementation of the primitive instructions of a level is delegated to programs belonging to lower levels. Each level is associated with a virtual machine that operates on the resources and through the language of the level.

The typical architecture of a computing system is composed of a hardware machine, a firmware machine, an assembler machine, an OS and a set of applications (Figure 3.1). The OS, located between the applications and the machine levels, plays the role of an interface between the application programs and the system resources.

The OS manages all the system resources (memory, files, I/O devices, processors), and optimizes the availability of these resources for the different application programs. The **OS functions** can be summarized as follows:

- *Process and processor management*. This function is supplied by the OS *kernel*, which supports concurrent processes of both user and system with the goal of optimizing the system performance and the usage rate of system resources.
- *Resource management*. The OS allocates the system resources (memory, files, I/O devices) to the applications requesting them for their tasks. The OS solves possible conflicts among different programs requesting the use of the same resources, according to criteria of system efficiency and of processing speed optimization. For this purpose, the OS exploits the kernel functions.

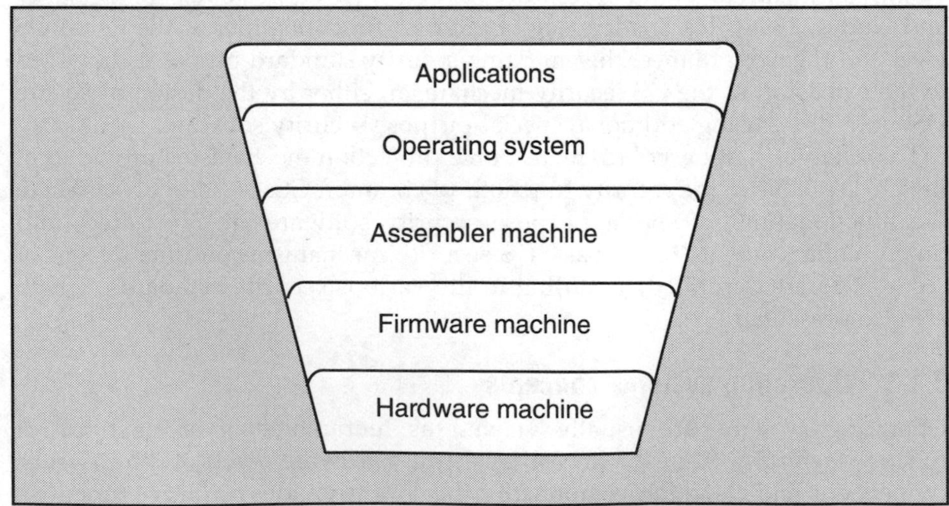


*Figure 3.1* Levels of a processing system.

- *Supervision.* In its function as supervisor, an OS directly interfaces the application programs, supporting the implementation of the different application languages (by supplying a virtual machine) and scheduling the processes corresponding to the running application programs. The OS also controls the running programs: it avoids any improper use of the system resources, and prevents any fraudulent or accidental interference, either among memory areas assigned to programs, or between areas assigned to programs and the OS memory area.

OSs have been continuously evolving, starting from simple programs for control transfer among programs, to complex systems supporting multitasking, real-time processing, multiprocessor and distributed architectures. According to the type of system, resource management by the OS can pursue different purposes and policies bound to the application category and to the system architecture.

Generally, an OS provides some **data protection functions**. In a processing system, data is contained in a resource (for example, memory, file, I/O device); for an OS, data protection means checking that only authorized users access the resource (object) containing the data. To illustrate the *functions* of an OS in supporting security, Figure 3.2 shows the basic phases of a user work session in a multi-user system. The user activity starts with a connection request to the system *(login phase):* users are identified uniquely by the OS via identification and authentication techniques. Once this phase is passed successfully, the user can execute his activities: for example, working on files *(file system management)*, or running programs *(program execution)*. Program execution needs a reserved area in primary memory for that program; this must be protected from interference by other programs, and from outside *(memory protection)*. A running program can execute input and output operations, which are managed by the OS *(I/O management)*. Owing to the presence of different users, an OS supports concurrent resource access by programs, thus solving possible conflicts *(resource allocation, access control to resources)*. Run-time errors cause the OS to terminate the program *(unsuccessful termination)* in order to limit possible damage to the system or to other user programs *(error detection and management)*. Furthermore, an OS keeps a track of all the operations executed by the user (and by all users) on the system resources *(accounting)*, possibly filling in an audit trace *(auditing)*. Upon termination of his activities, the user will close his work session and be disconnected from the system *(logoff phase)*.

Besides service functions (such as program execution, file management, I/O operations, resource allocation, error detection and management), some OS functions are explicitly oriented to security support, namely:

- User identification/authentication
- Memory protection
- Access control to resources
- Flow control
- Auditing.

The first four functions are examined in detail in this chapter. Auditing is treated extensively in Chapter 6.

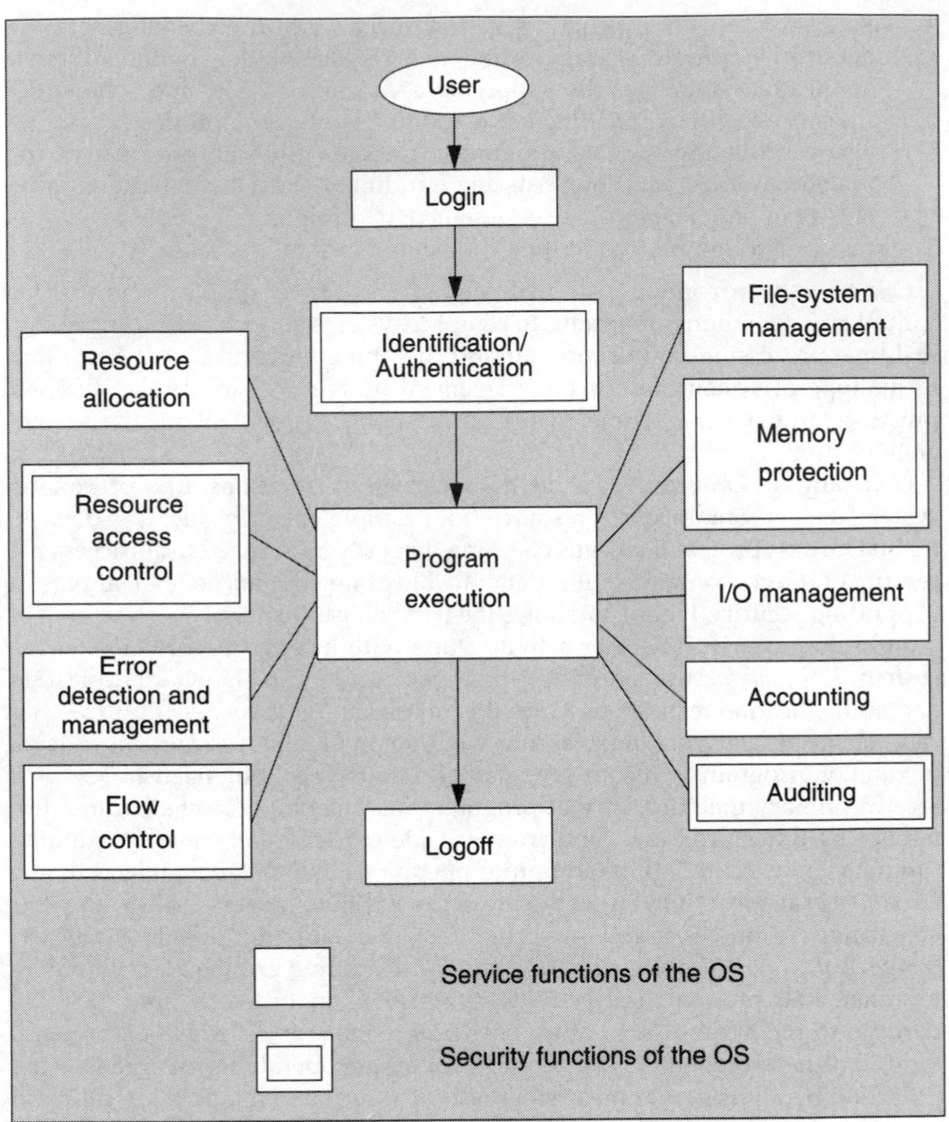


*Figure 3.2* User work session.

## 3.2 User identification/authentication

The premise for a security system is the correct identification of users; to this purpose, authentication mechanisms validate the user identity through some object, or information, known to the user, through something owned by the user, or through a combination of these modes. Authentication systems based on *information known to the user* are:

- *Password-based systems.* A user is identified through a secret string (password) known exclusively by this user and by the system.
- *Query-answer-based systems.* A user is identified on the basis of his or her answering a set of questions posed by the system. Questions are specific for each user and, generally, based on mathematical functions to be computed by the system after receiving entry values from the user. Sample functions are:
  - polynomial functions (the value of a variable $x$ is provided by the system) whose result (for example, $f(x) = x^3 + x^2 - x + 4$) is to be computed by the user;
  - functions based on the transformation of strings of characters: the system gives the user a string of characters to be changed according to a known scheme (for example, $f(a_1a_2a_3a_4a_5) = a_4a_3a_5a_2a_1$);
  - functions based on simple cryptographic algorithms, where a crypto value is given by the system: the user deciphers and uses it to compute a function, then enciphers the result, for example, $f(E(x)) = E(D(E(x))^2)$.
- *Double authentication systems (hand-shaking),* where the system introduces itself to the user, and the user authenticates himself back to the system. Authentication by the system occurs through information known only to the user (for example, date, time, and code of the last work session). User authentication is password based.

Authentication systems based on *information owned by the user* are basically *card-based systems*: a magnetic card contains a bar or magnetic strip code, or a microprocessor. Authentication occurs upon acceptance of the card inserted in a proper reader, sometimes coupled with a secret code.

Authentication systems based on *'something a user is'* are:

- *Computerized facsimile systems.* The user image is stored; identification occurs by matching the person with his or her stored image shown on the screen;
- *Fingerprint-based systems.* Identification is the result of a match between the user's fingerprints with the stored ones;
- *Hand-pressure systems.* Identification is made based on the user pressure in writing his or her signature on a suitable device;
- *Voice-recognition-based systems.* The user's voice is matched against its stored version;
- *Retinal features-based systems.* Identification is made by examining the features of the user's retina.

This last set of authentication systems has a higher degree of complexity than the previous ones because of the intricacies of the *matching* operations between the stored features of an individual and the actual ones. They incur a higher probability of denial to authorized users. Costs are also a relevant consideration, and the technologies involved (voice/image recognition) make these systems expensive. Therefore, their use is only appropriate in highly security-critical environments.

Not all the mechanisms mentioned are implemented at the OS level: password-based mechanisms are the most common ones and we will examine these in detail next.

### 3.2.1 Password-based authentication

A password is a secret string of characters (numerical and alphanumerical), which is known only to its owner (a system user) and the system; hence, the system is enabled to identify a user uniquely upon password validation. Problems in the use of **passwords** depend on the **initial choice**, on the possible disclosure by malicious individuals with fraudulent purposes, and on password **management**.

Choosing a hard-to-detect password proves a serious issue: the use of trivial words as passwords makes an illegal disclosure a rather easy event. Analysis of various attacks on password secrecy has led to the formulation of criteria for the selection of passwords that are able to withstand such attacks and reduce the probability of their success. The basic criteria for 'secure' passwords are:

- Use at least eight characters, in general long passwords;
- Use both numerical and alphanumerical characters;
- Use both capital and small letters (if the system implements the difference);
- Use special keyboard symbols as well (for example, &, @, %);
- Concatenate two non-correlated words and cut off the resulting word to a length equal to $n-1$, where $n$ is the admitted length of the password, then insert a special symbol;
- Choose foreign words;
- Use keyboard character sequences that can easily be stored (for example, the last four characters of the second row; the letters in the third column of the keyboard, etc.);
- Choose terms related to one's hobby or sporting activities and concatenate them;
- Always choose easy-to-remember terms.

Some examples in Table 3.1 show the construction of passwords according to the above criteria.

Actions should be taken to focus the users' attention on the relevance of a careful choice of password, and of its correct use. In particular, users should:

- Choose their passwords bearing in mind the previous criteria;
- Memorize their own passwords, never write them;
- Never reveal their passwords;
- Change their passwords frequently and regularly.

Some systems automatically invalidate passwords upon an expiration period, thus forcing the users to modify them regularly.

**Table 3.1** Construction of secure passwords.

| First word | Second word | Special character | Resulting password |
|---|---|---|---|
| town | pick | _ | town_pi |
| brain | stormy | & | brain&sto |
| dog | hot | ! | hot!dog |
| domestic | chestnut | 2 | dom2ches |
| felix | soon | @ | fel@soon |

Regular alternations of the same passwords should be avoided: some systems automatically check and avoid this.

A password must be known only to its legal user and to the system; ownership of a password grants connection to a system and use of its resources. **Password disclosure**, therefore, should not occur.

Attempts can be made to detect valid passwords for fraudulent connections, for example by entering several combinations of characters (exhaustive attacks). To deter this type of attack, the number of password insertions can be limited (for example, three attempts). Users are then disabled, and should report to the security officer for password re-initialization.

Usually, a large number of passwords must be stored in a multi-user system for subsequent authentication operations. Therefore, passwords are stored in a file managed by the OS, where each user identifier has its associated password(s). Entered passwords are matched against stored ones for verification.

Valid passwords can also be discovered by reading the password file, which therefore needs high protection: storage of passwords in a memory area accessible only by the OS can be a solution, but it also means that all the OS modules are enabled to access the password file. Malicious users, taking advantage of erratic OS modules *(bugs* or *trapdoors),* could still access the contents of the password file. A further step is to have only some specific procedures accessing the password file (for example, the *login* procedure). Still, malicious individuals succeeding in reading the whole memory could also access the memory area containing the password file. A Trojan Horse in the login procedure of a system can record all the passwords used at login time (each time a user/system connection takes place).

Drawbacks of this type have been overcome in some systems by enciphering passwords through cryptographic algorithms (Denning, 1982). Upon creation, passwords are enciphered and stored in the password file which can be read by all users, but modified (insert, erase, update operations) only by the OS. Protection is achieved by choosing enciphering algorithms requiring complex and expensive deciphering operations, in terms of both time and computation.

If two users accidentally choose the same password, two identical enciphered texts would exist in the password file. As users know the clear text of their own password, both users might automatically know each other's password. Mechanisms are needed that implement code uniqueness of a password. For instance, a *salt-based* technique is used in UNIX (Wood and Kochan, 1985).

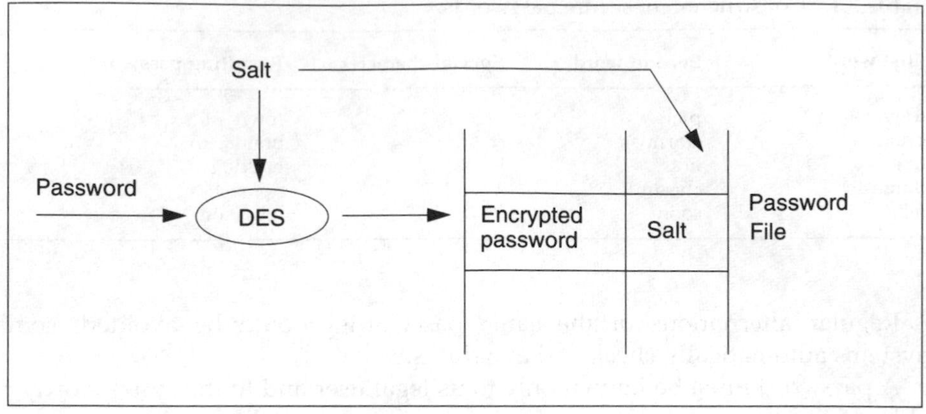


*Figure 3.3* Salt mechanisms.

A salt is a 12-bit number that is added as an extension to a password. Upon creation, a password is associated to its salt which is generated on the basis of the creation time and of the identifier of the running process (Figure 3.3). Since these two parameters usually differ from user to user, the uniqueness of passwords is ensured.

The DES (Data Encryption Standard) enciphering algorithm is applied in UNIX to the 'password/salt' combination; the result is stored in the password file together with its related salt. Each time a user inserts his password, this is combined with the stored salt, enciphering is performed, and the result is matched with the stored one (Figure 3.4). Thus, by employing a control system for accessing the password file and a cryptographic algorithm for enciphering its contents, the OS protection level increases against the risk of illegal password disclosure.

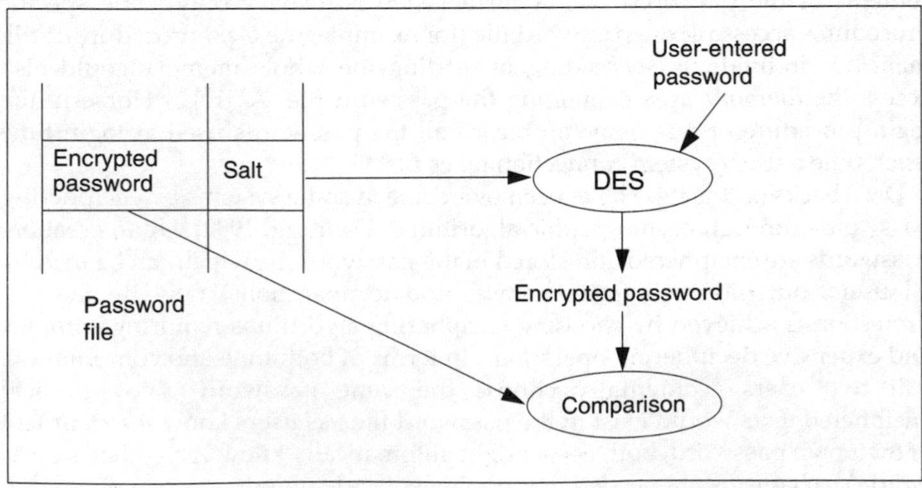


*Figure 3.4* Password creation and validation in UNIX.

In spite of all these measures, the risk of fraudulent intruders persists. Studies have shown that the illegal disclosure of passwords through repeated attempts is still feasible today, and with acceptable computation times, also due to the use of massive parallelism (several processors for the same program); these technologies, combined with a negligence in the selection and management of passwords, increase the exposure to intrusions.

## 3.3 Memory protection

In multiprogrammed environments, the primary memory of a system is partitioned and assigned to the data and programs of different users. This requires protection from mutual interference (among application programs, or among application and system programs). Moreover, the same resources need to be shared among different users. Various sharing levels exist, ranging from *no sharing* (complete isolation) to *uncontrolled sharing* (whatever access is allowed to whatever object). Intermediate levels of sharing can be chosen, such as *sharing of object copies*, where the users work on their own object copies while the master copy is periodically updated; or *sharing of original objects*, where a unique object copy is available to all users.

Usually, sharing involves originals of data and programs for space saving (unique object copy), and for time saving (no need of duplication or periodical updates of the copies for consistency maintenance). With a unique copy, the object state is always updated and consistent.

The implementation of a controlled sharing mechanism needs sophisticated protection at the OS level for management of issues relating to:

- *Concurrent access* (access queries for the same object, from different users, at the same time). Simultaneous work on the same object must be prevented by means of serialization operations.
- *Confinement* (for programs only). A program is said to be confined (Lampson, 1973) when it is prevented from copying its parameters. Thus, a shared program (for example, a text editor) is prevented from copying and transferring into system files confidential information from input data. Should this be possible, a program such as, for example, a text editor containing a Trojan Horse, could make data copied from the program invoked by this text editor accessible to unauthorized users. Shared programs must then be confined to prevent these types of threat.

The following types of *hardware mechanisms* for protection and controlled memory sharing are described here (Silberschatz and Peterson, 1983; Pfleeger, 1989):

- Fence address
- Relocation
- Bound registers (base/bound)
- Paging
- Segmentation.

### 3.3.1 Fence address

A *fence address* marks the bound between the memory area reserved to the OS (generally the lower memory region) and the memory area available for a user (Figure 3.5).

Assuming the OS is assigned the lower memory, a fence-address-based mechanism verifies that each address generated by a program refers to the higher region of the memory. Addresses generated by user programs are matched against the fence value: an address value higher than the fence value is a correct reference to the user area, whereas a lower value is incorrect: the program is terminated, and an error message is reported to the user (Figure 3.6).

A fence address can be specified as a constant, inserted directly in the hardware, or can be loaded into the *fence register*. In the first case, the fence address value is contained in a set of memory addresses; the OS is assigned a fixed memory area. The disadvantage is that the OS size might vary (an OS is a set of modifiable software programs): its memory area might become insufficient, or be partially unused.

The fence register solution stores the fence address in a register loaded by the OS through privileged instructions; the fence value can vary dynamically according to variations in the OS size (the new values are loaded into the register by the same OS). Addresses in the user programs are matched against the value in the fence register for validation.

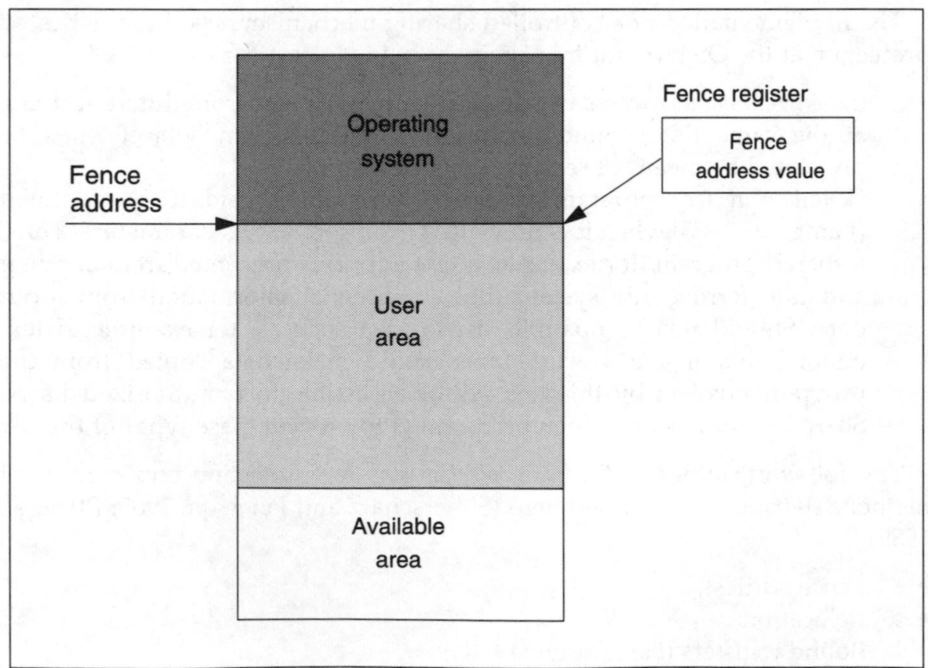


*Figure 3.5* Fence-based protection.

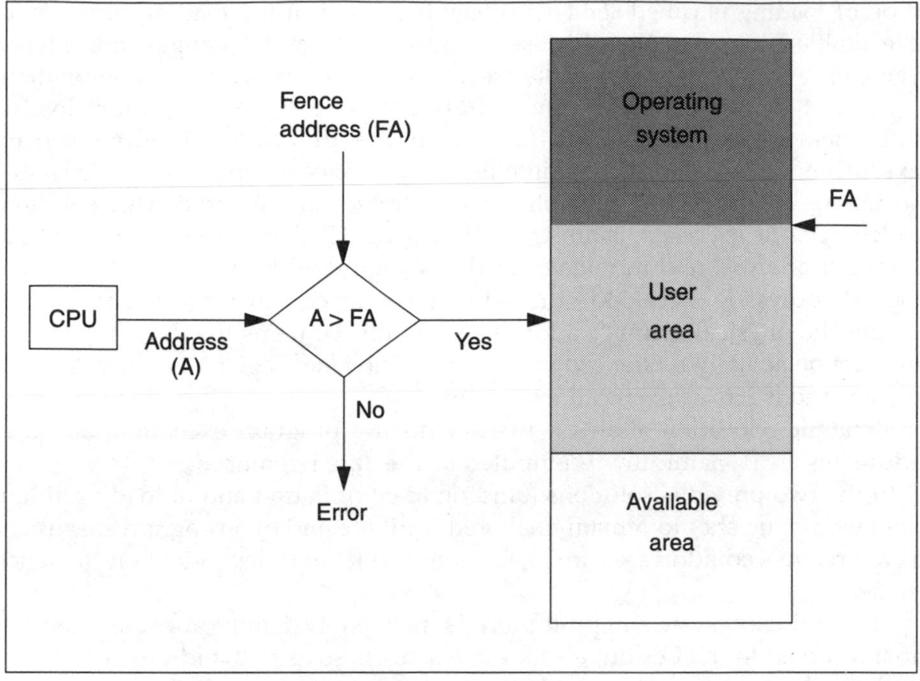


*Figure 3.6* Access to memory by fence address.

Variations in the fence value have consequences on program development. The logical addresses of an executable program progress from the 0 address onwards. Physically, the addresses in an executable program can be in absolute or (more frequently) in relocatable format.

### 3.3.2 Relocation

Assuming *K* is the value of the fence address, the physical address of a user program is obtained by adding *K* to the logical address. Modifications to the logical addresses of an executable program into physical memory addresses *(binding)* can occur at compilation time, at loading time or directly during program execution.

In the case of **binding** during **compilation**, addresses in an executable program are in *absolute format* which is computed starting from a specific memory location. The *loader program* loads the executable code into a precise memory area. Practically, the executable code starts from the address following the fence address. Changes to the fence value imply that all programs must be recompiled to generate new executable programs in absolute format.

When **binding** occurs **during program loading** into memory, for each instruction, the address values of a program are modified by adding the fence value to each address. Addresses in the object code are in *relocatable format*. This type of loading is called *static relocation*: the result of the loading phase is an executable program with addresses in absolute format. Changes to the fence value only require reloading of the executable programs, without recompilation.

In the two previous cases, the addresses of an executable program loaded into memory are in absolute format. In the third case, **binding during execution**, a program is loaded into memory in relocatable format. Relocatable addresses are translated into physical addresses at run time. This solution, called *dynamic relocation*, is illustrated in Figure 3.7. A program starts from the 0 logical address, and terminates at the $N$ logical address. At run time, each logical address $R$ is added to the value in the fence register (for example, $K$), giving the physical memory address $R + K$; this contains the data item or the instruction actually referenced by the CPU. The fence register is called the *base register* and it acts as a relocation register.

Dynamic relocation allows $K$ to vary during program execution; absolute addresses are dynamically recomputed as they are referenced.

In the two previous solutions (binding at compilation and at loading time), the fence value should remain unaltered until the end of a program execution, as the referenced addresses are in absolute format and dependent on the fence value.

In multi-user systems, protection is needed not only for the memory area reserved to the OS, but also for users' areas so as to avoid unauthorized/undesired accesses.

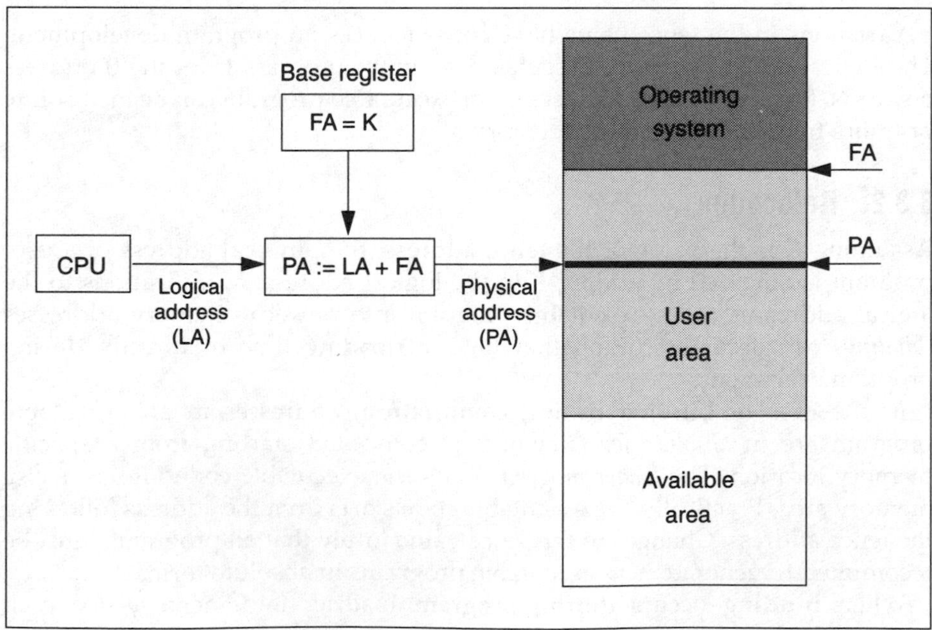


*Figure 3.7* Dynamic relocation.

### 3.3.3 Register-based protection

By this technique, a user's memory area is delimited by a pair of values, stored in proper registers, that mark the area bounds. Each user has an associated pair of registers. Bound values can be expressed in two different ways:

(1) *Bound registers.* Each program is assigned a memory area, delimited by a lower and an upper limit; two registers *(bound registers)* store these limits. Each address generated by the CPU is first matched against the lower limit and then, if accepted, against the upper limit. An address is accepted if it falls within the limits, otherwise the program is terminated for erroneous reference to memory (Figure 3.8). Bound registers support static relocation (at compilation or loading time) because matched addresses are physical addresses.

(2) *Base/limit registers.* For a user area, the start physical address and its limit are specified; the limit corresponds to the value of the largest logical address of a program. Base and limit values are stored respectively in the base and in the limit register. An address generated by the CPU is matched against the value contained in the limit register. If it is lower, the address is added to the base register, producing the physical memory address; if greater, the program will be terminated for incorrect reference to memory (Figure 3.9).

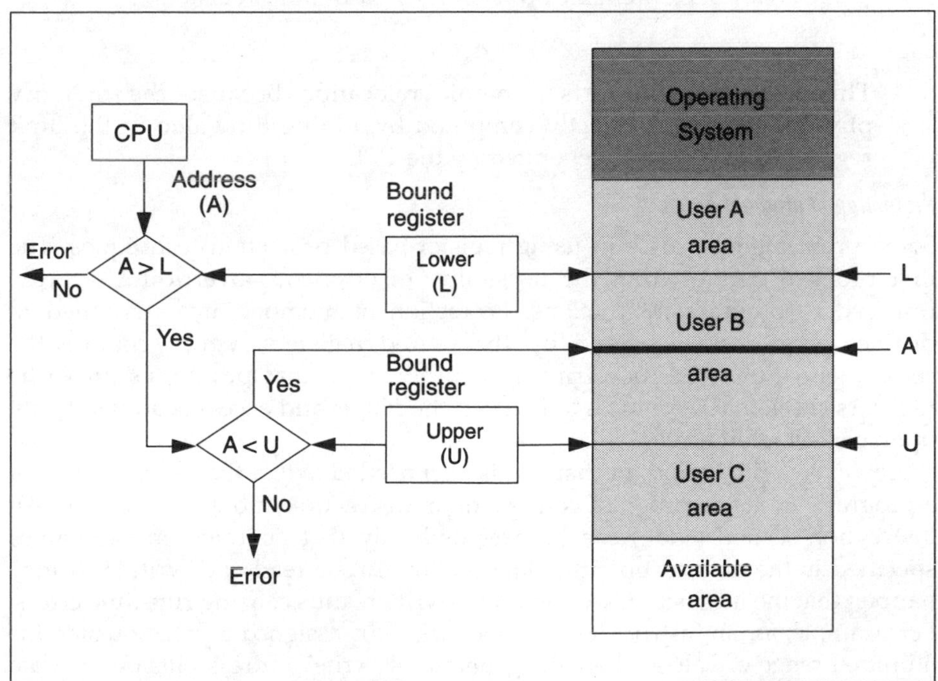


*Figure 3.8* Protection by bound registers.

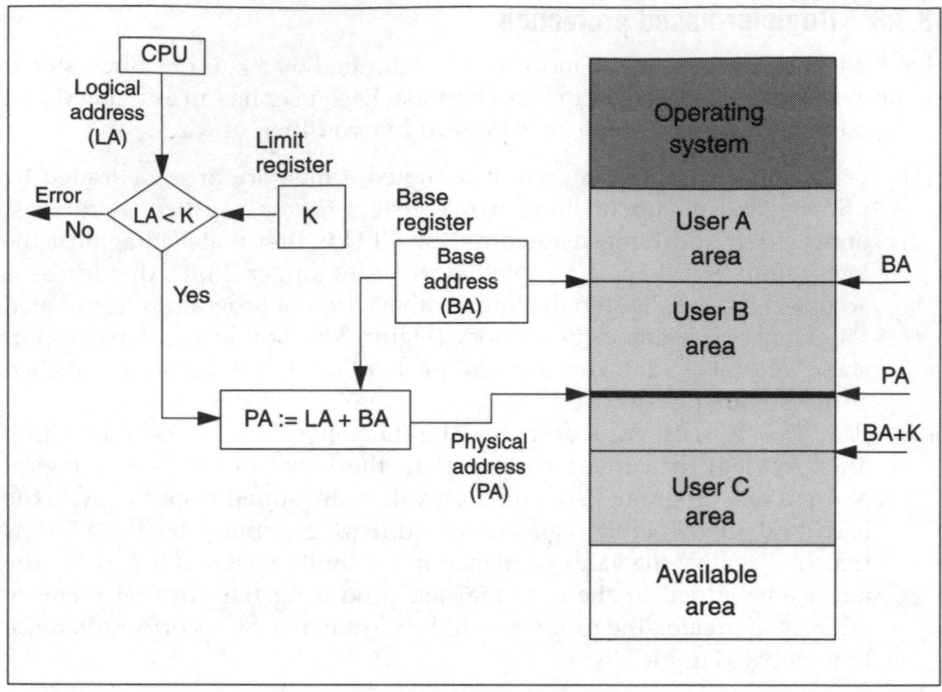


*Figure 3.9* Memory protection by base/limit registers.

This technique supports dynamic relocation because the memory physical address is directly computed by adding the value in the limit register to the address generated by the CPU.

***Protection of program areas***

Some problems may arise in using register-based protection techniques. The first problem derives from the possibility of erroneous overriding of areas reserved to program instructions. Protection of memory areas assigned to distinct programs is ensured by the bound registers, which confine the consequences of errors occurring in a program to that program's area (the registers check that references fall within the range, and access is allowed only upon correct reference).

However, a protection mechanism is also needed *within* the memory area of a program. In fact, a program consists of an instruction and a data section. An instruction section (code) can be executed only if it operates on the values specified in the data section; the data section can be read and written. It may happen that the instruction section is overwritten, thus causing run-time errors. For example, for an instruction where a variable is assigned a value outside the admitted range of values, the CPU generates a 'write' address outside the data area (for example, belonging to the code section of the program); hence, this section could be overwritten and improperly altered.

To prevent these types of error, data sections must be separated from instruction sections, and the operations allowed on each of them have to be defined. In particular, it must be stated that program instructions can only be executed (execute operation); data can be read and modified (read and write operation). Authorization checks on operations cannot rely solely on bound registers, which do not distinguish between code and data sections. If the generated address is correct, its contents can be accessed via any operations. The distinction between operations executable on the contents of a memory area (rights) can be implemented through mechanisms such as:

- Two pairs of registers
- Tagged architecture.

In the first case, the memory area reserved to a program is split into a code and a data section. The distinction between an instruction address (next instruction to be executed) and a data address (read/write a value) can be made by the CPU. Therefore, **two pairs of bound registers** can be used for code section control and for data section control respectively (Figure 3.10). The pair

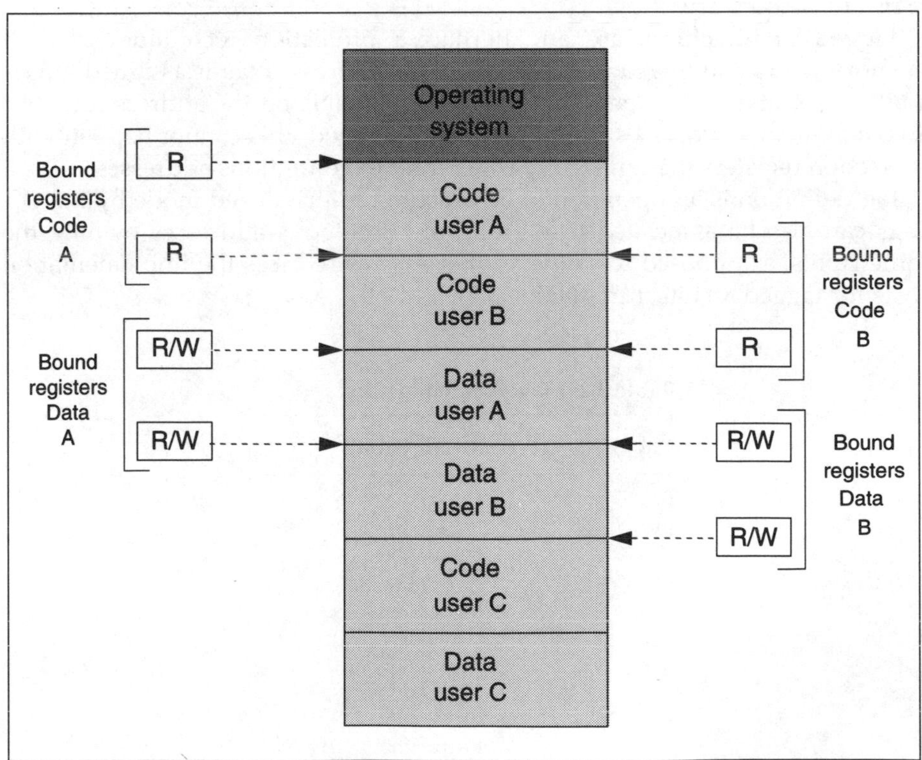


*Figure 3.10* Using two pairs of bound registers.

of registers for the code section is declared as *'read-only'*; thus, instructions cannot be modified. The pair of registers for the data section is declared as *'read/write'* and data here can be modified during program execution.

Two categories alone (data and instructions) are not sufficient to guarantee protection for all types of object inside a program. In addition to modifiable read/write data, other objects can be read-only data (for example, a constant). Following the same principles illustrated so far, a memory area reserved to a program could be divided into three sections: a code section, a modifiable data section and a read-only data section, each protected by a pair of registers.

Using more than two pairs of registers makes the selection of sections more complex. When referring to an item, the proper data section must be specified to identify the corresponding memory section (and consequently the register pair). The CPU has to specify the section for each memory reference, and this overloads the mechanism. Therefore, two pairs of protection registers are normally used, one for code and one for data.

Use of registers provides the whole memory with homogeneous protection: only the whole code section can be executed, only the whole data section can be read and written. In fact, registers provide a global protection: that is, they protect the whole contents of a memory section in the same mode. If a higher degree of protection is required, then a correspondingly higher number of registers is necessary.

**Tagged architectures** are an alternative protection technique: to each memory word, and therefore to each memory address, a tag is assigned: this is a bit set specifying the operations (rights) executable on the address contents. Two contiguous addresses can be differently tagged; this cannot happen with protection registers that uniformly cover a set of contiguous addresses.

Tag definition is an operation to be executed in privileged mode by the OS. Tags can also be associated to a group of contiguous addresses owning the same rights, as opposed to single addresses; this reduces the implementation costs for tagged architectures (Table 3.2).

**Table 3.2** Tagged architecture.

| Tag | Memory word |
|---|---|
| R | Data item |
| RW | Data item |
| X | Instruction |
| RW | Data item |
| X | Instruction |
| R | Data item |
| RW | Data item |
| X | Instruction |
| X | Instruction |
| X | Instruction |
| X | Instruction |
| X | Instruction |

***Sharing of memory areas***

A further issue in protection by bound registers involves different users sharing the same memory area. The same values (of addresses limiting the shared area) are stored in all the registers of these users. Problems arise when users are enabled to execute their operations on the contents of the shared area: as a matter of fact, a user can access the area contents in any mode, because, once the correct address has been checked, no control occurs on admitted operations by the bound registers. Sharing of utility programs/procedures (such as compilers or editors) necessitates measures of control on the operations executed on the shared code section in order to prevent write operations that could damage this code.

Two pairs of registers have proved a useful mechanism for controlled sharing, supporting separation between the code and data sections of a program: it is possible to share only the code section. The data section is reserved for single users, thus allowing different programs to use the same code with private data. Moreover, since the register pair controlling the code section is 'read-only', shared instructions cannot be modified by any user.

## 3.3.4 Paging

The paging technique is based on partitioning the physical and logical memory into fixed-size portions. For physical memory, these are called *frames*; for logical memory, they are called *pages* (Figure 3.11). The mechanism of mapping logical

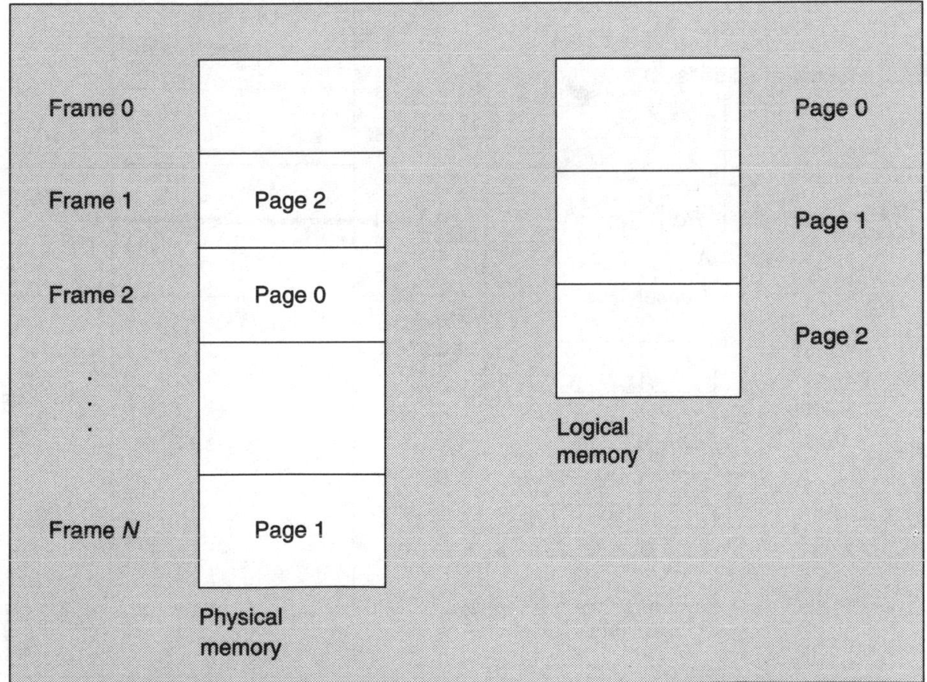


*Figure 3.11* Partitioning of logical and physical memory into pages.

addresses generated by the CPU into memory-absolute addresses is based on the *page table*, which is directly managed by the OS. In the table, an entry contains the value of the start address of the memory frame where a page is contained. The page table can be kept in dedicated registers (if small sized), in fast-access associative registers, or in cache memory.

A logical address is interpreted as a pair ⟨*Pn, Po*⟩: that is, ⟨Page number, Page offset⟩. *Pn* is used as an index for table scanning. *Po* is added to the frame start address of the selected page. This determines the exact position of the physical address within the frame. Page (and frame) sizes are fixed by the hardware, and generally correspond to a power of two. If *Sp* is the size of a page, and *L* the logical address ⟨*Pn, Po*⟩, the following relations hold:

$$Pn = L \text{ DIV } Sp$$
$$Po = L \text{ MOD } Sp$$

where DIV is the integer division operator and MOD the modulo operator. Assuming the page size is $2^m$, *Po* is represented by the value of the last *m* bits of the logical address; the remaining bits represent the value of *Pn*.

The hardware mechanism for paging is shown in Figure 3.12. Operations allowed (that is, rights) on the contents of a page are expressed through a set of

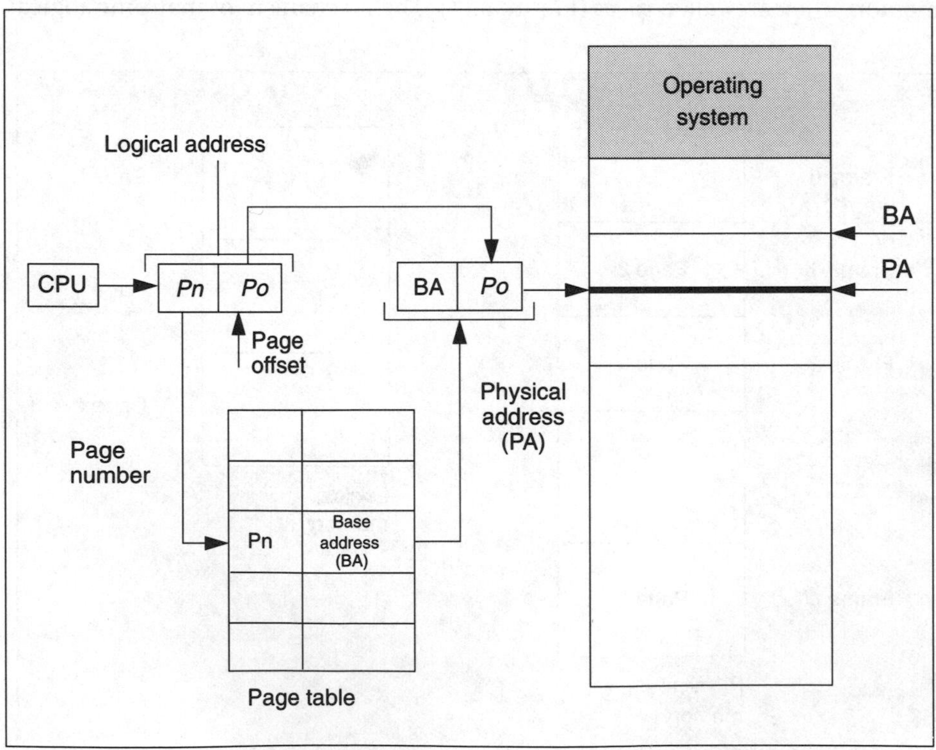


*Figure* 3.12 Paging mechanism.

protection bits stored, for each page, in the page table. Protection bits may specify 'read-only' pages, 'read/write' pages, 'execute-only' pages. When referring to the address of a certain page, a check is carried out to ensure that no conflicts exist between the requested operations and the rights for that page (for example, write attempt on a 'read only' page). Should a conflict emerge, the program should be terminated with an error condition.

Paging supports program sharing, since different users can refer to the same memory frames containing the shared programs. The page tables of these users store (corresponding to the pages of the shared program) the same base value of the memory frames where the shared program code is stored. Each user has his own private data area (memory frame) containing data accessed by the shared program (for example, a compiler code that is unique and operates in turn on different data).

In order to be shared, a code must be 'pure': that is, not self-modifiable when executed ('read only' code). Thus, the protection bit associated to pages of shared code must specify read-only operations.

Generally, the definition of rights associated to a program page may turn out to be rather difficult due to the page decomposition mechanism of a program, which is independent of the page contents. According to this mechanism, the first page stores the first $K$ instructions of a program, the second page the next $K$ instructions, and so on. Therefore, it may happen that a procedure, which should be a logical block both as a structure and for access rights, is split if its size exceeds the page size; alternatively, the same page might contain both data and instructions. For this reason, it is hard to protect the contents of a page through protection bits because the page may contain objects holding different rights.

### 3.3.5 Segmentation

Segmentation consists in partitioning a program into parts, named *segments*, corresponding to the logical entities of a program. A logical entity is a set of homogeneous objects: for example, all the instructions of a procedure or function, the instructions of the main program, or all elements of an array. Usually, a program is decomposed into as many segments as the number of its logical entities. Each segment has its own length, thus the size of segments is variable. Each segment takes an amount of memory equal to its size, starting from an initial address.

It is the compiler's task to create the segments for a program. In fact, their definition depends on the features of the programming language (program structuring in units depends on the programming language). The physical and logical structure of the memory in a segmentation-based system is shown in Figure 3.13.

For segmentation also, the mechanism that maps logical addresses into physical adresses is a table, the *segment table*. Table rows correspond to segments resident in memory. Each segment in the segment table corresponds to a base/limit value. The base value is the start address of a segment in

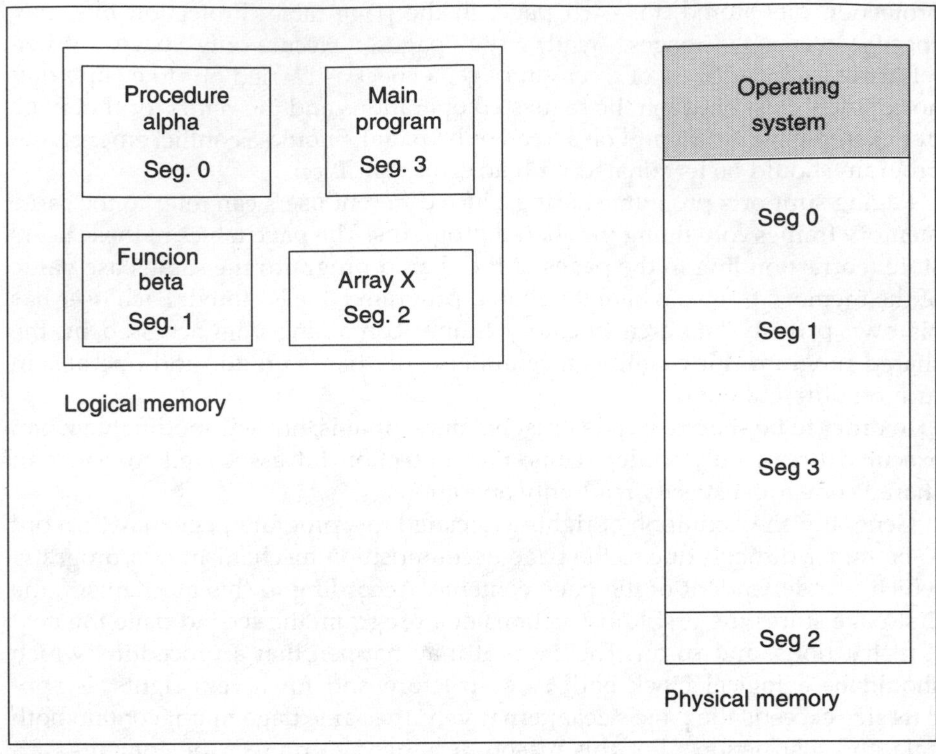


*Figure 3.13* Partitioning of logical and physical memory in a segmentation-based system.

memory. The limit value represents the segment size. A segment table exists for each system user. The segment table can be kept in fast-access registers or in cache memory.

A logical address is a pair ⟨*Sn, So*⟩, where *Sn* is the segment number, and *So* the segment offset. *Sn* is used for scanning the segment table. Upon identification of a segment, *So* is matched against the segment bound value (which is specified in the table). If *So* is lower than the bound value, it is added to the base to determine the memory physical address. If *So* is greater than the segment bound value, the memory reference is incorrect and the program will be terminated on the grounds of an error.

The hardware mechanism of segmentation is shown in Figure 3.14.

So far as protection is concerned, rights on the segment contents are expressed through protection bits. Segments can be read only, read/write, or execute only. Since each segment is a logical unit, its whole contents hold the same characteristics and rights; this overcomes the limitations of paged systems. Protection bits for segments are stored in the segment table; access requests are matched against the rights.

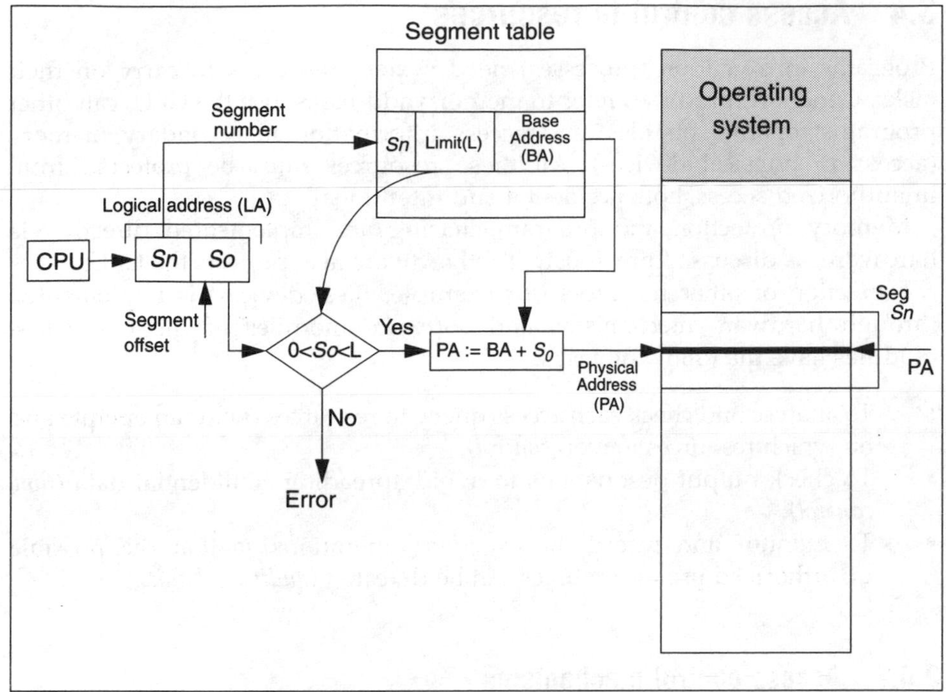


*Figure 3.14* Segmentation mechanism.

Segmentation allows for sharing of segments containing data, programs, or procedures and functions. Shared procedures must be pure code (non self-modifiable): that is, must be 'read only' segments.

***Paging versus segmentation***

From the viewpoint of protection, segmentation allows objects (data, instructions) with homogeneous protection requirements to be grouped in a unique segment. Rights associated to a segment are valid for the whole contents of the segment.

With paging, it is a complex task to express rights for a whole page because the page contents have heterogeneous protection requirements owing to the sequential mechanism of program partitioning. Such a mechanism allows both data and instructions, with different rights, to be merged in the same page.

Better results in the differentiation of rights can be achieved by separating instruction pages from data pages: code pages are 'read only', while data pages are 'read/write'.

From the perspective of sharing, segmentation is more powerful than paging. Both support program sharing, but segmentation also allows for procedure and function sharing, by declaring them as segments. A fundamental premise for both page and segment sharing is that pages or segments must contain pure code.

## 3.4 Access control to resources

Programs in execution (processes) need system resources to carry on their tasks. Generally, processes refer to memory addresses, use the CPU, call other programs, operate on files, and access information in secondary memory (access to physical devices). All these resources must be protected from unauthorized access, both accidental and intentional.

Memory protection and program sharing are implemented directly via hardware, as discussed previously. The hardware also protects the CPU.

Protection of other resources (for example, files, devices) is implemented through hardware mechanisms and software modules of the OS. These modules have the following tasks:

- To analyse and check each access query to resources (who can operate and on which resources) *(access control)*;
- To check output destinations to avoid spreading confidential data *(flow control)*;
- To monitor and record the executed operations so that the possible unauthorized use of resources can be detected *(audit mechanisms)*.

### 3.4.1 Access control mechanisms

Access control to a resource requires that the resource be univocally identifiable. **Resource identification** methods vary according to different resource types.

*Process identification* is based on identifiers *(user-id)* of the user who initiated the process. Therefore, an indirect reference to the creator always appears. The terms 'process' and 'process owner' are considered as synonyms.

The *memory* is seen as a set of addresses, assigned to different processes and to the system software. Different memory areas can be identified through pairs of bound registers, transformation tables and other mechanisms (as already discussed). *Devices* and the CPU are identified via hardware. *Files* are identified through their names. *Programs (procedures)* are identified through their names and their start address. *Users* are identified through authorization techniques during the login phase.

A set of authorized **resource operations** is associated with each type of resource. In particular, the following operations are generally allowed for the corresponding resources:

- CPU: *execute*
- Memory segments: *read/write*
- Input devices: *read*
- Output devices: *write*
- Tapes: *read/write*
- Data files: *create, open, read, write, append, close, delete*
- Program files: *read/write, execute.*

Resource protection means preventing both accidental and intentional accesses to resources by unauthorized users. This can be assured by the capability of verifying authorizations, and then allowing each authorized process to access only the resources needed for its completion *(minimum privilege principle)*. According to this principle, a program is granted access only to essential resources, that is, those necessary to the completion of its tasks, rather than to the whole set of resources it can be authorized for during its lifetime. This limits possible damage deriving from faults of the protection mechanism. For example, when calling a procedure P, only the main program variables referred from inside P (and not all the main program variables) can be accessed by P. For files, only those used by P can be accessed by P; the other ones of the main program should remain inaccessible for P. Protection from unauthorized access also makes it necessary to verify the consistency between required operations and resource types (for example, no read operations for output devices).

Access control mechanisms operate according to two different modes:

- *Access hierarchies.* Rights are associated to different protection levels.
- *Protection matrix* (or access matrix). Rights are associated to subjects (active entities of a system).

### *Access hierarchies*

Mechanisms based on access hierarchies use **privileged modes** or **nested program units**. According to privileged mode mechanisms, processors can operate in different *modes* (states), each corresponding to a set of authorizations associated with sets of executable instructions. For most systems, two execution modes exist: a *privileged mode* (supervisor) and a *user mode*. A bit is associated to each process to indicate its execution state.

The difference between these two modes is due to the types of instruction a processor can execute. Instructions executable in 'privileged mode' are those crucial for system management (for example, I/O instructions, halt, state change).

A finer-grained distinction of privileges is given by protection-level hier-archies: each level has its own set of access privileges. The privilege set within a level forms the *access domain* of that level. Access domains decrease for the outermost levels. The innermost level (level 0) holds the maximum privileges; the outermost level ($N - 1$) is the minimum privilege level (Figure 3.15). More generally, the protection domain of level $i$+1 is a subset of the domain pertaining to level $i$. With $N$ protection levels, an integer $i$ between 0 and $N - 1$ is associated to each process, denoting its protection level. A process has the same access domain as the protection level wherein it executes.

A hierarchy of protection levels is contrary to the minimum privilege principle, because programs always hold all the rights associated to their execution level. In particular, at level 0, programs can access all the system objects.

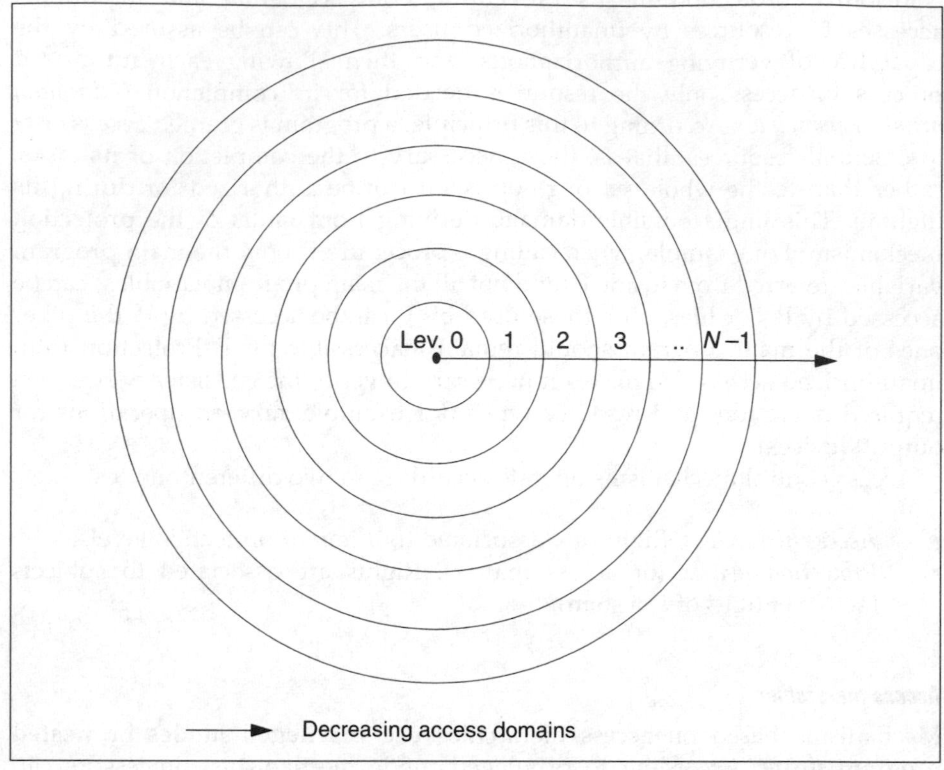


*Figure 3.15* Protection levels hierarchy.

Some languages (Pascal, ALGOL, PL/1) allow a program to be structured into subprograms (procedures), which can access objects according to fixed-scope rules; the basic rule states that a procedure P can access objects declared in P, and global objects declared in the main program.

The mechanism based on **nested program units** generalizes the scope concept of structured languages. A program unit can access global objects of all the units containing that program unit, as well as its own local objects (excluding those of the units it contains). Considering the following nesting of five program units:

<*U*5 <<<*U*1> *U*2 > *U*3 > <*U*4> >

the innermost unit *U*1 owns access rights upon all objects declared inside *U*1, and on all objects inside the units containing *U*1 (*U*2, *U*3, *U*5). *U*1 cannot access *U*4's objects, *U*4 being neither a sub-unit nor a super-unit of *U*1. Through this mechanism, units can access only those objects that are essential to task completion, as required by the minimum privilege principle.

#### Protection matrix

As described in Chapter 2, access rights granted to subjects on objects can be expressed through an access matrix $A$, where the rows $S_1 \ldots S_M$ represent the system subjects, the columns $O_1 \ldots O_N$ represent the system objects, and $A[S_i, O_j]$ is the set of rights held by $S_i$ on $O_j$ (Table 3.3). An access matrix, as defined in Harrison *et al.* (1976), is a suitable structure to represent access authorizations in an OS: objects are the processing system resources to be protected (such as files, devices, programs), while subjects are the system users, and the processes initiated by them.

Various implementation techniques are possible for $A$:

- Table
- Access lists
- Capability lists
- Authority-item lists
- Lock-key mechanism.

Access control will be variously enforced by the OS according to the implementation method employed.

Using the table-based method $A$ is implemented as a table of ordered triples $\langle S_i, O_j, A[S_i, O_j] \rangle$, where $A[S_i, O_j]$ is the set of rights held by subject $S_i$ on object $O_j$ (Table 3.4).

When a process $S_k$ requires an operation $M$ on an object $O_r$, the OS looks for a triple $\langle S_k, O_r, A[S_k, O_r] \rangle$ in the table. If this triple exists, it checks whether $M \in A[S_k, O_r]$. In the affirmative case, access is granted and $M$ is executed; otherwise access is denied and the program terminates with an error condition.

The main disadvantage of this method is the great size of the table, which makes it impossible to keep it wholly in main memory. Virtual memory techniques are necessary to transfer the required table blocks from secondary to main memory and vice versa. Moreover, for each object, there are as many triples as there are subjects holding rights on that object.

**Table 3.3** Example of protection matrix.

| | $O_1$ | $O_2$ | $O_3$ | $O_4$ | $O_5$ | ... | $O_N$ |
|---|---|---|---|---|---|---|---|
| $S_1$ | R | | | | | | |
| $S_2$ | | R | W, R | | X | | X |
| $S_3$ | | | | | | | |
| $S_4$ | | X | | | | | |
| $S_5$ | | | | | | R | |
| . | X | | | X | | | |
| . | | | | | R, W | R | |
| $S_M$ | | X | | | X | | |

R = read; W = write; X = execute

**Table 3.4** A protection matrix stored with the table-based method.

| Subjects | Objects | Rights |
|---|---|---|
| $S_1$ | $O_1$ | $A[S_1, O_1]$ |
| $S_1$ | $O_2$ | $A[S_1, O_2]$ |
| . | . | . |
| $S_k$ | $O_r$ | $A[S_k, O_r]$ |

Using access lists, $A$ is implemented by columns. For each object $O_j$, the list $\langle S_i, A[S_i,O_j]\rangle$ is specified. It is the list of pairs of subject identifiers and rights they are granted on $O_j$ (Figure 3.16). The non-empty entries of each column of $A$ are reported on the **access list** of the corresponding objects, thus saving memory space. An access list is also called an *A*-list.

An *A*-list is maintained by the OS for each protected resource: upon access requests, the OS finds the needed *A*-lists and loads them into memory.

When a subject $S_k$ requires to access an object $O_r$ in $M$ mode, the OS checks whether the *A*-list of $O_r$ contains the pair $\langle S_k, A[S_k,O_r]\rangle$, and whether $M \in A[S_k,O_r]$.

If so, the OS executes the required operation, otherwise the program terminates with an error condition.

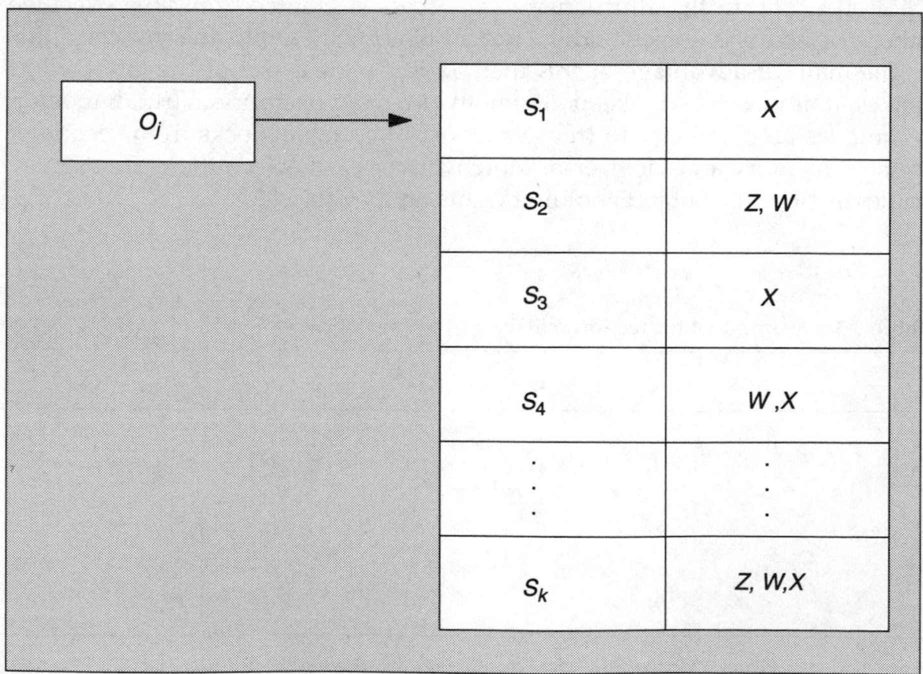


*Figure 3.16* Sample *A*-list.

$A$-lists support the specification of a set of default rights (that is, access rights valid for any process or resource type). Default rights are managed by the OS by looking for the pair $\langle S_k, A[S_k,O_r]\rangle$ both in the $A$-list of $O_r$ and in the default set of rights (for search efficiency, the default list is scanned first). If $M$ is not contained in any list, then access is denied and the program terminates with an error condition; if $M$ is included in at least one list, then $M$ is executed. Once loaded, the $A$-list of an object can be processed rapidly upon access requests.

Upon object deletion, the corresponding $A$-list is removed. Updates to the $A$-list owing to the deletion of a subject and/or modification of rights are rather complex: as a matter of fact, the $A$-lists of all objects must be scanned, so that all rights owned by the deleted user on different objects can be cancelled and/or modified.

Using capabilities, $A$ is implemented by rows: a **capability list** (C-list) is associated with each subject $S_i$ (Figure 3.17). A capability is a pair $\langle O_j, A[S_i,O_j]\rangle$ composed of a pointer to the object (address, identifier) and of a set of operations executable on an object. To be enabled to execute an operation $M$ on $O_j$, $S_k$ must specify $M$, and the pointer to $O_j$. By owning a capability for $O_j$, $S_k$ is entitled to access this object.

Capabilities must be managed only by the OS so as to avoid improper modification, copy, or creation by processes. Capability-based protection can be

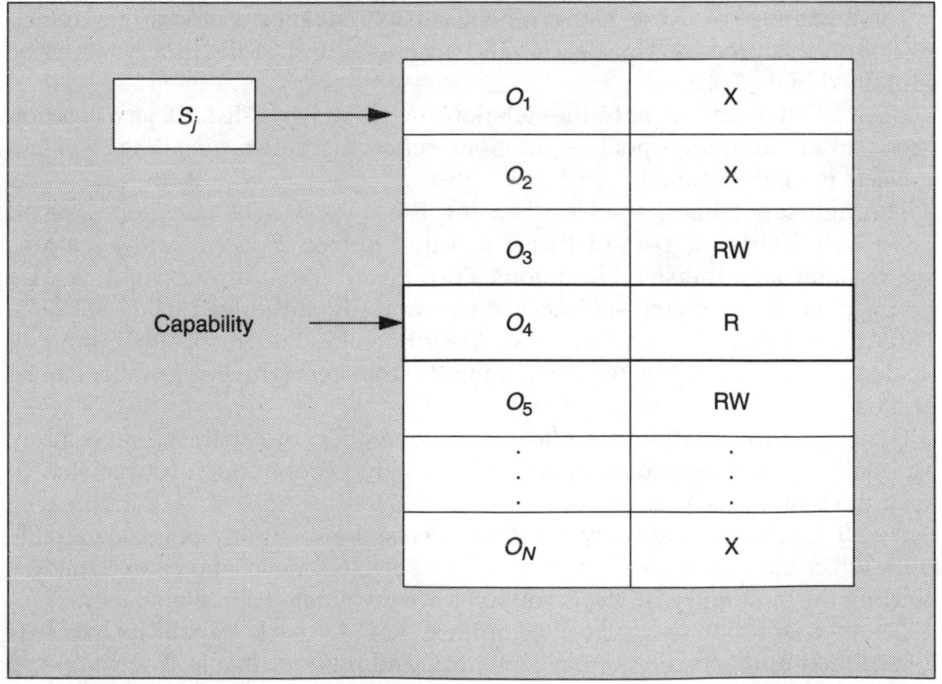


***Figure 3.17*** Sample C-list.

variously implemented depending on the system architecture. For example, the memory reserved to a process could be partitioned into two parts: one reserved for data and instructions and accessible by the process; the other reserved for storage of the process's C-lists and accessible only by the OS. This solution is supported in a straightforward way by memory segmentation techniques.

An alternative solution is based on 'tagged' architectures: capabilities are distinguished from other values in memory through labels which are accessible to the OS only. A one-bit label is sufficient to distinguish the capabilities, considering the 0 label for data items and the 1 label for capabilities (labels of more than one bit allow different types of value to be identified, for example integers, floating point, capability, Booleans, characters, pointers, instructions). Under this approach, capabilities are stored either in a stack or in registers, depending on the system architecture (stack-based system or register-based system).

Capabilities, as objects needing protection, are endowed with a set of executable operations. Possible operations are: *creation, copying and revocation.*

Creation is executed upon subjects creating new objects: rights owned by other subjects on the new object are defined. The OS creates the corresponding capabilities and updates the C-lists of the involved subjects.

Copying occurs when an authorized subject $S_i$ transfers (part of) his or her rights to other subjects. A copy of the capability of $S_i$ containing the transferred rights is created by the OS and inserted in the C-list of the receiving subject.

Capability revocation is used to delete capabilities related to objects.

The advantage of C-lists is that all objects accessible by a process are associated with this process. Thus, each valid access request of the process must be contained in its C-lists.

User deletion entails only the deletion of his or her C-list. Object deletion needs more complex update operations since the C-lists of all the system subjects must be scanned.

Through capabilities, a subject holding the *transfer right* can propagate all his or her rights (or part of them) to other subjects: access authorizations are dynamically transferable among subjects. If the transfer right is also propagated, the receiving subjects can dynamically authorize further subjects. Thus, the number of capabilities available for an object is practically unlimited. By denying the possibility of propagating the transfer right, this number can be limited.

Dynamic authorization complicates the operation of capability revocation, especially when propagation of the transfer right is unbound: it is necessary to keep track of all the capabilities referring to the same subject. A solution is to make all capabilities indirectly point to objects: the capability points to a table entry which contains a pointer to the referenced object. Revocation is executed by deleting the table entry: all the capabilities are invalidated simultaneously.

Another solution associates a unique key to each capability; this is determined upon creation of the capability and not modifiable. The same key is associated to the referenced object. Revocation consists in modifying the object key, thus altering its correspondence with the capability.

By this method, each subject is associated with a set of **authority-items** (*A-I*), each expressing the rights held by a subject on an object. The *A-Is* referring to the same object are linked together by a chain of pointers (Figure 3.18). Basically, an *A-I* corresponds directly to an implementation based on C-lists and, indirectly, to an implementation based on *A*-lists through the chain of pointers. This overcomes the difficulties encountered in update operations.

Access control by the OS is obtained as for the C-lists.

Finally, through the **lock-key** method, the access matrix *A* is implemented by associating a bit string to each object *(lock)* and to each subject (*key*) (Figure 3.19). Thus, a subject $S_j$ can access only objects with a matching key/lock (i.e., $O_r$). Key/lock matching must be verified by the OS before access is granted. Subjects must obviously be prevented from directly modifying the set of keys for subjects and objects.

This method falls in between the C-list and *A*-list methods; its flexibility and efficiency depend on the length of the selected keys (locks).

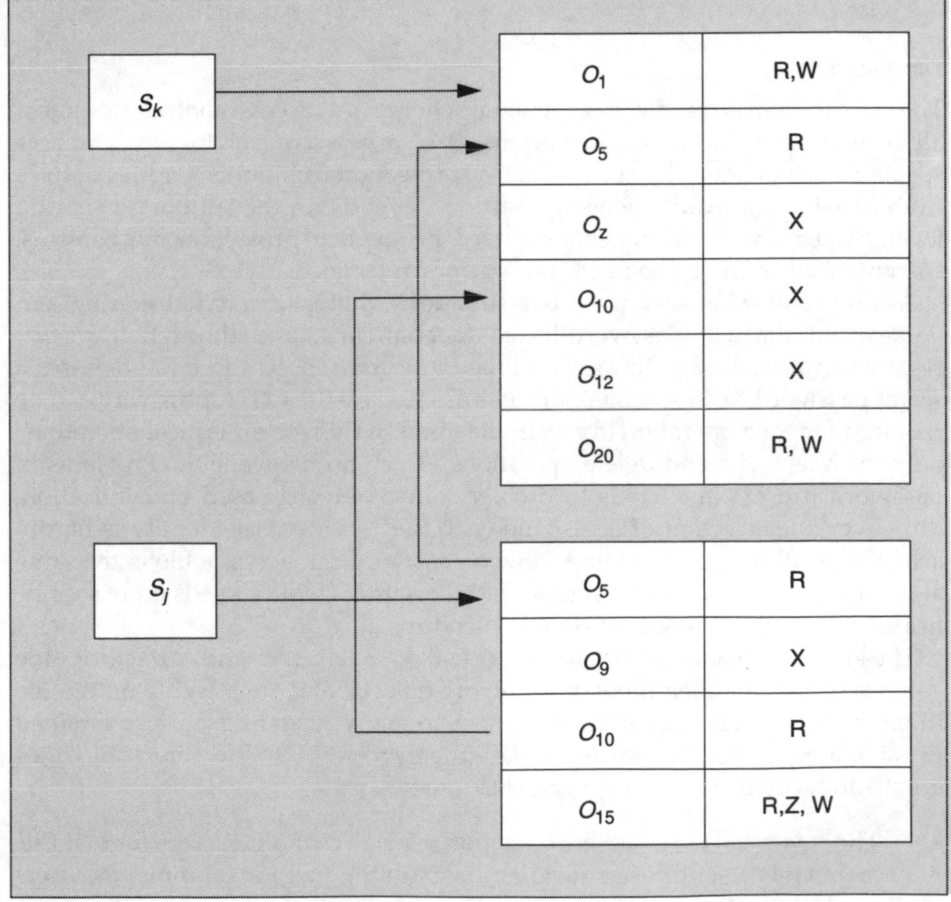


*Figure* **3.18** Authority-item.

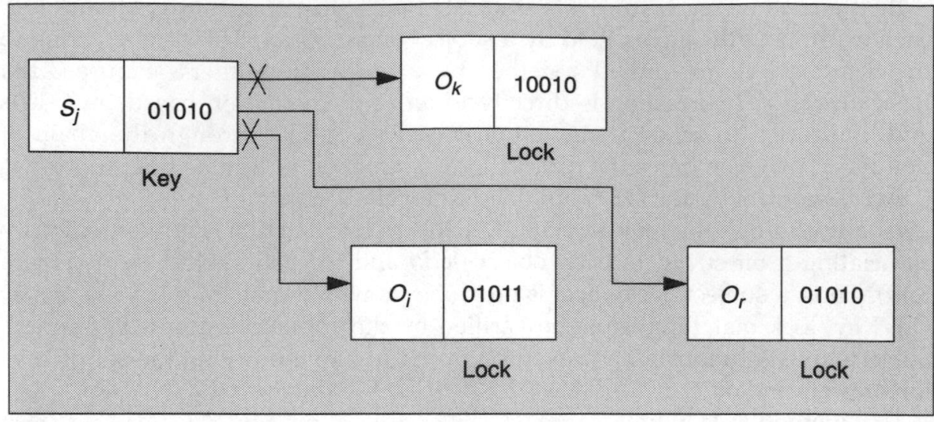


*Figure 3.19* Lock-key.

***File protection***

The access matrix model is a general scheme for access control to almost all object types. However, in various OSs, access control to files employs specific mechanisms. The need for *ad-hoc* protection techniques for files derives from file-sharing requirements; protection depends on the supported sharing level. Systems with no file sharing need no explicit protection mechanisms. Uncontrolled sharing also needs no type of protection.

A compromise between these two situations, that is, controlled sharing, can be realized through **password-based mechanisms**, and through *techniques based on right ownership*. In the first type of systems, access to a file requires a secret password to be specified; this is validated by the OS. A password can be required for each operation (for example, read, write), or for critical operations only, such as write and delete operations which are irreversible. Problems in password use are analogous to problems in password-based authentication. Moreover, the selection of access modes based on the user identity is hardly achievable: all the users holding a given password can access a file in the same access mode. Selection of operations based on user identity needs more sophisticated mechanisms based on right ownership.

These mechanisms associate an *A*-list to each file and directory; the *A*-list specifies the identifiers of different subjects, and their rights on the file (directory). In order to limit the *A*-list size, in many systems users are classified in categories, and rights are associated to categories. Usually, three categories are distinguished: *owner, group* and *other users.*

- The *owner* can create a file and define the rights of other users for that file.
- A *group* is a set of users needing to share the file: for example, the users working on the same project.
- *Other users* includes system users other than owners and group members.

A *field* associated with each category specifies the rights assigned to the category members. The *A*-list of a file is composed of three fields: a user identifier and a group identifier are associated with each user and rights can thus be expressed using these identifiers. Upon file access requests, identifiers are used to recognize the user category and the deriving rights for that user on the file.

This type of file control mechanism is implemented in UNIX. Categories are: *user, group, world*. Admitted rights are: read **(r-read)**, write **(w-write)**, execute **(x-execute)**. Each field associated with a category is composed of three bits, one for each type of allowed operation. For forbidden operations, the '-' symbol is specified. Globally, a nine-bit string is associated with a file. For example, the string 'rwx r-x r--' for a file F denotes that the owner can execute all the operations on F (first triple rwx); that the owner group members can read and execute F, but cannot modify it (second triple r-x); finally, all the other users can only read F (triple r--).

A mechanism based on right ownership supports rights differentiation on the same file, and the definition of the number of users sharing the same file. Implementation is straightforward because it does not need additional protection data, being based on user identifiers.

## 3.5 Flow-control mechanisms

Access-control mechanisms are responsible for checking users' authorizations for resource access: only granted operations are executed. Flow-control mechanisms are responsible for verifying the final destination of an operation output, in order to avoid the spread of reserved data.

A *flow* occurs when information moves from a source object into a destination object. We distinguish two types of flow: *explicit flows*, occurring as a consequence of assignment instructions, such as $y := f(x_1, \ldots, x_n)$, and *implicit flows* generated by conditional instructions, such as: if $f(x_{m+1}, \ldots, x_n)$ then $y := f(x_1, \ldots, x_m)$. *Flow-control mechanisms* must verify that only authorized flows, both explicit and implicit, are executed. Referring to the mathematical structure of the lattice model (see Chapter 2), a set of rules must be satisfied to assure secure information flows. Rules are expressed using flow relations among classes (assigned to information), stating the authorized flows within a system. These relations can define, for a class, the set of classes where information (classified in that class) can flow, or can state the specific relations to be verified between two classes to allow information flow from one to the other. In general, flow-control mechanisms implement the controls by assigning a label to each object, specifying the security class of that object. Labels are then used to verify the flow relations defined in the model.

A general mechanism for flow control can be obtained by extending access controls based on the axioms of the Bell–LaPadula model with multilevel protection requirements (see Chapter 2). Assuming that system objects have a fixed classification ('tranquility principle'), let us denote with $\underline{p}$ the clearance of a process $p$, and with $\underline{o}$ the class of an object $o$. By imposing $\underline{o} \leq \underline{p}$, the *ss*-property prevents information from being read by processes lacking clearance for that operation. The *-property prevents flow transfers towards lower or non-comparable security levels, by imposing that $p$, allowed to read $o$, be granted also to write into an object o', if $\underline{o} \leq \underline{p} \leq \underline{o}'$. Mechanisms to implement these axioms, combined with access control, operate by assigning to each process $p$ a clearance $\underline{p}$, by specifying the highest security class of an object which can be read by $p$, and the lowest security class of an object which can be written by the process. The mechanism grants $p$ the read mode to objects $o_1, \ldots, o_m$, and the write mode to objects $o'_1, \ldots, o'_n$ if the following relation:

$$\underline{o}_1 \oplus \ldots \oplus \underline{o}_m \leq \underline{p} \leq \underline{o}'_1 \oplus \ldots \oplus \underline{o}'_n$$

holds among the classifications of the involved objects.

On the basis of this relation, the mechanism is unable to operate a distinction between the differently classified objects a process could read: in fact, the classification of the read objects is computed as the least upper bound ($\oplus$ operator) of all objects classifications. Therefore, although a process can read both 'low' and 'high' classified data, 'write' operations can occur only into objects classified as 'high', since the mechanism is unable to distinguish which information is being transferred through write operations. In this way, mechanisms can be secure, but not precise (Denning, 1982), since they prevent possible executable flows (for example, a process could write 'low' data which can be written into 'low' objects, and not necessarily into 'high' ones). In general, we have mechanisms assuring system precision (meaning that the flows that are allowed, and so executed, by these mechanisms coincide with all the authorized flows), and mechanisms assuring system security (allowing execution of only a subset of the authorized flows).

More sophisticated controls can be obtained with flow-control mechanisms operating at execution time and at compile time. They are briefly described in the following.

### 3.5.1 Control mechanisms at run time

These mechanisms verify the flow correctness upon execution of instructions. Unauthorized flows cause the corresponding instructions not to be executed. Control mechanisms at run time operate both on fixed-class objects (*static link* between a class and an object), and variable class objects (class-object *dynamic link*). With *static links*, an object is assigned a security class permanently. With regard to explicit flows, each flow $x_i \rightarrow y$ must be authorized. The mechanism works on the labels associated with the involved variables. In particular, the following relations must be verified:

$$\underline{x}_1 \oplus \ldots \oplus \underline{x}_n \leq \underline{y}$$

For implicit flows, the mechanism has to check both the explicit flows of the assignment instruction and the implicit flows $x_i \rightarrow y$, ($i$=$m$+1, …, $n$) bound to the conditional part. In order to have all implicit and explicit flows secure, the following relation:

$\underline{x}_1 \oplus \ldots \oplus \underline{x}_m \oplus \underline{x}_{m+1} \oplus \ldots \oplus \underline{x}_n < \underline{y}$

must be verified upon execution of the assignment instruction.

It has to be noted that error messages reporting an unexecuted assignment due to unauthorized flows can possibly provide information on the value of the condition variables (this is true for specific types of condition, such as the disjunction condition). In these cases, an error message informs the user that the assignment has been tried, and values of the variables in the condition can be inferred; otherwise, if the condition is false, no message is reported, since the execution of the assignment has not even been tried. To prevent inference due to error messages, all the messages related to unauthorized flows can be recorded (logging) or, alternatively, a mechanism working at compile time to detect all unsecure flows can be employed.

For *dynamic links*, the security class of objects varies depending on the object contents. The class $y$ of the variable $y$ in assignment and conditional instructions has to be properly determined, taking into account the classes of the involved variables, and in a way that the flow relations on them result to be verified. The following rules are used to compute the resulting class to be assigned to $y$. Upon execution of assignment instructions $y := f(x_1, \ldots, x_n)$, $y$ is assigned the class $y$ computed as follows:

$\underline{x}_1 \oplus \ldots \oplus \underline{x}_n.$

This guarantees that the explicit flows deriving from the assignment are secure, since the relation $\underline{x}_1 \oplus \ldots \oplus \underline{x}_n \leq \underline{y}$ is verified because of the way $\underline{y}$ is computed.

For conditional instructions of the form if $f(x_{m+1}, \ldots, x_n)$ then $y := f(x_1, \ldots, x_m)$, the execution of the assignment causes a new class $\underline{y}$ to be computed for $y$ using the following rule:

$\underline{x}_1 \oplus \ldots \oplus \underline{x}_m \oplus \underline{x}_{m+1} \oplus \ldots \oplus \underline{x}_n.$

Although all the classes of the variables in the condition are evaluated, and a new class is obtained for $y$ (therefore ensuring the explicit flows), all the implicit flows involving $y$ in the program are not guaranteed to be secure. In fact, when the conditional part is false, $\underline{y}$ does not change: the implicit flows involving $y$ exist anyway, independent of the execution of the assignment instruction, and these flows may be insecure (Denning, 1976; Lampson, 1974; Lampson *et al.*, 1977).

### 3.5.2 Control mechanisms at compile time

These control the flow caused by programs during program compilation. For each instruction, all the relating flows are checked, specifying for each flow the relations that must hold on the security classes of the involved objects. All instructions are processed at compile time, and the relating relations are generated. Instructions are categorized as *assignment, sequence, condition, iteration or procedure call*. In the following, for each type of instruction, the relations to be verified for the flows associated with the instruction are specified.

For the assignment, instruction $y := f(x_1, \ldots, x_m)$, the relation is:

$$\underline{x}_1 \oplus \ldots \oplus \underline{x}_m \leq \underline{y}$$

That is, it is secure if each flow $x_i \rightarrow a$ is secure.

The sequence instruction:

```
begin I1; … ;In end
```

is secure if all the flows associated to each instruction `Ii (i= 1..n)` are secure.

For conditions such as:

```
if f(x1,…,xn) then I1 [else I2]
```

the relation is:

$$\underline{x}_1 \oplus \ldots \oplus \underline{x}_m \leq \underline{z}_1 \otimes \ldots \otimes z_m$$

That is, it is secure if the execution of I1 and I2 is secure, if the explicit flows of both I1 and I2 are secure, and if the implicit flows $x_i \rightarrow z_j$, $i = 1..n$, $j = 1..m$ are secure ($z_j$ ($j = 1..m$) being a variable target of a flow in I1 (or I2)).

For the iteration:

```
while f(x1,...xn) do I1
```

the following relation is defined:

$$\underline{x}_1 \oplus \ldots \oplus \underline{x}_m \leq \underline{z}_1 \otimes \ldots \otimes \underline{z}_m$$

That is, it is secure if the cycle terminates, if I1 is secure and if the implicit flows $x_i \rightarrow z_j$ are secure ($z_j$ ($j = 1..m$) being a variable target of a flow in I1).

A procedure call instruction has the form `procedure-name (a1,…,am, b1, …bn)`, for procedures of the following form:

```
procedure procedure-name (x1, …, xm; var y1, …, yn);
var z1, … zp; *local variables*
begin
procedure body
end;
```

where $x_1, \ldots, x_m$ are formal input parameters, $y_1, \ldots, y_m$ are the formal input/output parameters, and $a_1, \ldots, a_m$ and $b_1, \ldots, b_n$ are the corresponding input/output actual parameters. A procedure call is secure if the procedure name is secure and the following relations are verified:

$$\underline{a}_i \leq \underline{b}_j \text{ if } \underline{x}_i \leq \underline{y}_j \quad \underline{1 \leq i \leq m} \text{ and } \underline{1 \leq j \leq n}$$
$$\underline{b}_i \leq \underline{b}_j \text{ if } \underline{y}_i \leq \underline{y}_j \quad \underline{1 \leq i \leq m} \text{ and } \underline{1 \leq j \leq n}$$

That is, a procedure call is secure if the procedure `'procedure-name'` is secure, namely: if each flow $a_i \rightarrow b_j$ is authorized (also if the corresponding $x_i \rightarrow y_j$ flow is authorized) and if each flow $b_i \rightarrow b_j$ is authorized (also if the corresponding $y_i \rightarrow y_j$ flow is authorized).

A mechanism using the modalities previously described can be integrated with a compiler: during parsing, classes are assigned to the different instructions (following the above rules), and relations are verified between the classes according to the instruction types. A *deductive system*, which can also check the functional correctness of a program, has been proposed by Andrews and Reitman (1980) to prove flow security of a program, based on a set of *assertions*. Assertions are used to express the requirements for authorized flows. These requirements are based on the values and security classes of the objects involved in flows. An assertion is expressed as a first-order logic predicate. A program is viewed as a set of procedures, made, in turn, of instructions, like the previous types. For a procedure and for each instruction, relations that must be verified in the initial state are expressed by assertions named *preconditions*; relations to be verified in the final state are expressed by *postconditions*. Each program object $v$ is assigned a class variable $\underline{v}$ expressing the *state of information* in $v$ at a certain instant in the procedure lifetime. Assertions are formulated referring to the state of information contained in the different program objects. Proving a procedure security with respect to its flows consists in proving that if the procedure's precondition is verified when the procedure starts, its postcondition Q is verified at the end of the execution of the procedure.

The proof can be based on implication among subsequent assertions and on *demonstration rules* and *axioms* defined over the language instructions.

## 3.6 Isolation

Isolation denotes the possibility of limiting the consequences of possible security violations by preventing them from affecting other system elements. Isolation is achieved by splitting hardware and software into modules that operate independently from one another (that is, in isolation). Isolation may require duplication of some hardware/software modules. Isolation relies on the multiple-space-based method and on the virtual-machine-based method.

The **multiple-space method** exploits a virtual main memory for each system user. Main memory areas and user programs, shared among several users, are duplicated; the OS, the system programs and auxiliary memory devices are not duplicated (Figure 3.20). The uniformity of protection mechanisms is guaranteed by the existence of a unique copy of the OS; however, attempts to violate protection mechanisms do not avoid potential damage to all the user memory areas.

Using the method based on the *concept of* **virtual machine**, different work environments can coexist on the same computer: groups of users operate in their environment in isolation. Through a control program, which is a monitor of the virtual machine, copies (virtual machines) of the same system are emulated, each working in an isolated environment (Figure 3.21). User

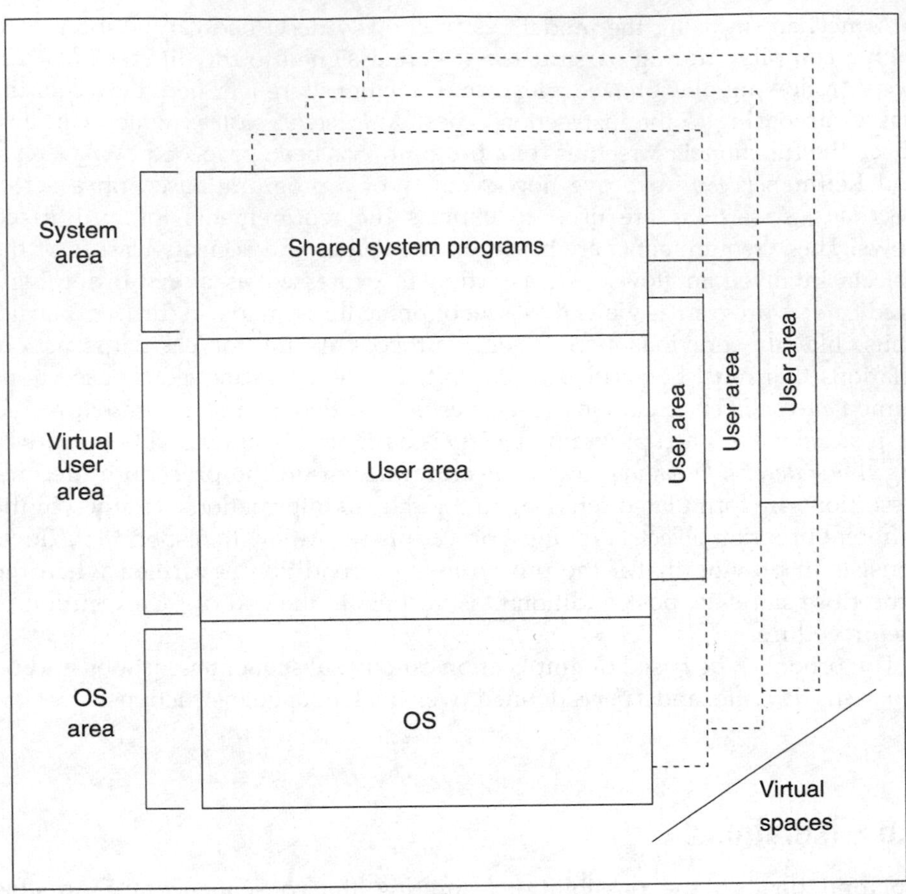


*Figure 3.20* Isolation based on a multiple machine.

programs and related files within the environment are separated (isolated) from other users. The system software and the hardware devices are replicated. Each element embeds its own protection requirements such that possible violation attempts within one environment do not affect other work environments.

The advantage of virtual machine techniques is that different environments can share the same machine, each employing different protection requirements and resource-handling policies. Moreover, damage is restricted in that the effects of failures or violations to security mechanisms are not propagated. No object sharing is allowed because isolation avoids the risk of program communication.

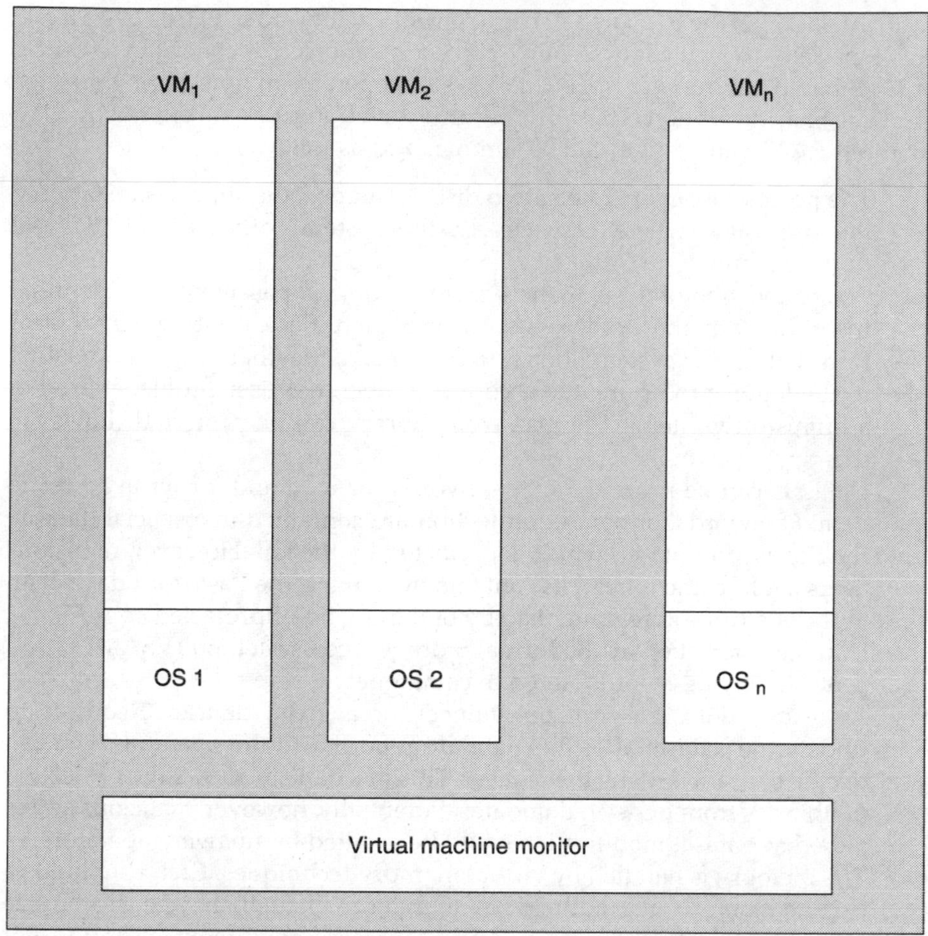


*Figure 3.21* Isolation based on a virtual machine.

## 3.7 Security functions in some operating systems

The basic security features of common operating systems, such as IBM MVS, UNIX, VAX/VMS, VM/SP, OS/400 are described in the following.

### 3.7.1 IBM MVS

MVS (Multiple Virtual Memory Space) is the IBM OS used on computers of the 370 series (Enterprise System Architecture 370 (ESA/370) or SYSTEM/370). Security functions comprise access control, virtual memory management and access auditing. Increased protection can be obtained by integrating an add-on security package; the Resource Access Control Facility (RACF) (see Chapter 4), was especially conceived for resource protection and access control to resources of MVS-based environments. The MVS system operates in timesharing through the Time Sharing Option (TSO). The security functions directly offered by MVS (without RACF integration) can be summarized as follows:

- The processor can operate in two distinct modes, the supervisor state and the user state where, respectively, the system software and the user programs run.
- The connection of users to the system occurs via password and identifier (userid). Both the user password and identifier are stored in a clear form within the system library `'SYS1.UADS'`, together with data relating to the logon procedure, the account number, the user profile, and other administrative items. The password library can be protected (however, this rarely occurs).
- Datasets can be protected by passwords for read and/or write access to data. Passwords for dataset protection are contained in a special dataset, the Password dataset, which is protected by the OS. However, malicious users could come to read its contents by making the Password dataset an input of a dump program, thereby obtaining an unprotected copy.
- Datasets controlled by the Virtual Storage Access Method (VSAM) can be protected by passwords stored in catalogues.
- An 'expiration date' can be defined for a given dataset. Requests to update the dataset after this date are reported to the operator, who can decide to grant or deny the request. This mechanism allows the protection of libraries from undesired updates. Potentially, however, malicious access aimed at dataset modification could be granted by unaware operators.
- The memory is handled by virtual memory techniques. Each user holds a private memory area (address space) that can virtually have the same size as the actual global memory. Address spaces of different users do not interfere with one another. The OS is resident in the user's virtual space (Figure 3.22). The paging technique is used for memory handling. Protection of the contents of each memory area is provided by a mechanism based on 4-bit keys that are associated with each page (a 4096-byte page). Upon access to a memory page, the access key of a program (inside the program status word) must match with the block key. Special programs, allowed to access all memory blocks, have a key of four zeros.

### 3.7.2 UNIX

The UNIX OS, developed in the 1970s at the Bell Laboratories, was conceived to be used in 'friendly' environments, such as research centres and universities, which characteristically employ resource-sharing policies and have no special security needs.

UNIX has now come to be widely used in industrial environments as well, and has become a standard of reference in the OS field. Currently, it works on

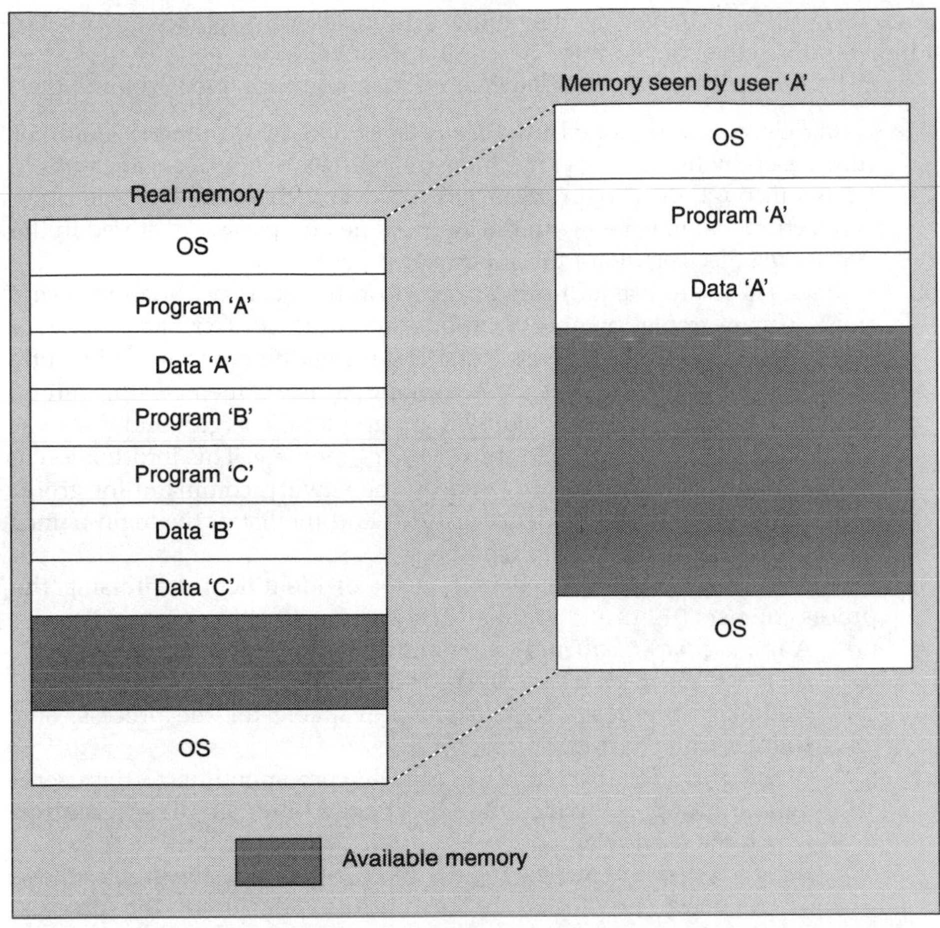


*Figure 3.22* Memory management in MVS.

a variety of hardware configurations, providing a uniform environment for both production and software development.

For security, UNIX is endowed with mechanisms able to keep trace of connected users, to authenticate users upon connection, to separate users' files and to control access to resources. By these same mechanisms, unauthorized users can be denied system access: an indicator of the creator is associated to processes and file access is allowed only if the requesting user belongs to a category owning the necessary rights for the required access. A *superuser*, or *root*, that is, a user endowed with unlimited authorization, is a UNIX user in charge of system administration and therefore allowed to access all the system resources. The presence of an unlimited authority poses some security problems: successful attempts from malicious users to acquire the root account lead to unlimited power being obtained. Therefore, in some UNIX versions (for example, Posix, Utix/23S), the unique administrator is replaced by a set of administrators contained in three different accounts.

In UNIX, the security-relevant elements are: users, groups, processes and files.

(1) *Users*. Users are identified by a *login name* and by a numeric identifier (uid), used by the low-level mechanisms of the system. Users are authenticated through their login name and password: these are typed in upon connection and matched with the login name and password stored in the */etc/passwd* file. The uid of the superuser is zero.
(2) *Groups*. These are lists of users grouped on the basis of common access rights (for example, owning a unique account). A user can belong to several groups but, at a given instant, he must be associated with one group only. Through the *newgrp* command, a user's membership can be modified. Groups are identified by a group identifier (gid) and information about all groups is stored into the */etc/group* file. This information is the group name, the password used by the newgrp command for group access, the group numeric identifier (gid) and the list of the login names (separated by ',') of the group members.
(3) *Processes*. These are associated with a set of identifiers, expressing the process owners (users and groups). They are:
    (a) A *real user identifier* (ruid) corresponding to the process owner;
    (b) *An effective user identifier* (euid) corresponding to the user whose discretionary privileges are currently available for the process, and usually equal to ruid;
    (c) A *real group identifier* (rgid) originally corresponding to the user's default group, but which may be changed into any other group to which the user belongs;
    (d) *An effective group identifier* (egid), corresponding to the group whose discretionary privileges are currently available for the process, usually equal to rgid.
(4) *File*. Each file is associated with a 16-bit structure called the *i-node*, which contains all the information relating to the file and its protection. In particular, the first 12 bits contain protection information for the file; the remaining 4 bits specify the file type. Protection bits are: the *setuid*, the *setgid*, and the *sticky bit*, and the nine bits expressing the privileges held respectively by the file owner, by his group, and by other users.

The *setuid* and *setgid* bits, if 'on' for an executable file, cause the creation of a process having the *euid* element equal to the *euid* of the file owner, rather than equal to that of the user requiring the execution (default). The *setgid* mechanism is analogous: it operates on *egid*. The *setuid/setgid* mechanism is used both to allow the superuser to propagate some privileges in a controlled way and to construct protected domains, where a *setuid/setgid* program controls accesses to a (set of) file(s) owned by the same group/user as the program owner.

For example, in the case of controlled propagation of rights, a user can visualize the current state of his active processes by accessing the kernel image represented by the */dev/kmen* file. This file is visible only to the superuser, while users can get information therein contained only via the */bin/ps* program which is *setuid* and belongs to the superuser (that is, it is *setuid* to *root*).

For protected domains, consider an archive of messages which is accessible only by a special program, named *mailx*. A directory is constructed owned by the mailx program and accessible only by this program. Within this directory, subdirectories *(mailboxes)* are available for users of the mail system; these users are the owners, but their mailboxes can be accessed and modified also by mailx (mailx can add or erase messages). A mailbox contains a file for each message that can be read and modified only by the recipient user. Initially, mailx has the *ruid* of the user executing the program and the *euid* of the mailx pseudo-user, and accesses the mail spool directory. According to the *ruid*, it accesses the mailbox of a specific user, setting that directory to its work directory, *euid* is set to *ruid*, losing the privileges of the mailx user and taking those of the executor, who is now enabled to access his messages (Figure 3.23).

The *sticky bit* 'on' for an executable file maintains the image of the executing process in the swapping area, even when the execution is terminated.

#### Security considerations on the 'setuid' mechanism

Although powerful, the *setuid/setgid* mechanism can entail serious security violations, especially when a file is *setuid* to *root*: in fact, during file execution, all users get the superuser's privileges (Bunch, 1987).

A *setuid/setgid* program getting parameters (files, object names) from users must be realized as a secure program. This means that files belonging to owners of a *setuid/setgid* program must be protected against this same program. As an example, the UNIX mail program of the first six versions used to be executed with the *setuid* option set to superuser, thus enabling it to write into the users' private mailboxes. An option was added later to allow a user to

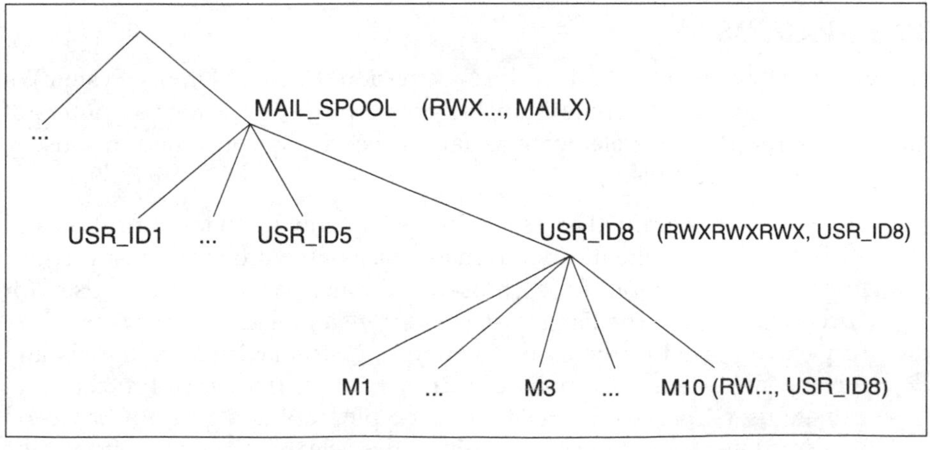


*Figure 3.23* *Setuid/setgid* mechanism.

define a file as an input for the mail program; however, no control was added to verify the user authorization to that file. Therefore, with the privileges of the root, this user could obtain copies of any file in the system, by sending the file to himself by mail.

The *setuid/setgid* mechanism is also vulnerable to Trojan Horses. A Trojan Horse program can access the files of its executor, and can also read and save data on behalf of the malicious creator of the Trojan Horse. Thus, by creating a child process, where *euid* and *ruid* are equal, the program can get both its owner's discretionary privileges and those of the executor.

Some restrictions have been put in place to face these problems: 'write' operations are forbidden on files containing *setuid* programs; the *setuid* protection modality can be set only through explicit user commands that reach the kernel along a secure channel; the *setuid/setgid* modality is disabled when writing a file. These modifications make it impossible for a user to modify a *setuid* program, or for a Trojan Horse to compromise users' privileges by creating *setuid* programs. Generally, a system administrator should verify that the *setuid* bit is 'on' only for known programs, and that *setuid/setgid* programs are not placed in directories that can be written by all users, thereby preventing users from transferring a *setuid/setgid* program into their directories and thus making it inaccessible to its owner (moving files around the file system keeps the state of the file bits unaltered).

Various extensions to the standard UNIX protection mechanisms have been proposed, mainly for building kernels for which security is provable. Extensions followed two approaches: emulation and restructuring/extension. In the emulation approach, an OS consists of a secure kernel, a set of trusted processes (with functions which are security-relevant), and a UNIX emulator. Kernel functions implement a mechanism (a reference monitor) that acts as an intermediary for all system accesses.

Under the restructuring/extension approach, the UNIX kernel is modified so that both new and old security policies can be handled.

### 3.7.3 VAX/VMS

The VAX/VMS system (Virtual Address eXtension/Virtual Memory System) of the Digital Equipment Corporation is a general-purpose OS for computers of the VAX series. Relevant elements as far as security is concerned are: users, groups, processes and files.

- *Users.* Users are granted access to the system only upon identification and authentication. Authentication is made via a password mechanism requiring a private password for each user, and other passwords to be used for special cases. In particular, a *system password* and a *secondary password* are respectively used in the case of connections to particular terminals and for crucial system operations (which are rather frequent). Protection of private users' passwords relies on a cryptographic algorithm based on unidirectional functions: obtaining the clear password from the enciphered password is made computationally hard.

- *Groups*. Each system account is associated with a User Identification Code (UIC) composed of two parts: a group number and a user number. A group collects the accounts of users performing the same tasks and therefore needing access to the same information. For the group members, specific access privileges can be granted by file owners.
- *Processes*. A successful user/system connection creates a process holding the UIC of the user's account; access requests to files are checked on the basis of the UIC of the requesting process. The reference monitor matches the process's UIC against the privileges defined for the file and the directory where the file is located, in order to determine the process authorization for file access.
- *Files*. Files and directories have an associated set of protections expressing rights of the owner, of the group and of the remaining users on the file/directory. In the discretionary policy implemented by VMS, rights held on the resources by each user class are established by the file owner. For example, a file owner can state that 'write' and 'erase' operations can be performed only by himself, while group members can only 'read' the file. The set of rights held on a file/directory is kept in an A-list, specifying the various UICs of users and groups holding access authorization, together with the related access rights. Process requests for files/directories are processed by the reference monitor which checks whether the process UIC (and therefore the user's UIC) is in the access list of the requested file/directory.

  Through access lists, unauthorized access attempts can be reported in real time to the security manager, or can be recorded in a log file. Under VMS, the contents of an erased file cannot be read by unauthorized processes. Erasing a file removes the file descriptor, not the file contents which are maintained and *marked* as erased. Malicious processes could be created to read disk areas containing marked files, or to systematically scan the disk contents *(scavenging)*. Techniques used by VMS to prevent such events are: *high-water marking* (a user cannot read beyond the space he or she is assigned for 'write' operations); *overwriting* of data through erase strings *(erasure pattern)*.
- *Log file*. VMS can record all relevant events concerning security into a log file; this can be read from the console by the security manager. Some classes of event are systematically recorded, others only on request by the security manager. Recorded event elements are: time, type of alarm, user name, and identifier of the generating process.

### 3.7.4 IBM VM/SP

The IBM OS VM/SP (Virtual Machine/System Product) was conceived for management of other OSs (for example, DOS, DOS/VS, DOS/VSE, OS/VS1, OS/VS2, SVS, MVS/SP, VM/370).

VM/SP handles a multiprogramming environment, where user groups can have their own OS, and all OSs are resident on the same computing system (this is an example of isolation architecture based on a virtual machine). Users of each OS work on a virtually dedicated system *(stand-alone)* with its own resources (CPU, memory, peripheral units). Actually, a 'control program' emulates a dedicated environment (a virtual machine) for each OS: virtual machines work 'in mutual isolation', apart from shared resources. This is shown in Figure 3.24.

The tasks of the control program are:

- Management of the CPU of the actual machine, giving each virtual machine a time slice.
- Memory management of the actual machine, and management of its secondary memory which supports the virtual memory of the virtual machines; for this purpose, paging and segmentation techniques are used, each segment being composed of 16 pages of 4K each. The address generated by the CPU is decomposed into three parts: the first indicates the segment number (8 bits), the second the page number (4 bits), and the last part denotes the offset in the page (12 bits). A segment table and a page table are used for page transfer from secondary into main memory. Logical addresses are translated into physical addresses in hardware (Dynamic Address Translation – DAT). This way, the address spaces of programs are handled and protected.

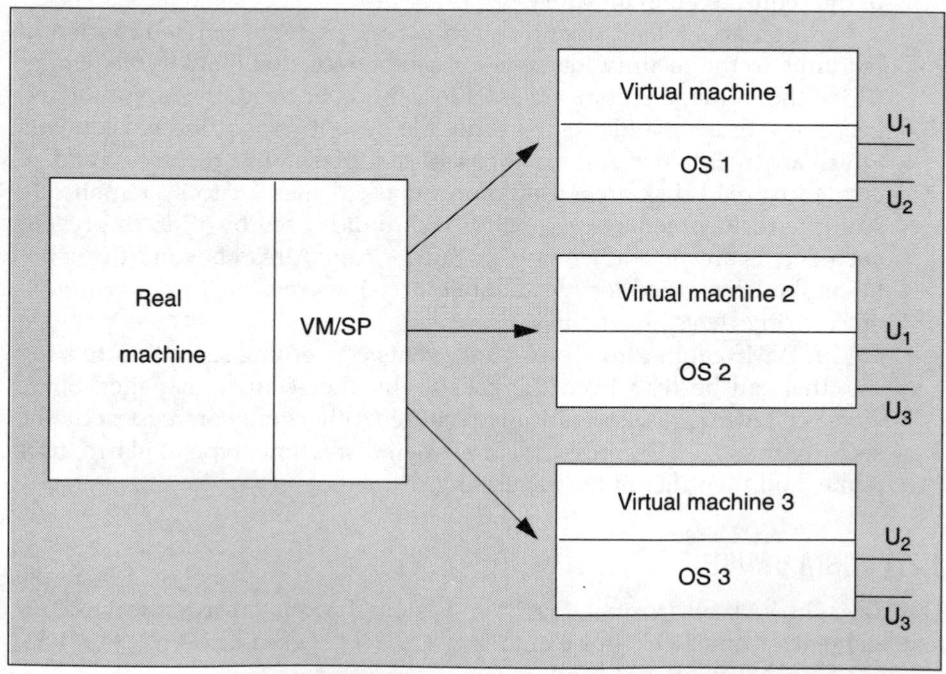


*Figure 3.24* VM/SP operating system.

- Management of peripherals. Each virtual machine can have dedicated peripheral units (for example, tapes), partially dedicated units (for example, mini-disks), and virtual units (shared among various virtual machines through mechanisms such as spoolers for printers).
- Activation of a virtual machine by a logon command, which can be sent from an active terminal under VM. The logon phase requires a password, controlled by the control program. During the logon, after password validation, the control program builds the segment and page tables for the virtual machine, and allocates the resources needed by the machine.

The control program is size-limited, which makes it difficult to penetrate and easy to maintain, thus offering remarkable advantages for security. Besides, the mutual independence of logically separated OSs limits the consequences of possible attacks to the subsystem where the attack takes place.

### 3.7.5 OS/400

OS/400 (Operating System 400) is the IBM OS for the AS/400 system series. The peculiarity of this system is that security is centred around the 'object' concept; an object is any storable item on which operations can be performed. Therefore, all the physical resources and information to be protected are considered as objects in OS/400. The features of users and of the access control mechanism in OS/400 are now described.

- *Users.* Each user has an associated profile, containing the following fields: *user class, special authorizations, and restricted possibilities*. The user class field contains the class to which a user belongs. Possible values are:
  - SECOFR: the authority maximum level defined for the system administrator;
  - SECADM: the authority level for the security manager;
  - PGMR: the authority level for the user programmer;
  - SYSOPR: the authority level for the system operator;
  - USER: the authority level for a generic user.

  The *authorizations* field specifies the set of authorizations defined for a user. User classes have an associated set of default authorizations, which can be chosen via the *userclass* option. These special authorizations define privileges relating to typical and usual operations of the user class assigned to a user (for example, privileges for defining user profiles, and authorizations for the SECADM class; or grants for save and recovery operations for the SYSOPR class).

  The *restricted possibilities* field is used to forbid some OS commands to the user. Therefore, it limits the set of default privileges of a user. Programs get the same authorizations as the users requesting execution. A particular mechanism, the 'presumed authorization' (similar to the setuid mechanism in UNIX), allows authorizations associated with a program to vary during the execution phase. At run time, a program that was compiled in the 'assumed authorization' modality gets the authorizations of its owner, rather than of its user. Considerations about security of the 'assumed authorization' are analogous to those regarding the setuid mechanism (see the paragraphs on security considerations on the setuid mechanism in Section 3.7.2).

- *Groups*. A group concept exists in OS/400. A user can belong to one group only. Groups have a *group profile*: that is, a user profile where security features of the group are specified. Each group member owns both personal and group authorizations.
- *Objects*. An object is any storable item on which operations can be performed. The name, type, access authorizations, and the data possibly contained in the object are associated to an object. Each object has an owner, generally the creator. Suitable commands can modify the owners. Authorizations are distinguished into owner's authorizations and public authorizations (relating to users who are not the owner). Specific authorizations (different from these two types) for particular users/groups that must be referenced can be specified inside the object. The authorizations defined for an object can be distinguished as follows:
  - Object authorizations: permit operations on the object (OBJOPR authorization), allow other users/groups to be granted authorizations on the object (OBJMGT authorization), and allow the physical erasure of the object (OBJEXIST).
  - Data authorizations: these allow access to data contained in the object in 'read' mode (READ authorization), in 'record update' mode (UPD authorization), in 'record insert' mode (ADD authorization), and in 'record delete' mode (DLT authorization).

Owner's authorizations and public authorizations are a combination of object and data authorizations. They are contained in the object and can be modified by the security managers. Objects can be grouped and authorization lists defined for them. Authorization lists contain authorizations granted to subjects on a group of objects, thus reducing the set of authorizations to be specified.

User authentication is password based. Functionalities for password control and handling are supplied (for example, duration, rotation, and disabling controls). Passwords are stored within an inaccessible password file.

Access control is implemented in firmware, by examining the combination of authorizations in the object and in the user profile, and by checking any authorization lists defined for the object (Figure 3.25).

Object control is automatically executed upon every access request (thus it cannot be modified or circumvented). Moreover, auditing functions are provided for the accesses executed.

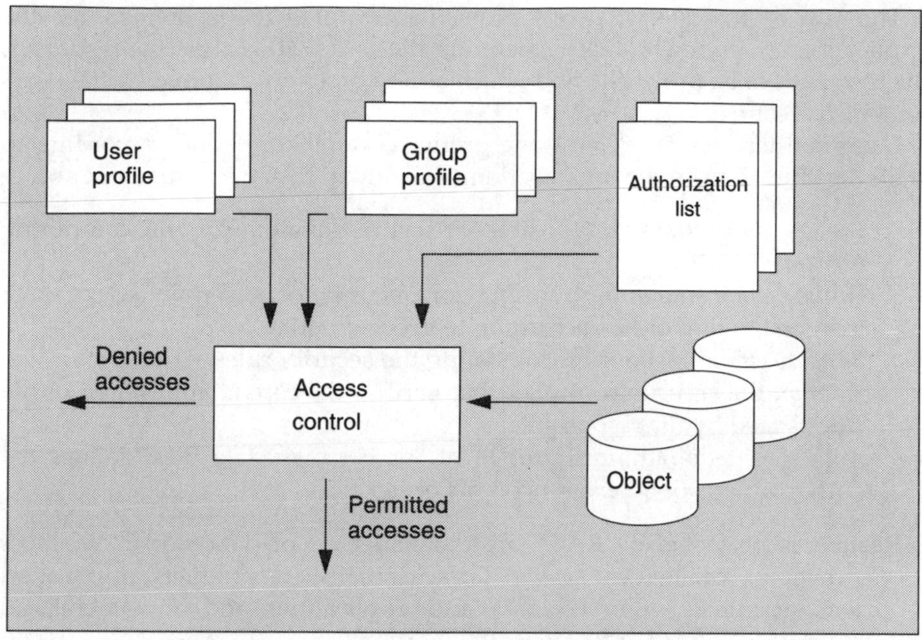


*Figure 3.25* Access control in the OS/400 system.

## 3.8 Security packages

Special-purpose security software consists of a set of security packages that can be integrated into existing environments to provide additional functions for security. These functions are typical of secure systems: therefore, they can be considered as security systems since they implement access control functions.

Among the various packages on the market, IBM's RACF (Resource Access Control Facility) and Computer Associates' CA-ACF2 (Access Control Facility 2) and CA-TOP SECRET are described in the following.

### 3.8.1 RACF

RACF is a security system for MVS systems (MVS/ESA and MVS/XA) and VM systems (VM/SP and VM/XA SP). The security functions provided by RACF are (Paans, 1991):

- User authentication, through password;
- Access control on resources;
- Logging and reporting of events related to security (violations, and access requests).

The use of RACF first needs protection features to be defined for the application environment: that is, defining the users who access the resources, the resources to be protected, and which access types are required by the users on which resources.

**Users** are inserted in at least one group. Groups are defined according to skills and functions in the organization. Skills in an RACF environment are:

- *System administrator*: responsible for security of all data in the computing centre;
- *Group administrator*: responsible for security of a certain set of data assigned to him or her, according to given criteria;
- *Security officer*: responsible for stating the security rules;
- *Auditor*: the security controller that verifies the correct application of the rules stated by the responsible;
- *Data owner*: the administrator of his or her own data files; defines the authorizations of other users on his or her files.

**Resources** protected by RACF are datasets (sets of data stored on direct access devices), catalogues, system libraries, software products, application programs, terminals, reserved data and applications and, in general, all resource classes defined at RACF installation time.

In RACF, *user profiles, group profiles, and resource profiles* are used to describe the features of resources and users.

- *User profiles*. These contain a set of information related to users, such as identifiers (userid), passwords, groups, sets of attributes that further specify the users' authority levels, and users' names. Authority is stated at different levels:
  - *special*: this level is associated with the RACF administrator and gives control on all RACF profiles;
  - *auditor*: this level is associated with the security controller to verify the correct application of security rules;
  - *operations*: enables the associated users to perform operations on the resources protected by RACF (for example, operations on files);
  - *class authority (clauth)*: allows the creation and modification of resource profiles for predefined classes of resources (for example, terminals, tapevol, dasdvol, opcclass, dsnr);
  - *create*: allows the creation and modification of dataset profiles for groups of datasets;
  - *revoke*: prevents users from accessing RACF protected resources.
- *Group profiles*. These describe the groups' features and the relationships among different user groups. Groups are organized in a hierarchical structure reflecting skills and functions within the organization. Users and datasets are defined for each group. The authority of single members inside a group is defined in a subsequent phase of users/groups connection. Resource administration may be decentralized, by defining group administrators. Resources may have an owner, who can administer his or

her own resources. There may be a group owner: this is the only user enabled to operate on the group composition and on members' access rights.

- *Resource profiles*. These describe the features of generic resources and datasets. In general, they specify the name of a dataset (or of a resource), the 'universal access authority' (UACC), and an access list of all users and groups of users granted access authorizations to the dataset (or resource) with the related authorizations. Dataset profiles may be specific (a profile for each dataset) or generic (a profile for each group of datasets holding a common prefix, for example, SYS1.*, referring to names starting with SYS1 for all datasets in the system). The UACC field is used to specify users neither included in the access list nor defined for RACF, but still enabled to access a resource.

The user (group) access modes for resources are the following:

- *Alter*: full control of a resource
- *Update*: read/write access
- *Read*: read-only access
- *None*: no access to a resource.

In the early versions of RACF, no resource protection was enforced until an explicit definition of protection rules was entered. Recent versions provide default protection for all the resources, according to different modes defined by the RACF administrator through the *setropts* (set racf options) command. According to parameters accepted by setropts, the modes are the following:

- *Setropts noprotectall*: allows the creation and use of resources holding no RACF protection, which can be accessed by all system users.
- *Setropts protectall (warning)*: upon access requests to a resource for which any valid profile exists, both the user and the console are sent a message signalling the missing protections. This protection mode is a transition mode useful during the refinement of the security requirements for resources.
- *Setropts protectall (failures)*: prevents users from creating non-protected resources and from accessing them (even although they already exist). The system administrator or group administrator must provide the profile definition in order to allow the accesses.

Access control is based on the classification of users and resources according to security levels and security categories. Security levels are hierarchically ordered from 1 to 254 (higher levels for higher security) and can have associated names (for example, 10 = internal use).

Security categories are not hierarchically ordered: they express possible relations between user groups and resource groups (for example, 'administration' category datasets can be accessed only by the same category of users). Access control is based on a comparison between the security levels and the categories defined for the users and resources involved. The user security level must be higher in the hierarchy than the level of the accessed resource. The security levels and security categories are defined in the *'seclevel'* and *'category'* profiles of the *secdata* class, which can be accessed only by the system administrator through the *ralter* command (resource alter).

The operation modalities are shown in Figure 3.26.

A user request for access to a resource is sent to RACF for validation. The user and resource profiles are consulted by RACF to verify the user authorization to access the resource. Incorrect requests cause access denial: the event would be recorded on an audit file, causing the abnormal termination of the process (code 913, abnormal end). The RACF user interface is the Resource Manager of the OS; it forwards the access requests (command) for their validation.

The user authentication mechanism is based on an identifier/password combination. If this combination is recognized, the user is accepted with his or her authority level. Passwords are ciphered using the Data Encryption Standard (DES) algorithm, and are stored in a ciphered form. The system administrator can also specify rules referring to the use of passwords through the *setropts password*: this allows, according to the specific parameters, different controls to be defined, for example on history, duration, number of attempts, length. The purpose is to prevent old passwords being reused, to limit the password validity or the number of attempts to enter passwords, or to pose requirements on the password length.

In particular, the *setropts* command recognizes the following parameters:

- *Setropts password (history (number of previous passwords)).* A list of used passwords is specified to prevent both rotation and reuse of passwords;
- *Setropts password (interval (number of days)).* A number of days is stated for password validity, thus forcing users to change their passwords periodically;
- *Setropts password (revoke (number of invalid passwords)).* Number of available attempts in the case of missing passwords;

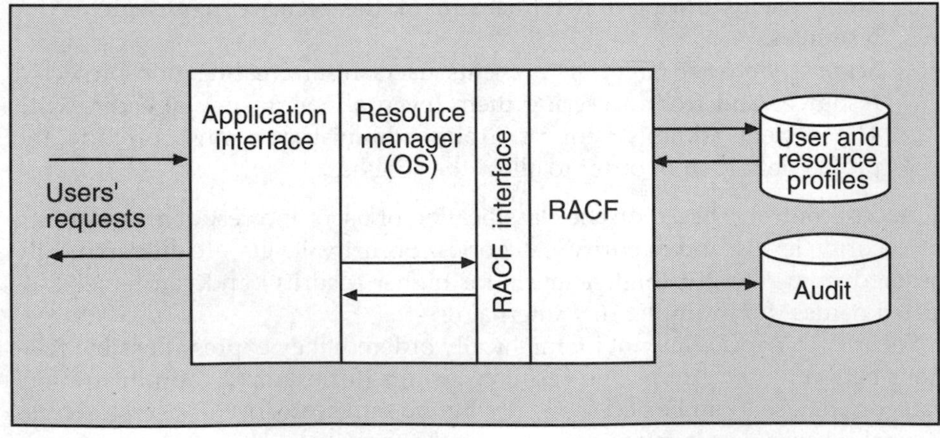


*Figure 3.26* RACF operational schema.

- *Setropts password (RuleN (Length(m)contents(position))).* This allows the definition of up to eight rules for building new passwords, defining, for each position, the contents of the position inside the password (numerical character, alphanumerical character, special symbol). Thus, the use of special symbols inside a password can be enforced.

The MVS OS contains System Management Facilities (SMF) for recording, in a suitable format, the events occurring in the OS and in the applications, keeping track of the users who caused the event. SMF is used by RACF for recording access attempts to resources, warning messages, and relevant events involving security (for example, access operations, procedure calls, system commands). Recording modalities (for example, for datasets, groups of datasets, security levels) can be defined by auditors, identifying a set of parameters. Reports can be also generated about the state of the system security mechanisms.

### 3.8.2 CA-ACF2

The denomination CA-ACF2 refers to a set of security products for VM, MVS, VS1 and VSE. CA-ACF2 is examined in detail for VM. CA-ACF2 protects crucial and relevant resources in VM, such as minidisks, CMS files, IUCV, VMCF, and the DIAL command. The design philosophy is the feature that distinguishes CA-ACF2 from RACF. CA-ACF2 has been designed to provide default resource protection. Thus, access authorizations need not be explicitly defined; users are denied access to resources by default. As a consequence, rules for resource sharing have to be defined.

The architecture of CA-ACF2, depicted in Figure 3.27, comprises three databases:

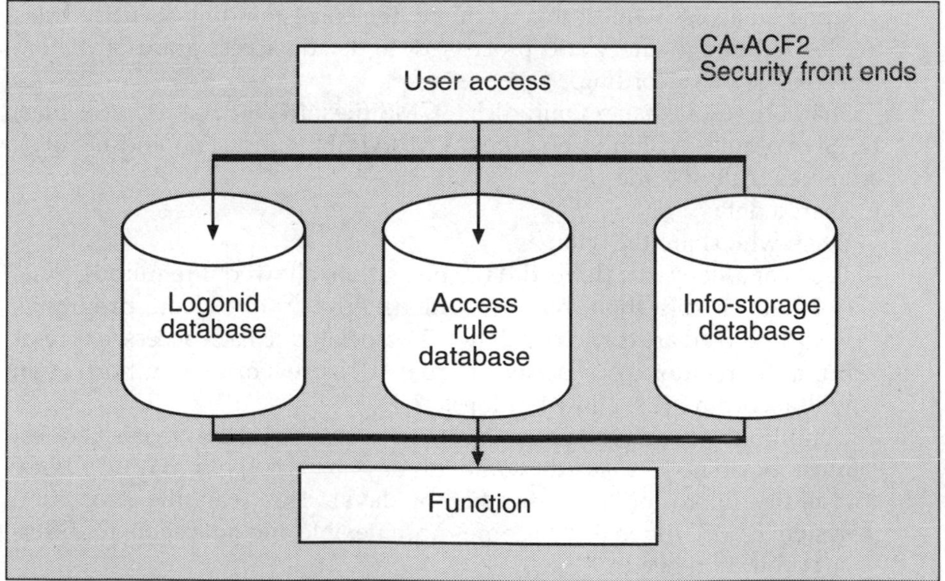


*Figure 3.27* Architecture of CA-ACF2.

- *Logonid database*. This stores the Logonids (logon identifiers) of all system users and enforces access control. Each user or virtual machine has an identifier (Logonid) which is, in turn, associated to a Logonid record protected by a password. The Logonid contains the user's privileges, attributes and restrictions. Upon connection to the system, a user enters his or her Logonid and password; these are matched against the Logonid record to validate the user and his or her privileges. A successful result enables the connection; otherwise, access is denied and the event is recorded. The password protects its associated Logonid. Password cryptography is a security precaution. Password discovery is further reduced through stating, for example, a minimum length, a maximum validity interval (in days), and invalidation after a certain number of wrong insertions. The attributes contained in the Logonid record specify the user's classification(s):
  - *Security*: to grant privileges and define access to data, and can access data and resources without any authorization;
  - *Account*: to create Logonid records;
  - *Audit*: to monitor the ACF2 activities;
  - *Leader*: to display and update specific data in Logonid;
  - *Consult*: to display specific data in Logonid database;
  - *User*: is the default, automatically assumed by ACF2 for all Logonids.
- *Access rules database*. This contains access rules defined for resource sharing. Owing to default protection, resource sharing needs to be explicitly defined through access rules; their definition can be a function only of the security officer (centralized administration), or of all users (or selected subsets of users) (decentralized administration).

  Upon an access request to a resource, the corresponding security rules are loaded into memory and processed, to decide access grant or denial, or access grant/recording.

  Sharable resources are: minidisks, CMS files, MVS datasets, VSE files, DASD volumes, volumes on tapes, VMBATCH (subsystem and facility). An access rule specifies:
  - Shared data;
  - Users who share the data;
  - Types of access: *read* (to read data; execution, allowed if required); *write* (for data modification; read is denied); *execute* (to execute programs; write and read are denied). A letter is associated to each access, expressing authorization (A – allow), denial (P – prevent), or authorization with recording (L – allow but log).
  - Conditions on access types: *location* (from where the access request must be issued); *time* (the time of day, or the week day); *until/for* (validity up to, or for a number of days). This way, the protection system can be tuned and become more flexible and adaptable to different protection needs.

  The UID string can be used in the definition of access rules; hence, user groups sharing a resource can be concisely defined, describing their features and Logonid through the string characters.

- *Information database*. This controls the use of the system resources, possibly defining further access restrictions. Protection is given to resources through rules and the Logon record: these must be stored in the database. The rules express control on access to resources (CIP, DIRMAINT commands and the other resources protected by CA-ACF2 ). The database records allow restrictions to be specified on user access (for example, connection time, from which terminal), and on user privileges. The rules and records referring to a resource, contained in the information database, are loaded into memory upon access requests to that resource.

The normal functions of VM are not altered by the installation of the CA-ACF2 package; however, they are intercepted because CA-ACF2 plays the role of a front end. The security procedures of CA-ACF2 are invoked upon access requests, and access can be granted if in accordance with information in the databases.

CA-ACF2 can operate in various 'modes', allowing for a gradual increase of the protection level provided by CA-ACF2. In increasing order, the **operation modes** are:

- *Quiet*. Only user authentication occurs in the Logon phase. No access control is performed.
- *Log*. Access violations are recorded, without blocking the access operation. Records are available for analysis by the security officers, to simplify and improve the definition of access rules.
- *Warn*. Access violations are recorded, and signal messages are sent to the users involved, still without blocking access operations. Again, these cases are used to tune the security rules.
- *Abort*. All security controls are on. Thus, access violations are recorded, signal messages are sent to the users involved, and access is denied.
- *Rule*. This provides more flexible protection, specifying access modes for different resources (DASD volume, CMS file, tape volume, and so on). A rule is a combination of the other modes.

An audit functionality is also offered by CA-ACF2. The audit mechanism records:

- All access violations, including attempts to enter wrong passwords;
- All events related to accesses for which denial, or authorization with recording, have been specified;
- All the updates on the three databases used by CA-ACF2.

Audit records are used to produce reports (for example, a report on the total number of records and violations, a report on variations in the security environment, a report on invalid connections to the system).

A CA-ACF2 product is also available for security in networked MVS and VAX/VMS systems; in addition, a version for personal computers exists, connected to MVS systems via a hardware board.

### 3.8.3 CA-TOP SECRET

The term CA-TOP SECRET refers to a set of products for security in MVS, VM and VSE environments. CA-TOP SECRET ensures protection of the following elements: resources, facilities and data. Thus, it controls the users' access requests, preventing the disclosure and unauthorized modification of the protected elements. In addition, it supplies auditing and on-line report functionalities for the security administrator.

CA-TOP SECRET needs the protection requirements of its application environment to be defined during the installation phase (which users can access which resources, how and when; the type of security – centralized or decentralized; the priority assigned to each resource).

The *primary security administrator* is responsible for the definition of the security requirements. He or she interacts with CA-TOP SECRET through the TSS (Top Secret System) command, which is a protected command. The TSS command is issued each time the protection requirements change.

**Users** are subjects accessing protected resources. Each user is associated with a set of access authorizations, defining accessible resources and access modes. Access authorizations are granted according to the user role within the organization. Each user (or process) has an associated ACID (Accessor ID), which is a string of characters used by CA-TOP SECRET to uniquely identify users and the associated access authorizations upon an access request.

Users (see Figure 3.28) belong to a *department*, depending on their work role; departments belong to *divisions* (if any). A department ACID and a division ACID respectively is associated to each department and division. In a department, users may belong to one or several groups. Access authorizations for users or groups of users are defined by the primary security administrator through the TSS command. Since users are grouped according to common access needs, common access authorizations are grouped into profiles. The profile is connected with each user ACID.

The **resources** protected by CA-TOP SECRET are the typical MVS resources: terminals, programs, datasets, volumes (tape and DASD), commands (TSO – Time Sharing Option, and all commands specified by the primary security administrator in the installation phase), transactions (CICS, IMS, IDMS and all transactions specified by the primary security administrator during the installation phase), databases and all typical MVS resources as specified in the product installation phase. Generally, resources needing protection are identified by a generic prefix, or by their complete name. As far as databases are concerned, access is controlled at the field level, which is identified by its logical name. Control can also depend on the contents, type and size of the accessed field. The CPUs can also be defined as resources needing protection: usage requests must thus be controlled and validated.

Security administration may be centralized or decentralized. In the first case, the primary security administrator is the only person responsible for security in the whole system. In the second case, secondary administrators can be appointed by the primary administrator: thus responsibilities are distributed. A

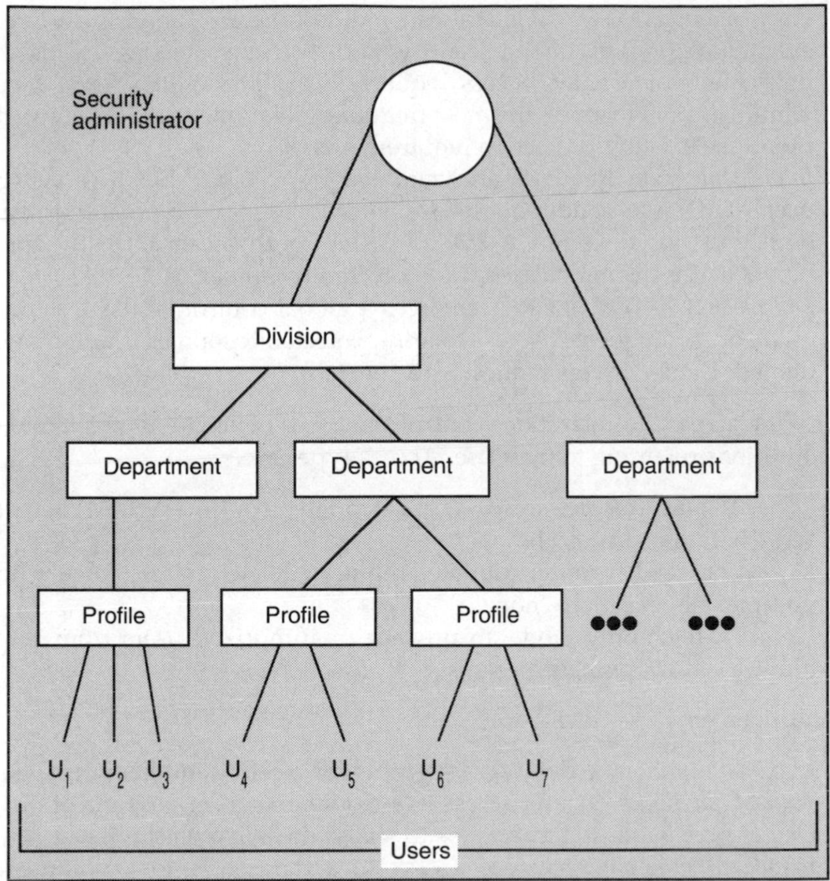


*Figure 3.28* Relationships between users, profiles, departments and divisions in CA-TOP SECRET.

user-owner of resources can be nominated; he or she can define access authorizations on his or her owned resources for other users. However, the tasks that always pertain only to the primary security administrator are: the definition of departments, divisions, and auditors; the identification of users and the assignment of ACIDs; the adding of resources; the appointment of owners and of secondary security administrators; and the supervision of the whole security system.

Four **operation modes** exist in CA-TOP SECRET, useful in the different phases of the products' application:

- *Dormant mode*. CA-TOP SECRET is installed, but control is not yet operating for validation. The TSS command is used to define protection requirements enabling the subsequent implementation of access controls.

- *Warn mode*. CA-TOP SECRET can validate access requests and record events (logging) involving security, with warning messages to users for non-valid but granted access requests. This phase allows the security administrators to study the most frequent violations, and consequently to refine the existing protection requirements.
- *Implement mode*. Requests are validated by CA-TOP SECRET using the user ACID; non-valid requests are denied. Users with no authorizations (and thus not needing CA-TOP SECRET control) can normally operate; however, they cannot access the protected resources.
- *Fail mode*. CA-TOP SECRET enforces a global control on the system, and on all access requests. Access to non-protected resources is automatically denied. Denied access requests are aborted.

For data, access authorizations control the types of access allowed, and specify conditions retaining to their use. Access types are:

- *Datasets* and *volumes*: read, write, update, control (VSAM), creation, scratch, non-creation, all none;
- *Databases*: read, browse, update, replace, delete, purge, force, end-of-volume, all operations, none;
- *Libraries*: fetch-only mode, to prevent unauthorized users from reading libraries and copying programs.

Conditions on access levels are:

- *Maximal duration*: to deny access grants for a certain number of days;
- *Time-of-day limits*: to limit access to a resource to a certain time of day;
- *Day-of-week limits*: to limit access to stated days in a week;
- *Privileged programs*: to force access to a dataset or to a volume only through a specific program, which must be fetched from the library of the resource owner.

For the other resources needing protection, CA-TOP SECRET checks, through the corresponding ACID, whether the user (process) should be granted access to the resource. For access to be granted, users must connect to the system and be authenticated. Authentication is governed by passwords; passwords also protect the ACIDs. General organizational rules are employed to reduce the risk of password disclosure. Some of these rules involve:

- Assignment of limits to password validity;
- Maintenance of a password history, to forbid reuse;
- Assignment of rules on password composition (for example, minimum length, non-trivial terms);
- Definition of limits on the number of attempts: passwords are disabled beyond the chosen threshold number of attempts;
- Implementation of an algorithm for random password generation.

All security information is stored in the *security file*, which is shared by all the CPUs of the system and contains records of all the features and access authorizations of all the users. After successful user authentication and connection, the users security record is loaded into memory (into the user memory area) until disconnection time.

CA-TOP SECRET also supplies a set of audit functions, supporting the activities of the security administrators and auditors (specific auditor tasks include the display of users activity and the analysis of audit data). Events are recorded on the *Audit/Tracking* shared file, and are notified to the primary security administrator. From audit records, information can be obtained about violations of access controls. In addition, recorded events can be manipulated according to specific selection criteria, in order to supply reports concerning, for example, resources, time of day, date, type of access, and types of events.

The description of CA-TOP SECRET given here refers to the MVS OS. Analogous functions exist for other systems that can be linked to CA-TOP SECRET. A version of the package is available for VMS (VAX Digital) connected via a network to CA-TOP SECRET MVS; another version is available for personal computers (DOS) connected to MVS via a hardware board.

## 3.9 Security standards

From the viewpoint of both security vendors and developers and users of security packages, the need is arising for security standards as a reference for product development and certification. Many organizations and agencies have proposed standards to these purposes (Russel and Gangemi, 1991)

The very first efforts at security standard definition date back to the late 1970s, when a number of **initiatives** were undertaken **in the USA**. The US DoD promoted the *DoD Computer Security Initiative* in 1977, launched in 1978. The US Government and private concerns were involved through a series of meetings and seminars aimed at stating the status of security and at studying the available tools for building secure systems; a further concern was the analysis of existing or envisioned certification techniques for security.

An analogous initiative was undertaken in those years by the National Bureau of Standards (NBS, now called NIST – National Institute of Standards and Technology). After publication of the *Brooks Act* in 1965, the NBS became responsible for the development of standards for acquisition and use of federal computing systems. It supported the federal agencies interested in the enforcement of the standards. All the federal standards of the NBS relating to information processing, in general, and to security, in particular, are published in the Federal Information Processing Standards collection of publications (FIPS PUBs).

The NBS focused on two initiatives for security, one oriented to *cryptography standards*, the other to the *development* and *evaluation process* for secure systems. Under the first initiative, in 1973 the NBS invited the constructors to submit technical proposals for enciphering unclassified federal data and for sensitive commercial data. After a set of seminars sponsored also by the Institute of Computer Science and Technology (ICST, now called the National Computer

Systems Laboratory), the Data Encryption Standard (DES) technique was designated as the standard for cryptography, based on the DES algorithm. In 1977, the DES became the official technique for protection of unclassified federal data; later, it was adopted as a standard by the American National Standards Institute (ANSI).

Concerning the evaluation of secure systems, from 1968 up to the present day the NBS has stimulated researchers, constructors, vendors, software developers, and users to undertake the definition of certification standards. Conferences and workshops were held between 1972 and 1977, concentrating on the issue of certifying the security and the level of trust of a given system through the definition of techniques to evaluate the security level of a system with respect to the target environment and to its proposed use. In the case of insufficient security, the standards should propose and guide a set of interventions aimed at reaching the level identified as necessary. The reports, produced as a result, outlined the need for explicit *security policies* and for *security mechanisms* able to enforce these policies. They also mentioned the need to have a list of certified security products as a support for users. Finally, the need to develop standardized and formal tools to measure and evaluate the global security of a system was outlined.

In 1979, the Mitre Corporation was entrusted with producing an initial set of criteria to evaluate the security of a system handling classified data. Public seminars organized by the Office of the Secretary of Defense about the *DoD Computer Security Initiative* contributed to consolidate the initiative proposed by the DoD, and in 1981 the Computer Security Center (CSC) was founded within the National Security Agency (NSA). The goal was to support the DoD initiative. The CSC was officially nominated through the *Computer Security Evaluation Center* document.

In August 1985, the NCSC (National Computer Security Center) was constituted, grouping the CSC and all the US federal agencies. The Center, whose basic publications referenced here are National Computer Security Center (1987a, 1987b, 1988a, 1988b, 1988c, 1988d, 1989a, 1989b, 1989c, 1991), was founded with the following basic aims:

- To provide the technical support of the governmental agencies and a reference for systems handling classified data;
- To define a set of criteria for the evaluation of security of computing systems and for the assessment of available security products;
- To encourage and perform research in the field of security, also in distributed systems;
- To favour the availability of secure systems;
- To develop verification and testing tools to be used in the certification of a given security system;
- In general, to spread the sensibility and culture of security in both federal agencies and private companies.

A well-known result of the NCSC is the *Trusted Computer System Evaluation Criteria* (TCSEC) document, known as the *Orange Book* (see section 3.9.1) (Department of Defense, 1985). In this document, criteria are collected to evaluate the security of a system; the criteria are defined on the basis of previous issues developed at Mitre. The products assessed as secure belong to the *Evaluated Product List*. After the Orange Book, some reports were published to interpret the requirements of the Orange Book in particular areas. These reports are known as the *Rainbow Series*. In particular, the Trusted Network Intepretation (TNI), published in 1987, is the interpretation of the TCSEC for network environments, also called the *Red Book* (National Computer Security Center, 1987a), and the Trusted DBMS Interpretation (TDI), recently published (National Computer Security Center, 1991), represents the TCSEC interpretation for database environments.

Some research centres and some organizations do not totally agree with the specifications defined in the Orange Book, in particular with its being regarded as a reference specification for evaluating the trustworthiness of security systems. On this point, the debate is still open, although the Orange Book is still the reference standard for secure systems (Barker and Pfleeger, 1990).

In 1985, the National Security Agency unified its researches on security and on communications under the Deputy Directorate for Information Security Systems, INFOSEC.

In **Europe**, several **initiatives** have been undertaken to define security standards (UK-IT, 1990; Commission of the European Communities, 1991; Jahl, 1990). In particular, a centre has been founded aimed at studying issues related to security in information systems, called the Commercial Computer Security Centre (CCSC) of the Trade and Industry Department (TDI) in Germany. In order to be able to consider both commercial/industrial environments and military environments, other organizations have been involved: the Central Computer and Telecommunications Agency (CCTA) for commercial/industrial environments and the Communications–Electronics Security Group (CESG) for military environments handling classified data. Other European countries (United Kingdom, France, The Netherlands) have collaborated with Germany in the definition of the European standards for security.

In 1990, the CCSC published the *Criteria for Security Product Evaluation for Information Systems*, known as the *White Books*. This standard is based on both the Orange Book and some European standards (Branstad *et al.*, 1991). The White Books define a set of *system typologies*, rather than a hierarchy, each corresponding to, and responsible for, a set of security requirements, depending on the computing system considered (for example, in some target environments secrecy is more relevant than integrity).

Another environment where security requirements strongly need to be defined is the distributed environment. The International Standards Organization (ISO) is in charge of defining these standards.

The European Computer Manufacturers Association (ECMA), grouping about 50 European manufacturers, is also involved in the definition of security standards (ECMA, 1988). Its aim is the definition of criteria for distributed processing and data exchange for the execution of private applications and public services (such as e-mail systems, or data retrieval services). The ECMA reference architecture is based on security *domains, tools* and *techniques*. A security domain is a set of network connections of private and public computers and applications, controlled by a network manager. Security is regarded within a domain as a set of tools and techniques related to authentication, security authorization management for subjects and objects, authorization-based access control, domain status save operations, record of security-relevant events, saving the system after an attack, and data cryptography. At a higher level, the *network security domain* considers network-wide security problems caused by the network computers sharing the objects of one domain, and data exchange between network computers.

The work of ECMA is specifically oriented to the network domain and, in particular, to the definition of network security policies for access control to objects (machines/applications) of the various domains. At a lower level, the security policies of the domains have to be designed to be consistent with the network policies; this way, a separation is achieved between users, applications, data, system functions, and communication functions, creating a 'shell' of security tools and techniques. Within each shell, different security policies can be defined and, consequently, different security functions, too. The communication protocols among the various security services of a network conform to the OSI standards.

**Other initiatives** include the X/Open Organization, founded in 1984, which involves a group of European and US producers in the definition of standards for open systems based on an integrated environment, the Common Application Environment (CAE). The effort of X/Open is directed at combining the existing standards into one integrated environment where applications are portable at the source code level. The *X/Open Security Guide* describes the interface security standards which promote portability. A family of X/Open products, named XPG, is available in different versions (XPG1, XPG2, XPG3). An XPG family is an integrated set of products (XPG Specifications, XPG Verification Suite, XPG Descriptive Guides, and XPG Trademark Licensing Materials) for the development and implementation of open systems.

The American National Standards Institute ANSI **(ANSI)** is responsible for standard approval. Presently, various ANSI Committees are developing standards for cryptography and authentication of messages.

The International Federation for Information Processing **(IFIP)** groups multinational professional and technical organizations working in the area of information systems. The n.11 Technical Committee (TC-11) of IFIP for Information Systems Protection and Security has the task of promoting internationally interest in and attention on security issues, and of proposing and promoting standards.

The Institute of Electrical and Electronics Engineers **(IEEE)** is an international professional organization whose tasks are, among others, the development of standards to be submitted to ANSI for approval. Among the IEEE standards, the most relevant are:

- The standard for application portability in open systems (Portable Operating System Interface for Computer Environments – POSIX). POSIX was developed in collaboration with ISO;

- The standard for developing a secure system according to the POSIX criteria; this is still under study by the IEEE 1003.6 Security Extensions Committee.

Studies are ongoing to define standards regarding discretionary and mandatory access control, privileges and audit activities.

### 3.9.1 The DoD criteria

The evaluation of the protection level provided by a system is a central problem of research in security. Criteria and evaluation tools should be available to both developers and end users to enable the trust level of a security mechanism to be stated. In this perspective, the criteria defined by the US Department of Defense (DoD) (Department of Defense, 1985) provide a reference for both the development and the evaluation of secure systems.

The DoD criteria were defined to supply:

- *Users* with evaluation metrics to assess the reliability of the security system for protection of classified or sensitive information when:
  - the security system is not developed internally to an organization, but a commercial product is employed: criteria are needed to evaluate a security product;
  - the security system is developed internally, and criteria are needed to check whether all the security requirements have been considered and implemented;
- *Developers/vendors* with a design guide showing the security features to be included in commercial systems in order to make available trusted off-the-shelf products that meet the security requirements of sensitive applications;
- *Designers* with a guide for the specification of security requirements.

Although conceived for military systems (protection of classified information), the focus directed by the DoD criteria on security system design is also suitable for commercial systems. Systems are classified by the DoD according to a set of criteria or requirements, which can be grouped into broader categories concerning, respectively, the protection level offered by the system *(security policy)*; the accountability of the users and user operations to support the security policies *(accountability)*; and the assurance of the reliability of the system, with reference to both the system development and operation *(assurance)*. System development should follow the traditional system engineering practices, and the system should operate without circumvention of the security features. The system should be well documented through a set of documents providing detailed information about the security features, the design characteristics, and the test cases of the system *(documentation)* (Chokhani, 1992).

The DoD requirements refer to the Trusted Computing Base (TCB), namely the set of hardware, software and firmware mechanisms enforcing the system security features. In addition, the criteria are centred around the concept of a *reference monitor*, responsible for mediating all accesses by subjects to objects, and for verifying that only authorized access is performed (Figure 3.29).

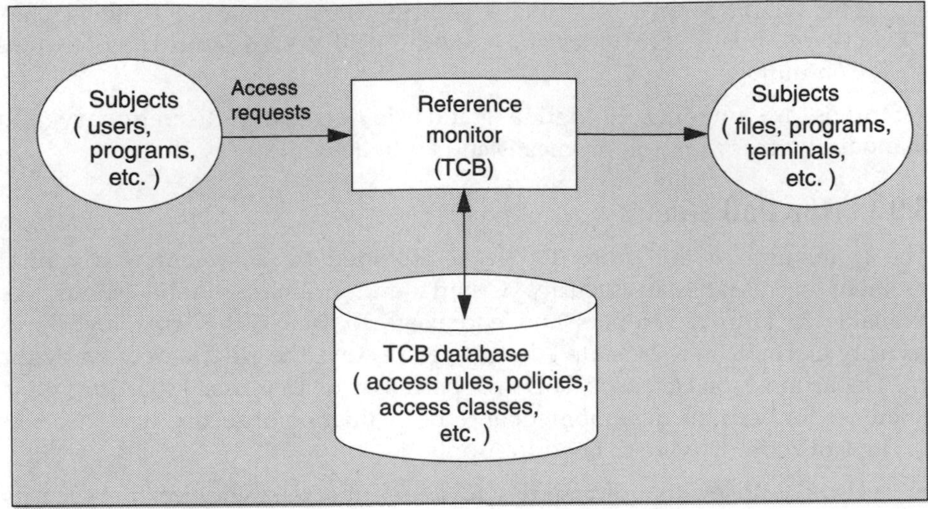


*Figure 3.29* Reference monitor in the DoD criteria.

In the following, the requirements categories mentioned above are examined.

(1) *Security policy*. This requirement groups a set of security requirements concerning the definition of the policies regulating the accesses of users to information, according to the organization policies and rules. Subjects, objects and rules for subject access to objects must be defined. According to the DoD, a security system should support both discretionary access control (DAC) and mandatory access control (MAC), as well as a label mechanism and the possibility of reusing memory. In particular, the following capabilities are requested:

(a) *DAC*. According to DAC, subjects can protect their own objects, and can grant or deny access permissions to other subjects (users or groups of users), specifying also the access mode (that is, the operation executable on the object).

(b) *MAC*. According to MAC, subjects can read/write objects for which they have the required clearance. MAC operates using security labels, assigned to both subjects (security clearances) and objects (security classification). Security labels specify a hierarchical classification level and a set of non-hierarchical categories that together state the clearance of the subject and the level of sensitivity of the information stored in the object. According to MAC, subjects can read objects at the same or lower classification, and write objects at the same or higher classification, than that of the subject.

(c) *Labels*. Security labels must be associated with subjects and objects, in order to support MAC. The system should be able to attach to each subject/object a label, composed of a hierarchical classification level and a set of non-hierarchical categories that together state the clearance of the subject and the level of sensitivity.

(d) *Reuse of objects*. According to this requirement, basic storage elements, such as memory pages and disk sectors, must be cleared before being released to a new user, to prevent intentional/accidental data scavenging.

(2) *Accountability*. This issue includes the features of identification/authentication, audit, and trusted path.

(a) *Identification/authentication*. System subjects (users) must be identified and authenticated, to ensure that only authorized users have access to data. This is a crucial feature, since all access requests will be evaluated on the basis of subject identity. Identification is the process of the user identifying himself to the TCB, making use of user name, user ID, and so on. The authentication process consists in verifying the user identity through authentication mechanisms (for example, password based).

(b) *Audit*. The system TCB should record security-relevant events, such as logins, operations on objects, and logouts. Audit records must be maintained and protected, making possible subsequent analysis for threat detection and identification.

(c) *Trusted path*. The TCB must be sure that no users are attempting to access the system fraudulently (for example, a Trojan Horse could simulate the login procedure to catch the user password).

(3) *Assurance*. The system must contain reliable hardware/software/firmware components that can be evaluated separately to ensure the system can meet the requirements listed above. The assurance requirements can be partitioned into two further categories related to *operation reliability* and *development reliability*:

(a) *Operation reliability*. This category deals with reliability during system operation, with the purpose of assuring trusted execution of security features. The following requirements are involved:

(i) *System architecture*. This requirement deals with the development process and the usage of the security system. In particular, the system should be developed following modularization and abstraction principles (layered architecture, data abstraction, information hiding). During system operation, it is desirable to have the system TCB isolated from user processes, as well as the security kernel isolated from non-security-critical portions of the TCB.

(ii) *System integrity*. This refers to the correct operation of the system hardware and firmware, usually verified through special-purpose software (diagnostic software).

(iii) *Covert channel analysis*. This requires that no covert channels exist in the system: that is, users have no means to acquire unauthorized information through observation of authorized information (for example, variables, attributes). This requirement states that the system should be verified against the presence of covert channels in order to eliminate them.

(iv) *Trusted facility management*. This requirement concerns the separation of duties, namely the distinction of the roles of system administrators and system operators.

(v) *Trusted recovery*. This means the capability to recover the security features after TCB crashes/failures.

(b) *Development reliability*. This category of requirements concerns system reliability during the development process. It should be achieved using formal development methods and techniques (software engineering and formal testing/verification of security features). The following requirements are involved:

(i) *System testing*. This requires that the system security features have been tested and verified.

(ii) *Design specification and verification*. This requirement concerns the system design and implementation. It requires that the system has been correctly designed and implemented with reference to the requirements of the security policy. In particular, the TCB formal specifications should be proved to be consistent with the security policy model.

(iii) *Configuration management*. This deals with the configuration management of all the system components (hardware, software, firmware) and of the related documentation.

(iv) *Trusted distribution*. This requirement deals with ensuring that the security system components (hardware, software, firmware) do not undergo unauthorized modifications/alterations during transit from vendor to client. This can be gained through trusted couriers, registered mail, physical seals, and so on.

(c) *Documentation*. This requirement concerns the documentation that should be provided for the system. The system must be well documented, through a defined set of documents. The minimal set of documents includes: a Trusted Facility Manual, a Security Features User's Guide, test documentation, and design documentation, compiled under the responsibility of administrators, operators, users, developers and maintainers. Other documents can be required for divisions from B upwards (see the DoD hierarchical classification below): configuration management, system architecture, covert channel analysis report, formal model, and formal and descriptive top level specifications, providing information about the formal analysis and specification of the system and of the security features. They precisely describe the features of the system with reference to security-relevant features, design methods and techniques, test cases and architectural features.

### The DoD hierarchical classification

On the basis of these requirements, security systems can be classified according to four hierarchical divisions (D, C, B, A). Within each division, one or more hierarchical classes are defined. 'Hierarchical' refers to the fact that for each division (class), the level of protection offered by the systems in that division (class) is higher than the level of protection provided by the systems in lower divisions (classes), and lower than that provided by the systems in higher divisions (classes). Systems range from the D division, with no security requirements, to more complex systems (C, B, A divisions).

Table 3.5 shows the requirements of each class. For each category of requirements (described above), the table shows how these requirements are fulfilled by DoD classes. Note that in the table, for the *security policy* category, additional requirements have been indicated concerning label management and dissemination of classified information; these are a consequence of the MAC policy.

The features of each division and each class are now described, with reference to the contents of the original DoD document, the Orange Book (from the colour of its cover).

- *Division D – Minimum protection.* No subclass. Systems in this class are those lacking any requirements needed for higher classification.
- *Division C – Discretionary protection.* Systems in this class supply DAC and object reuse policies. In addition, they can supply identification/authentication and auditing mechanisms. Two classes are defined in division C.
  - *Class C1 – Discretionary security protection.* Systems in this class provide DAC and identification/authentication security features. In this class, it is not strictly required that the systems enforce DAC and/or accountability on single users, rather systems can operate on groups of users. For this reason, the C1 class is sometimes considered of little use.
  - *Class C2 – Controlled access protection.* Systems belonging to this class provide DAC, single-user accountability and object reuse. C2 systems refine the control mechanisms of class C1, by accounting single users and by enforcing auditing mechanisms.
- *Division B – Mandatory protection.* The primary requirement of B systems is the MAC and security labels. The most relevant data structures in the system must be assigned labels. The TCB must preserve sensitive labels' integrity. The developers must provide a model of the security policy on which the TCB is based, provide the TCB specifications and certify that a reference monitor exists in the system. There are three classes in B division. In order to be evaluated as a B (or over), a system must be developed with security features in mind from its initial design, using formal modelling and analysis techniques.
  - *Class B1 – Labelled security protection.* Systems belonging to this class own the same features as C2 systems, augmented by MAC and labels. Labelling must also be enforced for input information. B1 systems supply an informal description of the security policy model. Flaws discovered during the testing phase must be removed.

**Table 3.5** DoD evaluation criteria.

| | D | C1 | C2 | B1 | B2 | B3 | A1 |
|---|---|---|---|---|---|---|---|
| **Security policy** | | | | | | | |
| Discretionary access controls (DAC) | ★ | ◆ | ◆ | ✳ | ✳ | ◆ | ✳ |
| Object reuse | ★ | ★ | ◆ | ✳ | ✳ | ✳ | ✳ |
| Labels | ★ | ★ | ★ | ◆ | ◆ | ✳ | ✳ |
| Label integrity | ★ | ★ | ★ | ◆ | ✳ | ✳ | ✳ |
| Classified data dissemination | ★ | ★ | ★ | ◆ | ✳ | ✳ | ✳ |
| Dissemination across multilevel resources | ★ | ★ | ★ | ◆ | ✳ | ✳ | ✳ |
| Dissemination across monolevel resources | ★ | ★ | ★ | ◆ | ✳ | ✳ | ✳ |
| Printings and output classification | ★ | ★ | ★ | ◆ | ✳ | ✳ | ✳ |
| Labels of subject sensitivity | ★ | ★ | ★ | ★ | ◆ | ✳ | ✳ |
| Device labels | ★ | ★ | ★ | ★ | ◆ | ✳ | ✳ |
| Mandatory access controls (MAC) | ★ | ★ | ★ | ◆ | ◆ | ✳ | ✳ |
| **Accountability** | | | | | | | |
| Identification and authentication | ★ | ◆ | ◆ | ◆ | ✳ | ✳ | ✳ |
| Audit | ★ | ★ | ◆ | ◆ | ◆ | ◆ | ✳ |
| Trusted path | ★ | ★ | ★ | ★ | ◆ | ◆ | ✳ |
| **Assurance** | | | | | | | |
| *Operation reliability* | | | | | | | |
| System architecture | ★ | ◆ | ◆ | ◆ | ◆ | ◆ | ✳ |
| System integrity | ★ | ◆ | ✳ | ✳ | ✳ | ✳ | ✳ |
| Covert channels analysis | ★ | ★ | ★ | ★ | ◆ | ◆ | ◆ |
| Trusted facility management | ★ | ★ | ★ | ★ | ◆ | ◆ | ✳ |
| Trusted recovery | ★ | ★ | ★ | ★ | ★ | ◆ | ✳ |
| *Development reliability* | | | | | | | |
| System testing | ★ | ◆ | ◆ | ◆ | ◆ | ◆ | ◆ |
| Design specification and verification | ★ | ★ | ★ | ◆ | ◆ | ◆ | ◆ |
| Configuration management | ★ | ★ | ★ | ★ | ◆ | ✳ | ◆ |
| Trusted distribution | ★ | ★ | ★ | ★ | ★ | ★ | ◆ |
| **Documentation** | | | | | | | |
| Security Features User's Guide | ★ | ◆ | ✳ | ✳ | ✳ | ✳ | ✳ |
| Trusted Facility Manual | ★ | ◆ | ◆ | ◆ | ◆ | ◆ | ✳ |
| Test documentation | ★ | ◆ | ✳ | ✳ | ◆ | ✳ | ◆ |
| Design documentation | ★ | ◆ | ✳ | ◆ | ◆ | ◆ | ◆ |

★ : no requirements
✳ : no additional requirements (all and only the requirements of previous classes)
◆ : new or added requirements with respect to those of previous classes

– *Class B2 – Structured protection*. Starting with B2, the requirements stress the assurance. B2 systems must provide a formal model of security policies (both MAC and DAC), clearly defined and documented, and proven to be consistent with security axioms. The access control policies of the B1 class are extended to all system subjects and objects. Authentication mechanisms are implemented, and tools are provided both for system administration and for users to support configuration management. Concerning system assurance, the following requirements must be provided. The TCB must be accurately structured, separating security-critical portions from the the remaining software. The TCB interface must be clearly defined: its design and development must undergo severe tests and revisions. In addition, covert channels analysis must be performed, and possible covert channels identified and audited. A trusted path is provided for users to connect with the TCB in a secure mode. The system must be relatively penetration resistant, and penetration tests should be performed. Separation of system administrator and operator duties is also required.

  - *Class B3 – Security domains*. This class stresses the simplification and minimalization of the TCB, which must satisfy the reference monitor requirements (that is, it must mediate all access requests, be resistant to tampering, and be formally analysed and tested). Audit mechanisms are expanded with real-time monitoring and alerting mechanisms. Recovery procedures are required. B3 systems must be highly resistant to penetration attempts. Engineering techniques must be used in the design and implementation phases.

- *Division A – Verified protection*. Use of formal methods for system security verification is the main characteristic of this class. It must be formally verified that the TCB specifications are consistent with the security axioms of the formal policy model, and implement the stated security policies. Precise documentation is also required, proving that the TCB meets the security specifications in all phases, from design to implementation. Two classes are defined.
  - *Class A1 – Verification design*. From a functional viewpoint, A1 systems are equivalent to B3 systems: that is, no additional security features are provided. A main characteristic required for A1 systems consists in the use of formal and informal techniques to prove the consistency between the top-level specification of the TCB and the formal policy model. Formal methods must be employed to perform a formal analysis of the covert channels.
  - *Beyond Class A1*. This class is not described in the Orange Book. It refers to possible future systems for which formal verification techniques will be executed on source code against formal specifications and against the formal policy model.

#### The evaluation process

The evaluation process a system must undergo in order to belong to a given class consists of the following phases (Chokhani, 1992) (Figure 3.30).

- Preliminary Technical Review (PTR)
- Vendor Assistance Phase (VAP)
- Design Analysis Phase (DAP)
- Formal Evaluation Phase (FEP).

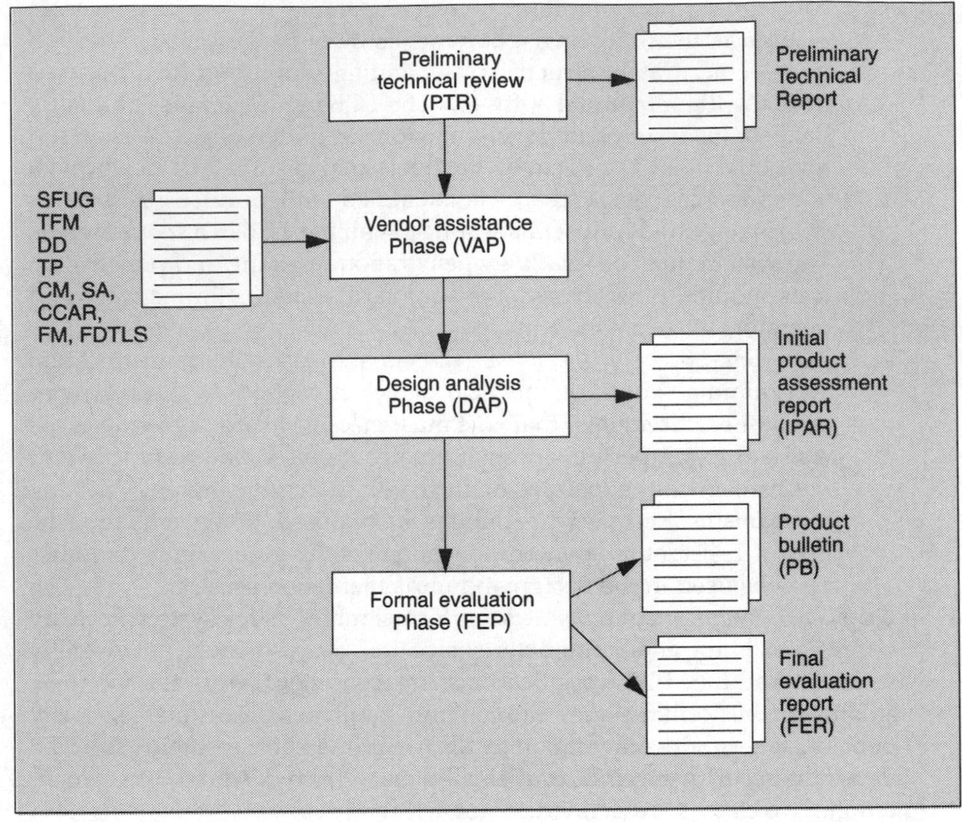


*Figure 3.30* Evaluation process.

Once rated, the system enters the Rating Maintenance Phase (RAMP) to maintain the rating.

The evaluation process is basically a manual analysis process, performed by a team of security evaluators from NCSC, who are responsible for analysing and assessing the security features of the system to be evaluated, at the request of the system vendor. In order to best support the evaluation process, the NCSC has compiled a couple of questionnaires (National Computer Security Center, 1989a). The first has the purpose of collecting information from the evaluators, related to the required tools and mechanisms, to refine the evaluation process. The other questionnaire helps evaluators, developers and vendors to acquire technical information about the target system, and is very useful during various phases of the evaluation process. Moreover, a Multics-based system is available, providing e-mail/bulletin board services, to simplify the interactions between vendors and evaluators. In the following, we describe how the evaluation process take place in each phase.

*Preliminary Technical Review (PTR)*

During this phase, two to three NCSC security evaluators are responsible for establishing if the target system is suitable for evaluation. They examine the documentation provided by the vendor and the architecture of the system with respect to the target rating. Results of the preliminary review are collected in the Preliminary Technical Report (PTR). This document has the purpose of describing the architecture potential for the target rating. It is about 20–40 pages long, and illustrates the hardware security relevant features provided by the system (for example, machine states, rings, privileged instructions, protection domains, and so on). Moreover, the subjects, objects, DAC, MAC, accountability, and other security relevant features are summarized, together with the engineering method and the schedule. At this point, evaluators can decide to accept, reject, or suggest changes before acceptance. Even if the PTR can be requested at any time during the system life cycle, the best time to perform it should be during product planning or initial development.

*Vendor Assistance Phase (VAP)*

Systems accepted for evaluation enter this phase. During VAP, a team of NCSC evaluators assist the vendor during system development, providing interpretation of security requirements needed for the target rating. The evaluator team performs a review of the documentation required for the evaluation process, consisting at least of the following documents: Security Features User's Guide, Trusted Facility Manual, design documentation, and test plan. If B division, or higher, is desired for the system, additional documents must be supplied by the vendor, namely, configuration management, system architecture, covert channel analysis report, formal model, and formal and descriptive top-level specifications, providing information about the formal analysis and specification of the system and of the security features. The VAP phase should ideally take place during the system design and implementation phases.

*Design Analysis Phase (DAP)*

Systems enter this phase when the evaluator team decides that the documentation provided is sufficiently detailed and organized. The evaluators increase (from five to eight), and they carefully study the documentation provided, together with undergoing formal training on the design and implementation of the system. The main security features provided by the system are understood and included in the Initial Product Assessment Report (IPAR). This document is about 100–200 pages long, and provides detailed information about the hardware and software architecture and the security-relevant features of the system. It specifies the team assessment for each security feature required for the target rating, providing motivations and explanations of why and how the vendor meets such requirements. IPAR also includes a list of the hardware and software components forming the TCB, and references to the documents related to system design and assurance. A Technical Review Board composed of security experts exists, to which the IPAR is delivered for review and comment. Finally, the evaluator team and the Technical Review Board make recommendations to the NCSC, for either acceptance of the system for its formal evaluation, or conditional acceptance after specific requirements are met, or review by another Technical Review Board for specific problems. The DAP should be performed after the system has been implemented, and has been successfully alpha or beta tested.

*Formal Evaluation Phase (FEP)*

This phase corresponds to a formal and public announcement, through a Public Bulletin, that a vendor has submitted its system for a specific rating. The NCSC evaluator team compiles the Final Evaluation Report. This document includes information from the IPAR, together with information about testing results. The team develops its own tests for the system, and for B2 rating upwards, reviews the code in order to verify consistency with the formal top-level specification and/or with the formal policy model. For A1 rating, the evaluator team reviews the proofs of consistency between formal top-level specifications, descriptive top-level specifications, and the formal security policy model. The team decides penetration test scenarios, and includes them in the test plan for the system. A test plan for a system consists of the vendor supplied tests, the team tests, and the team penetration test scenarios. The test plan is revised according to the Technical Review Board's suggestions. Then, the evaluator team performs all the tests, documents them, specifying the security anomalies detected, and conducts appropriate regression testing. Finally, test results are delivered to the Technical Review Board. On the basis of the Technical Review Board and team recommendations, the NCSC decides the rating for the system. All the evaluated systems are published in the Evaluated Product List, included in the NCSC's catalogue of INFOSEC products published quarterly. The final evaluation reports (FER) are also published, specifying technical details about the evaluated systems.

*Rating Maintenance Phase (RAMP)*

An evaluated system enters this phase as a consequence of minor changes or revisions to its configuration. Revised systems require to be re-evaluated, to assure that the stated rating still holds, even if system revisions do not affect security-relevant features. Since the evaluation is essentially manual, in order to reduce the resources needed, the NCSC has developed the so-called RAMP programme for C1–B1 systems (National Computer Security Center, 1989b). According to this programme, the vendor staff are responsible for system analysis for re-evaluation. The re-evaluation process take place by the vendor submitting a Rating Maintenance Plan, which describes the configuration management for the system hardware/software and documents. NCSC evaluates the Rating Management Plan and decides to start the configuration management process. This means that vendor analysts are trained in the security and technical features of the system, and also by the NCSC, which offers training for security vendor analysts. The security analysts task consists in reviewing the changes applied from old release to the newer, and stating the changes in terms of security and system rating. The analysts augment the test cases with scenarios specifically dealing with new changes, and document test results. Finally, the security vendor analysts meet the Technical Review Board to identify the changes and state their security relevance with reference to the DoD security requirements, documenting them with test results. Depending on the Technical Review Board's recommendations, the NCSC assigns the rating to the system under evaluation.

### 3.9.2 Classification of some systems according to the DoD criteria

In this section we illustrate how some commercial systems, either OS or special-purpose security packages, network systems and workstations are classified with reference to the DoD criteria. Table 3.6 summarizes the system classification.

For each system, we specify its classification, if it has already been evaluated, or the phase of the evaluation process the system is actually undergoing. For evaluated systems, the date the evaluation process took place is reported. We indicate that efforts are ongoing to increase the certification classes of many of the systems presented in the table and, in the meanwhile, some efforts might have been successfully completed.

#### *Considerations on the classification table*

The table shows that most systems have been evaluated as C2, while few systems have been classified at the B (B1, B2, and B3) and A1 levels. We can conclude that actually most systems provide the security features related to identification/authentication, DAC controls, audit, security testing and process isolation. For MAC protection and verified protection, classification levels higher than C2 are required, and only a few systems already provide them, while others are under evaluation.

The **MVS** OS with RACF, classified as C2, has recently been submitted for B1 classification. In order to become B1, MAC controls have been added, in addition to the existing DAC controls, as well as a label-based mechanism for subjects/objects.

The classification of the **UNIX** OS depends on the version considered. The original version, that is, a system suitable for friendly environments such as research centres or universities, can be classified as C1 (not shown in the table). Some versions, however, do not even match this level owing to the lack of documentation concerning both security aspects and the description of the procedures used for verification of the protection mechanisms.

Gould's Utx/32S system, installed on minicomputers, has been evaluated as C2. UNIX System V is under formal evaluation for a B2 classification. Efforts in the UNIX environment aim at higher classifications reaching B1 or B2. Some systems have been only theoretically evaluated as B1 on minicomputers and B2 on workstations. Implementation of MAC controls in UNIX might turn out to be rather difficult, since it is beyond the philosophy of UNIX design and development. From the implementation viewpoint, labelling of system subjects and objects (files, devices) can be obtained using the *i-node* structure. Extended (or

**Table 3.6** DoD classifications for commercial systems.

| System | Date | C2 | B1 | B2 | B3 | A1 | DAP | VAP | FEP |
|---|---|---|---|---|---|---|---|---|---|
| IBM MVS/RACF (very close to being a B1) | | • | | | | | | | |
| Computer Associates International ACF2/MVS | August 1984 | • | | | | | | | |
| Computer Associates International ACF2/VM | September 1987 | • | | | | | | | |
| Computer Associates International TOP SECRET | April 1985 | • | | | | | | | |
| IBM MVS with TOP SECRET | | | • | | | | | | • |
| Concurrent Computer Corporation OS-32 | | • | | | | | | | • |
| Convex Computer Corporation Convex OS/Secure 10.0 | | • | | | | | | | • |
| Control Data Corporation NOS | May 1986 | • | | | | | | | |
| Data General Corporation AOS/VS | December 1988 | • | | | | | | | |
| Digital Equipment Corporation VAX/VMS 4.3 | July 1986 May 1988 (RAMP) | • | | | | | | | |
| Encore Computer Corporation UTX/32S (Unix) | December 1986 | • | | | | | | | |
| Hewlett Packard MPE V/E | October 1988 | • | | | | | | | |
| IBM MVS/XA with RACF | June 1988 | • | | | | | | | |
| IBM VM/SP with RACF | September 1989 | • | | | | | | | |
| Prime Computer Primos | June 1988 | • | | | | | | | |
| Unisys Corporation A Series | August 1987 | • | | | | | | | |
| Wang Laboratories SVS/OS CAP 1.0 | September 1990 | • | | | | | | | |

**Table 3.6** continued.

| System | Date | C2 | B1 | B2 | B3 | A1 | DAP | VAP | FEP |
|---|---|---|---|---|---|---|---|---|---|
| Wang Laboratories SVS/OS CAP 1.01 | September 1991 (RAMP) | • | | | | | | | |
| AT&T System V/MLS Re:1.1.2 | September 1989 | | • | | | | | | |
| AT&T System V/MLS Re:1.2.0 | September 1990 (RAMP) | | • | | | | | | |
| IBM MVS/ESA (with RACF) | September 1990 | | • | | | | | | |
| Secureware CMW+ | January 1991 | | • | | | | | | |
| Unisys Corporation OS 1100 | September 1989 | | • | | | | | | |
| Unisys Corporation OS 1100/2200 Re: SB3R6 | September 1989<br>April 1991 (RAMP) | | • | | | | | | |
| AT&T Unix System Laboratory, Inc. Unix System V Release 4.1 | | | | • | | | | | • |
| Honeywell Information Systems, Inc. Multics | September 1985 | | | • | | | | | |
| Trusted Information Systems Trusted Xenix | January 1991 | | | • | | | | | |
| Verdix Corporation VSLAN 5.0 (evaluated as a B2 MDIA network component under TNI) | July 1990 | | | • | | | | | |
| Honeywell Federal Systems, Inc. XTS-200 | | | | | • | | | | • |
| Honeywell Information Systems, Inc. SCOMP | December 1984 | | | | | • | | | |

**Table 3.6** continued.

| System | Date | C2 | B1 | B2 | B3 | A1 | DAP | VAP | FEP |
|---|---|---|---|---|---|---|---|---|---|
| Boeing, SNS (evaluated as an A1 MI network component under TNI) | July 1991 | | | | | • | | | |
| Gemini Computer, Inc. Gemini Trusted Network Processor (evaluated as an A1 MI network component under TNI) | | | | | | • | | | • |
| **Unix-like trusted operating systems** | | | | | | | | | |
| Harris Corporation | | | | | | | • | | |
| CX/SX | | | | | | | B | | |
| Hewlett Packard | | | | | | | • | | |
| HP-UX B Level | | | | | | | B | | |
| Amdahal | | | | | | | • | | |
| UTS/MLSB | | | | | | | | | |
| Sequent Computer Systems | | | | | | | | • | |
| Silicon Graphics, Inc. | | | | | | | | • | |
| Trusted Information Systems | | | | | | | | • | |
| **Proprietary trusted operating systems** | | | | | | | | | |
| DEC, Security Enhanced VMS | | | | | | | B | | |
| Tandem Guardian-90 | | | | | | | C | | |
| IBM | | | | | | | | • | |
| **Network systems and network components** | | | | | | | | | |
| Boeing SNS+NM | | | | | | | A | | |
| Loral MLS 100 | | | | | | | B | | |
| Cray Research, Inc. | | | | | | | | • | |

**Table 3.6** continued.

| System | Date | C2 | B1 | B2 | B3 | A1 | DAP | VAP | FEP |
|---|---|---|---|---|---|---|---|---|---|
| **Compartmented mode workstations** | | | | | | | | | |
| Addamax | | | | | | | B | | |
| DEC | | | | | | | B | | |
| IBM | | | | | | | B | | |
| SUN Microsystems | | | | | | | B | | |

Efforts are ongoing to increase the certification classes of many of the described systems in the DoD hierarchical structure. In the meanwhile, some efforts might have been successfully completed.

VAP Vendor Assistance Phase
DAP Design Analysis Phase
FEP Formal Evaluatiuon Phase
RAMP Rating Maintenance Phase
TNI Trusted Network Interpretations (of TCSEC)

Bold face words denote different systems.
Double lines are used to separate systems of the same type at different evaluation classes/phases.

additional) i-nodes are traditional i-nodes with information about labels added. Finally, difficulties might also arise from end users who chose UNIX as an open system.

**VAX/VMS** is classified as C2. User identification/authentication and DAC controls are supplied via a reference monitor mediating all user access queries to protected resources. Each resource owner can grant access to the group members and to all the system users. Access rights are defined on the basis of the 'need-to-know' principle, because accounts are functionally grouped (users performing the same tasks should access the same data), and each account has different privileges (the minimum privileges for a task are provided to an account). An audit functionality is also supplied, allowing user requests to be recorded on a log file. In addition, mechanisms to avoid scavenging are supplied: that is, mechanisms whose purpose is to prevent unauthorized users from reading the contents of a memory area reserved for erased files (in fact, the deletion of a file affects the file header, not the file contents).

The **VM/SP** OS, classified as C2, has a version called kernelized VM, which is a secure OS evaluated as A1. Its design matches the DoD requirements. In particular, a reduced-size kernel has been implemented, interacting with a set of trusted processes for user authentication and login, and for object access control.

**Other certifications** are **ongoing.** MVS/XA and VM/SP, together with RACF, were initially certified as C2. B1 evaluation is presently ongoing for MVS/ESA, VM/SP and VM/XA SP with RACF. MVS with ACF2 and MVS with TOP SECRET have been submitted for B1 evaluation. The VM operating system, with CA-ACF2 version 3.1, has been certified as C2. Ongoing extensions aim at its certification as B1.

## 3.10 Design of secure operating systems

The protection level of current OSs is rather low with respect to DoD classification. Improvements are being studied for all of them. However, the integration *a posteriori* of security functions within an existing system may be very expensive (and very difficult). Security aspects should be considered as a part of the system development process.

In many OSs, the different protection mechanisms (user authentication, memory protection, access control to files, resources and objects in general, support mechanisms for resource sharing, and interprocess communications) are often provided by modules added *a posteriori*: these are scattered inside the system code to preserve the structure of the existing system (Tanenbaum, 1988). This approach is shown in Figure 3.31. On the other hand, grouping all the security functions in one module can alter the OS modularity and may lead to the construction of a large module that cannot easily be verified. In general, the introduction of security functions complicates the validation and formal verification of the protection mechanisms, as required at high (DoD) classification levels, owing to the size and complexity of the security code.

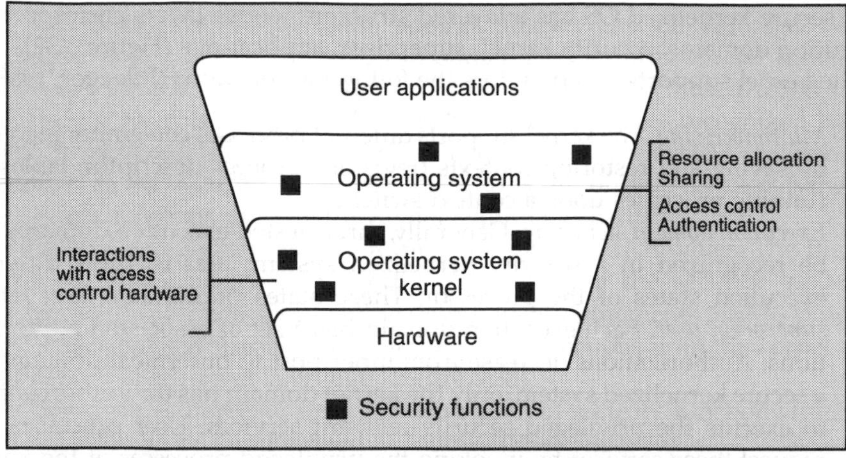


*Figure 3.31* Security functions without a security kernel.

This section illustrates the architecture of some secure OSs, that is, those where security functions have been a primary design concern.

## 3.10.1 Kernel-based approach

The kernel-based approach tries to reduce the size and complexity of the security mechanisms by grouping the security functions inside a *security kernel*. This is formally verifiable and is the first layer of the OS immediately above the hardware. A subset of all OS functions is provided by the security kernel (Ames *et al.*, 1983).

Security is considered in the early stages of design: first, the security kernel is developed, then the OS is defined on the basis of the kernel. The *reference monitor* concept is realized by the security kernel, because it controls all the access operations and executes all the security-relevant functions. The rest of the OS provides all the functions where security is not involved.

The security kernel must satisfy the following properties:

- *Completeness:* by mediating all accesses to system information;
- *Isolation:* the kernel must be tamper-proof;
- *Verifiability:* the kernel code must be verifiable to prove that it implements the security requirements and policies described by the security model.

The construction of a kernel needs formalized security policies. These policies state what must be resident in the kernel, and what can be left outside (the part of the OS outside the kernel is called the 'supervisor'). Functions that are not security-relevant or supply user services are part of the supervisor (except when some of them are inserted into the security kernel for efficiency or functionality reasons).

The use of a security kernel has some disadvantages. The basic drawback is the reduction in system performance, especially when using unsuitable hardware. In practice, a kernel is difficult to modify: changes might alter its correct working and the requirements would no longer be met. System performance can be downgraded, since the kernel adds a further intermediate level between the user programs and the OS resources. Moreover, it is difficult to implement a small-size and reduced-complexity kernel, since it is hard to isolate the security functions (dependences usually exist between security and non-security functions); moreover, a precise level of formal specifications and a limited set of protection requirements are required.

Experience has shown that the size of kernels is usually considerable; consequently, some systems use trusted processes to implement those functions for which less strict security controls are needed, and which are not included in the kernel to avoid the increase in kernel size.

Verifying that a kernel correctly enforces the protection requirements of the security model means examining all the possible violations of kernel security. There can be direct violations (the kernel grants access to unauthorized subjects) or indirect violations (unauthorized subjects get information through resource sharing). Indirect violations in multilevel security are, for example, transfers of high-classified information to low-classified users (the kernel is used as a communication channel). The verification process should identify all possible direct and indirect violations of the kernel. The formal verification of a security kernel can take place through formal specification techniques, proving that:

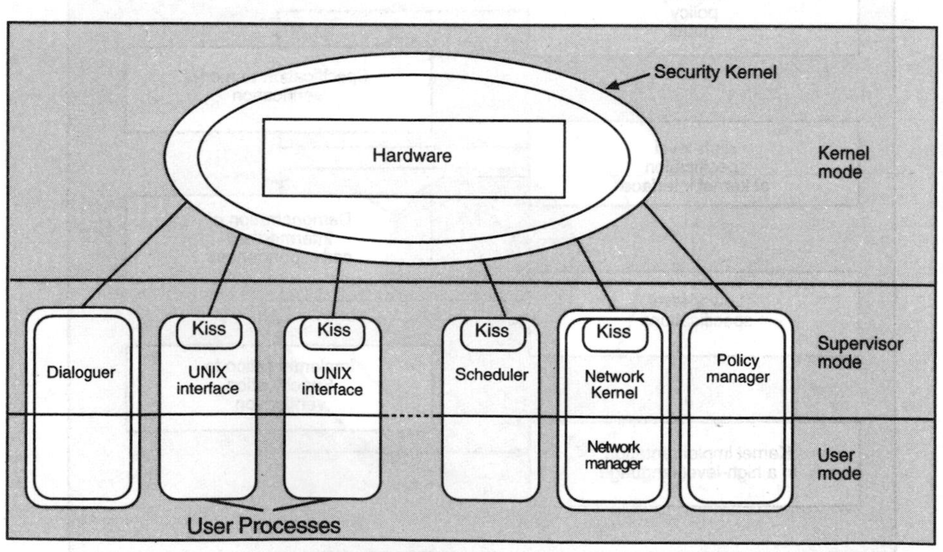


*Figure 3.34* UCLA Secure UNIX architecture.

- High-level specifications of the kernel interface meet the formal specifications of the security model;
- Subsequent refinements of high-level specifications are correct with respect to these same specifications;
- The kernel code is correct with respect to the implementation specifications (this is the last refinement level).

Special languages and programs have been developed for proving the correctness of kernels.

As an example, the main features of the following kernelized secure OSs are described below: UCLA Secure UNIX, the Kernelized Secure Operating System (KSOS) and Secure Xenix, which were all designed to extend the basic UNIX protection mechanisms (Bach 1986; Bunch, 1987); and the VAX Security Kernel, the Digital Equipment Corporation kernel for VAX machines.

### 3.10.2 UCLA Secure UNIX

UCLA Secure UNIX (Popek *et al.*, 1979) was designed following a formal approach which allowed the system correctness to be formally verified. The architecture of UCLA Secure UNIX is shown in Figure 3.34. It consists of a set of correlated modules. Security functions are implemented by the double-circled modules. These are: the Security Kernel, the Policy Manager, the Dialoguer and the Network Kernel. The usual service functions of an OS are implemented by the remaining modules.

The **Security Kernel** is written in Pascal – about 760 lines of code – to which the code for I/O management must be added – about 600 lines, describing an interface independent of the devices and of the various drivers for each supported device. The kernel is small, as required by the DoD criteria, for easy verification of its correctness. Four types of abstract data types are realized by the kernel; only some given primitive operations, which can be invoked by user processes, can be executed on these.

The four types of abstract data types are:

- *Processes*. These are objects consisting of a page of memory and of state variables. The process virtual memory is not included. Available operations are execution, suspension, initialization, virtual memory modification, and forwarding and reception of interrupts. All kernel primitives related to processes are controlled via capabilities.
- *Pages*. These are objects representing abstract memory units. Pages have a fixed location in secondary memory which is maintained when the page is allocated into main memory. Access to memory pages from processes occurs on the basis of capabilities. A process needs to hold a capability for access to pages. Available operations on page objects are: page copying from secondary into main memory; version updating in secondary memory so that the version is kept consistent with version changes in main memory; page deletion in main memory.

- *Devices*. These represent the various connected devices. All I/O operations on them are subjected to capability-based control. Devices implementing both read and write operations (for example, terminals) are treated as two devices, needing separate read and write capabilities, respectively, for read and write operations on the same terminal. Available operations on devices are: start of I/O operations, interruption for completion (end of I/O operations), and signalling the state of a running operation.
- *Capabilities*. These represent protection information related to the different objects. A capability consists of: the object name, possible access rights on the object, and a set of information used by the kernel for managing the capability. Each process has a capability list (C-list) containing the capabilities this process holds on the different objects. A process's C-list is stored in pages. For capabilities, the only operation is 'grant', by which a capability is added to the C-list of a process, in a given position. Control on this 'grant' operation is made by capabilities. Revocation of a capability occurs by inserting a null entry.

The **Policy Manager** is the basic process for security, because it is responsible for shared file system management, process initialization (following each fork, namely each UNIX primitive needed in process creation) and implementation of the security policies supported by the system. The Policy Manager functions aim at protection of shared files. In particular, file protection labels are expressed by differently combined 'colours'. Users have a list of colours determining their access rights. A user is granted access to files holding protection labels covered by that user's colour list. Processes generated by users have associated profiles, which are subsets of the users' colour lists. Different profiles are defined for file read and write operations.

The **Kernel Interface SubSystem** (Kiss) is an intermediate interface between the kernel and the OS interface. It manages the process environments by realizing virtual machines for different processes.

The **Dialoguer** process enforces the authentication functions as well as performing other relevant security functions, such as process profile modification by users. The Dialoguer can authenticate itself to the user, who can hence be assured of his correct interaction with the Dialoguer (secure user-terminal connection). For this, a user must connect his terminal with the Dialoguer by typing in a predefined string of control characters.

The **UNIX Interface** constitutes a user interface as similar as possible to the standard UNIX interface. Its task is to handle the primitive calls from user processes, by executing them from within itself, if possible, or by forwarding them to the kernel. In particular, the UNIX interface behaves in the same way as the usual UNIX file system, supporting search operations, control of the work directory, and all the other usual UNIX operations on the directories.

The tasks of the **Scheduler** and the **Network Manager** are, respectively, to select the executable processes and to enforce security for the distributed environment, when the computer operates in a networked environment.

In UCLA Secure UNIX, three **execution domains** are recognized: the *user*, the *supervisor*, and the *kernel*. A user process is initially executed in the user domain. Upon the request of a system functionality, the process enters the supervisor domain; if the requested functionality refers to a primitive related to objects managed by the kernel, control passes to the kernel domain. Access rights in each domain are expressed in *C-lists* managed by the security kernel.

Techniques for formal verification have been developed to prove the system security. The security kernel-based approach has allowed the implementation of a relatively small and simple kernel, thus simplifying the phase of formal verification.

### 3.10.3 Kernelized Secure Operating System (KSOS)

KSOS (McCauley and Drongowski, 1979) was developed with the primary goal of certifying its security, meaning that both the design process and mechanisms are oriented to proving the system correctness according to DoD requirements. The approach was kernel-based. KSOS is capable of managing information at different security levels, as in military environments. It was conceived for minicomputers. The design methodology is multiphase, as described in this chapter. Security requirements have been formally expressed as *properties* that need verification. The design was described in a non-procedural language (SPECIAL). Design properties were tested through demonstration of theorems derived from this same design and from the security model. A suitable language was chosen, aimed at supporting formal testing of the specifications.

The structure of KSOS is shown in Figure 3.35. KSOS is composed of a *Security Kernel*, a *UNIX Emulator*, and *System Software* external to the kernel (both trusted and untrusted).

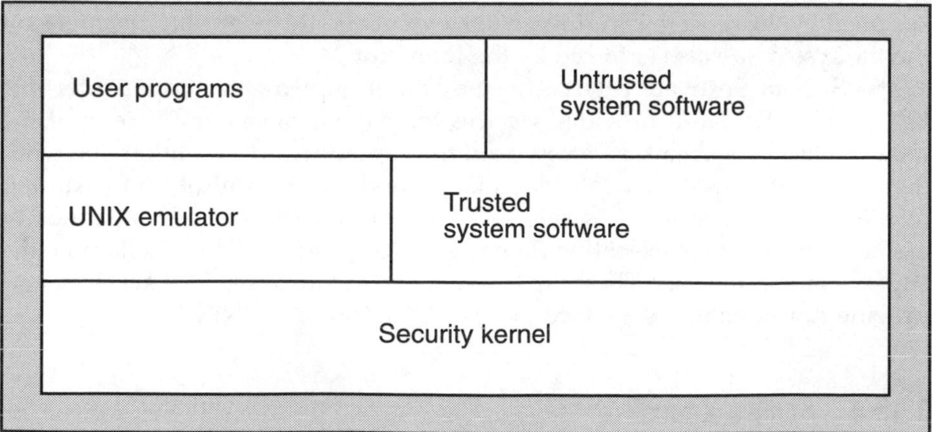


***Figure 3.35*** KSOS architecture.

The **Security Kernel** implements the reference monitor concept, because it is the mediator of all accesses to the system objects, and because it is tamper-proof. Starting from system resources, a set of objects is created by the kernel. The supported objects are:

- *Processes.* These are the only active agents of KSOS. There are some trusted processes holding privileges and requiring a limited amount of controls from the kernel. Process privileges are assigned on the basis of the minimum privilege principle.
- *Segments.* These are portions of the process virtual space. They have a variable size and can be shared by several processes.
- *Files and devices.* The file structure is uniform, meaning that nothing is assumed by the kernel about their contents and internal structures. Directories and other high-level constructions are located outside the kernel. Devices are special files, as in UNIX.
- *Subtypes.* The subtype mechanism supports the selective encapsulation of a file class. Each file is a member of one or several subtype classes (for example, UNIX directory files belong to the 'Directory UNIX' subtype class). Access to subtypes can undergo restricted conditions (for example, a restriction to the 'UNIX Directory' class can be: 'read is granted to everybody, write operations are granted only to processes holding the Directory Manager identifier').

The kernel access control policies conform to the DoD control policies. Precisely, the 'ss-property' and '*-property' of the Bell–LaPadula model (Chapter 2); the integrity policies for changes to programs and databases; the discretionary policies of standard UNIX allowing users to grant and revoke access to objects they own, are enforced.

The task of the **UNIX Emulator** is to transform the UNIX system primitives into sequences of kernel primitives. A primary function for UNIX interface support is file system creation (starting from the initial system configuration supplied by the kernel). Directory management and further utility functions on the file system are also enforced by the Emulator.

The **System Software** external to the kernel implements support tools for KSOS. In particular, it provides services for the management of user and file security levels; systems services needing continuity in execution (network demon, printer spooling, intruder mail); services for control and restoring of file system consistency; services supporting the system administrator in system control. Three execution domains are possible in KSOS: the kernel, the supervisor and the user. These are typical of all secure kernelized systems, and provide functionalities similar to those of UCLA Secure UNIX.

### 3.10.4 Secure Xenix

Secure Xenix was conceived to integrate the security mechanisms of the Bell–LaPadula model within the Xenix OS (Gligor *et al.*, 1986; Luckenbaugh *et al.*, 1986).

The interpretation of the Bell–LaPadula model in Xenix is as follows.

- *Subjects.* These are processes. Each process is associated with a user, identified by the login name and by his group;
- *Objects.* These are files, devices, directories, named pipes, semaphores, shared memory areas, messages and processes;
- *Access privileges.* These are read, write, execute rights, and no privilege. The semantics of these operations differs according to the referenced object (for example, the 'execute' right on a directory is interpreted as the search operation);
- *The set of current accesses of a subject.* This is the set of privileges held by a process, associated with the file descriptors;
- *Access matrix.* This is represented by access control lists (ACL), namely by columns;
- *Maximum security level.* This is assigned to a special user, the security administrator. Current levels of the system subjects and objects are assigned by the kernel upon creation of subjects;
- *Multilevel objects.* Only directory objects can contain objects with different classifications (multilevel objects).

Compared with Xenix, the distinguishing aspects of Secure Xenix are the use of ACLs and the modification of the *setuid* mechanism.

ACLs are associated with the system objects and consist of a pair <main identifier, access privileges>. The main identifier is composed of a user identifier and a group identifier expressing the group a user must belong to in order to be given the privileges on the protected object. The '*' symbol can apply to any identifier. Pairs are ordered inside ACLs: the first positions pertain to pairs with a specific user identifier; pairs with the generic user identifier '*' follow.

These last pairs are ordered analogously, in that the pairs with a specific group identifier appear first, followed by pairs with the '*' generic group identifier. Removing a user from an ACL is implemented either by inserting a 'null privilege' into this user pairs, or by omitting all the pairs with the user identifier as 'user identifier'; or by omitting the pairs containing the name of any group this user belongs to as 'group identifier'. Grant and revocation of access privileges are performed by the object owner.

Modifications to the setuid mechanisms increase security and overcome the weaknesses of UNIX, such as the use of the setuid mechanism by a Trojan Horse to alter the privileges. In particular, write privileges on files containing setuid programs is forbidden; besides, the setuid modality can be set only through explicit commands from users sent to the kernel through a trusted channel.

### 3.10.5 VAX Security Kernel

The Virtual Machine Monitor (VMM) Security Kernel is a security kernel designed for VAX architectures, with the objective of being certified as A1 (Karger *et al.*, 1991). The design started in the early 1980s, supported by DEC.

After a first prototype on VAX 11/730, and some extensions on VAX 8800 machines, the first VAX security kernel was installed in the UK, January 1988, at the European ULTRIX Engineering Group. It was afterwards successfully tested by a group of government and aerospace companies. The design is interesting both for the methodology (trying to achieve strict conformance to the DoD guidelines) and for the technological solutions adopted.

The VMM Security Kernel supports several virtual VAX machines (each using its own VMS or ULTRIX-32 OS) working on one physical machine; the virtual machine ensures isolation and controlled resource sharing. The design and development had a double objective: A1 certification and commercial assent. In particular, the security kernel offers satisfactory performance, is usable on current hardware (needing no substantial modification), and offers consistency with applications of different OSs (VMS and ULTRIX-32). It can also be used on VAX 8530, 8550, 8700, 8800 and 8810 machines. The VAX Security Kernel is a Virtual Machine Monitor (VMM): that is, it supports the virtualization of VAX architectures (virtualization could not exist without microcode extension). Virtualization code is kept separate from code related to security functions, in order to reduce the kernel complexity. In this sense, the virtualization code is partly a security kernel. The implementation of a security kernel in the form of a VMM derives from the necessity of both making it compatible with existing software and reducing the development costs, according to the initial requirements. Development was partly dedicated to virtual VAX architecture, through code modifications properly tested and verified with a view to A1 certification. In particular, the partition into protection levels is virtual, so that sensitive instructions, or instructions referring to sensitive data, can be executed in the privileged state of the processor. The VAX Security Kernel supports both mandatory and discretionary access controls. For mandatory access controls, system subjects and objects have an access class, composed of a secrecy class and an integrity class, according to the Bell–LaPadula and Biba models (see Chapter 2). Access control is implemented through access control lists associated to the different objects requiring protection.

The Vax Security Kernel is a multi-user OS working on virtual machines and disks. Its **subjects** are both virtual machines and users. A virtual machine is considered an untrusted subject, working through its own OS. During the phase of connection with the security kernel (login phase), a trusted connection (session) between the user terminal and the user server process is stated by the VMM. Server processes are trusted processes working inside the kernel (differently, for example, from KSOS).

The users interact with the OS of a virtual machine in the usual modes (login phase, work session, logout phase). A user trying to attack the OS security is limited to the system involved (possibly to the virtual machines sharing disks), thus avoiding damage to the security of other virtual machines working concurrently and to the security kernel. A user could request the use of a different virtual machine by sending his server the *connect* command, specifying the name of the virtual machine. The result of this command is the set-up of a new session, interrupting the current one, if the connection is authorized (if unauthorized, the new connection is denied).

Virtual machines can be considered both as system subjects and objects depending on the operations involved. In the case of users requesting to start a new session on a virtual machine, the machine is the object, and the users the subjects.

The VAX Security Kernel considers physical devices, volumes and security kernel files as protected **objects**. Physical devices include all devices containing or transmitting information, such as disk and tape devices, printers, terminal lines and network lines. The main memory is also considered as a protected object, and memory allocation to a virtual machine occurs upon connection.

Disk and tape volumes are another category of object to be protected. Two classes of disk volume are distinguished.

- *Exchangeable volumes* which can be exchanged with other systems that use conventional OSs are entirely under the control of the virtual machine, such as volumes containing the file system structures.
- *VAX Security Kernel volumes*, containing the files of the security kernel. These can neither be exchanged nor accessed by the OS in order to avoid manipulations possibly damaging the security kernel.

Files contained in the *VAX Security Kernel* volumes are used for different functions, such as maintenance of information related to authorizations and auditing, and creation of virtual disk volumes. (A virtual disk volume is a portion of a whole disk. This solution is adopted in the case of virtual machines needing limited disk space.) Excluding log files, error files and crash dump files, other files contained in the VAX Security Kernel volumes are considered parts of the TCB, so they cannot be directly accessed by virtual machines. Tape volumes are all interchangeable.

Each system subject and object has an associated **access class**, consisting of a *secrecy* and an *integrity class*. Each of these components is, in turn, composed of a *level*, expressing the hierarchical classification, and a set of non-hierarchical categories. The kernel supports 256 secrecy/integrity levels and 64 secrecy/integrity categories. According to the Bell–LaPadula model, a subject is allowed to read (write) an object if the subject access class dominates (is dominated by) the object access class, following the dominance relation for access classes defined in the model.

Specific categories of users (system administrators, security officers, operators) are associated a set of privileges, allowing these users to further restrict subject access grants on objects that were defined on the basis of mandatory access classes. *User privileges* (only executable through a trusted path) and *virtual machine privileges* (held by virtual machines) are distinguished.

**Server processes** are trusted processes running inside the security kernel. They are associated with users upon requests of using a virtual machine. The privileges of a server process are determined on the basis of the minimum/maximum access class of the user and terminal involved, of the users' discretionary authorizations and privileges, and of the privileges held when using that terminal.

The VAX Security Kernel was implemented following the *levels* of *abstraction* approach, to reduce its complexity and to determine clear specifications, as required by the DoD criteria for A1 certification. The approach based on abstraction levels states that a system has to be developed using a set of abstractions which are implemented by each level, partly using services offered by lower levels (without using any upper-level service). This reduces the system interactions and the global complexity of the system. The layers composing the VAX Security Kernel are shown in Figure 3.36.

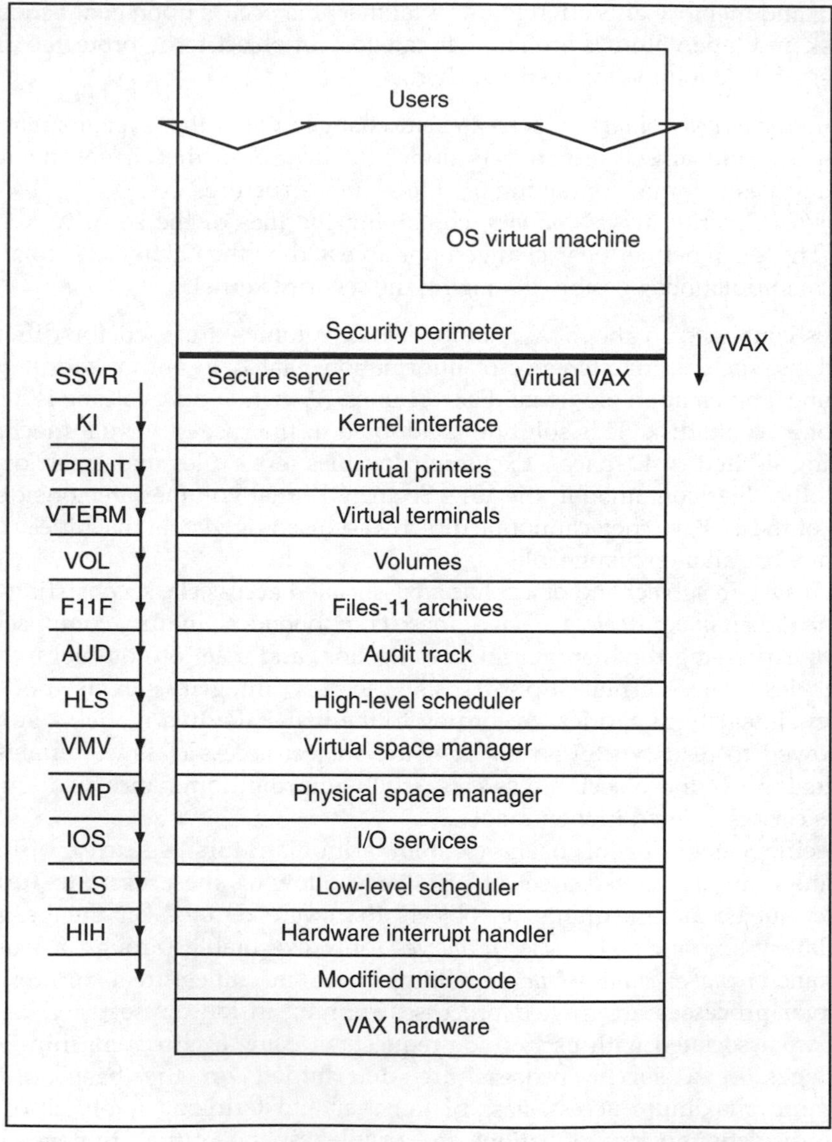


*Figure 3.36* VAX Security Kernel.

The kernel is structured into processes. As shown in Figure 3.36, all trusted processes are included within the security perimeter, and in system specifications. In particular, the layers, from the bottom up (starting above the VAX hardware and the microcode modified for the virtual machine), are:

- *Hardware-Interrupt Handler (HIH).* This contains interrupt-handlers for I/O devices and CPU-specific codes.
- *Lower-Level Scheduler (LLS).* This creates abstraction of virtual level 1 processors (vp1) that form the basic unit of scheduling; assigns and revokes the CPU to level 1 processors. There are dedicated vp1 (containing software for devices handling), linkable vp1 (which can be associated to virtual processors of level 2 (vp2), used by a higher-level scheduler), and addressable vp1 (which can be associated to vp2, therefore to virtual machines). These last have an unrestricted addressing space; the others operate outside the global address space of the kernel. An event counter mechanism exists at this level, used as a kernel synchronization mechanism.
- *Input/Output Services (IOS).* This realizes the software for handling and control of I/O devices (terminals and secondary memory).
- *Virtual Machine Physical space manager (VMP).* This manages the actual memory, assigning it to different virtual machines.
- *Virtual Machine Virtual space manager (VMV).* This realizes the mechanism for virtual memory management for the virtual machines (based on pages). This mechanism allows actual memory, required by an active virtual machine, to be resident. Through this strategy, the number of virtual machines working contemporaneously is limited, while the code of the security kernel is simplified (the demand-paging mechanism is not present).
- *Higher-Level Scheduler (HLS).* This creates the abstraction of level-2 virtual processors (vp2). There are dedicated vp2 (used by the Server Process level), and linkable vp2 (used for the virtual machines).
- *AUDit Trail (AUD).* This realizes audit and security alarms management functions.
- *Archives Files-11 (F11F).* This realizes a subsystem of the ODS-2 file system, also used in VMS for the security kernel; it requires files to be pre-allocated and contiguous, to reduce the kernel complexity.
- *Volumes (VOL).* This realizes the exchangeable volumes and the VAX Security Kernel volumes.
- *Virtual Terminals (VTerm).* This realizes virtual terminals for each virtual machine. It manages the physical lines of the actual terminals, allows the opened user sessions to be connected to different virtual machines, and supports the connections of the virtual machines to the network.
- *Virtual Printers (VPrint).* This realizes virtual printers for different virtual machines by multiplexing the real printers.
- *Kernel Interface (KI).* This realizes virtual controllers for I/O virtual devices, and control functions on the devices.

- *Virtual VAX (VVAX).* This completes the virtualization process.
- *Secure Server (SSVR).* This supplies administrative functions related to security. It implements a trusted path between users and the security kernel; in addition, it provides users with system connection and disconnection. Each terminal line is associated with a 2-level virtual processor, so that each user has an associated server process.
- *Virtual Machine Operating System (VMOS).* This is the OS of the virtual machine.
- *Users (USERS).* This is the level of users connected to the system through trusted paths, and of untrusted application programs to be executed upon request.

The DoD criteria for reduced size and complexity of a security kernel are satisfied through the abstraction levels-based approach. However, commercial requirements have demanded the development of a friendly user interface.

A proper user interface needs a lot of code, thus increasing the kernel size and complexity. This problem was solved in the VAX Security Kernel by implementing the user interface through two sets of commands, the *Secure Server commands* and the *SECURE commands*. The first set is located in the security kernel trusted code; the second set is interpreted by the OSs (VMS and ULTRIX-32).

The Secure Server commands represent a direct user/security kernel interface, supporting the creation of a trusted path with the server process, using a suitable keyboard key: the *Secure Attention Key*. This key is always active; it cannot be intercepted by untrusted software in the system. Therefore, the *connect, disconnect, resume,* and *show sessions* commands are available for user session handling. The SECURE commands are realized through the same modalities as for other OS commands (MVS and ULTRIX-32), and are interpreted by the command interpreter of these systems. Their execution causes a call to the kernel. There are two classes of SECURE commands: *VM SECURE* and *User SECURE,* both of administrative type. Only the VM SECURE commands must be trusted commands. These are guaranteed to be trusted by the system, which supplies them with an individual accountability. After receiving a valid User SECURE command, the system requires this user to type in the Secure Attention Key and the command is validated, thus preventing unauthorized users (for example, a Trojan Horse) from having a command executed by the system.

A1 certification of a system needs **formal verification**, proving and documenting that software engineering techniques have been followed in system design and development. In addition, documentation must be clear and understandable to users, to simplify system use. In the VAX Security Kernel, the Formal Development Methodology (FDM) has been used for requirements specification and formal verification. A high-level formal specification and the security model (defined in the form of criteria and constraints, and of high-level specification) have been written in the Ina Jo formal specification language. The FDM theorem prover has been used to prove that the high-level specification verifies the security policies and the model specification.

**Covert channels** were exaustively analysed during VAX Security Kernel development, causing the most evident channels (first of all, memory channels) to be eliminated early in the design phase. Time channels were eliminated through the innovatory dual-clock analysis: this technique is based on the principle that, in order to draw some advantages from a time channel, a very precise clock and a Trojan Horse are needed, monitoring the clock to get information from it. This technique is also based on the consideration that time channels can be identified by localizing all potential precise clocks inside the system. Through the fuzzy time technique, the accuracy of these clocks is slightly modified in order to cancel the time channel effects.

Specific protection techniques against possible damage during hardware and software installation have been studied, to guarantee that the system is not damaged during delivery (trusted distribution).

For the documentation, nine manuals and a reference card have been produced following the DoD requirements for A1 classification.

## References

Ames S.R., Gasser M. and Schell R.R. (1983). Security kernel design and implementation. *IEEE Computer*, **16** (7)

Andrews G.R. and Reitman R.P. (1980). An axiomatic approach to information flow in parallel programs. *ACM Trans. Prog. Languages and Systems*, **2** (1)

Bach M.J. (1986). *The Design of the UNIX Operating System*. Prentice-Hall

Barker W.C. and Pfleeger C. P. (1990). Civil and military applications of trusted systems criteria. In *Proc. 13th National Computer Security Conf.*, October (1991).

Branstad M.A., Brewer D., Jahl C., Kurth H., and Pfleeger C. (1991). Apparent differences between the US TCSEC and the European ITSEC. In *Proc. 14th National Computer Security Conf.*, October

Bunch S. (1987). The SETUID feature in UNIX and security. In *Proc. 10th National Computer Security Conference*, Baltimore

Chokhani S. (1992). Products evaluation. *Comm. ACM*, **35** (7), July

Commission of the European Communities (1991). Information technology security evaluation criteria (ITSEC): provisional harmonized criteria, version 1.2. Luxembourg: Office for Official Publications of the European Communities, June

Denning D.E. (1976). A lattice model of secure information flow. *Comm. ACM*, **19** (5)

Denning D. E. (1982). *Cryptography and Data Security*. Addison-Wesley

Department of Defense (1985). *Trusted computer system evaluation criteria* (*DoD 5200.28-STD*). December

ECMA (1988). Security in Open Systems: a Security Framework. *ECMA Technical Report/46*. European Comp. Manufacturers Ass., July

Gligor V.D., Burch E. L. *et al.* (1986). On the design and the implementation of Secure Xenix workstation. In *Proc. IEEE Symp. on Security and Privacy*, Oakland, April

Harrison M.A., Ruzzo W.L. and Ullman J.D. (1976). Protection in operating system. *Comm. ACM*, **19** (8)

Hsiao D.K. and Kerr D.S. (1978). Operating system security – A tutorial of current research. *Proc. of the IEEE*

Jahl C. (1990). Europe pursues different computer security approach: a harmonized evaluation applies to products, systems, application areas. In *Proc. 6th Annual Computer Security Applications Conf.*, December

Karger P.A., Zurko M.E., Bonin D.W., Mason A.H. and Kahn C.E. (1991). A retrospective on the VAX VMM security kernel. *IEEE Trans. Software Eng.*, **17** (11)

Lampson B.W. (1973). A note on the confinement problem. *Comm. ACM*, **16** (10)

Lampson B.W. (1974). Protection. *ACM Operating Systems Rev.*, **8** (1)

Lampson B.W., Needham R.M., Randall B. and Schroeder M.D. (1977). Protection, security, reliability. *Operating System Rev.*, **2** (1)

Landwehr C.E. (1983). The best available technologies for computer security. *IEEE Computer*, **16** (7)

Luckenbaugh G.L., Gligor V.D., Dotterer L.J. and Chandersekaran C.S. (1986). Interpretation of the Bell–LaPadula model in Secure Xenix. In *Proc. DoD-NBS Conf. on Computer Security*, September

McCauley E.J. and Drongowski P.J. (1979). KSOS – The design of a secure operating system. In *Proc. National Computer Conference*

National Computer Security Center (1987a). *Trusted Network Interpretation of the Trusted Computer System Evaluation Criteria (NCSCV-TG-005 Version 1)*. July

National Computer Security Center (1987b). *A guide to understanding discretionary access control in trusted systems (NCSC-TG-003 Version 1)*. September

National Computer Security Center (1988a). *A guide to understanding configuration management in trusted systems (NCSC-TG-006 Version 1)*. March

National Computer Security Center (1988b). *A guide to understanding audit in trusted systems (NCSC-TG-001 Version 2)*. June

National Computer Security Center (1988c). *Computer security subsystem interpretation, NCSC-TG-009 Version 1*, September 1988

National Computer Security Center (1988d). *A guide to understanding design documentation in trusted systems (NCSC-TG-007 Version 1)*. October

National Computer Security Center (1989a). *Guidelines for formal verification systems (NCSC-TG-014 Version 1)*. April

National Computer Security Center (1989b). *Rating maintenance phase-program document (NCSC-TG-013 Version 1)*. June

National Computer Security Center (1989c). *Trusted products evaluation questionnaire (NCSC-TG-019 Version 1)*. October

National Computer Security Center (1991). *Trusted database management system interpretation of the trusted computer system evaluation criteria (National Computer Security Center, NCSC-TG-021, version-1)*. April

Needham R.M. (1974). Protection – A current research area in operating systems. A. Gunther et al. (eds.), North-Holland

Paans R. (1991). *With MVS/ESA security labels towards B1. Computers and Security,* Elsevier Sc. (North-Holland), **10**(4)

Pfleeger C.P. (1989). *Security in Computing.* Prentice-Hall

Popek G., Kamper M., Kline C., Stoughton A., Urban M. and Walton E. (1979). UCLA Secure Unix. In *Proc. National Computer Conf.*

Russel D. and Gangemi G.T. (1991). *Computer Security Basics.* O'Reilly Associates Inc.

Silberschatz A. and Peterson J.L. (1983). *Operating System Concepts,* 2nd edn. Addison-Wesley

Silberschatz A. Peterson J.L. and Galvin P. (1991). *Operating System Concepts.* Addison-Wesley

Spooner D.L. and Gudes E. (1984). A unifying approach to the design of a secure database operating system. *IEEE Trans. Software Eng.,* **10** (4)

Tanenbaum A.S. (1988). *Operating Systems Design and Implementation.* Prentice-Hall

*UK IT Security Evaluation and Certification Scheme* (1990) (UKSP 01,02). July. Communications–Electronics Security Group, Government Comm. Headquarters & Dept. of Trade and Industry (UK)

Wood C. C. and Kochan J. J. (1985). *UNIX System Security.* Hayden Press

# 4 Database security design

## 4.1 Introduction

The previous chapters have defined the concepts of logical database security, illustrated the formal security models, surveyed the basic security mechanisms at the operating system level, and described the functionalities of security software packages.

Logical database security tackles the security problems (secrecy and integrity) through a set of rules establishing the authorized accesses to the database information and resources. These rules have to be properly defined and enforced on the basis of the security requirements and policies of the organization, avoiding inconsistencies and errors that would expose the system to possible attacks. Logical security has to be regarded as an integral part of the global security system of the organization.

This chapter is devoted to the design of logical database security measures. Logical design of a security system means designing the *security software* and the *security rules* (Jones and Wulf, 1975). The security software comprises security packages, such as secure operating systems, secure DBMSs, and *ad-hoc* security procedures. Its design should take advantage of the existing security standards, such as those described in Chapter 3, using them both as an input guideline for the design process and as a basis for subsequent project certification. The security rules have to be defined correctly and consistently, taking into account the different security requirements of users and trying to balance the secrecy and integrity aspects of a system. In addition, the design of security rules has to be harmonized with the database design activities, in order to achieve a coherent design of the database and its logical security, also taking into account the priorities given to the different technical/organizational perspectives of the target application environment.

Since the security rules for a database are more complex than simple access control lists, or tables, the design of a set of security rules turns out to benefit from a *design methodology*. In fact, the base of the security rules may be regarded as a database itself; therefore, the use of a methodology for security rule design (analogous to database design methodologies: Batini *et al.*, 1992), by separating the concerns into conceptual design aspects, logical design (DBMS-dependent) aspects, and physical design aspects, allows the achievement of an incremental, good-quality, and testable/verifiable security design. More generally, the well-known phases of analysis, conceptual design, detailed design implementation, testing and maintenance of the system development life cycle are also to be applied to the security system development.

This chapter first illustrates methods for secure DBMS design; some research prototypes and commercial secure DBMS products are described. Then, a methodological approach to the design of security rules is illustrated.

## 4.2 Secure DBMS design

A database is a collection of data organized and managed by specific software, the DBMS. Database security is achieved through a set of mechanisms at both the DBMS and the OS level.

In the implementation of security requirements, some security functions enforced at OS level can be exploited by the DBMS. In particular, I/O management functions and shared resources management prove useful to security in DBMS environments (Spooner, 1988; Wood, 1988). However, DBMS security functions should not be considered a simple extension to the underlying OS functions. As far as security is concerned, the differences between OSs and DBMSs can be listed as follows (Henning, 1988):

- *Object granularity.* The degree of granularity in an OS is the file level. The granularity of objects in a DBMS is finer (for example, relations, rows, columns, fields). A finer granularity for data sharing is also required at DBMS level.
- *Semantic correlations among data.* Data in a database has a semantics and is related through semantic relationships. Consequently, different types of access controls should be enforced, depending on object contents, context and access history, in order to assure a correct implementation of security requirements, and avoid security violations related to semantic correlations among data (for example, inference threats).
- *Metadata.* In a DBMS, metadata exists, providing information about the structure of the data in the database. Metadata is usually stored in data dictionaries separated from data. For example, in relational databases, metadata describes attributes, domains of attributes, relationships between attributes, and the location of database partitions. Metadata requires protection, as the usual data does. Metadata can, in fact, provide sensitive information about database contents (data types and relationships) and can be used as a method for controlling access to underlying data (for example, the SQL 'view' statement for creating sanitization views should itself be protected). No metalevel descriptions exist in an OS.
- *Logical and physical objects.* Objects in an OS are physical objects (for example, files, devices, memory, processes). Objects in a DBMS are logical objects (for example, relations, views). DBMS logical objects are independent of OS physical objects, and this requires security requirements and mechanisms specifically oriented to database object protection.

- *Multiple data types.* Databases are characterized by a variety of data types, for which multiple access modes are required (for example, statistical mode, administrative mode). At OS level only the physical access exists, for read, write and execute operations.
- *Static and dynamic objects.* Objects managed by the OS are static and correspond to actual objects. In databases, objects can be dynamically created (for example, as query results) and may have no actual corresponding objects. For example, in relational databases views are dynamically created, as virtual relations derived from base relations actually stored in the database. Specific protection requirements should be defined to deal with dynamic objects.
- *Multilevel transactions.* In a DBMS it is often necessary to perform transactions involving data at different security levels. The DBMS must assure that multilevel transactions are executed in a secure way. At OS level only basic operations (for example, read, write, execute) are executed, involving data having the same security level.
- *Data life cycle.* Data in the database has a long life cycle, and the DBMS must assure protection throughout the whole lifetime of the data.

## 4.2.1 Security mechanisms in DBMSs

Analogously to what happens for OSs, the DBMS should be designed with security in mind, to make security a DBMS feature considered from the earliest development stages, rather than an additional feature.

Data security is concerned (see Chapter 1) with the *improper disclosure or modification* of information, where modification is intended as insertion of spurious data items, or deletion of, or changes to, existing data. Various functionalities are required in a general-purpose DBMS to achieve the security requirements of an information system. The DBMS plays a central role in this task because it handles complex relationships among data which are useful when dealing with complex security policies. Obviously, some kernel security functions must be provided by the underlying OS, while the application-specific security constraints are to be handled by the DBMS: it will then be delegated to prevent applications from disclosing or corrupting the data.

The main security requirements that a DBMS should provide are related to the following issues:

- *Different degrees of granularity of access.* The DBMS should ensure access controls at various degrees of granularity. For relational databases, access controls can be applied to the following degrees of granularity: database, collections of relations, one relation, some columns of one relation, some rows of one relation, some columns or some rows of one relation.
- *Different access modes.* Access controls must be differentiated with respect to the operation they apply (for example, an employee can be authorized to read a data item, but not to write it). In relational databases, access

modes are expressed in terms of the basic SQL statements (for example, SELECT, INSERT, UPDATE, DELETE).

- *Different types of access controls.* Access requests can be processed using different types of controls. Name-dependent controls are based on the name of the object to be accessed. Data-dependent controls make the access dependent on the contents of the object to be accessed. Context-dependent controls grant or deny access depending on the value of some system variables (for example, date, time, requesting terminal). History-dependent controls consider information about query sequences (for example, query types, returned data, requesting user's profile, frequencies). Finally, result-dependent controls make the access decision dependent on the result of auxiliary control procedures which are executed at query time. In relational databases, data-dependent access controls are usually implemented through either view-based or query modification mechanisms. Views are virtual relations derived from base relations (that is, relations actually stored in the database) and other views, according to selection criteria for tuples and attributes. Using a query modification technique, the initial query requested by the user is properly restricted according to user's authorizations.
- *Dynamic authorization.* The DBMS should support the modification of users' authorizations while the database is operational. This reflects the minimum privilege principle, since it is possible to modify the authorizations according to the user's tasks.
- *Multilevel protection.* When required, the DBMS should enforce multilevel protection through the mandatory policy. Mandatory access controls are based on security labels associated with both objects (that is, data items), and subjects (users). In military environments, security labels are composed of a *hierarchical component* and a possibly empty set of non-hierarchical *categories*. Access controls are enforced using a set of axioms that state the relations to be verified between security labels of the subjects and objects involved (see Chapter 2). The DBMS should provide mechanisms to define security labels and to assign labels to objects and subjects. Using security labels, the DBMS should enforce multilevel protection, in that different security labels can be assigned to different data items in the same object. For example, in relational databases, it should be possible to have relations with a given security label containing attributes with their own security labels (possibly different from the relation label) which, in turn, store values with their own security label.
- *Covert channels.* The DBMS should be covert channel-free: that is, users should not be able to obtain unauthorized information through indirect methods of communication. Even if mandatory controls are provided by the DBMS, unfortunately this is not sufficient to guarantee that the system does not have covert channels.
- *Inference controls.* Inference controls must prevent users from drawing inferences from information they obtain from the database. In a database system, inference problems are usually related to *aggregation* problems

and *data association* problems (see Chapter 1). The DBMS should provide a means of assigning classifications to aggregate information, reflecting the level of sensitivity of the aggregation with respect to the data items involved in the aggregation. Thus, situations where the information about relationships among data items, or about the collection of data items, is more sensitive than the single data items individually considered must be correctly managed. The DBMS should avoid, through inference controls, users knowing about high-classified aggregate information by using low-classified data items. In a relational DBMS, query restriction techniques are usually used to avoid inference. Such mechanisms can either modify the initial query to generate a modified query, evaluated only on data dominated by the security level of the user, or abort the query. Polyinstantiation and audit techniques can also be used for this purpose (see below). Finally, a special type of inference is that occurring in statist-ical databases, where users must be prevented from inferring individual data items from aggregated statistical data obtained through statistical queries. This type of inference is extensively described in Chapter 5.

- *Polyinstantiation.* This technique can be used by the DBMS to prevent inference, by allowing the database to contain multiple instances of the same data item, each one having its own classification level. Polyinstantiation occurs as a consequence of the mandatory policy. In a relational DBMS, it is possible to have different tuples with the same key, each at a different classification level, if, for example, a high-classified row already exists, and a low-classified user requests the insertion of a new row having the same key. This prevents the low-classified user from inferring the existence of the high-classified row in the database. For a detailed discussion of polyinstantiation in relational databases see Chapter 2.
- *Auditing.* Security-relevant events occurring while the database system is active should be reported, possibly in a structured format such as system journals, audit trails, and system logs. The audit trail is useful for subsequent analysis, to detect possible threats to the database. Audit information is also useful for inference control, in that the history of the queries made by a user can be examined to determine whether the response to a new query, correlated with the responses to previous queries, could result in an inference violation (see Chapter 5).
- *Flow controls.* Flow controls check the destination of the output obtained through an authorized access (see Chapter 3).
- *No back doors.* Access to data should occur only via the DBMS. The absence of hidden access paths must be guaranteed.
- *Uniformity of mechanisms.* General mechanisms should be used to support the different policies and all the security-related controls (integrity and secrecy controls).
- *Reasonable performance.* Security controls entail additional execution time; this should be minimized to preserve the system performance.

Moreover, there are various basic principles for **information integrity**, which are independent of the DBMS context and the application characteristics. The principles mentioned here are elaborated by Clark and Wilson (1987, 1989) and in the NIST workshops (Ruthberg and Polk, 1989; Sandhu, 1988; Sandhu and Jajodia, 1990). The principles translate into concrete measures when considering the DBMS mechanisms. The benefit of these 'abstract' principles is that they provide an evaluation ground for informal DBMS evaluation and, similarly, a ground for evaluation of the security policies of a specific information system.

- *Well-formed transactions.* This principle, also called constrained change, states that data can be modified only via well-formed transactions, rather then via arbitrary procedures. Well-formed transactions are certified to be correct with some (usually qualitative) degree of assurance.

  Well-formed transactions translate into DBMS mechanisms ensuring the following properties for transactions: atomicity of failures, serializability, progress, and correct state transform. These properties, usual in the DB transaction management terminology, assure that either all or none of the effects of a transaction occur, that both upon failures and upon regular termination, the system is in a correct state, and that no infinite blocking occurs. The DBMS must ensure that updates are executed *exclusively* via transactions *(encapsulated updates)*, recalling that the DB must be encapsulated within the DBMS by the OS.

  As far as transaction installation and modification are concerned, well-formed 'transaction maintenance' transactions should be provided.

  Finally, we note that correct state transform can be achieved by considering also the semantics of the applications, and is complicated by the general undecidability of the correctness problem. Correct state transform can be achieved partly by using software engineering techniques (application developers' responsibility) and partly by using the DBMS consistency constraints mechanisms (such as entity integrity or referential integrity, or domain constraints and various dependency constraints in the relational model). In practice, although theoretically rich, the set of constraints usually enforced by relational DBMSs is limited to domain and entity constraints.
- *Authenticated users.* This principle states that changes should be executed only by users whose identity has been authenticated as proper for that task.

  Authenticating users is the responsibility of the OS and need not be duplicated in the DBMS. Authentication (see Chapter 3) underlies some of the other principles listed here (least privilege, separation of duty, delegation of authority), which become meaningful only if authentication is possible at the granularity of individuals.
- *Least privilege.* This is the well-known principle of limiting users to work with the minimal set of privileges and resources necessary to carry out their tasks (as described in Chapter 1). In the integrity context, this principle is also named 'need-to-do'. The difficulty in applying it consists

in balancing the user's least privileges with the task's (process's) privileges, since users and processes are two differently long-lived entities.

Least privilege translates into DBMS mechanisms for 'read' and 'write' operations. For 'read' operations, fine-grained mechanisms exist (for example, view based or query-modification based) which are not equally applicable for 'write' controls. Access rules described in Chapter 1 (Fernandez *et al.*, 1981) as triples might become:

<user, transaction, relation>

to control the execution of transactions, or, with higher selectivity:

<user, transaction, relation, attribute>

A sample authorization tuple is:

<Smith, Increase-5%, Employee, Salary>

which states that user Smith is authorized to increase the salary of employees by 5%. A 5-tuple is necessary if the update is to be restricted to the Salary attribute of a specific tuple – say, the tuple describing employee Perridge:

<Smith, Increase-5%, Perridge, Employee, Salary>

This 5-tuple takes a key, relation and attribute to specify the actual parameter of the transaction.

More generally, transactions have *N* parameters (for example, the source account number and the destination account number during a money transfer order) that will be mapped at run time into a list of actual parameters. The parameters specify the data item authorized for the update using the following identifiers: 'relation'; 'relation, attribute'; 'key, relation, attribute'. Each case gives a different granularity level of update control.

- *Separation of duties.* Briefly stated, this principle establishes that no single individual should be able to corrupt the data on his own, but rather several individuals should collude at some key point of an action chain, leading to data integrity violation.

  Separation of duties is concerned with controls on sequences of transactions. Currently, various mechanisms are available, but they have not been designed for integrity purposes and are therefore awkward. A technique proposed in Sandhu (1988) is called transaction-control expressions. It exploits the differences in the lifetime of objects involved in transactions (some data items are transient, for example, a voucher; some are persistent, for example, an account). Since transient objects carry a complete story of a session (unit of service), separation of duties can be enforced using transient objects (while persistent objects are regarded as a simple side-effect of a transaction). This idea is taken from the paper-based world where processing steps are coded in rules and have to be executed by different people.

- *Continuity of operation.* This problem has received great attention in theory and practice, and solutions based on replication of data have been proposed. In the face of devastating events beyond the organization's control, the system operations should be maintained to some properly defined extent (physical security measures are considered by this principle).
- *Reconstruction of events.* This principle states that improper behaviour should be detected, thus deterring privilege misuse. Since, practically, the least privilege principle rarely applies, reconstruction of events is useful to account users of misuse of extra privileges.

  Reconstruction of events in a DBMS is based on *audit trails.* Reconstruction can occur at different levels of detail and can mean different things: to keep a complete history of each modification to the value of an item, or to store the identity of each individual making a change, for each change. Techniques such as before-image and after-image are useful. In general, the ability to trace who has accessed what data, when, and in what order, depends on the database activity model used in the DBMS. The problem of querying a large quantity of data in the audit trail is also relevant. Some recent proposals use expert-system techniques to store and interpret audit trails; these techniques are presented in Chapter 6.
- *Reality checks.* A periodic check with the real-world entities contributes to maintaining correct data values in the system.

  Reality checks go beyond the duty of the DBMS; the DBMS has the responsibility to maintain an internally consistent view of the database which is the base for external inspections.
- *Ease of safe use.* The easiest way to operate a system should also be the safest. This means that the security procedures should be simple, user-friendly, known, and fault-free.

  Ease of safe use translates into an evaluation of the DBMS, rather than a function provided by the DBMS. User friendliness of the DBMS interface can contribute to enforcing this principle.
- *Delegation of authority.* This concerns the assignment of privileges in the organization, based on the policies. It states that the assignment procedures should reflect the organization's rules and be flexible, thus avoiding the perception by the users that security is a burden and should be circumvented.

  Delegation of authority should be flexible enough to be adequate to the policies; broadly speaking, typical organizational situations translate into mandatory and discretionary mechanisms.

  In discretionary mechanisms, delegation is generally achieved through the concept of *ownership*. The owner of an object, by default the *object creator*, can grant and revoke authorizations on the owned object to other users. Delegation of authorizations is enforced through discretionary policies, supporting grant/revoke of authorizations. Special privileges should exist in the DBMS, conferring on a restricted number of users special authorities on database users (that is, Database Administrator privileges).

The possibility of granting authorizations to other users, different from the creator, could pose problems when granted authorizations must be revoked. The DBMS should provide mechanisms for managing cascading revocation (see the detailed description of the System R revocation mechanism in Section 4.2.2). Authorization delegation is an essential capability for reflecting the hierarchical structure of the organization, and should be done in compliance with the rules defined within the organization. Delegation supports decentralized authorization, particularly useful in distributed environments. Delegation of authority in a relational DBMS is usually enforced through the SQL GRANT/REVOKE statements.

In particular, concerning integrity for a DBMS, in Sandhu and Jajodia (1990) principles are grouped as follows:

- *Group 1:* well-formed transactions, continuity of operation. These principles are properly covered by current DBMS mechanisms (except for the 'current state' concept).
- *Group 2:* least privilege, separation of duties, reconstruction of events, and delegation of authority. New mechanisms are required for this group, and several promising approaches extending the DBMS mechanisms are emerging.
- *Group 3:* authenticated users, reality checks, and ease of safe use. The DBMS mechanism can contribute in a limited way: authentication is the OS responsibility, reality checks depend on organizational security, while ease of use is contributed by the DBMS through its data manipulation languages.

### 4.2.2 The System R authorization model

To illustrate how some of the previous issues have been implemented in one of the very first DBMSs, we present the authorization model defined by Griffiths and Wade (1976) and later revised by Fagin (1978), in the framework of the relational DBMS System R, developed at the IBM Research Laboratory in San Jose.

The authorization model of System R considers, as objects to be protected, tables of the database. These can be either base tables or view tables (see Chapter 1). Subjects of the model are the users who can access the database. The privileges considered by the model are the access modes applicable to the tables of the database. In particular, the following access modes are considered:

**Read** to read tuples (rows) from a table. The authorization for the read privilege entitles a user owning it also to define views on the table.
**Insert** to add tuples to a table.
**Delete** to delete tuples from a table.
**Update** to modify existing tuples in a table.
**Drop** to delete an entire table from the system.

All the access modes refer to a table as a whole with the exception of the update privilege which can refer to specific columns inside a table.

The model supports a decentralized administration of authorizations. In particular, any database user may be authorized to create a new table. When a user creates a table, he or she is solely and fully authorized to execute privileges on the table (this is not completely true if the table is a view, as we will see later on). As owner, the user is also the only one entitled to drop the view. The owner can grant other users the privileges on the table. When a user grants another user a privilege on a table a new authorization is inserted among the set of authorizations held in the system. Privileges can be granted with the grant option, meaning the receiver is allowed to grant privileges, and the grant option, to other users. Each authorization can be characterized as a tuple $\langle s, p, t, ts, g, go \rangle$ where:

*s* is the subject (user) to whom the authorization is granted (that is, the *grantee*);
*p* is the privilege (access mode);
*t* is the table to which the authorization refers;
*ts* is the time at which the authorization was granted;
*g* is the user who granted the authorization (that is, the *grantor*);
$go \in$ {yes, no} indicates whether *s* has the grant option for *p* on *t*.

If the privilege in the authorization is 'update', the columns on which the privilege can be executed must also be indicated. The grant option is similar to the copy flag of the access matrix model. If a user holds the authorization for a privilege on a table with the grant option, the user can grant other users the privilege on the table as well as the grant option on it.

For example, tuple <B, select, T, 10, A, yes> indicates that user B can select tuples from table T, and grant other users authorizations to select tuples from table T, and that this privilege was granted to B by user A at time 10. Tuple <C, select, T, 20, B, no> indicates that user C can select tuples from table T and that this privilege was granted to C by user B at time 20. The authorization does not entitle user C to grant other users the select privilege on T.

The reason why, in each authorization, the grantor and the time the authorization was granted are indicated, is to enforce a special type of revoke procedure as we will illustrate later.

The data definition, manipulation and control language of System R, named SQL, has been extended to the consideration of statements allowing the user to require execution of grant and revoke operations.

The grant command of SQL has the form:

```
      { ALL RIGHTS              }
GRANT { ⟨privileges⟩            } ON ⟨table⟩ TO ⟨user-list⟩ [WITH GRANT OPTION]
      { ALL BUT ⟨privileges⟩    }
```

The user granting a privilege on a table may also specify the keyword PUBLIC instead of the ⟨user-list⟩ to which the privilege is being authorized. In such a case, all database users are granted the privilege on the table.

Every user who has the authorization for a privilege on a table with the grant option can also revoke the privilege on the table. However, a user can revoke only those authorizations that were granted by him. In particular, the revocation of a privilege on a table from the revokee by the revoker does not have any effect on possible authorizations for the privilege on the table that the revokee may have received from users different from the revoker.

The revoke command of SQL has the form:

```
REVOKE { ALL RIGHTS     } ON ⟨table⟩ FROM ⟨user-list⟩
       { ⟨privileges⟩   }
```

The next section discusses the revoke mechanism.

***Revocation of authorizations***

The System R authorization model enforces recursive (or *cascading*) revocation. The semantics of the recursive revocation of privilege $p$ on table $t$ from user $y$ by user $x$ is defined to be as if all the authorizations for $p$ on $t$ granted by $x$ to $y$ had never been granted. Therefore, all the effects brought about by the presence of the authorizations being revoked have to be eliminated. In particular, all the authorizations for $p$ on $t$ which could not have been granted if the revokee had never received any authorization for the privilege on the table from the revoker will also have to be deleted.

As an example, consider the sequence of grant operation for privilege $p$ on table $t$ illustrated in Figure 4.1(a), where every node represents a user and an arc between node $u_1$ and node $u_2$ indicates that $u_1$ granted the privilege on the table to $u_2$. The label of the arc indicates the time the privilege was granted: that is, the timestamp of the authorization. Suppose now that user $B$ revokes the privilege on the table from user $D$. According to the semantics of recursive revocation, the resulting authorization state has to be as if $D$ had never received the authorization from $B$. If $D$ had never received the authorization from $B$, he could never have granted the authorization to $E$ (his request would have been rejected by the system). Analogously, $E$ could not have granted the authorization

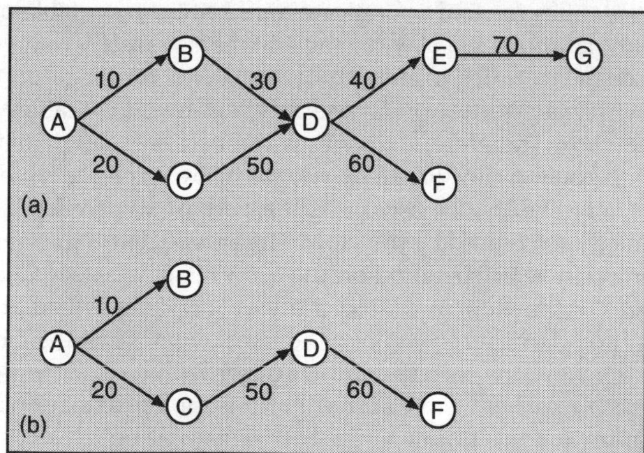


*Figure 4.1* An example of a revoke operation: (a) B has granted a privilege to D, who has passed it to E, who has passed it to G; (b) authorization state after B revokes D's privilege.

to *G*. Therefore, the authorization granted by *D* to *E* and by *E* to *G* must also be deleted upon the revocation. By contrast, the authorization granted by *D* to *F* does not have to be deleted. Indeed, this authorization could have been granted anyway even if *D* had never received the grant option for the privilege from *B*. Then, after the revocation, the set of authorizations holding in the system should be as if the sequence of grant operations had been as in Figure 4.1(b).

The revocation algorithm works as follows (Fagin, 1978). Suppose user $x$ revokes privilege $p$ from user $y$. If there is no authorization for the privilege on the table granted by $x$ to $y$, then the revoke operation is ignored. Otherwise, every authorization for privilege $p$ on table $t$ granted by $x$ to $y$ is deleted. If at least one of the deleted authorizations was with the grant option, then the authorizations granted by $y$ may also need to be revoked. Let $ts$ be the minimum timestamp of $y$'s remaining authorizations for privilege $p$ on table $t$ with the grant option (if no such authorization still appears, then let $ts = \infty$). Then, each grant by $y$ of privilege $p$ on table $t$, with timestamp smaller than $ts$, is deleted from the authorization table. The procedure is repeated for each user from which any authorization is revoked.

### Views

System R allows users to define views on top of base tables and other views. Views, which are defined in terms of queries on one or more base tables or views, represent a single and effective mechanism to support content-dependent authorizations. For example, suppose user *A* creates table *T* and wants to give user *B* the authorization to read the tuples of *T* for which the value of attribute $a_1$ is greater than 1000. Then, *A* can define a view of the form "select * from *T* where $a_1 > 1000$" on top of *T*, and grant *B* the read authorization on the view.

The user defining a view is the view owner and is therefore entitled to drop the view. However, he may not be authorized to exercise all privileges on the view. The authorizations that the owner of a view owns on the view depend on the view semantics (certain operations may not be executable on the view) and on the authorizations the user has on the tables directly referenced by the view. In particular, in order to be authorized for a privilege on a view, the owner must own an authorization for the privilege on all the tables directly referenced by the view. Therefore, if a view is defined on a single table, the user can be authorized on the view for all privileges he owns on the table. If the view is defined on a set of tables, the user is authorized for all privileges he owns on every table directly referenced by the view. The privileges on the view, however, may be further restricted depending on the view semantics (see Chapter 1).

The privileges of the view owner on the view are determined at the time of the view definition. For every privilege the user owns on all the tables directly referenced by the view, the corresponding authorization on the view is defined. Although the user may have more authorizations for a privilege on a table, only one authorization for the privilege on the view will be derived. If the user defining the view is authorized for a privilege on all the underlying tables with the grant option, the grant option for the privilege on the view will be given to the user. The grantor of the authorizations derived for the owner of a view on the view is the view owner himself. The timestamp is the time of the view definition.

For example, suppose user *B*, who is authorized for the read privilege on tables $T_1$ and $T_2$ with the grant option, defines view *V* on top of the two tables. User *B* receives the authorization for the read privilege with the grant option on the view.

If a user receives the authorization for a privilege on a view with the grant option, he can grant other users the privilege, possibly with the grant option, on the view. In order for these users to use the privilege on the view, it is not necessary to be authorized for the privilege on the tables directly referenced by the view. For instance, with reference to the example just mentioned, if user *B* grants *C* the read privilege on the view, *C* can select tuples from *V* even if he or she does not have the read authorization on tables $T_1$ and $T_2$.

If, after having defined a view, the view owner receives additional privileges on the underlying tables, these will not be passed on to the view: that is, the user will not be authorized for them on the view. By contrast, if after having defined a view, the view owner is revoked a privilege on any of the underlying tables, the privilege may need to be revoked also on the view. For instance, with reference to the example just mentioned, if *B* is revoked the read privilege on $T_1$, *B*'s authorization on *V* and, as a consequence, the authorization on *V* granted by *B* to *C* will also have to be deleted.

#### *Implementation of the model*

Information of users' authorizations to access database tables are stored in two relations named SYSAUTH and SYCOLAUTH. Relation SYSAUTH has the following attributes:

**Userid** indicates the user to which the authorizations are referred.

**Tname** indicates the table to which the authorizations are referred.

**Type** indicates the type of table *Tname*. This attribute has value "R" if the table is a base table and "V" if the table is a view table.

**Grantor** indicates the user who granted the authorizations.

**Read** indicates the time at which the grantor granted the grantee the read privilege on the table. If there is no authorization given by the grantor to the grantee for the read privilege on the table, the attribute has value 0.

**Insert** indicates the time at which the grantor granted the grantee the insert privilege on the table. If there is no authorization given by the grantor to the grantee for the insert privilege on the table, the attribute has value 0.

**Delete** indicates the time at which the grantor granted the grantee the update privilege on the table. If there is no authorization given by the grantor to the grantee for the update privilege on the table, the attribute has value 0.

**Update** indicates the columns on which the update privilege is granted. It can have the value "All", meaning all columns can be updated, "None", meaning no update privilege, or "Some", meaning the privilege can be exercised only on some columns of the table.

**Grantopt** indicates whether the privileges indicated have been granted with the grant option.

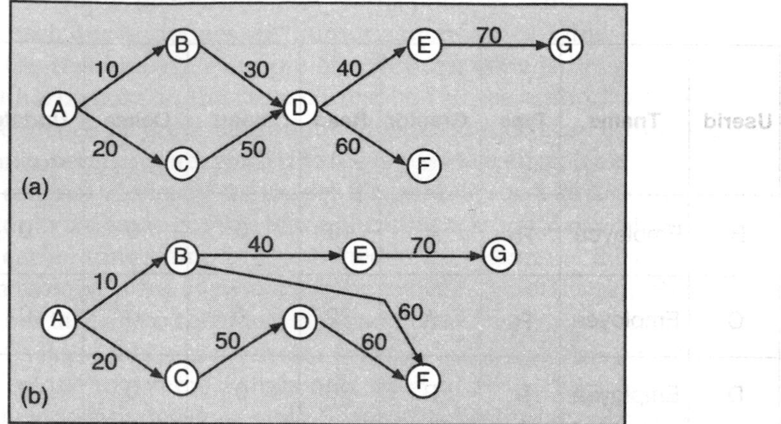


*Figure 4.3* Example of a non-cascade revoke operation: (a) B has granted a privilege to D, who has passed it to E, who has passed it to G; (b) the authorization state after B revokes D's privilege.

The second extension concerns *negative authorization*. Most DBMSs use the *closed world* policy. Under this policy, the lack of an authorization is interpreted as a negative authorization. Therefore, whenever a user tries to access an object, if no proper authorization is found in the system catalogues, the user is denied the access. This approach has a major problem in that the lack of a given authorization for a given user does not prevent this user from receiving this authorization later on. Suppose that a user *U* is not meant to access a given object. In situations where authorization administration is decentralized (like System R) it might happen that a user, possessing the right to administrate that object, grants *U* the authorization on that object. Indeed, in a system like System R, several users may have the right to administrate the same object. Therefore, it is not possible to enforce the constraint that a user is not supposed to access an object. In recent works, explicit negative authorizations are proposed as an approach for handling that type of constraint. An explicit negative authorization expresses a *denial* for a user to access an object under a specified mode. *Negative* authorizations are stronger than *positive* authorizations (that is, authorizations permitting access). Therefore, whenever a user has both a positive and a negative authorization on the same object, the user is prevented from accessing the object. Note that, even if a positive authorization is granted after a negative authorization has been granted, the user is still denied the access. Moreover, the consideration of negative authorizations allows exceptions to authorization to be specified. For example, it makes it possible to grant an authorization to all members of a group, except for one specific member, by granting the group the positive authorization for the privilege on the table and the given member the corresponding negative authorization.

### 4.2.3 Secure DBMS architectures

In this section we describe the main features of secure DBMS architectures. Secure DBMSs operate according to two possible modes, the 'system high' mode and the 'multilevel' mode.

In system high DBMSs, all the users are cleared to the highest security level and, before releasing data, a human responsible (guard) must review such data, in order to properly release them. This approach allows one to use existing DBMS technologies without changes, but generates additional costs owing to the clearance procedure and the manual review of data. This mode would augment risks for security, since all the users are cleared to the highest clearance level.

With multilevel mode, different types of architectures are possible, based on the use of both trusted and untrusted DBMSs. The multilevel architectures are the *Trusted Subject Architecture* and the *Woods Hole architectures*, proposed in the Woods Hole Summer Study on Multilevel Data Management Security in 1982. The Woods Hole architectures are the Integrity Lock, the Kernelized, and the Replicated architectures. In the Trusted Subject Architecture both a trusted DBMS and a trusted OS are used, while in the Woods Hole architectures an untrusted DBMS is employed with an additional trusted filter. Thus, the Trusted Subject Architecture requires either the development from scratch of a new DBMS, or the extension of the security features of an existing DBMS.

Table 4.1 gives an overview of the architectures used in some commercial DBMSs, and in some DBMS research prototypes.

**Table 4.1** Architectures of DBMS prototypes and commercial products.

| Architecture | Research prototypes | Commercial DBMS |
|---|---|---|
| Integrity Lock | Mitre | TRUDATA |
| Kernelized | SeaView | Oracle |
| Replicated | NRL | – |
| Trusted Subject | A1 Secure DBMS (ASD) | Sybase |
| | | Informix |
| | | Ingres |
| | | Oracle |
| | | DEC |
| | | Rubix |

***The Trusted Subject Architecture***

The Trusted Subject Architecture is shown in Figure 4.4.

A set of untrusted front ends (UFE) is used to interface the users with different clearances, here simply shown as Low and High. A trusted DBMS is employed, acting as a trusted subject with respect to the OS, also trusted, which performs the physical accesses to the database. To act as a trusted subject of the OS means to be exempt from one or more aspects of the security policy of the OS and, in general, from mandatory controls. The DBMS and the OS must be considered as an entity (together they constitute the TCB of the DoD criteria) and, as such, evaluated to determine the protection level offered. In this architecture, the DBMS is responsible for multilevel protection of the database objects. The security lattice is structured in such a way that the High level dominates the Low level, and a DBMS level, incomparable with

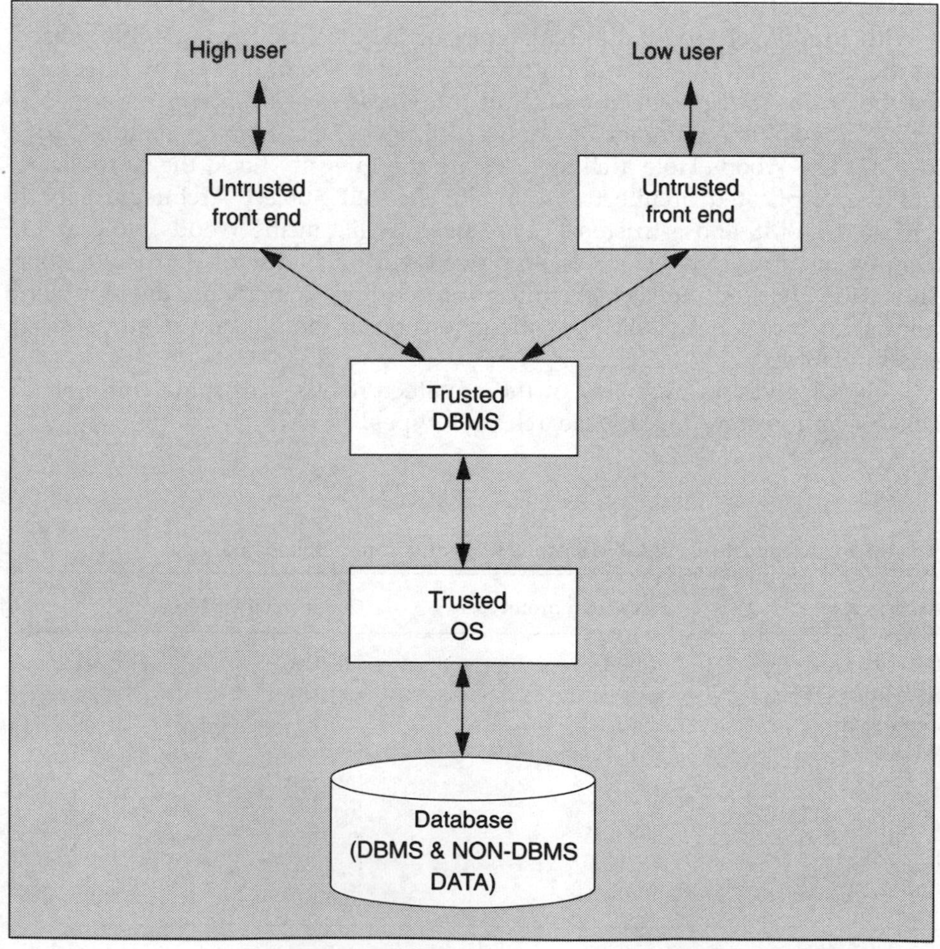


*Figure 4.4* Trusted Subject Architecture.

High and Low, is defined. A DBMS label is assigned to both objects and subjects. Only DBMS subjects can execute code and access data with a DBMS label. Moreover, subjects having a DBMS label are considered trusted subjects and, consequently, are exempt from OS mandatory controls. In this approach, it is possible either to group elements at the same sensitivity level and store them in one object at a coarse granularity level, assigning only one label to this object (thus reducing label overhead), or to assign a label to each object (for example, tuples, values). The Sybase DBMS adopts this solution, with a client/server architecture. Sybase implements a tuple-level labelling. A version on VAX computers (submitted for B2 classification) and a version with a secure UNIX OS (submitted for B1 classification) are available.

### The Woods Hole architectures

The Woods Hole architectures were illustrated in a document from the National Research Council in 1982 (Committee on Multilevel Data Management Security, 1982), and are classified as follows:

- Integrity Lock architecture (or spray paint architecture)
- Kernelized architecture
- Replicated architecture (also called Distributed architecture).

They can be described by the general architecture shown in Figure 4.5.

We recognize a set of untrusted front ends (UFE) interfacing users operating at various clearances, here simplified as High and Low. UFE, in turn, interact with a trusted front end (TFE), which acts as reference monitor: that is, it cannot be bypassed. The TFE interfaces an untrusted back end DBMS (UBED), responsible for accessing data in the database. In the following, we describe the characteristics of each architecture.

#### Integrity Lock architecture

The Integrity Lock architecture is shown in Figure 4.6 (Graubart, 1984).

In this approach, users are connected via untrusted front-end interfaces, performing pre- and post-processing of queries (namely, query parsing, optimization, projections). A trusted front end (TFE) (also called a trusted filter) is inserted between the UFEs and the untrusted DBMS. The TFE is responsible for enforcing security functions and multilevel protection, acting as a TCB. The TFE enforces multilevel protection by attaching security labels to database objects, in the form of stamps. A *stamp* is a special field of an object, storing information concerning the security label and other relevant control data in an encrypted format, generated using a cryptoseal mechanism called Integrity Lock (which gives the name to the architecture). The TFE performs the creation and validation of stamps, respectively, when data is stored in and retrieved from the database. Stamps are generated by the TFE using checksum techniques (it makes use of secret cryptographic key(s), known only to the TFE), are bounded to data, and stored in an encrypted format into the database. At the moment of retrieval, stamps are recomputed by the TFE and matched against the stored version, to detect possible mismatches, before data is

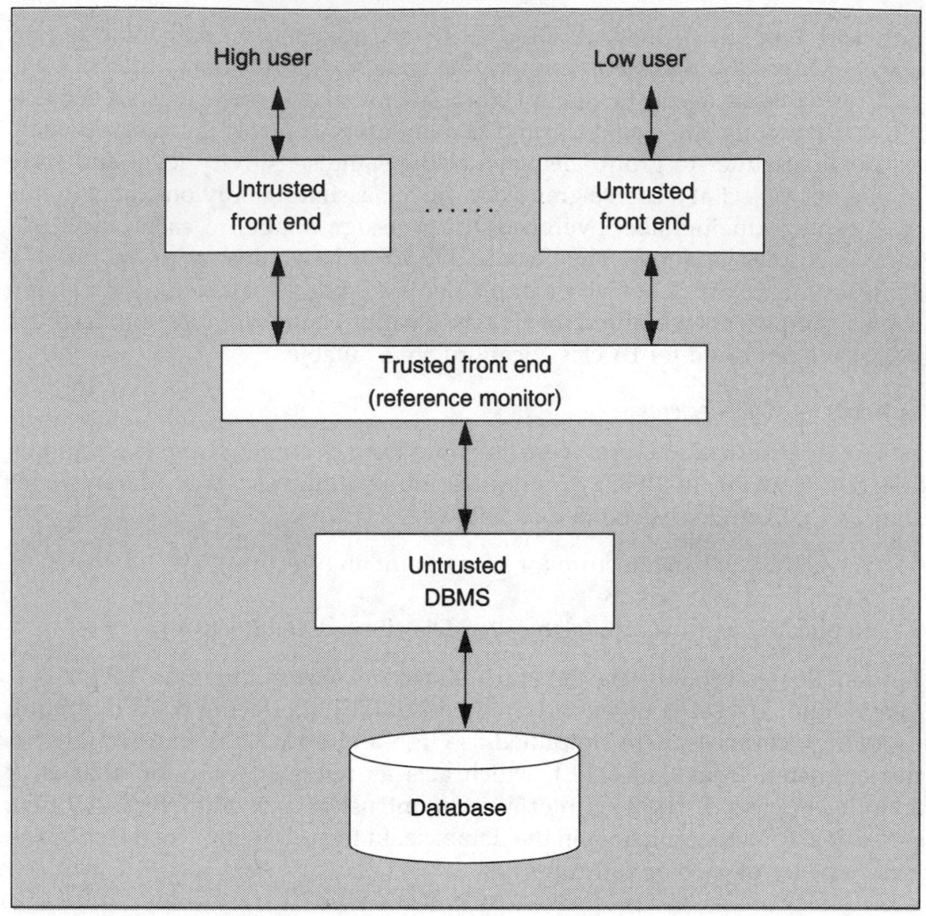


*Figure 4.5* Woods Hole architectures.

released to the user (corrective actions are required upon mismatch detection). The TFE is also responsible for the generation of its own audit records, possibly with the same format as the audit records generated by the OS, to guarantee the availability of a homogeneous audit trail.

Even if a stamp-based mechanism is correctly enforced, this is not sufficient to guarantee security. In fact, it guarantees that situations involving direct access to unauthorized data and the release of unauthorized information with incorrect classification by Trojan Horses do not happen. With this type of architecture, the database can be exposed to inference risks, as well as to Trojan Horse leakage risks. To avoid these threats, selections, projections, subquery handling, query optimization and statistical operations must be placed in the TFE or in the UFE, and not in the DBMS, which is only responsible for storage and retrieval operations. This way, the TFE sees all the data required to answer a query, and is enabled to eliminate from the returned data view those data for which the user is not cleared.

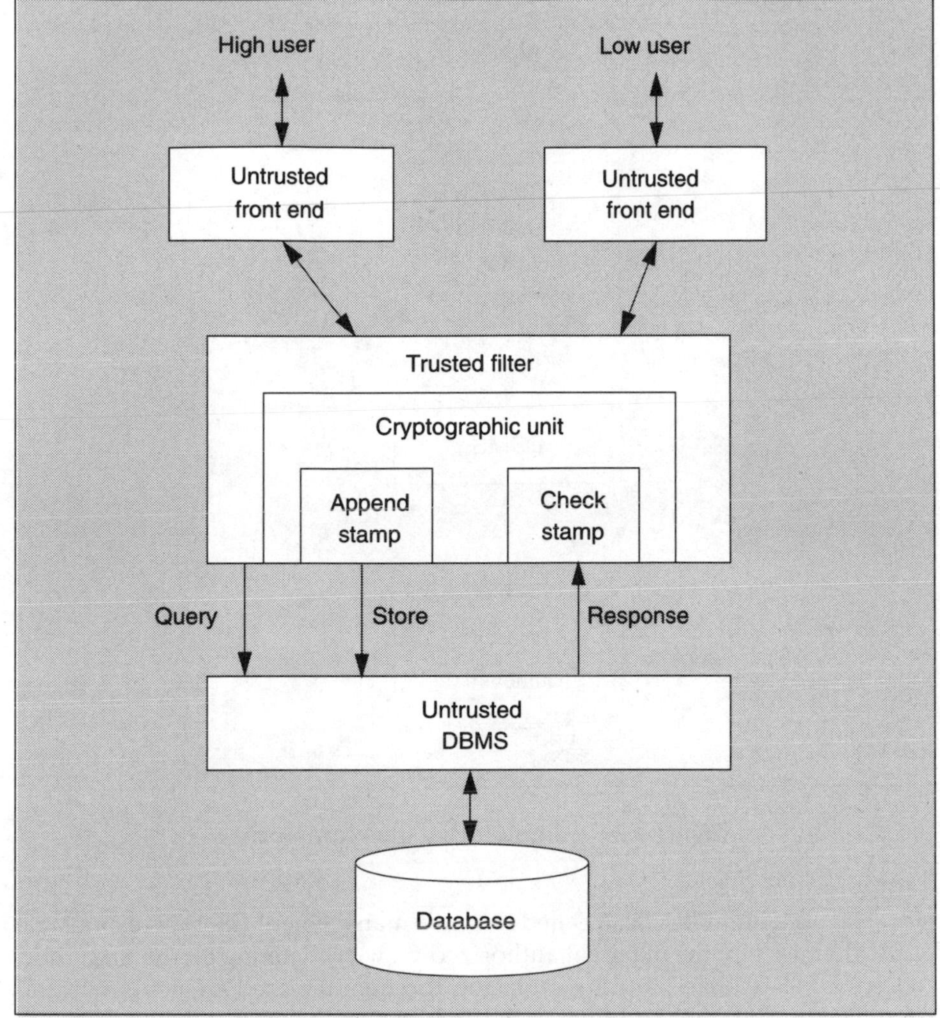


*Figure 4.6* Integrity Lock architecture.

An approach to eliminate inference risks has been proposed in Denning (1985), where a commutative filter is inserted between the users and the DBMS (see Figure 4.7), assuring the elimination of the inference threat, provided that the DBMS is free of Trojan Horses that leak data. This solution is derived from the Maximal Authorized View approach proposed in Downs and Popek (1977), shown in Figure 4.8, by commuting the DBMS and the back-end filter of Figure 4.8, and by defining only one trusted front-end filter, combining the two filters.

With the Maximal Authorized View approach, each query *q* is evaluated against a view of the database consisting only of the data the user is cleared for (called the maximal authorized view, which is a subset of the data stored in the database), giving origin to a query *qsec*, that avoids inference on unauthorized

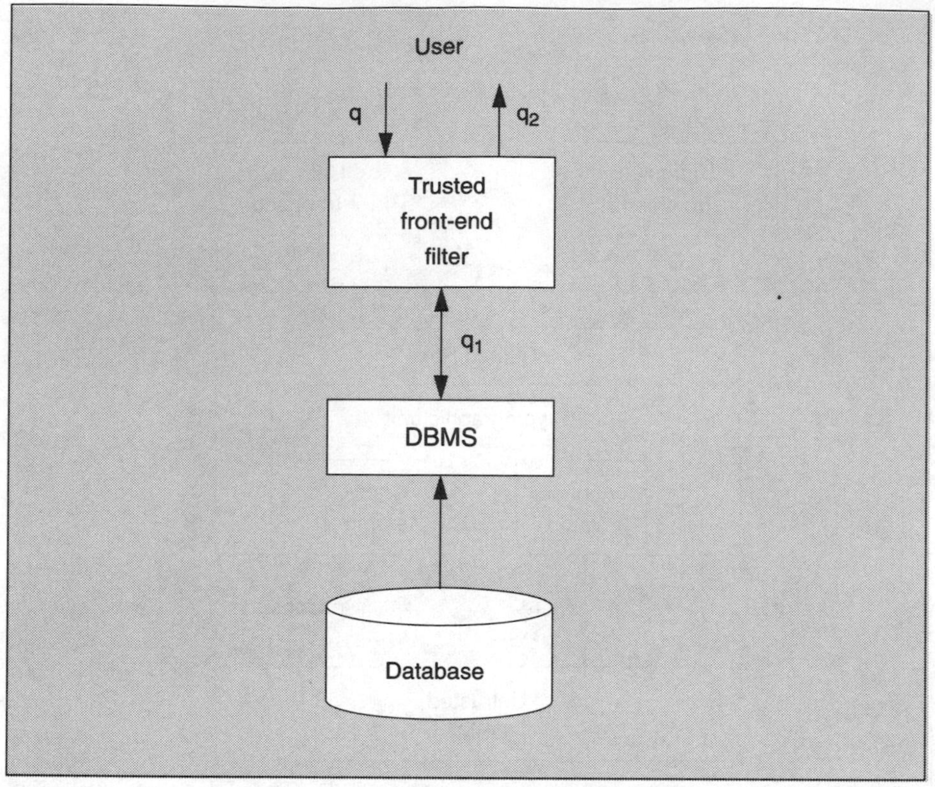


*Figure 4.7* Commutative filter approach.

data. The back-end filter (also called the data management filter) is responsible for the definition of the maximal authorized view, by deleting all the unauthorized records/attributes, and by replacing the unauthorized elements with nil value. The trusted front-end filter of the architecture in Figure 4.7 works in such a way that the query $q_2$ returned to the user is equivalent to the query *qsec* of the architecture in Figure 4.8, by augmenting the initial user query $q$ with the stamp information (giving origin to $q_1$), and filtering $q_2$ from the response for $q_1$. The Integrity Lock architecture has been adopted by the commercial product TRUDATA from Atlantic Research Corporation/Professional Services Group (ARC/PSG), running on AT&T 3B2/UNIX System V MLS and Sharebase relational database engine.

#### *Kernelized architecture*

The kernelized architecture is shown in Figure 4.9.

Here a trusted OS is used, which is responsible for the physical accesses to data in the database, and for enforcing mandatory protection. Users operating at High level interact with a High DBMS, through a TFE, as the Low users do with a Low DBMS. Their requests are then passed to the underlying OS, which

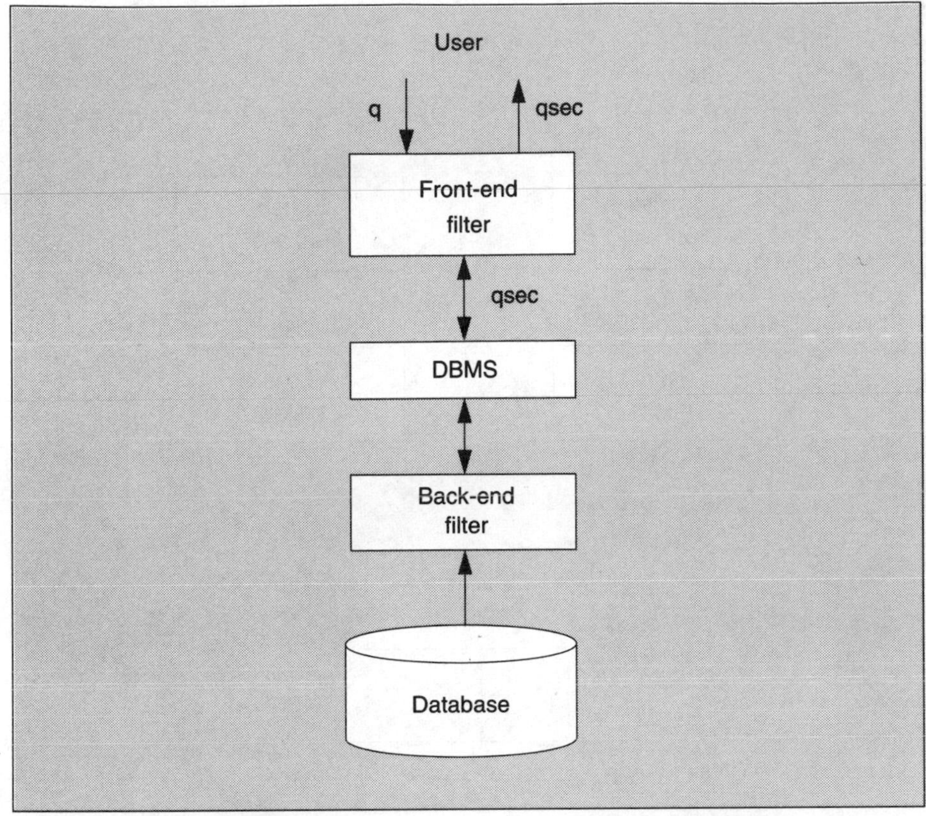


*Figure 4.8* Maximal Authorized View approach.

retrieves the proper data from the database. In this approach, database objects having similar security labels are stored in trusted OS objects (acting as containers of database objects). Thus, the trusted OS performs security controls on these latter objects. Multilevel relation decomposition and recovery processes are required. The decomposition process consists in transforming a multilevel relation into several single-level relations, containing only data at a given security level, which are stored in operating system objects. Recovery is performed on single-level relations when they are retrieved, to generate a multilevel view containing only the data the user requesting the query is cleared for. Decomposition and recovery algorithms must be properly defined, to guarantee correctness and system efficiency. Audit records are generated by the trusted OS for operations concerning access to OS objects, and other audit records must be generated for DBMS operations and recorded in a system high audit trail, possibly with the same format as the OS audit records. This architecture is used by the research prototype SeaView (Lunt, 1988), and by the commercial DBMS Oracle.

*Replicated architecture*

The replicated architecture is shown in Figure 4.10.

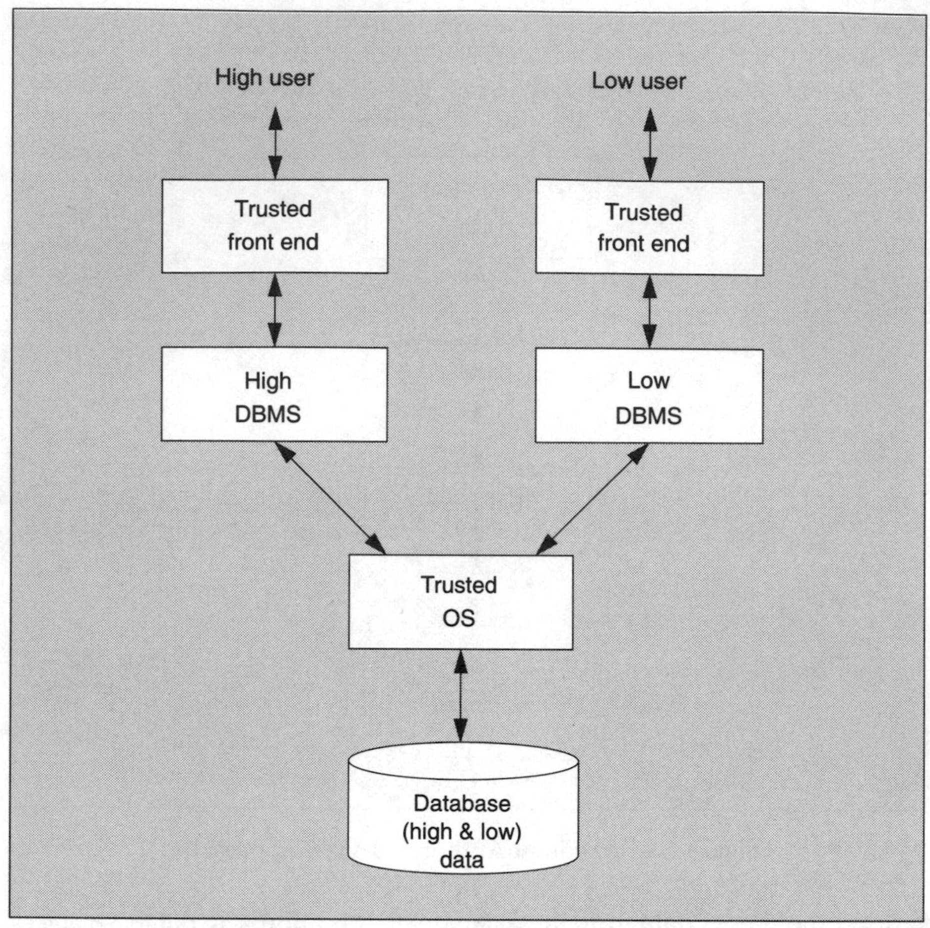


*Figure 4.9* Kernelized architecture.

In this solution, low data is replicated in the database. This way, Low users are allowed to access only the Low database, with no possibility of modifying high data. To enforce this approach, secure synchronization algorithms for consistent replication are required, and costs owing to replication increase with the size of the security lattice. No commercial DBMS uses this architecture, since it is expensive because of duplication of data; only the NRL research prototype uses this solution.

***Remarks on secure architectures***

The secure architectures described are suitable for different purposes, according to the characteristics and the requirements of the target application domain. For example, the Kernelized architecture fits environments requiring single-level tables, because it is the most economical and easy to implement. For environments characterized by a DBMS requiring label flexibility and a high degree of integration between the DBMS and the underlying OS,

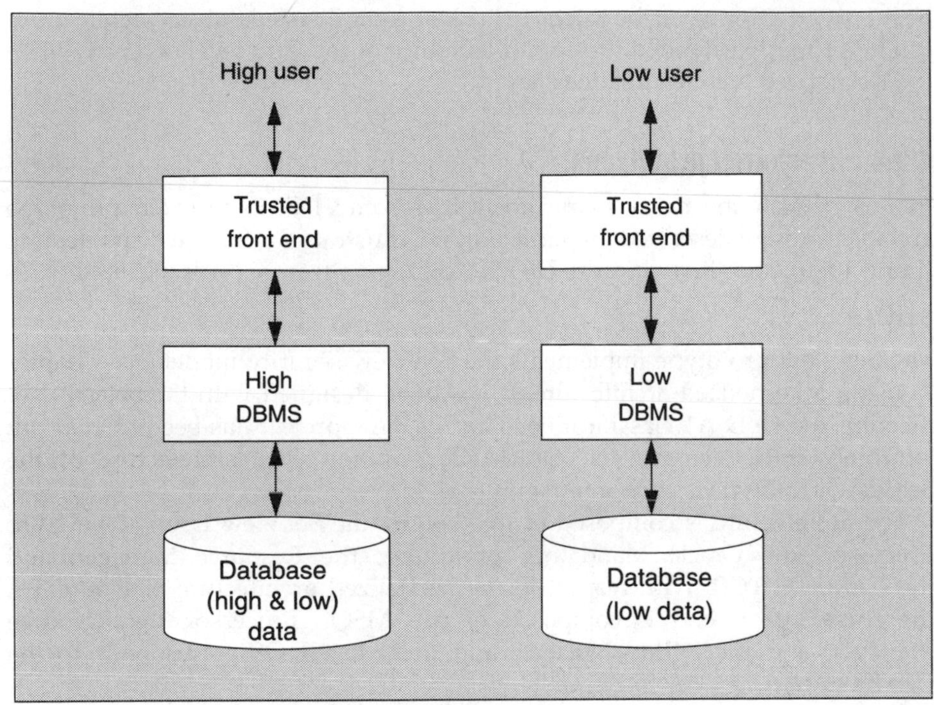


*Figure 4.10* Replicated architecture.

the Integrity Lock architecture should be preferred. The Trusted Subject Architecture is suitable for application domains where a trusted path can be assured from applications to the DBMS.

Concerning the evaluation of the level of trust of the architectures, that is, which architecture is most conducive to the production of trustworthy systems, it has to be noted that the complexity of the evaluation problem depends on the architecture. For example, the Integrity Lock architecture is easiest to validate, while the Trusted Subject is more complex. Indeed, while in the former we have a small-size filter, in the latter a trusted DBMS has to be evaluated, including services normally provided by a trusted OS. The kernelized architecture is in the middle, but if additional trusted software is added to operate securely in a multilevel environment, the evaluation task becomes harder.

Another issue concerns the degree of dependency between the DBMS and the underlying trusted OS. The Integrity Lock and the Kernelized architectures both rely on the secure services provided by the underlying trusted OS, while the Trusted Subject Architecture presents a lower level of dependency and integration. Concerning labelling granularity, that is, the smallest database object that can be assigned a label, architectures behave differently. For example, the Integrity Lock and the Trusted Subject architectures provide row labelling, while the Kernelized architecture relies on labelling provided by the trusted OS, on its container objects, thus reducing the storage overhead. This latter labelling mechanism is, however, not suitable if many multilevel tables have to be managed. Moreover, the Integrity Lock and the Trusted Subject architectures can be properly extended to support labelling at the field level of a row, while the Kernelized architecture does not.

### 4.2.4 Research prototypes

In this section the main characteristics of some DBMS research prototype architectures are described. In particular, we illustrate the SeaView architecture (Lunt, 1988), and the A1 Secure DBMS (ASD) architecture (Wilson, 1989).

#### *SeaView*

The SeaView prototype implements the SeaView security model (see Chapter 2) using a kernelized architecture. It has been designed with the objective of meeting the DoD A1 classification. The SeaView project has been carried out jointly by SRI, Gemini, and Oracle Corporation. The architecture of the SeaView prototype is shown in Figure 4.11.

The architecture is composed of five layers: the SeaView Users, the MSQL Processor, the Oracle Mandatory prototype, the Resource Manager, and the GEMSOS TCB. With respect to the kernelized architecture in Figure 4.9, the trusted front-end is composed of the MSQL Processor, the Resource Manager, and the DBMS Nucleus, and the trusted OS corresponds to the GEMSOS TCB.

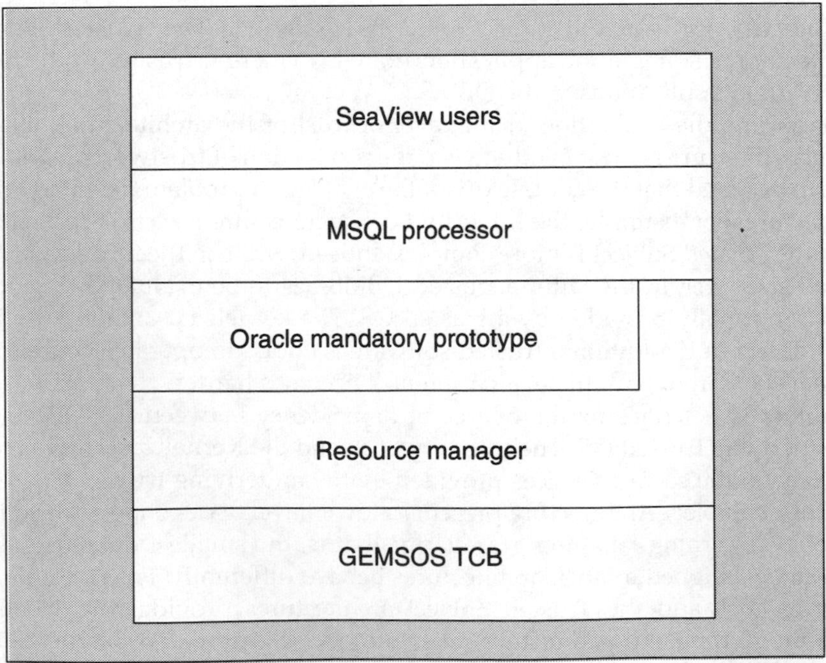


*Figure 4.11* SeaView architecture.

At the lowest layer, there is the GEMSOS TCB, composed of a Mandatory Security Kernel and the Non-mandatory TCB. The Mandatory Security Kernel is the GEMSOS security kernel. It implements the abstractions required for mandatory policy (namely, subjects, segments, devices, objects). The Mandatory Security Kernel enforces the mandatory security policy through a label-based mechanism. Moreover, it enforces user identification/authentication, trusted path, management of tables containing user clearances, and an interface for the mandatory security administrator. The GEMSOS mandatory security kernel has eight protection rings. Ring attributes are assigned to each object, and a ring number is assigned to each subject. A subject can access an object if the ring attributes of the object are consistent with the ring number of the subject. The non-mandatory TCB is responsible for discretionary access control to the database, and provides an interface for security audit and group administration. The mandatory security kernel and the non-mandatory TCB can be evaluated as A1.

The *Resource Manager* is responsible for providing the functions required to support the Oracle DBMS and SeaView. It is a special-purpose operating system, outside the TCB, since the TCB must have minimal design, as required to be certified as A1. The Resource Manager is responsible for functionalities like creation of the file system, high-level device drivers, mapping of the high-level objects of the DBMS to the low-level objects managed by the GEMSOS TCB, and so on. Some Oracle software modules have been rewritten (for example, the modules for data resource locking), and they have been included in the Resource Manager.

The *Oracle Mandatory Prototype* is responsible for the management of single-level relations. It is composed of the Oracle run-time environment; the Oracle utilities and software have not been rewritten. In particular, the ORACLE preprocessor has been maintained, preparing programs containing embedded SQL statements for compilation and execution.

The *MSQL Processor* allows users to deal with multilevel relations. It supports the transformation of programs containing embedded MSQL statements into equivalent programs containing embedded SQL statements, which can be given as input to the ordinary Oracle preprocessor. MSQL is an SQL specifically developed for SeaView, extended with capabilities to deal with multilevel relations. In particular, MSQL has a type to model the access class lattice and operators to compare values of that type. MSQL requires an apparent primary key to be defined for all multilevel real relations. It enforces multilevel entity integrity by creating unique indexes on the keys of the underlying single-level relations.

The *SeaView Users* layer is composed of those functions required to manage the database that can be left untrusted. It manages the user interface.

### A1 Secure DBMS

The *A1 Secure DBMS (ASD)* is a multilevel secure relational DBMS being developed under the Advanced Secure DBMS Internal Research and Development Project of the Defense Systems Group of the TRW (Lunt, 1992b). A prototype of the system is available. The development of the A1 Secure DBMS is mainly guided by the objective of meeting the criteria of the DoD, specifically those of A1 classification. It is developed in the Ada language, partly because the ASD has been developed by exploiting the Ada code of an existing relational DBMS. The system is targeted to run on top of an A1 secure OS, although currently the prototype works in a UNIX environment.

The main feature of the project is the fact that the ASD allows interconnection between trusted and untrusted systems, since it guarantees that data is protected via both mandatory and discretionary access control rules. Moreover, only one copy of the shared data is stored within the system; this copy is accessible to multiple users at different security levels, thus improving data integrity.

The architecture of the ASD is shown in Figure 4.12.

The system can operate in three different modes: as a *DBMS server* on a local area network, as a *back-end DBMS* for a host computer (both single-level and multilevel), or as a *host-resident DBMS* within a multilevel host under an A1 secure operating system. With reference to Figure 4.12, we can distinguish between trusted and untrusted code, the difference being in the potential

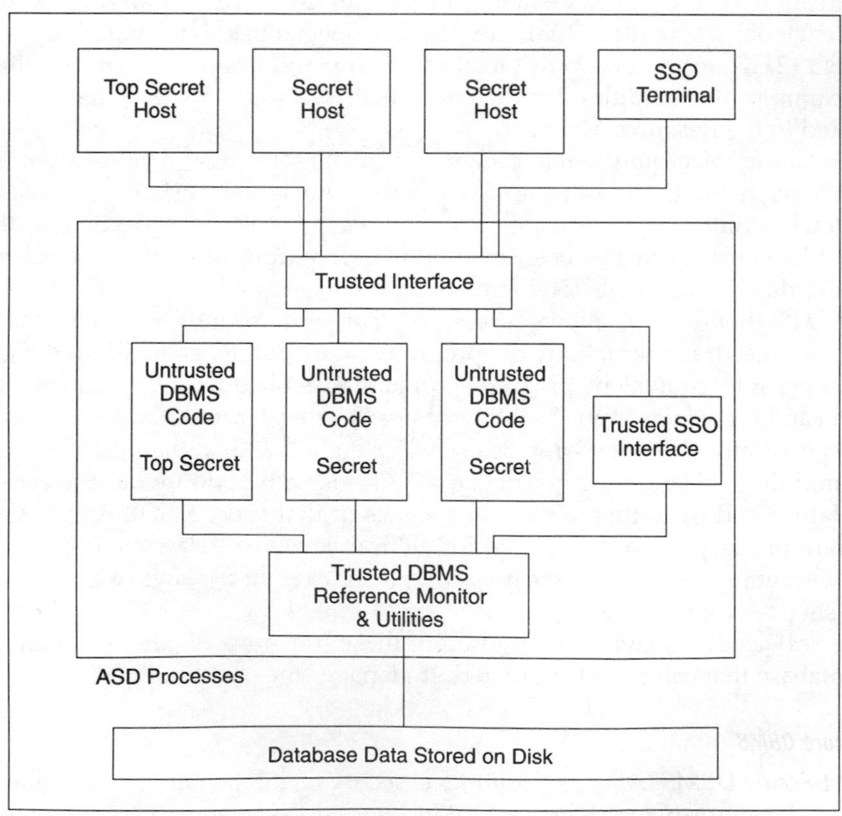


*Figure 4.12* Architecture of A1 Secure DBMS.

damage that could derive from incorrect code operations. More precisely, the trusted code constitutes the Trusted Computing Base (TCB) or Reference Monitor, and is the code that might lead to the disclosure of classified information if an incorrect operation occurs. The Gypsy Verification Environment Methodology, approved by the NCSC, has been employed to formally verify the correctness of the trusted code, as requested by the A1 classification. The code, whose incorrect operation cannot lead to classified information disclosure, is left untrusted. The untrusted code is instantiated into several different untrusted processes, holding the security level of the application process being supported. In fact, for each user of the DBMS, an untrusted process exists, inheriting the security level of the corresponding user session. The classification of the user session depends on the mode according to which the user accesses the DBMS.

Communication between untrusted processes is managed by the TCB of the ASD, which guarantees that processes send and receive information only at their security level. The Trusted Interface supports interactions with the users of the DBMS. In particular, when a user issues a query, the Trusted Interface receives the query and dispatches it to the appropriate untrusted DBMS code, with respect to the security levels involved. A set of trusted utilities are used to support the database creation and maintenance functions, which are responsible for accesses to the data stored on the disk files. Data accesses must satisfy both mandatory and discretionary controls. Mandatory protection is enforced at the tuple level. The Bell–LaPadula secrecy properties and the Biba integrity properties are enforced. In particular, the database file is assigned the 'DBMS high' security level, the same level at which the DBMS kernel works, and a special integrity compartment, enabling only the DBMS kernel to modify the data and its security labels. Discretionary authorizations, stating both permissions and denials of access, are defined for tables, while tuples inherit the authorizations from the table they belong to. Authorizations can be specified for users, groups, and public, for select, insert, update, and delete operations. The DBMS data file can be accessed only by the 'DBMS' special user.

In addition to the mandatory and discretionary protection of the file storing the database, the secure OS provides other kinds of services to the DBMS, namely: the separation of processes (trusted/untrusted, untrusted/other); secure communication services between untrusted processes and the DBMS kernel; user authentication; and the trusted path.

### 4.2.5 Commercial products

In this section, the security features provided by commercial DBMS products are described. In Table 4.2 the features of some commercial products are summarized, in particular those of Ingres, Oracle, Sybase, Informix, and SQLBase.

The table columns specify the security features examined, while rows correspond to the DBMS examined. In general, the discretionary policy is traditionally enforced by all the DBMSs, while, for the mandatory policy, mechanisms are under development to enforce multilevel protection in most of them. The security features summarized in the table are related to the following functionalities.

**Table 4.2** Overview of security functionalities in commercial DBMS products.

| DBMS Server | Authentication by password | Authentication by OS | CREATE ALTER DROP Users/ object types | Super-user operations | SELECT INSERT UPDATE DELETE tables & views | ALTER INDEX tables | REFERENCES | Column-level control | EXECUTE | GRANT OPTION | ADMIN OPTION | Groups ≠Public | Roles | Auditing |
|---|---|---|---|---|---|---|---|---|---|---|---|---|---|---|
| Ingres | | ❍ | ❍ | ❍ | ❍ | | | Update | ❍ | | | ❍ | ❍ | ❍ |
| Oracle | ❍ | ❍ | ❍ | ❍ | ❍ | ❍ | ❍ | Select Update Refer. | ❍ | ❍ | ❍ | | ❍ | ❍ |
| Sybase | ❍ | | ❍ | | ❍ | | | Select Update | ❍ | | | ❍ | | |
| Informix | | ❍ | ❍ | | ❍ | ❍ | ❍ | Select Update Refer. | ❍ | ❍ | | | | |
| SQLBase | ❍ | | ❍ | | ❍ | ❍ | | Update | | | | | | |

- *User identification/authentication.* User identification/authentication is enforced either via the OS, or via a password. Except for Oracle, which provides both the mechanisms, the DBMS servers provide one or other of them.
- *System authorizations.* This functionality concerns the definition of authorizations for operations on the object types of the database (database, tables, views) and on the users. All the DBMS servers examined provide privileges to create, alter, and drop object types and users. Other types of system authorizations are provided by some DBMSs for superuser operations (namely, the start-up and shut-down of the database server).
- *Data authorizations.* These authorizations specify the operations that can be executed on the data stored in the objects of the database. All the DBMS servers have SELECT, INSERT, UPDATE and DELETE privileges for tables and views, while only some of them provide the ALTER, INDEX and REFERENCES privileges for tables. The REFERENCES privilege is supported in those DBMS servers where the referential-integrity constraint holds (except for Gupta Sybase, which does not support the REFERENCES privilege, but does support referential-integrity constraints), and the EXECUTE privilege in those systems where it is possible to execute a database procedure. Some DBMSs provide a column-level control, meaning that they support control at the column level of the tables for some privileges (specified in the table). These privileges are granted to users through the SQL GRANT statement, possibly with the GRANT OPTION. The GRANT OPTION allows users who are granted privileges to transfer, in turn, these privileges to other users. Only some DBMS servers provide this functionality, and the Oracle server also provides the ADMIN OPTION facility, specially defined for system privileges.
- *Management of the authorizations.* This functionality is related to the possibility of granting authorizations, reflecting the need for delegating responsibilities and authority within an organization. Traditionally, the delegation mechanism is based on the concept of ownership, and is enforced through the SQL GRANT and REVOKE statements. The administration of authorizations takes place by partitioning the users into groups and roles, on the basis of their security requirements. In general, a group 'Public' exists in all database servers, and every user is a member of this group. Some DBMSs allow the administrator to define other groups on the basis of database users' security requirements. Each group is assigned a name, and the privileges are granted to the whole group; consequently, they hold for all the group members. Roles, when supported, are used to specify sets of authorizations, associated with given applications. Thus, a role can be created with a name and given the set of authorizations necessary to execute an application; users acquire such privileges when they execute the application. In practice, when a user executes an application, its role is enabled and the associated privileges are active in the user session; the privileges will be deactivated by the server at the end of the application usage.

- *Auditing of security-related events.* Database servers generally provide auditing functionalities by recording security-related events, generating a so-called audit trail which is useful for subsequent analysis and reconstruction of events. For this purpose, DBMSs provide mechanisms to select the events to be audited (to avoid recording audit data indiscriminately), and to organize the audit trail in a manner that supports easily formed queries.

In the following, the security features of the commercial DBMSs Sybase, Ingres, Oracle and DB2 are described in more detail.

### *Sybase Secure Server*

The Sybase Secure SQL Server (SYSSS) is a server of databases in network environments. This is a commercial DBMS product which comes in both B1 and B2 classified versions. The B1 version uses a B1 secure UNIX OS. The B2 version is directly installed on bare hardware, without an underlying OS. In the following we refer to the B2 system. Besides security functions, SYSSS supplies the functions of the most recent relational DBMSs, together with user-oriented utilities (friendly interface); therefore, both industrial and commercial security needs are assured.

The security functions offered by SYSSS refer to:

- User identification/authentication;
- Mandatory/discretionary access control;
- Auditing of security-related events;
- Differentiation of user responsibilities and user roles in the database system (security officer, database administrator, database owner, generic users).

B2 certification needs to separate the 'untrusted' software from the 'trusted' software (the system TCB) which must have a minimal size. In SYSSS, an execution domain of the TCB (*TCB Domain*) and an execution domain of the untrusted software, called the *User Domain*, are recognized. The TCB domain is in turn divided into two domains, the *I/O Domain* for low-level functions and the *Policy Domain* for the code implementing the security policy and the index/page management. Each domain has its own hardware domain, distinct from other domains' hardware; this reduces the risk of possible bypass actions and/or sabotaging actions against the protection mechanisms. Furthermore, protection mechanisms for the physical integrity of the database are supplied by SYSSS. The Cyclic Redundancy Check (CRC) mechanism is used as an integrity field for data pages, to protect against inadvertent errors. SYSSS assures secure end-to-end transmission of data over an untrusted network by interfacing with network encryption devices.

**Objects** needing protection are the data contained in a database. They are divided into *primary and secondary objects*. Primary objects correspond to table rows, and represent the smallest object that can be assigned a security label. Secondary objects are tables and databases. Secondary objects are associated to lists of discretionary access (ACL, see Chapter 3) in which identifiers of authorized users (or user groups) and allowed operations (*insert, delete, update, select*) are specified. The ACLs of secondary objects and the mandatory security labels of primary objects are stored in the Data Dictionary, which is accessible only by the TCB trusted software.

**Subjects** are users and user groups querying the database, using the Sybase Transact-SQL query language. A specified user role (security officer, database administrator, database owner, generic user) can be assigned to a user. According to the roles taken at connection time, different types of operation are available.

A user forwards his connection request to the server, through his server protocol. The security officer, as a special user, must grant connection using a trusted interface for the security officer. The connection procedure (Login procedure) that receives the connection requests is part of the TCB; thus it is a piece of trusted software. When receiving a connection query, the Login procedure executes the user identification/authentication steps (authentication is password based) and verifies the validity of the user role and the security level requested at connection time. A maximum clearance level is assigned to each user and stored in the DBMS, which represents the maximum security level this user is granted for accesses and operations in the system. Therefore, the Login procedure verifies that the maximum clearance level of the user 'dominates' (see Chapter 2) the security level requested at connection time. For each connection granted, the TCB creates a non-trusted process, which operates at the same security level assigned to the user at connection time; then it transfers control to the command interpreter and loops in the 'available' state for further commands.

The user **operations** (commands) are Sybase Transact-SQL requests (SELECT, UPDATE, INSERT, DELETE). The command interpreter of the non-trusted user processes receives Sybase Transact-SQL commands. In order to have a limited-size TCB, an SQL parser and an SQL compiler (which are non-trusted software) have been introduced; they translate the user requests into a reduced set of binary format instructions (called a *procedure*), whose security properties can be verified in the execution phase, ready for execution from the trusted TCB software. A procedure contains details of the tables needed for the request, the indexes required, and the types of operation on data requested. The TCB is the executor of the procedures, enforcing the mandatory properties and the discretionary authorizations defined for the requester. The TCB trusted software is responsible for access control to data: first, it transfers the procedure from the user memory area to a reserved memory area accessible only by the TCB; then, it verifies that all the procedure addresses and pointers reference the user memory area, to avoid the overflow of memory bounds. Access control is first mandatory then discretionary. The mandatory part is based on labels assigned both to objects and subjects of the database.

For **access control** it is first verified that a user is cleared to read and/or write the requested objects on the basis of his system security level (the security level he has been assigned at connection time), and on the basis of the classifications assigned to the primary objects involved, according to the mandatory policy. In particular, a user can access a (primary or secondary) object if his classification 'dominates' the object classification. After verifying the mandatory authorization, the TCB verifies the discretionary privileges, and in particular, the user authorization for the requested operations on the secondary objects. Discretionary controls are performed only on the tables and on the database, using the ACLs contained in the Data Dictionary.

Users requesting execution of a procedure or the use of a view must be discretionarily authorized to access all tables to which this procedure or view refers. If the discretionary controls are successful, the tables are recovered and then submitted to a further mandatory control. This control has the purpose of verifying, for each table row, that the user should be mandatorily granted access on the basis of the classifications he received and on the basis of the different rows (primary objects). Only the accessible rows are selected and returned to the requester. Should some control step be unsuccessful, the control procedure is suspended and its operations recorded in the audit file. For multilevel protection, polyinstantiation occurs on insertion and update operations if the relaxation property is off, and does not occur if that property is on, because data elements are overwritten.

'Trusted' operations can also be executed; these do not require compilation, being immediately transferred to the TCB for execution. Trusted operations can be executed only through proper trusted paths: that is, via direct connections between a terminal and the TCB of the Sybase Secure SQL Server. Trusted paths are available on the trusted interfaces for the security officer and for trusted users (System Security Officer Trusted Interface and User Trusted Interface). Trusted operations executable by the security officer (through the proper interface) relate to database security management, users' roles, recording of security events in the audit trail, and table deletion.

The interface for trusted users is used by:

- System administrators, for trusted operations in storage device handling;
- Database owners, for definition/modification of database owners, definition/updating of user groups, enabling/disabling user access to the database, and forcing the 'dump' of the database and database log files;
- Table owners, to define access authorizations and access modes (operations) allowed to other users of their tables.

For **auditing**, the recorded security-related events, selected by the security officer, are forwarded to a printer and recorded in a system table, *Sysaudits*. This table can be accessed through normal SQL requests by the security officer. Events that occur because of system inconsistencies are always recorded. Other events related to users, rows, tables, databases and access modes can be turned on selectively. Violations of discretionary access control and the execution of trusted operations are always automatically recorded.

### *INGRES*

In INGRES, security is characterized as follows.

**Subjects** are users and user groups querying the database. Users are partitioned into groups and roles, on the basis of their security requirements. The Public group exists, and every user is a member of this group. Other groups can be created by the administrator, grouping database users having common security requirements. Each group is assigned a name, and the privileges are granted to the whole group. Users can be members of one or more groups, and can have a default group, whose privileges are automatically activated at connect time. Roles are defined by the administrator to specify sets of authorizations, associated with given applications, and are associated with applications by developers. A role is created with a name and given the set of authorizations necessary to execute an application. When executing an application, users are asked for the role name and the password, in order to acquire the role's privileges. In practice, when a user executes an application, its role is enabled and the associated privileges are active in the user session; they will be deactivated by the server at the end of the application usage.

**Objects** to be protected are database objects: that is, databases, catalogues, tables, views, procedures.

The GRANT command is used to define the **operations** executable on database objects and on users. The administrator can grant privileges for SELECT, INSERT, UPDATE and DELETE operations on tables and views, and for the EXECUTE command for executing a procedure. Ingres supports column-level control only for the UPDATE privilege. Since no referential constraint is supported by the server, no REFERENCE privilege can be granted. Moreover, the GRANT OPTION for granting privileges to other users is not supported. Ingres has the Accessdb utility, whereby the administrator can create, alter and drop system users, and decide who performs superuser operations (namely, start-up and shut-down of the database server). Still using Acessdb, with a form of the SQL GRANT command, the administrator can define privileges on database objects and procedures.

To **audit** security-related events, the AUDITDB command is available in Ingres, enabling the administrator to inspect the audit file where security-related events have been recorded. This command records audit data related to a specific database, table, user and time stamp in a table or a file, provided that the administrator enabled journalling for the database, and the specific tables.

### *ORACLE*

Oracle DBMS, a product of the Oracle corporation, is available for several operating systems, and in different versions (for example, single-user, multi-user, networked, distributed). Two versions of Oracle have been certified at different security levels. A UNIX version exists certified as B1, and a GEMSOS version certified as A1.

**Subjects** are users and user groups querying the database. Oracle provides the SQL CREATE (ALTER, DROP) USER command to create (respectively, alter and drop) users in the system. During creation, the administrator can choose between password-based and operating-system-based authentication of users, using the IDENTIFIED BY clause of the corresponding SQL command. The special ADMIN OPTION is available in Oracle, by which an administrator can grant system privileges to users who, in turn, can grant such privileges to other users. Only the Public group exists in Oracle, and several roles. By using the ANSI/ISO SQL3, an administrator defines a role, grants privileges to the role, and then grants the role to the users. In Oracle it is possible to grant roles to other roles, allowing a hierarchical organization of privileges, thus producing an organization similar to that of user groups. The SET ROLE statement is used to assign a created role to an application, which is enabled via password. Users have a default role, active at login time. Oracle databases have user accounts characterized by a username and password. Three basic privileges are defined, called Connect, Resource, and DBA. The *Connect* privilege allows users to connect to the database, and to access and update the tables to which they have been properly granted access; they may not create tables, only views. The *Resource* privilege allows users to create tables, and to grant access to other users for them. The *DBA* privilege is the highest privilege of the database, enjoying all privileges, included the creation of user accounts. Three special accounts are installed with the Oracle system, called Sys, System, and Public. The first two both have the DBA privilege. Public corresponds to the basic group of Oracle, and all the privileges granted to Public are automatically granted to all user accounts.

The **objects** to be protected are the database objects, as in Ingres. Labels are associated with objects, at the relation level.

For **operations**, the SELECT, INSERT, UPDATE, DELETE, ALTER, INDEX and REFERENCE privileges are available on tables, but only the first four are available on views. The EXECUTE privilege is available for procedures. The GRANT OPTION is supported, enabling the granted users to transfer the acquired privileges to other users. Column-level control is supported for the UPDATE, INSERT and REFERENCE privileges.

The AUDIT command of Oracle is used by the administrator to **audit** operations related to any privilege, for both successful and unsuccessful statements. Audit records can be stored in either a database or operating system audit trail.

### *DB2*

IBM's DB2 (Database 2) is a relational DBMS for the MVS operating system. Several subsystems exist on MVS – IMS (Information Management System), CICS (Customer Information Control System) and TSO (Time Sharing Option) – and users of DB2 first log into one of the subsystems. DB2 carries out user identification through a system administrator, assigned an authorization identifier (ID). User authentication is performed by each subsystem, using the local mechanisms available for this purpose. Objects to be protected are the database tables, and the metadata in the system catalog, also stored as tables in the database. SYSTABLES and SYSCOLUMNS are special tables. SYSTABLES stores data concerning every base table, namely its creator, name, number of columns and other relevant data. SYSCOLUMNS stores data concerning columns, namely the column name, the name of the table the column belongs to, and the column domain. User accesses to objects are based on authorization IDs. The current authorization ID is referred to by the system keyword USER. The system keyword PUBLIC refers to all the authorization IDs. The SYSADM (system administrator) privilege is associated with one authorization ID, and is the highest privilege in the system, including all privileges. A DBADM privilege is also available, to execute any privilege on a specific database of the system. Accesses to base tables and the system catalogue are regulated by views. DB2 access controls can be either disabled, if desired, or used in combination with those of MVS, IMS, CICS and TSO to augment system protection.

## 4.3 Design of secure databases

Database security can either be seen as a secondary requirement to be added to existing systems, or it can be regarded as a primary need, and therefore considered as a relevant requirement from the initial system design stages (Wood, 1988).

In most cases, security is not a primary concern in system development. In these situations, the systems are enriched with add-on security packages, providing the basic security features at OS level (user authentication, access control, auditing). This happens with many widely used OSs, such as MVS, VMS, and VM where security is supported by RACF, Top Secret, and CA-ACF2 packages (see Chapter 3). In some environments (for example, military environments), the security system needs to be designed *ad hoc* and protection requirements verified in a formal way. In any case, facing the design of secure database security systems is a serious and crucial problem, and various research issues are still open (Lunt, 1992a).

The DoD criteria constitute useful reference standards for secure software system classification, while also providing a guide for security design. In fact, at each classification level, a set of requirements is described that, if considered during system design, can assure the desired rating. In particular, the DoD criteria clearly outline a set of key requirements to be taken into account during system design, concerning the need for defining a conceptual model of the system protection requirements and system security policies (both mandatory and discretionary) that can be verified and tested, possibly using formal verification techniques. Moreover, the DoD criteria explicitly refer to a TCB which is used to enforce the policies and to mediate all accesses to data (the reference monitor concept), and whose correctness against the policy requirements must be formally verifiable.

From these considerations, it turns out that security is achieved by clearly stating the protection requirements of a system, and then implementing security mechanisms using methods and techniques aimed at simplifying the task of demonstrating their correctness.

A methodological approach where explicit reference to the DoD requirements is made is a possible answer to the problem of designing secure databases with security features in mind from the initial development phases.

A multiphase methodology represents a valid approach to the design of database security, allowing the designers to state precisely the security requirements of an environment, independently of the security software and mechanisms actually available to enforce them. In fact, approaching secure database design by starting from the security functions offered by commercial OSs and DBMSs is inadequate, although specific security packages and products are available and can be considered. Analogously, nowadays no one would design a database starting from a specific DBMS.

So far, we have described models, mechanisms and packages specifically oriented to security problems. The models constitute a formalized means of describing system security requirements and policies; the OS mechanisms provide the basic security functions (for example, identification/authentication, access control); finally, off-the-shelf security packages and secure DBMSs extend the OS functions to manage database security requirements. In this paragraph, models, mechanisms and secure products are framed in an integrated multiphase methodology, supporting a coherent development of database security systems from the initial analysis and design phases. In particular, the methodology guides the developers during security requirement analysis, selection of security policies and definition of a security model, and the design of security mechanisms to implement the model, also taking into account the actual OS and DBMS security functionalities. The methodology we propose for secure database design, based on the guidelines offered by the DoD criteria, consists of the following phases:

(1) Preliminary analysis
(2) Security requirements and policies
(3) Conceptual design
(4) Logical design
(5) Physical design.

as shown in Figure 4.13.

This methodology shows analogies with the usual methodologies for database design (Batini, 1992), thus allowing security system design to be integrated with database design (Fugini and Martella, 1987; Fugini, 1988). A multiphase development methodology has various benefits. First, it is possible to separate the design process (in general, a complex task) into subtasks, thus allowing the developers to focus on particular security aspects in each task. Moreover, a methodological approach allows security policies to be separated from security mechanisms. Policies are high-level guidelines to be followed in security system design, implementation and management. They express protection requirements and possible strategies for information protection in organizations. Different access control policies are available, expressing different protection needs/strategies (not in mutual conflict), suitable for different environments. Security mechanisms are a set of hardware, firmware and software functions enforcing the policies. Mechanisms should be verifiable against security requirements, to prove that they actually enforce the given policy specifications. Moreover, the mechanisms should have linear usage costs, and

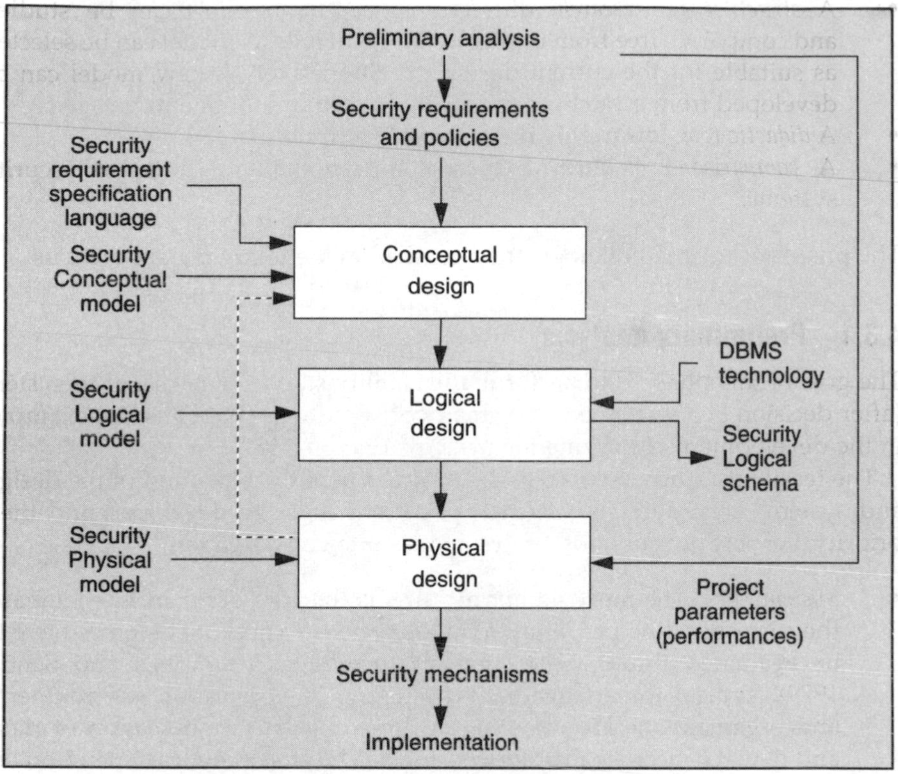

*Figure 4.13* Design methodology for database security.

should be able to enforce several policies. The separation between policies and mechanisms in security system development yields advantages, such as:

- The capability of defining access control rules and reasoning about them independently of their implementation (with no burdens about implementation details);
- The possibility of comparing different access control policies, or different mechanisms for the same policy;
- The capability of designing mechanisms supporting different policies. This advantage becomes a strong need when policies change as a consequence of changes in the organization requirements (replacement or modification of the whole system would otherwise be required).

Second, a multiphase methodology, being based on a conceptual security model, has the advantage of making security provable during system design. System security can be proved by proving the correctness of the security model against the requirements, and by proving the correctness of the mechanism specifications against the security model. The security model is:

- A *design tool,* to guide the system design;

- A *structure for research*; different conceptual models can be studied and compared, free from implementation details. A model can be selected as suitable for the current design or, alternatively, a new model can be developed from scratch, *ad hoc* for the system requirements;
- A *didactic tool*, to simplify the system description;
- A *comparison/evaluation tool*, to compare/evaluate different security systems.

The phases of the methodology are described in the following subsections.

### 4.3.1 Preliminary analysis

The goal of this phase is to perform a feasibility study for the security system (after decision at a strategic level), analogously to what happens, for example, in the development of information systems (Parker, 1984).

The feasibility study consists in the evaluation of the risks, and of the design and system costs, defining which applications must be developed and their priority. For this purpose, the analysis takes into consideration:

- *System risks.* The most significant threats that can occur in the database, the corresponding perpetration modes and the consequent losses have to be evaluated through risk analysis techniques (Campbell and Sands, 1979). Typical threats generally occurring in application environments and organizations are unauthorized reading and modification of data, and denial of access to authorized users. The attack modes depend on the type of threat. For example, unauthorized read and modification could be realized through access to physical storage, or through improper use of application programs (for example, Trojan Horses), or through access to data schemas.
- *Features of the database environment.* These affect protection requirements and related mechanisms. For example, multilevel protection systems are suitable for military environments, but could be unsuitable for commercial ones, where data/user security levels can be difficult to define.
- *Applicability of existing security products.* Convenience must be considered in choosing between available commercial products and the development of a security system from scratch. The choice depends both on the typology and level of protection, and on whether security is to be considered as an inherent feature of the database or as an additional feature.
- *Integrability of the security products.* This refers to the possibility of integrating the security mechanisms with the actual hardware and software mechanisms.
- *Performance of the resulting security system.* The performance of the security systems has to be compared with the actual system, or with the new system without any security mechanisms and controls.

The result of this analysis is a set of threats to which the system is exposed, ordered by priority. Moreover, commercial security products' level of applicability and integrability with the existing mechanisms are evaluated, possibly requiring *ad hoc* mechanisms to be developed from scratch.

The next phase of the methodology is undertaken if the cost/benefit analysis gives a positive result.

### 4.3.2 Requirement analysis and security policy selection

The analysis of security requirements starts from a precise and accurate study of all possible threats to which the system can be exposed. This allows designers to define the security requirements correctly and completely, according to the real protection needs of the system.

Protection needs for different **types of risk** are different for different database systems. A first difference derives from information *sensitiveness* and relevance, and from possible laws and regulations. Further, systems may be classified as *high- or low-risk* systems on the basis of elements such as the level of data correlation, data sharing, data accessibility, staff skilfulness, and selected technologies. *Correlation* occurs when data is mutually related, and changes in a data item imply changes to other data items. Correlation occurs also when read operations on an item reveal the value of other items. *Sharing* occurs when the same data item is used by several applications (or users). In particular, in databases this poses concurrency problems caused by contemporaneous access to data. Data sharing also involves secrecy and integrity issues. Regarding secrecy, different processes accessing the same data item could come to know information previously inserted by other processes, thus giving rise to an information flow. Data integrity could be altered by incorrect modification of data (intentional or accidental), thus affecting the correctness of other processes using that data. High levels of data sharing and correlation imply higher security needs. Analogous considerations hold for data dependence. To summarize, low-risk systems are those where data is highly partitioned and processes are decentralized, avoiding correlation and sharing and even introducing some redundancy. On the other hand, data redundancy poses greater secrecy problems, and problems related to data consistency, too (however, consistency problems can be easily managed nowadays).

*Data accessibility* concerns the issue of who can access which data for which purposes. Accessibility to different types of data must be stated, taking into consideration different aspects such as privacy, security, confidentiality, legal implications and authorizations. In addition, users requesting access to data should be granted access rights in such a way that control over their activity can be maintained (accountability). With respect to accessibility, systems where privacy, confidence and accountability policies are employed prove to be low-risk systems. Risks increase in systems where access occurs in real time because all data is accessible to all users.

System protection is also affected by the *number and type of users*. On the one hand, skilful users make security systems more reliable; however, on the other hand, attacks on security come more frequently from users abusing their authorizations. From this viewpoint, skilled users expose the system to higher risks of bypassing control. Ignorance, in this case, might represent a security guarantee. Also, users' reliability is relevant: in military environments security is strictly bound to user identity rather than to the reliability of the security system.

Further, security relies on the *selected technologies*. Low-risk systems use certified hardware and software supplied by certified suppliers. Lack of certification could be replaced by widely tried and tested systems (no certification authority is yet available in some countries). Risks are higher for new technologies and obviously so for unreliable suppliers.

During requirement analysis, the system's *degree of vulnerability* should be determined by considering the most significant attacks (intentional/accidental) to which the environment is exposed. The most common attacks are unauthorized data disclosure and modification, or denial of access to data.

A systematic approach to threat analysis and system vulnerability encompasses the following:

- *Value analysis.* The data held and the applications accessing that data are analysed to determine their level of sensitiveness. Access controls increase proportionally to the sensitiveness of data.
- *Threat identification.* Possible threats and modes typical of different applications are identified, as well as the possible penetration techniques.
- *Vulnerability analysis.* Weak points in the system are identified, related to the previously identified threats.
- *Risk analysis.* Possible threats, system weakness and penetration modes are matched against possible violations of the system security and integrity (unauthorized disclosure of data, data manipulation, resource use and denial of service).
- *Risk evaluation.* On the basis of proper weights, the probability of each undesired event occurring is evaluated, together with the system's capability of reacting to or facing these events.
- *Requirement definition.* Security requirements are defined based on evaluated threats and undesired events, and on the probability of their occurrence.

Protection policies are stated on the basis of the identified **protection requirements**. This phase aims at defining protection requirements for the database: that is, at defining the subjects' modes of accessing the system objects. User classes are defined, each holding specific access authorizations on the database. As a result, a set of informal sentences expressing the security requirements are listed, such as: 'Authorization is centralized'; 'Transactions that update salaries must be activated by a specific terminal'; 'Marketing information is accessible only to marketing personnel'. The selection of policies follows the stated requirements.

#### Security policy selection

The purpose of a security policy is the definition of authorized accesses for each subject to the different objects in the system, through a set of guidelines. The security policies that best match the defined security requirements are selected, defining in detail the access modes (for example, read, write) to be used by each subject (or group) on each object (or object set).

The basic security policies were presented in Chapter 1. They can be combined, rather than be considered as alternatives, in order to better meet the security requirements. Besides, for different application environments, the policies may be more or less 'suitable' rather than 'better' or 'worse' (for example, university and military environments respectively constrain security in a different manner).

To assist in choosing security policies that best match the security requirements, some policy selection criteria are (Abrams and Olson, 1990):

- *Secrecy versus integrity versus reliability.* Secrecy is paramount, for example, in military environments; integrity and reliability in commercial environments. A balance has to be achieved for other environments.
- *Maximum sharing versus minimum privilege.* According to minimum privilege (need-to-know), users are granted access only to information strictly needed for their tasks; this suits military environments well. Environments like research centres or universities, however, should look for a maximum sharing policy. A good combination might be 'maximum sharing on a restricted set of information'.
- *Granularity of control.* The first meaning of granularity refers to the extent of the controls, in relation to the number of subjects and objects controlled. Global control (on all system entities) is achieved through mandatory policies; partial control (only on some system entities) is provided by discretionary policies. A second meaning refers to the granularity of the controlled objects. In dedicated systems, users need only the capability to access the system in order to gain access to its resources; in multi-user systems, a higher control granularity is required for validation of accesses to directories, files, and data items. A third meaning refers to the level of distribution of control. In some systems, control of all the system files occurs within a unique area (security is simplified, but possible faults concentrate in that unique area). In other systems, security is more complex, but controls and responsibilities are spread throughout different areas of the system.
- *Attributes used for access control.* Security decisions are based on subject/object attributes and/or on access request context. The basic attributes (sometimes called predicates) are: subject/object classification, location, time, state of some system variable(s), access history. Security policies must be selected according to the control needs of the environment involved.
- *Integrity.* Specific security policies and models apply to environments where integrity is a primary concern: for example, database environments (see Chapter 2).

- *Priorities.* Conflicts among the rules expressing the security policies may arise; rule priorities can help. A typical example refers to group membership: authorizations can be individual, or can relate to group membership. Individual authorizations may hold priority over group authorizations ('more specific rule' criterion); or denial of access may hold priority over any other authorization ('priority be denied' criterion). This refers both to the denial specified for the individual, and to the denial specified for the group to which this individual belongs.
- *Privileges.* Access privileges state through which modes (read, write, execute, delete, insert) a subject can access an object. Default privileges must be defined as well as how privileges can be modified. There are a certain number of default privileges that depend on the selected policies. For example, no default privilege exists for mandatory policies, because these are used only in stating granted access. In many systems, read/write operations are stated as default privileges by discretionary policies used in combination with mandatory policies. As to privilege management, grant/revoke privileges must be explicitly defined.
- *Authority.* A policy must define the different types of roles, authorities and responsibilities within a system. Common roles are: user, owner, security administrator. In addition, there are user groups: these are useful for users sharing common access requirements in the organization (e.g., shared design tasks within a development team, or members of the same department). A policy must state the group composition criteria, the group partitioning suitable for the environment, the membership of an individual in one or more groups, and how possible conflicts of privileges held by individuals can be resolved (see the *Priorities* point above). Access control levels are different: Level 1 refers to the proper access control from subjects to objects; Level 2 refers to access control on information used for access control; Level 3 refers to information defining who can access information used for access control. In mandatory policies, Levels 2 and 3 are typically assigned to the security administrator. In discretionary policies, Level 2 is typical of a resource owner. In general, roles must be defined together with the access rights for the different levels of access control.
- *Inheritance.* This refers to the propagation of access rights from objects to their copies, or derivations. Although not explicitly stated, access rights propagation does not occur in discretionary policies, while it does in mandatory ones.

Using these criteria, high-level guidelines can be translated into rule format, suitable for formalization and subsequent design phases. Selected protection requirements and security policies are the input for the next phase of conceptual design.

### 4.3.3 Conceptual design

In this phase, requirements and security policies defined in the previous phase are conceptually formalized. 'Conceptual' refers to the fact that implementation details are not yet considered. Rather, the focus is on semantic aspects, providing a separation between policies and mechanisms. A conceptual security model is a tool used for the formalization of requirements and policies.

A **conceptual security model** is defined through:

- Identification of the subjects and objects relevant from a security viewpoint; subjects/objects playing the same role in the organization are grouped;
- Identification of the access modes granted to different subjects on different objects, recognizing possible constraints on access;
- Analysis of the propagation of authorizations in the system through grant/revoke privileges. This analysis is particularly relevant for checking that the minimum privilege principle is respected.

Through the above steps, requirements are represented as

$$\langle \textit{subject, access right, objects, predicate} \rangle$$

quadruples, where the predicate describes the possible access conditions. These quadruples represent the access rules.

The basic features of a conceptual security model should be:

- To be a representation of the semantics of database security. This means that security and integrity of a certain data item are expressed in terms of the information contained in this item, and of its modality of use and relationships with other items, deriving from the actual reality represented by the data item.
- To support the analysis of authorization flows, that is, the consequences of grant/revoke authorizations.
- To be a support for the Database Administrator, allowing him to pose queries on the current state of authorizations and to check the consequences of variations in authorizations. These checks are easier to do at a conceptual level rather than at the level of security mechanisms.

A model maps the informal requirements into security rules. A conceptual security model allows requirements and policies (that is, the desired behaviour) to be clearly represented, and some properties of the security system to be verified. Following the DoD criteria, the high levels of security system classification require a model of the security system to be defined; the model should contain a unique structure grouping all the system properties, and should provide a valid support to the subsequent phases of design, validation and documentation.

A conceptual security model represents subjects, objects, operations and access modes granted according to the defined polices. The model of a given system must be:

- *Complete*: the model meets all the security requirements initially stated;
- *Consistent*: inconsistency in a system occurs, for example, when an unauthorized user cannot access an object directly, but can reach the object through another path, or set of operations. In this case, there is no

guarantee that the only executable actions in the system will be those that are authorized.

As far as the **use of the model** is concerned, several phases are often needed to obtain a complete and consistent model. As a final result, a model must guarantee that all requirements have been specified and no conflicts and redundant situations exist (a set of requirements must be minimal). Possible conflicts and/or ambiguities in requirements can be solved by referring to the guidelines represented by the security policies.

The various security models were described in Chapter 2. Yet, they seem still to be far from fully complying with the requirements stated early in this chapter for a security model. The cause is that generally the proposed models are selective with respect to security problems. Models may be abstract or concrete, depending on whether they are intended to prove the properties of the system or to be a development guide for secure systems. An approach to the selection of the most suitable model consists in adopting a basic model which matches the initial requirements, then (if needed) creating a combination with other suitable models. However, the process of combining security models might cause the loss of some security features of the models involved. In fact, the model must define the global behaviour of the security system: a rigid modelling of distinct operations and their combination does not guarantee the security of the model so obtained. For this reason, the final model should always undergo validation and verification.

In general, the choice of a model depends on the type of system to be represented, that is, on the type of protected resources; it also depends on the intended formal verifications foreseen for the system (for example, completeness of requirements, inconsistencies).

### 4.3.4 Logical design

In this phase, the conceptual security model is translated into a logical model supported by the specific DBMS that will be used. For example, considering a relational DBMS, view-based and query-based security techniques are commonly used for access control, and the rules of the conceptual model have to be suitably translated to support such techniques. The external schemas are defined, with respect to the views granted to the applications, according to the system security policies.

Moreover, in this phase, security rules are specified in the logical security model taking into consideration the OS-level mechanisms and the functionalities offered by possible security packages. The purpose is to determine which security requirements, policies, constraints and axioms represented in the conceptual security model can be fulfilled by existing mechanisms, and which have to be designed *ad hoc*. For this purpose, using the information about security features defined in the conceptual phase, the developers establish which security requirements can be provided by existing mechanisms, either at the OS level or the DBMS level, or by specific security packages, if available. If some security requirements stated in the conceptual model cannot be enforced using available mechanisms, the developers should design specific mechanisms to meet the requirements.

### 4.3.5 Physical design

Details concerning storage organization and implementation/integration modes for the security mechanisms required are considered in this phase. Starting from the logical security model, the detailed design of security mechanisms is dealt with, namely the design of the physical structure of access rules, their relationships with the physical structures of the database, the related access modes for required access controls, and the detailed architecture of the mechanisms that will enforce the security requirements and policies. The goal is to assign each security task the correct level of enforcement.

Possible feedbacks from physical design return to conceptual and logical design, requiring modifications to model elements of rules, are due to implementation issues (Figure 4.13).

### 4.3.6 Implementation of security mechanisms

A set of guidelines can be useful to support developers in selecting and/or implementing from scratch *ad hoc* security mechanisms, to avoid subsequent serious problems (some of them were identified by Saltzer and Schroeder (1975), for evaluating the quality of a mechanism). In the following we illustrate such guidelines and discuss the implementation problems.

The guidelines for mechanism selection/implementation are listed below.

- *Economy of mechanisms.* Mechanisms should be as simple as possible, thus simplifying the correctness of the implementation and the code inspection in case of failures (for example, detection of trapdoors). In general, relevant advantages are an immediate reduction in costs, higher reliability, and easier testing and audit system phases. The lower the (hardware/software) architectural level where these mechanisms are located, the easier the achievement of the security target.
- *Efficiency.* Mechanisms should be efficient, especially considering that they are often invoked at run time. A kernel-based approach does not fully satisfy this requirement owing to overload and burdens in terms of performance.
- *Linearity of costs.* After the installation phase, the operation costs should be proportional to the actual use of the mechanism.
- *Privilege separation (responsibilities).* Wherever possible, several control mechanisms should be layered, making access dependent on many conditions (complexity would be a further security defence). Privilege

separation can be obtained through both different mechanisms and repeated use of the same mechanism, as in distributed systems where there are several password levels. The degree of protection can be increased by organizing the design and application of controls so that they form a cascade to achieve concentric protection levels. The depth of controls thus achieved reduces the possibility of attacks.

- *Minimum privilege.* Programs and users should be confined to the minimum level of privileges. This requires the 'need-to-know' principle to be considered in policy selection, and applied to the system components. The advantages are:
  - *error confinement:* consequences from faulty components are minimized; as a matter of fact, limiting the amount of memory a component can access limits the possible damage;
  - *maintenance:* consequences of component modification can be easily estimated on a reduced number of components;
  - *defence from Trojan Horses:* the range of action for Trojan Horses contained in a confined program is limited;
  - *demonstration of correctness:* since the purpose is to prove that unauthorized situations do not arise, restricted privileges simplify the formal verification process.
- *Complete mediation.* Each access to each object must undergo authorization control.
- *Known design.* The security techniques adopted should be well known. The secrecy component must rely on keys and passwords, rather than on the mechanism: hence the relevance of key-handling techniques (generation, storing, distribution). In other words, the system's degree of security should not depend on potential intruders being ignorant of the design principles.
- *Security by default.* If options are not specified by users, default protection options should always be in favour of security. The access decisions should be based on grants rather than on denials. Therefore, a closed system policy is preferred, which proves more secure than an open policy.
- *Minimum common mechanisms.* According to this principle, the design must encourage mutual independence between mechanisms, in such a way that the correct working of one mechanism should not depend on the correct operation of another one. For example, different mechanisms should be employed for physical and logical access control: this way, the consequences of unauthorized access from intruders are as limited as possible. If, instead, a single control mechanism exists (that is, if logical control is based on the correct operation of physical access control), intruders gaining physical access would be enabled to access the system resources.
- *Psychological acceptability.* Mechanisms must be easy to use, allowing users to employ them correctly. Heavy or unnecessary restrictions should be avoided. Access authorizations should also be easy to define: thus, users

are encouraged to prefer protection, rather than disabling the control mechanisms.

- *Flexibility.* Different policies should be enforced by a security mechanism. Mechanism flexibility also involves maintenance of protection against intentional or accidental attacks. Design, in this sense, should guarantee the correct and continuous operation of the mechanism even in the case of events arising from intentional or accidental attacks. Furthermore, the design should follow a 'hostile environment' philosophy: mechanisms should be assured to work in the worst conditions. Therefore, intentional/sophisticated attacks from strongly determined/skilled users have to be considered as common events, while accidental attacks derived from errors or faults can be assumed to be rare and improbable events.
- *Isolation.* The security mechanism must be isolated from other system components, and be resistant to tampering.
- *Verifiability.* The security mechanism must be proved to match the security policy requirements. A methodology of formal development is an efficient tool in this aim.
- *Completeness and consistency.* The security mechanism must be complete, that is, complying fully with design specifications, and consistent, that is, with no inherent contradictions. The degree of completeness is stated by foreseeing how many, and which type of, attacks the mechanism might undergo. Protection should be specified both as a set of 'positive' specifications (the mechanism protects against) and as a set of 'negative' specifications (the mechanism does not protect against).
- *Observability.* The mechanism and the possible attacks against the mechanism must be controllable. This allows possible weaknesses or design errors to be pointed out. Log files, audit trails, journals, and similar tools are generally used to keep track of the mechanism operations.
- *Problem of residuals.* Residuals are pieces of information used by a process that might be kept in memory after the process terminates. Secrecy of data can be compromised if unauthorized subjects can examine the residuals. Residuals should always be erased by proper security mechanisms responsible for memory management.
- *Invisibility of data.* Unauthorized users who are denied access to data stored in an object should not get information about the structure (schema) or the existence of the object. Therefore, besides the objects' contents, the existence of these objects should be hidden from users to prevent inference (for example, by reading object names inside the system).
- *Work factor.* Circumventing a security mechanism should be a difficult operation requiring much effort (work factor). The quality of a mechanism can be evaluated by comparing the effort required to bypass the mechanism with the resources of a potential intruder. Generally, a high level of effort corresponds to a good protection level (this occurs, for example, with cryptographic/authentication techniques). The effort needed for circumvention is often difficult to define, owing to the logical impossibility of expressing the effort required in terms of systematic

attacks. However, several modes for circumventing a security mechanism exist (for example, a hardware error, or implementation errors).

- *Intentional traps.* A mechanism might be designed with intentional internal bugs, designed to be easy for malicious users to detect. The bugs can then be kept under control during the system lifetime, to detect possible penetration attempts and to observe and monitor the behaviour of intruders exploiting the bugs. This method is useful to get information about the possible types of attack and to learn about the behaviour of intruders. This procedure might, however, infringe existing laws or regulations, and should be used with legal precautions and certifications.
- *Emergency measures.* The mechanism should be designed with 'disable' modalities (in case of particular organizational needs or disasters requiring the system to be rebuilt or reconfigured). To support such circumstances and, generally, to increase the mechanism's flexibility, a set of trusted persons should be allowed either to switch the controls off or to temporarily modify the execution modes of the controls.
- *Secure hardware.* This requirement refers to the protected system, rather than to the security mechanism. The hardware must be reliable, because hardware/software bugs can be easily used by intruders to skip access control. Save and restore facilities might be missing, relying solely on the access control mechanism.
- *Programming language.* Various considerations need to be taken in account regarding the programming language. The compiler of the language used to program the mechanisms must be reliable. The correct use of a conventional programming language, together with the use of a compiler that has been repeatedly used for a large number of programs, is preferred. Skilled programmers contribute to assuring the system reliability, as well as its maintainability and the possibility of detecting errors. In the process of coding the security mechanism, the model specifications have to be rigorously complied with. In fact, vulnerability may derive from variations to the design during the programming phase, owing to performance constraints or the need to reduce the development costs. Necessary variations should be clearly identified and minimized. In addition, in the case of code modifications (which can occur not only in the initial phase, but also during system maintenance), the specifications should be updated in parallel.
- *Correctness.* The model must be exactly interpreted by the mechanisms, otherwise the mechanisms are considered incorrect. Incorrect mechanisms are worse than missing mechanisms, because they offer a false protection. Incorrect mechanisms can be over- or under-protective: in the first case, authorized operations are denied, in the second case unauthorized accesses are granted. This last case is by far the most dangerous for system security, causing possible damage to the secrecy/integrity of data.

Mechanisms to be developed from scratch can be implemented via hardware, software or firmware (Laferriere, 1990). When deciding on technologies during the implementation phase, a hardware/software compromise is advisable, taking into consideration the complexity, size and efficiency required for the final system. At one extreme, the choice can be to implement all the functions as hardware mechanisms, which should therefore prove reliable and secure as they are entirely responsible for the system's security. At the other, software-only mechanisms would produce rather large mechanisms acting as interpreters of the users' instructions. A good choice is to implement the mechanisms partly in hardware and partly in software, balancing the system and user needs (degree of protection, performance, reliability, mechanism size, and so on). In any event, mechanisms must be able to manage interprocess communications, memory protection, the concept of an execution domain (privileged mode or user mode) and the mediation of I/O requests.

In this phase, models of secure system architectures are needed. Architecture models represent the relationships between the system modules and the module interfaces with respect to the execution of security functions: that is, how the modules communicate when security functions are executed. These models also show how security functions are assigned to the DBMS and to the OS, and emphasize the role of the TBC in the system mechanisms. Secure DBMS architecture models have been discussed previously in this chapter. Following this architecture, different solutions can be adopted, according to the specific requirements of the environment, as discussed above.

In order to implement software mechanisms, it has to be noted that the transformation of the formal security model into the corresponding implemented mechanism is not direct. In fact, the model does not generally provide implementation specifications directly, although the model allows the designer to derive the functions the mechanism is expected to implement. Thus, the mapping between the formal model and the implementation level should proceed via successive refinement transformations, from formal specifications to the actual coding of mechanisms.

As well as mechanisms, in this phase issues related to system performance are taken into account, bearing in mind the expected throughput. Security controls require additional time in data processing: quantitative parameters of the security mechanism, such as the response time, the time/space of data storing/update, as well as qualitative parameters (for example, flexibility, adaptability, convertibility to new environments, recovery capability), are considered.

### 4.3.7 Verification and testing

Exactly as for software system development, a representation of the system obtained during one phase of the development method must be properly translated into the representation at the next stage of detail, and eventually into a correct software product. For security, the 'correctness' of the developed security software can mean different things, depending on the required level of trust expected from the software. In general, the purpose of this phase is to verify that the security requirements and policies have been correctly implemented by the software product. To this aim, formal and informal methods are available, respectively based, or not based, on mathematical notations (Kemmerer, 1990; Wing, 1990).

Informal methods are based on:

(1) cross-control of requirements/source code, or requirements/behaviour at run time (to prove that each security requirement defined in the analysis phase is enforced by the software);
(2) revision of the software code for errors/inconsistencies detection;
(3) analysis of the program behaviour according to different parameters, to examine the different execution paths and the corresponding variations of the program parameters;
(4) thorough testing, debugging, etc.

Generally, informal methods can be quickly applied; besides, no formal security model needs to be predefined (a model defining access requirements in a natural language is generally sufficient). With informal methods, it is possible to state the software behaviour in certain situations, but it is not possible to state that unauthorized actions are not executed by the system. Another verification technique consists in submitting the software to repeated attacks from specialized groups of skilled users (tiger team), to detect possible weak points or flaws in the code examined. Usually, these experts exploit their knowledge about typical bugs/flaws of the systems to try to penetrate the security mechanisms. Also in this case, results of the penetration tests cannot guarantee security against all types of attacks. Indeed, even if the system does not fail the attacks, it is not proved to be error-free.

Formal methods are more sophisticated, since they are based on formal (mathematical) notations and methods. The formal model of the security requirements has to be analysed for correctness using correctness tests, such as proving security axioms. High-level formal specifications are refined into intermediate levels until generation of low-level specifications for the software development phase is reached. With these techniques, it can be proved that the model is secure, and that the mechanism is secure, by proving the correctness of the formal specifications against the formal model. To be precise, each intermediate refinement specification level must be proved to be consistent with the previous level of specification, until the consistency of the high-level specifications with the formal security model is verified. Some specification languages and verification tools have been developed for security-critical systems (Watson, 1990); other techniques use 'clean development environment' requirements, reaching a *semi-formal* degree of verification (McDermott, 1990).

## References

Abrams M.D. and Olson I.M. (1990). Computer access control policy choices. *Computers & Security*, Elsevier Sc. (North-Holland), **9**(8)

Batini C., Ceri S. and Navathe S. (1992). *Conceptual database design*. Benjamin-Cummings

Bertino E., Samarati P. and Jajodia S. (1993). Authorizations in relational database management systems. In *Proc. 1st ACM Conf. on Computer and Communication Security,* Fairfax, November

Campell R.P. and Sands G.A. (1979). A modular approach to computer security risk assessment. In *Proc. AFIPS Conf.,* **48**

Clark D.D. and Wilson D.R. (1987). A comparison of commercial and military security policies. In *Proc. IEEE Symp. on Security and Privacy,* Oakland, April

Clark D.D. and Wilson D.R. (1989). Evolution of a model for computer integrity. In *Report of the international workshop on data integrity. (NIST Special Publ. 500–168)* (Ruthberg Z.G. and Polk W.T., eds), September

Committee on Multilevel Data Management Security (1982). Multilevel Data Management Security. *Technical Report,* Air Force Studies Board, National Research Council

Denning D.E. (1985). Commutative filters for reducing inference threats in multilevel database systems. In *Proc. IEEE Symp. on Security and Privacy,* Oakland, CA, April

Downs D. and Popek G.J. (1977). A kernel design for a secure data base management system. In *Proc. 3rd Conf. on Very Large Data Bases*

Fagin R. (1978). On an authorization mechanism. *ACM Trans. Database Systems,* **3**(3)

Fernandez E.B., Summers R.C. and Wood C. (1981) *Database Security and Integrity.* Addison-Wesley

Fugini M.G. (1988). Secure database development methodologies. In *Database Security: Status and Prospects* (Landwehr C.E. ed.). Elsevier Sc. (North-Holland)

Fugini M.G. and Martella G. (1987). Conceptual modeling of authorization in database systems. *Journal of Systems and Software,* **7**(1), Elsevier Sc.

Graubart R. (1984). The integrity lock approach to secure database management. In *Proc. IEEE Symp. on Security and Privacy,* Oakland, April

Griffiths P.G. and Wade B. (1976). An authorization mechanism for a relational database system. *ACM Trans. Database Systems,* **1**(3)

Henning R.R. (1988). The functional security responsibilities of a database management system and an operating system. In *Database Security: Status and Prospects* (Landwehr C.E. ed.). Elsevier Sc. (North-Holland)

Jones A.K. and Wulf W.A. (1975). Towards the design of secure systems. *Software – Practice and Experience,* **5**(4), October/December

Kemmerer R.A. (1990). Integrating formal methods into the development process. *IEEE Software,* September

Knode R. and Hunt R. (1988). Making databases secure with TRUDATA technology. In *Proc. 4th Aerospace Computer Security Applications Conf.*

Laferriere C. (1990). A discussion of implementation strategies for secure database management systems. *Computers & Security,* Elsevier Sc. (North-Holland), **9**(3)

Lunt T.F. (1988). A near-term design for the SeaView multilevel database system. In *Proc. IEEE Symposium on Security and Privacy,* April

Lunt T.F. (1992a). Security in database systems: a research perspective. *Computers & Security,* Elsevier Sc. (North-Holland), **11**(1)

Lunt T.F. ed (1992b). *Research Directions in Database Security.* Springer (Berlin)

McDermott J.P. *et al.* (1990). Informal top-level specification for trusted application systems. In *Proc. 6th Annual Computer Security Applications Conf.,* December

Melton J. ed. (1990). ANSI X3H2-90-309, *(ISO/ANSI working draft) Database Language SQL2.* August

Parker D.B. (1984). Safeguards selection principles. In *Proc. 2nd IFIP Intl. Conf. on Computer Security,* Toronto, September

Ruthberg Z.G. and Polk W.T. eds (1989). Report of the invitational workshop on data integrity. *NIST Special Publ. 500-168,* September

Saltzer J.D. and Schroeder M.D. (1975). The protection of information in computer systems. *Proc. IEEE,* **63**(9)

Sandhu R.S. (1988). Transaction control expressions for separation of duties. In *Proc. 4th Aerospace Comp. Security Applications Conf.*

Sandhu R. and Jajodia S. (1990). Integrity mechanisms in database management systems. In *Proc. 13th NIST-NCSC Nat. Comp. Sec. Conf.,* October

Spooner D.L. (1988). Relationships between database security and operating system security. In *Database Security: Status and Prospects* (Landwehr C.E. ed.). Elsevier Sc. (North-Holland)

Watson J and Amoroso E. (1990). A trusted software development methodology'. In *Proc. 6th Annual Computer Security Applications Conf.,* October

Wilms P.F. and Linsday B.G. (1982). A database authorization mechanism supporting individual and group authorization. In *Distributed Data Sharing* (van de Riet R.P. and Litwin W. eds.) North-Holland

Wilson J. (1989). A security policy for an A1 DBMS (a trusted subject). In *Proc. IEEE Symp. on Security and Privacy,* Oakland

Wing J.M. (1990). A specifier's introduction to formal methods. *IEEE Computer,* **23**(9)

Wood C.C. (1990). Principles of secure information systems design. *Computers & Security,* **9**(1), Elsevier Sc. North-Holland

# 5 Statistical database security

## 5.1 Introduction

In the previous chapters, we have described models and mechanisms for securing databases against unauthorized accesses to information stored therein. A database can also be used for statistical purposes, namely for acquiring information of a statistical nature about entities of the real world, represented in the database. In this case, the term statistical databases is used.

A *statistical database* (SDB) is a database that is used for statistical queries (for example, averages, counts) on subsets of the database entities. Statistical databases may be *special purpose or general purpose*. The former are used only for statistical computations (for example, census SDBs). The latter are ordinary databases (for example, hospital, bank, commercial, academic SDBs) which can be used both by the usual applications accessing individual entities through queries (key-based queries), in which case the access control mechanisms described in the previous chapters are sufficient to guarantee protection, and by statistical applications, in which only statistical queries are allowed. For this second type of query, special protection techniques must be developed, in order to deal with threats typical of the statistical environment.

The main problem in SDB protection is the achievement of a compromise between the privacy needs of individuals and the right of organizations to know and process information (Palley, 1986). This entails the right to release statistical information, while at the same time assuring that confidential information about the individuals represented in the SDB is maintained. Protecting an SDB means preventing and avoiding **statistical inference**. Inference in an SDB means the possibility of obtaining confidential information on single entities, by taking advantage of (sequences of) statistical queries issued against a set of entities stored in the SDB.

A first security measure consists in building a *statistical filter*, which permits only statistical queries and which prevents direct access to specific entities in the SDB. For example, referring to commercial SDBs, a filter would allow the 'count' query for the number of employees whose salary is higher than a certain threshold but deny queries that select single individuals having this characteristic.

However, a statistical filter is not sufficient to prevent inference. Since the released statistics always maintain a trace of the data that have been used in the computation, skilled users can get unauthorized information. Consider, for example, a user first querying the SDB about the average salary of the women employees of a certain department, and then the same user querying the number of women employees. If this count returns the value 1, then the user obtains (*infers*) the salary of that woman employee by means of legal (namely, allowed by the filter) statistical queries.

When this happens, an SDB is said to be positively compromised. An SDB is *positively compromised* if a user finds out that an individual has a specific characteristic (that is, the individual represented in the SDB has certain attribute values). An SDB is *negatively compromised* if a user finds out that a given individual does not hold a certain characteristic.

Protection from statistical inference cannot be achieved through the protection techniques discussed in the previous chapters, but requires *ad-hoc* techniques, as illustrated in this chapter. However, mechanisms for user identification/authentication are still required, to identify the users requesting information from the SDB. Design and implementation of special-purpose techniques for inference protection is a complex task, and the following issues have to be taken into account.

- *Characteristics of the SDB to be protected.* SDBs may be *on-line* – in this mode users get real-time responses to their statistical queries, or *off-line* – users do not know when their statistics will be processed, making compromise more difficult. Also, SDBs may be *static* or *dynamic*. Static SDBs do not change during their lifetime (namely, no insertion or deletion operations occur – in census databases, for example), and possible changes give rise to new static databases. Dynamic SDBs undergo modifications due to the insertion and deletion of entities in order to reflect the dynamics of the real world. Protecting a dynamic SDB is more complex, since variations in the database state provide additional information to malicious users, and specific techniques have to be designed. For example, a user requesting a statistical sum of the salaries of the individuals in the SDB who have certain characteristics, before and after the insertion of a new individual *I* who has those characteristics, can infer the salary of *I*, by subtracting the first sum value from the second one. SDBs may be *centralized* or *distributed*. In the latter case, inference controls are more complex because of the necessity of applying controls at each site, and of having integrated management of the users' profiles. Finally, SDBs may be oriented to *single applications* or may serve a set of *heterogeneous applications*. Protection is obviously more complex in heterogeneous environments, given the large number and different types of applications that interact with the SDB.
- *Additional knowledge of the users.* Users can have additional knowledge of the individuals represented in the SDB; this knowledge can be properly exploited for inference purposes. In Denning (1982) a distinction is made between *supplementary knowledge* and *working knowledge*. Supplementary knowledge is the set of information items (usually not supplied by the SDB) owned by the user, both confidential (for example, the salary of an

employee) and non-confidential (for example, the qualifications of an employee). Working knowledge is the set of information items the user has about the attribute values in the SDB (for example, the values of the 'Qualification' attribute of an Employee SDB), and about the types of statistics available in the SDB. Inference is easier when users have supplementary knowledge, since this knowledge can help the user to interpret the results of statistics. For example, suppose that only one male employee works in a certain department. A statistical query asking the total salaries of the male employees of that department could lead to discovering the salary of the employee only if the user knows the name of the employee involved. Techniques are more reliable as they succeed in taking supplementary knowledge into account.

- *Types of attacks.* The capability of developing a good inference control technique also depends on the knowledge the developer has about the techniques exploited by snoopers attacking the SDB. In the face of sophisticated attack techniques, protection mechanisms need to be more sophisticated. Moreover, a combination of techniques can be required to protect an SDB against inference, since a single technique is generally designed to overcome specific attack techniques.

This chapter deals with the inference problem in SDBs, with special attention to the protection techniques available. In particular, the basic protection techniques are discussed, which are based either on the restriction (that is, no release) of requested statistics that could enable the user to infer confidential information, or on the modification of the data used for computing the requested statistics, thus releasing modified results. Finally, a comprehensive evaluation of the features of the techniques presented is given. (The chapter does not illustrate or demonstrate in detail theorems and formulas, which are instead presented with the purpose of showing how they can be applied in the various cases.)

## 5.2 Basic concepts and assumptions

The reference SDB structure considered in this chapter is the relational form (see Chapter 1). According to the relational form, an SDB can be represented as a two-dimensional table whose rows are records describing real-world entities or individuals, and whose columns are the attributes describing properties of the entities or individuals. (The terms *entity* and *individual* will be used interchangeably.) Formally, let $N$ be the number of individuals represented in the SDB and $M$ the number of attributes of the SDB schema, $A_1, \ldots, A_M$ characterizing each individual. In Figure 5.1 the reference form is shown, where $x_{ij}$ denotes the value of the $j$-th attribute $A_j$ for the $i$-th record in the SDB.

Each attribute $A_j$ $(1 \leq j \leq M)$ has $|A_j|$ possible values. For instance, in an SDB storing data about employees, the attribute *Dept-Code* can assume the values *Dept1*, *Dept2*, and *Dept3*, corresponding to the departments of interest. A

| Record | $A_1$ | • | • | • | $A_j$ | • | • | • | $A_M$ |
|---|---|---|---|---|---|---|---|---|---|
| 1 | $X_{11}$ | • | • | • | $X_{1j}$ | • | • | • | $X_{1M}$ |
| • | • | • | • | • | • | • | • | • | • |
| • | • | • | • | • | • | • | • | • | • |
| • | • | • | • | • | • | • | • | • | • |
| • | • | • | • | • | • | • | • | • | • |
| i | $X_{i1}$ | • | • | • | $X_{ij}$ | • | • | • | $X_{iM}$ |
| • | • | • | • | • | • | • | • | • | • |
| • | • | • | • | • | • | • | • | • | • |
| • | • | • | • | • | • | • | • | • | • |
| N | $X_{N1}$ | • | • | • | $X_{Nj}$ | • | • | • | $X_{NM}$ |

***Figure 5.1*** Conceptual model of an SDB.

distinction is usually made between (multi) numerical (for example, 'Salary') and (multi) non-numerical (for example, 'Sex'), also called categorical, attributes.

Generally, special-purpose SDBs, such as census SDBs, release statistics in the form of two-dimensional tables, called *macrostatistics*, providing summary statistics (for example, counts and sums) on the individuals in the SDB who hold certain attribute values. In this case we talk about the tabular form for SDBs. An example of macrostatistics is shown in Figure 5.2, where a three-dimensional table for the *Count* statistic is shown, computed on the 'Birth-Year', 'Sex', and 'Dept-Code' attributes of an Employee SDB.

| BSD Table | | | | |
|---|---|---|---|---|
| Birth-Year | Sex | Dept-Code | | |
| | | Dept1 | Dept2 | Dept3 |
| 1941-1951 | M | 10 | 12 | 0 |
| | F | 1 | 0 | 3 |
| 1952-1962 | M | 12 | 10 | 5 |
| | F | 20 | 2 | 8 |
| >1962 | M | 15 | 0 | 1 |
| | F | 20 | 10 | 0 |

***Figure 5.2*** Example of macrostatistics.

The tabular form will sometimes be considered in the following, since some inference control techniques have been specifically developed for SDBs that release statistics in tabular form.

The case of statistics calculated at the time they are requested, through query languages, is more usual. With these languages, statistical queries can be issued through either keys or characteristic formulas. A *key-based statistic* is requested by specifying the set of entities (in general, fixed) involved in the statistic via a set $C$ of keys, $C = (C_1,...,C_M)$, where the values of these keys are the identifiers of the SDB entities. A sample key-based summing query can be, for example, *sum(C,Salary)*, with C = (Smith, Johnson, Brown); the query returns the total salary of the employees Smith, Johnson, and Brown, under the hypothesis that the last name of employees is used as the entity identifier. Inference control techniques have been specifically studied for key-based statistical queries such as sums (Schlörer, 1977), maximum (Davida *et al.*, 1976), and medians (De Millo *et al.*, 1977), but they will not be described in the book, owing to their limited practical interest.

More generally, statistics are formulated through characteristic formulas, defined as follows (Denning, 1982).

*Characteristic formula.* A characteristic formula (or, simply, a characteristic), generally indicated by a capital letter ($A, B, C, ...$), is a logical formula where the attribute values are combined through the Boolean operators OR, AND, NOT ($\vee, \wedge, \neg$, listed in increasing order of priority). An example of a characteristic formula is:

$$A = (\text{Sex} = \text{F}) \wedge ((\text{Dept-Code} = \text{Dept1}) \vee (\text{Dept-Code} = \text{Dept2})) \wedge (\text{Birth-Year} < 1965)$$

specifying all the female employees of departments 'Dept1' and 'Dept2' born before 1965.

A characteristic formula identifies a set of records in the SDB called a query set.

*Query set.* The query set of a characteristic $C$ is the set of records matching that characteristic. The query set of $C$ is indicated by $X(C)$. The number of records in $X(C)$ is $|X(C)|$.

*All* is a special characteristic whose query set contains all SDB records. In general, for each characteristic formula $C$, the relationship $X(All) \supseteq X(C)$ holds, meaning that the query set of any characteristic $C$ is a subset of the whole SDB.

Elementary sets are a special type of query set, since they are not further decomposable. Elementary sets correspond to characteristic formulas of the type:

$$\bar{C} = (A_1 = a_1) \wedge ... \wedge (A_M = a_M)$$

where $A_j$ ($j = 1,..., M$), is an attribute of the SDB, and $a_j$ is one of the $|A_j|$ values of the attribute $A_j$. The number $E$ of elementary sets in an SDB with $A_1, ..., A_M$ attributes is:

$$E = \prod_{j=1}^{M} |A_j|$$

and some of them may be empty. Records belonging to the same elementary set are not distinguishable because their attributes hold the same values. If $g$ indicates the size of the largest elementary set, a relationship can be defined between the total number $N$ of records in the SDB and the number $E$ of elementary sets. Precisely, if $N \leq E$, then $g = 1$.

The main statistical **queries** available to users for requesting information in an SDB are: *Count*, *Sum*, *Rfreq*, *Avg*, *Median*, *Max* and *Min*. These are now illustrated in detail.

- $Count(C) = |X(C)|$: used to count the records in a query set of a given characteristic formula $C$.
- $Sum(C,A_j) = \Sigma_{i \in X(C)}\, x_{ij}$: used to compute the sum of the values of a given numerical attribute $A_j$ for all the records of the query set $X(C)$.
- $Rfreq(C) = {}^{Count(C)}/_{N} = {}^{|X(C)|}/_{N}$: used to compute the relative frequency of the query set $X(C)$, with respect to the total number of records in the SDB.
- $Avg(C,A_j) = {}^{Sum\,(C,A_j)}/_{Count\,(C)}$: used to compute the mean (that is, average value) of a numerical attribute $A_j$ in the query set.
- $Max(C,A_j) = Max_{i \in X(C)}\, x_{ij}$: used to determine the maximum value of a numerical attribute in a query set.
- $Min(C,A_j) = Min_{i \in X(C)}\, x_{ij}$: used to determine the minimum value of a numerical attribute in a query set.
- $Median(C,A_j) = \lceil |X(C)| \rceil /2 \rceil$: used to compute the median value in an ordered set of numerical values of an attribute $A_j$ (the values are in increasing order). The median value of an attribute $A_j$ is the value located in the position $\lceil |X(C)| /2 \rceil$ in the query set associated with $C$ (when the the query-set size is even, the median is the lowest of the two middle values, rather than their average); $\lceil x \rceil$ denotes the smallest integer greater than x.

For statistical queries the concept of order can be defined. A statistic involving values of $m$ distinct attributes is called an $m$-order statistic. For example, the statistic *Count* ((*Sex* = *F*) $\wedge$ ((*Dept-Code* = *Dept1*)) is a 2-order statistic, since the attributes Sex and Dept-Code are specified. *Count*(*All*) is the only 0-order statistic.

An important concept in SDBs is the concept of sensitive statistics. A *sensitive statistic* is a statistic that can lead to identifying confidential information on a single individual represented in the SDB. Sensitive statistics must be restricted: that is, they should not be released. A statistic computed on a confidential attribute in a query set of size 1 is sensitive by definition.

## 5.3 Inference protection techniques

Inference protection techniques, also called inference controls, aim at preventing users from inferring confidential information about individuals represented in the SDB, thus causing the SDB to be *compromised*. Let $A_i$ be either a non-numerical confidential attribute (the value of a non-numerical attribute is 1 if an entity holds the property described by the attribute; 0 otherwise) or a numerical attribute, and $x_j$ a record describing an entity in the SDB. Depending on the type of information on $A_i$ gained by the user, exact and partial (or approximate) compromise are distinguished (Adam and Wortmann, 1989; Denning and Schlörer, 1983), defined as follows:

- *Exact compromise*. Exact compromise occurs if a user, through one or more statistical queries, can state for the attribute $A_i$ the value 1 (in the case of a non-numerical attribute) or the exact value (in the case of a numerical attribute), for a record $j$ in the SDB.
- *Partial compromise.* Partial compromise occurs if a user, through one or more statistical queries, can state for the attribute $A_i$ the value 0 (in the case of a non-numerical attribute), or obtain an estimator $\hat{A}$ of the actual value (in the case of a numerical attribute), such that its variance satisfies the relationship:

  $Var(\hat{A}) < k^2$

  for a record $j$ in the SDB, where $k$ is a parameter defined by the database administrator (DBA).

  (This definition of compromise is quite general, and most protection techniques refer to this definition; when necessary, specific definitions of compromise will be introduced.)

A general classification of inference protection techniques is presented in Denning and Schlörer (1983), Adam and Wortmann (1989), where a distinction is made between *conceptual*, *restriction-based* and *perturbation-based* techniques.

The conceptual techniques address the inference problem at a conceptual level, dealing with a conceptual data model of the SDB. These techniques will be described in Section 5.3.1.

Restriction-based techniques provide inference protection by restricting (that is, not releasing) some statistical queries, such as, for example, those identifying query sets containing a very small/large number of records, or query sets that have several common records. If the number of statistical queries denied is too great, these techniques, although assuring inference protection, heavily limit the usability of the SDB. The main restriction-based techniques will be illustrated in Section 5.3.2.

Perturbation-based techniques provide inference protection by introducing modifications to the information used for answering statistical queries. The information to be modified can be either the data stored in the SDB (thus generating a new perturbed SDB), or the computed result, before releasing it to the user.

A crucial problem for this class of techniques is the bias introduced in the responses as a consequence of the modifications, which should be as small as possible to assure both inference protection and accuracy of responses. Moreover, the modifications must guarantee the consistency of the released results (for example, repeated queries must always have the same result, to avoid skilled users drawing real data by averaging the different responses). The principal perturbation-based techniques will be illustrated in Section 5.3.3.

When necessary, some examples of possible attacks will be provided during the presentation of inference controls.

### 5.3.1 Conceptual techniques

In this section we describe the main conceptual techniques for inference protection, namely the lattice model (Denning and Schlörer, 1983), and the conceptual partitioning technique proposed in Chin and Ozsoyoglu (1981) for partitioning the SDB individuals into populations, in the conceptual design phase of the SDB.

#### *The lattice model*

This model is considered a conceptual-level model since it provides a conceptual representation of the records stored in an SDB, based on the lattice structure of $m$-dimensional tables, or $m$-tables organized at different levels of abstraction (Denning and Schlörer, 1983). An example of an $m$-table is presented in Figure 5.2, where the three-dimensional table for the *Count* statistic is shown, computed on the 'Birth-Year', 'Sex', and 'Dept-Code' attributes of the Employee SDB.

The tabular form is also very similar to the release format used for special-purpose SDBs, such as census SDBs. The US census statistics have usually been released in the form of *macrostatistics*, namely two-dimensional tables containing related *Count* and *Sum* statistics.

In general, an $m$-dimensional table represents a collection of correlated statistics of $m$ order, namely, computed on $m$ SDB attributes $A_1, ..., A_m$. If each attribute $A_i$ has $|A_i|$ values, then the total number $S_m$ of the table elements is given by:

$$S_m = \prod_{i=1}^{m} |A_i|$$

and the possible statistics that can be derived from the table are $2^{S_m} - 1$.

The tabular form does not correspond to the actual data organization in the SDB, previously illustrated (see Section 5.2). It is rather a view of the SDB, and can be derived through the *microaggregation* process from the relational model. Let us consider $M$ attributes $A_1, ..., A_M$ of the SDB, each having a finite set of values $\{1... |A_i|\}$. The set of attribute values that characterize the entities are grouped into classes or categories. Using $M$ attributes for categorization, the data about the SDB entities are described using an $M$-dimensional table, where the entities belonging to the same categories for all attributes are classified in the same elementary entry of the $M$-dimensional table. An elementary entry contains summary statistics computed over the entities of that entry. The cells of an $M$-table correspond to query sets specified through $M$ distinct attributes, and not less than $M$, called $M$-sets. An SDB characterized by $M$ attributes gives rise to $2^M$ $m$-dimensional tables: that is, as many as the possible attribute subsets.

The set of $m$-tables related to a given statistic give rise to a lattice structure. In Figure 5.3, a lattice structure is shown for the *Count* statistic, starting from

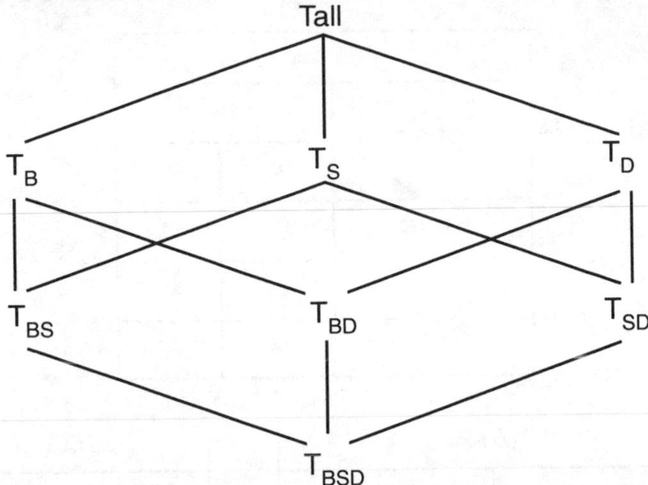


*Figure 5.3* The table lattice on Birth-Year, Sex, Department-Code attributes.

the three-dimensional table shown in Figure 5.2. The lattice is built through the aggregation mechanism (sum) with respect to an attribute, obtaining tables of size smaller than $m$, until a 0-dimensional table that represents the *Count* statistic computed on the whole SDB is obtained.

For example, by aggregating the three-dimensional table of Figure 5.2 (that is, *Birth-Year*, *Sex*, and *Dept-Code* attributes), the two-dimensional tables *BS*, *BD*, and *SD* depicted in Figure 5.4 are obtained for the *Count* statistic.

The *use of the lattice model* has provided a valid framework for studying and comparing different inference controls, such as those based on query restriction and on data modification (to be examined in the following sections).

Using the tabular form of the lattice model, inference control techniques to restrict sensitive statistics have been studied. (In general, a statistic is *sensitive* when it may lead to the disclosure of confidential data on single individuals in the SDB, even in negative form: that is, showing that the entity does not have certain characteristics.) In particular, the $n$-respondent, $k$%-dominance criterion has been generally used for determining when a statistic is to be considered sensitive. According to this criterion, a statistic is sensitive if $n$ or fewer records represent more than $k$% of the total. The parameters $n$ and $k$ are fixed and kept secret.

Consequently, a statistic holding a query set of size 1 is sensitive. Then, in the $m$-tables the cells for the *Count* statistics that hold the value 1 are sensitive. Also, the *Sum* statistics computed on these unitary cells turn out to be sensitive, because they give the exact value of the attribute on which the *Sums* have been computed for the individuals represented in those unitary cells. By exploiting the existing relationships among the $m$-tables in the lattice structure, one can discover that additional cells turn out to be sensitive, in spite of the definition of sensitivity. In fact, by using operations involving cells of $m$-tables at different

BS Table

| Birth-Year | Sex | |
|---|---|---|
| | M | F |
| 1941–195 | 22 | 4 |
| 1952–1962 | 27 | 30 |
| >1962 | 16 | 30 |

BD Table

| Birth-Year | Dept-Code | | |
|---|---|---|---|
| | Dept1 | Dept2 | Dept3 |
| 1941–195 | 11 | 12 | 3 |
| 1952–1962 | 22 | 12 | 13 |
| >1962 | 35 | 10 | 1 |

SD Table

| Sex | Dept-Code | | |
|---|---|---|---|
| | Dept1 | Dept2 | Dept3 |
| M | 37 | 22 | 6 |
| F | 41 | 12 | 11 |

*Figure 5.4* Two-dimensional tables for the Count statistic on the Employee SDB.

levels of abstraction, the user can disclose sensitive statistics. In general, given a lattice structure, it is possible to permit a *Count* statistic in an *m*-table of the lattice if the individual is not identified in some parent table of that *m*-table in the lattice. The problem of determining all the cells that have to be considered sensitive in an *m*-table, and thus to be suppressed from the table, will be described in Section 5.3.2, subsection 'Cell suppression'.

***Conceptual partitioning***

This technique has been proposed in Chin and Ozsoyoglu (1981), and addresses the inference protection problems during the conceptual design phase of the SDB. It is based on the definition, at the conceptual level, of the set of entities, called *populations*, of the SDB on which statistics can be released, and of the conditions that must be verified to avoid inference. Precisely, the *Data Abstraction (D-A)* model (Smith and Smith, 1977), based on the *aggregation* and *generalization* abstractions, is used to model the sets of entities of the SDB on which statistical queries can be computed. Aggregation allows object relationships to be represented as aggregated objects. Generalization allows object classes to be represented as generic objects. The real world is then represented through generalization and aggregation hierarchies, whose intersections are the abstract objects (aggregated and generic).

For statistical purposes, generalization hierarchies are of interest, since they allow the designers to describe, at different levels of genericity, the real-world individuals to be represented in the SDB. Thus, in a generalization hierarchy, different levels of generic objects can be defined, partitioning the individuals according to their property values. A set of SDB entities holding common properties is referred to as a population. Moving from the root to the leaves in a generalization hierarchy, populations are decomposed into sub-populations, down to the *atomic* populations (*A*-populations): that is, populations that cannot be further decomposed, which are the leaves of the hierarchy. Each non-atomic population consists of disjoint *A*-populations. Disjoint sub-populations holding a common parent in the generalization hierarchy form a cluster.

In Figure 5.5 the conceptual model of an Employee SDB is shown, where the Employee population is decomposed into five sub-populations, according to the 'Sex' and 'Dept-Code' attributes.

Intermediate populations form two clusters, *Sex* = (*Male*, *Female*) and *Dept-Code* = (*Dept1*, *Dept2*, *Dept3*). The leaves of the tree represent the *A*-populations: that is, the atomic populations composed of the employees of a given sex in each department.

This *conceptual model of a statistical database* is used to define which statistics can be released and yet avoid inference. In particular, for each population of the model, the designer defines which statistical queries (for

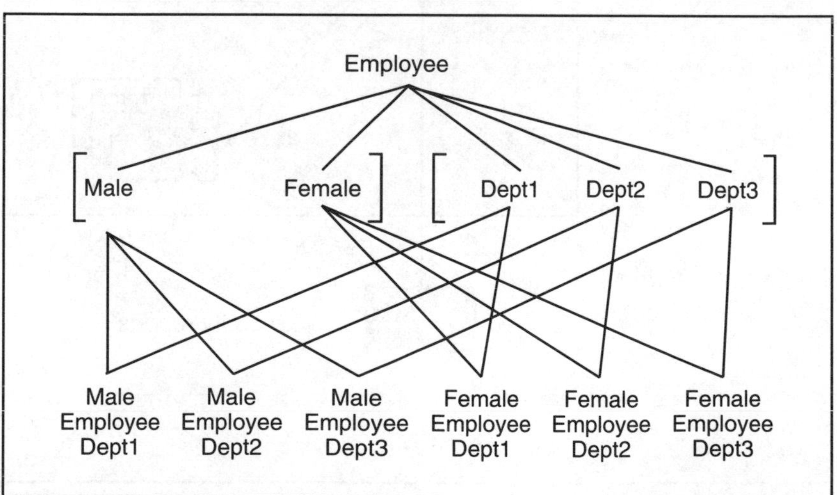


***Figure 5.5*** The conceptual model applied to the Employee SDB.

example, sums, averages) are permitted on which properties of the population. Moreover, the designer specifies whether the *Count* statistic can be applied to the whole population. To improve the definition of statistical security requirements, the concept of *security atom populations* (*SA*-populations) is introduced. An *SA*-population groups one or more *A*-populations into a logical population for which no statistical information involving any property can be released, and this is true also for any of its proper subsets. The term *security atom value set* (*SA*-value set) is used to indicate the set of property values to be protected for the properties of an *SA*-population.

To support the definition of statistical security requirements in this conceptual model, the *Statistical Security Management Facility (SSMF)* system has been proposed, whose architecture is shown in Figure 5.6.

SSMF consists of three modules, namely the *Population Definition Construct*, the *User Knowledge Construct*, and the *Constraint Enforcer and Checker*.

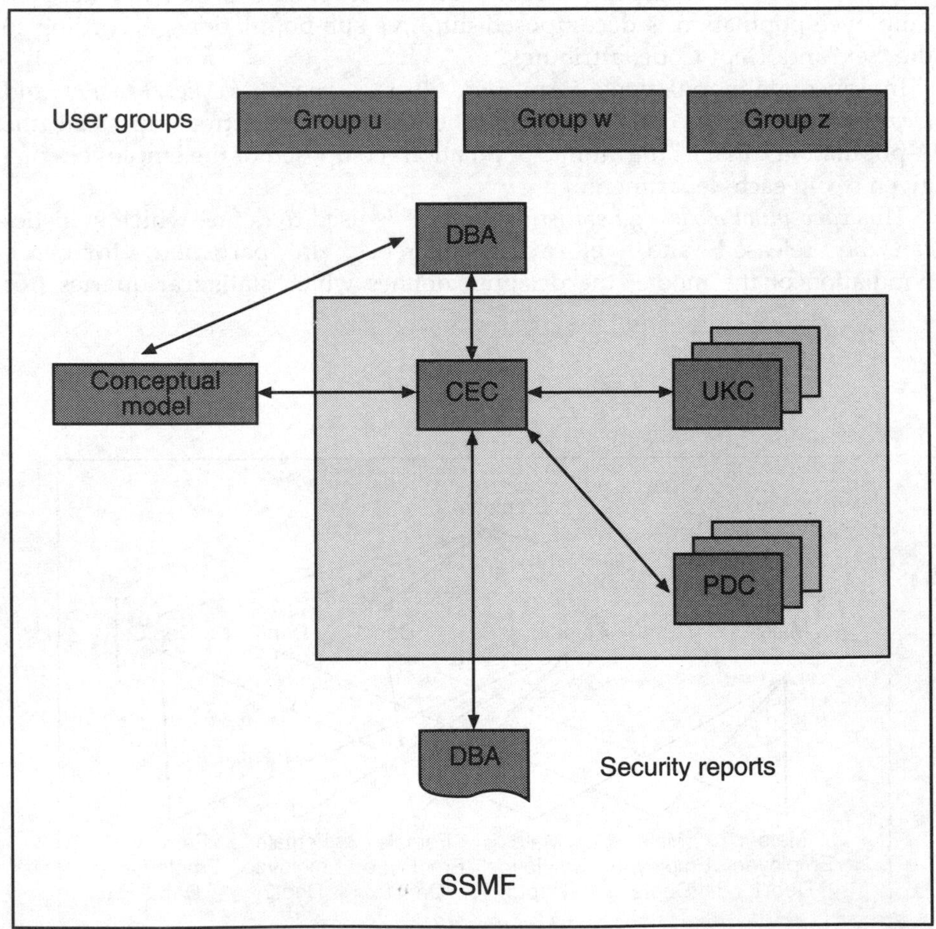


***Figure 5.6*** SSMF system architecture: DBA = Database Administrator; CEC = Constraint Enforcer and Checker; UKC = User Knowledge Constraint; PDC = Population Definition Construct; SSMF = Statistical Security Management Facility.

The *Population Definition Construct* (PDC) is associated with each population of the model and describes the population characteristics. In particular, for a population $P_j$ of the model the PDC describes:

- the characteristics of $P_j$, and its relationships in the hierarchy (parents, children, siblings);
- the user groups that are authorized to access $P_j$;
- how to manage changes on $P_j$ data, as a consequence of the changes occurring in the real world;
- the set of properties of $P_j$ for which statistical information can be released, and the statistics permitted for each property. Let $p_{ij}$ be the *i*-th property of population $P_j$, $Q(p_{ij})$ the set of permitted statistics on $p_{ij}$, and $C$ the cluster $P_j$ belongs to. For permitted statistics the following rules must be satisfied:
  - (i) The set of the permitted statistics on a property $p_{ij}$ must be identical for the same property of all populations belonging to the same cluster. Formalizing:
    $\forall$ cluster $C$, $\forall\, i, j, h$: $P_j, P_h \in C \Rightarrow Q(p_{ij}) = Q(p_{ih})$
  - (ii) The set of permitted statistics for a property $p_{ij}$ of any population $P_j$ must be a subset of the set of permitted statistics on the corresponding property (if existing) $p_{ij}$ of the population $P_{j'}$ parent of $P_h$. Formalizing:
    $\forall\, i, j, h$: $P_h$ parent of $P_j \Rightarrow Q(p_{ih}) \supseteq Q(p_{ij})$
- if the *Count* statistics can be released for $P_j$;
- the constraints deriving from the dynamics of the real world and from relationships between populations, relevant from the security viewpoint. If $P_j$ is a normal population, *global constraints* can be defined, to be applied to all individuals belonging to $P_j$ and to all individuals belonging to populations including $P_j$ in the hierarchy (*global constraints of type* 1), or for the individuals of $P_j$ and to individuals of a population located in other parts of the hierarchy (*global constraints of type* 2). If $P_j$ is an *SA*-population, specific constraints, called *SA-constraints*, can be specified, stating conditions that must be verified on the values of the *SA*-value sets of $P_j$.

The *User Knowledge Construct* (UKC) describes for each user group the supplementary knowledge the group members have about the SDB individuals. This knowledge refers to both the knowledge derived from query sequences to the SDB, and to information owned *a priori* on single individuals of the population.

For each population, *Identifiable Dynamics*-labelled information is maintained, related to the knowledge the group members have about the population dynamics (namely, individual insertions, deletions, updates). The level of protection obtainable on populations directly depends on the number of operations visible to the group. For example, users authorized for both insert and delete operations seem more dangerous than users authorized only for the insert (or delete) operation.

For *SA*-populations, *Change Sequence*-labelled information is also maintained, storing all the information held by the group concerning the *SA*-population dynamics: that is, insert, delete and update of *SA*-population individuals. Moreover, for *SA*-populations, the upper and lower values of the *SA*-set of a property and/or of a specific individual are also specified, if the group knows them.

The *Constraint Enforcer and Checker (CEC)* module includes algorithms to be executed when the SDB is queried. Thus, it is the module for inference protection, allowing only those queries that obey the security constraints defined for the populations involved in the statistical queries. For each statistical query, the CEC retrieves the global constraints and *SA*-constraints to be verified to assure inference protection, using the information contained in PDC and UKC; if necessary, suitable modification procedures are executed before releasing the statistic. In addition, it updates the UKC corresponding to the user who requested the statistic.

The CEC is invoked for any insert, delete or update operation, to modify the security constraints and the Change Sequence field of the UKCs concerned. The CEC also supports the DBA in studying changes in security constraints following variations in user groups, in populations and in the users' additional knowledge. In addition, it is invoked in the case of change operations on the data conceptual model to modify the security constraints and the contents of the different UKCs. The CEC supplies the DBA with information related to inference events, in the form of security reports that specify the values of the security parameters, the constraints involved, and both involved and non-involved users.

The techniques for inference protection discussed so far address the inference problem at a conceptual level. In the following sections, we describe inference protection techniques that operate at a lower level, namely, on the set of records actually stored in the SDB, with the purpose of either restricting some queries (restriction-based techniques) or modifying data used for query processing (perturbation-based techniques).

### 5.3.2 Restriction-based techniques

These techniques protect against inference by restricting (that is, not releasing) the statistical queries that could reveal to the user confidential information on single individuals represented in the SDB. In this way of working, the set of released queries is, in general, a subset of the set of those requested. In the following, techniques are described that: restrict statistical queries by considering the size of the query set; control overlapping between successive query sets; maintain a user profile that keeps track of the query history (auditing); limit the number of attributes involved in the issued query; and take into account predefined undecomposable groups of SDB records.

#### *Query-set size control*

A very simple restriction technique controls the size of the query set associated with a statistical query. Precisely, a statistic $q(C)$ is permitted only if its query set $X(C)$ satisfies the following relation:

$$k \leq |X(C)| \leq N-k$$

where $N$ is the number of SDB records and $k \geq 0$ is a fixed parameter. Note that $k$ must satisfy the condition $0 \leq k \leq N/2$, in order to release statistics, and that $q(All)$ is not allowed (it can in any case be computed as $q(All) = q(C) + q(\neg C)$ for each characteristic $C$ such as $k \leq | X(C) | \leq N-k$). This control prevents simple attacks based on very small or very large query sets, such as the following.

Suppose, for example, that a user knows that a certain individual satisfies a given characteristic formula $C$. If the statistic $q_1 = Count(C)$ returns the value 1, the user has uniquely identified that individual in the SDB. The user can disclose additional information on the individual under examination, by issuing the statistic $q_2 = Count(C \wedge C')$, where the characteristic $C'$ involves the additional attributes of interest on the individual. If $q_2$ returns the value 1, the individual also satisfies $C'$; if $q_2$ returns the value 0, the individual does not satisfy $C'$.

By applying the query-set size control, the statistics $q_1$ and $q_2$ are not released and, consequently, the user cannot infer confidential information about single individuals. Very large query sets are restricted, too, since the information on a small query set specified by a characteristic $C$ can also be obtained using $q(\neg C)$, specifying a query set of size $N-k$, where $k$ is the size of $X(C)$.

Although this control prevents trivial attacks, because of its simplicity it can be easily circumvented by more sophisticated attacks, such as the so-called trackers (Schlörer, 1980; Denning, 1982). A *tracker* is a set of characteristic formulas that can be used to pad out small-size query sets with additional records, thus making their size fall into the allowed range $[k, N-k]$. With trackers, restricted statistics are computed through combinations of allowed statistics that take advantage of the padding effect operated by the tracker. This effect is then suppressed, finally giving the desired value of the restricted statistics. To clarify this way of operating, let us show a very simple example of tracker-based attack. Let us suppose that the characteristic:

$$C = (Dept\text{-}Code = Dept1 \wedge Sex = F \wedge Birth\text{-}Year = 1951)$$

uniquely identifies the employee Brown in the Employee SDB, and that the query-set size control mechanism has parameter $k$ set to 3. Consequently, the statistic $Count(C)$ is not permitted. A tracker is obtained by defining a characteristic $A = (Sex = F)$, a second characteristic

$$B = (Dept\text{-}Code = Dept1 \wedge Birth\text{-}Year = 1951)$$

and a third characteristic $T = (A \wedge \neg B)$. Such a tracker is called an individual tracker, since it is constructed using the user's knowledge about a certain individual represented in the SDB, and allows the user to obtain additional confidential information about such an individual (for example, the employee Brown). In our case, the forbidden statistic:

$$q(C) = Count(C) = Count\ (Dept\text{-}Code = Dept1 \wedge Sex = F \wedge Birth\text{-}Year = 1951)$$

can be computed using the tracker in the following way:

$Count(C) = Count(A) - Count(T)$

Moreover, it is possible to infer additional information about Brown's salary, by issuing the following query:

$Count(C \wedge Salary \geq 20) = Count(T \vee A \wedge Salary \geq 20) - Count\ (T)$

If the result of this query is 1, the user infers information about Brown's salary (here the salary is expressed in thousands of dollars).

More sophisticated types of tracker can be defined, namely *general trackers, double trackers* and *union trackers*, that operate with success although the parameter $k$ of the query-set size control has a value very close to $N/2$. Moreover, general and double trackers have the advantage of not requiring supplementary knowledge about a specific individual represented in the SDB, such as is required with individual trackers. An in-depth study on possible tracker-based attacks is given in Denning (1982), and in Schlörer (1980) a procedure to generate trackers automatically is described, which takes at most $O(log_2E)$ queries to find a tracker, where $E$ is the number of elementary sets in the SDB.

Another type of attack that can be used to subvert the query-set size control is the linear system attack, which requires solving a system of equations of the form:

$HX = Q$

where $X = (x_1, ..., x_N)$ is the vector of the SDB records; $Q = (q_1, ..., q_m)$ is the vector of the issued statistics; and $H$ is the incidence matrix, namely a matrix of size $(m \times N)$, where the element $H[i,j]$ is 1 if $x_j \in X(C_i)$, and 0 otherwise, where $X(C_i)$, $i$=1,..., $m$ is the query set associated with the statistic $q_i$. For example, suppose that, in the Employee SDB, the statistic $q_1 = Sum(Sex = F \wedge Dept\text{-}Code = Dept3, Salary)$, requesting the salary of the female employees working in Department 'Dept3', returns the value 33 (in thousands of dollars), and that the statistic $q_2 = Sum((Sex = F \vee Sex = M) \wedge Dept\text{-}Code = Dept3 \wedge Birth\text{-}Year = 1968, Salary)$, requesting the total salary of the employees of the department 'Dept3' born in 1968, either male or female, returns the value 37. A possible linear system is the following:

$$x_1 + x_3 + x_4 + x_6 + x_7 + x_8 + x_9 = 33$$
$$x_1 + x_3 + x_4 + x_5 + x_6 + x_7 + x_8 + x_9 = 37$$

where the records involved in each statistic are listed. Suppose that the statistic $Sum(Sex = M \wedge Dept\text{-}Code = Dept3 \wedge Birth\text{-}Year = 1968, Salary)$ is sensitive, its query set being of size 1, and that it denotes the salary of the employee Donald; this statistic is then restricted by the query-set size control. Using the previous linear system, Donald's salary can be computed solving the system by $x_5$: that is, $x_5 = q_2 - q_1 = 4$.

#### *Expanded query-set size control*

As previously seen, the basic mechanism of the query-set size control is not sufficient to guarantee inference protection, since sensitive statistics can still be computed through a set of permitted statistics, properly defined to make their query sets fall in the allowable range $[k, N-k]$. This control can then be improved, to face attacks like those previously described.

From the analysis of tracker-based and linear-system-based attacks, we can note that the characteristic formulas used in these attacks present some form of relationship to each other. A possible extension of the query-set size control consists in augmenting the number of query sets to be controlled to decide whether a statistic is allowed and, possibly, whether it can be released. More precisely, given a characteristic formula $C$, we can define for it the so-called *implied query sets* (Friedman and Hoffman, 1980), namely query sets identified by characteristics directly derived from $C$ by different logical combinations of $C$'s attributes; these query sets must also be controlled in deciding whether the statistic can be released.

Given an $m$-order statistic of the form:

$$q(A_1 = a_1 \wedge A_2 = a_2 \wedge \ldots \wedge A_m = a_m)$$

or of the form:

$$q(A_1 = a_1 \vee A_2 = a_2 \vee \ldots \vee A_m = a_m)$$

there exist $2^m$ implied query sets corresponding to the following statistics:

$$\begin{array}{l} q(A_1 = a_1 \wedge A_2 = a_2 \wedge \ldots \wedge A_m = a_m) \\ q(A_1 = a_1 \wedge A_2 = a_2 \wedge \ldots \wedge \neg A_m = a_m) \\ \vdots \\ q(A_1 = a_1 \wedge \neg A_2 = a_2 \wedge \ldots \wedge \neg A_m = a_m) \\ q(\neg A_1 = a_1 \wedge A_2 = a_2 \wedge \ldots \wedge A_m = a_m) \\ \vdots \\ q(\neg A_1 = a_1 \wedge \neg A_2 = a_2 \wedge \ldots \wedge \neg A_m = a_m) \end{array}$$

An $m$-order statistic is allowed iff all the $2^m$ implied query sets obey the query-set size control: that is, if they fall in the range $[k, N-k]$. In practice, it is sufficient to check that each implied query set has at least $k$ records, to guarantee that none of them has more than $N-k$ records. By extending the query-set size control to the implied query sets, attacks like those described in the previous section can be prevented. Given the characteristic:

$C$ = (*Dept-Code* = *Dept1* $\wedge$ *Sex* = *F* $\wedge$ *Birth-Year* = 1951),

the query set corresponding to the characteristics:

$T$ = (*Sex*= *F* $\wedge$ $\neg$*Dept-Code* = *Dept1* $\wedge$ $\neg$*Birth-Year* = 1951)

is checked too, since it is an implied query set for $C$, and, consequently, the attack is prevented.

It has to be noted, however, that, since the number of implicit query sets to be checked grows exponentially with the order of the statistic, increasing the number $m$ of attributes makes this control very expensive, and may, consequently, be impractical with high-order statistics. Besides, sensitive statistics can be derived anyway, by analysing all their implicit query sets, as in the following example (Denning, 1982).

Let us consider two attributes $A_i$ and $A_j$ of the database entities. If the attribute $A_i$ has $n$ values $a_{i1}, ..., a_{in}$ and the attribute $A_j$ has $p$ values $a_{j1}, ..., a_{jp}$, the SDB records are partitioned in $(n \times p)$ subgroups, featured by characteristics of type $(a_{it} \wedge a_{jq})$, $t = 1,..., n$ and $q = 1,..., p$. Let us suppose that $q(a_{i1} \wedge a_{j1})$ is a sensitive statistic and that all the remaining statistics $q(a_{it} \wedge a_{jr})$, $t = 2, ..., n$ and $r = 2, ...,p$ are not sensitive. The expanded query-set size control checks the implied query sets of $q(a_1 \wedge b_1)$, and prevents queries based on these query sets, thus avoiding attacks like the following:

$$q(a_{i1} \wedge a_{j1}) = q(a_{j1}) - q(\neg a_{i1} \wedge a_{j1})$$

However, the sensitive statistic $q(a_{i1} \wedge a_{j1})$ can be computed using allowed statistics, such as the following:

$$q(a_{i1} \wedge a_{j1}) = q(a_{j1}) - [q(a_{i2} \wedge a_{j1}) + ... + q(a_{in} \wedge a_{j1})]$$

where the user makes use of statistics not involving both the values $a_{i1}$ and $a_{j1}$ at the same time.

To prevent this type of attack, it is necessary to further augment the number of query sets to be checked to include all the elementary sets determined by the values of all the attributes involved in the statistic.

#### *Query-set overlap control*

Another way to improve the query-set size control is to act on the number of common records that the characteristics used in tracker-based and linear-system-based attacks usually exploit for inference. As we can also see from the previous examples, these attacks are characterized by consecutive statistics whose characteristics have a very high number of common records. The idea underlying the query-set overlap control technique is that successive queries must be checked against the number of common records they have, to prevent those that have a number of common records greater than a given threshold. Precisely, the *query-set overlap* control technique permits a requested statistic $q(C)$ only if:

$$| X(C) \cap X(D) | \leq \alpha, \alpha > 0$$

that is, only if the number of common records between the query set of $q(C)$ and the query set of all the statistics $q(D)$ already released is less than or equal to $\alpha$ ($\alpha$ being the system threshold denoting the maximum number of common records allowed for the query sets of two successive queries).

Let $k$ be the parameter of the query-set size control and $\alpha$ the overlap threshold; in Dobkin *et al.* (1979) it was proved that a lower bound $e$ for the number of queries needed to compromise the SDB is given by $e = 1+ (k - 1) / \alpha$.

Even if this control succeeds in preventing attacks such as the linear-system-based attack previously described, it can be circumvented by properly designed attacks in the form of sequences of successive queries that satisfy the overlap control, such as in the following example, where a linear system is used to deduce $x_3$ using three queries, with $x = 2$ and $r = 1$:

$$q_1 = x_1 + x_2$$
$$q_2 = x_2 + x_3$$
$$q_3 = x_1 + x_3$$

Then

$$x_3 = (q_3 + q_2 - q_1)/2$$

This control turns out to be poorly effective, since it requires a lot of comparisons (each new query must be checked against each previously released query to verify the overlap condition on their respective query sets), and, more importantly, it can limit the usefulness of the SDB, in that statistics involving a set and its subsets cannot be released (thus, for example, queries on the set of female employees, and on the set of female employees with a birth year higher than a certain year, are restricted). The additional time required for processing each new query for the overlap condition is $O(N)$, where $N$ is the number of SDB records. Moreover, the control can be easily circumvented, as previously shown, by properly defined linear system attacks (Denning, 1982), and also by using key-specified queries (see Davida *et al.*, 1978).

#### Audit-based controls

The query-overlap control suggests more comprehensive types of control, aimed at detecting inference threats by comparing each new statistical query issued with queries previously released. Audit-based controls have been developed in this direction, which keep track, in user profiles or logs, of the history of the queries issued by users, and match each new query with queries released in the past, to decide if the new query could lead to compromising the SDB (Schlörer, 1976; Chin and Ozsoyoglu, 1982; Sicherman *et al.*, 1983). For example, in Sicherman *et al.* (1983) an approach based on the use of *censors* is presented, assuming that queries can be expressed as sentences: that is, as well-formed formulas in first-order logic with all variables quantified. A censor is a function used for deciding if the user's queries can be answered, on the basis of the issued query, and on the basis of the actual knowledge of the user, stored in the so-called *assumed information base*. This keeps track of what the user knows about the SDB contents, and is continuously updated with the knowledge acquired from each released answer.

In the following, we describe the Audit Expert system (Chin and Ozsoyoglu, 1982), which can detect possible inferences by matching each new query with the previously released queries, using a suitable representation of the queries in memory.

#### The Audit Expert system

The *Audit Expert (AE)* system is based on auditing techniques for inference control. This system has been specially designed for small-size SDBs; it is also suitable for large SDBs, if combined with a partitioning technique with which the individuals of the SDB can be partitioned into groups that have the same protection requirements. In this case auditing techniques are applied to each group of individuals. 'Expert' refers to the system's capability of being able, when processing a new requested statistic, to check that it does not lead to compromise, using efficient checking procedures and, at the same time, trying to maximize the number of released statistics. The system's reliability turns out to be rather low, in that statistics related to SDB subsets containing a reduced number of records can be released. Also, AE requires some work because of the need for complex algorithms to be implemented for analysis and checking. AE can be considered a secure system, in that it releases only secure statistics with respect to the history of the users; in addition, it operates without requiring any relevant intervention from the DBA, and it has been designed to be independent of specific DBMSs, since it can be added to an existing database system with few modifications.

AE may be used in two modes:

- *on-line:* statistics are processed one by one as they are issued, to check, for each statistic, if the SDB is compromised;
- *off-line:* a batch of statistics is processed, with the purpose of avoiding compromise while, at the same time, maximizing the number of released statistics.

AE uses the concept of *knowledge space (KS)* to indicate the knowledge actually held by a user. Such knowledge is determined by the set of the *answered queries (AQ)*. In Chin and Oszoyoglu (1982) the statistical query *Sum* is considered, which can be defined as a vector of the following type:

$$q = \sum_{i=1}^{N} a_i \, x_i$$

with $a_i = 1$ if $x_i \in X(q)$, and $a_i = 0$ otherwise. $X(q)$ indicates the query set associated with the statistical query $q$; $a_i$ is an attribute value on which the *Sum* is computed. Thus, AQ is defined as a set of vectors:

$$\{(a_{j1}, a_{j2}, \ldots, a_{jN}) \mid \sum_{i=1}^{N} a_{ji} \, x_i \text{ is a response to a user query}\}$$

The knowledge space *KS* is the vector space spanned by the set of vectors in AQ, namely:

(1) if $\overline{q} \in AQ$, then $\overline{q} \in KS$
(2) if $\overline{q} \in KS$, then $\mu\overline{p} \in KS$
(3) if $\overline{q}$ and $\overline{q_1} \in KS$, then $\overline{q} + \overline{q_1} \in KS$
(4) no other vector belongs to *KS*.

AE uses the following definition of compromise. A compromise occurs if a vector exists in *KS* of the form:

(i) $(0, 0, \ldots, a_i, 0, \ldots, 0)$, with $a_i = 1$

The SDB is secure if all the vectors in *KS* are not in form (i).

AE keeps in memory a representation of *KS* and, for each new requested statistic $q$, it checks whether $q$ may lead to SDB compromise (on-line mode), or inserts the statistic into a batch of statistics and executes the check on the whole batch, trying to maximize the released information (off-line mode). To check whether the release of a statistic $q$ can lead to a compromise, the Check procedure is used (see Figure 5.7).

```
Procedure Check (q) ;
   begin
      if (q∈KS) then notify the database to answer q
         else
            if (the database is secure when q is added to AQ)
               then
                  notify the database to answer q;
                  include q in KS
               end; (*if*)
         else
      notify the database to ignore q
        end; (*if*)
   end; (*procedure*)
```

*Figure 5.7* The Check procedure.

In **on-line mode**, each new issued statistic $q$ is checked against the knowledge actually possessed by the user: that is, against the vectors of *KS*. The efficiency of the checking procedure in the on-line mode is strictly dependent on the representation of *KS* in memory. A 'good' representation of *KS* must be minimal and non-redundant; it must contain complete information about the user knowledge; and it must be efficient both for checking new query redundancies and for updates with information related to new requested statistics.To meet the requirements for a 'good' representation, *KS* is represented as a matrix $H$ of size $k \times N$, whose rows are linearly independent vectors of AQ, called base, that is:

$$H = \begin{bmatrix} a_{11} & \dots & a_{1N} \\ . & \dots & . \\ . & \dots & . \\ a_{k1} & \dots & a_{kN} \end{bmatrix}$$

with $a_{ij} = 0$, or $a_{ij} = 1$, for $1 \le j \le k$, $1 \le i \le N$.

Then, the matrix $H$ is transformed into a matrix $H'$ of the form $[I_k \mid B]$, where $I_k$ is the $k \times k$ identity matrix, and $B$ is a matrix of size $k \times (N-k)$, that is:

$$H' = \begin{bmatrix} \overline{h}_1 \\ \overline{h}_2 \\ . \\ . \\ \overline{h}_k \end{bmatrix} = [I_k \mid B]$$

$H'$ is a 'good' representation of *KS* in memory, since it is simple to verify, using the *Check* procedure, whether a new statistic $q$ belongs to *KS*, and, consequently, to verify SDB's security. Each new statistic either belongs to *KS* (in this case, $q$ is redundant and can be expressed as a linear combination of the *KS* vectors) or does not belong to *KS* and has to be inserted in *KS*; *KS* is normalized and the new matrix is checked for compromise.

To formally demonstrate how the checking is enforced with the matrix $H'$, let us consider the new requested statistic $q = (a_1, \ldots, a_N)$, with $a_i = 1$ if $x_i \in X(q)$, $a_i = 0$ otherwise. To test if $q$ belongs to *KS*, a theorem has been defined stating that:

$$q \in KS \quad \text{iff} \quad q = \sum_{i=1}^{k} a_i \bar{h}_i$$

where $\bar{h}_i$ denotes the $i$-th row of $H'$. If the new statistic $q$ does not belong to *KS*, $q$ is inserted in *KS*, giving rise to a new matrix $H'$, of size $(k + 1) \times N$. If a user has supplementary knowledge about the SDB (for example, the value of a statistic, although the statistic was not released), this information must be stored in *KS*, in the same way as requested statistics are inserted.

To verify the SDB's security, a second theorem has been defined, stating that the SDB is secure if and only if there does not exist a row $\bar{h}_i$ in $H'$ such that $h_{ij}= 0$ for all $j$, with $k < j \leq N$, where $H'= [h_{ij}]$.

It has been proved that the AE takes no more than $O(N^2)$ to process a new query. To check if $q$ belongs to *KS* takes no more than $O(kN)$ and, if $q$ does not belong to *KS*, to check the resulting matrix $H'$ takes no more than $O(kN)$. Since $k$ can assume at most the value $n-1$, then AE takes no more than $O(N^2)$ to verify security of the system.

*KS* is represented in memory through a matrix, where rows represent already answered non-redundant statistics and columns represent SDB records.

To further improve the representation of *KS*, it can be noted that records holding similar characteristics (similar attributes) in the SDB tend to appear together in queries, and their columns in the *KS* matrix tend to be identical. Identical columns can then be grouped in a single column, thus reducing memory occupation and matrix size. Individuals presenting similar characteristics can be grouped into a basic group, and the *KS* matrix can be organized according to the basic groups. In this case, the *Check* procedure is applied on the basic groups, and the SDB is secure if no basic group contains just one individual. When operating with the basic groups, it must be verified that a new statistic does not split an already existing group, in which case new columns must be created in the matrix. The *Split* procedure has been developed for this purpose, able to re-organize, and possibly create, the basic groups of the *KS* matrix (Chin and Ozsoyoglu, 1982). The *Split* procedure requires $O(N)$ time and memory to create a new set of basic groups.

In **off-line mode**, a batch of statistical queries $q_1, \ldots, q_t$ are processed together with the *Check* procedure, trying to release the largest set of queries with no SDB compromise. The simplest algorithm to check for compromise consists in applying the procedure *Check* to each query $q_i$, $i = 1, \ldots, t$, to verify if $q_i \in KS$. This algorithm requires $O(tkN)$ steps. The algorithm can be refined by applying the *Check* procedure to all the statistics of the batch together, by defining a new statistic $\bar{Q} = q_1 + Kq_2 + K^2q_3 + \ldots + K^{t-1}q_t$, choosing the constant $K$ sufficiently large so that the various statistics do not interfere with each other. The check is then executed on $\bar{Q}$, and it is demonstrated that $\bar{Q}$ belongs to $KS$ if and only if all the statistics $q_i$ belong to $KS$, that is:

$$\bar{Q} \in KS \text{ iff } q_i \in KS, 1 \le i \le t$$

If all the statistics $q_i$ belong to $KS$, then all the requested queries are released to the user. On the contrary, if some query $q_i$ does not belong to $KS$, the *Check* procedure is executed on that specific query.

The problem of maximizing the number of queries to be answered from a batch of queries turns out to be an *NP*-complete problem (a problem is *NP*-complete if no algorithm exists that can solve this problem in polynomial time).

The description given so far of AE operation refers to static databases: that is, SDBs where insert, delete and update operations are not executed.

The AE system can also be used for **protection in dynamic environments**, properly modifying the matrix representing the knowledge space $KS$ (under the assumption that the *Sum* query is the unique available statistical query). The insertion of a new individual is managed by adding a column of zeros to the matrix representing $KS$, and this does not affect the security of the individuals already represented in the SDB.

As for the delete operation, if the attribute value of the suppressed individual needs no protection, then the column corresponding to that individual in the $KS$ matrix can be deleted. Otherwise, the matrix is not modified, and queries are processed as if suppression had not occurred; however, this individual is not considered in any statistics.

The update of a value $x$ to a new value $x'$ for an individual is managed as an insert–delete (or delete–insert) combination. If $x$ is an attribute needing protection, the matrix of $KS$ will have two columns, one for the old value $x$ and the other for the new value $x'$. These two columns can be merged into one column only and the matrix is left unchanged. However, this update implementation does not protect the amount of the change; that protection can be obtained by adding to the $KS$ matrix a new column corresponding to the difference between $x$ and $x'$. Each time the value $x'$ is involved in a query, the values $x$ and $(x-x')$ are considered, providing protection also to $x'$.

### *Techniques based on the number of attributes*

In this subsection we briefly describe two techniques that enforce inference control by considering the number of attribute values involved in a statistical query.

The *order control* restricts any statistical query that involves too many attribute values, and has been derived from experiences performed on real SDBs. In particular, in Schlörer (1975) it was noted that in augmenting the number of attributes used for specifying a query, the percentage of records that can be identified in the SDB is also augmented. Thus, this basic control forbids high-order statistics, and precisely those statistics that have a number of attributes greater than a threshold $d$. The threshold $d$ is properly defined by the DBA, and depends, in general, on the dimension of the SDB to be protected.

The $S_m/N$ *criterion* (Denning, 1982) restricts the statistics requested on a number of attributes partitioning the database records into too many subsets, against the total number $N$ of records. Let $C$ be a characteristic defined over the attributes $A_1, \ldots, A_m$, and $S_m$ the number of elementary sets defined over these attributes, that is:

$$S_m = \prod_{i=1}^{m} |A_i|$$

A statistic $q(C)$ is restricted if the following condition holds:

$$S_m/N > t$$

where $t$ is a properly defined threshold (for example, $t = 0.1$).

#### *Partitioning*

The partitioning technique is a restriction technique that ensures inference protection by grouping database records at the physical level into disjoint subgroups, called *atomic populations* (Yu and Chin, 1977; Chin and Ozsoyoglu, 1979). Thus, the SDB consists of a set of atomic populations, identified by specific values of the attributes of the SDB schema. Some conditions must be verified on atomic populations to avoid inference. More precisely, each atomic population must contain 0, 2, or more, but always an even number of SDB records. Populations of size 1 are forbidden, in order to prevent attacks based on small and large query sets. To guarantee that the conditions on the size of atomic populations are verified also in dynamic environments, insert and delete operations are allowed only for pairs of records at the same time. In Chin and Ozsoyoglu (1981) the authors propose delaying the processing of single insertions (deletions) until a second insertion (deletion) is requested on the same atomic population, although this mode can contrast with the requirement, for dynamic SDBs, of providing users with updated statistics reflecting as much as possible the dynamic of the real world. Moreover, it has been observed in real databases that there are several atomic populations of size 1. To deal with this problem, techniques have been studied to augment the size of unitary populations to an acceptable size. A possibility is to cluster atomic populations of size 1 with larger atomic populations, causing information loss (Ozsoyoglu and Chin, 1986). Another possibility consists in inserting dummy records in the SDB, introducing bias in released statistics (for example, in *Avg* or *Rfreq*).

Using the partitioning technique, the only released statistics are those characterized by a query set involving one or more atomic populations. If the requested statistic involves several records, belonging to different atomic populations $AP_1, \ldots, AP_t$, then the statistic $q(AP_1 \vee \ldots \vee AP_t)$ is released.

A variant to partitioning is the *microaggregation* technique, which still groups the SDB records, but with the purpose of defining a number of synthetic *average individuals* (Denning, 1982). The statistical queries are computed on these synthetic individuals rather than on the real ones.

To facilitate the identification of atomic populations, especially in the case of relational dynamic SDBs, it is useful to address the partitioning starting from the design phase of the SDB, using the conceptual partitioning approach described in Section 5.3.1, which is suitable for modelling the atomic populations as distinct types of entities at the conceptual level of the SDB design.

### Cell suppression

This technique has been designed for SDBs that release statistics in two-dimensional tables of macrostatistics (for example, census statistics). The cell suppression technique consists in suppressing from the tables all the cells corresponding to sensitive statistics and the cells corresponding to statistics that could, indirectly, lead to disclosure of sensitive statistics (*complementary suppression*).

A criterion is needed to state when a statistic **(cell)** is **sensitive**, or can lead to the revelation of sensitive statistics. For *Count* statistics, the sensitivity criterion generally used considers the minimum query-set size (for example, query-sets of size one). The statistics (cells) that have a value lower than or equal to this minimum are suppressed. In the case of cells of size 1, a technique has been proposed for dealing with them (which is also used in the partitioning described in the previous subsection), consisting in merging a cell of size 1 with a cell of size greater than 1. This approach, however, can produce significant information loss (about 50%), and so is rather inefficient for general-purpose SDBs. For *Sum* statistics, the sensitivity criterion generally used is the $n$-respondent, $k$%-dominance rule. According to this criterion, a statistic is sensitive if $n$ or fewer values contribute to form more than $k$% of the total (Cox, 1980). The parameters $n$ and $k$ are stated by the DBA and kept secret.

#### An example

Suppose $n = 1$ and $k = 90\%$, and consider the two-dimensional table of macrostatistics shown in Table 5.1, reporting the sums of salaries of Male and Female employees of departments 'Dept1', 'Dept2', and 'Dept3', in the Employee SDB.

If only one male employee works in department 'Dept3', that is, *Count(DeptCode = Dept3* $\wedge$ *Sex = M)* = 1, the entry (1,3) in the previous table must be suppressed, because the salary of that employee contributes 100% of the total sum. Also, the entry (2,3) must be suppressed (complementary suppression), because, if subtracted from the total of column 3, it would reveal the salary of the male employee of the department 'Dept3'. The table resulting from the application of the cell suppression technique is shown in Table 5.2.

**Table 5.1** Sum statistic for the Employee SDB.

| **Sex** | **Department** | | | **Sum** |
|---|---|---|---|---|
| | Dept1 | Dept2 | Dept3 | |
| M | 135 | 80 | 4 | 219 |
| F | 120 | 360 | 33 | 513 |
| **Sum** | 255 | 440 | 37 | 732 |

**Table 5.2** Result of cell suppression on Table 5.1.

| Sex | Department | | | Sum |
|---|---|---|---|---|
| | Dept1 | Dept2 | Dept3 | |
| M | 135 | 80 | – | 219 |
| F | 120 | 360 | – | 513 |
| **Sum** | 255 | 440 | 37 | 732 |

Complementary suppression is also required on Table 5.2, since the suppressed entries can still be inferred from the actual cells of the table. Indeed, in Table 5.2, by subtracting the entries in row 1 or those in row 2 from the total sum of the respective row, we can find out the value of the already suppressed sensitive cells, producing Table 5.3.

Consider the statistic $q(C) = sum(C, A_j)$ and the parameters $k$ and $n$ of the '$n$-respondent, $k$%-dominance' criterion. In Denning (1982) a method to state if $q(C)$ is sensitive is described, based on a relationship between the total value of the sum (that is, $q(C)$) and the partial sum computed on the first $n$ dominant values.

The sum computed on the values of the attribute $A_j$ is $q = a_{j1} + \ldots + a_{jn} + \ldots + a_{jN}$. Let $a_{j1} + \ldots + a_{jn}$ be the first most dominant values in the computation of the sum, with: $a_{j1} \geq \ldots \geq a_{jn} \geq \ldots \geq a_{jN}$.

Posing $d = a_{j1} + \ldots + a_{jn}$ and $q = a_{j1} + \ldots + a_{jn} + \ldots + a_{jN}$, the statistic $q(C)$ is sensitive if $d > (k/100)q$. Posing $q^+ = (100/k)d$, $q(C)$ is sensitive if $q < q^+$.

Concerning complementary suppression, the problem is more complex. A possible approach has been proposed to deal with it, based on estimates of sensitive statistics and on the definition of an interval of estimate for a statistic $q$ (Denning, 1982). Statistics that derive unacceptable estimates are suppressed from the table. In particular, denoting with $\hat{q}$ an estimate of a sensitive statistic $q(C)$, an acceptable upper estimate $q^+$ and an acceptable lower estimate $q^-$ for $q(C)$ are determined:

$$q^+ = (100/k)d$$
$$q^- = (n/m)(100/k)^2 d \quad \text{if } m > n$$
$$q^- = 0 \quad \text{if } m \leq n$$

**Table 5.3** Complementary suppression on Table 5.1.

| Sex | Department | | | Sum |
|---|---|---|---|---|
| | Dept1 | Dept2 | Dept3 | |
| M | – | 80 | – | 219 |
| F | – | 360 | – | 513 |
| **Sum** | 255 | 440 | 37 | 732 |

where $m$ is the size of the query set $X(C)$ associated with $q(C)$. The interval estimate $I = [L_{\hat{q}}, Q_{\hat{q}}]$ for the statistic $q(C)$ is acceptable if it falls below $q^-$, above $q^+$, or if it contains the interval $[q^-, q^+]$.

A modified version of the simplex algorithm of linear programming has been studied to determine the confidence intervals for complementary suppression in two-dimensional tables. Cell suppression might become an intractable technique as tables grow larger. Moreover, the problem of determining a minimum set of cells to be complementary suppressed has a high degree of computational complexity. The main disadvantage of this technique is that it is impractical for general-purpose SDBs where arbitrary statistical queries can be requested through the query system. It would be interesting to study its possible association with a random sampling or data modification technique. In the next subsection we will see how cell suppression has been used in a combined inference protection technique.

### A combined technique

In this subsection we describe the *partial suppression* technique, a restriction-based technique which combines the concepts of the partitioning, query-set size and cell suppression techniques in an integrated approach, with the aim of providing the DBA with a less restricted inference protection technique, releasing a higher number of statistics than those released by the restriction-based techniques separately considered (Chin and Peng, 1987).

Partial suppression operates as follows. First the SDB records are partitioned into a number of distinct subsets (query sets), on the basis of the values of selected indexed attributes (in a relational schema, an attribute is indexed if an index is associated with it, for fast access on records in files; this technique uses only the indexed attributes of the SDB schema for record partitioning); then the query sets whose size does not satisfy the query-set size control are identified and, finally, some predefined conditions are evaluated to decide which query sets must be suppressed.

Let $q(C)$ be a requested statistic; its query set $X(C)$ is called a *basic query set* (BQS) if it corresponds to a single subset resulting from the partitioning technique. A BQS is called an *insufficient query set* (*IQS*) if its size does not verify the query-set size control (that is, if $|X(C)| < k$, see the discussion on query-set size control in Section 5.3.2), and a *sufficient query set (SQS)* otherwise. To graphically show how the partitioning takes place in the SDB, in Figure 5.8 an example of a partition tree is shown, where the records of an *Employee* SDB are partitioned according to the indexed attributes *Sex, Dept-Code* and *Birth-Year*.

The query set corresponding to the characteristic $C$ = (*Sex* = *F* $\wedge$ *Dept-Code* = *Dept1* $\wedge$ *Birth-Year* = *1951*) is an IQS, since its size is 1. The query set corresponding to the characteristic $C$ = (*Sex* = *F* $\wedge$ *Dept-Code* = *Dept1* $\wedge$ *Birth-Year* = *1952*) is an SQS.

After partitioning the SDB records, and identifying the IQSs, some conditions are evaluated to establish which query sets must be suppressed in partial suppression. The conditions are the following:

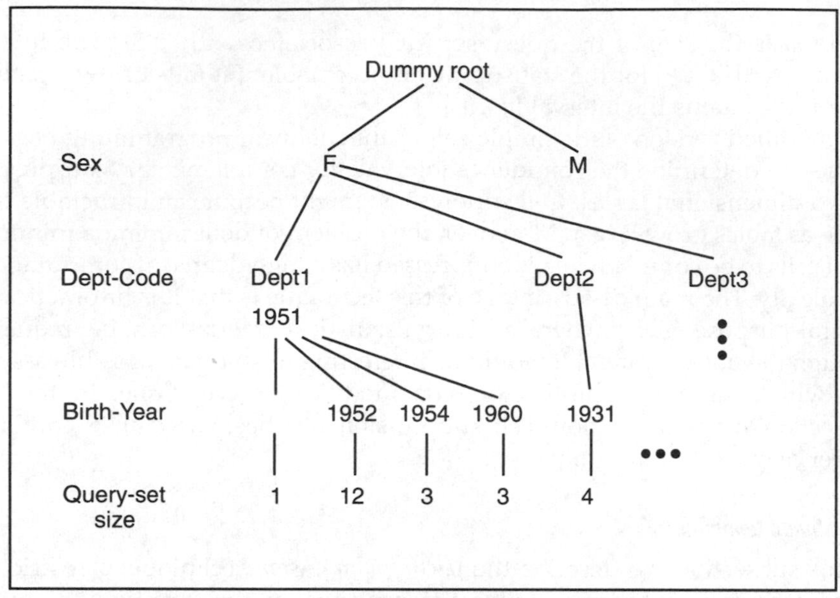


*Figure 5.8* Example of partition tree.

(1) If the characteristic $C$ has either $m$ indexed attributes or $(m-1)$ indexed attributes (not including the $m$-th attribute) connected by $\wedge$ operator, then an IQS is suppressed.

For example, let us consider the IQS of size 1, corresponding to the characteristic $C$ = (*Sex* = *F* $\wedge$ *Dept-Code* = *Dept1* $\wedge$ *Birth-Year* = *1951*). The condition says that this IQS is always suppressed, using both the cell suppression and the partial suppression techniques. If we ask for the query:
$q(C_1)$ = *Count(Sex* = *F* $\wedge$ *Dept-Code* = *Dept1)*
using the cell suppression technique, the response released to the user is 19 (see Figure 5.8). Using the partial suppression technique, the response returned to the user is 18, which is inaccurate, but has the advantage of allowing one to release more statistics. Indeed, the following query:
$q(C_2)$ = *Count(Sex* = *F* $\wedge$ *Dept-Code* = *Dept1* $\wedge$ $\neg$*Birth-Year* = *1951)*
must be suppressed using cell suppression, since, combined with $q(C_1)$, it reveals the size of the sensitive suppressed IQS (that is, $q(C_1) - q(C_2) = 1$). Using partial suppression, the statistic $q(C_2)$ can be released, since the answer released for $q(C_1)$ cannot be used for inference (that is, $q(C_1) - q(C_2) = 0$).

(2) If C involves $(m-1)$ indexed attributes, and the $m$th attribute is one of these $(m-1)$ attributes, an IQS can be released if both the following conditions hold:

(a) there are one or more basic query sets

(b) these basic query sets and the IQS have the same value for the $m$-th attribute.

Let us consider the query $q(C_3)$ = *Count(Sex = F ∧ Birth-Year = 1951)*, containing two indexed attributes. With reference to the partition tree in Figure 5.8, we have that the number $m$ of indexed attributes is $m = 3$, and that the third attribute is *Birth-Year*. Thus, the characteristic $C_3$ specifies both an IQS (that is, (*Sex = F ∧ Dept-Code = Dept1 ∧ Birth-Year = 1951*)), and a basic query set (that is, (*Sex = F ∧ Dept-Code = Dept2 ∧ Birth-Year = 1951*)). As we can note, the two subconditions are verified, and the IQS is not suppressed.

(3) If C involves 1, 2,..., or ($m-2$) indexed attributes, and conditions (1) and (2) are verified, then an IQS can be released.

The partial suppression technique is an attempt to improve the cell suppression technique, by introducing some additional conditions that allow some statistics (that would be suppressed using cell suppression alone either for being sensitive or for complementary suppression) to be released. The drawback is the lack of precision, since some statistics are released with inaccurate answers. To assure acceptable accuracy, an error rate threshold must be defined by the DBA (the error rate threshold can depend on the dimension of the SDB, the size of the query set, and desired magnitude of the error), and the statistics with an error rate greater than the threshold must be restricted, just as with cell suppression. Imprecise statistics satisfying the threshold can be released, assuring protection against inference on the IQSs used for computing the statistics.

### 5.3.3 Perturbation-based techniques

This class of techniques prevents inference by introducing some type of modification during the processing of a statistical query, with the aim of releasing more statistics than the restriction-based techniques. The modification can be applied either to the records stored in the SDB used for computing the requested statistic (*record-based* perturbation techniques), or to the correct result before releasing it to the user (*result-based* perturbation techniques).

Record-based techniques operate on the values of the record stored in the SDB, and generate new 'modified' data that is used as input for statistical query computation. Modification of database contents is enforced following different approaches. A first possibility considers the original SDB as a sample of a population, characterized by a given probability distribution. In this case, the modified SDB is either a different sample from the same distribution, or is the distribution itself. Another approach consists in taking a sample of the records specified by the characteristic formula of the requested statistic, and computing the query on this sample. Another way of working consists in modifying the attribute values in the original SDB, and using these modified values. These techniques may require the creation of a new 'modified' SDB, which is maintained together with the original SDB if the SDB serves general-purpose applications in addition to statistical applications, in order to allow general-purpose applications to work correctly.

Result-based techniques apply the modification to the correctly computed result of a requested statistical query, before releasing it to the user. Basically, they perform some type of rounding on the correct result.

Before illustrating the main perturbation-based techniques, it is necessary to discuss briefly some concepts typical of this class of inference controls, namely *bias* and *consistency*. Since a modification is introduced on the computed statistics, there is a difference between the true value and the released value of a statistic. Such a difference is called bias, and affects the accuracy and precision of the released statistics (Matloff, 1986). The bias should be as small as possible, better if zero, to guarantee high precision in the information provided to the user. The perturbation scheme should be properly designed to minimize the introduced bias. The bias problem will be studied when the specific techniques are described.

Another important concept for this class of techniques is consistency: that is, the absence of contradictions and paradoxes. Contradictions happen when, for example, linear equations are not verified between statistics (that is, the *Sum* statistic requested on a row in a table has a value different from the value obtained by requesting the *Sum* statistic on the single entries of the same row), or when repetitions of the same statistic have different results. Perturbed statistics must also be free of paradoxes, meaning that answers consistent with the semantics of the statistic must be released (for example, a *Count* statistic cannot be negative).

In the following subsections, we describe the main perturbation-based protection techniques.

#### *Data swapping*

This technique, also called *multidimensional transformation* (Schlörer, 1981), generates a modified SDB where the first $t$-order statistics (a $t$-order statistic is a statistic computed over $t$ attributes $(A_1,\ldots,A_t)$ of the SDB records) are correct (that is, they coincide with those of the original SDB), for some parameter $t$, and the higher ones are not necessarily correct.

The term data swapping derives from the fact that the technique exchanges attribute values between the records of the original SDB, in such a way that the resulting modified SDB has no records in common with the original SDB, while ensuring both inference protection and correctness of the released (first $t$-order) statistics.

The data swapping technique is based on concepts and properties defined for matrices, and then extended to SDBs, under the hypothesis that SDB records are not key-identified and that the SDB is of static type (this is commonly true for special-purpose SDBs). The extension is based on the possibility of mapping the records of an SDB into a matrix.

Let $D$ be an SDB consisting of a set of $N$ records, $D = (x_1,\ldots, x_N)$ characterized by $A_1, \ldots, A_M$ attributes. For each attribute $A_j$ having $c_j$ possible values in the set $M_j = \{a_{j1}, \ldots, a_{jcj}\}$, we define a function $f_j$ that maps the set $M_j$ of each attribute in the set of non-negative integers $N_0 = \{0,1, 2, \ldots\}$, namely:

$$f_j : M_j \rightarrow N_0 \mid f_j(a_{jk}) = k-1, j = 1 \ldots M, k = 1 \ldots c_j$$

Let $F$ be the set of the functions $f_j$, namely $F = \{f_j\}$.

$F(D)$ is called the *image matrix* of $D$ on the set $N_0$, which is a matrix of size $(N \times M)$. The image matrix is used as a reference for deriving the framework to formally demonstrate the hypothesis and theorems underlying the technique. In particular, let us see when matrix $M$ over the set $N_0$ (and, consequently, the SDB $D$ such that $F(D)=M$) is $d$-transformable.

*d-transformable matrix*. An $(n \times m)$-size matrix $M$ is *d-transformable* if at least one $(n \times m)$-size matrix $T$ exists, called d-transform, such that:

(i) $M$ and $T$ are $d$-equivalent, and
(ii) $M$ and $T$ are row disjoint, namely they have no common row.

Let us define the meaning of $d$-equivalence for matrices.

*Equivalent matrices*. Two matrices $A$ and $B$ are equivalent if a row permutation $\sigma$ exists such that: $\sigma(A) = B \leftrightarrow \sigma^{-1}(B) = A$

*Analogue matrices*. Let $A$ and $B$ be two $(n \times m)$-size matrixes. Let $A^p = (A^{j1}, ..., A^{jp})$ and $B^p = (B^{k1}, ..., B^{kp})$ two $(n \times p)$-size submatrices of $A$ and $B$, respectively, with $p = 1 \ldots m$, where $A^i$ $(B^i)$ is a column vector of $A^p(B^p)$. $A^p$ and $B^p$ are analogue submatrices of $A$ and $B$ if:

$j_i = k_i, i = 1, \ldots, p$

*d-equivalent matrixes*. Let $d \in \{0, 1, \ldots, m\}$. Two matrices $A$ and $B$ are $d$-equivalent if all the possible pairs of analogue $(n \times d)$-size submatrices are equivalent.

Thus, given a pair $\{M, T\}$ of mutual $d$-transformable matrices, also called *d-pair*, the SDB $D$ that has $M$ as its image matrix is $d$-transformable too: that is, it can be transformed into a new SDB $D'$, with $D' = F(T)$. Given a $d$-pair $\{D, D'\}$ of SDBs, their records have different contents, but the $k$-order statistics, with $1 \leq k \leq d$, are identical. Therefore, $D'$ can be used instead of $D$ to release the first $d$-order statistics, without losing statistical accuracy, and preventing inference. In practice, $D'$ is obtained from $D$ by swapping the attribute values among the records of $D$, preserving the statistics. For example, to preserve 1-order counts means that the same number of attribute values and the same values for a given attribute $A_j$ must exist in both $D$ and $D'$, and this facilitates the swap among the records.

Depending on the way the statistics are released, the data swapping technique can be physically applied or not. Precisely, with dedicated SDBs in tabular form, the original SDB is physically transformed into a $d$-transformed SDB, by properly swapping attribute values between records. This mode is not suitable for general-purpose databases, where the correctness and accuracy of released information is a crucial requirement, especially for non-statistical queries. In this case, it is sufficient to demonstrate that the SDB is $d$-transformable and to release only the $k$-order statistics, for $k = 0, 1, \ldots, d$, without applying the transformation. (Note, however, that efficient algorithms for testing if an SDB is $d$-transformable are not available.)

An SDB $D$ is $d$-transformable if the following conditions are verified:

- the records of $D$ must have at least $m \geq d+1$ attributes;
- $D$ must contain at least $N \geq (\bar{M}/2)2^d$ records, where $\bar{M}$ is the maximum size of the sets $M_j$, $j = 1, \ldots, M$ of the possible values of the attributes $A_1, \ldots, A_M$ of $D$.

An extension to the data swapping technique has been studied, called *approximate data swapping*, defined for non-numerical, and precisely Boolean, attributes, but applicable also to numerical attributes (Reiss, 1984). With this technique, studied for SDBs that release macrostatistics, a transformed SDB $D'$ of the original SDB $D$ is randomly generated considering a portion of $D$, record by record, with values taken from a distribution defined with the $k$-order statistics of the original SDB $D$.

To summarize, the level of protection offered by data swapping increases by decreasing $d$, while the statistical information the user can acquire from the SDB decreases. Efficient criteria and algorithms are needed to test an SDB for $d$-transformability, in order to apply the technique to dynamic on-line SDBs.

#### Random-sample queries

This technique draws inspiration from the random sampling principle used by the US Census Bureau agencies to protect their SDBs against inference, which consists in releasing statistics computed on small samples of the whole population. The *random-sample queries* technique adapts the idea of using samples to dynamic SDBs, by constructing samples from the query sets associated with statistical queries, instead of from the whole SDB (Denning, 1980). Inference protection is enforced by avoiding the user having control over the composition of query sets, which are randomly generated.

The basic mechanism of the random-sample queries technique consists in replacing the query set associated with a statistical query with a *sampled query set*, composed of a subset of properly selected records belonging to the original query set. The requested statistic is then computed on the sampled query set. A selection function $f(C,i)$ is defined for selecting records from the original query set associated with a requested statistic $q(C)$.

The function $f$ is designed in such a way that each record $i$ belonging to the query set $X(C)$ has a sampling probability $p$ of being selected, which can be defined by the DBA. The selection function is implemented using two functions $r(i)$ and $g(C)$, which map the records and the characteristic into sequences of symbols. In particular, the function $r(i)$ maps the $i$-th record $i$ into a random sequence of $m \geq k$ bits. The function $g(C)$ maps the characteristic C into a string of length $m$ over the alphabet $\{0,1,*\}$, where the symbol '*' denotes 'don't care'. This string includes exactly $k$ bits and $m-k$ asterisks. To implement functions $r$ and $g$, encryption algorithms (for example, DES) are suitable.

The inclusion of a record $x_i$ in the sampled query set is decided on the basis of the matching between $r(i)$ and $g(C)$. A match exists between $r(i)$ and $g(C)$ if each symbol different from '*' in $g(C)$ is identical to the corresponding symbol in $r(i)$.

The definition of the function $f(C,i)$ depends on the value of the probability $p$. More precisely, when $p < \frac{1}{2}$, the function is defined as follows:

$$f(C,i) \begin{cases} = 1 \text{ if } r(i) \text{ matches } g(C) \\ = 0 \text{ otherwise} \end{cases}$$

For $p > \frac{1}{2}$, the function is 1 if $r(i)$ does not match $g(C)$, and is 0 otherwise.

The sampled query set $X^*(C)$ is composed of all records selected from $X(C)$ using $f(C,i)$, that is:

$X^*(C) = \{i \in X(C) \mid f(C,i) = 1\}$

The sampling probability $p$ may be independent of the query-set size (fixed probability), or dependent on the query set (variable probability).

If $p$ is large and fixed, a minimum query-set size restriction should be imposed, for dealing with small-size query sets. Indeed, large values of $p$ lead to selecting all the records of small query sets, thus making inference probable. On the other hand, small values of $p$ are not suitable, since, to guarantee accuracy in the released statistics, a large number of records should be included in the sampled query set.

A possible solution consists in choosing a variable probability $p$, which proportionally decreases with the size of the query set. To implement this latter approach, different possibilities have been envisaged, whose choice depends on how the records are organized in the SDB. For example, it is possible first to determine the query set, together with the probability $p$, and then to compute the requested statistic on the sampled query set.

Another possibility consists in computing several answers for the requested statistic, corresponding to different values of $p$, and in selecting one answer among the set of computed answers, on the basis of the query set size of the requested statistic. A third possibility consists in assigning to $p$ a value proportional to the reciprocal of the number of examined records preceding the first record included in the sampled query set.

To guarantee the consistency of the released statistics, the selection function should be defined in such a way that equivalent statistics return the same result, to prevent averaging attacks. To guarantee that equivalent but lexicographically different queries generate identical query sets, characteristic formulas should be reduced to normal form. Reduction to normal form can be obtained, for example, by restricting the syntax of the queries (for example, to logical AND).

Let us discuss now the accuracy of the random-sample queries technique. Using the selection function $f(C,i)$ previously described, the relative frequencies and the averages computed on the sampled query sets hold the following values :

$$Rfreq^*(C) = (|\, X^*(C)\, |) \,/\, (pN)$$

$$Avg^*(C,A_j) = \frac{1}{|x^*(C)|} \Sigma_{i \in X^*(C)}\, x_{ij}$$

The expected value of $|\, X^*(C)\, |$ is $p \,|\, X(C)\, |$, and the expected value of the sampled frequency is $|\, X(C)\, | \,/ N$: that is, the real frequency. The values of $p$ and $N$ may be notified by the DBA, to enable the users to evaluate the accuracy of the obtained estimates. Using these known values, the user can compute also the true and sampled *Count* and *Sum* statistics, exploiting the sampled values *Rfreq** and *Avg**, and the relationships existing between these statistics (see Section 5.2).

The random-sample queries technique introduces an error in statistic computation, owing to the fact that the statistics are computed on sampled query sets. The relative error $f_c$ between the sampled frequency and a true frequency is given by:

$$f_c = \frac{Rfreq^*(C) - Rfreq(C)}{Rfreq(C)}$$

The sampled relative frequency is an unbiased estimator of the true relative frequency, since the expected relative error is zero. The root-mean-squared relative error $\hat{R}(f_c)$ is:

$$\hat{R}(f_c) = \sqrt{\frac{1-p}{p\,|X(C)|}}$$

That is, the relative error $f_c$ is a function of the sampling probability $p$, and of the query-set size $|X(C)|$. In general, for small query sets, the error might be unacceptably high. It can be decreased by increasing the value of $p$; however, high values of $p$ increase the risk of compromise, since the probability of a record being included in the sampled query set increases. A minimum query-set size restriction is then required, to avoid unacceptable errors in released statistics, affecting their accuracy.

Absolute errors for *Count* statistics are higher than the corresponding errors for *Rfreq* statistics by a factor of N, while the relative errors are comparable. The same holds for *Sums*.

The relative error $a_{c,j}$ between the sampled average and the true average is given by:

$$a_{c,j} = \frac{Avg^*(C,A_j) - Avg(C,A_j)}{Avg\,(C,A_j)}$$

The relative error for the *Avg* statistic is a function of the sampling probability $p$, of the query set size $|X(C)|$, and of the value distribution in the selected field. Let $E(x)$ be the mean of the values of attribute $A_j$ in the query set $X(C)$, that is, $E(x) = Avg(C,A_j)$, and let $Var(x)$ be their variance. The sampled value $Avg^*(C,A_j)$ is a biased estimator of the true value $Avg(C,A_j)$. The expected relative error is:

$$E(Avg^*(C,A_j)) = E\,(x)(1-(1-p)^{|X(C)|})$$

$Avg^*(C,A_j)$ can be divided by $(1-(1-p)^{|X(C)|})$ to obtain an unbiased estimator. Thus, for sufficiently large-size query sets the mean-square relative error is approximately:

$$\hat{R}(a_{c,j}) \cong Var(x)^{1/2}/E(x)\,\hat{R}(f_c)$$

where $Var(x)^{1/2}/E(x)$ is the coefficient of variation for the distribution of values of attribute $A_j$. Experiments have shown that, for uniformly distributed values, relative errors for the statistic *Avg* are about 40% lower than those of the *Rfreq* statistic. Moreover, for fixed $p$, the expected error of both statistics decreases with the square root of the query set size.

#### Specific attacks

The random-sample queries technique has been tested against possible attacks and, precisely, against attacks based on small-size query sets, and on error removal techniques. Tracker-based attacks have also been studied, and they were unsuccessful with the random-sample queries technique.

Now, an example illustrates how attacks based on **small-size query sets** (for example, query sets of size 0 or 1) can compromise the SDB with the random-sample queries technique. Suppose a user knows that an individual, represented by the record $x_i$ in the SDB, matches a characteristic *C*, and that *Rfreq(C)* = 1/*N*. The user can then discover whether that individual has an additional property *A* by requesting the statistic *Rfreq*($C \wedge A$), and examining the returned value. If this value is still 1/*N*, then the individual has the property *A*; if this value is 0, the property does not hold for the individual. These values are useful for compromising the SDB if the user can assume, with a high probability, that the sampled value *Rfreq*(C)* = 1/*N* (or 0) is a good estimate of the true *Rfreq(C)* = 1/*N* (or 0), and this is true for large values of *p*. Thus, to avoid these types of attack, a minimum query-set size restriction should be imposed, or a variable probability *p* should be adopted, as already pointed out.

The random-sample queries technique is exposed to those attacks that aim at **removing errors** due to the sampling mechanism. Let *q(C)* be a statistic characterized by a query set *X(C)*. Two types of attack have been studied.

One type of attack consists in requesting a set of equivalent statistical queries, namely, statistics specifying the same query set *X(C)* but different sampled query sets, and in averaging the responses returned by the system for such queries.

A second type of attack consists in averaging the responses returned by the system for a set of statistics specifying disjoint subsets of *X(C)*.

The statistics $q(C_1),\ldots,q(C_m)$ are equivalent to *q(C)* if their characteristic formulas $C_1, \ldots, C_m$ specify the same query set *X(C)*, but different sampled query sets, namely:

$$C_1, \ldots, C_m \mid X(C_i) = X(C), \text{ and } X^*(C_i) \neq X^*(C), i = 1 \ldots m$$

An estimate $\hat{q}(C)$ of the true value of *q(C)* is given by:

$$\hat{q}(C) = \frac{1}{m} \sum_{i=1}^{m} q^*(C_i)$$

that is, by averaging the sampled values returned for the equivalent statistics $q(C_1), \ldots, q(C_m)$.

For example, given the statistic *q(C)* = *(Sex = M)* $\wedge$ *(Dept-Code = Dept1)*, an example of equivalent statistics is the following:

$q(C_1)$ = *(Sex =* $\neg$ *F)* $\wedge$ *(Dept-Code = Dept1)*
$q(C_2)$ = *(Sex = M)* $\wedge$ $\neg$*((Dept-Code = Dept2)* $\vee$ *(Dept-Code = Dept3))*

To prevent this type of attack, the function *g* should reduce the characteristics to normal form, assuring that the same sampled query set is generated for equivalent characteristics (namely, *g(C)= g(D)* if *C* and *D* are equivalent). Unfortunately, the problem of reducing a characteristic to normal form is intractable.

Consider the statistics $q(C_1), \ldots, q(C_m)$ where the characteristics $C_1, \ldots, C_m$ specify disjoint subsets of the query set *X(C)*:

$$X(C_i) \cap X(C_j) = \emptyset, i \neq j$$

and

$$X(C) = X(C_1) \cup \ldots \cup X(C_m)$$

An estimate $\hat{q}(C)$ of the true value of $q(C)$ is given by:

$$\hat{q}(C) = \frac{1}{m} \sum_{i=1}^{m} \hat{q}(C_i)$$

namely, by averaging the values of the estimates $\hat{q}(C_i)$ of each statistic $q(C_i)$ defined over the disjoint subsets.

It has been proved that, using the first type of attack, a lower bound to the number $m$ of queries needed to achieve a sufficiently accurate estimate of the true value for a statistic *Rfreq* is given by the following value:

$$m \geq (3.92)^2 \left(\frac{1-p}{p}\right) | X(C) | > 15 | X(C) | \left(\frac{1-p}{p}\right)$$

For a fixed value of the sampling probability $p$, the function grows linearly with the query set size $| X(C) |$. Consequently, for small query sets few queries are required, while several queries are required for large query sets. For example, with $p = 0.5$, 10 queries are required for query sets of size 10, while more than 450 queries are required for query sets of size 30, and more than 1500 queries for query sets of size 100. Thus, a query-set size restriction technique is suggested to overcome the problems posed by small query sets.

For *Avg* statistics on variables uniformly distributed over the range $[1,s]$, it has been proved that a lower bound for the number $m$ of queries needed to achieve a sufficiently accurate estimate of the true value is given by the following value:

$$m \geq 128\ (1-p)/(p)\ | X(C) |$$

This means that more queries are required for *Avg* statistics than those required for *Rfreq* statistics, to estimate the true value of a given statistic.

In summary, with large query sets, the random-sample queries technique guarantees protection against attacks employing trackers. It also provides protection against manual attacks based on averaging the sampled responses, since the number of queries required to obtain accurate estimates is large enough. The control can be circumverted by automated averaging attacks, using a computer which systematically generates the necessary statistics. The possibility of using a sampling function $g$ able to transform the characteristics into normal form, thus recognizing equivalent characteristics, is required, to avoid attacks averaging the responses to equivalent statistics. Attacks averaging responses to statistics on disjoint query sets can still be a problem, and auditing mechanisms are necessary to keep track of and analyse the set of statistics required to perform such an attack.

#### Fixed perturbation

The fixed perturbation technique consists in modifying the values of the attributes used in the computation of statistics, and the statistics are computed using the perturbed values (Traub *et al.*, 1984). The perturbation does not vary from query to query.

This technique was studied for linear statistics and for numerical attributes, and its extension to generic queries requires further study. A linear statistic is a statistic $q(C)$ of the form:

$$q(C) = \Sigma_{i \in X(C)} x_{ij}$$

where $x_{1j},\ldots,x_{nj}$ are the values of a numerical attribute $A_j$ for each of the $n$ records belonging to the query set $X(C)$ of the requested statistic.

Let $N$ be the size of the SDB. According to the perturbation scheme, each true value $x_{ij}$, $i= 1,\ldots, N$ of an attribute $A_j$ is replaced by a perturbed value $x'_{ij}$:

$$x'_{ij} = x_{ij} + e_i, \quad i = 1, \ldots, N$$

The vector $e = (x' - x) = (e_1, \ldots, e_N)$ is a random perturbation vector, and $x = (x_{1j},\ldots,x_{Nj})$, $x' = (x'_{1j},\ldots,x'_{Nj})$ are the vectors of the true and perturbed values, respectively, of the records in the SDB, for attribute $A_j$. The components of vector $e$ are independent random variables, and the expected value of the vector is null. Each component of the vector $e$ has the following expected value and variance:

$$E(e_i) = 0, \text{Var}(e_i) = \sigma^2$$

Since the perturbation covers the whole SDB and is the same for all the queries, the estimation of a response cannot be improved by repeating the query.

Let us suppose that the perturbations $e_i$ are identically distributed, and let us consider a linear statistic $q(C)$. Owing to Chebyshev inequality, the probability that the error in the query exceeds a given bound ε is:

$$P(|q'(C) - q(C)| \geq |\varepsilon \mid X(C)|) \leq \frac{\sigma 2}{(|X(C)|\varepsilon 2)}$$

where $q'(C)$ indicates the statistic computed using the perturbed values.

The probability is defined in terms of the variance $\sigma^2$ of the perturbation, of the error bound ε, and of the size $|X(C)|$ of the query set of the involved statistic $q(C)$. A trade-off has to be achieved in choosing the value of σ, to cope with the needs both of the user, for accuracy of the released statistics (σ should be maintained small and modifications minimal), and of the DBA, for high SDB protection (σ should be maintained high to have large perturbations).

In general, we observe that the probability of error decreases with the size of the query set, and, thus, the larger the size of the query set, the higher the accuracy of the corresponding statistic. However, cases may occur where, given a perturbed vector $x'$, the difference $|q'(C) - q(C)|$ is relevant, even for very large query sets. To cope with these cases, a possible solution consists in checking the amount of the error $|q'(C) - q(C)|$ to verify whether it exceeds the fixed threshold. If the error is too high, and if $|X(C))|$ is greater than a certain threshold value $n_o$ (defined by the DBA), then a correction mechanism is invoked. This mechanism consists in adding to the true statistic $q(C)$ a random variable *Per(C)*, which has null mean and variance $\sigma_1^2$, selected so that $| Per(C) |$ satisfies the error bound.

By adopting this solution, studies have proved that the SDB is exposed to compromise. Indeed, compromise can be achieved by finding *compromising query sets*: that is, query sets whose size exceeds $n_o$, and by exploiting the correction mechanism invoked by such query sets. However, the number of queries required to find a compromising set is exponential, and makes the compromise of the SDB unfeasible.

The perturbation can be statically applied, that is, the attribute values are permanently modified in the SDB, or dynamically applied, that is, perturbed values are computed at the time they are accessed, for query computation. This second mode is suitable for general-purpose SDBs, where common applications are served in addition to the statistical ones.

Additive perturbation, described so far, can pose scale problems, owing to the magnitude of the attribute value to be protected and the value of the perturbation applied (for example, too small perturbations applied to very high attribute values can lead to compromise). To avoid such problems, multiplicative perturbations can be applied.

Fixed-perturbation techniques have also been studied for non-numerical attributes (Warner, 1965; Abul-Ela *et al.*, 1967). With these techniques, the DBA should balance the accuracy of released statistics and the protection level provided on the SDB, by properly setting the parameters employed to apply the perturbation to the attribute values.

#### *Query-based perturbation*

This technique generates a perturbation on the attribute values used for computing a query on the SDB, and the perturbation varies from query to query (Beck, 1980).

Let $x_{ij}$ be a value of attribute $A_j$ for the *i*-th record in the SDB. Given a statistic $q(C)$, this technique applies a modification function $f$ to each attribute value $x_{ij}$ of the records belonging to the query set $X(C)$ of $q(C)$, to generate a modified value $x'_{ij}= f(x_{ij})$, which is used for computing $q(C)$.

Before describing this technique in detail, we give the definition of 'compromise' considered by this technique. Owing to the modification applied by the technique, the user knows only an estimate $\hat{x}_{ij}$ of the true value $x_{ij}$ of an attribute. Let $\sigma(\hat{x}_{ij})$ be the standard deviation of such an estimate, and $E(\hat{x}_{ij}) = x_{ij}$ its expected value.

The SDB is said to be *compromisable* if a user can obtain an estimate $\hat{x}_{ij}$ of the true value $x_{ij}$ of an attribute $A_j$ such that:

$$\sigma(\hat{x}_{ij}) < f(x_{ij})$$

where $f$ is the modification function, depending on the true value $x_{ij}$, and, possibly, on other SDB parameters. An SDB is said to be *statistically compromisable* if:

$$\sigma(\hat{x}_{ij}) < c \mid x_{ij} - \overline{x}_j \mid$$

where $c$ is a constant for the SDB selected by the DBA, and $\bar{x}_j$ is the mean value of the attribute $A_j$.

To define the function $f$, issues to be taken into account involve the magnitude of the values to be modified (the applied modification is different, depending on the magnitude of the values to be protected); the nature of the values to be modified (the values far from the mean value $\bar{x}_j$ require more 'masking'); the supplementary knowledge of the user about the attribute values (the function $f$ should guarantee that the supplementary knowledge of the user is not further increased).

We describe the modification function and show how the technique works for the *Sum* and *Count* statistics.

Considering ***Sum* statistics** (that is, $q(C) = Sum(C,A_j)$, where $A_j$ is the attribute on which the sum is computed), let $n$ be the number of records of the query set $X(C)$. The mean value of $A_j$ in the query set is denoted by $\bar{x}_{Cj}$.

The mean value of $A_j$ over the entire SDB is denoted by $\bar{x}_j$. The statistic $Sum(C,A_j)$ is computed on the modified values $x'_{ij}$ of attribute $A_j$ of the involved records, originating the perturbed value $S'$:

$$S' = \sum_{i=1}^{n} x'_{ij}$$

with:

$$x'_{ij} = x_{ij} + z_1(x_{ij} - \bar{x}_{C_j}) + z_2$$

where $z_1$ and $z_2$ are independent random variables generated for each record. The expected values and variances of $z_1$ and $z_2$ are given by:

$$E(z_1) = 0 \quad Var(z_1) = 2a^2$$

$$E(z_2) = 0 \quad Var(z_2) = \frac{2a^2}{n}(\bar{x}_{C_j} - \bar{x}_j)^2$$

where $a$ is a parameter constant for all queries. The modified response $S'$ is an unbiased estimator for the true value $S$ of the requested sum, since its expected value is $S$:

$$E[S'] = E[\sum_{i=1}^{n} x'_{ij}] = \sum_{i=1}^{n} x_{ij} = S$$

exploiting the fact that the expected values of the random variables $z_1$ and $z_2$ are zero.

The variance of $S'$ is given by:

$$Var(S') = 2na^2s^2_C + 2a^2(\bar{x}_{C_j} - \bar{x}_j)^2$$

where $s^2_C = \Sigma(x_{ij} - \bar{x}_{C_j})^2/n$ is the sample variance computed over the query set $X(C)$.

The variance of $S'$ has the property of growing whenever the values $x_{ij}$ in the query set $X(C)$ become very different from each other ($s^2_C$ grows), and whenever the values $x_{ij}$ in $XC$ are very far from the average value ( $(\bar{x}_{C_j} - \bar{x}_j)^2$ grows).

A lower bound for the standard deviation of the estimator $S'$ is given by:

$$\sigma(S') > a \mid x_{ij} - \bar{x}_j \mid$$

for each record $i$ in the query set $X(C)$.

Considering the relationship previously given for statistical compromisability, posing $a \geq c$, the variance is sufficiently large to avoid compromise, and the minimum number of statistics required to compromise the SDB is at least $(a/c)^2$. Thus, by increasing the value of $a$, the number of statistics needed for SDB compromise grows, and compromise can be prevented. However, increasing the value of $a$ causes the variance of the perturbed responses also to increase. It is then necessary to find a trade-off between the level of protection offered by the technique and the accuracy of the released statistics. To this purpose, a method based on proper selection of the random variables $z_1$ and $z_2$ used for perturbation has been studied. As mentioned before, these variables are generated for each record of the query set and for each query. For each record in a query set consider the independent random variables:

$$z_1^{(1)}, z_1^{(2)}, \ldots, z_1^{(j)}$$

and

$$z_2^{(1)}, z_2^{(2)}, \ldots, z_2^{(j)}$$

By posing:

$$E(z_1^{(i)}) = 0 \qquad Var(z_1^{(i)}) = 2a^2$$
$$E(z_2)^{(i)} = 0 \qquad Var(z_2^{(i)}) = \frac{2a^2}{n}(x_{C_j} - \bar{x}_j)^2$$

with $1 \leq i \leq j$, and by taking for each record $x_i$ the quantities:

$$z_1 = \Sigma_{i=1}^{i} z_1^{(i)}$$
$$z_2 = \Sigma_{i=1}^{i} z_2^{(i)}$$

we obtain:

$$E(z_1)= 0 \; Var(z_1) = 2ja^2$$
$$E(z_2) = 0 \; Var(z_2) = \frac{2ja^2}{n}(\bar{x}_{C_j} - \bar{x}_j)^2$$

The variance of $S'$ is given by:

$$Var(S') = 2jna^2s_C^2 + 2ja^2(\bar{x}_{C_j} - \bar{x})^2$$

and therefore:

$$\sigma_{S'} > y\sqrt{j}\,(|\, x_{ij} - \bar{x}_j\,|)$$

That is, the standard deviation of $S'$ increases by $j^{1/2}$.

Using this method, the number of queries needed for compromise grows exponentially with $j$, while the standard deviation of the responses has a less than linear increase, under the following hypothesis:

- the random variables $z_1$ and $z_2$ are generated as the sum of $j$ random variables, where the parameter is decided by the DBA, taking into account that, by increasing the value of $j$, the number of queries required for compromise also grows;
- the values of $z_1^j$ and $z_2^j$ are modified for each query;
- for every $d = \lfloor (a/c)^2 \rfloor$ changes in $z_1^i$ and $z_2^i$, the values of $z_1^{i-1}$ and $z_2^{i-1}$ vary, too.

For ***Count* statistics**, let $n$ be the query set size. This technique must prevent users from obtaining an estimator $\hat{n}$ such that:

$$\sigma_{\hat{n}} < c_1$$

Setting $c_1$ to a sufficiently large value, the response is properly biased to avoid inference.

The perturbed value $n'$ returned to a *Count* statistic is computed as follows:

$$n' = \sum_{i=3}^{n} z_3$$

with $E(z_3) = 1$ and $Var(z_3) = a_1^2/n$, under the hypothesis that the values of $z_3$ are generated independently for every record $x_i$ in the query set $X(C)$ and for each query. Moreover, $z_3$'s values are not stored in the SDB.

The expected value and the variance of $n'$ are given by:

$$E(n') = n$$
$$\mathrm{Var}(n') = a_1^2$$

Under this perturbation scheme, the number of queries needed to compromise the SDB is at least $(a_1/c_1)$ queries.

Also with *Count* statistics, the protection level offered by the technique can be improved by properly generating the random variable $z_3$. That is:

$$z_3 = \sum_{i=1}^{j} z_3^{(i)}$$

with:

$$E(z_3^{(i)}) = \frac{1}{j}$$
$$Var(z_3^{(i)}) = \frac{a_1^2}{n}$$

Then, for $z_3$ we have that:

$$E(z_3) = 1$$
$$Var(z_3) = \frac{ja_1^2}{n}$$

In this case, the minimum number of queries required for SDB compromise $d_1$ increases exponentially: that is, $d_1 = (\lfloor (a_1/c_1)^2 \rfloor)^j$.

#### *A combined technique*

In this subsection we describe the PRD perturbation technique, which is a perturbation-based technique combining the concepts of partitioning, random-sample queries, and data perturbation in an integrated approach (Chin and Peng, 1987). With this technique, inference problems pointed out in the previously described techniques are avoided, since the sample is selected before the query is processed and, consequently, the responses are always consistent, regardless of the number of submissions of a query.

The PRD perturbation technique operates as follows. First, the SDB records are partitioned into query sets according to the values of selected indexed attributes. The partitioning principles used in this technique are the same as those of the partial suppression technique, described in Section 5.3.2, subsection 'A combined technique'.

On the resulting SDB partition, a query-set size control is applied, and Sufficient Query Sets (SQSs) are randomly sampled, while data of the records belonging to Insufficient Query Sets (IQSs) are perturbed.

The perturbation scheme used for data modification is similar to the scheme described in the previous subsection, namely:

$$x'_{ij} = x_{ij} + v\,[z_1(x_{ij} - \overline{x}_{C_j}) + z_2]$$

where $x'_{ij}$ denotes the perturbed value of attribute $A_j$ for the $i$-th record of the selected IQS; $x_{ij}$ denotes the true value; $\overline{x}_{C_j}$ is the mean value of the attribute $A_j$ in the IQS; $v = e$ when $|\, x_{ij} - \overline{x}_{C_j} \,| \leq b$, and $v = 1$ otherwise, with $e$ and $b$ parameters to be set by the DBA. The remaining items in the formula have the same meaning as those described in the previous subsection.

For example, let us consider the partition tree shown in Figure 5.8, with the query set size parameter $k = 2$.

If a user asks for the following *Sum* query:

$q_1(C) = Sum(Sex = F \wedge Dept\text{-}Code = Dept1, Salary)$

the basic query sets are sampled by a certain sampling rate (for example, 7/8), giving rise to the sampled partition tree shown in Figure 5.9.

The IQS corresponding to the characteristic $C = (Sex = F \wedge Dept\text{-}Code = Dept1 \wedge Birth\text{-}Year = 1951)$ is perturbed using the perturbation scheme previously illustrated, assuming $b = 1$, $e = 10$, $z_1 = 0.1$, and $z_2 = 0.2$. This way, the true value 15 is perturbed into 13.06, since $v = 1$, and $\overline{x}_{C_j} = 36.38$.

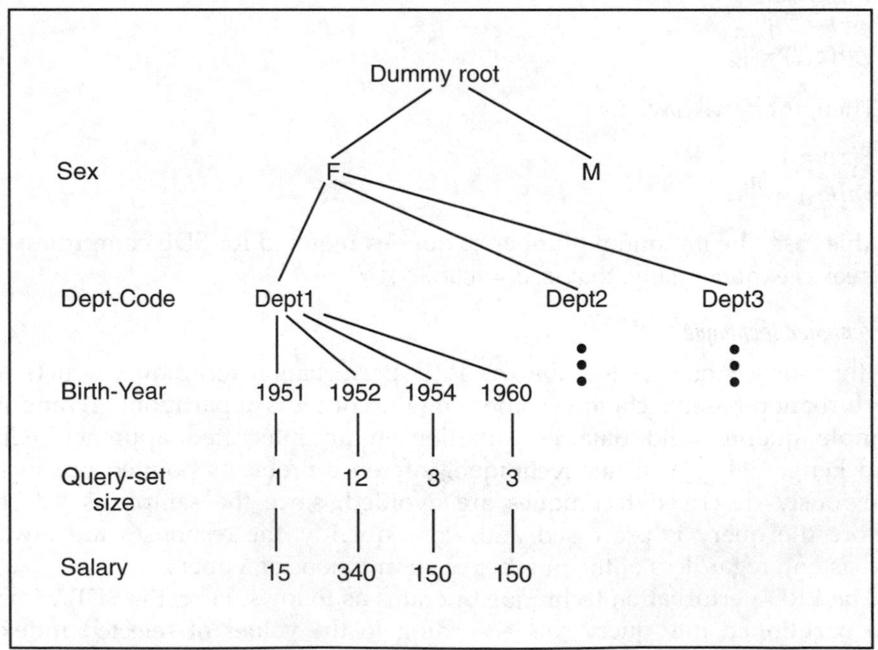


*Figure 5.9* Sampled partition tree.

The (perturbed) response to the query $q_1$ returned to the user is computed considering the salary data for the sampled SQS, and the perturbed data of the IQS, averaged on the sampled query set, times the true query set: that is, by computing

$$q_1(C) = [(13.06 + 340 + 150 + 150)/18] \times 19 = 689.34$$

with an acceptable error degree with respect to the true value (that is, the error degree is $(689.34-655)/655 = 0.052$, where 655 is the true value of $q_1$).

The main advantages of this technique are related to the following issues:

- The number of query sets to be sampled is reduced to only the SQSs, since a query-set size control is used to decide the query sets on which the sampling is to be applied.
- Inconsistencies arising from query repetitions are avoided (see 'Random-sample queries', above), since the sample is computed before the query is submitted, also reducing the query processing time.
- The time required for data perturbation is reduced with respect to the technique described in 'Query-based perturbation' above, since a query-set size control is used and the perturbation is applied only to IQSs.

### *Rounding*

This technique perturbs the response computed for a statistic, rather than the values used in determining the response, and it is considered a result-based perturbation technique.

The term 'rounding' derives from the fact that the response values are rounded before being released. Precisely, the true response $Q$ to a statistic $q(C)$ is rounded up or down to the nearest multiple of a certain base $b$ through a rounding function $r(Q)$ that produces a new modified response $Q' = r(Q)$. Depending on how the rounding function is defined, the following types of rounding are identified:

- systematic rounding
- random rounding
- controlled rounding

Let $Q'$ be the modified result computed for a requested statistic $q(C)$, $b' = \lfloor (b+1)/2 \rfloor$ ($\lfloor\rfloor$ denotes the rounding down to the nearest integer), and $d = Q \ mod \ b$.

Let us describe how the rounding function $r(q)$ is defined in each type of rounding technique.

In **systematic rounding**, $r(q)$ is defined as:

$$r(Q) = \begin{cases} Q & \text{if } d = 0 \\ Q-d & \text{if } d < b' \\ Q+b-d & \text{if } d \geq b' \end{cases}$$

From this definition of $r(Q)$, a user can deduce that the true value $Q$ is in the interval

$$[Q' - b' + 1, Q' + b'-1].$$

Taking advantage of these relationships, systematic rounding allows a user to go back to the true values of the responses, in special cases (for example, under the hypothesis that a set of *Sum* queries is requested over disjoint query sets, and that some relationships are verified between the intervals of such queries (Denning, 1982)). Studied have been performed on the possibility of circumventing systematic rounding through tracker-based attacks.

In **random rounding**, $r(Q)$ is defined as follows:

$$r(Q) = \begin{cases} Q & \text{if } d = 0 \\ Q-d & \text{with probability } 1 - p \\ Q+(b-d) & \text{with probability } p \end{cases}$$

In the case of $p = d/b$, this type of rounding is unbiased. However, by adopting this type of rounding, the SDB can be compromised using attacks based on averaging the modified responses to the same query, repeated many times, as well as tracker-based attacks.

In general, with systematic and random rounding, the sum of rounded statistics requested on disjoint query sets can differ from the rounded statistic on the union of the query sets. This can pose problems with statistics released in the form of macrostatistics. To overcome these problems, the controlled rounding technique has been studied.

**Controlled rounding** applies to SDBs in tabular form. With this type of rounding, whenever a systematic or random rounding is applied to an entry $x_{ij}$ of the table, the same rounding is applied to three other table entries, properly selected to preserve the true values of the statistics corresponding to the row and column involved (that is, the $i$-th row and $j$-th column of the table).

Let $X(C_1), ..., X(C_n)$ be disjoint query sets, and $X(C_{n+1}) = X(C_1) \cup ... \cup X(C_n)$ the query set resulting from their union. Let $r(q_1), ..., r(q_n)$ be the rounded values of each statistic computed on each query set, and $r(q_{n+1})$ the statistic computed on the query set $X(C_{n+1})$.

Using random and systematic roundings, we have:

$$r(q_1) + ... + r(q_n) \neq r(q_{n+1})$$

Using controlled rounding, the following relationship is imposed:

$$r(q_1) + ... + r(q_n) = r(q_{n+1})$$

In summary, rounding techniques release accurate statistics, since the responses are computed on true values before being released, but offer low protection to the SDB, since they can be circumvented by several attacks (for example, tracker-based, averaging-based). Still, rounding is an interesting technique to be used in combination with other protection techniques.

## 5.4 A general framework for comparing inference protection techniques

We discuss a set of criteria to be used for comparing all the examined techniques (Denning and Schlörer, 1983; Chin and Peng, 1987; Adam and Wortmann, 1989). Inference protection techniques can be classified and compared according to the following characteristics and related criteria:

- *Security* expresses the level of protection provided by the technique. This level can be evaluated by testing the protection technique against various types of attack (for example, attacks based on trackers, linear systems, error removal (Denning, 1982)) to find out whether the technique is exposed to compromise, either exact or partial. The exposure of the SDB increases if the user has supplementary knowledge about the SDB schema and contents. Criteria used for classifying protection techniques with respect to security are the following:
  - *Exact compromise:* indicates the possibility of a user exactly compromising the SDB, when the technique is used.
  - *Partial compromise:* indicates the possibility of a user partially compromising the SDB, when the technique is used.
  - *Robustness:* expresses the capability of the technique to take into account, in preventing inference, the user's possible supplementary knowledge.
- *Quality* expresses the global quality of the information released to the user in the presence of an inference protection technique. Criteria used for classifying protection techniques with respect to quality are the following:
  - *Information loss:* indicates, in general, the richness of information released to the user in the presence of the technique. For restriction-based techniques, information loss indicates the amount of non-sensitive statistics that are unnecessarily restricted by the technique to assure inference protection. For perturbation-based techniques, it is related to the variance of the error in the perturbed statistics provided to the user.
  - *Bias:* applies, in general, to perturbation-based techniques. It occurs when the estimator of the true statistic provided to the user has an expected value different from the true value. Unbiased estimators of the true statistics are highly desirable.
  - *Precision:* applies only to perturbation-based techniques. It can be measured by the variance of the estimator supplied to the user. The lower the variance is, the more precise and accurate the released statistic is. On the other hand, the higher the variance, the higher the protection level offered by the technique. A trade-off must be found between these requirements.

  - *Consistency:* applies only to perturbation-based techniques. It indicates the lack of contradictions and paradoxes caused by the perturbation introduced by a technique. A contradiction occurs, for example, when different perturbed responses are supplied to repetitions of the same statistic, or to equivalent statistics. A paradox occurs when a response inconsistent with the semantics of the requested statistic is returned to the user (for example, a negative value for a *Count* query).
- *Cost:* expresses the costs related to the implementation and usage of the technique. Criteria used for classifying protection techniques against cost are the following:
  - *Implementation cost:* indicates the costs related to the implementation of the technique, and to the setting of the required parameters.
  - *Processing overhead per query:* refers to the CPU time and storage requirements during query processing.
  - *User education:* refers to the costs incurred in training the user in the protection technique.
- *Suitability* is a set of criteria dealing with the applicability of a technique, with respect to the type and number of SDB attributes, and the type of the SDB itself. The criteria used to classify protection techniques against suitability are the following:
  - *Numerical/non-numerical attributes.* A technique can be applied either to only one type of attribute or to both.
  - *Number of attributes.* A technique can be applied to one or more attributes of the SDB schema.
  - *On-line dynamic SDBs.* A technique can be more or less suitable for inference protection in dynamic, on-line environments. The main requirements to be taken into account in such environments refer to the fact that statistical queries are computed at the time they are requested, and that statistics reflect the updates performed on the SDB records (that is, insertions, deletions, modifications). Consequently, depending on the way of working, we can have techniques that are well suited to this type of SDB, and other techniques that are not, since they have been specially developed for special-purpose SDBs, releasing statistics in the form of macro-statics.

A classification of the restriction-based and perturbation-based techniques according to these criteria is shown in Tables 5.4 and Table 5.5 (The symbol '–' is used when the criterion is not defined for the examined technique.)

From these tables, we can draw the following summary considerations.

Restriction-based techniques could lead to severe information loss (for example, query-set overlap control) in order to guarantee protection against exact compromise, and this could heavily limit the usefulness of the SDB. Moreover, these techniques can require a significant query processing overhead, especially with audit-based techniques, owing to the number of queries

**Table 5.4** Comparison criteria for restriction-based techniques.

| | Criteria | | | | | | |
|---|---|---|---|---|---|---|---|
| | Security | | | Quality | | | |
| Technique | Exact compromise | Partial compromise | Robustness | Information loss | Bias | Precision | Consistency |
| Query-set size | Yes | Yes | Low | High | – | – | – |
| Expanded query-set size | Yes | Yes | Low | Moderate | – | – | – |
| Query-set overlap | Yes | Yes | Low | Very high | – | – | – |
| Audit-based | No | Yes | Low | Moderate | – | – | – |
| $S_m/N$ criterion | Yes | Yes | Low | Moderate | – | – | – |
| Partitioning | No | Yes | Depends on size of A-populations | Moderate/high | Yes (with dummy entities) | – | – |
| Cell suppression | No | Yes | Low | Moderate | – | – | – |

| | Criteria | | | | | |
|---|---|---|---|---|---|---|
| | Cost | | | Suitability | | |
| Technique | Implementation cost | Processing overhead per query | User education | Numerical/ non-numerical attributes | Number of attributes | On-line dynamic SDBs |
| Query-set size | Low | Low | Very low | Both | ≥1 | Moderate |
| Expanded query-set size | High | High | Low | Both | ≥1 | Moderate |
| Query-set overlap | High | Very high | Low | Both | ≥1 | Moderate |
| Audit-based | High | Very high for large SDBs | Low | Both | 1 | Low |
| $S_m/N$ criterion | Low | Low | Low | Both | ≥1 | Moderate |
| Partitioning | Moderate (static SDB) Very high (dynamic SDB) | Very low (static SDB) | Low | Both | ≥1 | Yes |
| Cell suppression | High | None | None | Both | ≥1 | No |

**Table 5.5** Comparison criteria for perturbation-based techniques.

| Technique | Criteria | | | | | | |
|---|---|---|---|---|---|---|---|
| | Security | | | Quality | | | |
| | Exact compromise | Partial compromise | Robustness | Information loss | Bias | Precision | Consistency |
| Data swapping | No | Yes | High | No | Yes | Could be very low | High |
| Random-sample queries | Yes | Yes | Moderate | Low | No | Could be very low | Low |
| Fixed perturbation | No | Yes | Moderate | No | Yes | Balanced against security | Moderate |
| Query-based perturbation | No | Yes | Moderate | Low | No | Balanced against security | Low |
| Systematic rounding | Yes | Yes | Low | Const. prop. to the rounding base | Yes | Depends on rounding base | Low |
| Random rounding | Yes | Yes | Low | Const. prop. to the rounding base | No | Depends on rounding base | Moderate |
| Controlled rounding | | Yes | Low | Const. prop. to the rounding base | | Depends on rounding base | High |

| Technique | Criteria | | | | | |
|---|---|---|---|---|---|---|
| | Cost | | | Suitability | | |
| | Implementation cost | Processing overhead per query | User education | Numerical/ non-numerical attributes | Number of attributes | On-line dynamic SDBs |
| Data swapping | Very high | None | Moderate | Non-numerical | 1 | No |
| Random-sample queries | Low | Low | Low | Both | 1 | High |
| Fixed perturbation | Low | Very low | Very low | Numerical | 1 | Moderate |
| Query-based perturbation | Moderate | Moderate | Very high | Numerical | 1 or > 1 if independent | High |
| Systematic rounding | Low | Moderate | Low | Both | 1 | Low/moderate |
| Random rounding | Low | Moderate | Low | Both | 1 | Low/moderate |
| Controlled rounding | Moderate | Moderate | Low | Both | 1 | Low |

to be checked for compromise. On the other hand, such comprehensive controls are required in order to prevent malicious users from exploiting properly set sequences of queries to infer confidential information about individuals (for example, using tracker-based or linear-system-based attacks), which is more probable using memoryless techniques (for example, query-set size control, expanded query-set size). Here, the user is always provided with precise and consistent statistics, if they are released, since the statistics are computed on true values of the individuals represented in the SDB.

Perturbation-based techniques try to release more statistics than restriction based-techniques, reducing the information loss by introducing noise into the released statistics. The introduced noise, however, poses new problems, such as bias and consistency of the released statistics. However, the record-based perturbation techniques seem to be the most suitable inference controls for on-line, dynamic SDBs, since they can operate on the queries when they are submitted with moderate query processing overhead, and allow the DBA to balance the precision of the responses released and the level of protection on the confidential information in the SDB by acting on the technique's parameters. This way, such techniques can be adapted to the protection requirements of specific environments. The information loss is related to the variance of the error, which is proportional to the query-set size for record-based techniques, and a constant proportional to the square of the rounding base for result-based techniques. As far as implementation costs and the query processing overhead are concerned, for record-based perturbation techniques they are proportional to the query-set size, and are small for result-based techniques.

In general, we can conclude that no single protection technique alone provides high security and low information loss at low cost. Moreover, no technique that can prevent both exact and partial compromise exists. Since no one technique is superior to another in all aspects, the choice of suitable protection technique(s) should be guided by the protection requirements and the characteristics of the environment to be protected. There are techniques, such as cell suppression, which are especially suitable for static and off-line SDBs, publishing statistics in the form of macrostatistics. For static on-line SDBs, data swapping is suitable, while perturbation-based techniques such as random-sample queries, fixed perturbation and query-based perturbation are suitable for dynamic and on-line SDBs, provided that bias is made acceptable.

Combined techniques also seem very attractive, such as those described in Sections 5.3.2 and 5.3.3 under the subheading 'A combined technique'. Indeed, these techniques have the advantage of providing higher security and faster response time, even if, in general, they incur more costs than a single technique.

## References

Abul-Ela A.L., Greenberg B.G. and Horvitz D.G. (1967). A multi-proportions randomized response model. *J. Am. Stat. Assoc.*, **3319**(62), September

Adam N.R. and Wortmann J.C. (1989). Security-control methods for statistical databases: a comparative study. *ACM Computing Surveys*, **21**(4), December

Beck L.L (1980). A security mechanism for statistical databases. *ACM Trans. Database Systems*, **5**(3), September

Chin F.Y. and Ozsoyoglu G. (1979). Security in partitioned dynamic statistical databases. In *Proc. IEEE COMPSAC Conf.*

Chin F.Y. and Ozsoyoglu G. (1981). Statistical database design. *ACM Trans. Database Systems*, **6**(1), March

Chin F.Y. and Ozsoyoglu G. (1982). Auditing and inference control in statistical databases. *IEEE Trans. Software Eng.*, **8**(6), April

Chin Y.H. and Peng W.L. (1987). An evaluation of two new inference control methods. *IEEE Trans. Software Eng.*, **13**(12), December

Cox H.L. (1980). Suppression methodology and statistical disclosure control. *J. Am. Stat. Assoc.*, **75**(370)

Davida G.I. *et al.* (1976). Database Security. *Technical Report TR-CS-76-14, Dept. of Electrical Eng. and Com. Sc., University of Winsconsin*, July

Davida G.I., Linton D.J., Szelag C.R. and Wells D.L. (1978). Database security. *IEEE Trans. Software Eng.*, **4**(6), November

De Millo R.A., Dobkin D. and Lipton R.J. (1977). Even databases that lie can be compromised. *IEEE Trans. Software Eng.*, **4**(1), January

Denning D.E. (1980). Secure statistical databases under random sample queries. *ACM Trans. Database Systems*, **5**(3), September

Denning D.E. (1982). *Cryptography and Data Security.* Addison-Wesley

Denning D.E. and Schlörer J. (1983). Inference controls for statistical databases. *IEEE Computer*, **16**(7), July

Dobkin D., Jones A.K. and Lipton R.J. (1979). Secure databases: protection against user influence. *ACM Trans. Database Systems*, **4**(1), March

Friedman A.D. and Hoffman L.J. (1980). Towards a fail-safe approach to secure databases. In *Proc. IEEE Symp. on Security and Privacy*, Oakland, April

Matloff N.E. (1986). Another look at the use of noise addition for database security. In *Proc. IEEE Symp. on Security and Privacy*, Oakland, April

Ozsoyoglu G. and Chin F.Y. (1986). Information loss in the lattice model of summary tables due to cell supprression. In *Proc. IEEE Symp. on Security and Privacy*, Oakland, April

Palley M.A. (1986). Security of statistical databases compromise through attribute correlational modeling. In *Proc. IEEE Conf. on Data Engineering*

Reiss S.P. (1984). Practical data swapping: the first step. *ACM Trans. Database Systems*, **9**(1), March

Schlörer J. (1975). Identification and retrieval of personal records from a statistical data bank. *Methods Inf. Med.*, **14**(1), January

Schlörer J. (1976). Confidentiality of statistical records: a threat monitoring scheme for on-line dialogue. *Methods Inf. Med.*, **15**(1), January

Schlörer J. (1977). Confidentiality and security in statistical data banks. In *Data Documentation: Some Principles and Applications in Science and Industry; Proc. Workshop on Data Documentation* (Guas W. and Henzler R., eds.). Verlag Dokumentation

Schlörer J. (1980). Disclosure from statistical databases: quantitative aspects of trackers. *ACM Trans. Database Systems*, **5**(4), December

Schlörer J. (1981). Security of statistical databases: multidimensional transformation. *ACM Trans. Database Systems*, **6**(1), March

Sicherman G.L., De Jonge W. and Van De Riet R.P. (1983). Answering queries without revealing secrets. *ACM Trans. Database Systems*, **8**(1), March

Smith J.M. and Smith D.C.P. (1977). Database abstractions: aggregration and generalization. *ACM Trans. Database Systems*, **2**(2), June

Traub J.F., Yemini Y. and Wozniakowski H. (1984). The statistical security of a statistical database. *ACM Trans. Database Systems*, **9**(4), December

Warner S.L. (1965). Randomized response: a survey technique for eliminating evasive answer bias. *Journal Am. Stat. Assoc.*, **309**(60), March

Yu C.T. and Chin F.Y. (1977). A study on the protection of statistical databases In *Proc. ACM SIGMOD Int. Conf. on Management of Data*, August

# 6 Intrusion detection

## 6.1 Introduction

The purpose of computer misuse detection measures is to discover the basic categories of security violations: disclosure, integrity violation, denial of service and unauthorized access. As seen so far in this book, a first line of defence is the institution of formal access operations: that is, logical security measures that restrict access to the database system.

Since several issues limit the efficacy of these measures (such as human errors in applying them, difficulty in achieving a compromise between conflicting requirements – controls against performance, undetected vulnerabilities and misuse of legitimate privileges), a second category of security measures is the *maintenance and analysis of audit trails* of the system activities (Perry 1982; Perry and Warner, 1978). *Intrusion detection* is defined as the issue of identifying intrusions by individuals who are using a system without authorization ('crackers') and those who are authorized but abuse their privileges ('insider threat'). Examples of intrusions are unauthorized modifications of files to permit access to data, unauthorized access or modification of user files and information, modification of system tables (such as router tables in order to deny use of the network), creation of unauthorized accounts or unauthorized use of existing accounts (Litecky and Rittenberg, 1981).

The ability to detect computer misuse depends on the presence of an intrusion model. Currently, two types of model are generally employed by *Intrusion Detection Systems (IDSs)*:

- *Anomaly detection models*. These enable the profile of a user's normal behaviour to be statistically compared with the parameters of the current user's session; 'significant' deviations from the normal behaviour are reported to the security officer, where 'significant' is defined as a threshold set by the specific model or by the security officer.
- *Misuse detection models*. This second type of model supports comparison between parameters of the user's session and known techniques used by attackers to penetrate a system.

In general, controls on user behaviour in the system are tackled by tracking the requests performed by users and recording them in a suitable trail (audit). The analysis has the purpose of detecting whether a set of requests, performed by a given user or user group, may be considered as suspicious.

Audit controls in *traditional audit systems* have the drawback of being very complex, and of being executed *a posteriori*. The manual review of the large amount of audit data to be assessed limits the workability of the approach and leads these controls being performed only from time to time. Consequently, possible attacks on the system are not always detected, or can be detected long after they occurred. Therefore, the necessity arises of providing tools and systems which, automatically or semi-automatically, check the audit data and try to detect intrusions, possibly on-line, in real time.

A number of IDSs are based on the analysis of the audit trails offered by the host operating system (OS). Examples are SRI's Intrusion Detection Expert System (IDES), National Security Agency's MIDAS, Haystack Laboratories' Haystack System, Los Alamos National Laboratory's Wisdom & Sense (W&S), AT&T's ComputerWatch, and Planning Research Corporation's Information Security Officer's Assistant (ISOA). These systems employ techniques such as the evaluation of a weighted multinomial function to detect deviations from normal behaviour, a covariance matrix for profiling normal behaviour, and rule-based expert systems to detect security violations (Lunt, 1993).

Particular problems of intrusion detection are the need for real-time response, the large amount of data to be processed, the lack of available attack data to be analysed, and the large number of parameters that can be associated with audit data. Therefore, intrusion detection can borrow solutions from other fields such as artificial intelligence, statistics, information theory, or machine learning. These solutions need to be adapted to IDS design and operation, and the impact of these techniques on intrusion detection is yet to be fully understood.

It is the purpose of this chapter to show the advances in intrusion detection techniques, and to illustrate some basic systems.

## 6.2 Automated tools for intrusion detection

Intrusion detection systems are applied in conjunction with access controls to detect possible violations or violation attempts. The basic architecture of an IDS is depicted in Figure 6.1.

One purpose of automated tools for the security analysis of audit data is to *reduce the amount of audit data* to be manually reviewed. Alternatively, tools may *evidence attempts* to violate the system security either *off-line* or *on-line* (as studied on some prototypes). The threats that can be tackled using audit data are classified in Anderson (1980) as threats by *external penetrators* (unauthorized to use the system), by *internal penetrators* (authorized users who use the system resources in an unauthorized manner – for example, by masquerading or simply bypassing access controls), and by *misfeasors* (authorized users who mislead their access privileges). Each category can be detected by a category of actions on the system: failed logins for external penetrators, failed access to files or system resources, and deviation from usual behaviour patterns for resources for internal penetrators.

Among internal penetrators, particularly dangerous are 'clandestine users', defined as those who evade both access controls and auditing by use of system

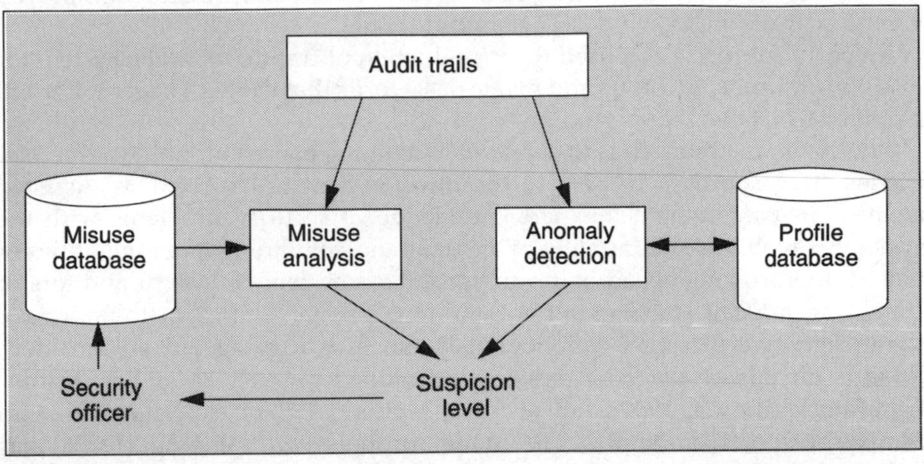


*Figure 6.1* Structure of an IDS (Proceedings of the Workshop on Future Directions in Computer Misuse and Anomaly Detection, University of California, Davis, March 1992).

privileges or by operating at a lower level than the audited level. Bypassing of auditing functions can be detected by recording in the audit data the functions that turn off auditing, or that change some auditing parameters. The problem bound to auditing levels can be solved by lowering the audit level (for example, to the kernel calls level). Moreover, in general, clandestine users can be detected by defining the normal usage pattern of some system parameters (CPU activity, memory and disk use) and comparing them with the actual values during system use (Anderson, 1980).

After this characterization given by Anderson, a number of projects were carried out on audit trails and automated tools for their analysis. The result is a set of Intrusion Detection Systems (IDSs) based on models enabling the audit data to be inspected and security violations to be detected, possibly in real time. Considering the base model, IDSs are programs that perform these types of analyses: some programs compare user actions to profiles (anomaly detection), others to known attack methods (misuse detection), while yet others have elements of both.

In general, an IDS accepts audit records from one (several) host(s), extracts features relevant to the analysis, and then generates a profile of the activities and compares this to its internal database. If this database is an *anomaly database*, the comparison is of statistical type; if it is a *misuse database*, the comparison uses pattern matching. Finally, the IDS employs comparison methods such as inference, predictive analysis, or other approximation methods. The result of the analysis can be stored in the IDS database and/or used to modify the audit record by adding/deleting a feature to be passed to the analysis component of the system, in order to allow the IDS to be tailored to the observed situations. This is done under control of the features employed for the analysis: that is, under a behaviour model.

An early approach proposed the introduction of trapdoors in the system for intruders (dummy accounts and magic passwords that trigger an alarm if used) (Anderson, 1980).

One common approach is to define *rules* defining behaviour patterns for user classes. This approach has led to the development of expert IDSs. Assisted analysis usually combines expert knowledge of security problems with the system's capability of accurately processing and combining large quantities of data: the processing speed helps an automated system to inform auditors of suspicious activities in time to trace and stop these activities, or to undertake some defensive measures autonomously (such as logging out an intruder). Projects on misuse detection systems developed in 1983/84 at Los Alamos Laboratory (Brown, 1984) and at SRI (Denning, 1987a) experimented with an expert system approach. The model proposed in Denning (1987a) has influenced other intrusion detection systems (for example, Halme and Kahn, 1988; Sebring *et al.*, 1988; Tsudik and Summers, 1990; Hochberg *et al.*, 1993). An anomaly detection component is used in most of these systems, which now includes an expert system component.

At SRI, experiments on an expert IDS followed the early studies aimed at producing algorithms for automating the analysis of audit trails. The analysis occurs *off-line*. One project used existing trails to study possible support task tools. Another project built special audit trails and a technique for their automated analysis. These projects provided evidence that it is possible to distinguish users from one another on the basis of their use patterns.

Subsequent work at SRI aimed at *real-time* intrusion detection systems. The resulting prototype, IDES (Intrusion Detection Expert System), detects intrusive operations in real time using the approach of detecting intrusions as deviations from normal user behaviours. IDES keeps statistics for user/intrusion-detection measure. The statistics form the user *profile* which is periodically updated based on the user's behaviour (adaptive learning).

Since the discrimination between 'normal' and 'abnormal' user behaviour is difficult, the approach of IDES and of other projects uses *expert systems* techniques. The knowledge of security experts (security officers, auditors, database authorizers) is coded in the form of *security rules* used to analyse the *audit data* to detect suspicious activities. The task of these rules is to *assist* the security officer rather than automate his tasks: the rules cannot be expected to be comprehensive. An alternative approach is to codify the *system vulnerabilities* and known attack scenarios into security rules, as done in some prototypes such as IDES. The rules do not depend on past user or system behaviour, but are fixed. A sample rule is that more than four consecutive attempts at login for one account within five minutes is an intrusion attack. Audit data derived from the monitored system are matched against this rule to determine suspicious behaviour.

In the rule-based approach, an event triggers a rule independently of whether the event is normal for the user. Therefore, intrusion scenarios that may not be anomalous for the user can be detected by proper rules. The limitation of the rule-based approach is that the audit data is searched for *known* attacks, while many intrusions can occur according to unknown modes. Moreover, writing a rule base is a complex knowledge engineering task, and the maintenance of the rule base is also difficult (rule consistency maintenance, rule ranking, facts deletion).

A further approach is to use *model-based reasoning*. This is based on the hypothesis that intruders use typical procedures to attack a system, such as systematic password attacks or access to privileged files. The approach develops specific models of predefined known attacks. The resulting intrusion detection system reasons on the basis of the model to correlate activities with observables: that is, the system searches for intruders by looking for actions belonging to a hypothesized attack scenario. The scenarios vary with the type of intruder and with the type of system. This approach is being evaluated at SRI in research studies (Garvey and Lunt, 1991): the system should be able to determine what action an intruder will execute next, under a given attack scenario. This is useful to select the audit data that should be collected and observed to predict the next step of an intrusive activity and to validate the hypothesis on possible intrusions.

One benefit of model-based reasoning for intrusion-detection is its selectivity about audit data: relevant data is focused, and therefore the amount of data to be examined is reduced. Moreover, preventive actions against intrusions can be undertaken, since the system is able to make predictions. As with expert systems, the approach is limited in that it looks for known intrusion scenarios, while many vulnerabilities and attacks may be unknown. The research tends to combine model-based reasoning with statistical anomaly detection.

Other approaches, not based on suspicion, define *acceptable behaviours* (Karger, 1987).

Recent proposals (deriving from studies at SRI) exploit the potential of *neural networks* to adaptively react to intrusion attacks. Neural networks solve the problem of the statistical methods: they do not require the assumption on the underlying distribution of user behaviour (for example, a Gaussian distribution of deviations from a norm). Currently, although promising, the approach is not sufficiently developed to substitute the statistical components of current prototypes.

With respect to special intrusions, that is, *viruses*, and to intrusions in general, existing systems are classified in Young (1987) as appearance monitors and behaviour monitors. *Appearance monitors* are static analysis tools aimed at detecting anomalies in source or executable files. They look at discrepancies such as increased executable image size, common or repeated code in files, or inconsistent coding styles. *Behaviour monitors* dynamically examine the behaviour of processes for dangerous actions (for example, reading a directory, or writing to an executable file). Under this classification, IDES is a real-time behaviour monitor, which identifies a set of auditable parameters, sets system and user profiles of the acceptable states and observes patterns of use. MIDAS also belongs to behaviour monitors: it monitors user commands and uses heuristic rules to identify various types of intrusions. These systems are among those described in this chapter.

## 6.3 Expert-systems-based approach: the IDES system

The basic reasons in favour of expert systems for intrusion detection can be stated as follows (Denning and Neumann, 1985; Neumann, 1985):

- Many existing systems have security flaws that make them vulnerable to penetration threats. It is often impossible to pinpoint or eliminate these flaws, for technical and economic reasons.
- Existing systems with known flaws cannot be easily replaced by secure systems because often these systems depend on the application system or the substitution requires considerable technical and economic efforts.
- The development of absolutely secure systems is extremely difficult, often impossible.
- Even highly secure systems are vulnerable to misuse by legitimate users.

The IDES (Intrusion Detection Expert System) system is a real-time system developed at SRI International, Palo Alto, which constitutes a reference milestone in the family of intrusion detection: its model has been at the heart of other systems, and the studies conducted in the project have led to results of overall interest in the field.

IDES monitors both external threats from users trying to penetrate the system and internal threats from users trying to abuse their authorizations. IDES belongs to the category of systems based on experience and learning obtained from watching the system, rather than on fixed rules. In addition, assuming that anomalies in usual behaviours may mean user threats, IDES is capable of learning and defining, by watching the system, the normal behaviour of each user.

### 6.3.1 Foundations

IDES uses an expert system approach, assuming that the exploitation of system vulnerabilities for system abuse leads to an *anomalous use* of the system. By watching user behaviour, it is possible to detect anomalous behaviours as departures from a defined *normal behaviour*; *evaluation rules* for anomalous behaviour detection are also defined, as well as actions to be monitored; the latter are both unauthorized and authorized requests (apparently legitimate).

#### *Threats–behaviours relationships*

The basic relationships between intrusion types and behaviour anomaly in IDES are:

- *Intrusion attempt*. Many login attempts using various passwords under the same account-id, or using the same password under different accounts;

- *Masquerading.* Intrusion via legitimate login (correct account and password, possibly stolen or copied) and then system usage patterns different from usual (for example, directory browsing instead of usual software development actions of editing, compiling, linking, and so on);
- *Penetration by legitimate users.* Authorized users who try to circumvent the security controls (they use programs different from those usually run). If the attempts are successful, owing to security flaws, the users get access to files or commands normally forbidden and, therefore, they exhibit anomalous behaviour;
- *Spreading of data by authorized users.* A user tries to access sensitive data by logging in at unusual times, by writing in an unusual manner (many read operations), by using remote printers, or by generating more copies than usual;
- *Inference by authorized users.* Confidential data is obtained by aggregation or inference (see Chapter 5);
- *Trojan Horses.* A Trojan Horse inserted into or substituted for a program can modify the usage rates of the CPU, memory, devices, and so on (for example, access to a directory could suddenly grow);
- *Viruses.* These can cause an increased frequency of rewriting into executable files, or an increase in memory used by executable files, or an increased number of runs of a certain program;
- *Denial of service.* An intruder who can lock a resource, for example, the network, thus preventing other users from employing that resource, can have a very high activity rate for that resource, if compared with other users.

#### *Analysis of behaviour anomalies*

The definition of the intrusion detection model requires *profiles* and rules to be determined. In particular, the definition of profiles can be given in terms of *metrics* and *statistical models*. A metric is a random variable $x$ representing a quantitative measure over a given observation period (either a fixed time interval or the interval between two correlated events). The observations, that is, user actions, which are sample points $x_i$ of $x$, are used in a statistical model to determine whether a new observation can be considered as 'normal'. The statistical model is independent of the distribution of $x$; hence, all the knowledge about $x$ can be obtained from the observations.

Let us look at the basic metrics and statistical models that can used for analysis of behaviour anomalies.

#### *Metrics*

Metrics describe how single observations of a user's behaviour can be grouped to produce a profile related to the user's behaviour. Some of the metrics that can be used are:

- *Event counter.* $x$ is the number of events, related to a given period, that meet given properties. For example, $x$ may describe the number of logins in an hour, the number of times a certain command has been executed in a session, the number of password failures in a minute, or the number of access violations to files in a day.

- *Time interval.* $x$ is the time interval between two correlated events: for example, the interval between two subsequent logins related to a single account.
- *Resource measurement.* $x$ is the quantity of resources used by a system action in a given period: for example, the total amount of pages printed by a user in one day, the total CPU time of a running program, or the number of records read in one day. Notice that the resource measurement is modelled in terms of event counters or time intervals. For example, the number of printed pages is an event counter.

***Statistical models***

Given a metric for a casual variable $x$ and $n$ observations $x_1, x_2,\ldots,x_n$, the purpose of a statistical model of $x$ is to determine if a new observation, $x_{n+1}$, is abnormal compared with the previous ones. Some statistical models that can be used for this purpose are:

- *Operational model.* This is based on the assumption that the anomaly can be determined by comparing a new observation of $x$ with a fixed limit. Although this model does not use the previous observations directly, it can be logically assumed that these will be used in determining the limit. This model is applicable to metrics for which experience has shown that threshold values exist that are related to intrusions. For example, upon three password failures, an intrusion threat is suspected; or an access performed through a login unused for two months can suggest an intrusion attempt on an old account.
- *Average and standard deviation model.* This is based on the assumption that a new observation is considered to be 'normal' if it lies within the confidence interval:
  $avg \pm d \times stdev$
  where the average *avg* and the standard deviation *stdev* are respectively:
  $$avg = \frac{x_1+\ldots+x_n}{n}$$
  $$stdev = \sqrt{\left(\frac{x_1^2+\ldots+x_n^2}{n-1} - avg^2\right)}$$
  and $d$ is a parameter.

  This model is applicable to all the metrics previously described. Its advantage is that no prior knowledge about normal user activity is required; instead, the model 'learns' from the observations and can easily distinguish between users, in that what is 'normal' for one user might be abnormal for other users.
- *Multivaried model.* This is similar to the average/standard deviation model, except for the fact that it is based on the correlation between two or more metrics. This model is useful in those cases where experience shows that a better degree of discrimination can be derived from the combination of correlated measures rather than from single measures: for example, the CPU time and the I/O devices used by a program, or the login frequency and the duration of a session.

- *Markovian model.* This model considers each type of event (user request) as a state variable, and uses a state transition matrix to characterize the frequencies of a transition between states. A new observation is defined as 'normal' if its probability, determined by the previous state and by the transition matrix, is high. This model, which is applicable only to the event counter metric, is useful to control the transitions between given commands, when the sequence of commands is relevant.
- *Time series model.* This model, using both the event counter and the measurement of resources and intervals metrics, takes into account the order and the interval times occurring between the observations and the values of these observations. A new observation is defined as 'abnormal' if the probability of its occurrence at that instant is too low. The advantage of this model is that it enables evolution of user behaviour to be measured and gradual but meaningful changes in behaviour to be understood. Its disadvantage lies in its high cost.

#### Profile characterization

Some profiles (behaviour aspects) that can be used to compare users' actual behaviour are described. For each, a metric and a statistical model are suggested.

The profiles are defined with respect to the subjects who execute actions, to the objects on which actions are executed, and to the type of action. *Behaviour profiles* can be defined for each subject on each object, or for classes of subjects and/or objects. Figure 6.2 shows all the possible subject/object combinations that can be monitored. In this figure, *system* means that the actions of whatever

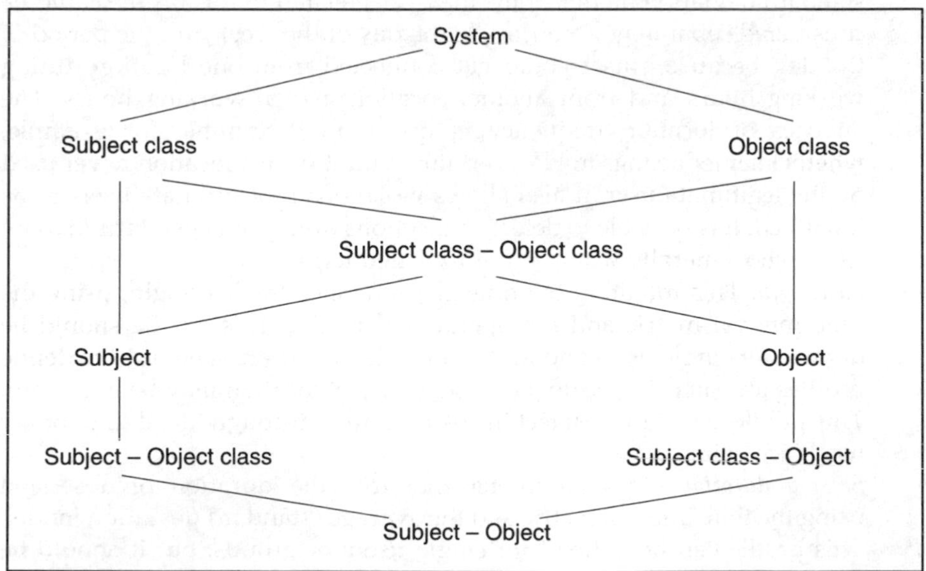


*Figure 6.2* Hierarchy of elements for which behaviour profiles can be defined.

subject on whatever system object are considered; *subject* means that the actions made by a given subject on whatever system object are considered; *object* means that the actions of whatever subject on a given object are considered. Other combinations have an immediate interpretation.

### Login and session activity profiles

Login and session activity profiles take into account the 'login'/'logout' actions executed by a subject (user) on the objects represented by the user login sites (terminals, workstations, networks, remote hosts, and so on). These profiles can be characterized in terms of:

- *Login frequency*. This monitors the login frequency by using the event counter metric and the average/standard deviation model. Since user behaviour can vary considerably during the work of, say, a week, the login occurrences can be represented as a vector of events parameterized with respect to the day of the week (considering a specific day, or distinguishing between a working day and the weekend) and to the period of the day (time, turn, morning/afternoon, evening/night). Login-based profiles can be used to detect users who generally get connected via an unauthorized account number during non-working hours, for example, when legitimate users are not expected to use the account. Login profiles can be defined for single users (or user groups), and object classes, which can be formed according to the type of location, connection, or by considering, together, all the locations;
- *Location frequency*. This parameter monitors the login frequency from different sites, by using the event counter metric and the average/standard deviation model. Some measures related to this profile could be considered separately, according to the day of the week and the period of the day, because a user could get connected from one location during working hours and from another location in non-working hours. The analysis of location frequency is useful to determine, for example, whether someone logs in via a certain account from a location never used by the legitimate user. It also allows violations by legitimate users to be identified. It is possible to detect connections from privileged terminals by users who generally work on unprivileged terminals;
- *Last login*. This monitors the time elapsed since the last login, using the time interval metric and the operational model. This profile should be defined for single users and for location classes. There is no need to define profiles for each single site, because the exact location may be irrelevant. This profile is useful to detect intrusion threats through 'dead' (no longer used) accounts;
- *Session duration*. This parameter monitors the duration of a session using the time interval metric and the average/standard deviation model. This profile can be defined for single users or groups, but it should be defined for object classes. Deviations from the standard behaviour are symptomatic of 'masking' attacks;

- *Session output*. This monitors the quantity of output produced from a terminal, over a session or a day, using the resource measurement metric and the average/standard deviation model. The definition of this profile for individual sites or classes of locations is useful to determine overloads of data transmitted to remote locations, which can be symptomatic of an illegitimate action of spreading sensitive data;
- *CPU per session, I/O per session, pages per session*, and so on. These parameters control the use of resources in a session using the resource measurement metric and the average/standard deviation model. These profiles are useful to determine masking threats;
- *Password failures*. This profile monitors the number of password failures related to a given login using the event counter metric and the operational model. This profile is very useful to determine intrusion threats. It can be defined for single users and for all system users. An attack performed via many password attempts from a given account should show a rather high, and therefore unusual, number of failures for a single user. An attack involving a single password attempt on various accounts should reveal an unusually high number of password failures with respect to a profile covering all users. Password failures can also be recorded against short time periods: for example, a few minutes. In fact, intrusion attempts generally occur during peaks of activity;
- *Location failures*. This last element monitors login failures using the event counter metric and the operational model. This profile can be defined for single users and for groups of locations. Groups of locations can be considered because, generally, a specific site is irrelevant for control purposes, whereas the fact that a location is unauthorized is very meaningful.

  This profile can be used to determine intrusion attempts, or attempts at connection from privileged terminals.

#### Command and program execution profiles

The command and program execution profiles control the 'execute' actions requested by users on programs. The commands can also be seen as called programs. In defining profiles, programs can be classified and aggregated, distinguishing between privileged programs (executable only by particular users accessing the system in a privileged mode) and non-privileged programs; between system programs and user programs; or between programs used by skilful users and programs used by novice users. It is unnecessary, although feasible, to consider profiles relating to each single program in the system. However, some programs might need specific profiles to determine masking, penetration threats or Trojan Horses. These profiles should be aggregated with respect to users. The programs possibly needing individual controls are privileged programs, security-relevant programs, programs performing browsing actions, and frequently used programs.

The program execution profiles can be featured in terms of:

- *Execution frequency*. This profile monitors login failures over a time period using the event counter metric and the average/standard deviation model. It can be defined for single users or for user classes, for single programs or for program classes. A profile for single users against single programs can be used to detect masking attempts (a user who penetrates the system with an account different from the usual one generally uses programs different from those employed by the legitimate user) or to detect successful penetrations by legitimate users (these users probably can have access to privileged programs which are not included in their profiles).

  A profile relating to all users for a single program is useful to detect Trojan Horses. In fact, the execution frequency of the original program changes owing to the actions expressed in the hidden code. Moreover, this profile is helpful to detect viruses appearing in a program call by executing a viral action.
- *CPU per program, I/O per program, and so on*. This monitors the use of resources by a program execution using the resource measurement metric and the average/standard deviation model. This profile can be defined both for single users/programs and for user/program classes. An abnormal value of one of these measures, applied to the whole user population, suggests possible insertions of Trojan Horses or viruses in the original programs, which invariably cause an increased CPU usage rate or I/O rate. Data accumulation on a time basis (for example, per day) or on an execution basis would be less meaningful or useful in determining possible intrusions.
- *Denied executions*. This monitors the number of attempts to execute an unauthorized program that have taken place over a certain time period, for example one day, through the event counter metric and the operational model. This profile, defined for single users, is useful to determine penetration attempts from particular users. It can also be defined for single highly sensitive programs.
- *Saturation of program resources*. This monitors the number of times a program terminates abnormally because of inadequate resources, using the event counter metric and the operational model. This profile can be measured on a per-day basis, and can be defined for single programs or program classes to monitor aborted programs (for example, due to spreading of data to the user through a covert channel based on the resource usage rate).

#### File access profiles

File access profiles consider 'read', 'write', 'create', 'delete', and 'append' operations executed on files. Files can be classified according to their type (text, executable program, directory, and so on), to their being user or system files, or to other properties. Since a program is also a file, the use of programs, besides being monitored with respect to their execution, can also be monitored by monitoring file access activities. The number of files in a system may be very high (millions), thus making individual controls often unfeasible.

Individual controls on security-relevant files are desirable, for example, on password files, files containing authorizations, files containing audit data or network routing tables.

File access profiles can be defined with respect to:

- *Read, write, create and delete frequency*. This controls the number of accesses and types of access modes, using the event counter metric and the average/standard deviation model. Access frequency profiles for 'read'/'write' operations can be defined for single users and files, or for user classes and files. Profiles for 'create'/'delete' operations are meaningful only for file aggregations, because each file is created or deleted at most once. Anomalies in 'read'/'write' access for single users can signal masking or 'browsing' threats. In addition, they can denote a successful penetration, because a user might access files that are usually inaccessible to him.
- *Read/written records*. This monitors the number of read/written records using the resource measurement metric and the average/standard deviation model. These profiles can be measured upon each access or on a per-day basis. They can be defined for single users or files, or for user and file classes. Anomalies can signal attempts to obtain sensitive data via inference or aggregation processes (for example, by requesting large quantities of correlated data).
- *Read, write, delete, create failures*. This monitors the number of access violations in a given time interval (for example, a day), using the event counter metric and the operational model. It can be defined for single users and files, or for user groups and file classes. Single-user profiles, with respect to a class containing all the files, are useful for detecting users who repeatedly try to access unauthorized files. Single-file profiles, with respect to all users, are useful for detecting unauthorized access to highly sensitive files.
- *File resource exhaustion*. This profile monitors the number of requests that failed because of missing memory, using the event counter metric and the operational model. This profile can be defined for single users against all files. An anomaly can mean a covert channel, into which the signalling process consumes the whole available disk space to store the flag bits.

#### Database access profiles

Database access can be treated like file access. In fact, since in relational database systems each relation is stored as a separate file, access to a relation is analogous to file access. However, the operations are different: in a database, 'retrieve', 'update', 'insert' and 'delete' access must be considered for the records in the relation, and the 'create' and 'delete' modes for the whole relation. 'Retrieve' operations on the database correspond to 'file read' operations; 'update', 'insert' and 'delete' operations correspond to 'file write' operations.

If the auditing function is executed at the relation level, then the profiles used to monitor the file activity can be used to monitor the database activity. If the auditing is executed at a lower level (for example, on single records), the same principles as apply to files can be used, but the DBMS must be provided with support for production of audit data at the record level. However, considering the large data volumes which are likely to be generated by separately checking the access to each record (a single 'read' may need to access millions of records to compute the average of their values), an intrusion detection system at the record level is not always feasible. For some systems, it is sufficient to monitor at the 'database' level, with no need to decompose the database into its constituent files. In this case also, the same principles as those used for files are applicable.

Using a database and a set of processes, IDES monitors:

- Intrusion threats;
- Masquerading;
- System penetration by external users;
- Inference and aggregation threats;
- Information spreading channels: two types of covert channel are monitored: memory channels, which can involve resource saturation and exception conditions; and time channels (which lead to inference using the system time properties);
- Denial of service;
- Side-effects: caused by viruses, worms, or similar programs involving denial of service or damage to data and software.

## 6.3.2 IDES model

The IDES security model comprises the following elements (Figure 6.3):

(1) *Subjects:* the initiators of activities in the monitored system. Typically, a subject is a *user*, but also a *process* that operates on behalf of users or *user groups*, or on behalf of the system. All the activities are initiated by user commands. Subjects can be grouped into classes (groups) in order to consider accesses to objects in the system by many users. The user groups, formed for this purpose, can intersect: that is, a user can belong to more than one group.

(2) *Objects:* the resources handled by the system: that is, the entities on which actions are executed. Objects are: *files, programs, messages, records, terminals, printers* and structures created by programs or users. The subjects on which actions can be executed, for example, the electronic mail system, are also considered as objects. Objects may be grouped into classes according to their type (for example, program or text files), or according to other relations (for example, records can be grouped into files or database relations, files into directories, and so on). The granularity of the controlled objects depends on the monitored system. For example, for some database applications, it is preferrable to treat the data at the record level; for other applications a file/directory granularity is sufficient.

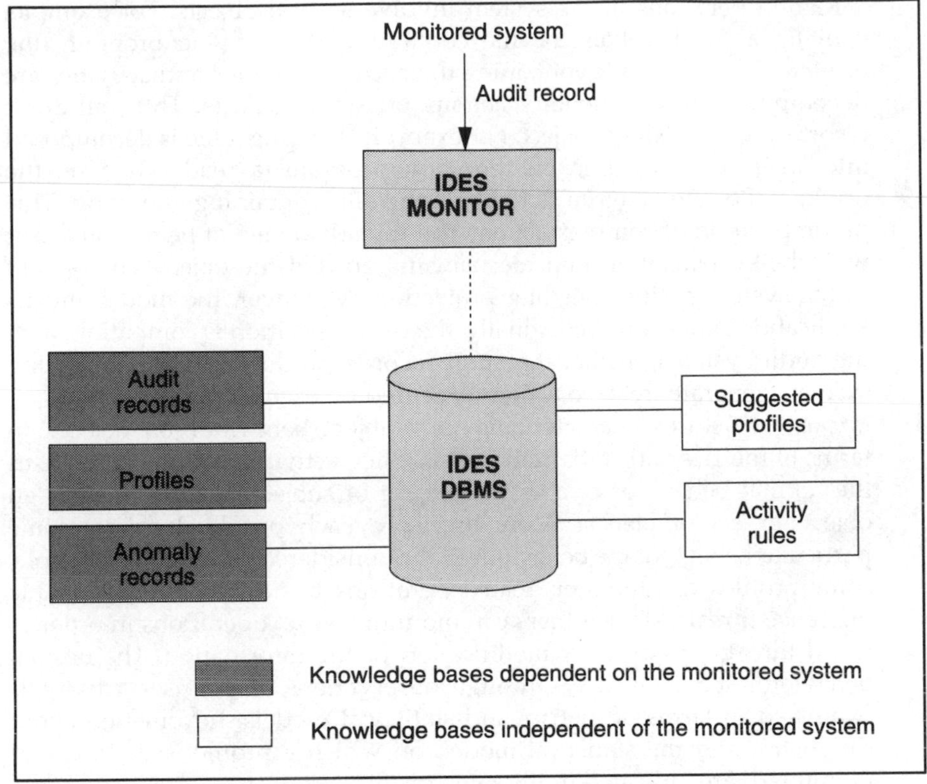


*Figure 6.3* IDES model elements.

(3) *Audit records:* records of the actions requested by users on the monitored system. Therefore, audit records represent accesses requested by users on objects. Each record is a 6-tuple of the type:

⟨subject, action, object, exception-condition, resource-use, time⟩

where:

- *Action:* an access operation (e.g., login, logout, read, execute);
- *Subject:* the subject who requested the action;
- *Object:* the object on which the action was requested;
- *Exception-condition:* describes a possible exception returned to the subject in the case of partial/total rejection by the system of the request to execute the action. This condition can be, besides the apparent justification for denying the service returned to the user, a further motivation which is not returned to the user for security reasons (the user might infer information from the given motivation);
- *Resource-use:* a list of quantitative elements, each providing the amount of usage of a certain resource. For example, the number of lines or printed pages, the number of read/written records, the CPU or I/O unit time used, the duration of a session;
- *Time:* the instant of action execution.

Many operations in the system involve several objects. For example, copying a file involves the file containing the copying program, the original file and the file containing the copy. All actions and activities are decomposed into elementary actions on single objects. Thus, all audit records refer to a single object. For example, copying a file is decomposed into an execution action on the copy program, a read action on the original file and a write action on the file containing the copy. This decomposition of complex actions has the advantage of being consistent with the system protection mechanisms, in that the objects correspond to the system entities needing protection. Moreover, the model and its applications are simplified. Finally, the decomposition is compatible with the audit systems, in that the audit records produced by other existing systems generally refer to actions executed on each single object.

(4) *Profiles:* structures characterizing the subject behaviour on objects, in terms of metrics and statistical models. Each activity profile characterizes the normal behaviour of a subject, or set of subjects, with respect to an object, or set of objects. More precisely, each profile describes some particular aspects of the behaviour of the considered subject. For example, some profiles can monitor 'read' operations in order to show possible inference threats, while others can monitor 'write' operations in order to avoid threats of improper modification of the information. The normal behaviour, stated by IDES through observations of the user activity, is expressed in terms of metrics and statistical models. Information about the metric and the statistical model, on which a profile is defined and monitored, are indicated in the same profile.

An activity profile is described by the 10-tuple:

⟨variable-name, action-pattern, exception-pattern, resource-use-pattern, period, variable-type, threshold, subject-pattern, object-pattern, value⟩

where:

- *Variable-name:* the name of a variable;
- *Action-pattern:* corresponds to zero or more actions in the audit record (for example, 'login', 'read', 'execute', and so on);
- *Exception-pattern:* corresponds to the exception-condition fields of an audit record;
- *Resource-use-pattern:* corresponds to the resource-use field of an audit record;
- *Period:* describes the length of the time period to which observations refer: for instance, day, hour, minutes. This component is null if the period is not fixed;
- *Variable-type:* defines the metric and the statistical model on which the profile is defined: for example, event counter and average/standard deviation model;
- *Threshold:* a parameter defining the limit (or limits) used in the statistical test to determine the anomaly. The interpretation of this field depends on the statistical model used, indicated in the

'variable-type' element. For example, for the operational model, this field represents an upper (lower) limit against which an observation is to be matched; for the average/standard deviation model, it describes the number of standard deviations acceptable with respect to the average;

- *Subject-pattern:* corresponds to the subject field of an audit record;
- *Object-pattern:* corresponds to the object field of an audit record;
- *Value:* the value of the most recent observations and of the parameters used by the statistical model to represent the distribution of the previous values. For example, for the average/standard deviation model, the parameters are the total number of observations, the sum of the values of the observations, and the sum of the squares of the values of the observations. An operational model needs no parameters, since it is not based directly on past observations.

The first seven fields of the activity profile are independent of the considered subject and object, while the remaining three fields are not. A profile is uniquely identified by the 'variable-name', 'subject-pattern' and 'object-pattern' fields, which respectively indicate the type of profile, and the subject and object for which the profile is defined. All the profile components are invariant, except for the value field which is modified each time an action is executed under the profile monitoring.

When IDES receives an audit record satisfying the 'variable-name' pattern, it updates the distribution of the variable and executes some controls in order to detect possible anomalies.

The activity profiles can be defined with respect to single subjects and objects or to groups of subjects/objects. The activity profiles are automatically generated by IDES when a subject uses an object for the first time. This way, only useful profiles are considered: that is, those corresponding to a real use of the system. The definition and management of profiles for all possible subject/object combinations, which are never involved in any access request, is thus avoided.

(5) *Anomaly records:* records describing illegitimate behaviour by users. They are generated on abnormal behaviours with respect to the defined behaviour profiles. Each time an audit record is generated or a period terminates, IDES updates the activity profiles and checks for possible behaviour anomalies through the activity rules. If this control denotes an abnormal behaviour, an anomaly record is generated describing the anomalous behaviour detected.

The anomaly records are defined by 3-tuples of the form:

$\langle$event, time, profile$\rangle$

where:

- *Event* indicates the event that originated the anomaly. It takes the 'audit' value if the anomaly was originated by a single audit record, that is, by a single action; it takes the 'period' value if the anomaly arose from a set of actions over a given period of time;

- *Time.* Where the anomaly refers to a specific audit record, this attribute indicates the time shown inside this record; otherwise, it indicates the end time of the period to which the anomaly refers;
- *Profile* is the activity profile with respect to which the anomaly has been determined.

(6) *Activity rules:* these describe the actions that must be executed when some given conditions are satisfied. Such actions may involve profile updating, abnormal behaviour detection, connections between the anomalies detected and suspicions of intrusion, and reporting.

An activity rule specifies the action to be executed when an audit or anomaly record is generated, or when a period of time expires. Activity rules are composed of a *condition* which, if satisfied, causes the rule execution, and a body.

The condition is specified as a match between a pattern and an event. Activity rules can be grouped into four classes:

- *Audit record rules.* These are activated when a new audit record satisfies the activity profile. They update the profile to reflect the action examined and control possible behaviour anomalies. If an anomaly is detected, the corresponding anomaly record is generated;
- *Rules for periodic updating of the activity.* These are activated upon termination of an interval equal in duration to the period component of an activity profile. They update the profile and control possible behaviour anomalies. In this case also, if an anomaly is detected, a corresponding anomaly record is generated;
- *Anomaly record rules.* These are activated upon generation of an anomaly record coincident with the rule patterns relative to the 'event' or 'profile' elements. They bring the anomaly to the attention of the security officer, indicating the type of the suspected violation;
- *Rules for periodic analysis of the anomalies.* These are activated periodically so that reports about the anomalies detected in a given reference period can be generated.

IDES delegates to the monitored system the task of producing the audit records and forwarding them to IDES. As far as the definition of audit records is concerned, it should be noted that available information on accesses, which will be inserted into the audit records, depends on the moment when these same records have been generated. In fact, if the audit record is generated upon the request for an action, it is possible to record both executed and failed actions (for example, aborted or terminated because of a system crash). If the record is generated on completion of the action, further information can be recorded: for example, the amount of resources used by the action, or the exception conditions that possibly caused the abnormal termination of the action. However, recording upon action completion has a drawback: it does not allow possible anomalies to be immediately detected, especially those linked to intrusion attempts or system crashes. For this reason, some activities, such as login actions, the execution of highly risky commands, or access to sensitive data, are checked at request time. This way, possible penetrations can be immediately detected. Information regarding resource usage during the execution of actions is added to the record upon completion of these actions.

#### *Profile models and activity profiles management*

Profile models are the patterns used for the definition of new activity profiles. They have the same structure as the activity profiles; however, subject/object patterns are defined differently. The patterns define the audit records to which the profile corresponds, and describe how the subject/object pattern to be inserted into the generated activity profiles can be determined. Therefore, each activity profile is created on the basis of a particular profile model, specifying the subject and object to which the profile refers. When a new audit record is received, this is matched against the activity profiles and the profile models. This way, all the existing profiles are examined as well as all the new ones generated from the models.

A new profile corresponding to the audit record is therefore generated by properly instantiating the subject/object patterns and by copying all the other patterns from the profile model. This profile is then matched against the existing ones. If its values are equal to those of an existing profile it is rejected, otherwise it is inserted. The profile corresponding to the audit record (generated or existing) is then submitted for evaluation.

### 6.3.3 System architecture

When an audit record is generated, it is controlled by IDES against the profiles. The matching of the patterns against this record determines the rules for profile updating, for behaviour anomaly control, and for drawing possible anomalies to the administrator's attention. The security officer takes part in the determination of the profile models in order to state the behaviour aspects to be controlled. However, both the rules and the profile structure are independent of the system under control.

The actions controlled by IDES are the standard operations on the monitored system: login, command and program execution, and accesses to physical resources and to files. The system does not consider complex actions exploiting possible system weakness (known or suspected). Since IDES is independent of the monitored system, it cannot know the possible vulnerabilities of a given system. A first prototype is described in Denning (1987b).

IDES has been developed as a prototype using the Oracle relational DBMS for management of all the IDES information. The implementation language is C. Database updating and profile matching operations are expressed in embedded SQL (OraclePro*C). The prototype consists of processes interacting via the Oracle relational DBMS handling the *IDES database*. This database contains (Figure 6.4):

- *Audit data*. This is related to the audit record sent to IDES by the monitored system. It is stored in a table and examined to update the active data and the anomaly data;
- *Active data*. This contains the amount of activities carried out by a user with respect to a particular variable under measurement. A table of the intrusions considered is used for each variable. This data is periodically used to update the user profiles relative to a given variable;
- *Archive data*. This is the audit records examined: that is, already considered for profile updating and anomaly analysis. They are stored in a table and periodically removed;
- *Profile data*. This defines the normal behaviour profiles of each user or user group. It is stored in a set of tables (one for the intrusions considered for each variable);
- *Schedule data*. This indicates the updating period of each profile and the date of the last profile update. It is stored in a set of tables (one for the intrusions for each variable measured);
- *Anomaly data*. This is the anomaly records seen in the model. They are stored in a set of tables (one for each type of anomaly).

The *processes* that implement IDES communicate with one another via the IDES database. They are:

- *Receiver*. This implements the IDES protocol. It deciphers, analyses and validates the audit records coming from the system. It inserts valid records into the audit data;
- *Anomaly detector*. This takes a record relating to the audit data and updates the active data. If the value of the measure under control, for a particular user, exceeds the acceptability threshold indicated in the active data, the anomaly data is updated. When an audit record has been examined, it is removed from the active data and placed in the archive data;
- *Archiver*. This periodically backs up the data;
- *Profile updater.* This process updates the profiles on the basis of the active data at the end of the time period relating to the profiles considered;
- *Resetter of active data*. This periodically updates active data. At the end of the time period over which data is controlled, the activity gathered during this period is merged into the global activity, the period number is incremented, and the activity is set to 0;
- *Administrator interface*. This provides the IDES administrator with a complete view of the monitored system. The IDES interface, based on a window system, supplies:
  - a *state monitor*, which shows the current state of IDES;
  - an *anomaly monitor*, which shows the abnormal behaviour determined in the system for a measure (or for all the measures) that occurred in the past or in the present;
  - a *query monitor*, which allows the administrator to access the IDES database, using predefined queries or SQL queries.

Figures 6.4 and 6.5 show the IDES prototype structure, and the interactions among its components.

Since the IDES model is independent of the monitored system, the application environment, the system's types of vulnerability and the types of intrusions to be checked, IDES turns out to be a general-purpose intrusion

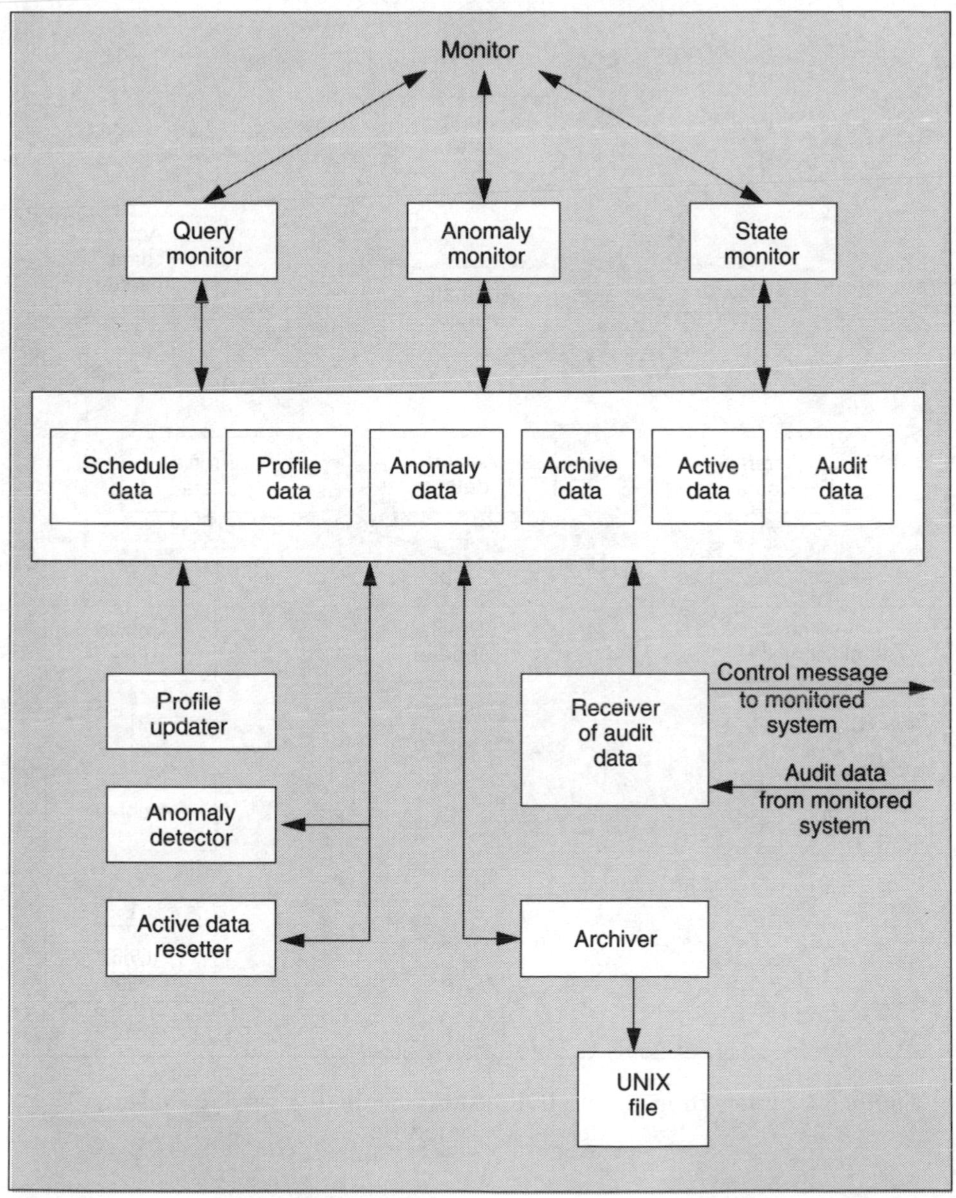


*Figure 6.4* Structure of the IDES prototype.

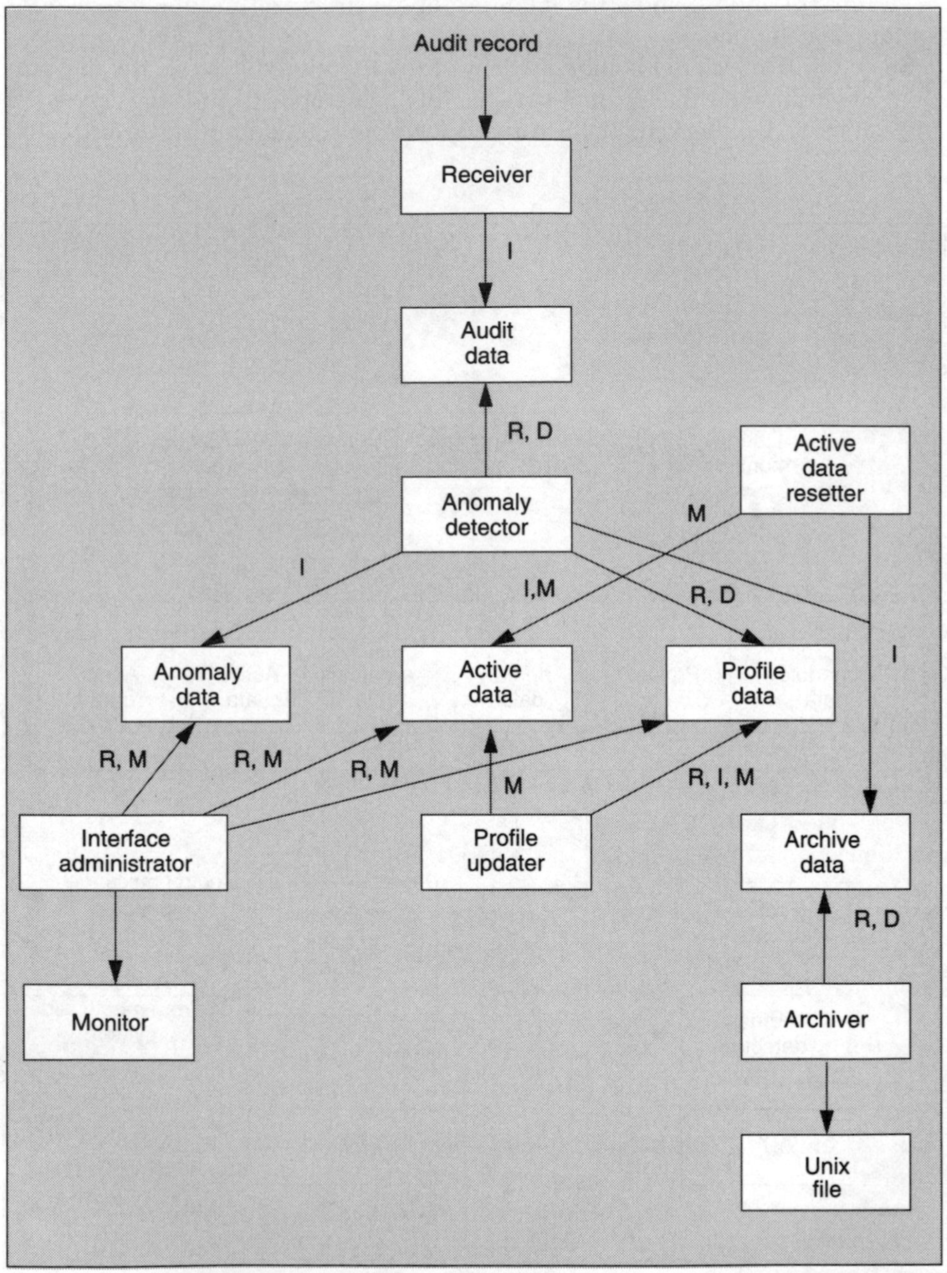


*Figure 6.5* Interaction among IDES components (R = read, I = insert, D = delete, M = modify).

detection system. The IDES prototype works on a different machine from that hosting the monitored system. This brings advantages in terms of:

- *Performance*. The presence of IDES does not increase the system response time;
- *Security*. IDES can be protected against the monitored system, so that a user of the system under control cannot access IDES to examine or alter it. Therefore, possible faults in the monitored system cannot compromise the secrecy or integrity of IDES;
- *Integration*. IDES can be easily adapted to different environments and integrated with various types of host system.

IDES has shown good powers of discrimination between normal and abnormal system use; the use of the prototype has shown a low number of false alarms and a rather satisfactory percentage of violation detections.

## 6.4 The Haystack system

Haystack (Smaha, 1988) is a prototype IDS in multi-user environments developed for the US Air Force computer systems. It was designed to help the System Security Officer (SSO) to detect and analyse in particular intrusions by authorized users (insiders). It uses behavioural constraints deriving from security policies and models of individual and user group behaviour.

The background of Haystack is constituted by the NCSC Trusted Computer System Evaluation Criteria TCSEC (see Chapter 3) about the B3 level upwards, which state that the TCB should also notify the Security Administrator when audited events go beyond fixed thresholds and terminate the events if they continue to exceed the thresholds. Its background is also the POSIX Committee IEEE P1003 standard for OS interface, and in particular the work done in security (Working Group P1003.6), including security auditing, which has a significant impact on security architectures.

Haystack reports on anomalous events in each day's audit trail files and is targeted at military systems, which, unlike most commercial systems, have explicit security policies. The target computer environment is a Unisys 1100/60 mainframe running OS/1100, which is the standard computing platform for all Air Force bases. The system handles unclassified but sensitive data; the primary threats to this data are data aggregation, violation of privacy, modification of logistic data and financial fraud (Smaha, 1988).

Haystack is designed to *augment* existing analysis tools and security personnel; it summarizes audit trail information into user behaviours, anomalous events and security incidents. Figure 6.6 shows the role of Haystack within the overall investigation process of the computer system.

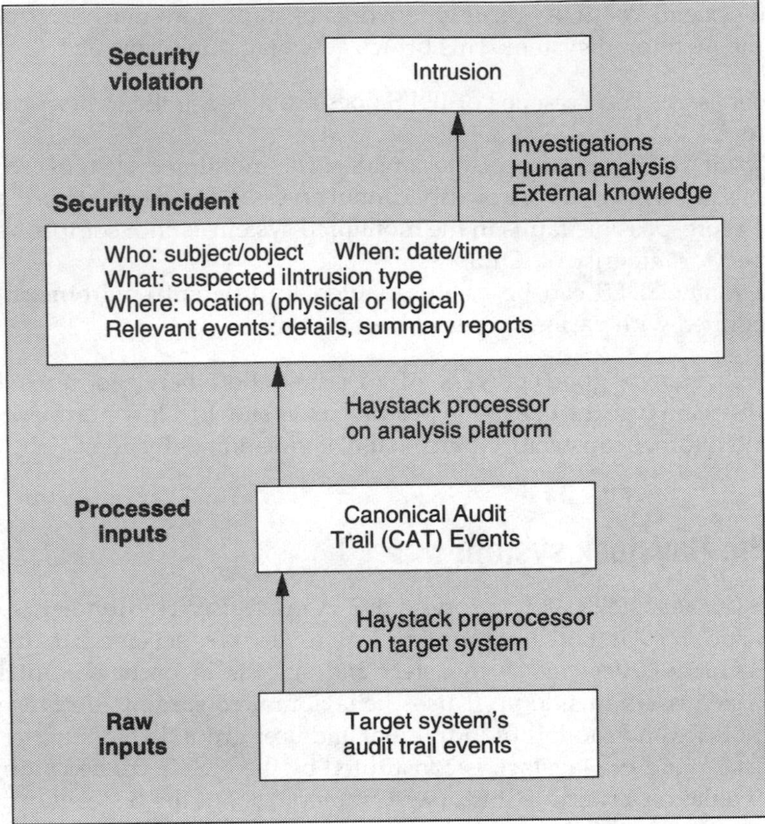


*Figure 6.6* Haystack's role in investigations (Smaha, 1988).

## 6.4.1 Intrusion types

Haystack has been designed to detect seven types of intrusion.

(1) *Attempted break-ins.* These are detected by monitoring the login attempts. A successful break-in occurs when an 'outsider' supplies a valid user identification and password, which can be detected by atypical behaviour profiles or violation of security constraints.

(2) *Masquerade attack.* This attack occurs when the intruder convinces the system that he or she is a certain user, generally one with higher privileges. These attacks are detected by atypical behaviour profiles or violation of security constraints.

(3) *Penetration of security system.* The intruder attempts to modify the security features of the system (for example, passwords). These attacks are detected by use of privileged logins or privileged system services.

(4) *Leakage.* Information is moved outside the system: for example, by printing a large number of files. The attack is detected by atypical usage of I/O resources.

(5) *Denial of service.* Resources are made unavailable to other users. This attack is detected by atypical usage of resources or by modification of privileges using special rights.

(6) *Malicious use.* This category includes various attacks, such as file deletion, resource misuse, and so on. It is also detected by atypical behaviour profiles, violations of security constraints, or use of special privileges.

(7) *Creation and propagation of viruses.* Although this is not a major design goal of Haystack, it is possible to detect some virus programs by exploiting some conditions met by the OS. Detecting modifications to executable files is one of the most effective detection techniques, which can be done if all executable files are marked by attributes of their names, or if the 'execute' right is maintained by the OS. Currently, none of these conditions holds in OS/1100.

### 6.4.2 Analysis of the audit trail

The amount of audit trail that can be dealt with at one time is based on the concept of *event horizon*. It is defined as the number of audited events the audit trail analysis system must remember in detail at one time while processing a series of events recorded in the audit trail.

Event aggregation is the technique used to reduce the amount of data to be analysed. In the simplest case, the horizon event is 1. In that case, each event is examined with no reference to details of preceding and succeeding events. Rather, information from an event is abstracted from the event data and stored as part of a data aggregate, such as a statistical element. The analysis of the event takes into account the recorded data aggregates obtained from the processing of previous events. The data aggregates are examined when all events have been aggregated.

In general, the IDS requires an event horizon greater than 1, for example, a horizon considering all the events in a user's session. An upper bound $B$ is needed for the number of events, which must be both reasonably small and meaningful for pattern matching. Such a value of $B$ is difficult to set – a session may contain a large number of events and it is difficult to find actual audited intrusions to be used as patterns. Haystack assumes an event horizon of 1.

### 6.4.3 Design principles and system architecture

The Haystack approach is similar to the approach of IDES (the model derives from Denning (1987a)); modifications have been made to adapt the model to the data available on the Haystack's target machine and to the security requirements of the US Air Force environment.

The design goals of Haystack can be summarized as follows.

- To improve the SSO's capabilities in a time-sharing processing environment.
- To provide suitable throughput with respect to a mainframe-based system.

- To monitor both time-sharing and batch users; users of specialized transaction processing applications are not monitored (these are controlled by application-level security systems, since audit data for these applications is inadequate for effective intrusion detection).
- To maximize the portability of the design (to ensure compatibility, for example, with POSIX standards, ANSI C, standard SQL).
- To design a friendly system, which does not discourage users.
- To use an available computing platform (based on an Intel 80286-like system, running MS-DOS).

The conceptual structure of Haystack is depicted in Figure 6.7.

Haystack is composed of two program clusters executing respectively on a mainframe and on a PC. At the highest level of the cluster, Haystack interacts with three entities: the OS, the SSO and the DBMS.

Moreover, Haystack maintains an evolving statistically based model of users; the model is adjusted to changes observed by the system in the user's work activity and according to user's new task requirements. It maintains data about past sessions in its database, thus helping the SSO look for tendencies in the user's behaviour over time. Some of the malicious 'training' that can be performed by a user (he modifies his behaviour gradually, training the system to learn the new behaviour and accept it as normal) can be detected as a statistical trend in user behaviour over time. The SSO can also apply 'ageing techniques' to take into account improvements gained by novice users, changes in task assignment, and usage frequency.

The OS/1100 audit trail is protected by access controls. Haystack's software, running on a PC, has password-based access control on the database (the PC is

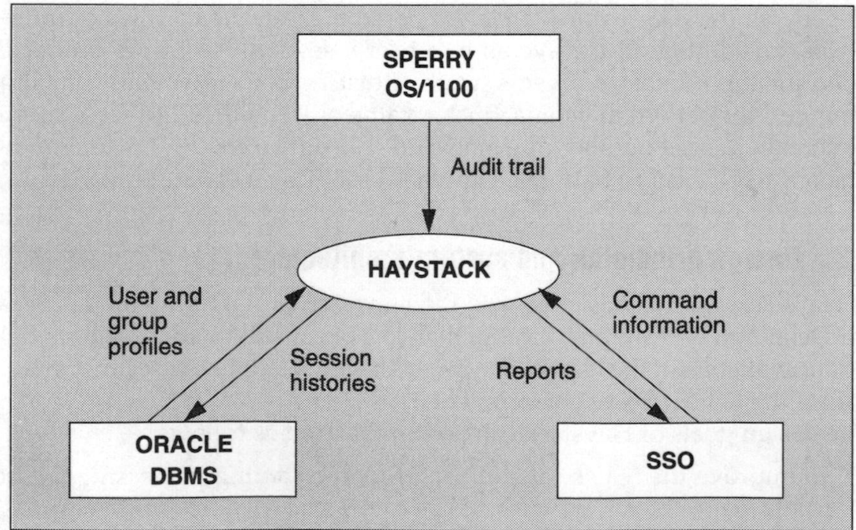


*Figure 6.7* Haystack's conceptual structure (Smaha, 1988).

also physically protected). Since the core of the audit processing is on a separate computer, the influence of the mainframe users on the audit system is limited. All SQL transactions, except the creation of new session history records, are audited to maintain a history of changes in Haystack and in its database.

## 6.5 The Multics Intrusion Detection and Alerting System (MIDAS)

The Multics Intrusion Detection and Alerting System (MIDAS) is an expert system developed for the US National Computer Security Center Multics-based networked environment (Sebring *et al.*, 1988). The design follows the guidelines of IDES: given the user and system statistical profiles, deviations form normal behaviour are detected. MIDAS has monitored the activity of more than 1200 users of the NCSC's Dockmaster network. MIDAS has been developed using an NCSC in-house expert system shell. Inference attacks are not considered. Trojan Horses and viruses belong to a single category, while denial of service and leakage are combined with misuse.

### 6.5.1 Rules

The rules (heuristics) in the rule base can be characterized according to the type of heuristics employed or to the monitored area.

The *types of heuristics* are:

(1) *Immediate attack.* These involve a small amount of data in the analysis, and use no statistical information. They detect audit log entries that are anomalous in themselves (that is, in isolation from other information).

(2) *User anomaly.* These employ statistical profiles to detect abnormal behaviours. They correspond to the SSO's intuition that 'something wrong is occurring' (for example, a user is logging in at unusual login time, therefore an anomaly record is generated).

(3) *System state.* These are analogous to anomaly heuristics but they define what is normal for the whole system. For example, these rules are responsible for detecting large numbers of failed logins system-wide, which denotes a possible attempt to penetrate the system.

The *areas of surveillance* are:

(1) *Attempted break-ins.* This area focuses on login failures; therefore rules in this category monitor excessive password failures on a system account.

(2) *Masquerade.* Detection is based on the assumption that the parameters of normal user–system interaction are useful for sampling activity attributed to that user but deviating from the user's statistical norms. Examples of factors characterizing the user are: connection origin, login time, resource usage.

(3) *Penetration.* This involves the detection of violations of security mechanisms. It is addressed by immediate attack, use anomaly and system state heuristics targeted toward access or attempted access of sensitive programs/data.

(4) *Misuse.* Abnormal resource usage reveals potential masquerades or valid users performing undesired activities. Inactivity is not reported as an attack. This area of concern also includes covert channel attacks: in Multics 11.0 all large covert channel sources have been eliminated, while medium and small covert channels are audited by the OS and also audited by MIDAS.

(5) *Trojan Horses and viruses.* Key factors are access violations on system sensitive objects and execution statistics violating the norms established for given commands. Access violations on sensitive objects denote the possible insertion of a virus; monitoring execution statistics attempts to detect their presence.

Most of the MIDAS rules are 'sensory rules' which detect anomalous activity and assert conclusions in the knowledge base representing the suspected problem. A set of 'secondary rules' operate only on the output of the sensory rules.

### 6.5.2 MIDAS operation

MIDAS constantly monitors user activity and the system state. The SSO may decide to work directly on the warning messages or analyse the recorded audit data in detail using the MIDAS interface (for example, querying the system or user state, or tracing some user activities). MIDAS is composed of the following parts (see Figure 6.8):

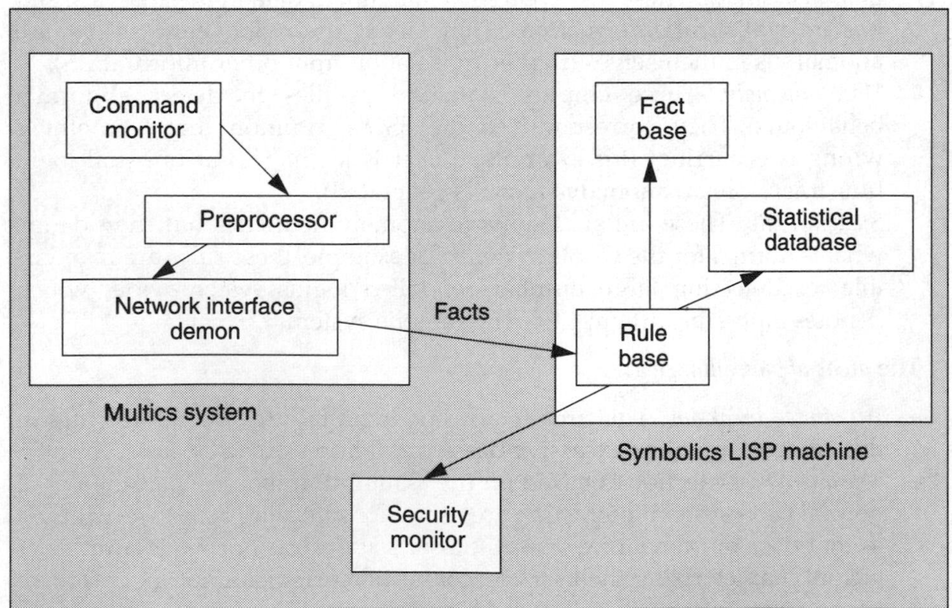


*Figure 6.8* MIDAS architecture (Sebring *et al.*, 1988).

- A command monitor that intercepts data resulting from command execution and not audited by Multics;
- A preprocessor that normalizes into a canonical form the audit log entries from the Dockmaster;
- A network interface demon;
- A statistical DB of the system and user statistics that have been recorded;
- A knowledge base composed of a base of current facts and of a rule base;
- A user interface for the SSO.

Upon generation of an audit record, the preprocessor filters out irrelevant data and constructs an assertion, which is forwarded to the network interface demon and passed to the expert system. The fact is inserted into the fact base; this causes a binding between the fact and all the matching rules in the rule base. Any such rules then fire; depending on the fact, a chain of rules fires giving various possible results (from warnings to the operator through to stop actions).

MIDAS statistics record the aggregation of monitored activities: the comparison between past activities and current actions determines whether the current activity is outside the norm. Statistics about users are updated when user behaviour changes. Session statistics are also kept by MIDAS for each user; these include some values used as thresholds for all the activities monitored for each user. For example, as described in Sebring *et al.* (1988), if a user's statistics indicate that during his 350 sessions he triggered an average of 20 errors, with a standard deviation of 20, the threshold of 58 is stored in the user's session statistics profile; 58 becomes the upper limit for his normal activity.

Audit data is preprocessed and data of the following form is obtained:

<subject> <object> <action> <exception> <time-stamp>

A *user pane* is provided at the interface consisting of the login time, userid, project, and tag for all the processes in the monitored system. A '?' flag indicates the user is suspected, the suspicion being generated as a result of the user having triggered some combination of rules, or by independent observation performed by the operator of the Dockmaster network. Another flag (denoted by 'M') indicates that a user session is being strictly monitored. The audit data is also reflected in the MIDAS *warning pane*, which displays the warning messages and MIDAS results obtained via rule execution. These messages are hierarchically grouped into classes of related messages. Finally, a *command pan*e is available to the MIDAS operator to allow him to modify system parameters or to generate different displays.

Initially, MIDAS was tested on 105 Dockmaster users (around 11% of the total user population). Under explicit simulated attacks, almost all anomalous activities were reported. In addition, a number of unexpected anomalies were detected and gave rise to a system review. MIDAS performs quickly because rules are compiled, because rules are generalized (whenever possible) and because many analysis functions are located in the user interface and can be triggered under operator control, rather than being placed in the rule base and being triggered autonomously by matching fact patterns.

## 6.6 Audit in Trusted Database Management Systems (TDBMS)

Extensive interviews with research and system development groups have given a set of security standards for the US government. The study, described in Schaefer *et al.* (1989), has contributed to providing guidance for TDBMS audit requirements and implementation strategies. The main result is that audit credibility is strictly coupled with the assurance that the TDBMS enforces its security policies correctly.

The TCSEC audit requirements state that a set of accountable events is defined, and each event must be associated with an accountable user and recorded in a protected audit log together with the proper event context (user-id, date, time, place, event type, and so on). It has been observed that, while an audit log is needed especially when security is lacking, the system may also lack the mechanisms for recording/detection of accountable actions or for protecting its audit data from observation, modification or erasure by intruders. The intelligent use of an audit mechanism can also reveal security flaws and weaknesses in the system.

Among the major findings of the study, the following key questions have been identified:

- *Audit data volume.* What effects do large data volumes have on the performance and operation of TDBMSs?
- *Application sensitivity.* In trusted OSs, the recordable facts are a function of the access control policy rather than of the application. Is it reasonable to expect that a TDBMS audit function should be adaptable to the applications (for example, to assure integrity or secrecy)?
- *Audit logs and transaction logs.* Most commercial DBMSs record DB 'modification' events and the transaction log is generally used to restore (part of) the state of a corrupted DB or to identify the accountable source of DB modifications. What portion of the security audit function can be fulfilled by the transaction/recovery log?
- *Verisimilitude and assurance.* What relationship exists between the recordable events on a TDBMS and what actually occurs on the system? For example, if the query text is recorded before its execution, how can it be concluded that the query was executed? Is it possible that the data returned to the query issuer is consistent with the query semantics?

The TCSEC requirements for audit in trusted systems address mostly the recording of access mediation decisions. Initially, the TCSEC requirements were oriented to auditing in trusted OSs where the primary security concern is *data confidentiality*. The extension to TDBMSs is linked to issues such as *complex access controls, additional vulnerabilities, finer granularity and volume, control objectives* and *abuse of authority* (for many TDBMSs, abuse of authority by authorized users poses a greater risk than abuses by unauthorized people).

### 6.6.1 Study results

The basic findings resulting from the study are:

- The goals of auditing depend strongly on the application, security policy and environment threats. However, the ability to capture data for auditing can be restricted to the TDBMS architecture. This means that the policy and the application determine what should be audited, while the system architecture determines what can be audited.
- Some TDBMS products provide audit data which is more relevant than that collected by their host OS. Moreover, much transaction data is collected, but little is analysed because of the lack of automated tools. Some capabilities have been included in some systems (for example, Rougeau and Sturms, 1987; Hunt and Knode, 1988; *Oracle RDBMS Data Administrator's Guide* Version 6.0) but need validation of their usefulness.
- Meaningful analysis requires the collection and correlation of audit data from various stages of query processing. This is applicable if access mediation is performed by various mechanisms at different architecture and abstraction levels.
- Intrusion detection technology has demonstrated some successes in OS audit trails, and may be extensible to analysis of TDBMS audit trails.
- Regarding the 'verisimilitude' of event recording in audit trails, the question arises about whether the audited event actually took place. It is concluded that a lack of credibility is sometimes symptomatic of basic weaknesses in assurance; thus, questions about audit data credibility provide a useful design testing technique for security.

*Problems* posed by *transaction management* derive primarily from the illusion that certain events (the component operations) that actually occurred on the DB, did not. This happens when a transaction is not completed and the DB is rolled back by the DBMS. Problems of confidentiality may arise. In fact, before being aborted, a transaction may try various read and write operations. Therefore, an accurate audit trail may need to include the *history of events* that occurred in aborted transactions. In other words, the audit system has to distinguish between audited events that were committed and those that were not and, for each event, the time of its effect. For example, the effect of a write attempt may have been delayed or cancelled by the transaction management mechanism in response to later events. Consequently, the audit analysis tools are required to *interpret* access events and their *sequence* in the context of transaction commitment events.

DBMS *developers* have taken various approaches in selecting mechanisms for auditing, depending on the tools intended to process the audit data (OS tools or a DBMS). *Vendors* have often implemented the audit trail as a table in the Data Dictionary, exploiting the use of SQL to retrieve and analyse the audit data.

In the general case of an untrusted back-end DBMS incorporated in system architectures including a trusted OS (which favours system performance) –

implementable according to the principles described in Chapter 4 – there are two fundamental issues about auditing:

(1) If the query is captured in the form of text and recorded by the OS/TCB before its passage to the back-end DBMS, how can it be determined that the DBMS response and the returned data are correct with respect to the formal semantics of the query?
(2) If a parsed (or compiled) version of the query is captured and recorded by the OS/TCB before its passage to the back-end DBMS, how can it be determined that the DBMS response and the returned data are correct with respect to the formal semantics of the query or its parsed/compiled form?

So far, there are no satisfactory answers to these questions. Instead, when considering monolithic DBMS security architectures, even with completely untrusted DBMSs (see Chapter 4), different results exist and several issues can be resolved.

- These architectures do not relegate the enforcement of mandatory access policy to any untrusted code, so the TCSEC MAC requirements should be preserved by these architectures.
- Deletion of relations/DBs can be validated by proving that the query (a user command) is captured by trusted code or by proving that there exists a mapping between the DB object and the OS objects, or by proving that the OS records its participation in the resulting deletion event.
- The granularity of the DBMS/OS object mapping relates also to audit relative to other forms of update, including object reuse requirements. If the OS/TCB has to protect individual relations or tuples, it could be determined which were modified or deleted as a side-effect of the query. Otherwise, coarser information could still be identified although its value for analysis purposes is questionable.
- There is still no evidence that full query semantics were related to the captured or recorded combined DBMS/OS execution history.

In conclusion, audit appears also to be of great utility for assessing the level of assurance and trust of DBMS system security architectures.

## 6.7 The Wisdom and Sense (W&S) anomaly detection system

The W&S system, developed at Los Alamos National Laboratory from 1984, is statistically based. It automatically generates rules from historical data using machine learning techniques, and employs these rules to identify transactions that represent a potential variance to fixed usage patterns (Vaccaro and Liepins, 1989).

### 6.7.1 Approach: the rule base

W&S has no rule templates but rather constructs its rules without human guidance, using inductive concept learning. It relies on its own examination of historical data. The form of the rules is determined by the system software capability to detect patterns in the data. The rules are often creative and non-intuitive and add to those that an expert might suggest. For example, some security flaws were detected in part by W&S-generated rules specifying that highly privileged users do not remain logged in for more than 12 hours, dial-up users no longer than 8 hours, and privileged users do not work over dial-up lines during working hours. One flaw was in the OS (the OS configuration did not terminate privileged sessions on dial-up lines): accidentally, a regular user received system privileges and remained connected for two days until he lost the phone connection because of line noise; the accident was detected by W&S via 'trivial' rules, disregarded by humans.

The rule base is large ($10^4$ to $10^6$ rules) and can be searched within 0.05 seconds. Therefore, W&S is capable of real-time detection of anomalies.

### 6.7.2 Data model

While other statistically based systems operate on continuous metric data, using 'categorical' or non-metric data mapped to some metric, W&S has a categorical view of data in that it sees the universe of possible transactions as a collection of events, rather than as a continuous ordered space. In fact, most of the available data is categorical, such as locations, object types, days of the week, names. Moreover, continuous data items are analysed, such as material weights, material processing times, CPU time usage and I/O volumes. Rather than creating metrics for non-metric data and treating the continuous data as unimodal normal data, the system includes heuristics for dealing with the data in its categorical form and for mapping skewed multimodal continuous data into categorical data.

This model for audit log records allows human-readable rule bases to be developed. Data is represented by unique character strings such as 'Smith' for a user, or 'FTN.EXE' for a program; continuous data is mapped to closed ranges (for example, from 10 to 100 seconds). Hence, the W&S rule base can be extended and substituted easily by human experts.

If behaviour differs from normal patterns, and if data indicating the difference is collected, it should be possible to compare new audit data with normal patterns and detect the anomaly. This problem can be solved by creating specialized profiles of users, terminals, executable programs, privileges, and so on, and determining whether the new data violates these profiles.

W&S receives audit data from the OS and periodically analyses it using a 'rule forest' where historically acceptable values are specified. The forest includes redundancy to interpret cases where part of the audit data is missing. Relevant issues are the significance of rule violations and the combination of elements across many rules.

### 6.7.3 Evaluation of rules for anomaly detection

Selected historical audit log data is used to generate a tree-structured forest describing historical behaviour patterns. The rule creation process is repeated for various combinations of conditioning values. For rule generation, the historical data is acquired, and then a rule base is generated in two steps. Experience with real data indicates that a scheduled rule base regeneration every 1–4 weeks is reasonable.

For *explanation*, one audit record is stored each time a process terminates, and includes data about the process invoker, the name of the executed process, its privileges, and the system resources used. A rule base creation program examines a history of audit log records to create instantiated rules. A rule base is applied to audit log data recorded either in batch mode or in real time to determine potential anomalies. The rule base also reflects the quality of the behaviour patterns it has learned. A *rule grade* is stored with the rule to indicate the conditions under which it applies.

A rule Left Hand Side has the form:

- field values (or value range);
- computed values based on data in a set of related records (for example, mean time between occurrences of a given event type);
- subroutines returning a Boolean value.

An anomaly record that violates many conclusions (Right Hand Sides) of rules is considered anomalous. If the record contains several anomalous fields or a highly anomalous field, the record is considered anomalous.

The *observation units* in W&S are the *transactions*, which are aggregated using the *thread* mechanism. A thread class is defined in terms of the data values of specific fields of audit records: for example, user/terminal thread class. Each thread class has an associated set of operations to be performed on a member's private data each time a new record is processed. The operations consist of computations such as event type counts, averages, differences, and so on.

An anomaly is detected for a thread when a new audit record for that thread is unusual and makes the thread member's score go beyond a threshold. The thread score is called its *figure of merit*. If a series of related records – for example, those for a particular user and terminal – are anomalous, the whole thread is considered anomalous.

### 6.7.4 Implementation

The basic design criteria of W&S are:

- to format raw audit data in usable forms;
- to store and use large base rules efficiently;
- to manage conflicting rules;
- to deal with errors, and with uncertain knowledge;
- to provide human-readable feedback of anomalies;
- to minimize the interferences with the monitored system;
- to generate a portable IDS.

The concepts of W&S are implemented through three components:

(1) *Data preprocessor.* This compacts historical transaction data. The VMS Audit Log Analysis Package version of W&S uses image termination records from the DEC VMS accounting log as its audit record source. W&S extracts 16 fields from the standard VMS image termination records, 13 of which are used for rule base generation (the remainder are used for display).

(2) *Rule base generator.* This processes the condensed historical data to produce the forest of rule trees. Rules in a forest require an average of 6–8 bytes each, which is achieved by sharing rule data and by using the data value dictionary created when the historical data is condensed.

(3) *Transaction analyser.* This is composed of a set of Sense modules which provide an interactive window-based interface to the kernel inference engine, to the transaction analysis tools, and to the configuration setting and rule base maintenance routines. Sense, the anomaly detection module, computes a transaction score (figure of merit (FOM)). Then, an *anomaly* is *detected* whenever either the transaction or thread FOM exceeds a limit set by the operator. Finally, *anomaly resolution* explains the meaning and likely cause of an anomalous transaction. The W&S transaction analyser supports:
   - Identification of the data in a record that apparently triggered the anomaly;
   - Listing of the violated rules that triggered the anomaly;
   - Provision of a thread history;
   - Suggestions of data fields that could avoid the anomaly determination.

W&S is undergoing operational tests with more and more complex intrusion scenarios. It seems applicable to various application types where large volumes of repetitive data are generated by plants or systems (for example, chemical, mechanical, electrical, or biological systems).

## 6.8 The Time-based Inductive Machine (TIM) approach

The intrusion detection approach presented in Teng *et al.* (1990) uses a domain-independent method and program called TIM for the incremental acquisition of symbolic patterns from observations of a temporal process. TIM discovers temporal patterns in the data using inductive generalization. A set of hypotheses (that is, temporal patterns represented as *rules*) generalized from observed data is maintained and modified dynamically. The hypotheses are generated or modified dynamically in order to keep good-quality rules in the rule base. A *high-quality hypothesis* must provide high accuracy in prediction and possess a high level of confidence (it is confirmed by many previous observations). The robustness of TIM is enhanced by the feature of producing partially accurate temporal patterns when no better patterns can be generated.

### 6.8.1 Input data and rules

Input data in TIM is called episodes, consisting of a sequence of events. An event is a snapshot of a temporal process at a given time.

TIM generates rules that can accurately predict the occurrence of given event types: given an event type to be predicted, the goal is to discover, from observations, a set of temporally related conditions that predicts the time of occurrence of the event relative to the conditions.

A session in an audit trail is an episode where each event is one single entry described in terms of a number of attributes, and where the events are considered as sequentially related ('next' or 'last' events are defined).

An event is described in terms of:

- *Time:* the sequence number of the event in a login session (or time stamp). An example is: Jan-18-1994 09:25:12
- *Description:* this is a set of attributes associated with the event:
  - *event-type:* for example, network access;
  - *image-name:* name of the executable image that has been executed (for example, disk:backup.exe);
  - *object-name:* accessed object (for example, disk:authorization.dat);
  - *object-type:* type of accessed object (for example, file);
  - *privileges-used:* the privileges used by the executable image (for example, SYSTEM);
  - *status:* status of the execution (for example, 'normal successful completion');
  - *process-ID:* identifier of the process (for example, 00000070).

Security event rules form the basis of a profile for each user (or group) and are generated by TIM. They describe behaviour patterns based on past security audit history. Each rule describes a sequential pattern that predicts the next possible events. For example, given five events $E_1$ to $E_5$, a possible rule is:

$$E_1 - E_2 - E_3 \rightarrow (E_4 = 95\%; E_5 = 5\%)$$

which indicates that if $E_1$ is followed by $E_2$ and $E_2$ is followed by $E_3$, there is a probability equal to 95% that $E_4$ will follow, and a probability equal to 5% that $E_5$ will follow, based on previous observations.

More generalized rules can be produced by TIM, and redundant rules are discarded.

### 6.8.2 Anomaly detection

TIM detects anomalies in two ways.

(1) *Deviation detection.* A deviation is detected if a sequence of events triggers the left-hand-side of a rule R, while the subsequent events deviate from the established pattern predicted in R. For each rule, an observed short-term pattern is matched against an observed long-term pattern to decide whether a deviation has occurred.

(2) *Detection of unrecognized activities.* When a sequence of events does not trigger the LHS of any rule, the sequence is considered as an unrecognized activity which can be presented to the security manager. The activity can generate new rules and update the profiles.

*Security management* is enabled to undertake different actions when unusual event sequences are detected, depending on the degree of deviation from typical profiles. Also, the security event patterns generated by TIM are a compression of all security events that occurred in the past and could be used to facilitate security management. For example, one rule can be recognized as a backup activity, another rule as a *project development activity*. Thus, instead of showing the security manager statistics about the activities of the group members, TIM may present textual descriptions of the observations. The benefits are that security managers only need to deal with reduced portions of the audit information and that security messages can be tailored to the monitored applications.

With respect to statistical methods, the inductive approach of TIM differs in that:

- The inductive approach uses a heuristic-based search to find the hypotheses that satisfy given criteria. Instead, the statistical approach is used for the evaluation of a selected hypothesis or for fitting a given class of models.
- The inductive approach uses logical expressions, while statistical approaches use analogue models.

### 6.8.3 System considerations

A prototype architecture has been developed for the TIM program, consisting of four modules:

- A data collection and conversion module
- A user profile generation module based on TIM
- An exception detection module
- A user interface module.

The system runs on a VAX 3500 computer with 32 megabytes. In tests, audit events were recorded with user consent; anomalies were detected within seconds of their occurrence. Profile generation proved very expensive in terms of computation; therefore, it was delayed for later processing. The analysis was conducted on the activities of two groups of users (Teng *et al.*, 1990): one group activated an average of 46 different executable images and accessed an average of 512 different files on a VAX/VMS system in a given time period, while the second group activated an average of 16 different executable images and accessed an average of 276 different files within the same period. The first group, in spite of a wider range of activity, showed stronger behavioural patterns in terms of sequences of activities. TIM generated rules for the first group with an entropy value less than 0.25 (9.5% of the rules), able to explain more than 63.5% of the security events over a given time period. Therefore, the first group had a consistent behaviour that could be described in terms of sequential rules, and consequently the anomaly detection sensitivity of the system was increased.

## 6.9 Trends in intrusion detection

Some research topics in auditing and in related areas, different from computer security, are ongoing and seem promising in terms of their ability to improve the approach to real-time intrusion detection described in this chapter. In particular:

### 6.9.1 Machine learning (ML)

As observed in Laird (1992), ML techniques can be used in IDSs to observe a given system and 'learn' to characterize 'normal' activities and thus detect abnormal conditions. Applications of ML techniques have been proposed in some studies and used, for example, in the Wisdom & Sense system. In particular, four areas of ML seem to have the greatest potential for IDSs:

- *Concept learning*. This is the task of training a system to classify elements into categories, which are fixed by the teacher, by considering the element attributes. A classification task in the field of misuse detection is to state whether a certain work session is intrusive or normal, using a variety of attributes available from the audit trail. Finding the relevant features among a multitude of irrelevant attributes is the major problem in concept learning. However, specific concepts, such as deciding whether a user is an abuser of a specific type, is a more feasible problem.
- *Clustering*. This consists of partitioning a collection of elements intro groups of related elements using some 'similarity' criteria. Clustering also includes the task of constructing the categories and the classification rules but in a different way from concept learning. For IDSs, classifying users, sessions, resource access requests and so on into sets of related elements is a possible application.
- *Predictive learning*. A temporal model of data is constructed giving the ability to learn about intrusion events from temporal data and sequences of discrete events. This method, based mainly on Markov and time-series models, usually incorporates additional knowledge about the specific application. The fewer bits *(compression ratio)* are required to represent a sequence of events, the more powerful the predictive model is. In misuse detection, a predictive model can be learned and characterized numerically by its compression ratio or mean rate of predictability: thus, if an observed sequence of events resists compression by a significant amount beyond the fixed measures, that sequence is likely to be anomalous. Compression is also useful during transmission of audit data along insecure channels.

- *Extraction of features.* The feature extraction problem (distinguishing the relevant from the irrelevant features, and combining the relevant features into a function that identifies an event, for example, an intrusion) is a problem of ML that limits the usefulness of standard techniques for concept learning and clustering. Some promising new approaches provide algorithms that ameliorate the effectiveness of feature extraction techniques (the Littlestone algorithm, the Pagallo and Matheus algorithm, or techniques applying genetic algorithms to the learning of effective classification functions).

Both concept learning and clustering, although limited by their complexity, are currently available as existing technologies. The challenge for the three categories is partly linked to complexity, partly to the ability to select appropriate criteria tailored to the application environment.

### 6.9.2 Software engineering techniques

Many system vulnerabilities that allow intruders to get or extend access privileges may be viewed as problems in software validation and verification. Moreover, operational/administrative flaws make even the best-designed system vulnerable if operated improperly. Therefore, better software construction and management techniques, by permitting the avoidance and detection of flaws that can be exploited by intruders, are a means of protection against intrusion attacks. In Spafford (1992) three types of flaws that expose a system to potential intrusions are identified:

- *Design flaws.* These derive either from an erroneous interpretation of requirements or an erroneous implementation of specifications. Software validation and verification techniques are appropriate methods.

  Common design errors include failure to validate the number, size or address of arguments provided to privileged calls, careless treatment of sensitive data in shared memory/heaps/directories, and failure to report abnormal conditions and errors and to provide safe fault recovery. Attacks against these problems can be *specific* (when a class of systems is known to contain a certain flaw) or *generic* (someone attempts to discover if a weakness exists). In both cases, monitoring helps to combat the attacks (for example, monitoring behaviour patterns such as repeated invocation of system calls with an incorrect number of argument).
- *Faults.* Faults or bugs derive from generation of code that does not implement the specifications. Many security flaws are the result of bugs: improper selection of data types, use of improper parameters, boundary condition faults, synchronization mistakes, abnormal termination of privileged routines, and so on. Since it is usually impossible to state when debugging and testing are complete, software systems are exposed to a number of either specific or generic attacks. For these flaws also, monitoring can help in detecting attacks.
- *Operational/administrative flaws.* Setting parameters to inappropriate or inconsistent values may lower the security of a system. Common

problems are poor choice of defaults delivered by the vendors, wrong software configuration for the hardware used, patches and upgrades, systems from different vendors put to work together, or systems administered with more than one security policy. Most of the flaws are specific, and are often well known; therefore, intruders attempting to exploit these flaws may be identified by monitoring the program areas where these weaknesses are present.

### 6.9.3 Neural networks

Since neural networks support a flexible pattern recognition capability, they can be used for intrusion detection, and damage assessment and removal. The advantages derive from adaptive modelling of the users' and system's behaviour, and from the ability to deal with unknown attacks (viruses or intrusions). Neural networks are proposed for IDSs to construct a front-end status monitor able to recognize unknown viruses and malicious users' behaviour patterns. In Fox *et al.* (1990) neural networks are proposed for IDSs for two potential uses: to learn specific virus patterns and take some actions if the virus appears, and to adaptively model the users' and system's normal state and take some action when anomalies are observed. Fox *et al.* (1990) describe a prototype architecture where neural networks of the 'Self-Organizing Feature Map' are used as a real-time background monitor to adaptively model normality; when deviations are noted, an operator is notified, who can activate an expert system to perform in-depth analysis. The network can be configured to notify the operator, log a report, or take more drastic measures. Its purpose is to learn the normal activities and adapt to *gradual* changes (*rapid* changes are caught by the expert system, which includes features taken from other systems, primarily IDES and MIDAS). A prototype system has been developed for a network arranged in a $12 \times 12$ vector developed on a Symbolics machine, on a VAX-like machine. Appropriate statistical simulations were developed for each of the 11 identified parameters (CPU usage, paging activity, mailer activity, disk accesses, and so on). There are drawbacks in that the network is itself subject to subtle attacks, and in the use of the system in networked environments.

## References

Anderson J.P. (1980). Computer security threat monitoring and surveillance. *Technical Report*, James P. Anderson & Co., April

Brown C. (1984). DOTTYE – An Interlisp program for the analysis of the network security controller files. *Technical Report*, Los Alamos National Lab., January

Denning D.E. (1987a). IDES – an Intrusion Detection Model. *IEEE Trans. Software Eng.*, **13**(2), February

Denning D.E. (1987b). A prototype of IDES – a Real Time Intrusion Detection Expert System. *Technical Report*, Computer Science Laboratory, SRI International, August

Denning D.E. and Neumann P.G. (1985). Requirements and model for IDES – a real time Intrusion Detection Expert System. *Technical Report,* Computer Science Laboratory, SRI International, August

Fox K.L., Henning R.R., Reed J.H. and Simonian R.P. (1990). A neural network approach towards intrusion detection. *Technical Report,* Harris Corp., Government Info. Systems Division, July

Garvey T D. and Lunt T.F. (1991). Model-based intrusion detection. In *Proc. 14th National Computer Security Conf.,* October

Halme L. and Kahn B. (1988). Building a security monitor with adaptative user work profiles. In *Proc. 11th National Computer Security Conf.,* October

Hochberg J., Jackson K. *et al.* (1993). NADIR: An automated system for detecting network intrusion and misuse. *Computers & Security,* Elsevier Sc. (North-Holland), **12**(3)

Hunt R.A. and Knode R.B. (1988). Making databases secure with TRUEDATA technology. In *Proc. 11th National Computer Security Conf.,* October

Karger P.A. (1987). Limiting the damage potential of discretionary Trojan horses. In *Proc. IEEE Symp. on Security and Privacy,* April

Laird P. (1992). Machine-Learning in intrusion and misuse detection. In *Proc. Workshop on Future Detections in Computer Misuse and Anomaly Detection,* Univ. of California, Davis, March

Litecky C.R. and Rittenberg L.E. (1981). An external auditor's review of computer controls. *Comm. ACM,* **24**(5)

Lunt T.F. (1993). A survey of intrusion detection techniques. *Computers & Security,* Elsevier Sc. (North-Holland), **12**(4)

Neumann P. G. (1985). Audit trail analysis and usage collection and processing. *Technical Report Project 5910,* SRI International, January

Nguyen T. *et al.* (1985). Checking an expert system knowledge base for consistency and completeness. In *Proc. 9th International Joint Conf. on Artificial Intelligence,* vol. 1

*Oracle RDBMS Database Administrator's Guide,* Version 6.0

Perry W.E. (1982) Developing a computer security and control strategy. *Computers & Security,* Elsevier Sc. (North-Holland), **1**(1)

Perry W.E. and Warner H.C. (1978). System auditability: friend or foe? *Journal of Accountancy,* February

Proc. Workshop on *Future Directions in Computer Misuse and Anomaly Detection,* Univ. of California, Davis, March 1992

Rougeau P.A. and Sturms E.D. (1987). The Sybase Secure Dataserver: a solution to the multilevel secure DBMS problem. In *Proc. 10th National Computer Security Conf.,* September

Schaefer M., Hubbard B., Sterne D., Haley T.K., McAuliffe J.N. and Wolcott D. (1989). Auditing: a relevant contribution to trusted database management systems. In *Proc. 5th Annual Computer Security Applications Conf.,* December

Sebring M., Shellhouse E., Hanna M. and Whitehurst R. (1988). Expert systems in intrusion detection: a case study. In *Proc. 11th National Computer Security Conf.,* October

Smaha S.E. (1988). Haystack: an intrusion detection system. In *Proc. 4th Aerospace Computer Security Appl. Conf.*, December

Spafford E.H. (1992). Common system vulnerabilities. In *Proc. Workshop on Future Detections in Computer Misuse and Anomaly Detection*, Univ. of California, Davis, March

Teng H.S., Chen K. and Lu S.C. (1990). Adaptative real-time anomaly detection using inductively generated sequential patterns. In *Proc. IEEE Symp. on Security and Privacy*, Oakland, May

Tsudik G. and Summers R. (1990). AudES – An expert system for security auditing. In *Proc. AAAI Conf. on Innovative Applications in AI*, May

Vaccaro H.S. and Liepins G.E. (1989). Detection of anomalous computer session activity. In *Proc. IEEE Symp. on Security and Privacy*, May

Young C. (1987). Taxonomy of computer virus defense mechanisms. In *Proc. 10th National Computer Security Conf.*, September

# 7 Security models for next-generation databases

## 7.1 Introduction

In presenting data security throughout this book, we have illustrated the 'traditional' security models: that is, models for the protection of operating systems and relational databases. We have shown that the definition and enforcement of security in database systems generates various problems, deriving from the granularity of database information and from the semantic meaning and relationships among data items. For example, the application of mandatory policies in relational databases generates inference and poly-instantiation problems.

These problems become more relevant when defining security models for data models endowed with a richer semantics, owing to the complexity of the correlations among data items and to the existence of inheritance principles among data (such as is-a, instance-of, part-of links). These aspects lead to new security requirements that are not satisfied by traditional security models.

In particular, when applying the mandatory policy it must be ensured that no illegal flow of information can occur through the semantic correlation among data. For example, in object-oriented models, if a class is defined as a subclass of a class with a higher classification, low-classified users accessing the subclass could come to know some information of the parent class. The classification of objects must therefore be controlled to prevent, on the one hand, users from inferring sensitive information, and on the other, the possible non-availability of data. This last case can occur, for example, when low-level information is stored in high-level objects, thus becoming inaccessible to authorized users.

As far as discretionary policies are concerned, relationships existing between protected objects must be evaluated since they may imply relationships between the authorizations.

Among new-generation systems for information management, we consider active and object-oriented database systems, because of the advances in technology, which resulted in the production of prototypes and commercial systems (Ullman, 1988), and because security models and techniques have given significant results for these systems.

In this chapter, the basic characteristics of active and object-oriented databases are given first (Sections 7.1.1 and 7.1.2 respectively). Then, discretionary and mandatory security models for active databases are described (Section 7.2). The remainder of the chapter is devoted to security of object-oriented systems (Bertino and Martino, 1991); work on security models for these databases, although in a preliminary stage for both discretionary and mandatory policies, has attracted various research efforts which have led to the systems illustrated from Section 7.3 onwards.

### 7.1.1 Elements of active databases

Active databases are characterized by a rule system that causes the database management system to react to events by triggering rules.

In active databases (Haas *et al.*, 1990; Stonebraker, 1992), a knowledge base of production rules can be associated to a database of facts; the rules describe the operations to be automatically executed when particular *events* occur and/or given *conditions* are satisfied.

The most general form for rules is a triple containing *Event, Conditions, Actions*: upon the occurrence of an Event, some Conditions are evaluated and, if these are satisfied, the Actions are executed. Thus, a database system can autonomously (without user intervention) execute some operations.

Various types of rule can be specified. Rules can describe the company's personnel policy, or the automatic production of reports. For example, when a time condition is verified, say, the last day of the month, the system executes the actions for report production, with no need for a specific user request.

Moreover, rules can be used to maintain database integrity constraints. These rules specify the conditions *('rule condition')* to be satisfied by the values of a (set of) certain attribute(s) and are activated upon a 'data modification' event (insert, delete, update operations) of the attributes under consideration. Rules indicate the actions to be executed if the integrity conditions are not satisfied. For example, the actions may indicate that the effects of an item update should be propagated to other data items, or that a requested update cannot be executed.

Further rules can be specified to maintain *derived data*: that is, views. In this case, the rules specify that when an operation (insert, modify, update) is executed on some data items, some operations must also be executed on other data items. For example, in a database relation describing the sum of the employees' salaries, a rule can be specified that, upon operations on the 'salary' of individual employee records, is activated to consistently update the attribute 'total amount of salaries'.

Two different approaches can be used to store the rules. The first consists of embedding the rules in an application program or storing them in a knowledge base managed by a rule management system. The second approach consists of coupling the rule system with a DBMS.

The fact that read, insert, update operations can be automatically activated by rules, and therefore without user intervention, implies new protection requirements, and new issues to be considered in the development of a protection system.

First, rules themselves need protection. This means that user knowledge about the rules existing in an active system must be controlled. Moreover, knowledge about parts of a rule (conditions, actions and effects of the rule) has to be taken into account for protection. The existence of rules in a system or their contents might need to be hidden, or it might be necessary to restrict user visibility of the effects produced by rule execution. These effects might allow unauthorized users to infer information. Also, a user might be authorized to know the existence of a rule but not to see its effects, or vice versa might be authorized for the rule effects but forbidden rule knowledge. In this last case, a user must ignore the fact that some information is produced by the execution of a rule.

The enforcement of mandatory policies requires control of the classification of the definitions of the rules, of their implementation and of the effects of the rules, in order to prevent possible illegal information flow. For example, an information flow can occur when the effects of a rule have lower sensitivity than the rule, or the actions observed by the rule.

The issue of *querying* the rule base is currently under investigation. In fact, commands that explain to the user the effects of his operations on the database are needed. The user would like to know what rules have been activated. For example, in Stonebraker *et al.* (1988) the 'describe' command can be used instead of 'retrieve': it returns the requested data only if it is actually stored as data; otherwise it returns the rule by which the value is derived. This explains to the user why a data element has a given value and, by iterating, the entire derivation path. If parts of this path are protected, limits should be imposed on the response returned to the query ('trace' command).

In active databases rules can be used to enforce security measures. In particular, rules can provide a means of specifying security constraints, such as in POSTGRES (Stonebraker *et al.*, 1988), where a rule like the following:

```
on retrieve to EMP.salary
then do append to AUDIT
  (name = current.name,
  salary = current.salary, user = user())
```

supports an audit trail.

### 7.1.2 Elements of object-oriented databases

Object-oriented databases (OODBs) have become very popular, because of their ability to support in a natural way advanced applications (for example, computer-aided design and engineering, hypermedia, office information systems, scientific applications) managing complex, possibly multimedia objects. OODBs are characterized by an object-oriented data model, allowing users to define static and dynamic properties of real-world objects (entities), constraints on them, and relationships between objects. OODBMSs are database management systems which directly support an object-oriented data model, providing object management functions. In the following, we describe the core concepts characterizing an object-oriented data model (Atkinson *et al.*, 1989; Bertino and Martino, 1991).

- *Object and object identifier.* Each real-world entity is modelled by an *object* associated with a unique identifier (called OID) that uniquely identifies the object in the database, independent of the values of its attributes.
- *Attributes and methods.* For each object, a set of *attributes* (instance variables), used to specify the object structure, and a set of *methods* (operations), used to specify the object behaviour, are defined. For a method, both a signature and an implementation are defined. The signature specifies the method name, the list of arguments, and the result. The method's implementation consists of code written in some programming language, realizing the service provided by the method.
- *Class.* A class is an abstraction mechanism, used to specify the definition of a set of similar objects sharing the same structure and behaviour, called the *class instances*, related to the class by means of the *instance-of* relationship. A class acts as a template for its instances, specifying a set of instance variables, a set of messages (that is, the external interface), and a set of methods, invoked by messages. Each object in the database is an instance of some class. The concept of class constitutes the basis on which queries on the database can be formulated, in analogy with relational databases, where queries are formulated against relations or sets of relations. Moreover, the concept of class enforces the integrity of an object-oriented database system, by providing type checking. In fact, specifying a class as a domain of an attribute (see complex objects below) makes it possible for the system to restrict the values that the attribute may take on the object instances of that class.
- *Complex objects.* Objects can be complex, in that the value of an attribute can be an object or a set of objects, allowing objects of arbitrary complexity to be defined. Moreover, the value of an attribute can be structured using *constructors* (for example, set, tuple, list). In terms of classes, the domain of the class attributes can be any class, with their own sets of attributes. Thus, the definition of a class results in a rooted directed graph, called the *class-composition hierarchy*. It is possible to superimpose the semantics of the part-of relationship on a complex object, introducing *composite objects*, for which a referenced object is actually a part of (or a component of) the composite object. Having part-of semantics on complex objects brings about some consequences on DBMS operations (for example, deletion of the composite object may imply the deletion of its components, too). The object-oriented paradigm allows complex objects to be directly represented by the model, with no need to flatten them into tuples as in the case of relational systems.

- *Specialization and inheritance*. A class can be defined as a specialization of one or more classes. A class defined as a specialization is called a *subclass* and inherits attributes and methods from its *superclass(es)*. A *class hierarchy* is used to capture the generalization relationship between a class and its direct and indirect subclasses, and an *is-a* relationship is defined between them. A subclass may override the definition of inherited methods and attributes. Therefore, inheritance lets a class specialize another class by *additions* and *substitutions*. Some systems support single inheritance: that is, a class can be the specialization of only one superclass. Some systems support multiple inheritance, allowing a class to be the specialization of more than one class.
- *Information hiding*. Values of the object attributes represent the object's status, accessible and modifiable only through *messages*, which invoke the corresponding methods of the object. The set of messages that an object can receive constitutes the object *interface*. According to the *information-hiding* principle, a separation exists between the status and the interface of an object. This allows *client* objects to use the services provided by the object with no knowledge about how the services are implemented. Thus, an object's implementation may change without affecting other objects or applications using the services provided by the object.

  The information-hiding capability also offers great potential for data security, as we will see, in that an additional layer is inserted between the object and its users, constituted by the object interface.

OODBMSs support the object-oriented data model, providing a set of functionalities to manage objects, either as extensions of the traditional functionalities or as new specific object management-oriented functionalities. OODBMSs provide capabilities for dealing with object persistence, secondary storage management, concurrency, recovery and *ad-hoc* query facilities.

For concurrency control and transactions, support must be provided to deal with long, cooperative transactions, characterized by a finer lock granularity, carried out by a group of users working together, typical of advanced applications (Barghouti and Kaiser, 1991).

Query languages in OODBMSs provide both a navigational mode and a query mode for accessing data. With the navigational mode, the OIDs are used to access objects in the database. Using the query mode, sets of objects can be selected (as in relational DBMSs where sets of tuples are selected), using query languages that are extensions of the relational languages. A query selects a set of objects on the basis of conditions specified in the query. Retrieved objects and their components are accessed by using the navigational mode.

Special functionalities are provided by OODBMSs, such as the capability of managing versioned objects (Kim, 1990). A *versioned object* can be seen as a hierarchy of objects, called a *version hierarchy*, where a derivation relationship holds among the hierarchy members. Each object in a version hierarchy (except for the root object) is derived from another object in the hierarchy by changing the values of one or more attributes of the second object. Objects in a version hierarchy have their own object-identifier (OID). Information about the version hierarchy is often stored as part of the root object, called the *generic object*. OODBMSs usually provide mechanisms to support management and inspection of version hierarchies. Some systems also provide support for specific (to a specific version of the hierarchy) and generic (to the root of the hierarchy) references to versioned objects, stable and unstable versions, version merging, and versions of classes. Moreover, OODBMSs should provide support for schema evolution management. Owing to the specific features of the object-oriented model, schema modifications are frequent (for example, ways to classify objects and their relationships vary during the schema lifetime). Taxonomies of schema changes have been proposed, which should be supported by the database system (Kim, 1990).

## 7.2 Security in active databases

Among the research efforts in security of active databases, this section describes a database system designed considering discretionary policies, the Starbust system (Gagliardi *et al.*, 1989; Haas *et al.*, 1990; Widom *et al.*, 1991), and a database system focused on mandatory security, the Multi Level Secure System (Smith and Winslett, 1992a, 1992b).

*Starbust* (Haas *et al.*, 1990) is a prototype extensible relational database system developed at the IBM Almaden Research Center. Its *attachment* mechanism permits procedure calls upon tuple-level operations; attachments are typed and can be managed using Starbust commands. The attachment mechanism is the basis for the tuple-oriented database rule system. Other mechanisms defined in Starbust are the *event queue*, for deferring the execution of parameterized procedures, and *table functions*, which extend the Starbust query language by allowing the registration of a function name, a parameter specification, a table schema, and a procedure for producing the tuples of the table function. Hence, the SQL `from` clause can contain a table function, which produces at run time a table with the schema declared in the table function.

Starbust's rule system includes a rule catalogue, global rule information, and rule-processing information pertinent to rules that execute within a transaction (such as which rules have been considered and when, and which rules are potentially triggered at a given instant). A set of rule execution modules permits the definition, attachment, and execution of rules.

In Starbust (Widom *et al.*, 1991), three distinct issues are considered for authorization:

- Authorization to create rules on a certain relation
- Authorization to create rules with given conditions and actions
- Authorization to modify or delete rules.

These issues have been addressed by the extensible authorization component of Starbust. A lattice of rights can be defined for database objects; rights are grantable/revocable.

In the lattice, higher types subsume rights of lower types. The highest right is *control*, lower rights are *write, attach* privileges, and then *read* privileges. The creator of a relation obtains the control right, which implies the discretionary ability to propagate lower rights.

A (linear) lattice of rights can also be defined for rules: the highest right is *control*, followed by *alter* and *activate/deactivate*. The rule creator receives the control right by default and can grant/revoke privileges on the rule. To create a rule on a relation, the user must have both attach and read rights on the relation. If the condition or action part of the rule being created does not match the creator's rights, the 'create rule' statement is rejected.

Analogous checks are executed at rule deletion time and at rule alteration time. Rules can be activated/deactivated upon possession of the *activate/ deactivate* rights.

During rule execution, rules are matched against the privileges of their creators. To this end the rights of a rule's creator are stored with the rule's condition and actions.

In multilevel secure active DBMSs, the mandatory security policy controls access privilege and accessibility for rule descriptions, rule execution and database transitions/events. Smith and Winslett (1992b) integrate the *Multi Level Secure (MLS) relational model*, proposed by the same authors in Smith and Winslett (1992a) (see Chapter 2), with an active database. The extension permits the definition and representation of MLS rules by giving explicit security classifications to rules and events via multilevel secure relations for each. Database rule descriptions are treated as MLS objects. New user-definable active compon-ents (rule actions, triggering demons) have associated mandatory security constraints for subjects. MLS rules follow the general event–condition–action rule model (McCarthy and Dayal, 1989). MLS rules are both set-oriented and SQL based (differently from the general production rules of expert systems). MLS rules fit the MLS environment in that:

- Rule descriptions and events are expressed in tuples with security labels;
- User-definable active components conform to the mandatory policies for subjects.

The MLS rules system executes in the context of atomic transactions and incorporates a triggering event limiting them to forward-chaining execution (to meet efficiency requirements for databases).

An SQL-like syntax is used in MLS; events, conditions and actions of rules pertain to sets of items described by MLS-SQL constructs. For example, a condition may refer to a set of employees (e.g., all employees whose salary is greater than 40k), or an action may perform a set of updates. The syntax of MLS rules is:

```
WHEN transition predicate /* event */
[IF condition predicate]  /* condition */
THEN operation block      /* action */
```

where the meaning of the elements is as follows.

(1) *Transition predicate.* A transition is a group of operations within a transaction; rules may execute at the end of each transition. A predicate can be UPDATED, INSERTED, or DELETED, followed by the name of a database relation; the predicate is evaluated 'true' if any of the specified events happened for the relation during a transition. A rule is triggered when its predicate is true. Predicates are evaluated at the end of each transition, rules are triggered during a transition. When an event matching a rule's transition predicate occurs, the rules become *pending*.

(2) *Condition predicate.* This is an arbitrary SELECT statement of the MLS-SQL language; the predicate is satisfied if the result is non-empty. SELECT may refer to the following main-memory system relations: INSERTED, DELETED, NEW UPDATED, and OLD UPDATED, which contain tuples affected in the named manner. SELECT may contain a BELIEVED BY clause if needed to restrict data to be selected to those at a given classification. For example, in the relation shown in Figure 7.1 (Smith and Winslett, 1992b), the first tuple contains the beliefs of level U about the entity *Smith U*. Level S agrees that *Smith U* (that is, the *Smith* 'believed by' level U) exists, and agrees with U regarding all data except project no. (believed, at level S, to be 40 instead of 20).

(3) *Operation block.* This is a non-empty sequence of MLS-SQL rule manipulation commands including a transition. Arbitrary actions can be used as long as mandatory security is respected. In particular, rule actions can affect only data at the security level of the executing rule.

MLS rules are multilevel entities and therefore can exist in multiple security levels simultaneously with the same id (rule polyinstantiation). Rules are stored in the relation:

*Rules (<u>Name</u>, <u>Transition</u>, <u>Table</u>, <u>KC</u>, Condition, Action)*

where the key fields are underlined, and where:

*Name* is the name given to the rule. *Transition* is one of DELETED, INSERTED, or UPDATED; *Table* is any relation in the user schema, or the Rules relation. *KC* is the level at which the rule was inserted. *Condition* is a piece of text specifying the condition to be satisfied for the rule execution. *Action* is a piece of text specifying the action to be executed when *Transition* happens to Table and the conditions are satisfied.

| Name | KC | Department | Project No. | Destination | Delivery date | Sector | TC |
|---|---|---|---|---|---|---|---|
| Smith | U | Engineering | 20 | Houston | 9-1-95 | Product X | U |
| Smith | U | Engineering | 40 | Houston | 9-1-95 | Product X | S |
| Wallace | U | Research | 30 | Bellaire | 31-7-96 | Product Y | U |

*Figure 7.1* An MLS relation in the MLS active data model.

Rules have an associated *state*, either descriptive (D) or active (A). A rule is in the descriptive state until it is activated by the ACTIVATE command; the DEACTIVATE command moves rules to the descriptive state. A rule can trigger and execute only in the active state.

Operations on the Rules relation must satisfy some constraints. Insertion is mediated by a rule parser which translates textual rules into Rules tuples; rules are assigned the descriptive state; the State field cannot be sent in the UPDATE, INSERT, or DELETE operations.

Further controls in the model are introduced by *discretionary security* which limits insertions, updates, and deletions to Rules (only the DBA may perform these actions).

The mandatory policy regulates rule activation. An active rule operates as an MLS subject with a security level equal to the Tuple Classification (TC) attribute. An attachment procedure is a demon executing rule installation. A subject has to issue the following ACTIVATE command:

```
ACTIVATE
WHERE p
[BELIEVED by L];
```

whose effect in terms of MLS-SQL UPDATE command on the Rules relation is:

```
UPDATE       Rules
SET          (Condition=Condition and Action=Action and State='A')
WHERE        P
BELIEVED BY L
```

where P is an MLS-SQL predicate and L a list of security levels.

The corresponding DEACTIVATE command has a similar syntax:

```
DEACTIVATE
WHERE P;
```

The command selects a set of active rules at the level of the command issuer, removes them from the DBMS runtime system, and sets their State field to 'D'.

The ACTIVATE and DEACTIVATE commands are subject to two integrity constraints (similar to Starbust (Widom *et al.*, 1991) described above):

(1) If a transaction entails an event on a relation, it can no longer activate/deactivate rules on that relation.
(2) If a transaction $t_1$ precedes $t_2$ in the commit order, rule activations/deactivations performed by $t_1$ must be visible in $t_2$, not vice versa.

The *execution model* of MLS rules is obtained by extending the MLS relational model in a way related to the Starbust rule execution model. Rules execute in the context of transactions. In particular, rules are labelled with the classification of the subject initiating the rules. Rules are treated as secure objects managed by the DBMS. A rule executes if it can 'see' the triggering event under the MLS constraints. For example, if a user cleared at level $L$ updates the table

*T* of Figure 7.1, the event UPDATE T is treated as an MLS object with security level *L*. An active action performed by a *U*-level subject triggering on the event UPDATE T would not see this event; an *S* activation of the same rule would see this event, and would be triggered by it.

Likewise, the predicates of MLS rule activations respect MLS constraints. This is managed within the SELECT clause: only the tuples with an access class dominated by the rule activation executing it are selected.

The execution of the 'operation block' also conforms to MLS access restrictions. Operations can write only at the classification level of the activation, and data is read only from dominated levels.

MLS rules are not allowed to lock data objects at lower levels in 'write' mode, because they are not allowed to write to lower levels. Since a rule $R_1$ may read from lower levels, it is not a direct violation of mandatory security for $R_1$ to acquire and hold a read lock on a lower-level data object. However, $R_1$ could use this lock to deny service, in this case the denial of the write access, to lower levels for an arbitrary period: this would also mean covert channels. The problems of denial of service and covert channels in MLS are discussed in Smith and Winslett (1992b).

In MLS, the problem of attribute polyinstantiation is considered: sometimes there is the need to automatically coalesce two MLS entities. When a user observes that two MLS entities represent the same real-world entity, he or she can decide to coalesce them into a single MLS entity. The decision depends on the application and on the user (therefore, the policy should not be coded in the DBMS).

In general, to simplify user interaction with the DBMS, external application programs can be run periodically to merge entities, while no user's policy on coalescence is enforced during the runs.

Exploiting rules, in MLS decisions on coalescence are encoded in rules to handle cases that are application-specific or not completely specified by the data model. These policy decisions are then enforced on the user's behalf by active rules when a given situation occurs, with no user intervention.

An MLS-SQL COALESCE command is defined:

```
COALESCE     R
WHERE        P
BELIEVED BY  L;
```

Some factors influence the decision to coalesce: for example, the aim to avoid inference.

## 7.3 Security in object-oriented databases

In this section we briefly review the main proposals to enforce security in Object-Oriented DBMS (OODBMS) by using discretionary or mandatory policy.

Regarding *discretionary controls*, very few OODBMSs, only Orion (Rabitti *et al.*, 1991) and Iris (Ahad *et al.*, 1992), provide authorization models comparable to those provided by current relational DBMSs.

In the Orion authorization model, authorizations to access objects can be specified for each group (role) of users. This authorization model takes into consideration semantic aspects of the object-oriented paradigm, such as inheritance hierarchy, versions, and composite objects. In particular, the model supports the derivation of new authorizations (called implicit) on some objects from the authorizations explicitly specified by the users on objects semantically related. Moreover, the model enforces derivation of implicit authorization on the basis of relationships between subjects and between access modes. The Orion model presented in Rabitti *et al.* (1991) has been extended in Bertino (1992b) to the consideration of content-dependent authorizations (i.e. including conditions to be satisfied by the values of the attributes of the objects to be accessed). Bertino (1992a) proposes a model where authorizations specify privileges for users to execute methods on objects. The model enforces the concept of *private* method to allow controlled execution of particular methods, and the concept of *protection mode* to grant users the privilege of executing a particular method *m* without the need to grant them the authorizations for all the methods that *m* may invoke during its execution. Ahad *et al.* (1992) present an authorization model based on controlling function evaluation. Authorizations can be specified for users, or groups of users, to execute functions: that is, methods over objects. *Specific function, guard function,* and *proxy function* concepts are used to enforce content-dependent authorizations and to restrict the execution of given functions to some users. Another model based on authorizations to execute methods on objects is presented by Richardson *et al.* (1992). In this model, the owner of an object can control who may invoke which methods on the object. Fernandez *et al.*, in Fernandez *et al.* (1989), Gudes *et al.* (1991) and Gal-Oz *et al.* (1993), present an authorization model which allows the specification of positive, negative, and content-dependent authorizations. The model also enforces, on the basis of the semantic relationships among data, the derivation of new authorizations from those specified by the users, and supports decentralized administration of authorizations.

Some work on limiting unconditional access to objects (Abdali *et al.*, 1986; Goldstein and Bobrow, 1980; Garlan, 1987; Habermann *et al.*, 1988; Minsky, 1987, 1991; Watt *et al.*, 1990) has also been performed in the area of object-oriented systems. Most of this work is based on the approach of providing multiple interfaces to objects, enforcing a sort of view mechanism. In Minsky (1987, 1991) access constraints to objects are expressed by rules, called *laws*, each of which defines the action the system must take when a message is sent from an object to another object. Possible actions include: let the message pass unaltered, send the recipient a different message, send the same or another message to a different object, or block the sending of the message. However, although all these approaches allow, in some way, the restriction or differentiation of access to objects, they do not really address the authorization problem.

Regarding *mandatory controls,* some work has been performed on the application of the Bell–LaPadula principles (see Chapter 2) to object-oriented systems. Meadows and Landwehr (1992) model mandatory access controls using the object-oriented approach in the context of the Military Message

System. Jajodia and Kogan (1990) and Jajodia *et al.* (1992) propose the use of a message filter, which corresponds to the reference monitor of the Bell–LaPadula model. The message filter mediates each and every message exchanged between objects, ensuring that no information flows from higher to lower levels. Other work on enforcing mandatory protection policies in object-oriented systems is presented in Keefe *et al.* (1988), Thuraisingham (1989a, b), Keefe and Tsai (1990) and Millen and Lunt (1992). There, the security properties of the Bell–LaPadula model are extended for their application to object-oriented systems. Moreover, new properties regarding the classification of data are introduced to avoid low users inferring high information through the relationships existing among data.

In the following sections of this chapter, we illustrate some of the above models for security of object-oriented systems. In particular, Section 7.4 illustrates discretionary protection models. Sections 7.5–7.8 illustrate models for the application of mandatory protection policies. The mandatory classifications used in these models and the relationship between them are the same as those illustrated for the Bell–LaPadula model, on which all these models are based. We refer to Chapter 2 for these issues. The chapter terminates with a discussion on open issues and research considerations.

## 7.4 The ORION authorization model

An authorization model for object-oriented database security has been proposed by Rabitti *et al.* (1991) in the ORION/ITASCA framework. The model enforces a discretionary protection policy which takes into consideration the relationships existing among the database objects, the access modes through which objects can be accessed, and the subjects that can access the objects. In particular, these relationships are used to derive new authorizations from the authorizations specified by users. Moreover, the model takes into consideration characteristics of object-oriented systems such as inheritance, composite objects and versioned objects.

### 7.4.1 Subjects

The model considers as subjects groups of users (*roles*) into which users are organized on the basis of the activities they execute in the organization. A user may belong to more than one role. Roles are related by means of an implication relationship. A role $R_1$ is in implication relationship with another role $R_2$ if, and only if, the authorizations associated with role $R_1$ subsume the authorizations associated with role $R_2$: that is, users belonging to role $R_1$ also belong to role $R_2$. For example, an implication link between the role 'accountant' and the role 'employee' indicates that accountants are also employees and therefore all authorizations specified for the role 'employee' are considered valid also for the role 'accountant'. According to the implication relationship, the set of roles forms a lattice, called a *role lattice*. An example of a role lattice is shown in Figure 7.2.

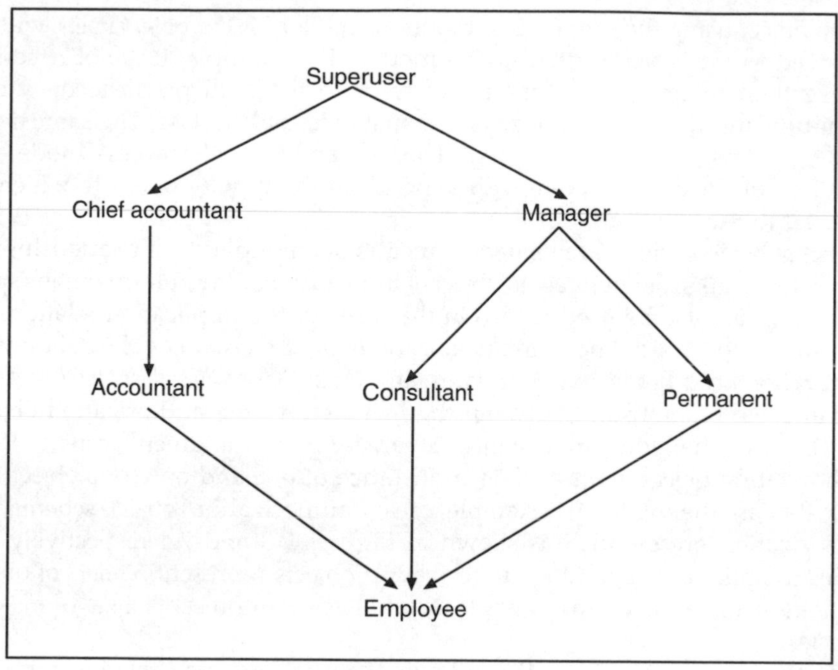


*Figure 7.2* An example of a role lattice.

An arc directed from role $R_1$ to role $R_2$ indicates that role $R_1$ is in implication relationship with role $R_2$. The root of the lattice (topmost role) corresponds to a role that has the authorizations of any other role in the system. The bottommost role corresponds to a role that has a set of basic authorizations executable by any role. On the basis of the implication relationship, and therefore of the role lattice, a partial ordering relationship ($\geq$) is defined on all subjects as follows.

Let $s_i$ and $s_j$ be two subjects. Then, $s_i > s_j$ if an implication link exists directed from $s_i$ to $s_j$ in the role lattice; $s_i \geq s_j$ if $s_i = s_j$ or $s_i > s_j$ or there exist subjects $s_1$, $s_2$, ..., $s_n$ such that $s_i > s_1 > s_2 > \ldots > s_n > s_j$.

For example, with reference to the role lattice shown in Figure 7.2, the following relationships hold:

Superuser > Chief accountant > Accountant > Employee.

### 7.4.2 Objects

The authorization model considers the following elements as objects to be protected: *databases*, *classes* in the database, *instances* of classes, and their components (*attributes*, *values* and *methods*). The model also considers, as protection objects, *sets of objects* of the same type that have a common root (for example, the set of instances of a class or the set of values of an attribute). This allows authorizations to be specified on the set of objects contained in a given object using the same access modes specified for the object itself, without the need to introduce further access modes. For example, it is not necessary to use two different access modes to refer to the read privilege on a class definition and the read privilege on the instances of the class. The same access mode (that is, read) can be used. The semantics of the access mode, and therefore of the authorization, will depend on the type of object to which the authorization is referred.

Like subjects, objects are related by means of an implication relationship. An implication link from object $o_1$ to object $o_2$ indicates that the authorizations specified on $o_1$ can also be used on $o_2$. On the basis of the implication relationship, two structures are defined: an *authorization object schema* (AOS), defining the implication links between object types, and an *authorization object lattice* (AOL), defining the relationships between the instances of the authorization objects. An AOL is therefore an instance of an AOS for a given system. Every authorization object in an AOL is an instance of one and only one object type indicated in the AOS. An example of an authorization object schema and authorization object lattice is shown in Figures 7.3 and 7.4 respectively. The nodes in italics correspond to authorization objects representing sets of objects of the next lower level (for example, *Setof-instances* represents a set of instance objects).

On the basis of the AOL, the following partial ordering relationship (≥) is defined:

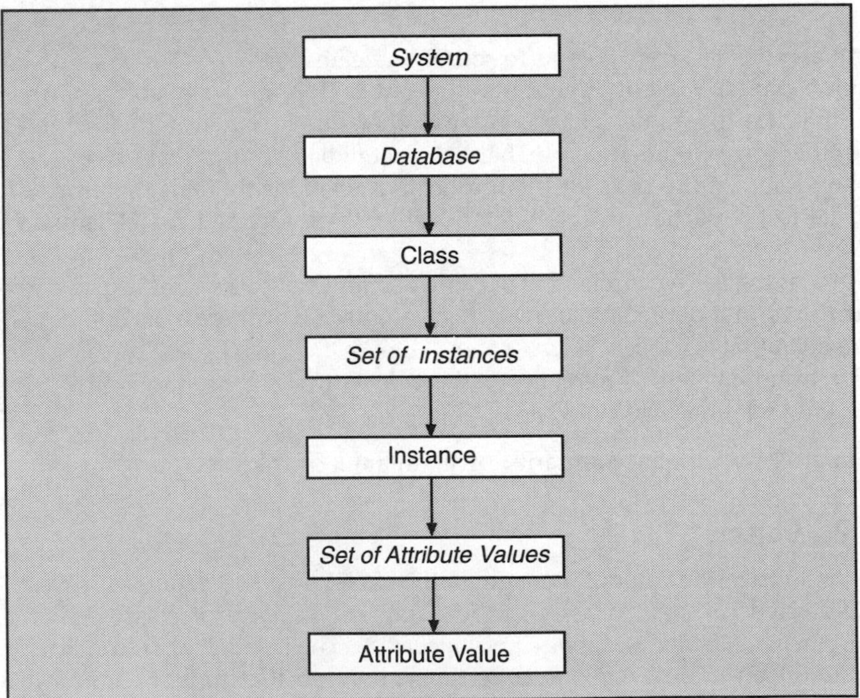


***Figure* 7.3** An example of an Authorization Object Schema (AOS).

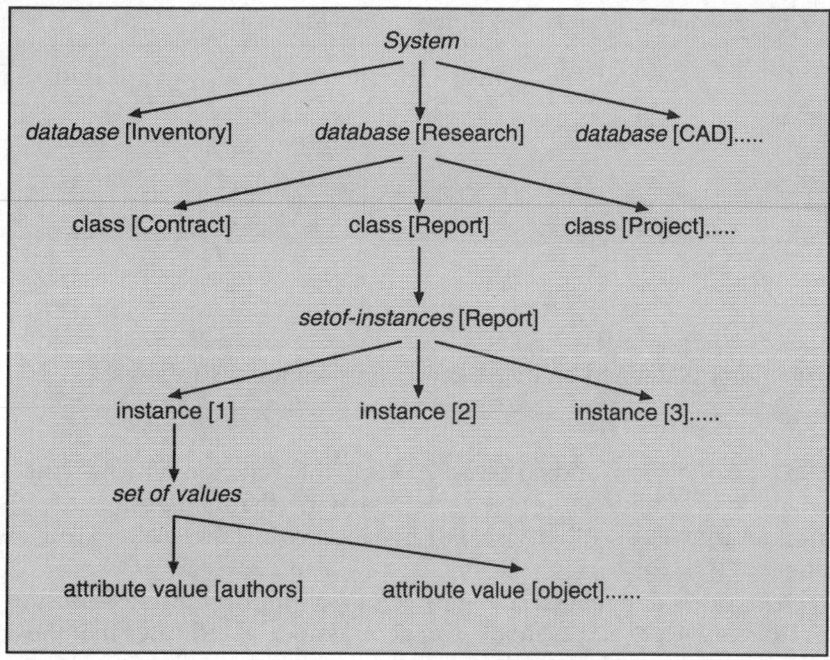


*Figure 7.4* An example of an Authorization Object Lattice (AOL).

Let $o_i$ and $o_j$ be two objects. Then, $o_i > o_j$ if an implication link exists directed from $o_i$ to $o_j$ in the authorization object lattice; $o_i \geq o_j$ if $o_i = o_j$ or $o_i > o_j$ or there exist objects $o_1, o_2, \ldots, o_n$ such that $o_i > o_1 > o_2 > \ldots > o_n > o_j$.

### 7.4.3 Access modes

The model considers the following access modes:

- *Write (W)* to write an object.
- *Write_Any (WA)* is analogous to the Write access mode. It allows an object to be written. It is considered for completeness purposes in the implication rules based on access modes.
- *Read (R)* to read an object. When referred to a method, it indicates that the method can be executed.
- *Generate (G)* to create instances of an object.
- *Read_Definition (RD)* to read the definition of an object.

Note that not all access modes are meaningful for every object. The access modes executable on an object depend on the object type. Given the access modes introduced earlier, an *access authorization matrix* (AAM) states, for every object type and every access mode, whether the access mode is executable on objects of that type. An example of an AAM is given in Table 7.1. The 't' value in entry *AAM*[*o*, *a*] indicates that access mode *a* is applicable to objects of type *o*. The 'f' value in entry *AAM*[*o*, *a*] indicates that access mode *a* is not applicable to objects of type *o*.

**Table 7.1** An example of an Access Authorization Matrix.

| | W | WA | R | G | RD |
|---|---|---|---|---|---|
| *System* | t | t | t | t | t |
| *Database* | t | t | t | t | t |
| Class | t | t | t | f | t |
| *Setof-Instances* | t | t | t | t | t |
| Instance | t | t | t | f | t |
| *Setof-Attr-Values* | t | t | t | f | t |
| Attribute-Value | t | t | t | f | t |

A function *c* is defined on objects and access modes as follows:

$c: O \times A \rightarrow$ (True, False)

Given a type of object *o* and an access mode *a*, this function returns 'True' if the access mode is applicable to objects of that type (that is, $AAM[o, a] = t$). The function returns 'False' otherwise. For instance, *c* (Instance, W) = 'True', while *c* (Instance, G) = 'False'.

Access modes are related by means of an implication relationship. An implication link from access mode $a_1$ to access mode $a_2$ indicates that the access mode $a_1$ on a given object implies the access mode $a_2$ on the same object. For example, the implication link between the access modes 'write' and 'read' indicates that the authorization to write an object implies the authorization to read the same object. The access modes, together with the implication relationship, form a lattice called the *authorization type lattice* (ATL). This lattice is shown in Figure 7.5.

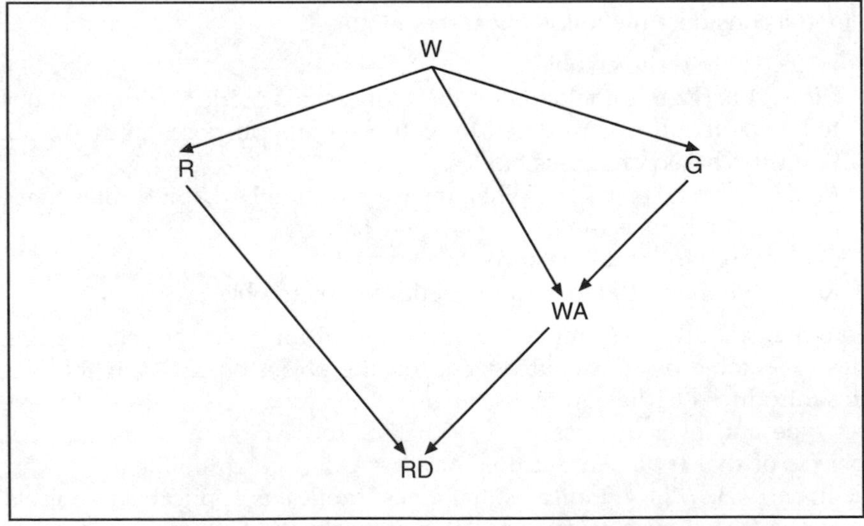


*Figure 7.5* Authorization Type Lattice (ATL).

On the basis of the ATL, a partial ordering relationship (≥) is defined on the access modes as follows. Let $a_i$ and $a_j$ be two access modes. Then, $a_i > a_j$ if an implication link exists directed from $a_i$ to $a_j$ in the access mode lattice; $a_i \geq a_j$ if $a_i = a_j$ or $a_i > a_j$ or there exist access modes $a_1, a_2, \ldots, a_n$ such that $a_i > a_1 > a_2 > \ldots > a_n > a_j$.

Moreover, authorization for an access mode on an object *o* can be propagated on different objects connected to *o* in the AOL. The objects to which authorizations are propagated depend on the access under consideration. In particular, access modes are grouped into three classes: *A.up*, containing all access modes that are propagated from low objects to higher objects in the AOL; *A.down*, containing all access modes that are propagated from high objects to lower objects in the AOL; and *A.nil*, containing all access modes that are not propagated. These groups are as follows:

- *A.up* = {*WA*, *RD*}. For example, authorization for the RD mode on the set of instances of a class, which allows their definition to be read, implies authorization for the RD mode on the class itself. Analogously, authorization for the RD mode on a class implies the authorization for the RD mode on the database to which the class belongs.
- *A.down* = {*W*, *R*}. For example, authorization for the R access mode on a class, which allows the class information to be read, implies authorization for the R access mode on the instances of the class, which allows the values of their attributes to be read.
- *A.nil* = {*G*}. The authorization to create objects cannot be propagated among objects related in the AOL.

### 7.4.4 Authorizations

Authorizations are specified by users. The model does not consider administrative privileges. Any subject authorized for an access mode on an object can grant other subjects authorization for the access mode on the object. Therefore, the authorization for an access implies the authorization to administer (that is, grant and revoke) the access.

From the authorizations specified by users, new authorizations are derived automatically by the system. The derivation of new authorizations is based on the implication relationships existing between subjects (for example, a manager can access the information his or her employees can access), between objects (for example, the authorization to read a class implies authorization to read all instances of the class) and between access modes (for example, the authorization to write an object implies authorization to read the object), as expressed in the respective lattices.

Authorizations specified by users are called *explicit*, whereas authorizations derived by the system are called *implicit*. Beside this classification, two other orthogonal classifications are introduced. These concern the distinction between *positive* authorizations, stating access privileges, and *negative* authorizations, stating denial of privileges, and between *strong* authorizations, which cannot be overwritten by other authorizations, and *weak* authorizations, which can be overwritten by other authorizations.

Authorizations are grouped into two sets: an *authorization base* (AB) composed of all strong authorizations, both positive and negative, and a *weak authorization base* (WAB) composed of all weak authorizations, both positive and negative. In the following, strong authorizations will be indicated in round brackets '( )', whereas weak authorizations will be indicated in square brackets '[ ]'.

#### *The strong authorization base*

The strong authorization base (AB, for short) groups all the strong authorizations, positive as well as negative, explicitly defined by users. A positive strong authorization is described as a triple $(s, o, a)$ indicating that subject $s$ can access object $o$ in access mode $a$. A negative strong authorization is described as a triple $(s, o, \neg a)$ indicating that subject $s$ cannot access object $o$ in access mode $a$.

From the explicit strong authorizations defined by the user, other strong authorizations, called *implicit* authorizations, are derived. Derivation of authorizations is based on implication rules which will be illustrated in Section 7.4.5. The implication relationship between strong authorizations is denoted by '$\rightarrow$'.

A function $i$, defined on the strong authorizations base AB, determines whether an authorization (or its negation) is explicitly contained in AB or may be derived from authorizations contained in AB. Function $i$ is defined as follows:

$i : S \times O \times A \rightarrow$ (True, False, Undecided)

Given a triple $(s, o, a)$, $i$ returns 'True' if $(s, o, a)$ belongs to AB or if an $(s_1, o_1, a_1)$ authorization exists in AB such that $(s_1, o_1, a_1) \rightarrow (s, o, a)$; 'False' if an $(s_1, o_1, \neg a_1)$ authorization exists in AB such that $(s_1, o_1, \neg a_1) \rightarrow (s, o, \neg a)$; 'Undecided' otherwise. In other words, given a subject, an object and an access mode, the function returns: 'True' if the corresponding authorization is in AB or can be derived from some authorization in AB; 'False' if its negation exists in AB or can be derived from some negative authorization in AB; 'Undecided' if nothing is explicitly specified in AB nor can be derived from AB with respect to the access.

The model requires the following two properties to be satisfied on the strong authorization base.

- **Consistency of the AB property**
  *For any $(s, o, a) \in AB$, with a positive or negative, if there exists an $(s_1, o_1, a_1)$ such that $(s, o, a) \rightarrow (s_1, o_1, a_1)$, there must not exist any $(s_2, o_2, a_2)$ such that $(s_2, o_2, a_2) \rightarrow (s_1, o_1, a_1)$.*

  This property asserts that no two authorizations can exist simultaneously in the AB such that one of them implies an authorization and the other implies the negation of that authorization.
- **Nonredundancy of the AB property**
  *If $(s, o, a) \in AB$, with a positive or negative, and $(s, o, a) \rightarrow (s_1, o_1, a_1)$, then $(s_1, o_1, a_1) \notin AB$.*

This property avoids the insertion of useless authorizations. An authorization is useless if it is already implied by another authorization.

#### *The weak authorization base*

The weak authorization base (WAB) groups all authorizations, positive and negative, that are classified as weak: that is, can be overwritten by strong authorizations or by more specific weak authorizations. A weak positive authorization is characterized by a triple $[s, o, a]$ stating that subject $s$ can execute access mode $a$ on object $o$. A weak negative authorization is characterized by a triple $[s, o, \neg a]$ stating that subject $s$ cannot execute access mode $a$ on object $o$.

As for strong authorizations, implication rules allow the derivation of further authorizations, called *implicit*, from those explicitly defined by users. Authorizations implied by weak authorizations are also weak. The implication relationship between weak authorizations is indicated with the symbol '$\mapsto$'.

A function $d$, defined on the WAB, determines whether a positive authorization (or negation) is contained in the WAB or can be derived from some authorization in the WAB. The function $d$ is defined as follows:

$$d : S \times O \times A \rightarrow (\text{True, False})$$

Given a triple $(s, o, a)$ $d$ returns: 'True' if $[s, o, a] \in$ WAB, or there exists $[s_1, o_1, a_1] \in$ WAB such that $[s_1, o_1, a_1] \mapsto [s, o, a]$; 'False' if $[s, o, \neg a] \in$ WAB, or there exists $[s_1, o_1, \neg a_1] \in$ WAB such that $[s_1, o_1, \neg a_1] \mapsto [s, o, \neg a]$.

Unlike function $i$ defined on the strong authorization base, function $d$ cannot return the 'undecided' value. Hence, for each authorization either the authorization or its negation must either exist or be derivable from the authorization base. This requirement is expressed by the following property.

- **Completeness of the WAB property**
  *For any authorization $[s, o, a]$, with a positive or negative, there must exist an $[s_1, o_1, a_1] \in WAB$ such that $[s_1, o_1, a_1] \mapsto [s, o, a]$.*

A further property requires the set of weak authorizations to be free from inconsistencies. This property is as follows.

- **Consistency of the WAB property**
  *For any authorization $[s, o, a] \in WAB$, with a positive or negative, if there exists $[s_1, o_1, a_1]$ such that $[s, o, a] \mapsto [s_1, o_1, a_1]$, then there must not exist any $[s_2, o_2, a_2] \in WAB$ such that $[s_2, o_2, a_2] \mapsto [s_1, o_1, \neg a_1]$.*

The property states that an authorization and its negation cannot both exist or be derivable from the set of weak authorizations.

Unlike strong authorizations, redundancy is allowed in the weak authorization base. In particular, an authorization can exist in the WAB even although it is implied by existing authorizations. Therefore, an authorization already implied by some authorizations in the WAB can be inserted into the WAB.

A further property, required on the union of WAB and AB, is that a weak authorization must not be denied, either as implicit or explicit, as a strong authorization. This property is as follows.

- **Coexistence of the WAB and the AB property**
  *For any authorization [s, o, a] ∈ WAB, with a positive or negative, there must not exist any* $(s_1, o_1, a_1) \in AB$ *such that* $[s_1, r_1, a_1] \mapsto [s, o, \neg a]$ .

The system ensures that this property is always satisfied. In particular, if the insertion of a new weak authorization would not satisfy the coexistence property, the weak authorization is not inserted. By contrast, if the insertion of a new strong authorization would not satisfy the property, the strong authorization is inserted and all weak authorizations that cause non-satisfaction of the property are eliminated.

### 7.4.5 Rules for the derivation of implicit authorizations and access control

Implication rules determine how implicit authorizations are derived from the authorizations explicitly defined by users. These rules are based on the relationships existing among subjects, objects and authorization types.

Implication rules, summarized in Figure 7.6, are defined for strong authorizations. Implication rules for weak authorizations are derived from the implication rules defined for strong authorizations. Authorizations derived from strong (weak) authorizations are also considered as strong (weak).

The implication rules for the derivation of strong positive authorizations can be summarized as follows:

**Rule 1** *Authorizations with access mode belonging to A.down are propagated for subjects at higher levels, and for objects and access modes at lower levels as described in the corresponding lattices.*
Since every subject, object and access mode is ≥ and ≤ itself, this rule allows the derivation, from an authorization, of authorizations involving the same or a different subject, object and access mode.

**Rule 2** *Authorizations with access mode belonging to A.up are propagated for subjects and objects at lower levels, and for access modes at higher levels as described in the corresponding lattices.*
Again, since any subject, object and access mode is ≥ and ≤ itself, this rule allows us to derive, from an authorization, authorizations involving the same or a different subject, object and access mode.

**Rule 3** *Authorizations with access mode belonging to A.nil, which do not propagate in the authorization object lattice, are propagated for subjects at higher level and for access modes at lower level as described in the corresponding lattices.*
Hence, starting from an authorization, new authorizations on the same object, with the same or different user and access mode, can be derived.

From these implication rules, according to the property that given two predicates $p$ and $q$: $p \rightarrow q \Leftrightarrow \neg q \rightarrow \neg p$, analogous implication rules for negative authorizations (Rules 4–6) are defined.

The implication rules for weak authorizations are the same as those for strong authorizations. The only difference is that, since weak authorizations can be overwritten, the derivation of authorizations from an explicit weak

| | |
|---|---|
| **Rule 1** | $\forall s_l, s_k \in S, o_i, o_j \in O, a_n \in$ A.down, $a_m \in A$: <br> $s_k \geq s_l, o_i \geq o_j, a_n \geq a_m \Rightarrow (s_l, o_i, a_n) \rightarrow (s_k, o_j, a_m)$ |
| **Rule 2** | $\forall s_l, s_k \in S, o_i, o_j \in O, a_n \in a_m \in A.$ up: <br> $s_k \geq s_l, o_i \geq o_j, a_n \geq a_m \Rightarrow (s_l, o_j, a_n) \rightarrow (s_k, o_i, a_m)$ |
| **Rule 3** | $\forall s_l, s_k \in S, o_i, o_j \in O, a_n \in$ A.nil, $a_m \in A$: <br> $s_k \geq s_l, o_i = o_j, a_n \geq a_m \Rightarrow (s_l, o_j, a_n) \rightarrow (s_k, o_i, a_m)$ |
| **Rule 4** | $\forall s_l, s_k \in S, o_i, o_j \in O, a_n \in$ A.down, $a_m \in A$: <br> $s_k \geq s_l, o_i \geq o_j, a_n \geq a_m \Rightarrow (s_k, o_j, \neg a_m) \rightarrow (s_l, o_i, \neg a_n)$ |
| **Rule 5** | $\forall s_l, s_k \in S, o_i, o_j \in O, a_n \in$ A, $a_m \in A.$ up: <br> $s_k \geq s_l, o_i \geq o_j, a_n \geq a_m \Rightarrow (s_k, o_i, \neg a_m) \rightarrow (s_l, o_j, \neg a_n)$ |
| **Rule 6** | $\forall s_l, s_k \in S, o_i, o_j \in O, a_n \in$ A.nil, $a_m \in A$: <br> $s_k \geq s_l, o_i = o_j, a_n \geq a_m \Rightarrow (s_k, o_i, \neg a_m) \rightarrow (s_l, o_j, \neg a_n)$ |

***Figure 7.6*** Implication rules for strong authorizations.

authorization terminates where another more specific explicit weak authorization starts.

To express this, the model introduces the concept of *scope* of weak authorizations. The scope of a weak authorization $[s_1, o_1, a_1] \in$ WAB denoted by $P[s_1, o_1, a_1]$ is the set of weak authorizations $[s, o, a]$ that are implied by $[s_1, o_1, a_1]$ and that are not overridden by exceptions. This is formalized as follows.

Let $[s_l, o_i, a_n]$, with $a_n$ positive or negative, be a weak authorization in WAB; its scope $P[s_l, o_i, a_n]$ is defined as:
$P[s_l, o_i, a_n] = \{[s, o, a] \mid s \in S, o \in O, a \in A, a$ positive or negative, such that $(s_l, o_i, a_n) \rightarrow (s, o, a)$ and there exists no $[s_k, o_j, a_m] \in$ WAB, such that $(s_l, o_j, a_n) \rightarrow (s_k, o_i, a_m)$, and $(s_k, o_j, a_m) \rightarrow (s, o, a)\}$

Therefore, the scope of a weak authorization terminates where the scope of a more specific authorization starts. Given the definition of authorization scope, the implication rule on weak authorizations is formulated as follows.

$\forall s_l, s_k \in S, o_i, o_j \in O, a_n, a_m \in A, a_n, a_m$ positive or negative:
if $[s_l, o_i, a_n] \in$ WAB and $[s_k, o_j, a_m] \in P[s_l, o_j, a_n]$ then $[s_l, o_i, a_n] \mapsto [s_k, o_j, a_m]$

To illustrate how the implication of authorizations works, consider the role lattice shown in Figure 7.2, the AOS shown in Figure 7.3, and the ATL shown in Figure 7.5, and suppose that the strong authorization base contains the authorization (Permanent, database[Research], W). Suppose now that authorization:

(*Manager, instance*[1] *of class[Report], R*)

needs to be checked. Along the subject domain, we have that 'Manager > Permanent'. Along the object domain we have that 'database[Research] > class[Report] > instance[1]'. Finally, along the authorization type domain we have:

'W > R', with W $\in$ *A.down*.

Therefore, by applying Rule 1, (Permanent, database[Research], W) $\rightarrow$ (Manager, instance[1] of class[Report], R). Hence, the authorization is satisfied.

The access control works as follows. Consider a request by a subject to exercise an access mode on an object. First, the strong authorizations are examined. If there exists a strong authorization, either explicit or implicit, that authorizes, or denies, the access, then the access is authorized, or denied, respectively. If there does not exist any strong authorization for the access, the weak authorizations are examined, and the access is either granted or denied on the basis of the outcome.

The access control can be expressed as a function that, given a request by *s* to access object *o* in *a* mode, returns 'True' if the access must be granted and 'False' if the access must be denied. This function can be expressed in terms of functions *i* and *d* defined on the AB and the WAB respectively as follows:

$$f(s, o, a): \begin{array}{l} \textbf{if } i(s, o, a) = \text{'Undecided'} \\ \textbf{then } f(s, o, a) = d(s, o, a) \\ \textbf{else } f(s, o, a) = i(s, o, a). \end{array}$$

### 7.4.6 Inheritance hierarchies, composite objects and versions

In this section, we illustrate how the ORION authorization model takes into consideration characteristics of object-oriented systems such as inheritance hierarchy, composite objects and versions.

#### *Inheritance hierarchy*

Regarding the inheritance hierarchy, when a class is defined as a subclass of another class, there are two approaches that can be taken concerning authorization on instances of the subclass.

The first approach is that authorizations on a class should not propagate to its subclasses. In particular, this implies that the creator of a class should not automatically receive implicit authorization on the instances of the subclasses of the class. For example, if a class TECHNICAL_REPORT is defined as a specialization of class REPORT, the creator of class REPORT should not be able to read or update the instances of class TECHNICAL_REPORT, unless explicitly authorized to do so by the creator of class TECHNICAL_REPORT (or other authorized users). This approach allows users to reuse existing classes without compromising the protection of the subclasses generated.

The second approach is that authorizations on a class are propagated to the subclasses. In particular, the creator of a class should have implicit authorizations on instances of all the subclasses of the class created by any user. For instance, in the above example, the creator of class REPORT will be implicitly authorized to update and read instances of class TECHNICAL_REPORT.

With respect to query processing, the first approach implies that an access request whose scope is a class and its subclasses will be evaluated only against those classes for which the user issuing the query has read authorization, whereas in the second approach, it would be evaluated against the class and all its subclasses.

The ORION authorization model adopts the first approach as default, and supports the second as a user option. This choice is motivated by the reason that under the second approach, a user wishing to derive a class from another class would not have any privacy on the instances of the subclass (which are readable by the creator of the superclass). Therefore, users could be discouraged from reusing existing classes, thus not taking advantage of the characteristic of inheritance.

When multiple inheritance is allowed, implicit authorizations along the class hierarchy may give rise to conflicts. Conflicts are handled as described in Section 7.4.4.

To allow the specification of authorizations to generate subclasses, the access mode *subclass-generate* (SG) is added to the set of access modes. A user authorized for the SG access mode on a class can define subclasses of the class. Access mode SG belongs to the set *A.nil*: that is, it is not propagated in the AOL. Moreover, the following relationships hold:

W > SG > RD.

Given these relationships, authorizations along the specialization hierarchy can be derived according to the rules given in the previous section. For example, if a user has the write authorization on a class, that user is implicitly authorized to generate subclasses from the class; if a user has the SG authorization on a class, that user implicitly has the RD authorization on the class. In order to create a subclass from a class C, a user must be able to read the definition of C. Therefore, the authorization to generate a class from a given class C implies the authorization to read the definition of C.

#### *Composite objects*

Composite objects are taken into account in the model by considering a composite object to be an authorization unit. This allows a single authorization, granted on the root of a composite object, to be propagated to all components with no need for additional explicit authorization. To allow this, the composite relationship among objects is represented in the authorization object lattice. Then, the implication rules defined in Section 7.4.5 can be used to derive authorizations along the 'composed-of' relationship. For example, if a user can read a composite object, then that user is automatically authorized to read its components. Note, however, that the implicit authorization holds only for the objects that belong to the composite object. For example, suppose a class C is defined on classes $C_1$ and $C_2$. Access authorization to instances of C implies authorization on instances of $C_1$ and $C_2$ that are components of some object of C. However, no authorizations for instances of $C_1$ and $C_2$ that are not components of any object of $C$ are derived.

Note that the implication of authorizations along the 'composed-of' relationship may introduce possible conflicts. For example, the positive authorization to read a composite object and the negative authorization to read one of its components cannot be present at the same time, unless the authorization on the component is a weak authorization and can therefore be overwritten. As in the case of inheritance hierarchy, conflicts are prevented as described in Section 7.4.4. Then, insertion of a new weak authorization is allowed only if the authorization does not conflict with authorizations already specified. By contrast, if a new strong authorization would conflict, the authorization is inserted and possible conflicting weak authorizations are deleted.

#### *Versions*

Authorizations can also be specified on versioned objects and on individual versions of an object. To represent the version hierarchy and enforce derivation of authorization along the hierarchy, the model extends the authorization objects (that is, the AOL and AOS) to include *generic instances* and *versions*. An implication link is defined between the generic instance of an object and the set of versions of the object. The implication rules defined in Section 7.4.5 can therefore be used to derive implicit authorizations on the basis of the 'version' relationship. For example, a read authorization on a generic instance of an object implies the same authorization on all the versions of the object. A write authorization on the set of versions of an object implies the same authorization on the versions described by the generic instance. The write authorization on the set of versions of an object allows users to create a new version from a working version of the object. The write authorization on a generic instance allows users to modify the generic instance (for example, by changing the default version) and implies the write authorization on the version objects described by the generic instance.

## 7.5 The Bertino–Weigand model

The authorization model proposed in Rabitti *et al.* (1991) has been extended and revised by Bertino and Weigand (1994). In the extended model, additional access modes have been introduced, and some implication rules for the derivation of implicit authorizations have been revised. An important extension is the consideration of content-dependent authorizations: that is, authorizations depending on some properties of the objects to be accessed. In Rabitti *et al.* (1991) a user is either authorized for or denied an access on an object. Instead, the extension makes it possible to specify that a user is allowed (denied) an access on an object only if some conditions on the object are satisfied. To allow this, authorizations are extended to the consideration of conditions that must be verified for the authorizations to hold. Conditions can be put on any of the object's attributes. In particular, they may involve class attributes: that is, attributes that characterize the classes themselves and are not inherited by instances, or instance attributes.

For example, consider a class Report, which has an attribute 'status'. An authorization could be specified by stating that role Employee can read only instances of class Report that have status 'released'.

The implication rules defined in Rabitti *et al.* (1991) are applied also to content-dependent authorizations. Authorizations derived from content-dependent authorizations are also content-dependent: that is, they inherit the conditions upon which access has to be controlled. Then, it is possible to specify content-dependent authorizations on a class to be evaluated against the instances of the class and to specify content-dependent authorizations on a versioned object to be evaluated against all versions of the object.

In the case of composite objects, the situation is a little different. Indeed, composite objects can have components of different classes and their types may be different. Therefore, it may not be possible to evaluate the conditions on all the components. In this case the conditions are considered only in reference to the components against which they can be applied.

A main problem of the model, introduced by the consideration of content-dependent authorizations, is how to evaluate conditions associated with authorizations efficiently in the model's implementation. Since conditions have to be evaluated over an object's attributes, which can change over time, they must be evaluated at run time, therefore increasing the response time of the system. In particular, enforcing satisfaction of the conditions expressed in the authorizations by filtering the data prior to user access would require a double access to the object (one to evaluate the conditions and the other to satisfy the user query). The solution considered in relational database systems is simply to add the conditions expressed in the authorization to the user query. This approach, known as the query modification mechanism, has the advantage of ensuring the satisfaction of the protection requirements and not overloading the access control. In object-oriented databases, where objects are accessed through methods, which can be nested, implementation of content-dependent conditions is not straightforward. A possible solution would be to incorporate conditions in the method. However, this approach has the drawback that method specification would be dependent on authorizations, and therefore a change in the authorizations would require a change in the specification of the methods.

Moreover, consideration of content-dependent authorizations introduces further complications. In particular, it is more difficult to determine the consistency and completeness of the authorizations. This is due to the fact that satisfaction of the conditions in the authorizations depends on the values of the objects' attributes and can therefore change over time. For example, consider the class Document having attributes 'date' and 'status'. Suppose then that subject Employee owns at the same time the positive authorization to read all documents with date later than 'October 12, 1993' and the negative authorization to read all objects with status 'protected'. If no objects exist with status 'protected' and date later than 'October 12, 1993', the authorization state is consistent. However, since attribute values can change and new objects can be added, authorizations may become inconsistent. Consistency and completeness criteria and mechanisms to satisfy them have therefore to be extended to the consideration of content-dependent authorizations. These problems have not been addressed by Bertino and Weigand who, in their paper, consider only positive authorization.

## 7.6 Authorization models based on methods

The models presented so far take into consideration many of the characteristics of object-oriented data models such as inheritance hierarchy, versions and composite objects. However, they do not exploit the potential of encapsulation typical of the object-oriented approach. In fact, all accesses made during method execution are further checked against the user who invoked (directly or indirectly) the method. For example, if, during execution of a method invoked by a user, an attempt is made to modify the attribute of an instance, the user's authorization to update the attribute must be checked. In some cases, where encapsulation is meant to provide protection, it is desirable not to give users the authorization to execute some accesses directly, but to allow those same accesses through the execution of some method. For example, users may not be authorized to write an attribute of an object but may be authorized to run a method that, during its execution, modifies the attribute. Therefore, since users should not be directly authorized for the access, no authorization enabling users to execute the access executed by the method should be provided. Two authorization models that take this principle into account are presented in the following paragraphs.

### 7.6.1 The Iris authorization model

An authorization model based on authorizations to execute methods has been proposed by Ahad *et al.* (1992) in the context of the Iris DBMS. In the Iris data model, both attributes and methods are represented as functions. In particular, attributes are defined as stored functions, while methods are defined as derived functions. Hence, objects (and their data) are encapsulated by a set of functions: that is, to access an object, users call the appropriate functions.

Accordingly, the authorization model considers authorizations that specify, for every user, the set of functions the user is allowed to call. Authorizations can be referred to single users as well as to groups of users. A user can belong to zero or more groups, and groups can be nested.

The model supports the concept of ownership. In particular, the user who creates a function is considered the *owner* of the function and can grant other users the authorization to call the function. Authorizations can also be specified with the grant option. If a user has the grant option on the authorization to call a function, the user can grant other users the authorization to call the function and the grant option on it. The grant privilege is also enforced as a function. In particular, the authorization for the grant privilege on a function $f$ is represented by the authorization to call the 'grant' function with $f$ as argument.

Moreover, functions, called *derived functions*, can be defined on other functions. Authorizations on derived functions can be defined as *static* or *dynamic*. If a user has a dynamic authorization on a derived function, then in order for the user to call the function, the user must have the call privilege on all the underlying functions. By contrast, in order to execute a derived function on which he has a static authorization, a user does not need to have the 'call' authorization on the underlying functions. When a user creates a derived function, the user must specify whether the authorizations on the functions on which the derived function is defined must be checked statically or dynamically. In either case, the creator of the derived function must have the authorization on all the under-lying functions. If the creator specifies that the function must have dynamic authorization, any user authorized for the derived function with the grant option can grant other users the authorization to call the function. By contrast, if the function is specified to have static authorizations, a user authorized for the derived function with the grant option can grant other users the authorization to call the derived function only if he has the grant privilege on all the underlying functions.

Derived functions can also be used to support content-dependent authorizations. In this case, users are not authorized directly for a function, but for a function derived from it that enforces some constraints. For example, consider class EMPLOYEE storing information about the employees and a function 'Salary', defined on EMPLOYEE, returning the employees' salaries. Although some employees can be authorized to read everyone's salaries, some employees could be restricted to seeing only their own salary. This condition can be enforced by defining a derived function 'Self_Salary' which takes into consideration the caller of the function and calls function 'Salary' to return the caller's salary. Since users cannot be authorized to call the function 'Salary' directly, the authorization to be specified on the function 'Self_Salary' is a static one. However, the application of a derived function to enforcing content-dependent authorizations has the drawback of embedding authorizations in the function implementation; therefore a change of authorizations would imply a change in the implementation of some derived functions.

The authorization model also takes into consideration the characteristic of polymorphism of object-oriented systems. Polymorphism allows the specification of functions, called *generic functions,* which are associated with a set of *specific functions* defined on different types (that is, classes). When a generic function is called, a specific function is selected for invocation (*late binding*). Authorizations can be specified on generic as well as specific functions. A user authorized to call a generic function is automatically authorized to call all specific functions associated with that generic function. When a user calls a generic function, the corresponding specific function is selected and the user is allowed to execute it only if he has the authorization on the specific function. The specific function can be selected regardless of the user's authorizations (authorization-independent resolution) or by taking the user's authorizations into account (authorization-dependent resolution). However, authorization-dependent resolution has the disadvantage that the query semantics is in this case dependent on the authorization policies.

Functions can also be specified as having a *guard* function. If a function *F* has an associated guard function, *F* can be executed only if the guard function returns 'true'. Guard functions can therefore be used to specify conditions that have to be satisfied before the users can execute some functions. Since guards enforce conditions by evaluating them prior to the execution of the guarded functions, they are really useful for evaluating preconditions: that is, conditions independent of the values returned by the guarded function. Indeed, in order to enforce conditions on values returned by the guarded function, the guarded function itself should be called and its results evaluated by the guard. To guarantee that no infinite loops will arise, the model requires that guard functions are not themselves guarded. Moreover, in order to guarantee the correctness of the computation, guard functions must not have any side-effects on the data: that is, they are read-only functions.

Another concept introduced by the model is that of *proxy* functions. Proxy functions provide different implementations of specific functions for different users. A function may have several associated proxy functions. When a user calls a function, the appropriate proxy is executed in place of the original function. Therefore, the result of a function may change depending on the user calling it. Hence, proxy functions can also be used to enforce conditions on accesses. Proxy functions have the advantage of allowing constraints on function execution by users to be enforced without any impact on the function implementation.

### 7.6.2 The Data-hiding model

Another model based on authorizations to execute methods has been proposed by Bertino (1992a). The model distinguishes between *public* and *private* methods. Private methods of an object can be invoked only by other methods of the same or different objects, whereas public methods can also be invoked directly by the users of the object (that is, end users, application programs, other objects). If a method is private, that is, can be accessed only by other methods, the declaration of the methods that can execute it is provided as part of the class definition to which the method itself belongs. The set of methods that can execute a specific private method is called the *invocation scope* of the method.

The model is based on authorizations for users to execute methods on objects. Authorizations specify, for each user, the set of methods the user can invoke on each object. Therefore, authorizations have the form $(o, u, m)$, where $o$ is an object, $u$ is a user, and $m$ is a method. The tuple $(u, o, m)$ specifies that user $u$ is authorized to execute method $m$ on object $o$. Authorizations can be specified only on public methods: that is, on methods directly invocable by end users. In order for a user to execute a method, the method must be public for end users and the user must have the authorization to execute the method. If both these conditions are satisfied, the user can execute the method. However, the fact that the user is authorized to run a method does not imply that the user will be able to execute all actions that are part of the method. Indeed, other methods can be invoked during execution of the method called by the user and, therefore, several access controls may need to be performed during the execution. In order for the user to complete the processing, all necessary authorizations for the different accesses must exist. In particular, suppose that during the execution of a method *m* another method *m*′ is invoked. The invocation must be checked against the existing authorizations. Then, if *m*′ is public for end users, the invocation is allowed only if the user has the authorization for *m*′. By contrast, if *m*′ is private, the invocation is allowed only if the invoking method *m* belongs to the invocation scope of *m*′.

Each object is associated with a creator: that is, the user who created the object. The creator of an object is always unique but can change during the lifetime of the object. In particular, the creator of an object may give the privilege of being creator to some other user. Since the creator must be unique, in so doing the first user loses the creator privilege on the object, which is passed to the other user. Moreover, each object is associated with a set of *owners*: that is, users authorized to administer authorizations on the object. The set of owners associated with an object can be modified (by adding or removing users) only by the creator of the object.

The model allows users to grant authorizations to execute methods to other users. A user can grant authorizations to execute methods on an object if the user is the object creator or if he or she is one of the owners of the object. Any user who can grant authorizations to execute methods on an object can also revoke authorizations to execute methods on the object. However, a user can only revoke authorizations that he or she granted.

The model also introduces the notion of *protection mode* for method execution authorizations. If user *u* grants user *u*′ the authorization to execute method *m* in protection mode, then when *u*′ executes *m*, all invocations of methods public for end users made by *m* are checked for authorizations not against *u*′, who called the method, but against *u*: that is, against the user who granted *u*′ the authorization on the method. In this way users can grant other users the privilege of executing some method *m* on an object without giving them the authorizations for the methods called (directly or indirectly) by *m*, not directly, but by using other methods. The concept of protection mode is very similar to the set *user-id on execution* concept considered in the UNIX operating system.

## 7.7 The message filter

The message filter, proposed by Jajodia and Kogan (1990) and revised by Jajodia *et al.* (1992), is a model for providing mandatory protection in object-oriented database systems. The model enforces access control by exploiting the encapsulation characteristic of object-oriented systems. In object-oriented systems, messages are the only means through which information can be exchanged among objects. Hence, information flow in object-oriented systems has a very concrete and natural embodiment in the form of messages and their replies. On the basis of this observation, the model proposed in Jajodia *et al.* (1992) controls information flow by mediating (filtering) the messages exchanged between objects.

### 7.7.1 Entities of the model

The model considers as objects/subjects of the protection model, objects of the object-oriented model. Hence, objects of the object-oriented model have a dual nature in that they are both objects and subjects in the Bell–LaPadula sense (see Chapter 2). They are objects in that they store information. They are subjects in that they can execute actions by sending messages.

A security level is assigned to each object at creation time. In the following, given object $o$, $L(o)$ indicates its security level. The level of an object is fixed for the whole object life cycle. This restriction corresponds to the tranquility principle of the Bell–LaPadula model (see Chapter 2). Moreover, the following restrictions must hold on the classification of objects:

- *If $o_j$ is an object of a class $c_j$ then $L(c_j) \leq L(o_j)$:* that is, the level of an instance object must dominate the level of the class of which the object is an instance.
- *If $c_i$ and $c_j$ are classes such that $c_j$ is a child of $c_i$ in the class hierarchy, then $L(c_i) \leq L(c_j)$:* that is, the level of a subclass must dominate the level of its superclass(es).

Note that these properties are not required for security reasons. Particularly also if the constraints above are not satisfied, the message filter ensures that no secrecy violation would be exploited. However, if these constraints are not satisfied users will not be able to use the system properly. For example, if the level of a subclass does not dominate the level of its superclass, then the subclass will not be able to gain access to the methods and properties it inherits from the superclass.

Users are seen as a particular type of object. A user object represents a user session in the system. User objects have the peculiarity that, besides invoking methods upon receiving messages, they can invoke methods spontaneously. This allows users to initiate their activities.

### 7.7.2 Information flow

As we have already noticed, messages are the only means by which information flow can be enacted in object-oriented systems. In particular, information flow among objects can take place when (1) a message is sent by an object to another object and (2) when a new object is created. In the first case, the information flow is *bidirectional*. The *forward* flow is carried through the parameters indicated in the message; the *backward* flow is carried through the return value. In the second case, information flows only forward: that is, from the creating object to the created object.

It is possible to have information flow between one object and another object even if no message is directly exchanged between the objects. Thus, information flow from one object to another object may be *direct*, if a message is sent from one object to another object, or *indirect* if the information flows between the first object and the second object through the mediation of one or more other objects. For example, suppose object $o_1$ sends a message to object $o_2$ which, in turn, sends a message to object $o_3$. There is a flow of information between objects $o_1$ and $o_3$ (and vice versa through the replies). However, no message has been exchanged between $o_1$ and $o_3$.

Note, however, that for information to be transferred to an object, the information has to be written into the object: that is, the values of the attributes of the object have to be changed accordingly. Thus, message reception does not necessarily entail information transfer to the receiving object. Indeed, if none of the attributes of the object is changed upon reception of a message, no information transfer has been enacted. In this case, the information flow is said to be *ineffective*.

Access to the internal attributes of an object (in order to read or write them) and to object creation are enforced by having the object send a message to itself. For this purpose, the following built-in messages are defined.

- A *read* message is a message sent by an object $o$ to itself to read any of the object attributes. The message is defined as $g$ = (READ, $(a_j)$, $r$), where $a_j$ is an attribute of $o$. The message has the effect of returning, as return value $r$, the value of attribute $a_j$. If the assignment is not possible, for example because the attribute does not exist, a *failure* is returned.
- A *write* message is a message sent by an object $o$ to itself to write any of the object attributes. The message is defined as $g$ = (WRITE, $(a_j, v_j)$, $r$), where $a_j$ is an attribute of $o$. The message has the effect of assigning value $v_j$ to attribute $a_j$; *success* is then returned. If the assignment is not possible, for example because the attribute does not exist or because the attribute cannot have that value, a *failure* is returned.
- A *create* message is a message sent by an object $o$ to itself to create a new object. The message is defined as $g$ = (CREATE, $((v_1, \ldots, v_k), S_j)$, $r$), where $S_j$ is a security level. The message has the effect of creating a new object with security level $S_j$. The new object inherits attributes and methods from $o$. Attributes are initialized with values $v_1, \ldots, v_k$. If the operation terminates successfully, the object identifier $i$ assigned by the system to the new object is returned as return value $r$. Otherwise a *failure* is returned.

### 7.7.3 Message-filtering algorithm

In the message filter model, messages are not allowed to flow directly from one object to another object. Instead, the message filter intercepts every message exchanged between objects and, based on the security levels of the sender and receiver and on some auxiliary information, decides how to handle the message. Possible actions the message filter can take are: leaving the message unaltered, blocking the message, or enforcing restriction on the execution of the method invoked by the message.

The message filter works by assigning each method execution $t$ a classification, named *rlevel*. The semantics of *rlevel* is that it keeps track of the least upper bound of all the objects encountered in a chain of method executions. In this way it is possible to control indirect flow among objects. Then, the messages are handled taking into consideration, as well as the classification of the sender and receiver, the classification (*rlevel*) of the execution sending the message. In particular, execution $t$ on object $o$ is said to be *restricted*, meaning write operations are not allowed, if its security level (rlevel($t$)) is higher than the security level ($L(o)$) of the object.

The message-filtering algorithm is illustrated in Figure 7.7. To illustrate the working of the algorithm, consider two objects $o_1 = (i_1, a_1, v_1, u_1)$ and $o_2 = (i_2, a_2, v_2, u_2)$, where $i_j$, $a_j$, $v_j$ and $u_j$ indicate respectively the identifier, the set of attributes, the set of attribute values and the methods in object $o_i$. Moreover,

```
% let g1 = (h1, (p1, ..., pk), r) be the message sent from o1 to o2
if o1 ≠ o2 ∨ h1 ∉ {READ, WRITE, CREATE} then case
% i.e., g1 is a non-primitive message
(1)  L(o1) = L(o2):   % let g1 pass, let reply pass
                      invoke t2 with rlevel(t2) ← rlevel(t1);
                      r ← reply from t2; return r to t1;
(2)  L(o1) <> L(o2):  % block g1, inject NIL reply
                      r ← NIL; return r to t1;
(3)  L(o1) < L(o2):   % let g1 pass, inject NIL reply, ignore actual reply
                      r ← NIL; return r to t1;
                      invoke t2 with rlevel(t2) ← lub[L(o2), rlevel(t1)];
                      % where lub denotes least upper bound
                      discard reply from t2;
(4)  L(o1) > L(o2):   % let g1 pass, let reply pass
                      invoke t2 with rlevel(t2) ← rlevel(t1);
                      r ← reply from t2; return r to t1;
end case;
if o1 = o2 ∧ h1 ∈ {READ, WRITE, CREATE} then case
% i.e., g1 is a primitive message
(5)  g1 = (READ,(aj), r): % allow unconditionally
                        r ← value of aj; return r to t1;
(6)  g1 = (WRITE,(aj, vj), r): % allow if status of t1 is unrestricted
                        if rlevel (t1) = L(o1)
                          then [aj ← vj; r ← SUCCESS]
                          else r ← FAILURE;
                        return r to t1;
(7)  g1 = (CREATE,(vi, ..., vk, Sj), r): % allow if status of t1 is unrestricted relative to Sj
                        if rlevel (t1) ≤ Sj
                          then [CREATE i with values vi, ..., vk, and L(i) ← Sj; r ← i]
                          else r ← FAILURE;
                        return r to t1;
end case;
```

*Figure 7.7* Message-filtering algorithm.

consider message $g = (h, p, r)$ sent by $o_1$ to $o_2$, where $h$ denotes the message name, $p$ the message parameters, and $r$ the return value of the message. Let $t_1$ be the method execution in $o_1$ which sent message $g$, and $t_2$ the execution of the method to be invoked upon reception of message $g$.

The first part of the algorithm (cases 1–4) considers the case where $g$ is a non-primitive message. The second part (cases 5–7) considers the case where $g$ is a primitive message.

Suppose $g$ is a non-primitive message. Then, if the sender and the receiver have the same security levels (case 1) the message and its reply are allowed to pass unaltered. Moreover, $t_2$ is assigned the same *rlevel* as $t_1$. If the sender and the receiver have incomparable security levels (case 2), the message is blocked and a *nil* reply is immediately returned to the sender. If the level of the sender is strongly dominated by (<) the level of the receiver (case 3) , then the message is passed through. However, a *nil* reply is immediately returned to the sender, while the actual reply from $t_2$ will be discarded. Moreover, $t_2$ is assigned *rlevel* equal to the least upper bound between the level of the receiver and the *rlevel* of execution $t_1$ which sent the message. Finally, if the level of the receiver strongly dominates (>) the level of the sender (case 4) the message and its reply are allowed to pass unaltered. Moreover, the *rlevel* of $t_2$ is set equal to the *rlevel* of $t_1$. In this way the execution invoked will not be allowed to execute write operations at a level which is not dominated by the level of the sender, thus preventing illegal information flow caused by writes down.

Consider now the case where $g$ is a primitive message. If the method invoked is *read* (case 5) then no restrictions are applied. Indeed no write up can occur because if the sender of the message does not dominate the level of the receiver a *nil* reply has already been returned to it and the real reply will be discarded. If the method invoked is *write* (case 6) or *create* (case 7), it will be executed only if the execution that sent the message has unrestricted status. Note that the restriction on the create operation guarantees that the security level of an object dominates the security level of the class of which this object is an instance.

### 7.7.4 Classification requirement representation

The application of the Message-filter model requires all objects to be single-level. Then, all properties and methods of an object must have the same classification. However, real-world entities are often multilevel.

In this section we illustrate the approach for modeling multilevel entities through single-level objects proposed by the authors of the message-filter model in Jajodia *et al.* (1992).

Suppose a multilevel entity $E$ has to be represented, containing properties with levels $L_1, \ldots, L_n$. Then, for each security level $L_i$ of some properties of the entity, an object $o_i$ is defined. Each object contains all the properties with level dominated by the level of the object. The properties in an object are then assigned the level of the object. Then, each object at level $L_j$ is defined as a child (is-a) of objects at levels directly dominating $L_j$ in the classification lattice. To illustrate, consider the following example.

Suppose entity EMPLOYEE is to be represented, with attributes 'name' and 'ssn' with level Unclassified (U), and 'salary' with level Secret (S). This entity can be represented as two class objects: class U_EMPLOYEE with level Unclassified, containing attributes 'name' and 'ssn', and a class S_EMPLOYEE with level Secret with the additional attribute 'salary'. An is-a relationship is then defined between class U_EMPLOYEE and S_EMPLOYEE. The resulting schema is as in Figure 7.8.

Now suppose entity MANAGER is to be defined as 'is-a' EMPLOYEE, with the additional attribute 'project' with level Unclassified. The resulting representation is illustrated in Figure 7.9.

Note that the *'is-a'* relationships between objects are determined by the data semantics (defined in the conceptual schema of the entities to be represented) as well as by security considerations (introduced because each multilevel entity is represented through several objects hierarchically connected). In both cases, the inheritance mechanism operates as the usual inheritance mechanism of object-oriented systems.

## 7.8 SORION model

SORION is a security model, proposed by Thuraisingham (1989b), which extends the ORION object-oriented model (Banergee *et al.*, 1987) by enforcing access controls based on a mandatory policy. The model is defined in terms of

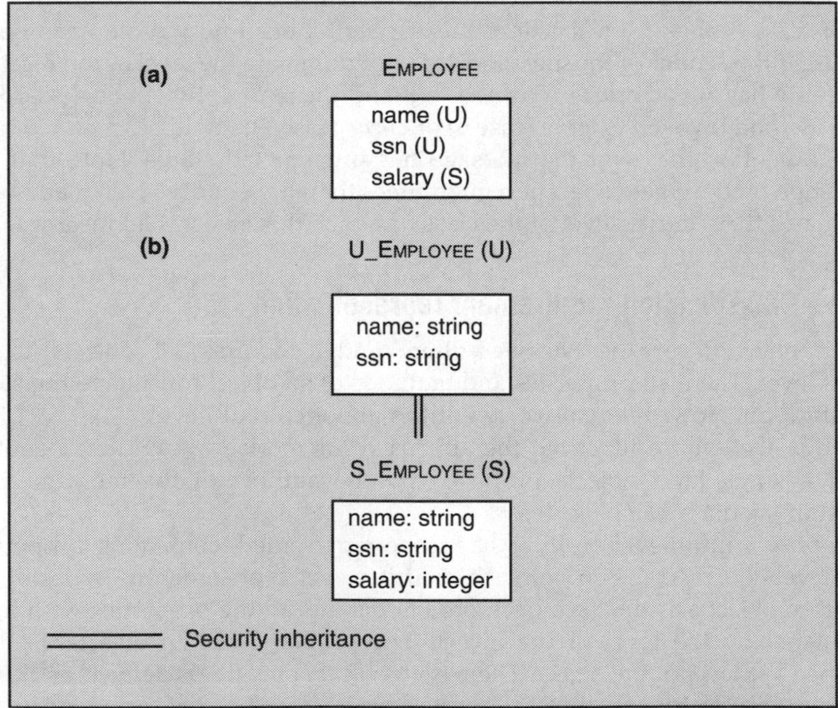


***Figure 7.8*** An example of representation of (a) a type of multilevel entity by (b) a hierarchy of classes of single-level objects.

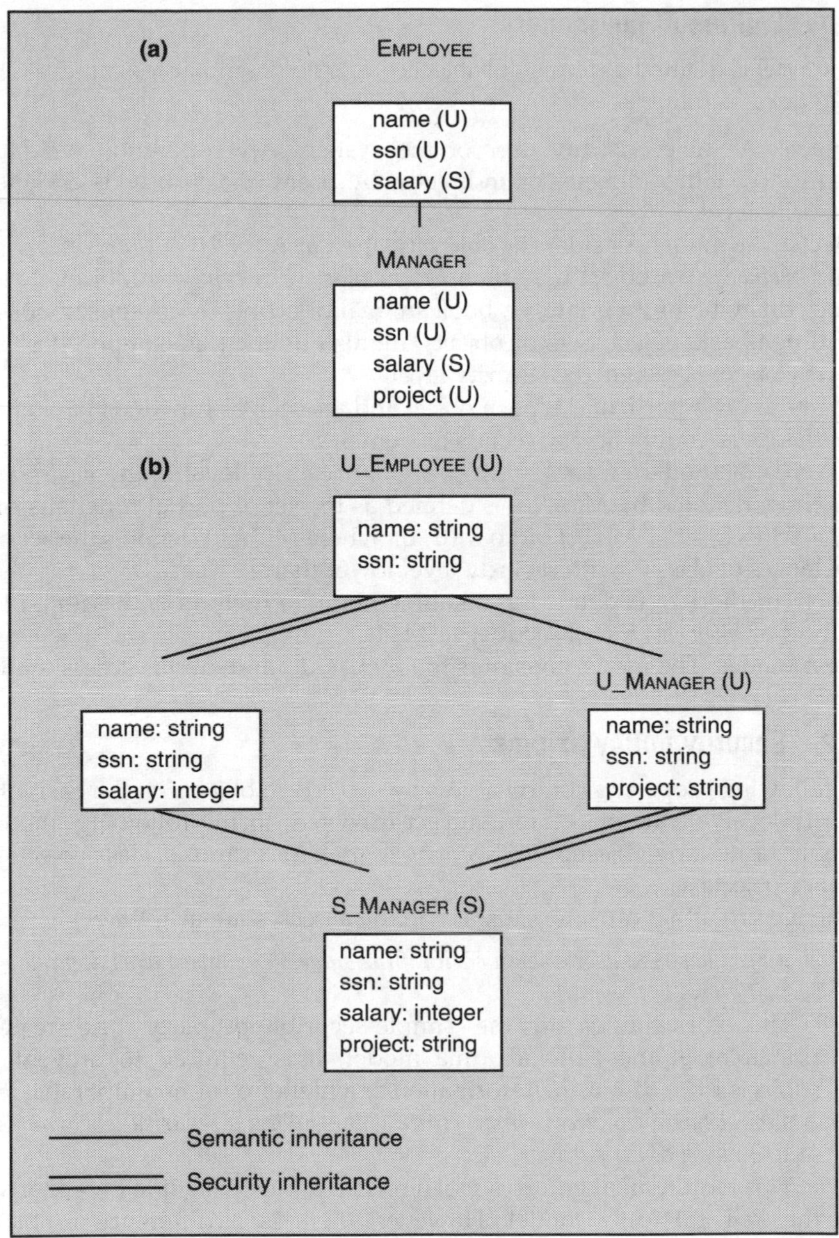


*Figure 7.9* An example of representation of (a) an *is-a* hierarchy of multilevel entities by (b) an *is-a* hierarchy of classes of single-level objects.

subjects, objects and access modes. Properties must be satisfied between the security levels of a subject and an object in order for the subject to access, in a given mode, the object. Moreover, further properties regulate the classification of objects.

### 7.8.1 Entities of the model

The model is defined in terms of subjects and objects, and access modes. These are defined as follows.

**Subjects:** A subject is any user of the system. Any operation on data is requested, either directly or indirectly, by users. Every user is assigned a security level.

**Objects:** The model considers as objects: *classes*, *objects* (*class instances*), *variables* and *methods*. An object may be a *basic* object or a *composed* object. A basic object may be of type integer, boolean, real or string. A composed object is any non-basic object. Sets of objects are also defined as composed objects. Every object is assigned a security level.

Methods are a particular type of object and are seen as functions having a set of classes as codomain and a class as domain.

Given a method $m$: $C_1 \times C_2 \dots C_n \rightarrow C$, at security level $L$, the *model* of the method, denoted by $M(m, L)$, is defined as the set of partial functions $M(C_1, L) \times M(C_2,L) \times \dots M(C_n,L)$ into $M(C, L)$, where $M(C_i, L)$ denotes the set of all instances of class $C_i$ with security level lower than $L$.

Then, method $m_1$ is defined as a submethod of a method $m_2$ if $M(m_1, L)$ is a subset of $M(m_2, L)$ for all security levels L.

**Access modes:** The model considers the *read*, *write*, and *execute* access modes.

### 7.8.2 Security policy axioms

The following properties control access by subjects to objects on the basis of the security levels of the object and subject involved. In the following, the term entity indicates any object of the security model: for example, class objects and instance objects.

The *properties* that must be satisfied on the accesses are as follows.

- *A subject has read access to an entity if the subject's security level dominates the security level of the entity.*

  This corresponds to the simple-security property ('no read-up' principle) of the Bell–LaPadula model. It is required to prevent low subjects from disclosing information at a higher or non-comparable level.
- *A subject has write access to an entity if the subject's security level equals the security level of the entity.*

  This requirement enforces the 'no write-down' principle (*-property) of the Bell–LaPadula model. However, there is a difference in that in SORION, write operations at higher levels are not allowed. Prevention of write operations at lower or non-comparable levels is maintained, to avoid illegal flows of information.
- *A subject can execute a method if the subject's security level dominates the security level of both the method and the type on which the method is defined.*

  This is a consequence of the read property. Indeed, because of the read property, a subject sees only methods that have a security level lower than that of the subject; and, indeed, a subject must not be able to execute a method if he cannot know of its existence.

- *A method executes at the security level of the subject who initiated the execution.*
  Since the method executes on behalf of the subject, it is given the access class of the subject to ensure that only accesses for which the subject has the necessary clearance will be allowed.
- *During the execution of a method $m_1$, if another method $m_2$ has to be executed then $m_2$ can execute only if the execution level of $m_1$ dominates both the security level of $m_2$ and the security level of the type on which $m_2$ is defined.*
- *If a new object has to be created as a result of executing a method, the object is created at the security level of the subject who initiated the execution of the method.*
  A create operation is a particular type of write operation. Consequently, this requirement is a particular case of the requirement that a subject can only write at its own level.

### 7.8.3 Classification axioms

The model requires properties to be satisfied on the classification of objects. This section illustrates the properties that must hold in the model. Properties are grouped according to the type of constraints they control.

#### *Object classification axioms*

The following *properties* must hold on the classification of instance objects.

- *If o is a basic object, then L(o) = system-low, where system-low denotes the bottom security level in the classification lattice.*
  This property requires basic objects of the system to be classified at the lowest security level. In this way all basic objects can be visible to any user in the system. If the property were not satisfied, there would exist some users (those whose level would not dominate the class of the basic objects) who would not be able to read the basic objects.
- *The security level of the name of an object must dominate the security level of the value of the object.*
  This requirement comes from the fact that values are interpreted as basic objects and therefore they must be assigned the lowest security level.
- *If o is a set object* $\{a_1, a_2, \ldots, a_n\}$, *then* $L(o) \geq lub(L(a_1), L(a_2), \ldots, L(a_n))$.
  This property requires the security level of an object defined as a set of other objects to dominate the security level of all the objects in the set. The satisfaction of this property prevents subjects from inferring high-level data by observing a low-level set containing the high-level data.
- *The security levels of the object variables of an object are the same as that of the object.*
  The model requires objects to be single-level. All variables in an object have the same level, which is the level of the object in which they are contained.

#### *Class classification axioms*

The following *properties* must hold on the classification of classes and their instances.

- *The security level of the instances of a class must dominate the security level of the class.*

  This property is a consequence of the read property. In particular, objects must have visibility of the class to which they belong.
- *Anyone who can read the name of a class should also be able to read the names of the instance variables of the class.*

  The security levels of the instance variables of a class must be the same as the level of the class where they are defined. However, if a user cannot read an instance of a class, then the user cannot read its variables.
- *The security level of a subclass must dominate the security level of the superclass.*

  This property is required to allow a subclass to inherit from its superclass(es).
- *The instance variables of a subclass (whether inherited or defined) have the same security level as that of the subclass.*

  Then, if the level of a subclass dominates the level of its superclass, the inherited properties are upgraded in the subclass.

#### Method classification

The *properties* that must be satisfied in the classification of methods can be summarized as follows.

- *If a method m is defined on* $C_1 \times C_2 \times \ldots C_n$ *and its range is C, then* $L(m) \geq lub(C_1, C_2, \ldots, C_n, C)$.

  The security level assigned to a method must dominate the security level of the classes in the domain and in the codomain of the method.
- *If* $C_1$ *is subclass of* $C_2$ *and* $m_2$ *is a method of* $C_2$*, then there is a method* $m_1$ *of* $C_1$ *with the same name as* $m_2$ *such that* $m_1$ *is a submethod of* $m_2$*. Moreover:* $L(m_1) = lub(L(m_2), L(C_1))$.

  This property regulates the classification of inherited methods. Since a subclass may have a security level greater than its superclass, the classification of the inherited methods may need to be increased (to avoid storing low-level methods in high-level classes).

#### Multiple inheritance

There is multiple inheritance if a subclass has more than one direct superclass. The following *properties* must hold in case of multiple inheritance.

- *Let C be a subclass of* $C_1, C_2, \ldots, C_n$*. Let the instance variable V be associated with* $C_1, C_2, \ldots, C_n$*. Class C will inherit the instance variable associated with class* $C_j$ $(1 \geq j \geq n)$ *such that* $L(C_j)$ *dominates the levels of the remaining classes. If there are more than one such* $C_j$*, then some* a priori *rule should be enforced to resolve the conflict.*

  The multiple inheritance property of the variables specifies that, in case of conflict, the variable contained in the higher classified class is inherited. Should this class not exist, because the levels of the different classes are not comparable, or should several classes have the same level, rules must be applied to resolve this conflict.

- *Let C be a subclass of $C_1, C_2, \ldots, C_n$. Let the instance variable m be associated with $C_1, C_2, \ldots, C_n$. C will inherit the method associated with class $C_j$ $(1 \geq j \geq n)$ such that $L(C_j)$ dominates the levels of the remaining classes. If there are more than one such $C_j$, then some* a priori *rule should be enforced to resolve the conflict.*
  This property is analogous to that required on the inheritance of variables.

#### Aggregate classes and objects

Classes may be related through the part-of relationship. Hence, class C may be defined as an aggregate of other classes $C_1, C_2, \ldots, C_n$. If a class C is defined as an aggregate of other classes $C_1, C_2, \ldots, C_n$, then each instance of C is an aggregate of instances of $C_1, C_2, \ldots, C_n$, respectively.

The following *properties* must be satisfied on the classification of aggregate classes and instances.

- *Let C be a class defined as an aggregate of classes $C_1, C_2, \ldots, C_n$. Then, $L(C) \geq lub(L(C_1), L(C_2), \ldots L(C_n))$.*
  The property requires the security level of the aggregate class to dominate the security level of the classes composing the aggregation. It ensures that a user will be allowed to access a composed object only if the user can access each single component of the object.
- *Let o be an instance of class C. Let $o_i$ indicate an instance of $C_i$, $1 \geq i \geq n$. Then, $L(o) \geq lub(L(o_1), L(o_2), \ldots L(o_n))$.*
  This is analogous to the above property, with the exception that it is required to hold on the instance objects.

#### Relationship

Relationships can be defined among objects. Example of relationship are the is-a relationship, connecting a subclass to its superclasses, and the part-of relationship, connecting a class to its components. The following property must be satisfied on the relationships.

- *Let R be a relationship object which describes a relationship between two objects $o_1$ and $o_2$. Then, $L(R) \geq lub(L(o_1),L(o_2))$.*
  The security level of a relationship object must dominate the security level of the objects connected by the relationship. Hence, if a subject cannot see any of the objects in the relationship, the subject must not see the relationship itself.

### 7.8.4 Classification requirement representation

The SORION model requires all objects to be simple-level. However, as we have already observed, real-world entities are often multilevel.

In this section we illustrate the representation of multilevel entities through single-level objects proposed in Thuraisingham (1989b).

The following three types of classification constraints are considered.

- *Simple constraint.* The attributes of a class have different security levels.
- *Content constraint.* The classification to be assigned to an attribute in a class depends on the value of the attribute.

- *Context constraint.* This deals with the classification to be assigned to aggregate objects.

Let us now illustrate them in detail.

Consider a simple constraint of a class C with instance variables $V_1, V_2, \ldots, V_n$ with different security levels. This is represented through single-level objects as follows. For each level for which there exist some instance variables, a class is defined. The class at a given level contains all instance variables at that level. Then, the classes are connected through the 'is-a' relationship. In particular, class C is defined as a subclass of $C_1$, if the security level of C dominates the security level of $C_1$.

For example, consider that a multilevel entity EMPLOYEE has to be defined containing attributes 'name' and 'ssn' (social security number) with level Unclassified and attribute 'salary' with level Secret (Figure 7.10(a)). This is represented by defining two classes, U_EMPLOYEE, with level Unclassified, containing instance variable 'name' and 'ssn', and S_EMPLOYEE with level Secret containing variable 'salary'. Class S_EMPLOYEE is then defined as is-a U_EMPLOYEE as illustrated in Figure 7.10(b).

There is a *content constraint* when the security level to be assigned to an attribute depends on the value of the attribute itself. In particular, a class C may have a variable V whose classification depends on the value of V or of other attributes of C. This situation can be represented as follows. A class C is defined containing all the variables except V. Moreover, for each possible level that can

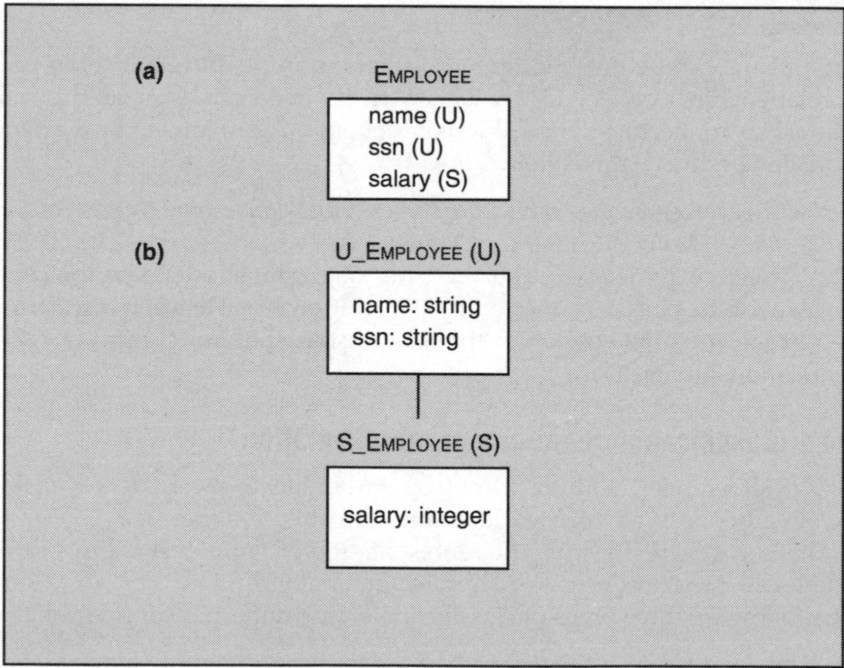


*Figure 7.10* An example of a simple constraint. Representation of (a) a multi-level entity by (b) a hierarchy of classes of single-level objects.

be assigned to variable *V*, a class is defined containing variable *V*. The value that the variable can assume in any of the subclasses is restricted according to the security level of the class. All these classes are then defined as subclasses of the first class.

For example, consider class EMPLOYEE has to be defined with attributes 'name' and 'ssn' with level Unclassified and the attribute 'salary' with level Unclassified for salaries up to 2000 and Secret for salaries greater than 2000 (Figure 7.11(a)). This is represented as follows. Class Emp is defined with level Unclassified containing variables 'name' and 'ssn'. Moreover, classes U_Employee(U) and S_Employee are defined as *is-a* Emp, with the additional variable 'Salary', and with constraints on the value that attribute 'salary' can assume. In particular, attribute 'salary' must be lower or equal to 2000 in class U_Employee and greater than 2000 in class S_Employee. This is illustrated in Figure 7.11(b).

*Context constraints* deal with the classification of aggregate objects. In particular a context constraint arises when aggregated information is more sensitive than the single pieces of information which compose the aggregate. This constraint is represented by defining a composed class with security level greater than the security level of the component. The class of the simple objects and the class defining their association are completely independent. For example, suppose attributes 'name', 'ssn', and 'salary' pertaining to Employee are all Unclassified. However, the association between an employee and its 'salary' has to be classified Secret (Figure 7.12(a)). This is represented as

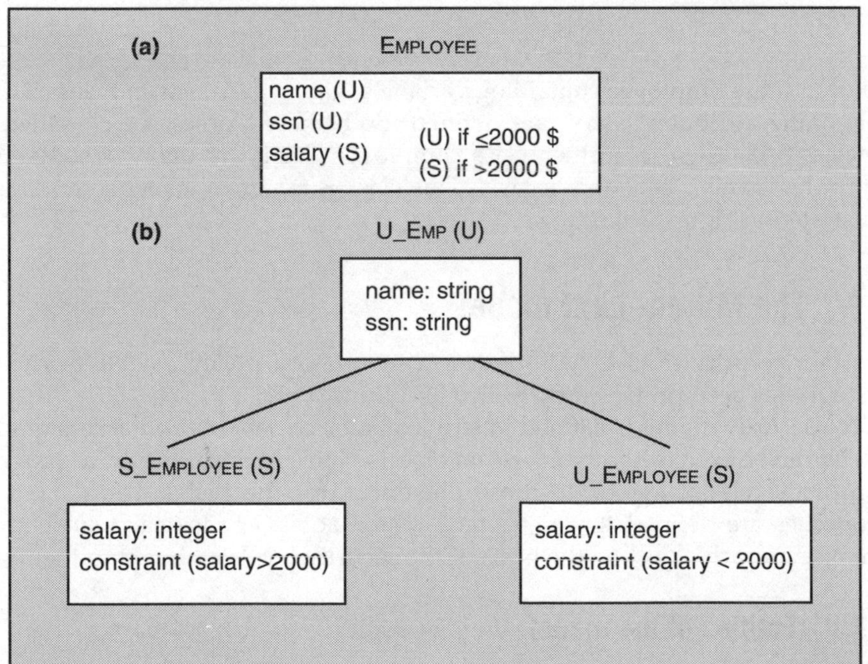


*Figure 7.11* An example of a content constraint. Representation of (a) a multi-level entity by (b) an *is-a* hierarchy of classes of single-level objects.

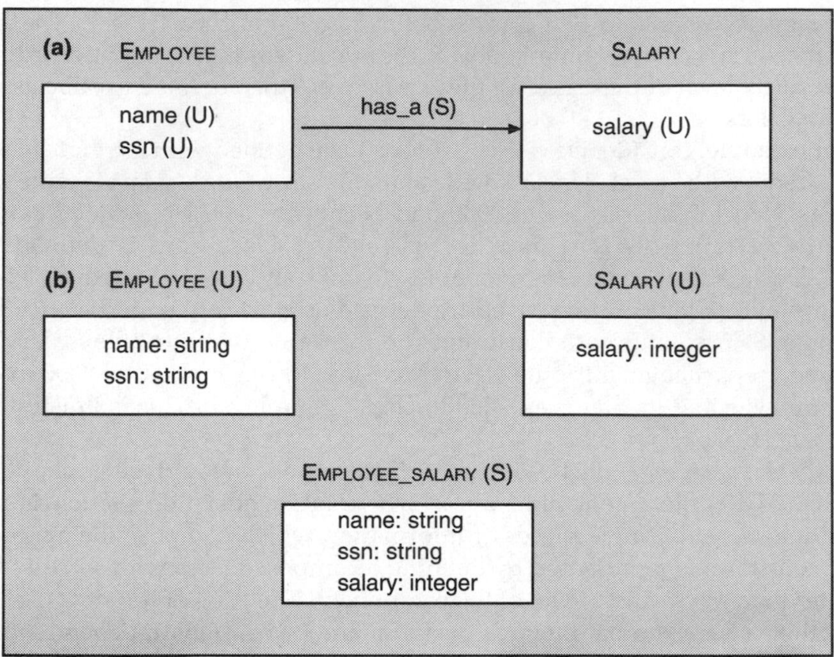


*Figure 7.12* An example of a context constraint. Representation of (a) classified relationship between entities by (b) classes of single-level objects.

follows. Class Employee containing variables 'name' and 'ssn' and class Salary containing attribute 'salary' are defined. Both these classes are classified as Unclassified. Then, a further class, Employee_Salary, is defined containing attributes 'name', 'ssn' and 'salary'. This class is assigned level Secret. This is illustrated in Figure 7.12(b).

## 7.9 The Millen–Lunt model

Another security model that enforces a mandatory policy in object-oriented systems has been proposed by Millen and Lunt (1992).

The security model is defined in terms of subjects, objects and access modes, which can be exercised by subjects on objects. Subjects and objects are assigned security levels analogous to those illustrated for the Bell–LaPadula model. Properties are defined that determine which access modes each subject can exercise on each object on the basis of the security levels assigned to them.

### 7.9.1 Entities of the model

This section describes the entities of the system which are taken into consideration in the definition of the model.

#### *Objects*

The objects of the security model correspond to the objects of the object-oriented model: that is, each object of the object-oriented model (classes included) is considered as an object of the security model. The model requires all objects to be single-level. Hence, a security level is assigned to each object. Properties (that is, attributes and methods) of an object do not have a classification by their own: they are classified at the same level as the object in which they are contained.

Objects are created using a method defined in the class root of the object hierarchy. A subject creates an object by sending a predefined message, named *create*, to the class of which the new object must an instance.

#### *Subjects*

A subject in the security model is an active entity that executes methods upon reception of messages and can also send messages. In other words, each subject corresponds to a method execution. Each time an object receives a message, a new subject is created. The object that created the subject is referred to as the *home* of the subject. The subject that sent the message is referred to as the *invoker* of the subject created to handle the message. The subject created by an object upon reception of a given message exists only to manage the message and execute the related method; it is deleted upon completion of the method. The subject is assigned a security level equal to the least upper bound of the levels of the invoker subject and the home object. A subject may also change its security level. However, the subject may only upgrade itself. Indeed, changing to a lower or non-comparable security level would lead to covert channels and is therefore not allowed.

#### *Access modes*

The model considers that users access objects by sending messages that require the execution of methods. The following predefined methods, referred to as *system methods*, allow access to the internal attributes of an object (in order to read or write them) and object creation:

- *Create* to create new instances of an object
- *Delete* to delete instances of an object
- *Addmessage* to add methods to an object
- *Getvar* to read attributes of an object
- *Setvar* to write attributes of an object.

### 7.9.2 Axioms

The model specifies properties that must be satisfied on the classification of subjects and objects and on the accesses subjects can execute on objects. Each request from a subject to execute a method or to write/read variables is allowed only if it satisfies the axioms.

The *properties* that must hold are as follows.

- **Hierarchy property**
  *The level of an object must dominate that of its class object.*
  This property is required to ensure that an object can inherit, without violating the no read-up principle, methods and variables defined for the class of which the object is an instance.
- **Subject level property**
  *The security level of a subject dominates the level of the invoking subject, and it also dominates the level of its home object.*
  A subject is assigned a security level equal to the least upper limit of the level of its home object and the level of the invoking subject. This classification meets the subject level property. Moreover, since a subject can only upgrade its classification level, possible changes to a subject level also satisfy the property.
- **Object locality property**
  *A subject can execute methods and read or write variables only in its home object.*
  This property restricts a subject to execute actions only on its home object. A subject can execute methods on an object different from its home object by sending the object a message. A new subject will be created by the recipient object for the execution of the corresponding method. This property corresponds to the encapsulation principle of object-oriented systems according to which an object has visibility only of its own variables and can access variables of other objects only by sending messages to them.
- ***-property**
  *A subject may write into its home object only if its security level is equal to that of the object.*
  This property is required to prevent subjects from writing down. Note that, according to the subject level property, the level of a subject dominates the level of the home object of the subject. Then, if the subject has the same level as the object, the subject can write information in the object. By contrast, if the level of the subject is higher than the level of the object, the subject will not be allowed to write into the object because this would entail an information flow towards lower levels.
- **Return value property**
  *A subject can send a return value to its invoking subject only if it is at the same security level as the invoking subject.*
  This property is required to avoid information flowing from higher subjects to lower subjects. A subject can send messages to any object, including objects with a higher or non-comparable level. However, in this case the security level of the subject created by the recipient object to handle the message will strictly dominate the security level of the invoker. In this case, the invoker will not be able to receive the reply.
- **Object creation property**
  *The security level of a newly created object dominates the level of the subject that requested the creation.*
  This property is required to avoid subjects writing down by creating lower objects. Indeed, creation of an object can be seen as a write operation. Then, the property is a particular application of the no write-down principle.

### 7.9.3 Classification requirement representation

In this section we illustrate the approach for representing the classification requirements proposed in Millen and Lunt (1992). The authors distinguish three different cases, according to different interpretations that the classification may have:

- The data itself (or the association among data) is classified;
- The existence of the data is classified;
- The reason, or rule, for classifying the data may be classified.

The authors propose two approaches for representing the classification of *data association* when the aggregate of data has a classification strictly greater than the individual data forming the aggregate. For example, consider that an employee entity has to be represented where each employee has a name, a social security number ('ssn'), and a 'salary'. Suppose that all attributes are unclassified but that the association between the name and ssn number of an employee and his salary is secret. A first approach consists in defining a new object representing the association between entities and assigning the new object a classification strictly greater than that of the entities themselves. With reference to the example above, three objects will be defined: object EMPLOYEE with attributes name and ssn, object SALARY with attribute salary, and object EMP-SALARY with two attributes whose values are the *oids* of classes EMPLOYEE and SALARY respectively. This approach is analogous to that proposed by Thuraisingham for the representation of context constraints (see Figure 7.12). The second approach consists in classifying one entity at the level of the association. This approach, which has the drawback of upgrading data that should be available at lower levels, can be used when the first solution does not completely protect against inference threats. For example, with reference to Figure 7.12, if the number of employees is small and their ranking is known, the association between each employee and his salary can be easily reconstructed. Figure 7.13 illustrates how this approach can be used in the example just mentioned. In the figure, object EMPLOYEE (with class U) has a variable 'salary' whose domain consists of *oids* of object SALARY (with class S). Therefore, an

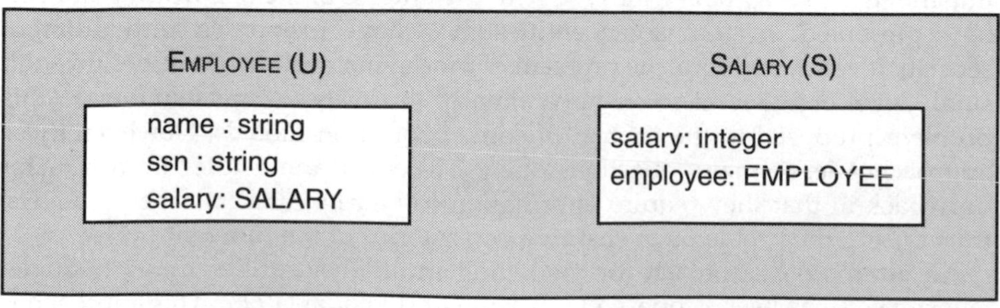


*Figure 7.13* An example of association classification when additional threats are likely.

unclassified subject can see that employees have salaries but cannot see their values (only their *oids*). Instances of class SALARY whose *oids* appear as values in EMPLOYEE objects must have been created by an unclassified subject. The values of their attributes are then entered by a secret subject. In this example, the existence of the object is classified at a level lower than the object itself (that is, the data stored in it).

The case where the *existence* of the object must be classified is dealt with by not allowing low objects to refer to higher objects. In particular, the model forbids the *oids* of high objects to be stored into lower objects.

The case where the *classification rules* must be classified is dealt with in a way analogous to that proposed by Thuraisingham for representing content constraints (see Figure 7.11).

The cases where the data, the association among data, and the rule for classifying the data are classified is dealt with as in the approach proposed in Thuraisingham (1989b) (see Section 7.8.4, Figures 7.10, 7.11 and 7.12 respectively); therefore we do not describe it further.

The model deals with the case where the existence of data is classified by hiding the existence of objects created by high subjects from lower subjects. In particular, in this case the model forbids objects to refer to (that is, to store *oids* of) higher or non-comparable objects. Note that, if the existence of an object is not to be hidden, the situation may occur where a low object has an attribute whose value is the *oid* of a higher object.

## 7.10 Modelling multilevel entities through single-level objects

A point common to the security models illustrated so far for the application of mandatory control to object-oriented systems is the requirement that objects be single-level: that is, all attributes of an object must have the same level. Indeed, directly supporting multilevel objects may be quite difficult and may lead to increased complexity in the design of the security monitor. By contrast, a model based on single-level objects has the important advantage of making the security monitor small enough so that it can be easily verified. However, as we have illustrated, this may not be the case with the entities of the real world that must be represented. In fact, some entities may have properties with different security levels. Therefore, the problem of modelling multilevel entities through single-level objects arises. We have already illustrated some solutions to this problem proposed in the context of some protection models. However, these approaches leave many questions open. Moreover, they suffer from a major drawback in that they require information to be replicated at different levels, thus raising the problems of ensuring consistency of the different copies.

An alternative approach for modelling multilevel entities through single-level objects has been proposed by Bertino and Jajodia (1993). This approach is based on the use of *composite objects*. In particular, instead of replicating low data in higher objects, a reference to the object containing the low data in inserted in the higher object. To explain, let $E$ be a multilevel entity containing properties with levels $L_1, \ldots, L_n$. Then, for each security level $L_i$ of some properties of the entity, a class $C_i$, with level $L_i$ is defined. Each class $C_i$ contains the properties with level $L_i$. Moreover, for each level $L_j$, with $L_j < L_i$, a composite attribute $a_j$ is defined in $C_i$ whose domain is a class $C_{Lj}$.

To illustrate, consider entity EMPLOYEE, with attributes 'name' and 'ssn' with level Unclassified (U) and 'salary' with level Secret (S). This entity can be represented as two class objects: a class U_EMPLOYEE with level Unclassified, containing attributes 'name' and 'ssn', and a class S_EMPLOYEE with level Secret containing attribute 'employee' with domain U_EMPLOYEE and attribute 'salary'. This is illustrated in Figure 7.14.

Note that entities may have properties that can assume more than one value at a time. Correspondingly, attributes in object-oriented data models can be multivalued: that is, more than one value may be associated with a given attribute. If a multivalued attribute has values at different security levels, the problem arises of properly storing these values. The approach proposed in Bertino and Jajodia (1993) is as follows. Suppose attribute $A$ may have values with security levels $L_1, \ldots, L_n$. Then, $n$ attributes $A_1, \ldots A_n$ with security levels $L_1, \ldots, L_n$ respectively are defined. The attributes are then stored in the appropriate class as illustrated above.

To illustrate, consider entity EMPLOYEE, with attributes 'name' and 'ssn' with level Unclassified (U), 'salary' with level Secret (S), and multivalued attribute 'projects' that can be either Unclassified or Secret. This entity can be represented as two class objects: a class U_EMPLOYEE with level Unclassified, containing attributes 'name', 'ssn' and 'u-projects' (containing the unclassified

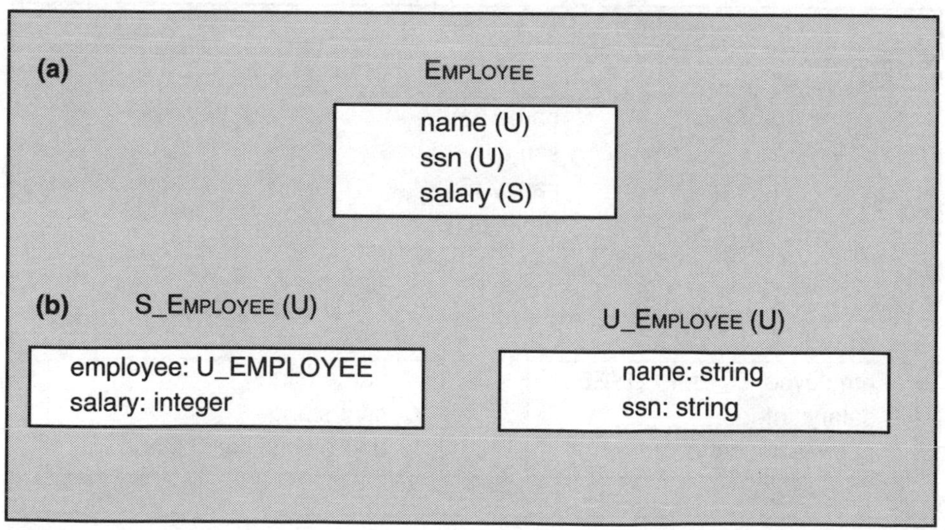


*Figure 7.14* An example of representation of (a) a multilevel entity through (b) composite objects.

projects), and a class S_EMPLOYEE with level Secret containing attribute 'employee' with domain U_EMPLOYEE, attribute 'salary', and attribute 's-projects' (containing the secret projects). An example of this is illustrated in Figure 7.15.

Note that in this approach the properties of an entity may be stored in different objects. Thus, in order for a user to completely see an entity more objects must be accessed. However, this can be provided by appropriate methods.

The model also extends the composite reference model (Kim *et al.*, 1989) to the consideration of additional types of references. In particular, the extended model allows one to require exclusive references to objects with respect to a given class (that is, an object cannot be referenced by more than one object of the same class). This allows enforcement of particular forms of semantic integrity without violating the security requirements. For example, with reference to the example illustrated in Figure 7.15 it is possible to require each instance of class U_EMPLOYEE to be referenced by one and only one instance of class S_EMPLOYEE.

## 7.11 Observations on OODBMS security

In this chapter we have illustrated some models for the protection of object-oriented database systems. All the models illustrated offer some solutions to the problem of protecting object-oriented systems. However, each of them addresses only some of the issues, therefore leaving many questions open.

For discretionary security models, an overview of the main issues which have to be addressed in order to provide an authorization model for object-

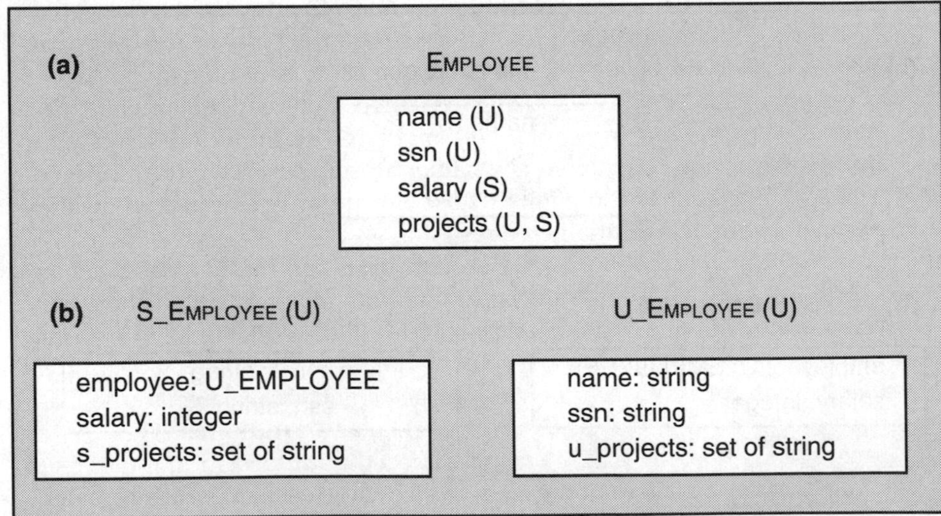


*Figure 7.15* An example of representation of (a) a multilevel entity with multi-valued attributes through (b) composite objects.

oriented systems has been given in Bertino and Samarati (1993). There, the following issues have been pointed out:

- *Authorization types.* In traditional access control models, access authorizations specify that a given subject (user, group of users, or program) can access an object (data or program) in a given mode (read, write, or execute). In particular, in order to read or write data in an authorization object, a user must have the necessary authorization for it. One of the main characteristics of object-oriented systems is the *encapsulation* property, meaning that objects can be accessed only by invoking predefined methods. Hence, considering only authorizations to read or write objects may be too restrictive. The authorization model should support the specification of authorizations to execute methods instead of authorizations to execute elementary read and write operations. Indeed, specifying authorizations as privileges of executing methods results in a more expressive authorization model. For instance, it is possible to allow a user to write in an object only by executing a given method, but still prevent the user from writing the object by using other methods.
- *Authorization subject.* In object-oriented systems, methods can invoke other methods. It would seem appropriate also to specify access authorizations with methods (not only users and groups of users) as subjects.
- *Authorization object.* Most of the authorization models proposed so far consider objects of the object-oriented model to be the unit of authorization. However, different levels of granularity should be provided. In particular, it should be possible to specify authorizations on single objects as well as on entire classes or databases.
- *Access control.* The access control determines whether an access request has to be granted or denied by the system on the basis of the authorizations specified. In object-oriented systems, users and applications access objects by calling methods. During execution, a method may invoke other methods on the same object or on other objects. An important issue which must therefore be considered is whether a user must have the authorization to execute all the methods whose execution is required in order to perform the method initially requested.
- *Administration of authorizations.* Different users can create objects belonging to the same class. The question therefore arises of establishing who can administer the privileges on the objects that are instances of the class. A particular issue concerns the control that the owner of a class can have on the authorizations other users can get on objects related to the class, such as instances and subclasses. In particular, the administration policy must specify how the class owner can affect the authorizations other users can get on the instances of the class (which these users may have created), on subclasses, or through the part-of relationship.
- *Propagation of authorizations.* Object-oriented systems allow the definition of subclasses from existing classes. The problem arises of determining

whether the authorizations a user owns on a class propagate along the class inheritance hierarchy. In particular, the authorization model must specify whether the authorizations that a user has on a class must also be considered valid on the subclasses of that class.

- *Conditional authorizations.* It should be possible to specify conditions that have to be satisfied for the execution of a given authorization. For example, authorizations referred to a class of objects can specify conditions that determine the subset of instances of the class on which the authorization can be used.
- *Interrelated authorizations.* Objects may be semantically related. This may require that in order to execute an operation on one object, some operations must be executed on other objects. For example, in order to execute a method on an object, the object's class must be accessible in some mode. This problem is solved in Rabitti *et al.* (1991) by enforcing derivation of implicit authorizations necessary for the execution of authorizations explicitly specified. For instance, according to this approach, if a user is authorized to read an object, the user is implicitly given the authorization for the read definition on the class of which the object is an instance. Another possible solution consists in requiring that in order to exercise an access, a user must be explicitly authorized for all the necessary related accesses. For instance, according to this approach, in order to read an object the user must own, besides the authorization to read an object, the authorization for the read definition on the class of which the object is an instance. An example of this approach, in the context of operating systems, is the UNIX operating system where, for example, to exercise any privilege on a file the user needs to have the execute privilege on the directory in which the file is contained.
- *Negative and positive authorizations.* The authorization model should support the specification of negative as well as positive authorizations. A policy for solving possible authorization conflicts should also be provided. The inclusion of both positive and negative authorizations in an authorization model may support exceptions to authorizations. For example, a user may be authorized to execute a given method on a class but at the same time denied execution of the same method on a superclass of that class.
- *Organizational aspects.* Some authorization models based on the role that users execute in the system have been proposed. Such an approach fits naturally with the object-oriented approach. User roles could be modelled as objects, and properties of those roles could be modelled as object attributes. Therefore, authorizations could be specified containing conditions on the subjects, in addition to conditions on the objects.
- *Formal model.* A formal authorization model should be devised and used for verifying the correctness of the authorization model. This task is particularly difficult owing to the lack of a standard reference model for object-oriented systems. Indeed, although all models are based on a set of common concepts, object-oriented systems have different characteristics which may affect the authorization model.

In the area of mandatory protection also, there are many issues that still need consideration. Some of them are the following:

- *Representation of real-world entities.* The security classifications may affect the way in which real-world entities must be mapped into the underlying object schema. For example, if the security model supports only single-level objects the mapping of multilevel entities to single-level objects must be provided.
- *Enforcement of classification requirements.* Classification requirements on real-world data must be properly represented in the stored objects. Then classifications on data, associations among data, aggregated and derived data must be supported. Classifications must be assigned with the assurance that no inference, covert channels, or leakage of information of any means will arise.
- *Supporting tools.* The number of entities and specialization hierarchies to be modelled may be quite large in real applications; therefore, tools to support the generation of the object-oriented schema that represents the real-world entities, their classification and the relationships between them should be provided.
- *Secure update and delete operations.* Objects may reference objects with a different security level. Therefore, particular care must be taken in the execution of update and delete operations. For example, if an object references a lower object, then if the lower object is deleted a dangling reference may result.
- *Polyinstantiation.* The problem of polyinstantiation has been extensively studied in the context of relational databases (see Chapter 2). Polyinstantiation occurs when an attribute has different values at different levels. Therefore, the problem arises of dealing with the existence of different values, each of which must be visible at the different levels. Moreover, the problem arises of distinguishing between correct information (that is, all the values at different levels are valid) and cover stories (that is, the values at lower levels represent a cover story to hide the data at a high level).
- *Sanitization.* It may be necessary to enforce methods that access high-level data but nevertheless return data at a lower level. This situation cannot be represented if the mandatory policy is strictly applied. Therefore, in some cases it may be necessary to relax the security constraints to support sanitization of information. This requires the provision of assurance that the sanitizing method will not leak high information: that is, no covert channel will arise.
- *Access synchronization.* High and low processes may concur in the access of low information. Since the low processes cannot be informed of computation at higher levels (otherwise a covert channel would arise), classical concurrency control mechanisms cannot be applied. Therefore, to guarantee correct computation some form of control on concurrent accesses must be provided.

- *Garbage collection.* The use of a garbage collection algorithm may introduce the possibility of covert channels. For example, if a low object is not collected because there are high objects referencing it, low users may infer the existence of the high object.
- *Identification of trusted components.* The amount of trusted code necessary to perform computation securely should be kept to the minimum possible. It is necessary to identify which components must be trusted, that is, verified to obey the security requirements, in order to ensure that the security system will perform properly.
- *Formal model.* A formal model should be provided and used for verifying the correctness of the security model. As already noticed, this task is particularly difficult owing to the lack of a standard reference model for object-oriented systems. Indeed, although all models are based on a set of common concepts, object-oriented systems have different characteristics which may affect the security model.

## References

Abdali S.K., Cherry G.W. and Soiffer N. (1986). A Smalltalk system for algebraic manipulation. In *Proc. ACM Conf. on Object-Oriented Programming Systems, Languages, and Applications (OOPSLA)*, Portland, September

Ahad R. *et al.* (1992). Supporting access control in an object-oriented database language. In *Proc. 3rd Int. Conf. on Extending Database Technology (EDBT)*, Vienna, Springer-Verlag Lecture Notes in Computer Science, vol. 580

Atkinson M. *et al.* (1989). The object-oriented database system manifesto. In *Proc. First Int. Conf. Deductive and Object-Oriented Databases*, Elsevier Science Publishers

Banerjee J. *et al.* (1987). Data model issues for object-oriented applications. *ACM Trans. Information Systems*, **5**(1), April

Barghouti N.S. and Kaiser G.E. (1991). Concurrency control in advanced database applications. *ACM Computer Surveys*, **23**(3), September

Bertino E. (1992a). Data hiding and security in an object-oriented database system. In *Proc. 8th IEEE International Conf. on Data Engineering*, Phoenix, Arizona, February

Bertino, E. (1992b). A view mechanism for object-oriented databases. In *Proc. Int. Conf. on Extending Database Technology (EDBT)*, Vienna, Springer-Verlag Lecture Notes in Computer Science, vol. 580

Bertino E. and Jajodia S. (1993). Modeling multilevel entities using single-level objects. In *Proc. 3rd Int. Conf. on Deductive and Object-Oriented Databases (DOOD'93)*

Bertino E. and Martino L. (1991). Object-oriented database management systems: concepts and issues. *IEEE Computer*, **24**(4), April

Bertino E. and Samarati, P. (1993). Research issues in discretionary authorizations for object bases. In *Proc. OOPSLA'93 Worskshop on Security for Object-Oriented Systems*, October

Bertino E. and Weigand H. (1994). An approach to authorization modeling in object-oriented database systems. *Data and Knowledge Engineering,* **12**(1) North-Holland

Fernandez E.B., Gudes E. and Song H. (1989). A security model for object-oriented databases. In *Proc. IEEE Symp. on Security and Privacy,* Oakland, May

Gagliardi R., Lapis G. and Lindsay B. (1989). A flexible and efficient database authorization facility. *IBM Research Rep. RJ 6826,* IBM Almaden Res. Center, May

Gal-Oz N., Gudes E. and Fernandez E.B. (1993). A model of methods authorization in object-oriented databases. In *Proc. Very Large Data Bases (VLDB) Conf.,* Dublin, Ireland, August

Garlan D. (1987). Views for tools in integrated environments. PhD *thesis,* Carnegie-Mellon, University, Pittsburgh

Goldstein I.P. and Bobrow D.G. (1980). A layered approach to software design. *Tech. Report CSL-80-5,* Xerox Palo Alto Research Center, December

Gudes E., Song H. and Fernandez E.B. (1991). Evaluation of negative and predicate-based authorization in object-oriented databases. In *Database Security IV: Status and Prospects* (Jajodia S. and Landwehr C.E., eds.), Elsevier Sc. (North-Holland)

Haas L., Chang W., Lohman G.M. *et al.* (1990). Starbust midflight: as the dust clears. *IEEE Trans. Knowledge and Data Eng.,* **2**(1), March

Habermann A.N., Krueger C., Pierce B., Staudt B. and Wenn J. (1988). Programming with views. *Technical Report,* Dept. of Computer Science, Carnegie Mellon Univ., Pittsburgh, January

Jajodia S. and Kogan B. (1990). Integrating an object-oriented data model with multilevel security. In *Proc. IEEE Symp. on Security and Privacy,* Oakland, May

Jajodia S., Kogan B. and Sandhu R. (1992). A multilevel-secure object-oriented data model. *Technical Report,* George Mason Univ.

Keefe T.F. and Tsai W.T. (1990). Prototyping the SODA security model. In *Database Security, III: Status and Prospects* (Spooner D.L. and Landwehr C.E., eds.). Amsterdam: North-Holland

Keefe T.F., Tsai W.T. and Thuraisingham M.B. (1988). A multilevel security model for object-oriented systems. In *Proc. 11th National Computer Security Conf.,* October

Kim W. (1990). Architecture of the Orion Next-Generation Database System. *IEEE Trans. Knowledge and Data Engineering,* **2**(1)

Kim W., Bertino E. and Garza J. (1989). Composite objects revisited. In *Proc. ACM-SIGMOD Conf. on Management of Data,* Portland, May

Meadows C. and Landwehr C.E. (1992). Designing a trusted application in an object-oriented data model. In *Research Directions in Database Security* (Lunt T.F., ed.). Berlin: Springer-Verlag

McCarthy D.R. and Dayal U. (1989). The architecture of an active Data Base Management System. In *Proc. ACM-SIGMOD, Conf. on Management of Data,* Portland, May

Millen J.K. and Lunt T.F. (1992). Security for object-oriented database systems. In *Proc. IEEE Symp. on Security and Privacy*, Oakland, May

Minsky N.H. (1987). A law-based approach to object-oriented programming. In *Proc. 2nd Int. Conf. on Object-Oriented Programming Systems, Languages, and Applications (OOPSLA)*, Orlando, October

Minsky N.H. (1991). Law-governed systems. *Software Engineering Journal*, September

Rabitti F., Bertino E., Kim W. and Woelk D. (1991). A model of authorization for next-generation database systems. *ACM Trans. Database Systems*, **16**(1), March

Richardson J., Schwarz P. and Cabrera L.F. (1992). CACL: Efficient fine-grained protection for objects. In *Proc. 7th Int. Conf. Object-Oriented Programming Systems, Languages, and Applications (OOPSLA)*, Orlando, October

Smith K. and Winslett M. (1992a). Entity modeling in the MLS relational model. In *Proc. 18th Conf. on Very Large Data Bases (**VLDB**)*, Vancouver, August

Smith K. and Winslett M. (1992b). Multilevel secure rules: integrating the Multilevel Secure and active data model. In *Proc. 6th WG11.3 Working Conf. on Database Security*, Vancouver, August

Stonebraker M. (1992). The integration of rule systems and database systems. *IEEE Trans. Data and Knowledge Engineering*, **4**(5)

Stonebraker M. *et al.* (1988). The POSTGRES rules system. *IEEE Trans. Software Engineering*, **14**(7)

Thuraisingham M.B. (1989a). A multilevel secure object-oriented data model. In *Proc. 12th National Computer Security Conf.*, October

Thuraisingham M.B. (1989b). Mandatory security in object-oriented database system. In *Proc. Conf. on Object-Oriented Programming: Systems, Languages, and Applications (OOPSLA)*, October

Ullman J.D. (1988). *Principles of Database and Knowledge-base Systems*. Computer Science Press

Watt S.M., Jens R.D., Sutor R.S. and Trager B.M. (1990). The Scratchpad II type system: Domains and subdomains. In *Computing Tools for Scientific Problem Solving* (Miola A.M., ed.). New York: New York Academy

Widom J., Cochrane R.J. and Lindsay B.G. (1991). Implementing set-oriented production rules as an extension to Starbust. In *Proc. 17th Conf. on Very Large Data Bases (VLDB)*, Barcelona, September

# Index

A1 Secure DBMS prototype 263–265
Abrams 279
abstract program, in lattice model 136–137
Abdali 395
Abul-Ela 328
access
  indirect 17
  granularity of 239
  hierarchy, *see* hierarchy
  lists 167 *see also* ACL
  policies 35
  requirements 35
  rules 28 *see also* rules
  set of current accesses, in Secure Xenix 227
  unconditional, to objects 395
access classes 97
access control 16, 18–32, 29
  discretionary 25
  in Wood *et al.* model 79
  in Sybase Secure Server 269
  mandatory 24
  mechanisms, *see* mechanisms
  request of 20, 21
  system 18–19, 21
  to resources 164–173, *see also* resource
  types of 240
Access Control List, *see* ACL
access limitation 20
access matrix 26–27, 45 (also authorization matrix)
  in ORION authorization model 399
  in Secure Xenix 227
access matrix model, *see* Harrison–Ruzzo–Ullman model
access modes 42
  in access matrix model 45–46
  in Acten model 60–61
  in Bell–LaPadula model 83
  in Biba model 88–89
  in Millen–Lunt model 427
  in ORION authorization model 399
  in Sea View model 98, 108
  in Take–Grant model 54
  in Wood *et al.* model 74–75
access rules management 28
accountability 14
accuracy of random-sample queries technique 323
ACL (Access Control List) 167, 168
  in access–matrix model 51, 52
  in Biba model 89, 91
  in Secure Xenix 227
Acten (Action–Entity) model 60–72
  active/passive entities 63
  authorization and protection states 62
  delegate/abrogate privilege 61, 71
  dynamic/static graph, privileges 63
  subordinated actions 68
Adam 297
address
  fence, *see* fence
  relocation, *see* relocation
ad-hoc security procedures 13
administrator
  application, *see* manager
  database, *see* DBA
  security 30, 43, *see also* security officer
Advanced Secure DBMS Internal Research and Development Project of the Defense Systems Group – TRW 263
aggregation abstraction 300
Ahad 410
All 295

Ames 219
Amman 53
Andrews 11, 177
Anderson 344, 345
anomaly
  behaviour 351
  database 345
  detection model 343, 378
ANSI (American National Standards Institute) 200, 202
ANSI/SPARC 7
  architecture 73, 74
    levels 73
assertions 177
assurance of security system 11
attachment mechanism 390
attribute
  confidential 296
  in OODB 388
  in relational model 8
Atkinson 388
Atzeni 8
availability 3
AUD (AUDit Trail), in VAX Security Kernel 231
Audit Expert (AE) system 309–313
audit
  trails 343, 367, 387
  data 346
  in DoD criteria 205
  in TDBMS 372–374
  records 357
auditing 14, 241
  in Ingres 271
  in Sybase Secure Server 270
auditor 32
authentication 15, 29
  in DoD criteria 205
  of user 146–151, 267
    double authentication (handshaking) 147
    password-based 147, 148–151
    query-answer-based 147
authority 280
Authority-item lists 167, 171
authorizer 20, 30, 73
authorization 43
  administration of,
    in access matrix model 48–50
    in Sea View model, in TCB 109–111
  centralized 20
  content-dependent 27, 409
    in SORION 425
  context-depedent 27
    in access-matrix model 45
    in SORION 425
  data-dependent, in access-matrix model 45
  history-dependent, in access-matrix model 45
  name-dependent 26
  time-dependent, in access-matrix model 45
  cooperative 22
  data 267
  dynamic 170, 240
  graph of, in Take–Grant model 57
  hierarchical decentralized 22
  indirect, in Acten model 70
  management of 20, 267
  negative/positive 252
  in Acten model 62–63
  in ORION authorization model 401
  in Starbust 390
  propagation of, in OODB 433
  revocation of, *see* privileges revocation
  rules of, *see* rules
  system (AS) 267, 303
  administration of, types of, in OODB
Authorization Type Lattice (ATL) 400
Authorization Object Lattice (AOL) 398, 399
Authorization Object Schema (AOS) 398
authorization base 402
  strong, weak, in ORION authorization model 402–404
Avg, statistic 296
axioms 23, 30, 44
  in Bell–LaPadula model 86–88
  in Biba model 89–92
  in Dion model 93–96
  in Millen–Lunt model 427–428
  in Sea View model 98–99
  in SORION, 420, 421

back doors 241
backup 30
Banergee 418
Barghouti 389

Barker 201
Batini 237
Beck 328
belief, in Smith and Winslett model 124
BELIEVED BY clause, in Smith and Winslett model 127
Bell 11, 82
Bell–LaPadula model 82–88
  interpretation of, in Secure Xenix 227
  principles 87
  secrecy level 82
Bertino 138, 250, 386, 408, 412, 431
Bertino and Weigand model 408–410
  content-dependent authorizations 409
  implication rules 409
  positive authorization 410
bias 320, 335, 337, 338
Biba 88
Biba model 88–92
  integrity level 88
  discretionary security policies 91–92
binding
  in lattice model 132
  in memory protection 153
  in flow control 175
Bobrow 395
Boebert 138
Bonium 14
Brooks Act 199
Brown 346
bugs 149
Bunch 183
Bussolati 27, 60

CA–ACF2 193–185
  access rules/logonid/information database 194, 195
  audit functionality 195
  modes 195
  sharable resources 194
CA–TOPSECRET 196–199
  modes 197–198
  resources 196
  users/departments/divisions 196
CAT (Canonical Audit Trail) 366
CCTA (Central Computer and Telecommunications Agency) 201
CAE (Common Application Environment)
cartesian product 10
capability
  lists (C-lists) 167, 169
  in access-matrix model 51, 52
  in UCLA Secure Unix 224
category 23
  in Bell–LaPadula model 83
  in Biba model 88
  in lattice model 132
  in VAX Security Kernel 229
  of instructions, in flow control 175
  of users: owner, group, other users 172
CEC (Constraint Enforcer and Checker) 302, 304
cell suppression 315
Central Computer and Telecommunications Agency, *see* CCTA
Cerniglia 26, 89
channels
  authorized 16
  covert 16, 233, 240,
  inference 17
  information spreading 356
  memory 16
  characteristic formula 295
Chebyshev inequality 327
checks reality 244
Chin 300, 314, 331
Chokhani 203
clandestine user 344
CICS (Customer Information Control System) 272
class
  of access, in VAX Security Kernel 229
  security 23
  in OODB 388
classification
  level 3
    of entities, in Acten model 63
    of methods, in SORION 422
    of subjects 23
    in Bell–LaPadula model 83
    in Biba model 88
    in lattice model 132
  class combination operator, in lattice model 132
clearance
  in Sea View model 105–107

*clearance continued*
in lattice model 132
clustering 380
COALESCE command, in MLS 394
Coates 33
commands, *see also* operations
ACTIVATE/DEACTIVATE, in MLS 393
AUDITDB, in Ingres 271
for rule manipulation, in MLS 392, 394
GRANT/REVOKE, in System R authorization model 246
in access matrix model 47–48
in Sybase Secure Server, *see* operations
in VAX Security Kernel 232
command pane, in MIDAS 371
Committee on Multilevel Data Management Security 255
Common Application Environment, *see* CAE
complementary suppression 315
compromise
exact 297, 337, 338
partial 297, 337, 338
positive, negative, in SDBs 292
Computer Security Center, *see* CSC
Computer Security Evaluation Center 200
Computer-Watch 344
condition,
context-dependent 45
data-dependent 45
history-dependent 45
time-dependent 45
confinement 15–16
connection 92
consistency
among rules, in Wood *et al*. model 79
in perturbation-based technqies 320
of inference protection techniques 336, 337, 338
Constraint Enforcer and Checker, *see* CEC
continuity of of operation 244
control
access 18–32, *see also* access control
audit-based 309
discretionary 30
in OODBMS 394
flow, 16–17, *see* flow control
granularity of 279
inference 16, 17–18
expanded query-set size 306–308
mandatory 30
in OODBMS 395
order 313
query-set overlap 308–309
query-set size 304–306
Conway 44
correlations
semantic, among data 238
cost of inference protection techniques 336, 337, 338
Count, statistic 294, 296
Courtney 2
Cox 315
crackers
cryptographic techniques 16
Cyclic Redundancy Check (CRC) 268
CSC (Computer Security Center) 200

D–A model 300
DAC(Discretionary Access Control) 22, 22
in DoD criteria 204
DAP (Design Analyis Phase) 209 , 211
data
association problem 241
correlated 17
derived, in active databases 386
description levels 6–7
invisibility of 286
life cycle 239
missing 18
models 3
Entity–Relationship 3–4
database
active 385, 386–387
ANSI/SPARC proposal 72 *see also* ANSI/SPARC
classified 32
commercial 33–34
design 3
entity, entity association 3
data description levels, *see* ANSI/SPARC
in government departments 32–33

misuse 345
object-oriented 385, 387–390 *see also* OODB
secure architectures 253–265
semantic of 33
unclassified 32
statistical, *see* SDB
Data Definition Language, *see* DDL
Data-hiding model 412–413
Data Manipulation Language, *see* DML
Date 1
Davida 309
Dayal 391
DBA (Database Administrator) 15, 20, 30, 32, 329, 330,
DBMS (Database Management System) 3
modules 4–6
multilevel secure architectures 34
relational 8
DB2 (Database 2) 272–23
DDL (Data Definition Language) 4
De Antonellis 8
delegation
of authority 244
De Millo 295
denial of service 3, 11, 356, 367
Denning 2, 16, 17, 18, 28, 33, 34, 44, 96, 131, 297, 306, 314, 348
DES (Data Encription Standard)
design
methodology, *see* methodology for secure database design
of database security 32–34,
based on DBMS security mechanisms 237–289
logical design 237
of secure databases 273–289
of secure DBMS 238–273
of secure OS 218–233
kernel-based approach 219–223
of a secure system 26
Design Analyis Phase, in DoD criteria, *see* DAP
detection of improper access 28
Deviation, standard 350
devices
in UCLA Secure Unix 224
in KSOS 226
Dialoguer, in UCLA Secure Unix 224
difference, 10
Dion 92
Dion model 92–96
security and integrity levels 92–93
Discovery
Discretionary Access Control, *see* DAC
division, in DoD criteria 207–209
DML (Data Manipulation Language) 4
Dobkin 2, 308
domain
access 165
execution domains, in UCLA Secure Unix 225
I/O, Policy, TCB, User, in Sybase Secure Server 268
network security, in ECMA 202
DoD (Department of Defense)
criteria 203–213, 273
accountability 203, 205
assurance 205
classes 207–209
designers 203
developers/vendors 203
division 207
documentation 206
reuse of objects 205
security policy 203, 204
users 203
DoD Computer Security Initiative 199
dominates relationship, in Sea View model 97
Downs 257
Drongowsi 225

ECMA (European Computer Manufacturers Association) 201
egid (effective group identifier) 182
entities
in Entity Relationship model 3
in Acten model 60–72
in Millen–Lunt model 426
in SORION 42, *see also* 'individual' in SDB errors
bugs in hardware/software 12
human 12
estimator 297
Evaluated Product List 201

evaluation process, in DoD criteria 209–213
events audit of security related 268
horizon of 367
in TIM 378
recontruction of 244
euid (effective user identifier) 182
European Computer Manufacturer Association, *see* ECMA

failures 13
fault
system 29
fence
address of 152
fence-based memory protection 152–153
FEP (Formal Evaluation Phase) 209, 211
Ferguson 138
Fernandez 2, 12, 19, 27, 30
file
in KSOS 226
protection 172
in VAX Security Kernel 229
filter
commutative 257, 258
statistical 291
FIPS (Federal Information Processing Standards) 199
flag,
copy, transfer, in access-matrix model 49
flow control 16–17
mechanisms 173–177
model (FM), *see* lattice model
at compile time 175–177
at run time 174–175
implicit and explicit 136–137, 173
of information, in message filter model 414
flow relation, in lattice model 132
Formal Evaluation Phase (FEP), *see* FEP
Fox 382
Friedman 307
functions
hidden 81
derived, guard, generic/specific, proxy
in Iris authorization model 410, 411, 412
mapping, in Wood *et al.* model 75
probability density (giusto?) statistical 18
Fagin 245
Fugini 39, 60, 72, 274
F11F (Archives Files-11), in VAX Security Kernel 231

Gagliardi 390
Gangemi 2
Garbage collection, in OODB 436
Garlan 395
Garvey 347
GEMSOS TCB 262, 271
generalization abstraction 300
Gligor 226
Graham 44
granularity
of objects 238
graph
dynamic and static in Acten model 63–65
in Take–Grant model 53, 57, 57
Graubart 138, 255
Griffiths 245
Gypsy Verification Environment Methodology 265

Haas 386, 390
Habermann 395
Hale 33
Halme 346
Harrison–Ruzzo–Ullman model 44–53, 143
extensions 52–53
implementation 50–52
Typed Access Matrix 53
Haystack 344, 365–369
conceptual structure 368
compatibility with standards 368
design principles 367–369
Henning 238
heuristics 369
hierarchy
access 165
classification, in DoD criteria 206
nested program units, *see* nested program units
of elements for profile characterization 351

of inheritance, in ORION authorization model 406
of protection levels 166
privileged modes, *see* privileged modes
HIH (Hardware-Interrupt Handler), in VAX Security Kernel 231
Hinke 11, 34, 42
HLS (Higher-Level Scheduler), in VAX Security Kernel 231
Hochberg 346
hostile agents 12
Hunt 373
Hruska 2
Hsiao 143

ICST (Institute of Computer Science and Technology) 199
*see also* National Computer Systems Laboratory
identification
in DoD criteria 205
user 146–151, 267
*see also* authentication
IDSs (Intrusion Detection Systems) 343
architecture 344
off-line/on-line 344
IDES (Intrusion Detection Expert System) 344, 348–365
analysis of behaviour anomalies 349
data 362
metrics 349–350
model 356
processes 362
profile characterization 351–352
statistical models 350
threats–behaviours relationship 348–349
IEEE (Institute of Electrical and Elctronics Engineers) 202
IFIP (International Federation for Information Processing) 202
independence of data
logical, physical 7
individual 293
average 314
inference
channel 17
control 17–18
attacks
types of 293
specific 324
statistical 18
inference protection techniques 296–334
audit-base, *see* control based on the number of attributes 313–314
based on query set, *see* query set
cell suppression, *see* cell suppression
conceptual 298–304
lattice model, *see* lattice models
partitioning, *see* partitioning
perturbation-based 319–335
data swapping 320–322
fixed perturbation 326–328
PRD perturbation 331–333
query-based 328
record-based 319
result-based 319
restriction-based 304–319
rounding 333
controlled 334
random 334
Sm/N criterion 314
information
change sequence-labelled 304
hiding of 369
flow of, *see* flow
identifiable dynamics-labelled 303
loss of 314, 335, 337, 338
non-vital 32
vital 32
Information Security Officer's Assistant, *see* ISOA
Informix 265, 266
Ingres 265, 226, 271
inheritance 389
multiple, in SORION 422
Institute of Electrical and Elctronics Engineers, *see* IEEE
integrity 3, 13
database class, in Sea View model 101
constraints 14
entity, in Jajodia and Sandhu model 112–114
inter-instance, in Jajodia and Sandhu model 114–115
multilevel entity, in Sea View model 102

*integrity continued*
multilevel referential, in Sea View model 102
no read-down, no write-up, in Biba model 91
null, in Jajodia and Sandhu model 114
null value, in Smith and Winslett model 124
operational, of data 14
polyinstantiation,
in Sea View model 104
in Jajodia and Sandhu model 115
semantic, of data 14
view class, in Sea View model 102
Integrity Lock (cryptoseal mechanism) 255
Integrity Lock Architecture 255
International Federation for Information Processing, *see* IFIP
International Standards Organization, *see* ISO
intersection 10
intruder 346
intrusion
detection 343
types 366
Intrusion Detection Expert System, *see* IDES
instance-of link 385
IOS (Input/Output Services), in VAX Security Kernel 231
Iris authorization model 410–412
is-a link 385
ISO (International Standards Organization) 201
ISOA (Information Security Officer's Assistant) 344
isolation 177–179
multiple-space method 177
virtual machine 177

Jajodia 2, 111, 413, 431
Jajodia and Sandhu model 111–123
join
natural 11
Jackson 2
Jones 39, 53, 59

Kahn 346
Kaiser 389
Karger 138, 227, 347
Keefe 396
Kemmerer 288
Kernel Interface Subsystem
Kernelized Architecture 258–259
Kernelized Secure Operating System, *see* KSOS
kernel
security 219
advantages 221
completeness, isolation, verifiability 219
functions 220
structures 220
in UCLA Secure Unix 223
in KSOS 225–226
Kernel Interface SubSystem (KISS), in UCLA Secure Unix 224
Kerr 143
KI (Kernek Interface), in VAX Security Kernel 231
Ki 389, 390
Knode 373
knowledge
additional, supplementary, working, in SDB 292
Kochan 149
Kogan 413
Korth 13
KSOS (Kernelized Secure Operating System) 225–226
architecture 225
security kernel, emulator, system software 225

label
in Dod criteria 204
security 22
Laferrier 287
Laird 380
Lampson 44, 143
Landwehr 26, 28, 33, 39, 395
LaPadula 82
lattice
authorization object lattice, in ORION 399
authorization Type Lattice, in ORION 400
derivation of 133–136
in Starbust 391

model 131–137, 298–300
ordered liner 135
role, in ORION 396
languages
Data Definition, *see* DDL
Data Manipulation, *see* DML
Query Language, *see* QL
leakage 366
least privilege 242–243
level
in ANSI/SPARC 73
of a processing system 144
of abstraction, in VAX Security Kernel 230
maximum security, in Secure Xenix 227
secrecy/integrity, in VAX Security Kernel 229
security, in Bell–LaPadula model 83
sensitivity 23
Levin 16
Liepins 374
Lindsay 250
link
static, dynamic 174
Lipner 33
list
A-list, *see* ACL
C-list, *see* capability
Litecky 343
LLS (Lower–Level scheduler), in VAX Security Kernel 231
lock-key mechanism 167, 171
locking
two-phase 14
Lockman 60
logging phase 30
Low-Water Integrity Audit Policy, Low-Water Mark Policy
for objects
in Biba model 90
for subjects
in Biba model 89–90
integrity audit policy
in Biba model 90
Luckenbaugh 226
Lunt 263, 273, 344, 347, 396

MAC (Mandatory Access Control) 22
in DoD criteria 204
model
in Sea View model 97
MacEwen 11
machine learning 380
of concepts 380
predictive 380
macrostatistics 294, 298
manager
application 30
concurrency 14
Mandatory Access Control, MAC
Martino 386
Matloff 320
McCauley 225
McCollum 138
McLean 2
Marshall 11
Martella 27, 39, 60, 274
masquerading 356, 366, 369
matrix
access, *see* access matrix
analog 321
d-equivalent 321
d-transformable 321
image 320
protection 167
implementation of 167–168
Max, statistic 296
Maximal Authorized View 257, 259
McCarthy 391
McDermott 289
McLean 39
Meadows 395
mechanims 11
access control 164–173
auditing 30
external 29
hardware 151–163
internal 29
minimum common 285
security 28–29, 143
user identification/authentication 146–151
Median, statistic 296
Melton 251
memory protection 151–163
*see also* protection
message filter model 413–418
classification requirement representation 417

message-filtering algorithm 415, 416
metadata 238
methods, in OODB 388
methodology for secure database design 237, 274, 275
  conceptual design 281–282
  implementation of security mechanisms 263–288
  logical design 237, 282–283
  phases 274
  physical design 283 preliminary analysis 276–277
  requirement analysis and policy selection 277–281
  verification and testing 288–289
microaggregation
  process 298
  technique 314
MIDAS (Multics Intrusion Detection and Alerting System) 344, 369–371
  architecture 370–371
  operation 370
  rules 369–370
Millen 26, 89, 396, 426
Millen–Lunt model 426–430
  classification requirement representation 429–430
  classification rules 430
  Min, statistic 296
Minsky 60, 395
misfeasors 344
misuse
  database 345
  detection models 343
  in MIDAS 370
MLS (Multi Level Secure System) 390
  execution model 393
MLS-SQL 391
models
  anomaly detection 343
  based on methods 410–413
  conceptual model of an SDB 294, 301
  conceptual security model 281
  Data Abstraction (D-A) 300
  Data-hiding model 412–413
  discretionary security models 39, 81–82
  mandatory security models 39, 137–139
  access matrix model 44–53
  Acten model 60–72
  Bell–LaPadula model 82–88
  Bertino and Weigand model 408–410
  Biba model 88–92
  Dion model 92–96
  Iris authorization model 410–412
  Jajodia and Sandhu model, *see* Jajodia and Sandhu model
  lattice model 131–137, 298–300
  message filter model 413–418
  Millen–Lunt model 426–430
  misuse detection models 343
  ORION authorization model 396–408
  Postgres 387
  Sea View model 96–111
  Smith and Winslett model 123–131
  SORION authorization model 418–426
  Starbust 390
  statistical models 350
    average and standard deviation 350
    Markovian 351
    multivaried 350
    operational 350
    time series 351
  System R authorization model 245–253
  Take–Grant model 53–60
  Wood *et al.* model 72–82
modes
  access, *see* access modes
  system high, multilevel, in secure DBMS 25
  user, privileged 165
monitors
  appearance 347
  behaviour 347
  of security, in MIDAS 370
  reference, *see* reference monitor
MSQL Processor 263
Multics 369, 370
multidimensional transformation 320
Multi Level Secure System, *see* MLS
multiple data types 239
MVS IBM 179–180, 272, 189, 213
Myers 28

National Computer Security Center, *see* NCSC

National Computer Systems Laboratory 199–200
National Security Agency, *see* NSA
NBS (National Bureau of Standards) 199, *see also* NIST
NCSC (National Computer Security Center) 200, 265, 369, 210
need-to-know, in lattice model 132
Needham 143
nested program units 165
Network Manager, in UCLA Secure Unix 224
Neumann 348
neural networks, in IDS 347
NIST (National Institute of Standards and Technology) 199, 242
NRL (National Research Laboratory) research prototype 260
NSA (National Security Agency) 200

Object Oriented Database Management System, *see* OODBMS
objects 24
  composite, in ORION authorization model 406
  in Bell–LaPadula model 87–88
  in OODB 388
    complex 388
  in security models 42
  in VAX Security Kernel 229
  in Biba model 88
  in Dion model 93
  in Millen–Lunt model 427
  in ORION authorization model 397
  in Sea View model 97
  in Wood *et al.* model 73–74
  in IDES model 356
  logical/physical 238
  static/dynamic 239
  in Ingres 271
  in Sybase Secure Server 268
  in Oracle 272
  in OS/400 188
  in Secure Xenix 227
    multilevel 227
  in SORION 420
  single-level 430
Object Oriented Database, *see* OODB
Olson 11, 279
OODB (Object Oriented Database) 387
OODBMS (Object Oriented Database Management System) 389
  security in 394–396
Operating Systems 143–146
  functions 144
  security functions 179–189
operation block 392
operations
  in access matrix model 46–47
  in Bell–LaPadula model 84–86
  in Jajodia and Sandhu model 116–123
  in Smith and Winslett model 127–131
  in Take–Grant model 54–57
  database, query and update 10
  Input/Output in a security kernel in Ingres 271
  in Sybase Secure Server 269
  in Oracle 272
Oracle 259, 265, 266, 271–272
  Mandatory Prototype 263
  RDBMS Data Adminsitrator's Guide 373
  in Haystack 368
Orange Book 200
ORION authorization model 396–408
  composite objects 407
  authorization base, weak authorization base 402–404
  authorization object schema 398
  derivation of implicit authorization 404
  implication rules 405
  versions 408
OS/1100 368
OS/400 IBM 187–189
  groups 188
  objects 188
  users 187
ownership 22, 244, 172
Ozsoyoglu 300, 314

pages
  in UCLA Secure Unix 223
paging 159
Palley 291
Parker 2, 276
partition tree 332
partial suppression technique 317
partitioning 314–315
  conceptual 300–304

*partitioning continued*
of logical and physical memory 162
part-of links 385
password 148
choice 148
encryption 149
disclosure 149
for file protection 172
management 148
PCS (Polyinstantiation for Covert Stories) 123
PDC (Population Definition Construct) 302, 303
penetrators
internal 344
external 344
Peng 331
Perry 2, 343
perturbation
of data 18
see inference protection techniques
Pfleeger 2, 151, 201
Policy Manager, in UCLA Secure Unix 224
policies 11, 43
access 19
closed world 252
minimum privilege 20
maximum privilege 20
ring, in Biba model 90, 92
security 19
discretionary 24–25
mandatory 22–24
strict integrity, in Biba model 91
for authorization management 20
support, *see* support policies
Polk 242
polyinstantiation 241
in Sea View model 103–104
in extensions to Jajodia and Sandhu model 123
Popek 223, 257
populations 300
atomic 301, 314
security atom (SA) populations 302
Population Definition Construct, *see* PDC
Posix 182
Committee IEEE P1003 standard 365
Postgres 387
precision
of inference protection techniques 335, 337
predicate, in MLS 392
Preliminary Technical Review, *see* PTR
prevention of improper access 28
privileged modes 165
privileges 24, 280
access, in Secure Xenix 227
administration/administrative 43
authorized, in discretionary and mandatory policies 26
minimum 284
ownership in access matrix model 45, 48
in Acten 65
in System R 248
propagation 24
revocation
of propagated rights 24
in access matrix model
in Take–Grant model
in System R 247
cascading 247
non-cascade revoke operation 252
separation 284
transfer of 50
probability
function, *see* probability function
error 327
density, *see* density function
space
procedures
auxiliary 28
of control, security mechanisms 19
processes
identification of 164
in UCLA Secure Unix 223
in KSOS 226
in VAX Security Kernel 229
multiple, in a security kernel
product, *see* cartesian product
profiles
activity 358, 361
behaviour 351
characterization 351
command and program execution 353
CPU per program, I/O per program 354
denied executions 354

execution frequency 354
saturation of program resources 354
database access 355
file access
read, write, create, delete frequency 355
read, written records 355
read, write, create, delete failures 355
file resource exhaustion 355
in IDES model 358
login and session activity 352
CPU per session 353
last login 352
location failures 353
login, location frequency 352
password failures 353
session duration 352
session output 353
models of 361
of users/groups/resources, in RACF 190, 191
projection 11
property
corruption, in Dion model 94–96
execute, in Sea View model 99
integrity, in Dion model 94–96
key and tuple classification, in Smith and Winslett model 125–127
in ORION authorization model 402
Authorization Base (AB) property, consistency, non-redundancy 402
Weak Authorization Base (WAB) property 403
completeness, consistency 403
coexistence of WAB and AB property 404
read, in Sea View model 98
read/migration, in Dion model 96
migration, in Dion model 94
simple security, in Bell–LaPadula model 86
security, in Dion model 94
discretionary security, in Bell–LaPadula model 87
visible data, in Sea View model 102
write, in Sea View model 99
write/corruption, in Dion model 96
protection
from inference, *see* inference protection techniques
from unauthorized accesses
multilevel 15, 240
of memory 151–163
of program areas 156
of sensitive data 15
requirements 12–16, 32
resource, *see* resource
prototypes
A1 Secure DBMS, *see* A1 Secure DBMS prototype
IDES 361
monitors, database, profile updater, anomaly detector, active data resetter, receiver of audit data, archiver 363
interaction among components 364
Mitre 253
NRL, *see* NRL prototype 253
Sea View, *see* Sea View prototype
PTR (Preliminary Technical Review) 209, 211

QL (Query Language) 4, 10
query controls 18
query set 295
basic 317
compromising 328
expanded 306
implied 307
insufficient 317
overlap 308
small-size 325
size 304, 306
sufficient 317
queries
key-specified 309
random-sample 322–323
statistical 296

Rabitti 408
RACF (Resource Access Control Facility) 189
modes 191
resources 191
setropts 192–193
users 191
RAMP (Rating Maintenance Phase) 210, 212

Rating Maintenance Phase (RAMP) *see* RAMP
reasoning, model-based in IDS 347
record
  audit 357
  anomaly 359
recovery system 13
Red Book 201
reference monitor 203, 204
  acceptance 347
  behaviour 347
  reference 203, 204
register
  protection based on 155–159
  bound 155
  base/limit 155
  two pairs of 157
Reitman 177
Reiss 322
relation 8
  attributes 8
  cardinality 8
  component 8
  degree 8
  entity integrity constraint 8
  multilevel,
    in Sea View model 99, 111
    in Jajodia and Sandhu model 112–123
    in Smith and Winslett model 125–127
  referential integrity constraint 8
  functional dependency 8
  schema
    logical 4
    logical data schema 7
    physical data schema 7
  SYSAUTH, SYSCOLAUTH 249
relational
  algebra 8
  model 8–11
  multilevel secure (MLS) 391
  schema 8
reliability, in DoD criteria 205, 206
relocation 153–154
Replicated Arhcitecture 259–260
reporting phase 30
residuals 285
resource
  identification 164
  operations 164
Resource Access Control Facility, *see* RACF
reversibility
  in Take–Grant model 58–60
Rfreq, statistic 296
rgid (real group identifier) 182
rights, *see* privileges
risks 276, 277
risk analysis 276, 278
Rittenberg 343
robustness
  of inference protection technique 335, 337
root, or superuser 181
Rougeau 373
ruid (real user idendifier) 182
rule base, in W&S 375
rules
  access 19
    in Wood *et al*. model 76–79
  activity 360
  audit record rules, for periodic updating of activity,
  anomaly record rules 360
  authorization 19, 21, 24, 25–28, 30
    of consistency and transformation, in Acten model 66–72
  implication, in Bertino and Weigand model 409
  management of 28
    in active databases 386
    in MIDAS 369
    in ORION authorization model 404–406
Russel 2
Ruthberg 242
Ruzzo 44

safety, in access matrix model 52
salt 149–150
Saltzer 2, 283
Sandhu 2, 52, 111, 243
Sandhu and Jajodia, extension to Jajodia and Sandhu model 123
SA-set (Security Atomic set)
Schaefer 42, 372
Scheduler
  in UCLA Secure Unix 224
Schematic Protection Model 52
Schlorer 17, 18, 297, 306, 313, 320
Schroeder 2, 283

SDB (Statistical Data Base) 291–296
  compromisable 328
  on–line/off–line, static/dynamic 291, 292, 337, 338
  positively, negatively compromisable 292
  special–purpose, general–purpose 291
  statistically compromisable 328
Sea View (SEcure dAta View) model 96–111
    administration of authorizations 109
    discretionary security policies, in TCB 107–108
    MAC model 97–99
    multilevel relations 99, 104, 111
    properties 101–104
    TCB model 99–111
SeaView prototype 262–263
Sebring 346, 371
secrecy 2–3
  in Bell–LaPadula model 82–83
  Secure Xenix 223, 226–227
security
  by default 284
  conceptual 281
  level of,
    external 32
    internal 32
  logical 32
  kernel, *see* kernel
  management, in TIM 379
  officer 20, 32
  packages 189–199
  physical 32
  mechanisms 28
    in DBMSs 239–245
  models, *see* models
  rules 237, *see also* rules
  software 237
  system
    development of 35
    multilevel 22
selection 11
segmentation 161–163
  in KSOS
separation of duties 243
setgid 182, 183
setuid 182, 183
Share 52
Sharebase relational database engine 258
Shell 33
side-effects 356
Silberschatz 13, 143
Sicherman 309
Smaha 365
Smith 123, 300, 390
Smith and Winslett model 123–131
SORION authorization model 418–426
  classification requirement
    representation 423
    constraints 423, 424, 425
Spafford 381
SPECIAL 225
specialization 389
Spooner 238
SQL (Structured Query Language) 8
SQLBase 265, 266
SSMF (Statistical Security Management Facility) 302
SSVR (Secure Server), in VAX Security Kernel 232
standards 199–218
  of Posix Committee IEEE P1003 365
  initiatives in Europe 201
  initiatives in the USA 199
  for cryptography 199
  for evaluation process 199
Star(*) property
  in Bell–LaPadula model 86–87
Starbust 390
statistic
  key-based 295
  sensitive 296, 299
Statistical Data Base, *see* SDB
Statistical Security Management Facility, *see* SSMF
state
  authorization
    in access matrix model 44
    in ACTEN model 62
    in Wood *et al*. model 76
    in Bell–LaPadula model
    in Take–Grant model 53
  protection
    in Acten model 62–63
  system
    in Bell–LaPadula model 84
Sterne 2
Stonebracker 386

Stoughton 138, 139
Sturms 373
Structured Query Language, *see* SQL
subjects 24
  in security models 42
  in VAX Security Kernel 228
  in Dion model 92–93
  in IDES model 356
  in Millen–Lunt model 427
  in Sea View model 97–98
  in Wood *et al.* model 73–74
  in Ingres 271
  in Sybase Secure Server 269
  in Oracle 271, 396
  in Secure Xenix 227
  in SORION 420
  subtypes
  in KSOS 226
suitability
  of inference protection techniques 336
Sum, statistic 296
Summers 2, 346
superuser, *see* root
surveillance, areas of, in MIDAS 369
swapping 320 *see also* multidimensional transormation
Sybase DBMS 255, 265, 266
Sybase Secure SQL Server (SYSSS) 268–271
SYSAUTH table, in System R 251
system
  classification of systems according to DoD criteria 213–218
  open 20, 21
  closed 20, 21
  operating, *see* Operating Systems
  database management, *see* DBMS
System Management Facilities (SMF) 193
System R authorization model 245–253
  extensions 250–253
  revocation of authorization 247
  timestamps 248
  views 248
System Software, in KSOS 226

tables
  implementation of access matrix 167
  in Acten model,
    of security classes 65
    of entity states 65
    of action hierarchy 65–66
  Sysaudits, in Sybase Secure Server 270
  Systables, Syscolumns, in DB2 272
tagged architecture 157, 158
Tanenbaum 218
Take–Grant model 53–60
  authorization graph 57
  extensions 58–60
  implementation 57
TCB (Trusted Computing Base)
  domain 268
  in Sea View model 99–111
TCSEC (Trusted Computer System Evaluation Criteria) 200, 365, 372
TDBMS (Trusted Database Mangement System) 372, 372
Teng 377, 379
threat 11–12
Thusaisingham 396, 418
TIM (Time-based Inductive Machine) 377–380
  architecture 379
  event 378
  input data and rules 378
Time-based Inductive Machine, *see* TIM
TNI (Trusted Network Interpretation) 201
tracker 305
  general 306
  double 306
  union 306
Trade and Industry department (TDI) 201
tranquility principle, in Bell–LaPadula model 87
transactions 13
  atomicity 13
  begin, commit, abort 13
  isolation 14
  lock, unlock 14
  management in TDBMS 373
  manager 30
  multilevel 239
  observation of 376
  serializability 14
  transport rights 54
  well-formed 242

transfer
of information 15
of privileges, in Take–Grant model 54–57
right of, via capabilities 170
traps, intentional 286
trapdoors 149
Traub 327
Trojan Horse 16, 81–82, 354, 369, 370
TRUEDATA 258
Trusted Computer System Evaluation Criteria, *see* TCSEC
Trusted Database Mangement System, *see* TDBMS
trusted filter, *see* Trusted Front End
Trusted Front End (TFE) 255
Trusted Network Interpretation, *see* TNI
trusted path, in DoD criteria 205
Trusted Subject Architecture 253, 254–255
TRW, *see* Advanced Secure DBMS Internal Research and Development Project of the Defense Systems Group Tsai 396
TSO (Time Sharing Option) 272
Tsudik 346
Turn 34

UCLA Secure Unix 222, 223–225
devices 224
pages 223
processes 223
*see also* kernel
UIC (User Identification Code) 302
UKC (User Knowledge Construct) 302, 303
Ullman 1, 385
union 10
Unix
classification according to DoD criteria 213
file 182
processes 182
security functions 180
salt-based technique in 149
System V MLS 258
user categories:owner, group, other users 173, 182
Unix Emulator, in KSOS 225
Unix Interface, in UCLA Secure Unix 224
Untrusted Front Ends (UFE) 254
user
authenticated 242
authentication, *see* authentication
authorized 12
identification, *see* identification
login and authentication 30
work session 146
User Identification Code, *see* UIC
User Knowledge Construct, *see* UKC
USERS, in VAX Security Kernel 232
Utix/23S 182

Vaccaro 374
VAP (Vendor Assistance Phase) 209, 211
Var, statistic
VAX Security Kernel 227–233
categories of users: 229
server processes: 229
VAX/VMS 184–185, 379
classification according to DoD criteria 218
files 185
groups 185
log file 185
processes 185
system password, secondary password 184
users 184
Vendor Assistance Phase, *see* VAP
verification, formal, in VAX Security Kernel 232
versions, in ORION authorization model 408
virtual machine 177
Virtual Machine Monitor, *see* VMM
views
logical 6
in System R authorization model 248
viruses 347, 354, 367, 370
VM/SP IBM 185–187, 189
classification according to DoD criteria 218
VMM (Virtual Machine Monitor) Security Kernel 227, 228
VMOS (Virtual Machine Operating System),

in VAX Security Kernel 232
VMP (Virtual Machine Physical space manager),
in VAX Security Kernel 213
VMV (Virtual Machine Virtual space Manager),
in VAX Security Kernel 231
VPrint (Virtual Printers), in VAX Security Kernel 231
VTerm (Virtual Terminals) 231
VOL (Volumes), in VAX Security Kernel 229, 231
VVAX (Virtual VAX), in VAX Security Kernel 232

Wade 245
Walter 138
Warner 343
warning pane, in MIDAS 371
Watt 395
Watson 289
Weigand 408
White Books 201
Wilms 250
Wing 288
Winslett 123, 390
Wisdom & Sense, *see* W&S
Wood 72, 238, 149, 273
Wood *et al.* model 72–82
Access Constraint Table 76
Conceptual Rule Table 76
Rules Table 78
consistency of rules 79
query modification 79
Woods Hole architectures 253, 255–260
Woods Hole Summer Study 253
Wortmann 297
W&S (Wisdom & Sense) 344, 374–377
data model 375
implementation 376
data processor 377
rule base generator 377
transaction analyzer 377
rule base 375
rule evaluation 376

Xenix, *see* Secure Xenix

Yu 314